INTERPRETING EXILE

Society of Biblical Literature

Ancient Israel and Its Literature

Steven L. McKenzie, General Editor

Number 10

INTERPRETING EXILE
Displacement and Deportation in Biblical and Modern Contexts

INTERPRETING EXILE

DISPLACEMENT AND DEPORTATION IN BIBLICAL AND MODERN CONTEXTS

Edited by

Brad E. Kelle,

Frank Ritchel Ames,

and

Jacob L. Wright

Foreword by Rainer Albertz

Society of Biblical Literature
Atlanta

INTERPRETING EXILE
Displacement and Deportation in Biblical and Modern Contexts

Copyright © 2011 by the Society of Biblical Literature

Library of Congress Cataloging-in-Publication Data

Interpreting exile : interdisciplinary studies of displacement and deportation in biblical and modern contexts / edited by Brad Kelle, Frank R. Ames, and Jacob L. Wright.
        p. cm. — (Society of Biblical Literature ancient Israel and its literature ; v. 10)
    Includes bibliographical references and index.
    ISBN 978-1-58983-604-4 (paper binding : alk. paper) — ISBN 978-1-58983-605-1 (electronic format)
    1. Jews—History—Babylonian captivity, 598–515 B.C. 2. Bible. O.T.—Criticism, interpretation, etc. 3. Exile (Punishment) in literature. 4. Exiles—History. I. Kelle, Brad E., 1973– II. Ames, Frank Ritchel. III. Wright, Jacob L.
    BS1199.B3 I58 2011
    221.8'305906914—dc22   2011039403

Printed on acid-free, recycled paper conforming to
ANSI/NISO Z39.48-1992 (R1997) and ISO 9706:1994
standards for paper permanence.

Contents

Part 4: Texts and Comparison

Abbreviations

AASOR	Annual of the American Schools of Oriental Research
AB	Anchor Bible
ABD	*Anchor Bible Dictionary*. Edited by D. N. Freedman. 6 vols. New York: Doubleday, 1992.
ABG	Arbeiten zur Bibel und ihrer Geschichte
ABRL	Anchor Bible Reference Library
ADPV	Abhandlungen des deutschen Palästinavereins
AfOB	Archiv für Orientforschung: Beiheft
AnBib	Analecta biblica
ANET	*Ancient Near Eastern Texts Relating to the Old Testament*. Edited by J. B. Pritchard. 3rd ed. Princeton: Princeton University Press, 1969.
Ant.	Josephus, *Jewish Antiquities*
AOAT	Alter Orient und Altes Testament
AOTC	Abingdon Old Testament Commentaries
ASOR	American Schools of Oriental Research
ATANT	Abhandlungen zur Theologie des Alten und Neuen Testaments
ATD	Das Altes Testament Deutsch
Atiqot	ʿAtiqot
BA	*Biblical Archaeologist*
BAIAS	*Bulletin of the Anglo-Israel Archeological Society*
BAR	*Biblical Archeology Review*
BASOR	*Bulletin of the American Schools of Oriental Research*
BBB	Bonner Biblische Beiträge
BETL	Bibliotheca ephemeridum theologicarum lovaniensium
Bib	*Biblica*
BibInt	*Biblical Interpretation*
BInS	Biblical Interpretation Series

BJS   Brown Judaic Studies
BMJ   *British Medical Journal*
BMW   The Bible in the Modern World
BN   *Biblische Notizen*
BTA   Bible and Theology in Africa
BTB   *Biblical Theology Bulletin*
BWANT   Beiträge zur Wissenschaft vom Alten und Neuen Testament
BWAT   Beiträge zur Wissenschaft vom Alten Testament
BZ   *Biblische Zeitschrift*
BZAW   Beihefte zur Zeitschrift für die alttestamentliche Wissenschaft
CAD   *The Assyrian Dictionary of the Oriental Institute of the University of Chicago.* Edited by Martha T. Roth. 21 vols. Chicago: The Oriental Institute, 1956–2009.
CBQ   *Catholic Biblical Quarterly*
CC   Continental Commentaries
CDC   Centers for Disease Control
CHANE   Culture and History of the Ancient Near East
COS   *The Context of Scripture.* Edited by W. W. Hallo. 3 vols. Leiden: Brill, 1997–2002.
CurBS   *Currents in Research: Biblical Studies*
DSM   *Diagnostic and Statistical Manual of Mental Disorders*
Dtr   Deuteronomistic (History; Writer)
EdF   Erträge der Forschung
EncJud   *Encyclopaedia Judaica.* 2nd edition. Edited by F. Skolnik. 22 vols. Detroit: Macmillan, 2007.
ErIsr   *Eretz-Israel*
FAT   Forschungen zum Alten Testament
FCB   Feminist Companion to the Bible
FEMA   Federal Emergency Management Agency
FOTL   Forms of the Old Testament Literature
FRLANT   Forschungen zur Religion und Literatur des Alten und Neuen Testaments
GCT   Gender, Culture, Theory
HALOT   Koehler, L., W. Baumgartner, and J. J. Stamm, *The Hebrew and Aramaic Lexicon of the Old Testament.* Translated and edited under the supervision of M. E. J. Richardson. 4 vols. Leiden: Brill, 1994–1999.

HALOT-SE	Koehler, L., W. Baumgartner, and J. J. Stamm, *The Hebrew and Aramaic Lexicon of the Old Testament*. Study edition. Translated and edited under the supervision of M. E. J. Richardson. 2 vols. Leiden: Brill, 2001.
HAR	*Hebrew Annual Review*
HBT	*Horizons in Biblical Theology*
HCOT	Historical Commentary on the Old Testament
Hen	*Henoch*
HSM	Harvard Semitic Monographs
HUCA	*Hebrew Union College Annual*
HUD	Department of Housing and Urban Development
IBC	Interpretation: A Bible Commentary for Teaching and Preaching
ICC	International Critical Commentary
IDP	Internally Displaced Person
IEJ	*Israel Exploration Journal*
Int	*Interpretation*
JAMA	*Journal of the American Medical Association*
JBL	*Journal of Biblical Literature*
JHS	*Journal of Hebrew Scriptures*
JHNES	Johns Hopkins Near Eastern Studies
JNES	*Journal of Near Eastern Studies*
JPT	*Journal of Pastoral Theoloy*
JRA	*Journal of Religion in Africa*
JSJSup	Supplements to the Journal for the Study of Judaism
JSOT	*Journal for the Study of the Old Testament*
JSOTSup	Journal for the Study of the Old Testament: Supplement Series
JSS	*Journal of Semitic Studies*
JTS	*Journal of Theological Studies*
KAI	*Kanaanäische und aramäische Inschriften*. H. Donner and W. Röllig. 2d ed. Wiesbaden: Harrassowitz, 1966–1969.
KAT	Kommentar zum Alten Testament
LAI	Library of Ancient Israel
LHBOTS	Library of Hebrew Bible/Old Testament Studies
LSJ	Liddell, H. G., R. Scott, H. S. Jones, *A Greek-English Lexicon*. 9th ed. with revised supplement. Oxford: Oxford University Press, 1996.
MMWR	*Morbidity and Mortality Weekly Report*

NEAEHL   Stern, Ephraim, ed. *The New Encyclopedia of Archaeo-
              logical Excavations in the Holy Land.* 4 vols. New York:
              Simon & Schuster, 1993.
NBBC   New Beacon Bible Commentary
NCB   New Century Bible
NEA   *Near Eastern Archaeology*
NIB   *The New Interpreter's Bible.* 13 vols. Nashville: Abingdon,
              1994–2004.
NICOT   New International Commentary on the Old Testament
NIDOTTE   *New International Dictionary of Old Testament Theology
              and Exegesis.* Edited by W. A. VanGemeren. 5 vols. Grand
              Rapids: Zondervan, 1997.
NRSV   New Revised Standard Version
OBO   Orbis biblicus et orientalis
OBT   Overtures to Biblical Theology
OTL   Old Testament Library
OTM   Oxford Theological Monographs
OTS   Old Testament Studies
PEQ   *Palestine Exploration Quarterly*
PNAS   *Proceedings of the Israeli National Academy of Sciences*
Proof   *Prooftexts: A Journal of Jewish Literary History*
PRSt   *Perspectives in Religious Studies*
PTSD   Post-Traumatic Stress Disorder
Qad   *Qadmoniot*
RANE   Records of the Ancient Near East
RB   *Revue biblique*
RevExp   *Review and Expositor*
RIMA   The Royal Inscriptions of Mesopotamia, Assyrian Periods
RSV   Revised Standard Version
SAA   State Archives of Assyria
SAHL   Studies in the Archaeology and History of the Levant
SBLABS   Society of Biblical Literature Archaeology and Biblical
              Studies
SBLAcBib   Society of Biblical Literature Academia Biblica
SBLAIL   Society of Biblical Literature Ancient Israel and Its Litera-
              ture
SBLBAC   Society of Biblical Literature The Bible and American
              Culture
SBLDS   Society of Biblical Literature Dissertation Series

SBLEJL	Society of Biblical Literature Early Judaism and Its Literature
SBLMS	Society of Biblical Literature Monograph Series
SBLRBS	Society of Biblical Literature Resources for Biblical Study
SBLStBL	Society of Biblical Literature Studies in Biblical Literature
SBLSymS	Society of Biblical Literature Symposium Series
SBLWAW	Society of Biblical Literature Writings from the Ancient World
SemeiaSt	Semeia Studies
SHANE	Studies in the History of the Ancient Near East
SHBC	Smyth & Helwys Bible Commentaries
SJOT	*Scandinavian Journal of the Old Testament*
SO	Symbolae osloenses
STAR	Studies in Theology and Religion
STW	Suhrkamp Taschenbuch Wissenschaft
SWBA	Social World of Biblical Antiquity
TA	*Tel Aviv*
Transeu	*Transeuphratène*
TynBul	*Tyndale Bulletin*
UF	*Ugarit-Forschungen*
UNFPA	United Nations Population Fund
UNHCR	United Nations High Commissioner for Refugees
VAB	Vorderasiatische Bibliothek
VT	*Vetus Testamentum*
VTSup	Supplements to Vetus Testamentum
YOSR	Yale Oriental Series, Researches
ZAW	*Zeitschrift für die alttestamentliche Wissenschaft*
ZDPV	*Zeitschrift des deutschen Palästina-Vereins*

Foreword

Rainer Albertz

The present volume, which emerged from the ongoing discussion of the SBL Warfare in Ancient Israel Section, is a remarkable enterprise. It intends to examine the exile of ancient Israel and Judah in conjunction with the general phenomenon of exile in its various ancient and modern manifestations. This enterprise, which tries to include a wide range of interdisciplinary and comparative explorations, promises to be fertile for producing both a better understanding of ancient Israel's exilic experience and a higher sensitivity toward modern refugees and migrant peoples through the means of biblical texts.

The main problem for a proper understanding of the exile of ancient Israel and Judah is the paucity and fragmented character of our historical sources. Nearly nothing is known about the deportees from the northern kingdom during the years 732-720 B.C.E. This is likewise true for the deportees from the southern kingdom of the year 701 B.C.E., who are mentioned in Sennacherib's inscription and illustrated on his famous Lachish relief, but not mentioned in the Bible and therefore almost forgotten. A little bit more is known about the Judean deportees under Neo-Babylonian rule (597, 587, and 582 B.C.E.), and our knowledge of their further destiny in Babylonia will perhaps increase once the cuneiform tablets from āl-Yaḫūdu and Našar have been published. But since this so-called "Babylonian exile" constitutes a lacuna in the Bible's historiographical texts, we know only some events of its beginning and its possible end, while the period in between is nearly unknown. Fortunately, archaeology can provide some estimations of how life went on in Judah during this period, although they are still disputed. Because of this historical uncertainty, some recent scholars have regarded the Babylonian exile as a mere myth and downplayed its significance. Yet the fact that this event provoked a sudden increase of biblical literature in Babylonia and Judah that tried

to cope with the catastrophe and find an orientation for a new beginning speaks against these recent assessments. The present volume, which
includes results from sociological, anthropological, and psychological
studies on the one hand and from cross-cultural migration, diaspora, and
disaster studies on the other hand, may not only help to fill some of the
gaps of our historical knowledge, but also provide us with the possibility
of a more realistic estimation of the economic, social, psychological, and
theological difficulties with which Judeans—both in exile and remaining
in the land—probably had to cope.

A deepened understanding of biblical texts that emerged from the
crisis of exile can also provide Jews and Christians with a higher degree
of sensitivity for dealing with comparable catastrophes and migration or
refugee problems in modern societies. Those who have learned to analyze
the hardship of the Judean exiles may be better prepared to distance themselves from their native societies and to sympathize with foreign refugees
or dislocated people. The present volume shows some impressive examples in this direction. When I wrote *Israel in Exile*, I did not consider that
I am a refugee of World War II. I have no memory of my home in Upper
Silesia, now Poland, from which my mother carried me westward when
I was one and a half years old. Nonetheless, the sense of being a refugee
that I felt throughout my life wherever I lived in Germany could have provided a little more sensitivity toward the severe psychological and religious
problems that the Babylonian exiles must have experienced, although they
seem to have been economically and legally integrated in a manner similar
to what I experienced. I had never thought of this conjunction before, but
the present volume revealed to me this possible hermeneutical predisposition.

A book that promotes such an interdisciplinary approach must cope
with many methodological questions. Archaeology, historiography, sociology, and psychology all have their own methods; their results have to be
brought into contact very carefully. Cross-cultural comparisons between
ancient and modern societies always need some critical reflection about
whether phenomena are truly comparable or can only be compared on
a rather abstract or metaphorical level, if at all. Daniel L. Smith-Christopher's contribution in this volume correctly states that "we all make social
and psychological assumptions when we interpret historical texts." An
advantage of this book is that it endeavors to explicate and clarify these
unconscious assumptions and reflect upon their appropriateness. I thank
the editors, Brad E. Kelle, Frank Ritchel Ames, and Jacob L. Wright, for

tackling this demanding project and hope that it will amplify our knowledge on the phenomenon of exile in all of its dimensions and foster the methodological reflections of such an explicitly interdisciplinary approach.

Rainer Albertz
Münster, June 2011

An Interdisciplinary Approach to the Exile

Brad E. Kelle

From the beginning to end, the Hebrew Bible may be considered as a series of narratives, tales, and depictions of deportation and displacement. ... the Bible is the great metanarrative of diaspora.[1]

Is it not true that the views of exile in literature and, moreover, in religion obscure what is truly horrendous: that exile is irremediably secular and unbearably historical; that it is produced by human beings for other human beings; and that, like death but without death's ultimate mercy, it has torn millions of people from the nourishment of tradition, family and geography?[2]

This article serves as both an introduction to the collection of essays that follows and an analysis of a particular facet of the past, present, and potentially future study of the Babylonian exile. Much has changed over the last three decades in the study of the exile. Since the late 1960s, scholars have often asserted that the exilic era (ca. 586–539 B.C.E.) was the primary formative time for much of the biblical literature, constituting the period during which a large portion of the material in the Hebrew Bible either came into being or received its most formative editorial shaping.[3] Even so,

---

1. Gregory Lee Cuéllar, *Voices of Marginality: Exile and Return in Second Isaiah 40–55 and the Mexican Immigrant Experience* (American University Studies Series 7; Theology and Religion 271; New York: Lang, 2008), 1.

2. Edward Said, "Reflections on Exile," in *Out There: Marginalization and Contemporary Cultures* (ed. Russell Ferguson et al.; New York: The New Museum of Contemporary Art; Cambridge: MIT Press, 1990), 358.

3. As a recent example, Rainer Albertz (*Israel in Exile: The History and Literature of the Sixth Century B.C.E.* [SBLSBL 3; Atlanta: Society of Biblical Literature, 2003], ix) proposes that "approximately half of the material" in the Hebrew Bible originated or received substantial formation during the exilic period.

most modern histories of ancient Israel written before the last three decades virtually ignored this era in their detailed reconstructions of Israel's past, providing only a one-dimensional or underdeveloped examination.[4] Since the 1980s, however, the study of the Babylonian exile has undergone a renaissance, with a significant increase in interest paid and critical issues considered, as well as new approaches to and reconstructions of the exile in its historical, social, and literary aspects.[5] A host of major studies of the history and literature of the exilic period have been published in the last three decades,[6] and by the end of the 1990s Daniel Smith-Christopher could remark, "Among the many historical-critical issues surrounding

---

4. To a large extent, this neglect may stem from the Hebrew Bible, which for all intents and purposes passes over this period as little more than an unfortunate parenthesis in the ongoing story of Israel, a story that proceeds almost directly from the destruction of Jerusalem to the return of exiled groups and the rebuilding of the temple. See discussion in Megan Bishop Moore and Brad E. Kelle, *Biblical History and Israel's Past: The Changing Study of the Bible and History* (Grand Rapids: Eerdmans, 2011), 334–95.

5. Recent scholarship has featured the pursuit of several questions, in particular: (1) how best to study the exile as both a literary element of the biblical story and a possible historical reality of Judean history; (2) how best to relate the Hebrew Bible's representations of exile(s) with historical realities in Israel's past; and (3) how best to conceive the historical period of the early sixth century B.C.E. in the Levant on its own terms, alongside (or irrespective) of the Hebrew Bible's association of the period with "exile."

6. E.g., Daniel L. Smith, *Religion of the Landless: The Social Context of the Babylonian Exile* (Bloomington, Ind.: Meyer-Stone, 1989); Hans M. Barstad, *The Myth of the Empty Land: A Study in the History and Archaeology of Judah During the "Exilic" Period* (SO 28; Oslo: Scandinavian University Press, 1996); Daniel L. Smith-Christopher, *A Biblical Theology of Exile* (OBT; Minneapolis: Fortress, 2002); Albertz, *Israel in Exile*; Oded Lipschits and Joseph Blenkinsopp, eds., *Judah and the Judeans in the Neo-Babylonian Period* (Winona Lake, Ind.: Eisenbrauns, 2003); Oded Lipschits, *The Fall and Rise of Jerusalem: Judah under Babylonian Rule* (Winona Lake, Ind.: Eisenbrauns, 2005); Jörn Kiefer, *Exil und Diaspora: Begrifflichkeit und Deutungen im antiken Judentum und in der hebräischen Bibel* (ABG 19; Leipzig: Evangelische Verlagsanstalt, 2005); Jill Middlemas, *The Templeless Age: An Introduction to the History, Literature, and Theology of the "Exile"* (Louisville: Westminster John Knox, 2007); Bob Becking et al., *From Babylon to Eternity: The Exile Remembered and Constructed in Text and Tradition* (London: Equinox, 2009); Ehud Ben Zvi and Christoph Levin, eds., *The Concept of the Exile in Ancient Israel and Its Historical Contexts* (BZAW 404; Berlin: de Gruyter, 2010); John J. Ahn, *Exile as Forced Migrations: A Sociological, Literary, and Theological Approach on the Displacement and Resettlement of the Southern Kingdom of Judah* (BZAW 417; Berlin: de Gruyter, 2011).

the study of the Hebrew Bible, the changing perspectives and assessment of the Babylonian Exile over the course of the twentieth century ought to be cited as one of the debates most impressive for dramatic swings of opinion and perspective."[7] The impact of these developments has not been limited to historical study. For many interpreters, the developments have elevated exile into a defining concept for conceptualizing the whole of the Hebrew Bible, the social dynamics and identity of ancient Israel, and the experiences of contemporary social and ethnic communities in a variety of modern settings—a notion expressed well by the quotation from Gregory Lee Cuéllar at the head of this essay.

Against this backdrop, the present article attempts to identify more clearly the nature of the changes that have occurred in the study of the exile over the last three decades and to propose that these changes point to specific ways in which future study of the exile—both as a part of the biblical literature and as a historical reality in Judah's history—should be undertaken.[8] To anticipate the conclusion: scholarship since the 1980s reveals a shift to consider the exile more broadly, not simply as an event in Judean history, but as a phenomenon (or set of related phenomena) that occurs in both ancient and modern settings and possesses sociological, anthropological, and psychological (not just military and political) dimensions at the heart of its realities and representations. These developments in exilic scholarship—and the insights they have yielded thus far—suggest that the most appropriate and fruitful future study of the exile must be thoroughly interdisciplinary in nature, making increased use of even broader interdisciplinary perspectives than have yet been employed, and expanding the boundaries of phenomenological comparison for Judah's exile(s) to include even more wide-ranging chronological, geographical, and cultural contexts of both the ancient and modern world. This article—and the essays within this volume—strive to demonstrate that such an analysis, while at points seemingly far afield from the traditional interests of biblical interpreters and Israelite historians, can provide scholars with new insights by recontextualizing Judah's exile as part of larger sociological, anthropological, and psychological phenomena of the

---

7. Daniel L. Smith-Christopher, "Reassessing the Historical and Sociological Impact of the Babylonian Exile (597/587–539 BCE)," in *Exile: Old Testament, Jewish, and Christian Conceptions* (ed. James M. Scott; JSJSup 56; Leiden: Brill, 1997), 7.

8. Significant portions of this discussion are drawn from my chapter on exile in Moore and Kelle, *Biblical History and Israel's Past*, 334–95.

past and present, and can thereby potentially overcome methodological dead ends that have plagued previous analyses.

1. The Changing Study of the Exile since the 1980s

1.1. Approaches to the Exile Before the 1980s

The scholarly study of the exile in the last three decades has featured a series of changes that share certain characteristics, especially when compared with previous analyses. Prior to the 1980s, scholarship tended to investigate the exile primarily as an event, with special focus on political and military aspects and/or the impact of the exile on the development of Israelite religious institutions, beliefs, and practices. Historians offered only brief assessments of the nature of the exile and typically paid no attention to the people and circumstances in the land of Judah between 586 and 539 B.C.E.[9] In short, the exile constituted an event that was significant, but narrow in scope.

The way that earlier scholars assessed the available sources for the Babylonian exile played a significant role in the development of this perspective. Past interpreters worked with a limited and fragmentary collection of relevant sources—a situation that remains unchanged today.[10] For instance, unlike the preceding eras of Israel's past, the Hebrew Bible's main historiographical texts contain no historical narrative that ostensibly covers the period of the exile. While scholars have often suggested that other kinds of biblical texts such as Ezekiel, Lamentations, and Daniel may provide indirect information, 2 Kgs 25 (see also Jer 39; 52) reports the destruction of Jerusalem and the essential emptying of the land of Judah, with only the poorest people left behind. The description in 2 Chr 36:17-21 goes further and depicts the land as rendered barren for seventy

---

9. E.g., John Bright, *A History of Israel* (3rd ed.; Westminster Aids to the Study of Scripture; Philadelphia: Westminster, 1989 [orig. 1959]), 344–46; J. Maxwell Miller and John H. Hayes, *A History of Ancient Israel and Judah* (2nd ed.; Louisville: Westminster John Knox, 2006), 479–97; J. Alberto Soggin, *A History of Israel: From the Beginnings to the Bar Kochba Revolt, AD 135* (London: SCM, 1985), 255. Perhaps as a noteworthy example of the prevalence of this treatment of the exile, one may note that the *ABD*, a standard, comprehensive reference work on biblical backgrounds published in 1992, does not include an individual entry for exile.

10. See the article by Bob Becking ("A Fragmented History of the Exile") in this volume, which stresses the fragmented nature of the available sources for the era.

years. Many scholarly reconstructions before the 1980s seemed to follow the lead of the biblical texts and gave the impression that the history of Judah temporarily ceased after 586 B.C.E., as the land of Judah sat virtually uninhabited and the exilic group in Babylonia simply marked time until their return to Judah, as told in the narratives of Ezra and Nehemiah.[11] Most comprehensive histories of Israel—even those written throughout the 1980s—jumped quickly from the collapse of Jerusalem to a few general comments about the life of the community in Babylonia to the return of Persian-period settlers to Judah.

Similarly, earlier scholars tended to handle the limited extrabiblical data for the exile in particular ways that led to the narrow perspective described above. The main archaeological data, for example, consists of evidence for destruction at major cities in Judah (e.g., Lachish, Ramat Raḥel, Beth-shemesh) during the final years of the kingdom (597–581 B.C.E.), with some data related to rural settlements and other elements of Judean culture such as certain house and tomb types. For many interpreters throughout the twentieth century, these archaeological findings seemed to reinforce the Hebrew Bible's presentation of a severe devastation and lack of significant resettlement in Judah throughout the mid-sixth century B.C.E.[12] Additionally, the majority of the extrabiblical texts that pertain to Judah and the Judeans bear directly only upon the historical events between 597 and 581 B.C.E.[13] The remainder of the relevant texts come from outside of Judah and are restricted in scope, speak only indirectly

---

11. Note that even the most descriptive biblical texts (2 Kgs 24–25; Jer 32–43; 52) taken together cover only a limited span of time (ca. 597–581 B.C.E.), leaving most of the exilic era unaddressed.

12. For the classic example of these ways of working with the archaeological sources, see William F. Albright, *The Archaeology of Palestine* (Baltimore: Penguin, 1949). More recently, see Ephraim Stern, *The Assyrian, Babylonian, and Persian Periods, 732–332 bce* (vol. 2 of *Archaeology of the Land of the Bible*; ABRL; New York: Doubleday, 2001), and Avraham Faust, "Social and Cultural Changes in Judah During the 6th Century BCE and Their Implications for Our Understanding of the Nature of the Neo-Babylonian Period," *UF* 36 (2004): 157–76.

13. E.g., the Babylonian Chronicle, Hebrew ostraca from Lachish and Arad, and the Egyptian Rylands IX papyrus. See Jean-Jacques Glassner, *Mesopotamian Chronicles* (SBLWAW 19; Atlanta: Society of Biblical Literature, 2004); *COS* 3.42:78–81, 3.43:81–85; Lester L. Grabbe, *Ancient Israel: What Do We Know and How Do We Know It?* (New York: T&T Clark, 2007), 190; Miller and Hayes, *History of Ancient Israel and Judah*, 441.

about the Judeans, or are removed chronologically and culturally from Judah and its people during the sixth century B.C.E.[14] Even so, scholars before the 1980s typically used these sources by creatively extrapolating and combining data that could then be applied by analogy to broader or earlier circumstances.[15] Overall, interpreters employed the archaeological and textual sources in conjunction with the Hebrew Bible's historiographical narratives for the primary purpose of reconstructing either the specific historical events of the final years of the southern kingdom or the nature of life in Babylonian exile for those deported from Judah.

The upshot of these ways of working with the available sources was that scholarship before the late 1980s generally approached the exile within the Hebrew Bible's literary and ideological framework. At the most basic level, scholars treated the exile as an event that called for the majority of attention to be paid to the reconstruction of the political dynamics and military happenings of the years leading up to and immediately following 586 B.C.E. Additionally, common interpretations of two other areas of inquiry concerning the exile became established in conjunction with this overall perspective by the second half of the twentieth century. First, working from the usual treatment of texts such as Jeremiah and Ezekiel, as well as the Babylonian assignment lists and *Murašû* documents, scholarship reached the consensus that life for those exiles in Babylonia was a reasonably tolerable experience in which the deportees maintained a decent level of freedom and even prosperity. Contrary to the impression one may have of life after deportation as marked by deprivation, oppression, or imprisonment, exile, it has been argued, was a relatively benign existence under circumstances in which most Judeans were able to maintain their communal identity and even participate in the kinds of social and economic activities suggested by Jer 29 and the *Murašû* archive. Although living as a subject population of outsiders, the Judean deportees were able to main-

---

14. E.g., cuneiform "assignment/ration lists" mentioning Jehoiachin and his sons (*ANET*, 308), cuneiform tablets containing the name "city of Judah/the Judahites" located near *Našar* in the area of Borsippa and Babylon and dating to 572–473 B.C.E. (see Grabbe, *Ancient Israel*, 190), tablets from the *Murašû* firm in Nippur that mention persons with Jewish names (ca. 464–404 B.C.E.) (see Matthew W. Stolper, *Entrepeneurs and Empire: The Murašû Archive, the Murašû Firm, and the Persian Rule in Babylonia* [Uitgaven van het Nederlands Historisch-Archaeologisch Instituut te Istanbul 54; Leiden: Nederlands Historisch-Archaeologisch Instituut te Istanbul, 1985]).

15. E.g., see Miller and Hayes, *History of Ancient Israel and Judah*, 491–97.

tain a cohesive family life, some self-government, and participation in economic and agricultural activities.[16] Second, scholars before the 1980s typically paid no attention to the people and circumstances in the land of Judah between 586 and 539 B.C.E., essentially reflecting the biblical picture of a virtually empty land. Their understanding was supplemented by the interpretation of archaeological excavations at major urban centers such as Lachish and Ramat Raḥel, and led to a common view that little meaningful population and few significant social structures or religious elements existed in the land of Judah after what was taken to be a severe devastation in the 580s B.C.E.[17] Even if most interpreters recognized that the territory of Judah was not completely devoid of inhabitants, the majority seemed to embrace, even if only implicitly, what has come to be called the "myth of the empty land."[18] They reckoned the remaining Judean population's number and significance to be minimal for the future shape of Israel's cultural and faith traditions.

1.2. Approaches to the Exile since the 1980s

Since the late 1980s, the most significant changes in the study of the exile have concerned the nature of the deportees' life in Babylonia and the character and conditions of life in the land of Judah between 586 and 539 B.C.E.

---

16. For expressions of this consensus view of life in exile in major historical treatments, see Bright, *History of Israel*, 345–46; Peter R. Ackroyd, *Exile and Restoration: A Study of Hebrew Thought of the Sixth Century B.C.* (OTL; Philadelphia: Westminster, 1968), 32; Bustenay Oded, "Judah and the Exile," in *Israelite and Judaean History* (ed. John H. Hayes and J. Maxwell Miller; OTL; Philadelphia: Westminster, 1977), 483; Ralph W. Klein, *Israel in Exile: A Theological Interpretation* (OBT; Philadelphia: Fortress, 1979), 3; Soggin, *History of Israel*, 253; Miller and Hayes, *History of Ancient Israel and Judah*, 493–94. Note, for instance, Martin Noth's assertion that "the exiles were not 'prisoners' but … were able to move about freely in their daily life, but were presumably compelled to render compulsory labor service" (Martin Noth, *The History of Israel* [trans. S. Godman; 2nd ed.; London: Black, 1960], 296). For a recent articulation of this older view, see Bob Becking, "In Babylon: The Exile as Historical (Re) Construction," in Becking et al., *From Babylon to Eternity*, 4–33.

17. E.g., Albright, *Archaeology*, 142; Bright, *History of Israel*, 343–44; Oded, "Judah and the Exile," 478–79; Soggin, *History of Israel*, 256.

18. The label seems to derive from Robert P. Carroll, "The Myth of the Empty Land," *Semeia* 59 (1992): 79–93. See also Barstad, *Myth of the Empty Land*.

As noted above, my interest here is to identify more specifically the nature of these changes and their implications for future study.

The first step toward new approaches in these areas was the critical reassessment of the character and proper use of the sources that had been known and employed in reconstructions of the exilic period throughout the twentieth century.[19] In the mid- to late 1980s, for example, scholars shifted their attention from the Hebrew Bible's historiographical accounts (e.g., 2 Kgs 24–25; Jer 39; 52) to the "indirect" biblical sources such as Ezekiel and Lamentations. While these nonhistoriographical texts had often played a supplementary role in the study of the exile, some interpreters moved them to the center of attention and emphasized an interdisciplinary reading, interpreting them through the lens of sociological, anthropological, and psychological data related to the experience of peoples who had undergone forced displacement, migration, or exile in both the ancient and modern worlds.[20] Likewise, scholarship took increasing account of methodological problems with the use of the extrabiblical textual sources from which historians had extrapolated and hypothesized the relatively benign picture of the exiles' existence in Babylonia. New emphasis fell on the fragmented and indirect nature of the sources, especially the chronological, geographical, and social distance of many of these sources from the actual circumstances of the Judeans in the early to mid-sixth century B.C.E., and the ways that earlier historians had combined evidence from sources that come from different chronological and geographical contexts.[21] Even the relevant archaeological sources underwent signifi-

---

19. In contrast to the changing study of other eras in Israel's past (e.g., the time of the Iron Age kingdoms of Israel and Judah), different evaluations of the sources for the exilic era did not result from dramatic new discoveries or new publications of sources. Rather, scholars reexamined the sources for the exilic period that had been known throughout the twentieth century and the ways they had been used by modern interpreters.

20. See especially Smith, *Religion of the Landless*; and Smith-Christopher, *Biblical Theology of Exile*—both discussed below.

21. See once again Smith, *Religion of the Landless*; and Smith-Christopher, *Biblical Theology of Exile*. The Jehoiachin ration texts and the "city of Judah" texts, for instance, share the general time period of the sixth century B.C.E. but provide no insight into the conditions of those outside the royal family nor explicit information concerning the status of those named in the Judean settlements. The "city of Judah" texts themselves come from a time span that covers 572–473 B.C.E. Similarly, the *Murašû* archive texts relate the activities of Jewish persons nearly a century after the time of the Babylonian

cant reassessment, especially as scholars looked beyond the indications of destruction and abandonment at major urban sites to evidence from rural towns and villages, and made sustained use of new methods related to archaeological surveys and demographic analysis (i.e., study of broad surface surveys, settlement patterns, levels of population growth, economic activity, and social structure).[22]

The scholarly investigations of the exile that began with the reassessment of the available sources eventually resulted in substantial new reconstructions.[23] In many cases, which will not be described in detail here, new reconstructions dealt with the specific historical details related to the political and military events of the final years of the kingdom of Judah between 597 and 581 B.C.E. In this area, which has traditionally been the focus of historical scholarship on the exilic era, scholars have continued to investigate the same basic issues as their pre-1980s predecessors—Judah's rebellions against Babylonia, the two captures of Jerusalem, the number of Judean deportees and deportations, the rise and fall of Gedaliah's administration[24]—with new proposals in recent works mainly constituting nuances or slight revisions of traditional views.

More substantial changes have occurred, however, in the two major areas of inquiry noted above. Changes in the first area, which deals with the nature of the Judean exiles' life in Babylonia, have revisited the prior consensus view that Judean life in exile was a relatively benign existence under the circumstances, allowing reasonable participation in the social and economic life of the empire.[25] By first questioning the relevance of

---

deportation from Jerusalem and under the control of the subsequent Persian Empire (ca. 464–404 B.C.E.).

22. See Barstad, *Myth of the Empty Land*; Lipschits, *Fall and Rise*; Israel Finkelstein and Yitzhak Magen, eds., *Archaeological Survey of the Hill Country of Benjamin* [Hebrew] (Jerusalem: Israel Antiquities Authority, 1993).

23. The following section draws upon my discussion of the exilic era in Moore and Kelle, *Biblical History and Israel's Past*, 334–95.

24. See the survey of reconstructions in Gary N. Knoppers, "The Historical Study of the Monarchy: Developments and Detours," in *The Face of Old Testament Studies: A Survey of Contemporary Approaches* (ed. David W. Baker and Bill T. Arnold; Grand Rapids: Eerdmans, 1999), 230–33.

25. Some dissenting voices that emphasized the onerous physical, social, and psychological experiences of disenfranchisement and destabilization did occasionally appear before the late twentieth century. See, e.g., J. M. Wilkie, "Nabonidus and the Later Jewish Exiles," *JTS* 2 (1951): 36–44.

the sources used in this traditional reconstruction (see above), interpreters in the last three decades have raised significant challenges to the consensus and produced new reconstructions that view the Judean experience of exile as a severe and traumatic personal, social, and psychological crisis that entailed suffering and domination and led the deportees into destabilizing recalibrations of their social and theological identity. Among all the factors involved in the development of these new perspectives, we may note especially the role played by an increase in interdisciplinary approaches. Smith-Christopher led the way in this regard with a series of works that used a cross-disciplinary approach to reexamine the traditional sources and broaden the comparative data on the Judean exile.[26] The first move here was to consider the available literary sources and the Judean experience of deportation through the lens of contemporary sociological, anthropological, and psychological studies of refugees, immigrants, displacement, forced migration, and trauma theory. The experiences of exiles, refugees, and immigrants in a variety of ancient and modern settings provides, it was argued, different data that illuminate different social realities, psychological experiences, and literary representations of the Judeans in the Neo-Babylonian setting.

Smith-Christopher's *Religion of the Landless* (1989), for example, examined how displaced and/or subordinated groups such as Japanese-Americans enduring internment in World War 2 and black South Afri-

---

26. See especially, Smith, *Religion of the Landless*; Smith-Christopher, *Biblical Theology of Exile*; Smith-Christopher, "Reassessing," 7–36. Of course, the type of interdisciplinary analysis (especially sociological and anthropological study of biblical texts) used by Smith-Christopher had found a place in the discipline before the 1980s, but the last three decades have seen the sustained application of those methods to the study of the exile. For others who have followed Smith-Christopher's lead in the use of sociological, anthropological, and psychological analysis for the experience of the Judean exile, see, e.g., Kathleen M. O'Connor, "Lamenting Back to Life," *Int* 62 (2008): 34–47; idem, "Reclaiming Jeremiah's Violence," in *Aesthetics of Violence in the Prophets* (ed. Julia M. O'Brien and Chris Franke; New York: T&T Clark, 2010), 37–49; Brad E. Kelle, "Dealing with the Trauma of Defeat: The Rhetoric of the Devastation and Rejuvenation of Nature in Ezekiel," *JBL* 128 (2009): 469–90; David G. Garber Jr., "Traumatizing Ezekiel, the Exilic Prophet," in *From Genesis to Apocalyptic Vision* (ed. J. Harold Ellens and Wayne G. Rollins; vol. 2 of *Psychology and the Bible: A New Way to Read the Scriptures;* Praeger Perspectives on Psychology, Religion, and Spirituality; Westport, Conn.: Praeger, 2004), 215–35; Nancy R. Bowen, *Ezekiel* (AOTC; Nashville: Abingdon, 2010).

cans and "Zionist" churches in the midst of apartheid reveal certain social values and practices, as well as coping strategies.[27] This data, he argued, reveals that dislocation and forced migration such as that experienced by the ancient Judeans had a traumatic nature that has been overlooked by historical scholarship, including the realities of deprivation, subjugation, and lack of access to resources and power. Seen through this kind of comparative sociological exegesis, even the biblical texts (e.g., Second Isaiah, Lamentations, Ezekiel) that had often been taken as indirect sources for the consensus view of life in exile point to a situation characterized by oppression—certainly not a benign experience.[28] These and other texts also indicate that the Judean exiles engaged in some of the same coping strategies commonly found among displaced communities, including the adaptation of patterns of ritual practice (such as the cultic legislation of the priestly passages in the Pentateuch, commonly dated to the exilic era) and the development of new folklore literature and heroes (such the "hero stories" of Daniel and Joseph).[29] From these starting points, Smith-Christopher and others have expanded the use of interdisciplinary and comparative analysis of exiles, deportees, and immigrants and examined ancient Judean realities and representations in light of contemporary fields such as forced migration, refugee studies, disaster studies, and trauma theory.[30] As a result, one now increasingly finds a reconstruction of life in Babylonian exile that emphasizes its traumatic physical, social, psychological, and theological impact as a "catastrophic and transformative event" and

---

27. Other comparisons included slave societies and religious responses in pre–Civil War U.S. and the forced movement of the Bikini islanders by the U.S. in the 1950s. See Smith, *Religion of the Landless*, 10–11.

28. See Smith-Christopher, "Reassessing," 24–33.

29. Smith, *Religion of the Landless*, 10–11.

30. E.g., Smith-Christopher was one of the first to use trauma theory and postcolonialist psychology to study the Judean exile. See Smith-Christopher, "Ezekiel on Fanon's Couch: A Postcolonialist Dialogue with David Halperin's *Seeking Ezekiel*," in *Peace and Justice Shall Embrace: Power and Theopolitics in the Bible: Essays in Honor of Millard Lind* (ed. Ted Grimsrud and Loren L. Johns; Telford, Penn.: Pandora, 1999), 108–44. Over the last two decades, this type of sociological exegesis has led to the production of books that attempt a full reconstruction of the social history of the Judean exile. See, for example, Rainer Kessler, *The Social History of Ancient Israel: An Introduction* (Minneapolis: Fortress, 2008).

thereby gives what Smith-Christopher calls a "more realistic picture of the trauma of the Babylonian Exile."[31]

Not all studies produced in the last three decades accept in full this new reconstruction, which has been especially slow to find its way into comprehensive history of Israel volumes. Yet the field overall now features increased attention to sociological, anthropological, and psychological considerations associated with viewing the exile in terms of broader analytical categories such as forced migration, conflict-induced displacement, and diaspora studies. The first full-length study devoted explicitly to this approach, John J. Ahn's *Exile as Forced Migrations*, appeared in 2011 and points to the shift by which new consideration of the realities of deportation and displacement has led scholars to reconfigure the basic categories in which they evaluate this era of Israel's past.[32]

The second area of inquiry into the exile—the constitution and character of life in the land of Judah between the destruction of Jerusalem in 586 B.C.E. and the settlement of the Persian province of Yehud after 539 B.C.E.— has seen even more dramatic changes in scholarship, especially since the 1990s. As mentioned previously, although most interpreters throughout the twentieth century acknowledged that the territory of Judah was not completely devoid of inhabitants after 586 B.C.E., the majority seemed to embrace, even if only implicitly, the notion of a functionally empty land in which the remaining population's significance was minimal for the future shape of Israel's cultural and faith traditions. The new approaches to the relevant archaeological sources described above, however, have led to a radical increase in attention to this topic in recent years. The use of new methods related to archaeological surveys and demographic analysis and new attention to evidence from rural towns and villages (rather than just destruction and abandonment evidence at major urban sites) have produced new historical reconstructions of life in the land that move significantly away from older conceptions.[33]

---

31. Smith-Christopher, *Biblical Theology of Exile*, 32; idem, "Reassessing," 10.

32. Ahn, *Exile as Forced Migrations*.

33. The new perspectives in the last three decades pick up on some voices from older scholarship that had previously argued for a minimal degree of population and culture disruption and a high degree of continued importance for the people remaining in Judah after the destruction of Jerusalem. See, for example, Martin Noth, *Überlieferungsgeschichtliche Studien: Die sammlenden und bearbeiten Geschichtswerke im Alten Testament* (2nd ed.; Tübingen: Niemeyer, 1957), 110 n. 1. For the English

The primary changes from earlier to more recent studies revolve around the degree of Judah's devastation and the significance of its remaining population. The data generated by the new methods and sources lead a number of scholars to propose that the deportations and destructions in sixth-century Judah occurred on a small scale overall, with the majority of the population remaining in the land, and that much of the longstanding Judean culture and religion continued virtually uninterrupted after the destruction of Jerusalem. The most significant type of analysis suggesting this emerging view consists of new interpretations of the archaeological data, with a special focus on the level of continuous occupation in various urban and rural areas around Judah.[34] Studies such as Robert Carroll's "Myth of the Empty Land" (1992), Hans Barstad's *The Myth of the Empty Land* (1996), and Oded Lipschits's *The Fall and Rise of Jerusalem* (2005), although differing on some specific points, provide analyses that conclude there is little evidence for widespread destruction or severe disruption of life outside of Jerusalem and its immediate vicinity or dependent areas. Beginning from the ambiguity within the biblical descriptions, these treatments distinguish between sites that show clear evidence of destruction (e.g., Jerusalem, Tell Beit Mirsim, Beth-shemesh, Lachish) and those that show signs of continued occupation and even growth, most notably, the Benjamin area north of Jerusalem (Mizpah, Ein-Gedi, Gibeon).[35] In addition to pottery evidence of unbroken material continuity,[36] surface surveys, settlement patterns, and demographic analyses lead these interpreters to conclude that a large percentage (perhaps 50 to 90 percent) of the Judean population remained in the land after 586 B.C.E.,[37] that Mizpah (Tell en-Naṣbeh) and other urban sites in the Benjamin region experi-

---

translation, see Martin Noth, *The Deuteronomistic History* (trans. Jane Doull et al.; JSOTSup 15; Sheffield: University of Sheffield Press, 1981). More recently, see Philip R. Davies, *The Origins of Biblical Israel* (LHBOTS 485; New York: T&T Clark, 2007).

34. For a full discussion, see Moore and Kelle, *Biblical History and Israel's Past*, 367–82.

35. Barstad, *Myth of the Empty Land*, 47–48.

36. See Lipschits, *Fall and Rise*, 192.

37. E.g., Lipschits (ibid., 270) suggests that Judah lost more than half of its population, although not all at once, yet still contained more than 40,000 people throughout the period. Other recent estimates propose higher figures. Albertz (*Israel in Exile*, 90), for instance, concludes that the deportees totaled only about 20,000 people, although he argues that the total people lost or killed through the entire Babylonian events may have equaled half the population, leaving about 40,000 people in the land.

enced planned development and population growth as new administrative centers for Judah, and that the sharp demographic and settlement decline after the Babylonian invasion was primarily limited to certain urban areas such as Jerusalem.[38] These reconstructions allow scholars to entertain the possibility that the seemingly continuous material culture was matched by continuity in cultural identity, social structures, and religious institutions. Current scholars may differ over the extent to which Judean political, social, and religious life continued in essentially the same way as it had previously,[39] but they share the emerging conclusion that a significant percentage of the population remained in the land after 586 B.C.E. and that this group continued elements of the long-established Judean society and religion that remained significant for the development of Judah's culture and faith.[40]

---

38. See Lipschits, *Fall and Rise*, 69, 217–45. For a primary survey used in several of the newer perspectives on the era, see Finkelstein and Magen, *Archaeological Survey*. Lipschits's specific demographic analysis illustrates some of the nuances present in the current conversation on this new reconstruction. He argues that Jerusalem and its immediate vicinity underwent an 89 percent decline in settlement during the sixth century B.C.E. and the peripheral areas of the kingdom in the Shephelah and Negeb, as well as the southern highlands below Hebron, suffered an 83 percent and 60 percent drop in settled areas, respectively, as a collateral effect of the central system's collapse (ibid., 217–30). By contrast, the major sites in the Benjamin region show evidence of full settlement continuity and growth, and the more rural area south of Jerusalem between Bethlehem and Hebron shows a significant enough settlement to suggest that that this territory is the place where the Babylonians resettled many of the people who remained in the land (ibid., 104, 237–45).

39. E.g., compare Barstad, *Myth of the Empty Land*, 42 ("life in Judah after 586 in all probability before long went on very much in the same way that it had done before the catastrophe") and Lipschits, *Fall and Rise*, 188.

40. Scholarship since the 1990s has also included some efforts to rearticulate the more traditional interpretation of a severe destruction and effectively empty or insignificant land. Many of these efforts come from archaeologists who see evidence for a significant gap in the population and material culture in Judah throughout the sixth century B.C.E. See especially Ephraim Stern, *Assyrian, Babylonian, and Persian Periods*; idem, "The Babylonian Gap: The Archaeological Reality," *JSOT* 28 (2004): 273–77; Bustenay Oded, "Where Is the 'Myth of the Empty Land' To Be Found? History Versus Myth," in Lipschits and Blenkinsopp, *Judah and the Judeans in the Neo-Babylonian Period*, 55–74; David S. Vanderhooft, *The Neo-Babylonian Empire and Babylon in the Latter Prophets* (HSM 59; Atlanta: Scholars Press, 1999); Faust, "Social and Cultural Changes," 157–76. While these more traditional reconstructions seem to be less nuanced in their evaluations and have fewer adherents, they indicate that the newer

Although the new reconstructions in these two areas of inquiry have attracted a significant number of followers, any talk of a consensus is premature.[41] To return to my first interest in this essay, however, the preceding survey allows one to identify more specifically the nature of the developments that have taken place in scholarship on the exile in the last three decades. First, the changes in the interpretation of the exile since the 1980s are predominantly interdisciplinary in character. An increase in cross-disciplinary approaches drawing especially from fields such as sociology, anthropology, and psychology stands behind many of the new reconstructions of both the nature of exile and the character of life in the land of Judah. These cross-disciplinary approaches feature an expanded range of vision that moves beyond a singular interest in politics, battles, and tactics to social, cultural, and human dimensions of the experience of deportation and displacement. On a broad level, this interdisciplinary character of the recent study of the exile represents the growth of seeds planted in the groundbreaking work of Susan Niditch on the study of war in general within ancient Israel and the Hebrew Bible.[42] As opposed to

---

interpretations of life in the land after 586 B.C.E. remain an emergent consensus, with significant dissenting voices that render the current scholarly conversation primarily an intra-archaeological debate. I have not detailed here another approach that has emerged in the wake of the changing evaluations since the 1980s. Some recent scholars undertake an ideological examination of the Hebrew Bible's concept of "exile" as a cultural myth or symbol created for particular socio-ideological purposes in the interest of certain groups in Judean society. The most accessible collection of such studies is Lester L. Grabbe, ed., *Leading Captivity Captive: "The Exile" as History and Ideology* (JSOTSup 278; Sheffield: Sheffield Academic Press, 1998).

41. Most discussions of life in the land after 586 B.C.E. have appeared in specific historical studies, and it remains to be seen how they will make their way into comprehensive histories of Israel and Judah. One of the first history volumes to incorporate elements of the newer reconstructions was Gösta Ahlström, *The History of Ancient Palestine* (JSOTSup 146; Sheffield: JSOT Press, 1993), 804–11. See also the revised edition of Miller and Hayes, *History of Ancient Israel and Judah*, 479–83, and the discussion in the more generally conservative Iain Provan, V. Philips Long, and Tremper Longman III, *A Biblical History of Israel* (Louisville: Westminster John Knox, 2003), 280–84. Some recent comprehensive studies of the exilic era also incorporate elements of the changes in the scholarly discussion. See Albertz, *Israel in Exile*, 90–96; Middlemas, *Templeless Age*, 16–18.

42. Susan Niditch, *War in the Hebrew Bible: A Study in the Ethics of Violence* (New York: Oxford University Press, 1993). A similar move toward social history in the study of war in the Hebrew Bible appears in T. R. Hobbs, *A Time for War: A Study of*

the often dominant trend of exploring warfare and its elements through the reconstruction of battles, weapons, tactics, and other logistics, Niditch appeals to a cross-disciplinary approach to ancient Israel's war practices and ideologies. Through this approach the biblical texts yield insight into social history, cultural maps, and general human experience. Seen in this way, warfare and its related experiences such as deportation and displacement are elements of social and cultural identity formation, and the proper study of such experiences demands an interdisciplinary methodology in which one must "immerse oneself in rich and complex debates among ethicists, political scientists, psychologists, anthropologists, biologists, and other students of war."[43]

On another level, the sustained use of interdisciplinary perspectives and the new insights that have resulted from them reveal that scholarship in the last few decades has increasingly approached the Babylonian exile not simply as an *event* in Judean history but as a *phenomenon* (or set of related phenomena) possessing sociological, anthropological, and psychological dimensions associated with the common human experiences of displacement, forced migration, and conflict-induced relocation from various times and settings. Recognition of the ways Judah's historical realities and the Hebrew Bible's literary representations share in the common experiences facing refugees, migrants, and other displaced peoples can illuminate them in new ways. When scholars attend to the widespread realities of exile and displacement for various peoples even in the modern period, they attain what Smith-Christopher calls a "wider lens," interpreting Judah's experience as another instance of the broader phenomenon.[44] As he states,

> Mass deportation is not itself an isolated or unique event in history, but, on the contrary, is a well-attested experience, whether on foot as the American Indian "Trail of Tears," or the tragically familiar historical image of train cars carrying Jews.[45]

Warfare in the Old Testament (Wilmington, Del.: Michael Glazier, 1989), which proposes that changes in Israelite social structure brought about changes in war practices and ideologies.

43. Niditch, *War in the Hebrew Bible*, 13.

44. Smith-Christopher, *Biblical Theology of Exile*, 29. For another example of the use of broader sociological and psychological dimensions to study the Babylonian exile, see Smith-Christopher, "Reassessing," 7–36.

45. Smith, *Religion of the Landless*, 69.

While the new interpretations do not claim that any of these instances of displacement precisely parallel the Judean exile, they identify in the instances a similar phenomenon with analogous experiences, patterns, and responses from a variety of social, cultural, ethnic, and historical contexts.[46]

The move to consider the exile not as a singular event but as a broader phenomenon with sociological, anthropological, and psychological dimensions connects to some longstanding observations within historical study. Historians have observed that the available sources do not allow one to identify a single "exile" with a clear beginning point, particularly given the multiple deportations that the Hebrew Bible associates with various Babylonian invasions in 597, 586, and 582 B.C.E. (2 Kgs 24–25), as well as Assyrian actions even earlier (e.g., 2 Kgs 17). The new evaluations of the people remaining in the land of Judah after the destruction of Jerusalem also connect with the longstanding debates over the nature and extent of any "return" to the land under the Persians and the realization that sources do not provide the exile with a clear ending point, or necessarily any definitive ending at all.[47] The significance of these longstanding factors simply became stronger when scholars like Smith-Christopher combined them with so-called "Fourth World" experiences and perspectives as a lens for the Judean exile—sociological and anthropological insights into migrants, refugees, and other displaced groups who lacked their own country and agency.[48] This connection, as well as the interdisciplinary investigations that have accompanied it, have helped to develop a conception of Judah's exile as "both a historical human disaster *and* a disaster that gave rise to a variety of social and religious responses with significant social and religious consequences," a phenomenon best understood in the terms of the "transhistorical conditions of diaspora."[49]

---

46. Ibid., 11, 69. For the broader phenomenon of forced migration, see Doreen Indra, ed., *Engendering Forced Migration: Theory and Practice* (New York: Berghahn, 1999). For a recent comprehensive attempt to apply the phenomenon of forced migration to the Judean exile, see Ahn, *Exile as Forced Migrations*.

47. See the discussion of the Persian period and the history of the so-called "return" from exile in Moore and Kelle, *Biblical History and Israel's Past*, 396–464.

48. Smith, *Religion of the Landless*, 8.

49. Smith-Christopher, *Biblical Theology of the Exile*, 6 (emphasis original). As a recent example of a treatment of the exile not simply as a historical event but as a cultural phenomenon and tradition that is repeatedly constructed, reinvented, and remembered, see Becking et al., *From Babylon to Eternity*.

Two recent studies of the history and literature of the exilic era—
Rainer Albertz's *Israel in Exile* and Jill Middlemas's *The Templeless Age*—
illustrate both the new reconstructions of the period and the interdisciplinary approaches and phenomenological perspective that gave rise to
them. Both works bear witness to a broader scholarly perspective on the
period as a whole, leading them to re-envision the era outside of the ideological categories of the biblical literature and beyond the scope of an
"event." For example, rather than characterizing the years between 586 and
539 B.C.E. simply as the "exile," effectively limiting interpretive attention
to circumstances and perspectives of the Babylonian deportees and their
descendants, these studies show a marked concern to discuss those years
under the broader designations of the "Neo-Babylonian period" or the
"Templeless Age" of Judah's past,[50] paying attention to the larger context
of Babylonian domination over the ancient Near East and its attendant
dynamics. Albertz and Middlemas then reframe their discussions of traditional historical issues for the exilic era (e.g., available sources, numbers of
deportees and deportations) by devoting significant space to the various
Judean groups who existed in both Judah and Egypt after the destruction
of Jerusalem. Thus, they expand the traditional focus on the Babylonian
deportees and stress the likely continuation of cultural, ritual, and literary
practices among others.[51] Additionally, rather than offering only a historical reconstruction of political and military events, Albertz and Middlemas
draw upon the interdisciplinary perspectives from anthropological, sociological, and psychological study, echoing the challenge made by Smith-
Christopher and others to the benign interpretation of the experience of
exile, and considering the human, psychological, and emotional challenges
involved.[52] These considerations lead them to structure their interpreta-

---

50. See especially Middlemas, *Templeless Age*, ix. Elsewhere she explains, "This
realignment in our terminology and conceptualization actually facilitates a more helpful assessment of the history and literature of the time. Exile implies an event and suggests nothing further about the period or what type of literature was generated. The
use of 'templeless' to define this age more accurately invites an understanding of the
diversity it entailed" (6). See also Albertz, *Israel in Exile*, 83. For similar moves, see the
designation of this era as the "Period of Babylonian Domination" in Miller and Hayes,
History of Ancient Israel and Judah, 478 (a designation that already appeared in the
work's first edition [1986]). Note also Middlemas's extension of the label "Templeless
Age" to cover the period from 586 to 515 B.C.E. (Middlemas, *Templeless Age*, 3–4).
51. Albertz, *Israel in Exile*, ix; Middlemas, *Templeless Age*, 16–22.
52. Albertz, *Israel in Exile*, 102–4; Middlemas, *Templeless Age*, 24.

tion of the various biblical texts associated with the exile in terms of the different conceptions of or reactions to the experience expressed by each text.[53] While these two recent works continue the use of many traditional perspectives and differ significantly from one another at various points, they exemplify a type of study that approaches the exile as a historical, social, and psychological phenomenon that generates a variety of human experiences and responses, many of which are represented by the Hebrew Bible's diverse literary traditions.

2. The Future Study of the Exile: Expanding Interdisciplinary and Comparative Explorations

The interdisciplinary and phenomenological nature of the changes that have occurred in the study of the exile over the last three decades, especially the dividends they have paid through new historical reconstructions and literary, theological, and social insights, point to some specific ways in which the most fruitful future study of the exile—both as a part of the biblical literature and as a historical reality in Judah's past—should proceed. This seems especially pressing since many of the new perspectives and reconstructions described above have not yet achieved the level of a new consensus nor appeared consistently in comprehensive histories of Israel. The following comments constitute only a gesture toward the kind of future study that recent developments suggest, rather than a comprehensive discussion. But they also form a theoretical framework for understanding the approach used in this volume, as well as the scope and content of the individual essays included herein.

2.1. Expanded Interdisciplinary Perspectives

At the most basic level, the developments sketched above suggest that future study of the exile should be decidedly, and even more broadly, cross-disciplinary in nature, continuing the trajectory that has emerged in scholarship since the late 1980s. The gains made in the last three decades indicate that future scholarship will benefit both by increasing the use of

---

53. For example, Middlemas (*Templeless Age*, ix) examines the literature and "thought" of the exilic period according to three reactions to the loss of the temple: (1) immediate reactions, (2) rationalization, and (3) recognition of restoration of divine commitment. See also Albertz, *Israel in Exile*, 2.

disciplines and methods that have already been brought to bear—especially following along with the developments occurring in those discreet fields of study—and by expanding the range of perspectives into even broader disciplines and methods. Such pursuit has the potential to fashion within biblical scholarship a working compendium of diverse interdisciplinary perspectives on the interpretation of the exile in Judean history and on the Hebrew Bible in relation to the various experiences of displacement and deportation from a broad range of times and settings. This development could also give biblical studies and its related fields a newfound significance for those seeking to deal with the realities of displacement and conflict-induced relocation for refugees in the modern world.

We have observed that the broad disciplines of sociology and anthropology have provided several fields of study that have already been significant for scholarship on the exile. The comparative research generated by these disciplines will likely lie at the heart of future and broader cross-disciplinary studies.[54] As a means of building upon the work already done, the particular fields of refugee studies and diaspora studies will likely continue to play the most pronounced role in future scholarship. The field of refugee (or forced migration) studies, for example, has developed significantly since the late 1980s, giving birth to major scholarly journals and focusing on comparative data related to the experiences of displaced and/or deported peoples and their repatriation in a wide variety of cultures and settings, both ancient and modern.[55] The field has paid particular attention to the larger social and human phenomenon of conflict-induced displacement, with an eye toward the various aspects that such an experience entails for the groups, cultures, and eco-systems involved. Questions include the ability of displaced persons to create sustainable identities in a new setting, as well as the different types of resettlements/returns (vol-

---

54. See especially Smith, *Religion of the Landless*; Smith-Christopher, *Biblical Theology of Exile*.

55. E.g., see the *Journal of Refugee Studies* and *Refugee Survey Quarterly*, as well as the recently established unit at the Annual Meeting of the Society of Biblical Literature entitled, "Exile (Forced Migrations) in Biblical Literature." For examples of the field, see Lynellyn Long and Ellen Oxfeld, eds., *Coming Home? Refugees, Migrants, and Those Who Stayed Behind* (Philadelphia: University of Pennsylvania Press, 2004); and B. S. Chimni, "From Resettlement to Involuntary Repatriation: Towards a Critical History of Durable Solutions to Refugee Problems," *Refugee Survey Quarterly* 23 (2004): 55–73. My comments on refugee studies here draw from the discussion in Moore and Kelle, *Biblical History and Israel's Past*, 388–90.

untary and imposed repatriation, "safe return," etc.) and their dynamics. Some recent works within biblical studies already make sustained use of refugee studies for reading literature associated with the exile. Fredrik Hägglund, for instance, employs insights from refugee studies to read Isa 52:13–53:12 as a discourse designed to deal with the dynamics of the repatriation of those Judeans coming to Judah from Babylonia after 539 B.C.E., urging those who had remained in the land to embrace the returnees as ones who had suffered on the remaining people's behalf.[56]

The related field of diaspora studies, which has already played a role in the new perspectives on the exile since the 1980s,[57] represents a broader and more developed field than refugee studies. Increased and sustained attention should benefit future study. The origins of the field lie in the study of the experience of the Jewish people in both ancient and modern settings, and that experience provided the traditional understandings of diaspora. But since the 1980s there has been increasing attention to the experiences of other groups (Armenians, Africans, etc.).[58] Over the last three decades, the field has achieved methodological and theoretical maturity. The traditional definition of "diaspora" as "the dispersion of a people from its original homeland," for example, has proved too general, and a host of major questions has come to occupy attention, including efforts to define "diaspora" and how it should be studied, to identify differences among types of dispersions, and to examine the variegated causes of diaspora in distinct settings and their implications (warfare, economics, geopolitical arrange-

---

56. Fredrik Hägglund, *Isaiah 53 in the Light of Homecoming after Exile* (FAT 2/31; Tübingen: Mohr Siebeck, 2008). For example, Hägglund examines the dynamics involved in the repatriation of returnees/refugees to Eritrea and Sarajevo. Some recent works proceed in the opposite direction, using the rhetoric of certain biblical texts to explore the experiences of contemporary refugees and exiles. See Cuéllar, *Voices of Marginality*.

57. E.g., see Smith, *Religion of the Landless*; Smith-Christopher, *Biblical Theology of Exile*.

58. For an overall survey of the field, see Kim D. Butler, "Defining Diaspora, Redefining a Discourse," *Diaspora* 10 (2001): 189–219. Note also the journal *Diaspora*, as well as Robin Cohen, *Global Diasporas: An Introduction* (Seattle: University of Washington Press, 1997) and Waltraud Kokot, Khachig Tölöyan, and Carolin Alfonso, eds., *Diaspora, Identity, and Religion: New Directions in Theory and Research* (New York: Routledge, 2004). For the Jewish Disaspora, see Daniel Boyarin and Jonathan Boyarin, "Diaspora: Generation and the Ground of Jewish Identity," *Critical Inquiry* 19 (1993): 693–725.

ments, etc.).[59] Already in the 1990s, some biblical scholars connected the Judean exile with diaspora studies, especially the field's emphasis on the dynamics of living simultaneously in different worlds while being at home in neither, and thus came to view exile/diaspora as a phenomenon and identity that could shape biblical and theological hermeneutics. Ancient Judean experiences and literature could provide insights into the dynamics of modern exiles and displacements, and contemporary experiences of diaspora could likewise provide themes, categories, and images for interpreting the Hebrew Bible and Judean history.[60] Fernando Segovia, for instance, employed the phenomena and experiences of diasporas and displacements such as those of ancient Judeans and modern Hispanic Americans to formulate a "diaspora hermeneutics"—a reading strategy and theology to serve in the ongoing struggle against colonization and for liberation. By emphasizing the dynamic of "otherness" in experiences of diaspora, Segovia developed a hermeneutic that attended to the multiple voices of persons, communities, and readers.[61]

The developments in the field of diaspora studies that have taken place in more recent years promise even further benefits for the future study of the Judean exile. For example, a recent listing of the defining aspects of the study of diasporas may provide fruitful categories for approaching the Babylonian exile: (1) reasons for and conditions of the dispersal, (2) relationship to the homeland, (3) relationship to the host lands, (4) interrelationship within communities of the diaspora, and (5) comparative studies

---

59. The quote is from Butler, "Defining Diaspora," 189. For discussion of new elements, see 189–90.

60. For examples of moves in both of these directions, compare Hägglund, *Isaiah 53* (which moves from contemporary experiences to the Hebrew Bible) and Cuéllar, *Voices of Marginality* (which uses the Hebrew Bible's depictions to address contemporary U.S.–Mexican immigration experiences).

61. Fernando F. Segovia, "Toward a Hermeneutics of the Diaspora: A Hermeneutics of Otherness and Engagement," in *Social Location and Biblical Interpretation in the United States* (vol. 1 of *Reading from This Place*; ed. Fernando F. Segovia and Mary Ann Tolbert; Minneapolis: Fortress, 1995), 57–73. This kind of hermeneutical appropriation of the notion of diaspora has also found a place in Jewish studies. Boyarin and Boyarin ("Diaspora," 693–725) propose the use of diaspora as a "theoretical and historical model" for the Jews, one that resists ethnic and political identities based on land control and national sovereignty and moves toward shared space and inclusivism (713).

of different diasporas.[62] The emerging concern within diaspora studies to distinguish between the elements and dynamics involved in forced and voluntary displacement may also offer scholars a broader consideration of the differing social processes and patterns that contributed to various Judeans being in exile, as well as the potentially different forms of existence therein.[63] Additionally, the conclusion among most current diaspora scholars that true "diaspora" entails the displacement of a people to at least two destinations (rather than simple deportation to a single new location) and the establishment of networks and interactions that join the different groups pushes the study of the Judean exile beyond the community in Babylonia to broader contexts such as Egypt and even forced population movements within the land of Judah.[64] Overall, the developing field of diaspora studies witnesses to a new emphasis on the widely varied nature of diaspora, moving beyond the singular notion of forced deportation (traditionally derived from a particular reading of the Jewish experience) to consider a wide range of types of diasporas and their corresponding elements.[65]

Some of the sociopolitical concerns of diaspora studies connect to elements of postcolonialism specifically associated with so-called "subaltern studies." This field's exploration of the dynamics and experiences that constitute the life of peoples ruled by physical or ideological coercion may illuminate the circumstances of nonelite, subordinated social groups such as refugees and exiles in a variety of settings.[66] The particular concern with

---

62. Butler, "Defining Diaspora," 195.

63. Ibid., 191–95.

64. Ibid., 192.

65. For an extended discussion aimed to broaden the understanding of diaspora beyond the Jewish paradigm to other "typologies," see Cohen, *Global Diasporas*. See also Said, "Reflections on Exile," 357–66.

66. The term "subaltern" is loosely derived from the Italian Marxist Antonio Gramsci, and the field originated with historians' efforts to write a new history of India that represents the points of view and experiences of the colonized and peasant classes and departs from the histories written from a colonialist and elitist perspective. See Ranajit Guha and Gayatri Chakravorty Spivak, eds., *Selected Subaltern Studies* (New York: Oxford University Press, 1988). The work of Gayatri Chakravorty Spivak has had a particularly strong influence on the development of the field. See, e.g., Gayatri Chakravorty Spivak, "Subaltern Studies: Deconstructing Historiography," in *The Spivak Reader: Selected Works of Gayatri Chakravorty Spivak* (ed. Donna Landry and Gerald Maclean; New York: Routledge, 1996), 203–36.

the political and social structures of subordination pushes historians of
the Babylonian exile to consider the material, economic, and ideological
dynamics that attend to marginalized groups in colonized or displaced settings. Moreover, subaltern scholars foreground the problematic issue of
sources by emphasizing that the available sources for writing subaltern
history are typically only those of the elite/colonizers.[67] The field's ongoing
discussion concerning how to deal with this reality may provide resources
for future historians of ancient Judah and lead them to formulate new
perspectives on the Babylonian texts commonly used for historical reconstruction of the exile, as well as on the Hebrew Bible as potentially the kind
of expression of subaltern perspectives not usually available from contexts
of subordination.[68]

The particular aspects of defeat and destruction involved in the experience of war-related exile and displacement point to other fields whose
interdisciplinary endeavors will likely benefit the future study of the
Babylonian exile. The field of "disaster studies" already contributed to
the new reconstructions that emerged in the late 1980s, providing sociological perspectives on the exile as a "crisis" and engaging the dynamics
associated with crises and disasters, as well as the cultural and religious
responses that often accompany them.[69] Contemporary disaster studies
now give increased attention to identifying a typology that distinguishes
among different kinds of disasters and responses, perhaps offering greater
interpretive specificity to the Judean experience.[70] The field of "trauma

---

67. See Spivak, "Subaltern Studies," 7–12.

68. E.g., Jacob L. Wright ("The Commemoration of Defeat and the Formation
of a Nation in the Hebrew Bible," *Proof* 29 [2009]: 433–72) has recently argued that
the Hebrew Bible literature underwent its most significant formulation in contexts of
defeat and represents the perspectives of those who have suffered victimization and
subordination.

69. See, e.g., Smith, *Religion of the Landless*, 49–50; and Smith-Christopher, *Biblical Theology of Exile*, 79–80. On disaster studies in general, see Michael Barkun, *Disaster and the Millennium* (New Haven: Yale University Press, 1974); Enrico L. Quarantelli, ed., *What Is Disaster? Perspectives on the Question* (London: Routledge, 1998);
and Havidán Rodríguez, Enrico L. Quarantelli, and Russell R. Dynes, eds., *Handbook of Disaster Research* (Handbooks of Sociology and Social Research; New York:
Springer, 2007).

70. From this perspective, one may identify the events of 586 B.C.E. more specifically as a group crisis caused by military actions and resulting in both forced and
voluntary relocation (Smith, *Religion of the Landless*, 53–54).

theory" from within the discipline of psychology provides a related means of focusing on the aspects of defeat and disaster involved in the exile that goes beyond the more common sociological and anthropological perspectives. As described above, this field played a significant role in the development of new reconstructions of life in exile beginning in the 1980s and seems poised to make new and extended contributions in the future.[71] When applied to the Babylonian exile, trauma theory highlights the typical human and psychological issues that are endemic to experiences of forced migration and displacement, centering on notions connected with the psychology of oppression and the dynamics of "posttraumatic stress disorder" (PTSD).[72]

The use of trauma studies within biblical scholarship has already developed to the point of providing an illuminating case study of the elements and results of this type of interdisciplinary approach. Several recent biblical scholars employ trauma theory to study the book of Ezekiel (and other biblical texts associated with the exile) and illuminate how it both reflects and addresses the traumatic psychological experiences involved in the Babylonian deportation. The recent commentary by Nancy Bowen, for example, provides the most developed attempt to engage Ezekiel through the lens of trauma. The typical personal and communal responses to traumatic stress provide a way to understand the prophet's bizarre behavior, sexually violent rhetoric, and depictions of nature's destruction.[73] Perspectives from trauma study also suggest that the book of Ezekiel represents the attempt to cope with trauma by establishing the framework of priestly holiness as an "alternative conceptual system to deal with the old shattered one."[74] Along with the rest of the methods mentioned in this section, such use of trauma theory illustrates the kind of broader and more sustained

---

71. Note the role played by trauma theory in Smith, *Religion of the Landless* and Smith-Christopher, *Biblical Theology of Exile*.

72. For these categories, see Smith-Christopher, "Ezekiel on Fanon's Couch," 108–44 and his use of Hussein A. Bulhan, *Frantz Fanon and the Psychology of Oppression* (PATH in Psychology; New York: Plenum, 1985) and Eduardo Duran and Bonnie Duran, *Native-American Postcolonial Psychology* (SUNY Series in Transpersonal and Humanistic Psychology; Albany: State University of New York Press, 1995).

73. Bowen, *Ezekiel*, xv–xvii. For similar recent approaches to Ezekiel, see Brad E. Kelle, *Ezekiel* (NBBC; Kansas City, Mo.: Beacon Hill Press, forthcoming); Kelle, "Dealing with the Trauma of Defeat," 469–90; Garber, "Traumatizing Ezekiel," 215–35.

74. Bowen, *Ezekiel*, xvii. For a similar approach to the book of Jeremiah, see O'Connor, "Lamenting," 34–47; and O'Connor, "Reclaiming," 37–49.

employment of interdisciplinary perspectives that can yield new insights for the future study of the exile.

2.2. A Broader Range of Comparisons

In addition to the need for broader interdisciplinary methods, the changes that have occurred in the study of the exile since the 1980s and the new insights they have produced suggest that future scholarship should expand the boundaries of phenomenological comparisons for the Babylonian exile to include realities and representations of exile and displacement from even more wide-ranging chronological, geographical, and cultural contexts of both the ancient and modern world. The discussion above detailed how the use of such a broader comparative range of vision has already played a significant role, as scholars' use of wide-ranging sociological and anthropological data led them to evaluate other evidence in new ways and to conceptualize the Judean exiles and their circumstances differently.[75] The simple recognition that experiences of forced migration, deportation, and displacement continue to endure and to arise in new contexts suggests that even modern experiences, though necessarily farther afield from those of the Judeans in the sixth-century B.C.E., may yield new insights into the social, cultural, psychological, and generally human dimensions that attend to all such realities and the responses they generate.[76]

There is, of course, a need for ongoing methodological rigor. Scholarship on the Hebrew Bible and Israelite/Judean history should maintain its moorings in the history, culture, and literature of the ancient Near East, and interpreters must not fall victim to a sloppy use of comparative data that ignores chronological and cultural particularities and simply maps the realities of one situation onto another. Nonetheless, expanding the comparisons for the Babylonian exile, some of which may seem far afield from the traditional interests of biblical scholars and historians, can provide new insights by recontextualizing Judah's exile as a part of ever-larger sociological, anthropological, and psychological phenomena of the past and present. I mention here only one contemporary work that provides a brief

---

75. See Smith, *Religion of the Landless*; Smith-Christopher, *Biblical Theology of Exile*; Smith-Christopher, "Reassessing," 7–36.

76. E.g., Cuéllar (*Voices of Marginality*, 5) cites a United Nations survey of "*International Labour Migration*" that estimates that eighty million people currently live as migrants in a country other than that of their origin.

case study. The recent examination of Isa 40–55 by Cuéllar approaches the expressions of "diasporic experiences" in Second Isaiah together with the experiences and expressions of contemporary Mexican immigrants in the United States.[77] The biblical and Mexican experiences and expressions, he argues, are mutually informing when viewed from the interdisciplinary perspective of diaspora studies. The exilic poems of Second Isaiah, for example, connect with the marginal voices of Mexican immigrants that appear in their *corridos* (ballads). Furthermore, he concludes that the Isaianic poems provide categories that readers can use to interpret a wide variety of contemporary instances of displacement and migration and their literary expressions, perhaps allowing the biblical literature to be a means toward the actual liberation of migrant peoples.[78]

The type of wide-ranging comparison represented by Cuéllar's work, which places Judah's realities and representations of exile into a broader context of similar war-related phenomena from multiple times and places, works at the level of phenomenological comparison rather than exact correspondence. The consideration of analogous realities can provide a deeper appreciation that allows interpreters to see more dimensions of the traditionally limited notion of "exile" that include family relationships and alterations, cultural changes, economic effects, and so on.[79] This might partly be accomplished simply by having the examination of other realities and representations of exiles, refugees, and immigrants stand beside studies of the Babylonian exile, allowing them to shape, even if only implicitly, the ways in which scholars conceptualize the various aspects of exile without necessarily drawing specific correlations. The present volume, which includes some essays that engage experiences and expressions of exile and displacement from wide-ranging settings such as the Jewish *Shoah* and the victimization of Sudanese children, may provide an example of the kind of compendium of resources that can suggest new vistas for scholars' approaches to the Babylonian exile.

---

77. Ibid., 2.

78. Ibid., 144–50.

79. See, for instance, Boyarin and Boyarin ("Diaspora," 693–725), who use the experiences and perspectives of those who continue to live in exile/diaspora to advocate that the most typical and fruitful response is to seek strategies for living faithfully in foreign settings rather than continually looking toward a return to a homeland.

3. The Orientation of the Present Volume

The volume for which this essay provides an introduction not only attempts to build upon the changes that have occurred in the study of the exile since the 1980s, but especially seeks to incorporate broader interdisciplinary perspectives and more wide-ranging comparisons that examine Judah's experiences in conjunction with the general phenomenon of exile and its various ancient and modern manifestations. The volume is organized according to methodological perspectives, including sections on archaeological, historical, sociological, psychological, and literary approaches to exile and its representations. Additionally, within many of these sections, the collection incorporates specific case studies of exile, deportation, and displacement drawn from settings as diverse as contemporary African-American experience and refugee crises in modern Sudan, some of which are written by scholars from outside the field of biblical studies. The result is a compendium of diverse interdisciplinary and comparative perspectives on the realities of exile in Judean history and their representations in the Hebrew Bible.

The first section includes essays that treat archaeological and historical aspects, illustrating different perspectives on the material evidence for the nature, causes, and effects of the exile and related experiences in Judah (Burke, "An Anthropological Model for the Investigation of the Archaeology of Refugees in Iron Age Judah and Its Environs"; Lipschits, "Shedding New Light on the Dark Years of the 'Exilic Period': New Studies, Further Elucidation, and Some Questions Regarding the Archaeology of Judah as an 'Empty Land'"; Faust, "Deportation and Demography in Sixth-Century B.C.E. Judah"; Wright, "The Deportation of Jerusalem's Wealth and the Demise of Native Sovereignty in the Book of Kings"). Marian Feldman's article complements these by examining the iconographic representations of the taking of booty ("Assyrian Representations of Booty and Tribute as a Self-Portrayal of Empire"). Bob Becking's essay concludes the section by providing an overall assessment of the available historical sources for the exile ("A Fragmented History of the Exile").

The essays in the second section of the volume build upon these elements to explore various sociological dimensions of the experience of exile. Frank Ames ("The Cascading Effects of Exile: From Diminished Resources to New Identities") examines the impact of exile upon constructions of family life, gender, and identity. Other essays expand the investigation beyond the boundaries of ancient Israel by drawing upon analyses of the devastation suffered by New Orleans during hurricane Katrina (Maier, "Lost Space and Revived Memory: From Jerusalem in 586 B.C.E. to New Orleans in 2009"; Homan, "Rebuilding That Wicked City: How the Destruction, Exile, and Restoration of New Orleans Elucidates Judah in the Sixth and Fifth Centuries B.C.E.") and the phenomenon of displacement among refugees in southern Sudan (Holton, "Imagining Hope and Redemption: A Salvation Narrative among the Displaced in Sudan"; Kamya, "The Impact of War on Children: The Psychology of Displacement and Exile").

The third section turns to the psychology of exile, including articles that center especially on the aspects of trauma involved in experiences of forced displacement. The essays begin with a focus on the Hebrew Bible and ancient Judean experiences (Smith-Christopher, "Reading War and Trauma: Suggestions Toward a Social-Psychological Exegesis of Exile and War in Biblical Texts"; Morrow, "Deuteronomy 7 in Postcolonial Perspective: Cultural Fragmentation and Renewal"; Carr, "Reading into the Gap: Refractions of Trauma in Israelite Prophecy"; Garber, "A Vocabulary of Trauma in the Exilic Writings"). The section also contains an inquiry into the possible healing of trauma with insights drawn from broader philosophical and psychological traditions (Rumfelt, "Reversing Fortune: War, Psychic Trauma, and the Promise of Narrative Repair").

The essays in the final section focus on the textual representations of exile in a variety of ancient and modern texts. Several articles examine Hebrew Bible texts related to exile (Balentine, "The Prose and Poetry of Exile"; Sharp, "Sites of Conflict: Textual Engagements of Dislocation and Diaspora in the Hebrew Bible"; Lemos, "The Emasculation of Exile: Hypermasculinity and Feminization in the Book of Ezekiel"), with some using broad interdisciplinary perspectives related to wide-ranging experiences and expressions (Meverden, "Daughter Zion as *Homo Sacer*: The Relationship of Exile, Lamentations, and Giorgio Agamben's Bare Life Figure"; Rambo, "Exiling in America: The American Myth and the Spectral Christ"). The volume's final essay constitutes the most explicit attempt to bring to bear upon the Judean exile the experiences and expressions of displacement that emerge from modern settings and literature far removed from sixth-century B.C.E. Judah. Nghana Lewis's examination of the dynamics of displacement in modern African-American experience and literature ("'There Was No Place for Cholly's Eyes to Go': [Black-on-Black] Crime and [Black Male] Displacement in Toni Morrison's *The Bluest Eye*") represents the kind of interdisciplinary dialogue partner that can place the Babylonian exile outside of the typical interpretive categories and into a broader comparative range of vision.

4. Conclusion

The conviction that the future study of the exile will benefit by being more thoroughly interdisciplinary and more expansive in its range of comparisons emerges from the changes that have taken place in the scholarship on the Babylonian exile in the last three decades and the new insights they have produced. While this kind of future inquiry will demand ongoing efforts to determine the appropriate methods and the proper employment of those methods, broader interdisciplinary and comparative approaches provide a way to overcome some of the methodological dead ends that have plagued previous study. In contrast to exilic study in the modern era, which characteristically has offered helpful but narrow treatments focused on textual interpretation and historical reconstruction, or has operated from one particular methodological perspective, the type of study envisaged here—and represented by the compendium of articles in this volume—goes beyond the conception of "the exile" that often limits interpretive attention to the circumstances of the Babylonian deportees in 586 B.C.E. and the ideological categories of the biblical presentation.

Broader interdisciplinary and comparative study recontextualizes the realities of exile within Israelite/Judean history and its representations in biblical and other literature by locating it more firmly as one manifestation of a sociological, anthropological, and psychological phenomenon known in diverse times and settings. In so doing, such study pushes historians and biblical interpreters to go beyond the simple reconstruction of events and offers new perspectives involving the social, psychological, and human dimensions of both the experiences and expressions of the exile. Seen in this way, aspects of the study of the Babylonian exile have a potential contribution to make to scholars working in a variety of disciplines and examining a range of past, present, and future instances of exile, displacement, and deportation. If future study is undertaken as suggested here, scholars from any field who aim to address adequately the kinds of far-reaching and complex dynamics that make "exile" in general an "unbearably historical" and ongoing "human" phenomenon—as Edward Said has stated[80]—

---

80. See Said, "Reflections on Exile," 358, quoted at the head of this essay.

will benefit from an interdisciplinary and comparative engagement with the Babylonian exile of Judah's past, the paradigmatic experience that has so often provided the categories of thinking about exile, displacement, and deportation throughout ancient and modern settings.

Bibliography

Ackroyd, Peter R. *Exile and Restoration: A Study of Hebrew Thought of the Sixth Century B.C.* OTL. Philadelphia: Westminster, 1968.

Ahlström, Gösta. *The History of Ancient Palestine.* JSOTSup 146. Sheffield: JSOT Press, 1993.

Ahn, John J. *Exile as Forced Migrations: A Sociological, Literary, and Theological Approach on the Displacement and Resettlement of the Southern Kingdom of Judah.* BZAW 417. Berlin: de Gruyter, 2011.

Albertz, Rainer. *Israel in Exile: The History and Literature of the Sixth Century B.C.E.* Translated by David Green. SBLSBL 3. Atlanta: Society of Biblical Literature, 2003.

Albright, William F. *The Archaeology of Palestine.* Baltimore: Penguin, 1949.

Barkun, Michael. *Disaster and the Millennium.* New Haven: Yale University Press, 1974.

Barstad, Hans M. *The Myth of the Empty Land: A Study in the History and Archaeology of Judah During the "Exilic" Period.* SO 28. Oslo: Scandinavian University Press, 1996.

Becking, Bob. "In Babylon: The Exile as Historical (Re)Construction." Pages 4–33 in *From Babylon to Eternity: The Exile Remembered and Constructed in Text and Tradition.* Edited by Bob Becking, Alex Cannegieter, Wilfred van de Poll, and Anne-Mareike Wetter. London: Equinox, 2009.

Becking, Bob, Alex Cannegieter, Wilfred van de Poll, and Anne-Mareike Wetter, eds. *From Babylon to Eternity: The Exile Remembered and Constructed in Text and Tradition.* London: Equinox, 2009.

Ben Zvi, Ehud, and Christoph Levin, eds. *The Concept of the Exile in Ancient Israel and Its Historical Contexts.* BZAW 404. Berlin: de Gruyter, 2010.

Bowen, Nancy R. *Ezekiel.* AOTC. Nashville: Abingdon, 2010.

Boyarin, Daniel, and Jonathan Boyarin. "Diaspora: Generation and the Ground of Jewish Identity." *Critical Inquiry* 19 (1993): 693–725.

Bright, John. *A History of Israel.* 3rd ed. Westminster Aids to the Study of Scripture. Philadelphia: Westminster, 1989.

Bulhan, Hussein A. *Frantz Fanon and the Psychology of Oppression.* PATH in Psychology. New York: Plenum, 1985.

Butler, Kim D. "Defining Diaspora, Redefining a Discourse." *Diaspora* 10 (2001): 189–219.

Carroll, Robert P. "The Myth of the Empty Land." *Semeia* 59 (1992): 79–93.

Chimni, B. S. "From Resettlement to Involuntary Repatriation: Towards a Critical History of Durable Solutions to Refugee Problems." *Refugee Survey Quarterly* 23 (2004): 55–73.

Cohen, Robin. *Global Diasporas: An Introduction.* Seattle: University of Washington Press, 1997.

Cuéllar, Gregory Lee. *Voices of Marginality: Exile and Return in Second Isaiah 40–55 and the Mexican Immigrant Experience.* American University Studies Series 7. Theology and Religion 271. New York: Lang, 2008.

Davies, Philip R. *The Origins of Biblical Israel.* LHBOTS 485. New York: T&T Clark, 2007.

Duran, Eduardo, and Bonnie Duran. *Native American Postcolonial Psychology.* SUNY Series in Transpersonal and Humanistic Psychology. Albany: State University of New York Press, 1995.

Faust, Avraham. "Social and Cultural Changes in Judah During the 6th Century BCE and Their Implications for Our Understanding of the Nature of the Neo-Babylonian Period." *UF* 36 (2004): 157–76.

Finkelstein, Israel, and Yitzhak Magen, eds. *Archaeological Survey of the Hill Country of Benjamin.* Jerusalem: Israel Antiquities Authority, 1993.

Garber, David G. Jr., "Traumatizing Ezekiel, the Exilic Prophet." Pages 215–35 in *From Genesis to Apocalyptic Vision.* Edited by J. Harold Ellens and Wayne G. Rollins. Vol. 2 of *Psychology and the Bible: A New Way to Read the Scriptures.* Praeger Perspectives on Psychology, Religion, and Spirituality. Westport, Conn.: Praeger, 2004.

Glassner, Jean-Jacques. *Mesopotamian Chronicles.* SBLWAW 19. Atlanta: Society of Biblical Literature, 2004.

Grabbe, Lester L. *Ancient Israel: What Do We Know and How Do We Know It?* New York: T&T Clark, 2007.

———, ed. *Leading Captivity Captive: "The Exile" as History and Ideology.* JSOTSup 278. Sheffield: Sheffield Academic Press, 1998.

Guha, Ranajit and Gayatri Chakravorty Spivak, eds. *Selected Subaltern Studies.* New York: Oxford University Press, 1988.

Hägglund, Fredrik. *Isaiah 53 in the Light of Homecoming after Exile.* FAT 2.31. Tübingen: Mohr Siebeck, 2008.

Hobbs, T. R. *A Time for War: A Study of Warfare in the Old Testament.* Wilmington, Del.: Michael Glazier, 1989.

Indra, Doreen, ed. *Engendering Forced Migration: Theory and Practice.* New York: Berghahn, 1999.

Kelle, Brad E. "Dealing with the Trauma of Defeat: The Rhetoric of the Devastation and Rejuvenation of Nature in Ezekiel." *JBL* 128 (2009): 469–90.

———. *Ezekiel.* NBBC. Kansas City, Mo.: Beacon Hill Press, forthcoming.

Kessler, Rainer. *The Social History of Ancient Israel: An Introduction.* Minneapolis: Fortress, 2008.

Kiefer, Jörn. *Exil und Diaspora: Begrifflichkeit und Deutungen im antiken Judentum und in der hebräischen Bibel.* ABG 19. Leipzig: Evangelische Verlagsanstalt, 2005.

Klein, Ralph W. *Israel in Exile: A Theological Interpretation*. OBT. Philadelphia: Fortress, 1979.

Knoppers, Gary N. "The Historical Study of the Monarchy: Developments and Detours." Pages 207–35 in *The Face of Old Testament Studies: A Survey of Contemporary Approaches*. Edited by David W. Baker and Bill T. Arnold. Grand Rapids: Eerdmans, 1999.

Kokot, Waltraud, Khachig Tölöyan, and Carolin Alfonso, eds. *Diaspora, Identity, and Religion: New Directions in Theory and Research*. New York: Routledge, 2004.

Lipschits, Oded. *The Fall and Rise of Jerusalem: Judah under Babylonian Rule*. Winona Lake, Ind.: Eisenbrauns, 2005.

Lipschits, Oded, and Joseph Blenkinsopp, eds. *Judah and the Judeans in the Neo-Babylonian Period*. Winona Lake, Ind.: Eisenbrauns, 2003.

Long, Lynellyn and Ellen Oxfeld, eds. *Coming Home? Refugees, Migrants, and Those Who Stayed Behind*. Philadelphia: University of Pennsylvania Press, 2004.

Middlemas, Jill. *The Templeless Age: An Introduction to the History, Literature, and Theology of the "Exile."* Louisville: Westminster John Knox, 2007.

Miller, J. Maxwell, and John H. Hayes. *A History of Ancient Israel and Judah*. 2nd ed. Louisville: Westminster John Knox, 2006.

Moore, Megan Bishop, and Brad E. Kelle. *Biblical History and Israel's Past: The Changing Study of the Bible and History*. Grand Rapids: Eerdmans, 2011.

Niditch, Susan. *War in the Hebrew Bible: A Study in the Ethics of Violence*. New York: Oxford University Press, 1993.

Noth, Martin. *The Deuteronomistic History*. Translated by Jane Doull et al. JSOTSup 15. Sheffield: University of Sheffield Press, 1981. Translation of *Überlieferungsgeschichtliche Studien: Die sammlenden und bearbeiten Geschichtswerke im Alten Testament*. 2nd ed. Tübingen: Niemeyer, 1957.

———. *The History of Israel*. Translated by S. Godman. 2nd ed. London: Black, 1960.

O'Connor, Kathleen M. "Lamenting Back to Life." *Int* 62 (2008): 34–47.

———. "Reclaiming Jeremiah's Violence." Pages 37–49 in *Aesthetics of Violence in the Prophets*. Edited by Julia M. O'Brien and Chris Franke. New York: T&T Clark, 2010.

Oded, Bustenay. "Judah and the Exile," Pages 435–88 in *Israelite and Judaean History*. Edited by John H. Hayes and J. Maxwell Miller. OTL. Philadelphia: Westminster, 1977.

———. "Where Is the 'Myth of the Empty Land' To Be Found? History Versus Myth." Pages 55–74 in *Judah and the Judeans in the Neo-Babylonian Period*. Edited by Oded Lipschits and Joseph Blenkinsopp. Winona Lake, Ind.: Eisenbrauns, 2003.

Provan, Iain, V. Philips Long, and Tremper Longman III. *A Biblical History of Israel*. Louisville: Westminster John Knox, 2003.

Quarantelli, Enrico L., ed. *What Is Disaster? Perspectives on the Question*. London: Routledge, 1998.

Rodríguez, Havidán, Enrico L. Quarantelli, and Russell R. Dynes, eds. *Handbook of Disaster Research*. Handbooks of Sociology and Social Research. New York: Springer, 2007.

Said, Edward. "Reflections on Exile." Pages 357–66 in *Out There: Marginalization and Contemporary Cultures*. Edited by Russell Ferguson, Martha Gever, Trinh T. Minh-ha, and Cornel West. New York: The New Museum of Contemporary Art. Cambridge: MIT Press, 1990.

Segovia, Fernando F. "Toward a Hermeneutics of the Diaspora: A Hermeneutics of Otherness and Engagement." Pages 57–73 in *Social Location and Biblical Interpretation in the United States*. Vol. 1 of *Reading from This Place*. Edited by Fernando F. Segovia and Mary Ann Tolbert. Minneapolis: Fortress, 1995.

Smith, Daniel L. *Religion of the Landless: The Social Context of the Babylonian Exile*. Bloomington, Ind.: Meyer-Stone, 1989.

Smith-Christopher, Daniel L. *A Biblical Theology of Exile*. OBT. Minneapolis: Fortress, 2002.

———. "Ezekiel on Fanon's Couch: A Postcolonialist Critique in Dialogue with David Halperin's *Seeking Ezekiel*." Pages 108–44 in *Peace and Justice Shall Embrace: Power and Theopolitics in the Bible: Essays in Honor of Millard Lind*. Edited by Ted Grimsrud and Loren L. Johns. Telford, Penn.: Pandora, 2000.

———. "Reassessing the Historical and Sociological Impact of the Babylonian Exile (597/587-539 BCE)." Pages 7–36 in *Exile: Old Testament, Jewish, and Christian Conceptions*. Edited by James M. Scott. JSJSup 56. Leiden: Brill, 1997.

Soggin, J. Alberto. *A History of Israel: From the Beginnings to the Bar Kochba Revolt, AD 135*. London: SCM, 1985.

Spivak, Gayatri Chakravorty. "Subaltern Studies: Deconstructing Historiography." Pages 203–36 in *The Spivak Reader: Selected Works of Gayatri Chakravorty Spivak*. Edited by Donna Landry and Gerald Maclean. New York: Routledge, 1996.

Stern, Ephraim. *The Assyrian, Babylonian, and Persian Periods, 732–332 BCE*. Vol. 2 of *Archaeology of the Land of the Bible*. ABRL. New York: Doubleday, 2001.

———. "The Babylonian Gap: The Archaeological Reality." *JSOT* 28 (2004): 273–77.

Stolper, Matthew W. *Entrepeneurs and Empire: The Murašû Archive, the Murašû Firm, and the Persian Rule in Babylonia*. Uitgaven van het Nederlands Historisch-Archaeologisch Instituut te Istanbul 54. Leiden: Nederlands Historisch-Archaeologisch Instituut te Istanbul, 1985.

Vanderhooft, David S. *The Neo-Babylonian Empire and Babylon in the Latter Prophets*. HSM 59. Atlanta: Scholars Press, 1999.

Wilkie, J. M. "Nabonidus and the Later Jewish Exiles." *JTS* 2 (1951): 36–44.

Wright, Jacob L. "The Commemoration of Defeat and the Formation of a Nation in the Hebrew Bible." *Proof* 29 (2009): 433–72.

Part 1
Archaeology and History

An Anthropological Model for the Investigation of the Archaeology of Refugees in Iron Age Judah and Its Environs

Aaron A. Burke

1. Introduction

In biblical studies the topic of exilic Jewish communities has received substantial scholarly attention, notably since the nineteenth century when great emphasis was first placed on the exile as a formative stage in the development of the Hebrew Bible.[1] Deportations have been viewed as prominent in the formation of exilic communities, and the role of self-exiled refugee communities is usually but a footnote in the biblical narrative. But deportation is only part of the story of exiled communities. Scholars have drawn attention to the divided nature of Israelite and Judean society, which reveals populations of different social, political, and religious loyalties. But the variety in refugee Judean communities remains an important line of inquiry that has yet to be explored. Alongside deportations are the forced migrations of refugees who to one degree or another chose to flee in the face of various situations. In what follows I will high-

---

1. I would like to thank Brad E. Kelle for the invitation to present a paper in the Warfare in Ancient Israel Section at the 2010 SBL Annual Meeting as well as Jacob Wright for his comments and suggestions. I am also grateful to William Schniedewind, Elizabeth Carter, Tammi Schneider, Moise Isaac, and Kyle Keimer for their insights during discussions of the topic throughout my research. This work represents the first in a series of articles on the archaeology of refugees in the ancient Near East. See also Aaron Alexander Burke, "Coping with the Effects of War: Refugees in the Levant during the Bronze and Iron Ages," in *Disaster and Relief Management in Ancient Israel, Egypt and the Ancient Near East* (ed. Angelika Berlejung, Ariel Bagg, and Gunnar Lehman; FAT; Tübingen: Mohr Siebeck, forthcoming).

light some of the biblical allusions to refugee populations from ancient
Israel and Judah and define the potential for archaeological inquiry concerning refugees.

A number of biblical texts expose both the existence and the plight
of refugees in the Levant during different periods and the importance of
the motif in biblical traditions, such as in the Exodus tradition and the
patriarchal narratives.[2] Notable examples of Iron Age refugee traditions
include the abandonment of Israelite towns in the wake of Saul's death
(1 Chr 10:7), the flight of David and his men from Saul into the wilderness (1 Sam 19–20), the flight of Hadad the Edomite (1 Kgs 11:14) and
Jeroboam son of Nebat (1 Kgs 11:40) to Egypt, Elijah's flight to the east (1
Kgs 17: 2–5), and Obadiah's hiding of refugee prophets in a cave (1 Kgs
18:4, 13). Such references reveal recurring trends in the refugee experience
in ancient Israel, such as the identification of places of refuge such as the
hills, the wilderness, Egypt, and caves. Refugee flight can be identified as
resulting from political, religious, and environmental phenomena. Later
references to Judean refugees in Ammon, Moab, and Edom in the book of
Jeremiah (Jer 40:11), and the flight to Egypt of surviving political refugees
from Judah after the Babylonian conquest (Jer 42–44; 2 Kgs 25:26) highlight the impact of Iron Age imperial conquests on Israelite and Judean
communities and the formation of refugee communities.

Despite the abundance of textual references to refugees in ancient
Israel and Judah, no study of the phenomenon of refugeeism in the Bible
has been undertaken. While it is certainly true that a number of factors
hamper the study of refugees in antiquity not only from a textual standpoint but also archaeologically, investigation of the subject reveals various
lines of evidence, especially in the archaeological record, that are suggestive of refugee phenomena and permit some attempt to reconstruct their
role. In this essay I begin by identifying a model that serves as a basis for
articulating an archaeology of refugees that can be employed to examine
the evidence for refugees in Judah and Philistia surrounding the fall of the
northern kingdom in 720 B.C.E.

---

2. Early biblical allusions to refugees include the patriarchal flights to Egypt (Gen
12:10; 46:1–7), the flight of the kings of Admah and Zeboiim into the hills (Gen 14:10),
and Jacob's flight from Laban (Gen 31:17–18).

2. The Characteristics of Refugee Phenomena

The anthropological study of refugees, which has focused predominantly on the work of NGOs in the Third World, has resulted in careful efforts to define refugee phenomena, and in the construction of at least one influential model that provides a useful starting place for historical and archaeological investigation of refugees in antiquity. To begin with, we may adopt for the sake of expediency and clarity the United Nations definition of a refugee:

> an individual who owing to well-founded fear of being persecuted for reasons of race, religion, nationality, membership of a particular social group or political opinion, is outside the country of his nationality and is unable, or owing to such fear, unwilling to avail himself of the protection of that country; or, who, not having a nationality or being outside the country of his former habitual residence as a result of such events, is unable or, owing to such fear, is unwilling to return to it.[3]

While this definition emphasizes the context for refugee formation, it provides no criteria for the identification of the characteristics of refugees that would permit their identification in, for example, archaeological contexts. In this regard the *Impoverishment Risks and Reconstruction* (IRR) model is particularly useful.[4] It was developed by Michael Cernea, who employed anthropological approaches to the study of refugees over the past several decades in an effort to identify strategies for the successful resettlement of refugees. It identifies universal risks encountered by refugees that must be addressed through relief efforts. These include *landlessness, joblessness, homelessness, marginalization, food insecurity, increased morbidity and mortality, loss of access to common property assets,* and *community disarticulation.*[5] These traits are also ordered to underscore, according to Cernea,

---

3. United Nations, "Article 1(2)," (U.N. Convention Relating to the Status of Refugees: United Nations, 1951).

4. See Michael M. Cernea, "Risks, Safeguards, and Reconstruction: A Model for Population Displacement and Resettlement," in *Risks and Reconstruction: Experiences of Resettlers and Refugees* (ed. Michael M. Cernea and Christopher McDowell; Washington, D.C.: World Bank, 2000), 11–55.

5. Ibid., 19–20, 22–35.

"how these subprocesses interlink, influence, and amplify each other."[6] Although the model was developed with different goals in mind,[7] I suggest that it can be employed, first, to articulate a number of archaeological phenomena associated with refugees and, second, to suggest the causal relationships between them.

To begin with, each of the phenomena associated with refugees identified by the IRR model can be correlated with a line of archaeological evidence; when taken together with other evidence, these can facilitate the identification of refugees in archaeological contexts:

(1) *Landlessness*, for example, may be reflected in the abandonment of sites or landscapes, rapid site growth in neighboring areas, and in settlement pattern shifts, in particular if they reveal abnormally rapid growth rates for entire regions or among particular settlements.

(2) *Joblessness* is likely to be reflected not in the absence of employment, which of course leaves no archaeological trace, but rather in the efforts made by polities to provide employment for newly arrived refugees on relatively short notice. Military conscription and mass labor projects are, for example, among the principal avenues for the employment of refugees, and one of the principal reasons that vassal treaties often stipulated the repatriation of refugees.[8]

(3) *Homelessness* will be reflected in the sudden growth of particular settlements, often extramurally at first, or even in whole quarters within settlements. By contrast with modern housing projects, most households in antiquity were built and maintained by their inhabitants and therefore are only distinct from other domestic structures insofar as the architectural traditions of the newcomers are themselves sufficiently distinct. However, all evidence in antiquity points to most refugee migrations being relatively short-distance phenomena (i.e., across the border to the nearest safe region). Thus, the sudden increase in domestic buildings at a site,

---

6. Michael M. Cernea and Christopher McDowell, "Reconstructing Resettlers' and Refugees' Livelihoods," in Cernea and McDowell, *Risks and Reconstruction*, 5.

7. Cernea suggest that the model has four functions: predictive, diagnostic, problem-resolution, and research. See Cernea, "Risks, Safeguards, and Reconstruction," 21–22.

8. Stipulations concerning refugees are a common theme, for example, among Hittite treaties where references to them are often translated in English as "fugitive," implying their outlaw status to certain political authorities; see Gary M. Beckman, *Hittite Diplomatic Texts* (2nd ed.; SBLWAW 7; Atlanta: Scholars Press, 1999).

often resulting in a substantial increase in the size of a settlement, would account for efforts to mitigate the homelessness facing refugees.

(4) *Marginalization* may be among the most difficult of the refugee's conditions to identify archaeologically. It may be reflected by the isolation of refugee communities to the periphery of settlements or within particular quarters within a settlement or, similarly, settlements in remote locations including caves. Otherwise, marginalization may be more readily detected in written sources such as inscriptions, which are often archaeological artifacts.

(5) *Food insecurity* is likely to be reflected by the adoption of a wide range of subsistence strategies that expose the inconsistency and unpredictability of food sources for refugees, including the intensification of agricultural production. The identification of these strategies requires, however, a high degree of resolution from archaeological excavations, and many earlier excavations simply cannot provide such data. Additionally, there may be evidence of malnutrition.

(6) *Increased morbidity and mortality* results from various types of stress such as food insecurity. The appearance of new cemeteries in areas previously unused at a period contemporaneous with the expansion of a settlement may corroborate the presence of refugees. As refugee studies indicate, given the varied economic levels of refugee communities it is impossible to predict the affluence of burials in these cemeteries. Furthermore, as with food insecurity, a certain quality of data collection is necessary to permit this type of assessment.

(7) *Access to common property assets*, such as "pastures, forested land, water bodies, burial grounds, quarries, and so on,"[9] would need to be replaced for refugees. Most notable among them is the establishment of new burial grounds and the need for access to new water resources and agricultural land, which may be reflected in the archaeological record. If unresolved, access to these needed resources can lead to increased social conflict, as Cernea notes.[10]

(8) *Community or social disarticulation* manifests itself in not only a breakdown in kinship bonds but also a loss of social capital, which can contribute to economic loss as well as social alienation. Albeit among the most challenging of the risks to identify archaeologically, indicators of

---

9. Cernea, "Risks, Safeguards, and Reconstruction," 29.
10. Ibid.

kinship relationships and markers of social integration may permit a dia-chronic investigation of the social disarticulation of households and kin groups.

3. Refugee Phenomena in Iron Age Judah

Having introduced the IRR model for addressing the challenges facing ref-ugees and the potential archaeological correlates of the risks facing refugees and responses to them, we may turn to a case study that permits consider-ation of these suggestions during the Iron Age. The context is well known to biblical historians and archaeologists, namely the tumultuous period of Assyria's direct military intervention in the southern Levant from the mid-eighth century, which resulted in the fall of the northern kingdom of Israel in 720 B.C.E. after three successive years of the siege of its capital, Samaria. In the book of Kings, we are informed of the vast numbers deported to other locales in the Assyrian empire (2 Kgs 17:6) and the introduction of a foreign population (2 Kgs 17:24). What is missing in the account, how-ever, is any reference to individuals and groups who escaped the Assyr-ian invasion, fleeing from Israel to neighboring Judah and places beyond, as would be in keeping with the biblical evidence noted earlier for other periods during which refugees, primarily in anticipation of an imminent military invasion, took refuge in neighboring lands.[11] Such individuals, at the least, included merchants and emissaries who were abroad at the time of the invasion, but also more substantial groups of individuals living near borders whose flight, even with short notice, was more feasible than that of many of their countrymen close to the targets of Assyrian military activity.

While the textual sources are silent about the flight of refugees from the northern kingdom, the issue of refugee flight was not unfamiliar to

---

11. Egon Kunz has classified the movements of refugees according to their loca-tion along a continuum between *anticipatory* movement (movement in anticipa-tion of crises) and *acute* movement (where there is little opportunity to prepare for flight and to arrange matters in advance). See Egon F. Kunz, "The Refugee in Flight: Kinetic Models and Forms of Displacement," *International Migration Review* 7 (1973): 131–32. There often is, unsurprisingly, a direct correlation between the wealth and social connections of groups and individuals and the nature of their movement. Those whose flight is anticipatory are often sufficiently well-connected socially to permit their acting upon their option to flee, while the less wealthy (agrarians, for example) would stand to lose most of their social and economic standing by fleeing and, there-fore, do so only as a last resort.

the Assyrians. The annals of Assyrian kings relate the pursuit of refugees into the mountains of Urartu, the mountains of Elam, and the marshes of southern Mesopotamia.[12] This scenario is evident in the archaeological record to date almost exclusively in Judah during the late eighth and seventh centuries B.C.E. Since the ordering of the eight principal risks outlined in the IRR model is intended to convey the interrelation of various risks experienced by refugees, the archeological data from Judah can be addressed in the same manner so as to illustrate the phenomena that provide direct archaeological correlates to the presence of refugees in Judah during this period.

The *landlessness* associated with the plight of refugees in the eighth century B.C.E. is nowhere more evident than in the abandonment of sites in the northern hill country of ancient Israel following Assyria's devastation of Samaria.[13] In addition to depletion of its population to warfare and the conquest of Samaria, some of its population undoubtedly fled Assyria's advance, most notably from areas along its southern border with Judah. Unfortunately, owing to the nature of refugee flight, the abandonment of a site rarely reveals the conditions under which it occurred, whether *acute* or *anticipatory*, to the extent that such conditions can be identified. It is only more rarely the case that anticipatory flight results in nearly emptied rooms, as at Zinçirli (the capital of the kingdom of Sam'al) in the seventh century, which according to its excavators appears to have been "evacuated in an orderly manner and swept clean."[14]

Magen Broshi was the first to suggest that Israelite and Judean refugees accounted for the rapid growth of Jerusalem in the late eighth century,[15]

---

12. See A. Kirk Grayson, *Assyrian Rulers of the Early First Millennium BC,* vol. 2: *(858–745 BC)* (RIMA 3; Toronto: University of Toronto Press, 1996). Flight into the mountains is mentioned on numerous occasions, including for the Aramean king of Bit-Adini who fled to a mountain stronghold (RIMA 3.102.6, 2:36), the Urartians (RIMA 3.102.8.41), and the Medes (RIMA 3.103.1). Others attempted flight across the Persian Gulf (RIMA 3.102.6, 2:36), and it is likely that during their flight they were defeated in the marshes of southern Mesopotamia.

13. Zertal cites a reduction from 238 to 95 sites in the wake of the Assyrian conquest (Adam Zertal, "Samaria [Region]: The Mount Manasseh [Northern Samarian Hills Survey]," *NEAEHL* 4:1311–12).

14. J. David Schloen and Amir S. Fink, "Searching for Ancient Sam'al: New Excavations at Zinçirli in Turkey," *NEA* 72 (2009): 214.

15. Magen Broshi, "The Expansion of Jerusalem in the Reigns of Hezekiah and Manasseh," *IEJ* 24 (1974): 21–26.

which is often cited as fourfold growth during a very short period. This observation rests on the fact that natural population growth cannot account for the expansion of Jerusalem westward from the City of David and Ophel. This in turn led to the conclusion that only refugees could account for such growth, and that they originated from Israel or Judah, or both.

The recent publication of Nahman Avigad's excavations of the Western Hill sustain this argument and corroborate the relative dates suggested,[16] namely the extramural resettlement of a substantial population on the hill to the west of the City of David that is identified with Stratum 9 (mid- to late eighth century B.C.E.).[17] Thereafter, this part of the site was enclosed by fortifications in Stratum 8, and while it is unclear exactly what span of time elapsed between these phases, as much as a decade is not unreasonable to assume. For Israelite refugees who did manage to flee south into Judah, I would argue that their *landlessness*, rather than a perception of Jerusalem's inviolability, served as the principal determinant in their choice of Jerusalem; their resettlement was, in fact, a pre-Zion theology phenomenon. In addition to the evidence concerning the belated construction of fortifications around the refugees of the Western Hill, the dense agricultural and horticultural claims over Judah's countryside in the late eighth century would have prevented refugee resettlement in new villages. They would also have required additional land for agriculture. Such an outright infringement on existing land use is likely not to have been tolerated by Judeans.

If the resettlement of Israelite refugees in Jerusalem did not resolve their landlessness, it did prevent their *homelessness* by addressing the *joblessness* of refugees. If refugees were responsible for the growth estimated

---

16. Nahman Avigad and Hillel Geva, "Area A—Stratigraphy and Architecture: Iron Age II Strata 9–7," in *Architecture and Stratigraphy: Areas A, W and X-2 Final Report* (vol. 1 of *Jewish Quarter Excavations in the Old City of Jerusalem Conducted by Nahman Avigad, 1969–1982;* ed. Hillel Geva; Jerusalem: Israel Exploration Society and the Institute of Archaeology, Hebrew University, 2000), 169–83.

17. See Nadav Na'aman, "When and How Did Jerusalem Become a Great City? The Rise of Jerusalem as Judah's Premier City in the Eighth–Seventh Centuries B.C.E.," *BASOR* 347 (2007): 21–56. Space does not permit a treatment of Na'aman's reassessment of Jerusalem in the eighth century. I disagree, however, with his conclusions concerning the stratigraphic sequence for the Western Hill and the conclusions that follow. I will evaluate elements of Na'aman's argument in a forthcoming work on the archaeology of refugees.

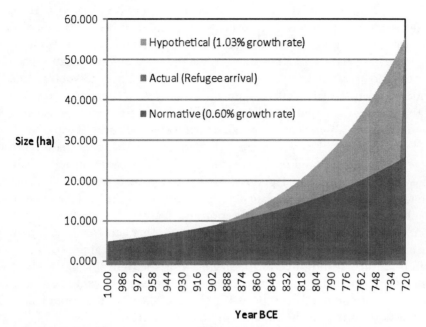

Figure 1. Projected growth rates for Jerusalem from ca. 1000 to 720 B.C.E. Lowest part of graph reflects the trend from the tenth century to start of ninth, which is taken as normative of growth at 0.6 percent. This trend is compared to the hypothetical trend required to achieve the attested size of Jerusalem by 720 B.C.E., which represents a significant departure from the earlier trend if it was sustained between ca. 900 and 720 B.C.E. The steep line on the right side of the chart reveals how the influx of refugees appears to have more than doubled Jerusalem's population within a short time ca. 720 B.C.E.

for Jerusalem in the late eighth century B.C.E., then it is arguable that more than half, at least 53 percent, of Jerusalem's population was comprised of refugees who arrived in the years leading up to 720 B.C.E. (fig. 1). This can be determined by comparing the growth trend for Jerusalem over the tenth century when the city gradually grew from the City of David to the Ophel. Taken as a normative growth rate for Jerusalem's population over the Iron Age (and it is important to remember that the city's growth appears to have been much more limited prior to the Iron II period), Jerusalem's attested size by the end of the eighth century vastly exceeds the anticipated growth of the city based on earlier trends. Thus the difference between the expected total settled area (the trend comprising the bottom half of the graph in fig. 1), and the actual settled area ca. 720 B.C.E. (comprising the top half of the graph) reveals that approximately 53 percent of Jerusalem's population arrived in the late eighth century. This arrival correlates with the expansion of Jerusalem onto the Western Hill (Stratum 9). Some have estimated a fourfold growth of Jerusalem by the late eighth century. To arrive at an estimate, however, it is necessary to subtract the prior population of Jerusalem, shown on the lower (normative) portion of the graph. The hypothetical trend (making no assumptions regarding the presence or absence of refugees), which traces the curve at top of both portions, consists of two separate growth rates: a 0.6 percent per annum growth rate during the first century of Israelite occupation of Jerusalem, followed by a more than 1 percent per annum growth rate that achieves the target population of the late eighth century B.C.E. In Iron Age demographics, however, the former is a more normative rate, while the latter exceeds normative growth rates and requires another explanation, namely, the arrival of an exogenous population over a short period at the end of the eighth century, as indicated by the steep line on the right side of the chart. Thus shortly after the arrival of refugees in the late eighth century, Jerusalem's citizens would only comprise 47 percent of the city's total population, despite accounting for the city's normative growth rate.

Two outcomes were theoretically possible, given the sudden influx of refugees. Either the refugees would become dependent upon the charity of the king to provide for their subsistence until they were naturally absorbed into the local economy, filling niches wherever possible, or work projects could be developed in which refugees would be employed while accomplishing important objectives for the state. Of these options the later is a more likely scenario. Indeed, a program of labor projects at the end of the eighth century can be identified that appears to account for Hezekiah's efforts to provide refugee assistance while benefitting from, if not exploiting, their labor.

The major labor projects include Hezekiah's tunnel and the so-called "Broad Wall" that encircled the Western Hill of Jerusalem (both mentioned in Isa 22:11 and Mic 3:9–10), which have already been the subject of much discussion in connection with Hezekiah's reign. These famous projects were therefore much more than a Judean strategy against future Assyrian attack, as is suggested by the many years that were undoubtedly required for digging the Siloam Tunnel, for example.[18] Rather, these proj-

---

18. Amihai Sneh, Ram Weinberger, and Eyal Shalev ("The Why, How, and When

ects can be viewed as shrewd efforts to provide gainful employment for Jerusalem's Israelite refugees, reminding us why refugees were viewed as *fugitives* by conquering powers, namely, their ability to aid and abet an enemy's resistance.[19]

The Siloam Tunnel inscription not only illustrates the nature of an eighth-century labor project, but also appears to identify the geographic origin of its author, and by extension the origin of some of Jerusalem's refugees, with the territory just north of Judah. In a recent article, Gary Rendsburg and William Schniedewind provide a new linguistic analysis of the Siloam Tunnel inscription, which was inscribed following the completion of this water system, presumably during Hezekiah's reign.[20] This inscription, which they argue is not a "royal display inscription," provides linguistic evidence of Israelian Hebrew, which includes features associated with Hebrew from as far south as Benjamin.[21] The inscription is thus an important piece of evidence in support of the identification of "refugees from southern Samaria who settled in Jerusalem," more precisely as those who came from "southern Ephraim and Benjamin," a region having experienced a considerable population disruption during this period.[22] The inscription's location and execution suggest that its Israelite author was likely a member of the workforce. Thus it supports identifying the tunnel's workers as refugees originating specifically in southern Israel and Benjamin. In this context we may observe that the Siloam Tunnel inscription also bears witness to the *marginalization* of those who inscribed it, a particularly difficult characteristic of the refugee experience to address from the archaeological record outside of epigraphic materials. Yet this can be suggested since the author felt no compunction to mention either the

---

of the Siloam Tunnel Reevaluated," *BASOR* 359 [2010]: 62) estimate at least four years for this project.

19. From as early as the Middle Bronze Age the Akkadian term for refugee was *munnabtu(m)*, which in many contexts is more appropriately translated as "fugitive," revealing that the identification of these individuals was largely dependent on the perspective of political authorities (*CAD* 10.2:203–5).

20. Gary A. Rendsburg and William M. Schniedewind, "The Siloam Tunnel Inscription: Historical and Linguistic Perspectives," *IEJ* 60 (2010): 188–203; see 2 Kgs 20:20; 2 Chr 32:3–4, 30; Isa 22:11.

21. The authors identify three substantive features of Israelian Hebrew: the form *re'ô* for "friend," the use of *hāyāt* rather than *hāyāh* for "there is," and *moza* for "spring" (ibid., 193).

22. Ibid.

king (who according to biblical writers commissioned the tunnel), a deity whom they may have regarded as their protector, or the name of the land in which they dwelt, that is, Judah. It might also be argued that the marginalization of refugees is evidenced by the peripheral and initially extramural settlement of refugees on Jerusalem's western side, thus correlating the location of refugee settlement with respect to previous settlement as a relative indicator of marginalization. But perhaps marginalization is best evidenced among Jerusalem's newest settlers in the construction of the "Broad Wall," which overran previously constructed houses on the Western Hill. Although arguments have been made on the basis of the strategic necessity of placing the wall in this location, it is still arguable that other solutions may have been possible for locating the wall. Elsewhere, marginalization is evident in cave occupation, which although not common during the late eighth and seventh centuries (Iron IIC) is still in evidence in the Judean Desert, as in later periods such as the Bar Kokhba revolt (132–135 c.e.).[23] Such occupation suggests a limited set of social relationships (i.e., relocation options) open to these refugees.

While the labor projects in Jerusalem may have contributed to short-term food security, they would not have alleviated long-term *food insecurity* and *loss of access to common property*, both of which would have been slow erosive processes in Jerusalem. To mitigate these underlying factors of refugee experience would have necessitated the intensification of agricultural production or the eventual resettlement of some of Jerusalem's population to other areas around Judah. There is now considerable evidence that new settlements were established in the Judean Desert during Hezekiah's reign in the late eighth century. Although assertions have been previously made about the absence of evidence for settlement in the region during the eighth century,[24] Andrew Vaughn's judicious examination of the evidence permits the identification of a number of previously disregarded

---

23. See Nahman Avigad, "The Expedition to the Judean Desert, 1960: Expedition A," *IEJ* 11 (1961): 6–10; idem, "The Expedition to the Judean Desert, 1960: Expedition A—Nahal David," *IEJ* 12 (1962): 169–83. This has also been suggested as the status of the author of the Khirbet Beit Leh inscriptions; see Simon B. Parker, "Graves, Caves, and Refugees: An Essay in Microhistory," *JSOT* 27 (2003): 259–88.

24. Israel Finkelstein, "The Archaeology of the Days of Manasseh," in *Scripture and Other Artifacts: Essays on the Bible and Archaeology in Honor of Philip J. King* (ed. Michael D. Coogan, J. Cheryl Exum, and Lawrence E. Stager; Louisville: Westminster John Knox, 1994), 175–76.

indicators of eighth- and early seventh-century settlement.[25] Among the indicators are *lmlk* jar handles that appear at nearly every one of the settlements he discusses. Furthermore, refinements to the chronology of Iron II ceramics reveal that ceramics from some settlements must be identified with the Lachish III assemblage and therefore suggest an earlier date in the eighth century B.C.E. for their initial occupation. This is true, for example, for sites within the Buqeiʻah Valley such as Khirbet Abu Tabaq, Khirbet es-Samrah, and Khirbet el-Maqari.[26] There is, however, no dispute about the discernible eighth century occupation of both Qumran and En-gedi, which should also be identified as part of this settlement trend. The need to resettle refugees throughout Judah can only have been further exacerbated by Sennacherib's devastating campaign against Judah in 701 B.C.E. The relatively rapid resettlement of sites such as Lachish, which rebounded during the seventh century (Iron IIC), may attest to the intense need for all available land despite the population losses that Judah incurred from warfare and deportations.

At this point it does not appear that there is any clear evidence in Jerusalem or elsewhere during the eighth and seventh centuries B.C.E. for *increased morbidity and mortality* associated with refugees. As hallmarks of refugee trajectories, these problems are associated with more impoverished refugees, for whom social and economic integration is traditionally more difficult. It may be argued, therefore, that the absence of evidence for increased morbidity and mortality points toward the relatively successful integration of refugees from the northern kingdom into Judah, as increased mortality would be associated with failure to meet subsistence needs or exposure to unsanitary and suboptimal environmental conditions.

While *social disarticulation* is also not particularly clear in Jerusalem, clues to its effect are evident in the archaeology of Ekron's Level IC settlement, which dates to the seventh century if not to the late eighth century B.C.E. Like Jerusalem, Ekron experienced radical growth, an eightfold increase that can only be attributed to massive resettlement of refugees.[27] A large number of olive oil presses were recovered from Ekron. These have been hypothesized by the site's excavators to reflect an Assyrian policy of

25. Andrew G. Vaughn, *Theology, History, and Archaeology in the Chronicler's Account of Hezekiah* (SBLABS 4; Atlanta: Scholars Press, 1999), 71–78.

26. Ibid., 75–78. See also Frank M. Cross, "Buqeiʻa, el-," *NEAEHL* 1:267–69.

27. Trude Dothan and Seymour Gitin, "Miqne, Tel (Ekron)," *NEAEHL* 3:1051–59.

economic development of the site.[28] However, David Schloen notes that they more likely indicate individual households of refugees who had lost access to shared common property, including olive oil processing equipment.[29] This, according to Schloen, explains why many of these presses were dismantled in the next phase of Ekron's settlement (Level IB), when intermarriage among refugee families established kinship bonds between neighboring households replacing those that were lost when these individuals fled from their settlements, which were very likely in Israel. Still, potential exists in a number of areas for further investigation of the experience of social disarticulation by refugees in this period. In places like Ekron, evidence of multiethnic communities, as suggested by Phoenicianizing inscriptions and four-horned altars of a type often associated with Israelite communities, points to the potential origin of these communities. A still more impressive indication of social disarticulation, also seen at Ekron and other Iron II sites, is the practice of hoarding.[30] In certain archaeological contexts, I would suggest that this is tied to the social disarticulation of refugees, who found themselves "in the company of unreliable strangers," as Schloen aptly characterizes the situation.[31] Rather than regarding hoarding as a last-minute affair, we may suggest that hoarding occurred in a variety of contexts of social disarticulation, which included both an impending flight from a site as well as the early phases of resettlement among refugee communities.

---

28. Seymour Gitin, "The Effects of Urbanization on a Philistine City: Tel Miqne-Ekron in the Iron Age II Period," in *Proceedings of the Tenth World Conference of Jewish Studies* (ed. David Assaf; Jerusalem: World Union of Jewish Studies, 1989), 277–84.

29. J. David Schloen, *The House of the Father as Fact and Symbol: Patrimonialism in Ugarit and the Ancient Near East* (SAHL 2; Winona Lake, Ind.: Eisenbrauns, 2001), 414.

30. For some well-known examples of hoards, see articles by Seymour Gitin and Amir Golani, "The Tel Miqne-Ekron Silver Hoards: The Assyrian and Phoenician Connections," in *Hacksilber to Coinage: New Insights into the Monetary History of the Near East and Greece* (ed. Miriam S. Balmuth; Numismatic Studies 24; New York: American Numismatic Society, 2001), 277–84, and Ephraim Stern, "The Silver Hoard from Tel Dor," in Balmuth, *Hacksilber to Coinage*, 19–26.

31. Schloen, *House of the Father*, 142.

4. Conclusions

Drawing on advances made in the study of ancient society in the past two decades, I have demonstrated in this paper that historical and archaeological study of ancient Near Eastern societies can benefit from the incorporation of anthropological lines of research as exemplified by the field of refugee studies. The *Impoverishment Risks and Resettlement* model offers one such avenue for greater consideration of the processes shaping ancient societies that have been largely overlooked in archaeological and textual approaches to date. The application of such models yields potential for better understanding the social context of ancient Israel and its neighbors.

Bibliography

Avigad, Nahman. "The Expedition to the Judean Desert, 1960: Expedition A." *IEJ* 11 (1961): 6–10.

———. "The Expedition to the Judean Desert, 1960: Expedition A—Nahal David." *IEJ* 12 (1962): 169–83.

Avigad, Nahman, and Hillel Geva. "Area A–Stratigraphy and Architecture: Iron Age II Strata 9–7." Pages 44–82 in *Architecture and Stratigraphy: Areas A, W and X-2 Final Report.* Vol. 1 of *Jewish Quarter Excavations in the Old City of Jerusalem Conducted by Nahman Avigad, 1969-1982.* Edited by Hillel Geva. Jerusalem: Israel Exploration Society and the Institute of Archaeology, Hebrew University, 2000.

Beckman, Gary M. *Hittite Diplomatic Texts.* 2nd ed. SBLWAW 7. Atlanta: Scholars Press, 1999.

Broshi, Magen. "The Expansion of Jerusalem in the Reigns of Hezekiah and Manasseh." *IEJ* 24 (1974): 21–26.

Burke, Aaron Alexander. "Coping with the Effects of War: Refugees in the Levant during the Bronze and Iron Ages." In *Disaster and Relief Management in Ancient Israel, Egypt and the Ancient Near East.* Edited by Angelika Berlejung, Ariel Bagg, and Gunnar Lehman. FAT. Tübingen: Mohr Siebeck, forthcoming.

Cernea, Michael M. "Risks, Safeguards, and Reconstruction: A Model for Population Displacement and Resettlement." Pages 11–55 in *Risks and Reconstruction: Experiences of Resettlers and Refugees.* Edited by Michael M. Cernea and Chris McDowell. Washington, D.C.: World Bank, 2000.

Cernea, Michael M. and Chris McDowell. "Reconstructing Resettlers' and Refugees' Livelihoods." Pages 1–8 in *Risks and Reconstruction: Experiences of Resettlers and Refugees.* Edited by Michael M. Cernea and Chris McDowell. Washington, D.C.: World Bank, 2000.

Finkelstein, Israel. "The Archaeology of the Days of Manasseh." Pages 169–87 in *Scripture and Other Artifacts: Essays on the Bible and Archaeology in Honor of Philip*

J. King. Edited by Michael D. Coogan, J. Cheryl Exum, and Lawrence E. Stager. Louisville: Westminster John Knox, 1994.

Gitin, Seymour. "The Effects of Urbanization on a Philistine City: Tel Miqne-Ekron in the Iron Age II Period." Pages 277–84 in *Proceedings of the Tenth World Congress of Jewish Studies*. Edited by David Assaf. Jerusalem: World Union of Jewish Studies, 1990.

Gitin, Seymour, and Amir Golani. "The Tel Miqne-Ekron Silver Hoards: The Assyrian and Phoenician Connections." Pages 27–48 in *Hacksilber to Coinage: New Insights into the Monetary History of the Near East and Greece*. Edited by Miriam S. Balmuth. Numismatic Studies 24. New York: American Numismatic Society, 2001.

Grayson, A. Kirk. *Assyrian Rulers of the Early First Millennium BC*, vol. 2: *(858–745 BC)*. RIMA 3. Toronto: University of Toronto Press, 1996.

Kunz, Egon F. "The Refugee in Flight: Kinetic Models and Forms of Displacement." *International Migration Review* 7 (1973): 125–46.

Na'aman, Nadav. "When and How Did Jerusalem Become a Great City? The Rise of Jerusalem as Judah's Premier City in the Eighth–Seventh Centuries B.C.E." *BASOR* 347 (2007): 21–56.

Parker, Simon B. "Graves, Caves, and Refugees: An Essay in Microhistory." *JSOT* 27 (2003): 259–88.

Rendsburg, Gary A., and William M. Schniedewind. "The Siloam Tunnel Inscription: Historical and Linguistic Perspectives." *IEJ* 60 (2010): 62–77.

Schloen, J. David. *The House of the Father as Fact and Symbol: Patrimonialism in Ugarit and the Ancient Near East*. SAHL 2. Winona Lake, Ind.: Eisenbrauns, 2001.

Schloen, J. David, and Amir S. Fink. "Searching for Ancient Sam'al: New Excavations at Zinçirli in Turkey." *NEA* 72 (2009): 203–19.

Sneh, Amihai, Ram Weinberger, and Eyal Shalev. "The Why, How, and When of the Siloam Tunnel Reevaluated." *BASOR* 359 (2010): 57–65.

Stern, Ephraim. "The Silver Hoard from Tel Dor." Pages 19–26 in *Hacksilber to Coinage: New Insights into the Monetary History of the Near East and Greece*. Edited by Miriam S. Balmuth. Numismatic Studies 24. New York: American Numismatic Society, 2001.

United Nations. "Article 1(2)." U.N. Convention Relating to the Status of Refugees: United Nations, 1951.

Vaughn, Andrew G., *Theology, History, and Archaeology in the Chronicler's Account of Hezekiah*. SBLABS 4. Atlanta: Scholars Press, 1999.

SHEDDING NEW LIGHT ON THE DARK YEARS OF THE "EXILIC PERIOD": NEW STUDIES, FURTHER ELUCIDATION, AND SOME QUESTIONS REGARDING THE ARCHAEOLOGY OF JUDAH AS AN "EMPTY LAND"

Oded Lipschits

1. INTRODUCTION

The Babylonian attack on the kingdom of Judah at the beginning of the sixth century B.C.E. brought about the desolation and utter destruction of Jerusalem and its immediate environs. The house of David ceased to reign; the temple was left in ruins; "the foxes walk upon it" (Lam 5:18). Furthermore, the western border of Judah was destroyed as part of the Babylonian military campaign, and the urban and administrative centers, the military forts, as well as many of the rural settlements in the region were crushed and deserted. In what was probably a longer, more complex process, the peripheral regions of the kingdom in the Negev to the south and in the Judean Desert, the Jordan Valley, and the western shore of the Dead Sea to the east all collapsed, with ruinous consequences. Many of the Judahites were exiled to Babylon, while many others escaped or were forced to leave their land and homes, or perished from the harsh penalties of the long war and the presence of the Babylonian forces in Judah. The small kingdom, which had existed for hundreds of years, turned into a province. A new period in the history of Judah had begun, its borders shrunk and its population sharply depleted. The social, theological and historical center of its gravity shifted to the community of deportees in Babylon. This is, at least, the gloomy, depressing picture that scholars have painted for decades of the "exilic period" of Babylonian rule over Judah (604–539 B.C.E.).

In recent years, new finds from the sixth century B.C.E., as well as new studies concerning the archaeology of Judah between the seventh and the fifth centuries B.C.E., have shed new light on our understanding of this period. Despite its harshness, the sixty-five-year interval has shown itself to be a period of administrative, economic, and cultural continuity, especially in the close peripheral circle to the north and south of Jerusalem. The dreary picture was not quite so bleak after all.

In this essay I will briefly present these new studies and new finds, and will discuss their meaning and implications for our understanding of the history of Judah in the sixth century B.C.E., and for our understanding of the biblical descriptions of the Babylonian destruction. This will be provide us with the basis for discussing and clarifying the problematic nature of the current methodologies for understanding the archaeological research of this period, the limitation of historical research based on archaeological material, and the motivation and "hidden polemics" of scholars studying the "empty land" in Judah.

2. New Studies and New Finds That Shed New Light on the Archaeology of the Sixth Century B.C.E. in Judah

2.1. The Continuation of the Judahite Administrative Center at Ramat Raḥel from the Late Iron Age to the Persian Period

The site of Ramat Raḥel provides a first case in point. The earliest building level at Ramat Raḥel (Aharoni's Stratum Vb) was settled in the late eighth, more probably in the early seventh century B.C.E.[1] Few architectural

---

1. Yohanan Aharoni, *Excavations at Ramat Raḥel: Seasons 1961 and 1962* (Serie archeologica 6; Rome: Università degli studi, Centro di studi semitici, 1964), 61–63, 119–20; Oded Lipschits et al., "Ramat Raḥel and Its Secrets" [Hebrew], *Qad* 138 (2009): 61–64; idem, "Palace and Village, Paradise and Oblivion: Unraveling the Riddles of Ramat Raḥel," *NEA* 74 (2011): 10–14. Aharoni (*Excavations at Ramat Raḥel: Seasons 1961 and 1962*, 119) dated this early level to the late eighth and early seventh centuries B.C.E. (see also Miriam Aharoni and Yohanan Aharoni, "The Stratification of Judahite Sites in the 8th and 7th Centuries B.C.E.," *BASOR* 224 [1976]: 73–90). The renewed excavations at the site (2005–2010) confirmed this date and demonstrated that this early building phase, which probably began only after the 701 B.C.E. Assyrian campaign to Judah, continued to exist without any break through the seventh century B.C.E. See Lipschits et al., "Ramat Raḥel and Its Secrets," 61–64; Oded Lipschits, Omer Sergi, and Ido Koch, "Royal Judahite Jar Handles: Reconsidering the Chronol-

remains belong to this phase, but a large quantity of pottery and about 225 *lmlk* stamped jar handles, most of which originated in fills under the second building level (Aharoni's Stratum VA), are a clear indication that already in this early phase the site served as a Judahite administrative center. The site was built near Jerusalem at the time when Judah was a vassal kingdom under Assyrian auspices, probably in order to collect goods in kind, mainly jars of wine and oil.[2]

In the second building phase (Aharoni's Stratum VA), dated to the last third of the seventh century B.C.E.,[3] an imposing edifice stood atop the mound.[4] This is one of the most impressive structures discovered in Judah, and it is no wonder that scholars have described it as either a palace for Judean kings,[5] or an Assyrian[6] or Judahite administrative center.[7] Its walls were of ashlar blocks, unique in Judahite architecture, and it was

---

ogy of the *lmlk* Stamp Impressions," *TA* 37 (2010): 3–32; idem, "Judahite Stamped and Incised Jar Handles: A Tool for Studying the History of Late Monarchic Judah," *TA* 38 (2011): 5–41.

2. Oded Lipschits and Yuval Gadot, "Ramat Raḥel and the Emeq Rephaim Sites—Links and Interpretations," in *New Studies in the Archaeology of Jerusalem and Its Religion: Collected Papers* (ed. D. Amit and G. D. Stiebel; 2 vols.; Jerusalem: Israel Antiquities Authority, 2008), 2:88–96; Lipschits et al., "Palace and Village," 16–20.

3. See Yohanan Aharoni, *Excavations at Ramat Raḥel: Seasons 1959 and 1960* (Serie archeologica 2; Rome: Università degli studi, Centro di studi semitici, 1962), 51–53; idem, *Excavations at Ramat Raḥel: Seasons 1961 and 1962*, 119–20, which dated this palace to the time of Jehoiakim (609–598 B.C.E.). But the renewed excavations proved that the date of this phase extends from the last third of the seventh century into the sixth century without any indication of destruction at the beginning of the sixth century B.C.E.

4. Lipschits et al., "Ramat Raḥel and Its Secrets," 64–70; idem, "Palace and Village," 20–34.

5. Aharoni, *Excavations at Ramat Raḥel Seasons 1961 and 1962*, 119–20; Ephraim Stern, *The Assyrian, Babylonian, and Persian Periods (732–332 B.C.E.)* (vol. 2 of *The Archaeology of the Land of the Bible;* New York: Doubleday, 2001), 69, 162; Gabriel Barkay, "Royal Palace, Royal Portrait? The Tantalizing Possibilities of Ramat Raḥel," *BAR* 32 (2006): 34–44 (39–42).

6. Nadav Na'aman, "An Assyrian Residence in Ramat Raḥel," *TA* 28 (2001): 260–280 (271–73).

7. Oded Lipschits, *The Fall and Rise of Jerusalem* (Winona Lake, Ind.: Eisenbrauns, 2005), 213–16; Lipschits and Gadot, "Ramat Raḥel and the Emeq Rephaim Sites," 88–96; Lipschits et al., "Palace and Village," 20–34.

decorated with volute (proto-Aeolic) capitals,[8] magnificent window balustrades, small limestone stepped, pyramid-shaped stones (probably part of the crenellation that topped the edifice wall), and other stone ornaments. Yohanan Aharoni assumed that the palace was surrounded by a wide, fortified courtyard extending over an area of about 2 hectares.[9] However, the renewed excavation project revealed that the edifice was surrounded on the south, west, and north by a magnificent garden, well built on artificially flattened bedrock. In and around this area large pools with high quality ashlars were built, surrounded by tunnels, channels, and other water installations covered with thick layers of plaster. This garden, as well as the edifice to its east, continued to exist until the Persian period, when the edifice was expanded on its northwestern corner. Of about 235 rosette stamp impressions known today, which date to the last decades of the Judean monarchy, forty-three were excavated at Ramat Raḥel, all of them above the floors of the second building phase, none of them below it.[10] This is a clear indication that the site continued to function as an important administrative center in Judah during the period when the large edifice and gardens were built.

Contrary to Aharoni's interpretation, there is no evidence for the destruction of Ramat Raḥel at the beginning of the sixth century b.c.e., or for a long occupational gap at the site.[11] The renewed excavations clearly demonstrated that the site continued to exist during the sixth century b.c.e., when Jerusalem was in ruins and Mizpah/Tell en-Naṣbeh was the capital of Judah.[12] Throughout this period, the second building phase at the site persisted without marked change.

---

8. Oded Lipschits, "Persian Period Finds from Jerusalem: Facts and Interpretations," *JHS* 9 (2009): 2–30.

9. Aharoni, *Excavations at Ramat Raḥel: Seasons 1961 and 1962*, 119.

10. Nadav Na'aman, "The Kingdom of Judah under Josiah," *TA* 18 (1991): 3–71 (31–33, 42–43, 57); idem, "An Assyrian Residence in Ramat Raḥel," 291–93; Ido Koch and Oded Lipschits, "The Final Days of the Kingdom of Judah in Light of the Rosette-Stamped Jar Handles" [Hebrew], *Cathedra* 137 (2010): 7–26.

11. Aharoni, *Excavations at Ramat Raḥel: Seasons 1961 and 1962*, 120.

12. Oded Lipschits, "Nebuchadrezzar's Policy in 'Hattu-Land' and the Fate of the Kingdom of Judah," *UF* 30 (1999): 473–76; Lipschits et al., "Ramat Raḥel and Its Secrets," 70; idem, "Palace and Village," 34–37.

Aharoni dated his next stratum, IVB, to the long period covering the Persian and Hasmonean eras.[13] Numerous small artifacts from these periods have been found, but only fragmented architectural remains. The renewed excavations at the site have uncovered valuable new evidence that illuminates Persian period Ramat Raḥel and emphasizes the continuum between the second and the third building phases, dated from the late sixth to the late fourth century B.C.E., with two main subphases. The remains of a new building, both sturdy and large, were exposed. Rectangular in shape, it was built on the northwestern side of the second-phase edifice complex, covers an area of about six hundred square meters, and comprises a new wing added to the existing complex, surrounding the largest pool of the second building phase. In the southeastern corner of the site, a huge pit was excavated that contained hundreds of pottery vessels, among them more than ten restorable jars, some of them bearing stamp impressions from the early *yhwd* types, and some with sixth-century "private" stamp impressions together with lion stamp impressions on body sherds. These finds, together with hundreds of stamp impressions on jar handles dated to the Persian and Hellenistic occupation periods at the site, are the best indication that Ramat Raḥel was the main center of the *yhwd* system in which the jars circulated. The possible involvement of the central Achaemenid government may be indicated by the intensive construction at the site and in the unusual creation of the additional wing on the northwestern side of the existing edifice, the style and strength of which are unparalleled by any other finds in the area in the same period.[14] As for the history of the site during the sixth century B.C.E., it seems that the continuous function of Ramat Raḥel as an administrative site is best attested by the continuity of use of the system of stamped jar handles, as indicated below.

2.2. The Continuation of the System of Stamped Jar Handles during the Sixth Century B.C.E.

The unique administrative nature of Ramat Raḥel is best reflected in its profusion of stamped jar handles. Over three hundred stamped handles from the late Iron Age have been found at the site, including *lmlk* and "pri-

---

13. Aharoni, *Excavations at Ramat Raḥel: Seasons 1961 and 1962*, 120–21; cf. Stern, *Assyrian, Babylonian, and Persian Periods*, 324, 436–37.

14. Lipschits et al., "Ramat Raḥel and Its Secrets," 70–72; idem, "Palace and Village," 34–37.

vate" stamp impressions (late eighth and early seventh centuries B.C.E.); concentric circle incisions (mid-seventh century B.C.E.), and rosette stamp impressions (late seventh to early sixth centuries B.C.E.). In the Persian and Hellenistic periods, too, Ramat Raḥel was the main center of stamped jar handles, with more than three hundred *yhwd* stamp impressions dated to the late sixth to mid-second centuries B.C.E., and *yršlm* stamp impressions (second century B.C.E.). All in all, this phenomenon takes in more than half a millennium of continuous, systemized administration of the collecting of jars of wine and oil. During long periods of this half millennium, Ramat Raḥel functioned as the main Judahite administration and collection center—as is evidenced by the presence at this small site of the large number of most of the different types of stamped handles excavated in Judah. No other Judahite site, not even Jerusalem, can challenge Ramat Raḥel's record.

2.3. The Lion Stamped Jar Handles and the Sixth-Century B.C.E. Administration in Judah

Wedged between the two systems of stamped jar handles—that from the Iron Age and that from the Persian and Hellenistic periods—another system existed in Judah, and mainly at Ramat Raḥel: the lion stamp impressions on the body or the handles of jars. Seventy-seven lion stamped jar handles were excavated at Ramat Raḥel, out of a total of about 110 stamped handles known to us to date. A modified typological classification demonstrates that two out of ten types were found solely at Ramat Raḥel, that one additional type was found at Ramat Raḥel and Nebi Samwil only, and that all the other types are represented mainly at Ramat Raḥel. Until recently, scholars dated the lion stamp impressions to the very beginning of the Persian period.[15] The reason is the absence of these stamped handles from the "classic" Persian period strata, and the historical assumption that they

---

15. Ephraim Stern, *Material Culture of the Land of the Bible in the Persian Period, 538–332 B.C.* (Warminster: Aris & Phillips, 1982), 209–10; idem, *Assyrian, Babylonian, and Persian Periods,* 541. Cf. Donals Tzvi Ariel and Yair Shoham, "Locally Stamped Handles and Associated Body Fragments of the Persian and Hellenistic Periods," in *Excavations at the City of David 1978–1985, IV* (ed. D. T. Ariel; Qedem 41; Jerusalem: Institute of Archaeology, Hebrew University of Jerusalem, 2000), 141. However, see H. G. M. Williamson, "The Governors of Judah under the Persians," *TynBul 39* (1988): 60–64.

cannot be dated to the pre-Persian period (i.e., to the "exilic period"). In addition, Ephraim Stern interpreted the "object"[16] or "indistinct signs"[17] forming part of a scene depicting a lion standing on his hind legs, with the two front legs stretched out wide, as an Achaemenid "fire altar." However, a new study of the iconography of this type hints at the connection of these objects with the Assyrian-Babylonian world.[18] Furthermore, petrographic analysis of the lion stamped handles made by Boaz Gross and Yuval Goren shows a resemblance to Iron Age patterns of the rosette jar handles (pottery production in the Shephelah of Judah and in the area of Jerusalem) rather than to Persian-period patterns of the *yhwd* jars (pottery production solely in the area of Jerusalem).[19]

The conclusion is that the lion stamp impression system belongs to an earlier and wider sixth-century B.C.E. administrative system and that it should be placed in the Babylonian period. This is the "missing link" in administrative continuity in Judah; it was part of the Babylonian administration that lasted until the beginning of the Persian period, at which point it was replaced by the *yhwd* stamp impression system.

The prominence of the lion stamp impressions is another indication that Ramat Raḥel continued to have a major administrative role during the sixth century B.C.E., while its second building phase continued to exist. Only one *mwṣh* stamp impression—which probably also dates to the mid-sixth century B.C.E.[20]—came from Ramat Raḥel, whereas thirty *mwṣh* stamp impressions were excavated at Tell en-Naṣbeh, the new capital of Judah after the destruction of Jerusalem.[21] This fact suggests that the administrative center that continued to exist at Ramat Raḥel had a different role and status from those of the capitals, whether Jerusalem or Mizpah.

---

16. Aharoni, *Excavations at Ramat Raḥel: Seasons 1961 and 1962*, 45.

17. James B. Pritchard, *The Water System of Gibeon* (Museum Monographs; Philadelphia: University of Pennsylvania, 1961), opposite of fig. 46.

18. Benjamin Sass, "The Lion Stamp Impressions from Sixth Century B.C.E. Babylon and Their Connection to the Lion Stamp Impressions from Judah" [Hebrew], in *New Studies on the Lion Stamped Jar Handles from Judah* (ed. O. Lipschits and I. Koch; Tel Aviv: Tel Aviv University Press, 2010), 13–14.

19. Boaz Gross and Yuval Goren, "A Technological Study of the Lion Stamped Handles—Preliminary Results," in Lipschits and Koch, *New Studies on the Lion Stamped Jar Handles from Judah*, 11–12.

20. Jeffrey R. Zorn, Joseph Yellin, John Hayes, "The *M(W)ṢH* Stamp Impressions and the Neo-Babylonian Period," *IEJ* 44 (1994): 161–83.

21. Lipschits, *Fall and Rise of Jerusalem*, 179–81.

2.4. The Continuation in Pottery Production in Judah between the End
of the Iron Age and the Persian Period

New discoveries at Ramat Raḥel have proven the theory that characteristics of the well known local pottery assemblages dating to the end of the
Iron Age and to the Persian period exhibit continuity, and therefore attest
to the existence of an unbroken tradition of pottery production in Judah
from the end of the seventh to the fifth and fourth centuries B.C.E.[22] There
is a time gap of 150 years between the well known pottery assemblages
from the late Iron Age, as discovered at Lachish Level II, City of David
Stratum 10, Tell Beit Mirsim Stratum 3A, Tel Arad Strata VII-VI; Tel ʿIra
Stratum VI; En-gedi (Tell Goren) Stratum V, and building levels 1 and 2
at Ramat Raḥel,[23] and the typical pottery assemblages from the Persian
period, as known from En-gedi Stratum IV, Stratum 9 of Area G in the
City of David, Jabel Nimra Stage II, building level 3 at Ramat Raḥel, and
sites in the region of Benjamin.[24] The new pottery assemblage from Ramat
Raḥel is the only one thus far that clearly fills this gap, and thus supports
the theoretical assumption that the local traditions of pottery production
continued throughout the sixth century B.C.E.

The best examples of this continuity are the store jars from the Persian period, characterized by an ovoid- or sack-shaped body, convex base,
narrow neck, rounded shoulder, thick, everted rim and four loop handles
that extend from the shoulder to the body (Type A, according to Stern).[25]
These jars exhibit the features of those jars characteristic of the end of the
Iron Age in Judah (known also as "rosette jars"), continued the tradition of
production, and were widespread only within the province of Judah.[26] The
fact that exactly this type of jar was recently discovered at Ramat Raḥel
with sixth century "private" and lion stamp impressions on the body of
the jars, with the same type of jars bearing the early types of *yhwd* stamp
impressions on their handles, all of them very similar in shape and proportion to the "rosette jars" from the late Iron Age, is a clear indication that

22. Ibid., 192–205, with further literature; Lipschits et al., *What the Stones Are Whispering: 3000 Years of Forgotten History at Ramat Raḥel* [Hebrew] (forthcoming).

23. Lipschits, *Fall and Rise of Jerusalem*, 192–93, with further literature.

24. See, e.g., ibid., 193, with further literature.

25. See Stern, *Material Culture of the Land of the Bible*, 103; Lipschits, *Fall and Rise of Jerusalem*, 199.

26. Stern, *Material Culture of the Land of the Bible*, 103.

jars of this kind continued to appear in Judah in the sixth century B.C.E. Later, in the Persian period, the jars with a more pronounced globular, sack-shaped body and those with two to four handles or with no handles at all (Types B and C, according to Stern)[27] gradually replaced this type of jar. On many of the handles of these jars, middle and late types of *yhwd* stamp impressions were discovered.

This is also the case with many other pottery vessels from the Persian period that continued to be produced from the late Iron Age into the sixth and early fifth centuries B.C.E. During the fifth century B.C.E. they began to demonstrate new features in terms of shape, processing technique, and material, probably due to influences of internal slow and gradual developments and interaction with both neighboring regions and cultures as well as with the culture of the Babylonian and Persian empires, and later on with the Hellenistic civilization. The characteristics common to almost all of the Persian-period vessels are the thickened, everted rim, trumpet base or raised disc base, globular sack-shaped body, and raised or "suspended" handles. These "classic" characteristics appear only in the fifth century B.C.E., and it seems that the sixth century B.C.E. serves, to some extent, as a transition period between the cylindrical-elliptical shape characteristic of the Iron Age and the shape characteristic of the Persian period. One main feature of the changes in the technique of pottery production is the disappearance of the polishing, especially of the bowls.[28]

This "intermediate" culture of the sixth century B.C.E. was not identified until now and did not get its typological and chronological definition because of its close similarity to the pottery assemblages that preceded and followed it. As will be discussed below, it was also not identified because scholars assumed that life ceased to exist in Judah during the "exilic period," and that pottery production and all other expressions of economy and administration could not be developed in Judah during this period. This assumption caused archaeologists to identify the "intermediate" material culture of the sixth century B.C.E. as representing the late Iron

---

27. Ibid., 103–4.

28. See Lawrence A. Sinclair, "Bethel Pottery of the Sixth Century B.C.," in *The Excavation of Bethel (1934–1960)* (ed. James L. Kelso and William F. Albright; AASOR 39; Cambridge: American Schools of Oriental Research, 1968), 71; and Nancy Lapp, ed., *The Third Campaign at Tell el-Ful: The Excavations of 1964* (AASOR 45; Cambridge: American Schools of Oriental Research, 1981), 84–85, who dated this change to the first half of the sixth century B.C.E.

Age (late seventh to early sixth centuries B.C.E.). This is so even in areas where there is a scholarly consensus that life continued in Judah in the sixth century B.C.E.[29]

The newly discovered, and not yet published, pottery assemblage from Ramat Raḥel stands as the clear marker for this group of sixth century B.C.E. pottery assemblage. Similar pottery assemblages can be found at a number of central sites, primarily in the Benjamin region, such as Tell el-Fûl (Stratum IIIb), several defined loci in Stratum I at Tell en-Naṣbeh, as well as well-defined pottery assemblages at Beitin and el-Jib.[30]

2.5. Continuation in the Rural Settlements to the North and South of Jerusalem

During the Babylonian period, a marked change took place in the characteristics of the settled areas. The settlement center of gravity moved from Jerusalem to the close periphery, and a new pattern of settlement was created in which the core was depleted and the nearby periphery continued to exist almost unchanged.[31]

---

29. See, e.g., the assumption of Finkelstein in Yitzhak Magen and Israel Finkelstein, *Archaeological Survey in the Hill Country of Benjamin* (Jerusalem: Israel Antiquities Authority Publications, 1993), 27.

30. Lipschits, *Fall and Rise of Jerusalem*, 193–94, with further literature.

31. There are two main changes in settlement pattern and characteristics in Judah following the Babylonian 586 B.C.E. campaign. Since the beginning of the 1950s, many scholars have noted the different fate that befell the Benjamin region and the archaeological reality that prevailed there after the destruction of Jerusalem. See, e.g., Abraham Malamat, "The Last Wars of the Kingdom of Judah," *JNES* 9 (1950): 218–28 (227); G. Ernest Wright, *Biblical Archaeology* (Philadelphia: Westminster, 1957), 199; Paul W. Lapp, "Tell el-Full," *BA* 28 (1965): 2–10 (6); Shmuel S. Weinberg, "Eretz Israel after the Destruction of the First Temple: Archaeological Report" [Hebrew], *PNAS* 4 (1970): 206; Joel P. Weinberg, "Demographische Notizen zur Geschichte der nachexilischen Gemeinde in Juda," *Klio* 54 (1972): 47–50; Stern, *Material Culture of the Land of the Bible*, 229; idem, "The Babylonian Gap," *BAR* 26.6 (2000): 51; idem, *Assyrian, Babylonian, and Persian Periods,* 321–23; Hans M. Barstad, *The Myth of the Empty Land: A Study in the History and Archaeology of Judah during the "Exilic" Period* (SO 28; Oslo: Scandinavian University Press, 1996) 47–48; idem, "After the 'Myth of the Empty Land': Major Challenges in the Study of Neo-Babylonian Judah," in *Judah and the Judeans in the Neo-Babylonian Period* (ed. Oded Lipschits and Joseph Blenkinsopp; Winona Lake, Ind.: Eisenbrauns, 2003), 6–9; Ianir Milevski, "Settlement Patterns in Northern Judah during the Achaemenid Period, according to the Hill Country of

The lack of definition of the sixth-century material culture and the continuation of the familiar late Iron Age material culture to the "exilic period" of the sixth century B.C.E. caused a phenomenon in which, at sites lacking archaeological evidence of the Babylonian destruction, especially in the small and rural sites, no distinction was made between strata from the end of the Iron Age and strata from the Babylonian and Persian periods. Even at sites where archaeological evidence of late Iron Age destruction was found, but life continued and another building level was located, the exact time of the destruction and settlement restoration could not be archaeologically located, and historical interpretation was used and presented as archaeological conclusion. This is the case mainly with the destruction of many sites in the Negev, the Southern Shephelah, the southern part of the Judean Hills, the Jordan Valley, and the Dead Sea area. On the basis of historical assumption, the destruction of many Iron Age sites in these areas was ascribed to Babylonian activity at the beginning of the sixth century B.C.E.; other options such as a gradual collapse before and after the fall of Jerusalem were never considered.[32] Furthermore, at many sites the finds from the Babylonian, Persian, and sometimes even Hellenistic periods were not separated, mainly because settlement continuity prevailed in the transition from Babylonian to Persian rule as well as in the transition to the Ptolemaic and Selucid periods, and there was difficulty in distinguishing between these periods.[33]

Benjamin and Jerusalem Surveys," *BAIAS* 15 (1996–1997): 7–29; Oded Lipschits, "The History of the Benjaminite Region under Babylonian Rule," *TA* 26 (1999): 155–90; idem, "Judah, Jerusalem and the Temple (586–539 B.C.E.)," *Transeu* 22 (2001): 131–35; idem, "Demographic Changes in Judah between the Seventh and the Fifth Centuries B.C.E.," in Lipschits and Blenkinsopp, *Judah and the Judeans in the Neo-Babylonian Period*, 346–51; idem, *Fall and Rise of Jerusalem*, 237–49; Oded, "Myth of the Empty Land," 71. It is probable that the same archaeological picture existed also in the area south of Jerusalem, between Bethlehem and Tekoa, and to a lesser extent in the area more to the south, as far as Beth-zur (Lipschits, "Demographic Changes in Judah," 351–55; idem, *Fall and Rise of Jerusalem*, 250–58; Lipschits and Gadot, "Ramat Raḥel and the Emeq Rephaim Sites," 88–96.

32. On the archaeological data and its interpretation, see Lipschits, *Fall and Rise of Jerusalem*, 224–37, with further literature.

33. See, e.g., the broad definition given to the "Persian-Hellenistic period" in Gezer (500 B.C.E. to 100 C.E.); to the "late Judahite period" in Jericho; to the "Hellenistic period" in Beth-zur (between the destruction of the First Temple and the Roman period); to the far-ranging characterization in Gibeon of all of the meager remnants between the sixth century B.C.E. and the first century C.E.; to the preliminary dating

During this time, the Judahite population that continued to subsist in the northern Judean highlands and in the Benjamin region preserved its material culture. There lies the great difficulty posed to archaeological research in discerning this culture and defining it. Many scholars have discerned the different fate of the Benjamin region and the archaeological reality in it after the destruction of Jerusalem.[34] The biblical description regarding the fate of this region during the Babylonian campaign against Jerusalem and after the destruction of the city, together with excavation data of the main sites explored in the Benjamin region and the data of surveys conducted there, attest that the region was not destroyed with Jerusalem. As a historical interpretation of this data, one may assume that already before the fall of Jerusalem the Babylonians had chosen Mizpah as the alternative capital of the Babylonian province, and appointed Gedaliah as the first governor.[35]

The area to the south of Jerusalem, with the Rephaim Valley in its center, probably had the same fate as the Benjamin region. The Rephaim Valley, with its rich alluvial soil and moderately terraced slopes, has historically been one of the prosperous agricultural districts in the environs of Jerusalem, vital to the economy of the city. The mounting archaeological data from this area, underscored by the many agricultural installations and small farmsteads found in and around the valley, confirms that those periods during which the Rephaim Valley flourished agriculturally are the same periods during which there was construction at Ramat Raḥel, that is, from the late Iron Age to the Persian period, with no sign of a hiatus (including, e.g., storage jars stamped with lion stamp impressions discovered at Khirbet er-Ras [not yet published]).

The site of Rogem Ganim was the main production center in the Rephaim basin.[36] It is located at the western edge of the upper part of the Rephaim catchment, about seven kilometers west of Ramat Raḥel. In addi-

---

of Stratum IV at Ramat Raḥel between the fifth century B.C.E. and the first century C.E., etc.

34. See Malamat, "The Last Wars of the Kingdom of Judah," 227; Wright, *Biblical Archaeology*, 199; Lapp, "Tell el-Full," 6; Weinberg, "Eretz Israel after the Destruction of the First Temple," 82; Nahman Avigad, "Two Hebrew Inscriptions on Wine Jars," *IEJ* 22 (1972): 8; Stern, *Material Culture of the Land of the Bible*, 229; idem, "The Babylonian Gap: The Archaeological Reality," *JSOT* 28 (2004): 273; Lipschits, "History of the Benjaminite Region," 155–90; idem, *Fall and Rise of Jerusalem*, 237–49.

35. Lipschits, *Fall and Rise of Jerusalem*, 98–112.

36. Raphael Greenberg and Gilad Cinamon, "Stamped and Incised Jar Handles

tion to a large tumulus (9 m high and 40 m across), Raphael Greenberg and Gilad Cinamon uncovered winepresses, storage caves, and plastered cisterns, but no architecture evidence of a site of agricultural industry and storage. The pottery discovered at the site included mostly jars, and most of the repertoire dates to the late Iron Age and to the Persian period.[37] According to the new assumptions concerning the lion stamp impressions and the sixth century B.C.E., the site may have continued to exist during the Babylonian period as well.[38]

All in all, it seems that Rogem Ganim was the main economic-agricultural site in the Rephaim basin, functioning in tandem with the administrative center at Ramat Raḥel.[39] Khirbet er-Ras, located on the slopes of a spur just above the riverbed of the Rephaim Valley, is the only site in the valley where private houses were discovered beside agricultural installations. During the surveys and the excavations, different structures and agricultural installations were discovered with pottery and other finds from the late Iron Age, with some scant remains from the Middle Bronze and Early Roman periods.[40] A *lmlk* stamped jar handle

---

from Rogem Ganim and Their Implications for the Political Economy of Jerusalem, Late 8th–Early 4th Centuries B.C.E.," *TA* 33 (2006): 229–43.

37. Ibid., 229.

38. Four *lmlk* stamped jar handles, four other handles with concentric circles, and three rosette stamped handles were discovered from the late Iron Age. Three lion stamp impressions were discovered from the sixth century B.C.E. From the Persian period two *yhwd* stamp impressions of the early types dated to the late sixth and fifth centuries B.C.E. and five *yhwd* stamp impressions from the middle types dated to the fourth and third centuries B.C.E. (see ibid., 231–33, 234 fig. 3, 240; Oded Lipschits and David Vanderhooft, *Yehud Stamp Impressions: A Corpus of Inscribed Stamp Impressions from the Persian and Hellenistic Periods in Judah* (Winona Lake, Ind.: Eisenbrauns, forthcoming). No Hellenistic remains come from the site, which dovetails with the absence of *yhwd* stamp impressions of the late types.

39. Gilad Cinamon, "The Tumuli South-West of Jerusalem and Their Significance to the Understanding of Jerusalem's Countryside in the Iron Age II" (M.A. thesis, Tel Aviv University, 2004); Greenberg and Cinamon, "Stamped and Incised Jar Handles," 229, 233–35; Lipschits and Gadot, "Ramat Raḥel and the Emeq Rephaim Sites," 88–96; Lipschits and Vanderhooft, *Yehud Stamp Impressions*.

40. Nurit Feig, "The Environs of Jerusalem in the Iron Age II" [Hebrew], in *The History of Jerusalem: The Biblical Period* (ed. S. Ahituv and B. Mazar; Jerusalem: Yad Yitshak Ben Tsevi, 2000), 387–409.

was discovered,[41] dated to the early seventh century B.C.E.,[42] and two lion stamp impressions were discovered at the site and at the slopes above it (not yet published), indicating the continued use of the site during the sixth century B.C.E. No *yhwd* stamped jar handles were discovered at Khirbet er-Ras, but according to the surveys Persian-period pottery is present at the site.[43]

These sites may also have functioned together with other small hamlets, farms, and agricultural installations in the area, all of them with late Iron Age and Persian-period pottery,[44] and probably attached to winepresses. These include, beside the farm at er-Ras,[45] a farm (?) and winepresses at Beit Safafa;[46] a cave site excavated near the Holyland Hotel in Jerusalem;[47] and probably also the sites at Manaḥat, Giv'at Massuah, and some other small sites.[48]

Although no continuous stratigraphic sequence exists at such small sites, Greenberg and Cinamon hypothesize, on the basis of the chronological distribution of the jar stamp impressions, that the area served as

41. Nurit Feig and Omar Abed-Rabo, "Khirbet er-Ras" [Hebrew], *Excavations and Surveys in Israel* 103 (1995): 65–66.

42. Lipschits, Sergi, and Koch, "Royal Judahite Jar Handles," 3–32.

43. Amos Kloner, *Survey of Jerusalem: The Southern Sector* (Jerusalem: Israel Antiquities Authority, 2000), 29.

44. Greenberg and Cinamon, "Stamped and Incised Jar Handles," 233.

45. Nurit Feig, "New Discoveries in the Rephaim Valley, Jerusalem," *PEQ* 128 (1996) 3–7; Gershon Edelstein, "A Terraced Farm at Er-Ras," *Atiqot* 40 (2000): 39–63.

46. Nurit Feig, "Excavations at Beit Safafa: Iron Age II and Byzantine Agricultural Installations South of Jerusalem," *Atiqot* 44 (2003): 191–238.

47. Sarah Ben-Arieh, "Salvage Excavations near the Holyland Hotel, Jerusalem," *Atiqot* 40 (2000): 1–24.

48. Greenberg and Cinamon ("Stamped and Incised Jar Handles," 234–36 and Table 2) mentioned thirty-five winepresses (eight wine presses at Rogem Ganim, sixteen at the nearby site of Manaḥat, five at Giv'at Massuah, four at Beit Safafa, and two at Khirbet er-Ras), together with numerous other installations connected to wine production such as plastered tanks and storage caves. The absence of silos like those discovered at the nearby site of Moẓa (Zvi Greenhut and Alon De Groot, "Moẓa—A Bronze and Iron Age Village West of Jerusalem" [Hebrew with English abstract], *Qad* 123 [2002]: 8–11; Zvi Greenhut, "Production, Storage and Distribution of Grain during the Iron Age and Their Linkage to the Socio-Economic Organization of the Settlement in Israel" [Hebrew] [Ph.D. diss., Tel Aviv University, 2006], 195–281), and of animal pens or corrals so common in other areas of the hill country also point to wine production as the raison d'etre for these sites. On this subject, see Avraham Faust, "Judah in the Sixth Century B.C.E.: A Rural Perspective," *PEQ* 135 (2003): 37–53.

Jerusalem's southwestern wine country from the late eighth to the fifth centuries B.C.E.[49] Following other scholars, they connected the development of the Rephaim basin in the latter part of the eighth century B.C.E. with the development of Jerusalem during the same period. Following Nadav Na'aman's suggestion and based on the detailed discussion by Oded Lipschits and Yuval Gadot,[50] Lipschits and David Vanderhooft[51] hypothesize that the development of the Rephaim basin was connected to the emergence of Ramat Raḥel as an administrative center in the region under Assyrian rule, and not as part of the development in Jerusalem. It follows logically that the development in the Rephaim basin in the hinterland of Jerusalem was connected with the organization of royal estates in the kingdom of Judah during the late eighth and seventh centuries B.C.E.,[52] probably after the period when Judah became an Assyrian vassal kingdom. The Rephaim basin appears to have been developed as a royal estate to supply local administrators, probably with wine. This explanation fits the centralized processing demonstrated by the concentration of winepresses not associated with village infrastructure, the process of organized decanting and shipping of the wine, and the function of Ramat Raḥel in all of the periods in question as an administrative center in the region. As with the Benjamin area to the north of Jerusalem, the administrative and economic nature of this area, its connection to the administrative center at Ramat Raḥel, and the archaeological evidence for its continuous use until the early Hellenistic period are clear indications of its existence under Babylonian rule as well.[53]

---

49. Greenberg and Cinamon, "Stamped and Incised Jar Handles," 236–38.

50. Na'aman, "An Assyrian Residence in Ramat Raḥel," 260–80; Lipschits and Gadot, "Ramat Raḥel and the Emeq Rephaim Sites," 88–96.

51. Lipschits and Vanderhooft, *Yehud Stamp Impressions*.

52. Israel Finkelstein, "The Archaeology of the Days of Manasseh," in *Scripture and Other Artifacts: Essays on the Bible and Archaeology in Honor of Philip J. King* (ed. Michael D. Coogan; J. Cheryl Exum, and Lawrence E. Stager; Louisville: Westminster John Knox, 1994), 169–87 (174; 177–78); Nili Sacher Fox, *In the Service of the King: Officialdom in Ancient Israel and Judah* (Cincinnati: Hebrew Union College Press, 2000), 216–40.

53. It is not clear to me why, in a series of papers, Avraham Faust insisted that the sites in this region did not continue to exist in the sixth century and during the Persian period, and even built a theory on the crisis of the rural settlement in Judah based on this data ("Jerusalem's Countryside during the Iron Age II-Persian Period Transition" [Hebrew], in *New Studies on Jerusalem: Proceedings of the Seventh Confer-*

In contrast with the settlement continuity in the northern area of the Judean Hills, the main and prominent change in the settlement, demography, and borders of Judah is the creation of the Idumaean province in the southern Judean hills, the southern Shephelah, and the Negev, previously parts of the kingdom of Judah.[54] It was probably a long and gradual change, set in motion by Sennacherib and the harsh Assyrian conquest of the region. The northern and southern Judean hills transformed into diverse settlement units. The northern unit was clearly allied with the areas north of it, and one must draw parallels between the settlement processes taking place there and those taking place in the Benjamin region. The southern unit was linked with settlement processes taking place in the Negev and the southern part of the Shephelah, and was separate from the settlement processes that took place in the northern highland.[55] In view of this settlement picture, one can understand why, when the array of border fortresses in the Beersheba-Arad Valleys collapsed (whether as part of the Babylonian attack or a gradual process that began before the final Babylonian attack and continued afterwards), the vast, relatively empty areas of the southern highlands of Judah became a lodestone for the Arab and Edomite tribes that had begun to invade from the south.[56] In any case, this region went through a different geopolitical and demographical process that cannot be compared with that which took place in the northern Judean hills and the region of Benjamin.

---

ence [ed. A. Faust and E. Baruch; Bar Ilan: Bar Ilan University Press, 2002], 83–89; idem, "Judah in the Sixth Century B.C.E.: a Rural Perspective," 37–53; idem, "Social and Cultural Changes in Judah during the 6th century B.C.E. and Their Implications for Our Understanding of the Nature of the Neo-Babylonian Period," *UF* 36 [2004]: 157–76; idem, "Settlement Dynamics and Demographic Fluctuations in Judah from the Late Iron Age to the Hellenistic Period and the Archaeology of Persian-Period 'Yehud,'" in *A Time of Change: Judah and its Neighbours in the Persian and Early Hellenistic Periods* [ed. Y. Levin; London: T&T Clark, 2007], 23–51; idem, "Judah in the Sixth Century B.C.E.: Continuity or Break," *ErIsr* 29 [2009]: 339–47).

54. Stern, "The Babylonian Gap: The Archaeological Reality," 274.

55. Oded Lipschits, "The 'Yehud' Province under Babylonian Rule (586–539 B.C.E.): Historic Reality and Historiographic Conceptions" [Hebrew] (Ph.D. diss., Tel Aviv University, 1997), 298–99.

56. Lipschits, "Demographic Changes in Judah," 334–38; idem, *Fall and Rise of Jerusalem*, 140–46, 181–84.

3. The Significance of the New Finds and the New Studies
for Understanding the Historical Reality of the Sixth
Century b.c.e. and the Biblical Description of the
"Exilic Period" in Judah

The meaning of the new finds from the sixth century B.C.E. and the new observations concerning the "exilic period" in Judah is that after the destruction of Jerusalem and the other main urban and military Judahite centers by the Babylonians at the beginning of the sixth century B.C.E., "the people who were left in the land of Judah" (2 Kgs 25:22) continued to live in close proximity to the north and south of Jerusalem, continued to maintain a rural economy, continued to pay taxes in wine and oil and other agricultural products in the same way and in similar stamped jars as they had previously, continued to produce pottery in the same Iron Age tradition, and continued to serve under the same administration. The administrative center at Ramat Raḥel continued to function as the collection center of the taxes, mainly in the form of jars filled with wine and oil, with no marked change, except for the new lion stamp impressions on the handles of the jars, which replaced the rosette stamp impressions on the same type of jars, even when the capital of the newly established province of Yehud moved to Tell en-Naṣbeh (Mizpah), which served as the *bîrah* for 141 years, from 586 B.C.E.,[57] through the Neo-Babylonian period,[58] until the time of Nehemiah (445 B.C.E.).[59] These observations confirm the conclusion that in many aspects the Babylonian empire continued the Assyrian ideology and administration, took over the Assyrian provincial system, and made only the minimal and necessary adjustments.[60]

---

57. Lipschits, "Judah, Jerusalem and the Temple (586–539 B.C.E.)," 129–42.

58. André Lemaire, "Nabonidus in Arabia and Judah in the Neo-Babylonian Period," in Lipschits and Blenkinsopp, *Judah and the Judeans in the Neo-Babylonian Period*, 292.

59. Joseph Blenkinsopp, "The Judean Priesthood during the Neo-Babylonian and Achaemenid Periods: A Hypothetical Reconstruction," *CBQ* 60 (1998): 42 n. 48; cf. André Lemaire, "Populations et territoires de Palestine à l'époque perse," *Transeu* 3 (1990): 39–40; idem, "Nabonidus in Arabia and Judah," 292.

60. See, e.g., Ronald H. Sack, "Nebuchadnezzar II and the Old Testament: History Versus Ideology," in Lipschits and Blenkinsopp, *Judah and the Judeans in the Neo-Babylonian Period*, 221–34 (229). A similar opinion was expressed by Ephraim Stern ("Assyrian and Babylonian Elements in the Material Culture of Palestine in the Persian Period," *Transeu* 7 [1994]: 51–62), as against later statements (see, e.g., Stern, *Assyrian*,

The major and most conspicuous archaeological phenomenon in sixth century B.C.E. Judah after the destruction of Jerusalem was the sharp decline in urban life, which is in contrast to the continuity of the rural settlements in the region of Benjamin and in the area between Bethlehem and Beth-zur.[61] This settlement pattern also continued throughout the Persian period when, despite the rebuilding of Jerusalem and the restoration of its status as the capital of the province, there was no strengthening of urban life in this area, and settlement in Judah remained largely based on the rural population.[62]

This sharp decline in urban life has other implications for the material culture, such as the disappearance of the typical family burial caves usually associated with urban and other elite classes in society.[63] This is a reflection of deep religious and social change. Since there is continued use of some of the burial caves in the area of Benjamin, in Jerusalem and other sites,[64] there is no need to connect it to the isolated crisis of 586 B.C.E., but rather to a broader and graduated change in religion and society that occurred during the sixth century B.C.E. and perhaps mainly at the beginning of the Persian period, when other changes, such as the disappearance

---

Babylonian, and Persian Periods, 307–8). See, in this line, also Joseph Blenkinsopp, "The Bible, Archaeology and Politics; or, the Empty Land Revisited," *JSOT* 27 (2002): 179–80. A different view was expressed by David S. Vanderhooft (*The Neo-Babylonian Empire and Babylon in the Latter Prophets* [HSM 59; Atlanta: Scholars Press, 1999], 90–114), but see against his views Sack, "Nebuchadnezzar II and the Old Testament," 226–27.

61. On this subject, see Charles E. Carter, "The Province of Yehud in the Post-Exilic Period: Soundings in the Site Distribution and Demography," in *Second Temple Studies 2: Temple and Community in the Persian Period* (ed. Tamara C. Eskenazi and Kent H. Richards; JSOTSup 175; Sheffield: JSOT Press, 1994), 106–45; Milevski, "Settlement Patterns in Northern Judah," 7–29; Lipschits, "'Yehud' Province under Babylonian Rule," 171–336; idem, "History of the Benjaminite Region," 155–90; idem, "Demographic Changes in Judah," 326–55; idem, *Fall and Rise of Jerusalem*, 250–58; Nadav Na'aman, "Royal Vassals or Governors? On the Status of Sheshbazzar and Zerubbabel in the Persian Empire," *Hen* 22 (2000): 43.

62. See Lipschits, "Demographic Changes in Judah," 326–55; idem, *Fall and Rise of Jerusalem*, 206–71.

63. Gabriel Barkay, "Burial Caves and Burial Practices in Judah in the Iron Age," in *Graves and Burial Practices in Israel in the Ancient Period* (ed. I. Singer; Jerusalem: Izhak Ben Zvi, 1994), 96–104.

64. Faust, "Judah in the Sixth Century B.C.E.: Continuity or Break," 341, with further literature.

of iconography in the stamp impressions on jar handles (the well dated change from the lion to the *yhwd* stamp impressions) occurred.

Other elements that emphasize the change in material culture from the Iron Age to the Persian period, such as the disappearance of the typical Judahite house, are probably part of a gradual change that had already begun during the seventh century B.C.E. and continued for hundreds of years afterwards, with some typical four-room houses still built during the sixth century B.C.E.[65] One should remember in this regard that, aside from the monumental building at Ramat Raḥel and the industrial site at En-gedi, there are only scanty architectural remains in Judah dated to the Persian period. The domestic architecture that can be compared with Iron Age Judahite architecture came from the Hellenistic period. From an archaeological perspective it is difficult to date the disappearance of the typical Judahite house and to connect it to a specific period when a sharp decline in urban life occurred but other aspects in the material culture continued to exist.

These new observations concerning sixth century B.C.E. Judah fit well with the biblical account of this period—both with the description of the destruction of Jerusalem and with the description of the days of Gedaliah in the short period afterwards. There are some clear clues in the biblical description about the destruction of the border fortresses and cities in the Shephelah (Jer 34:7), and this information fits well with the archaeological data concerning the destruction of these sites, as well as of many small towns, villages, and hamlets in the region,[66] and the mention of Azekah in Ostracon 4 from Lachish.[67] The biblical description of the period of the Babylonian destruction focuses, however, on the destruction of Jerusalem and the burning of the centers of government and religious ritual in the city (2 Kgs 25; Jer 37; 52), as well as the burning of "all of the houses of Jerusalem," and "every large house" (2 Kgs 25:9), and the total destruction of the city walls (25:10). This description accords with the archeological finds that were revealed in the excavations at the City of David, the Ophel, and the southwestern hill of Jerusalem.[68] It seems that the beginning of

---

65. Jeffrey R. Zorn, "Mizpah: Newly Discovered Stratum Reveals Judah's Other Capital," *BAR* 23 (1997): 29–38, 66.

66. Lipschits, *Fall and Rise of Jerusalem*, 218–23.

67. Harry Torczyner, *Lachish I: The Lachish Letters* (London: Oxford University Press, 1938), 76.

68. Lipschits, *Fall and Rise of Jerusalem*, 210–13.

the systematic destruction of Jerusalem, about a month after the king's flight and the surrender of the city, is evidence that this was not a spontaneous deed. It was a considered and conscious political act attesting to a strategic decision: to obliterate the center of rebellion and to prevent its future rebuilding, so as to eradicate, once and for all, the seeds of ferment and instability in Judah. Along the same lines, the biblical description of the destruction of the kingdom of Judah mentions only the deportation of the populace of Jerusalem (2 Kgs 25:11; Jer 39:9; 52:15), and does not mention deportations from other areas in Judah. This description accords with accounts given in 2 Kgs 25:12, Jer 39:10, and Jer 52:16, mentioning "the poorest people of the land" who were left by Nabuzaradan, the commander of the guard (2 Kgs 25:12; Jer 42:16), to be vinedressers and tillers of the soil.[69] This is a description deriving from the qualitative, economic, and class-oriented judgment of the elite deported to Babylon toward those who remained in the land, pronounced also in the tendentious summary generalization, "So Judah was carried away captive out of his land" (2 Kgs 25:21b; Jer 52:27b). There is only a semantic gap between this attitude toward the question of how many were deported and from where, and how many remained and where, and the attitude toward the same questions in the two versions describing the days of Gedaliah (2 Kgs 25:22–26; Jer 40:7–41:18). According to these verses those who remained in Judah were not "the poorest people of the land," but rather "the people who remained in the land of Judah" (2 Kgs 25:22a); "men, women from those who were not deported to Babylon" (Jer 40:7),[70] or even "a remnant for Judah" (40:11). They were left under the leadership of Gedaliah to continue the national life of the people in its land (2 Kgs 25:22b, 24b; Jer 40:7aβ–b; 10). Nebuchadrezzar, king of Babylon, is the one who left them (2 Kgs 25: 22a).

There are no details in the biblical description regarding how many people remained in Judah after the destruction of Jerusalem. Since the focus of the description is the deportation of the people from Jerusalem, it is reasonable to assume that the "remnant" was part of the rural population, especially in the regions around the city. Gedaliah was officially appointed

---

69. See a detailed discussion of these descriptions and expressions in ibid., 102.

70. In the Septuagint version, which at this point seems more reliable, "children and some of the poorest people of the land" are missing from the text. Thus, the text refers only to "men and women who were not deported from Judah." See J. Gerald Janzen, *Studies in the Text of Jeremiah* (HSM 6; Cambridge: Harvard University Press, 1973), 53; and Lipschits, *Fall and Rise of Jerusalem*, 118–22, with further literature.

over "those who remained in Judah" (2 Kgs 25:22b, 23aβ; Jer 40:7),[71] and this population had a well-defined status and place, probably in the region of Benjamin and the environs of Jerusalem.[72] The events described in the story of Gedaliah's period of rule in Judah are restricted, geographically, to a specific area around Mizpah, where "the land of Judah" (2 Kgs 25:22) or "the land" (v. 24) were mentioned. In the version in Jer 40–41, there are "the cities" around Mizpah (40:10) "in the land of Judah" (40:12). These cities include Gibeon (41:12, 16), and there is reference to the people living "in Geruth-Kimham, near Bethlehem" (41:17).[73] This is the reason for and the background to the description of the days of Gedaliah's rule in Mizpah. Gedaliah commanded the people left in the land and the refugees "who were in Moab, in Ammon, in Edom, and in all the countries" (Jer 40:11), who had returned "out of all the places to which they had been scattered" (v. 12a), to join the people that were left in Judah and "stay in the land and serve the king of Babylon, and it shall go well with you" (2 Kgs 25:24; Jer 40: 9–10).[74]

---

71. After Peter Machinist, "Palestine, Administration of (Assyro-Babylonian)," *ABD* 5:79, there is nothing to support the assumption that Gedaliah was appointed as a king. See Lipschits, *Fall and Rise of Jerusalem*, 88–92, contra J. Maxwell Miller and John H. Hayes, *A History of Ancient Israel and Judah* (Philadelphia: Westminster, 1986), 421–25; cf. Francesco Bianchi, "Zorobabele re di Giuda," *Hen* 13 (1991): 133–50; idem "Le rôle de Zorobabel et de la dynastie davidique en Judée du VIe Siècle au IIe Siècle av.J.-C.," *Transeu* 7 (1994): 153–65; André Lemaire, *Nouvelles inscriptions araméennes d'Idumée au musée d'Israël* (Supplément 3 à *Transeu*; Paris: Gabalda, 1996), 48–57. Cf. also Rainer Albertz, *Israel in Exile: The History and Literature of the Sixth Century B.C.E.* (SBLSBL 3; Atlanta: Society of Biblical Literature, 2003), 92–93 n. 166.

72. See Lipschits, *Fall and Rise of Jerusalem*, 339–44, with further literature.

73. For the meaning of the name "Geruth-Kimham," see Yair Hoffman, "Literature and Ideology in Jeremiah 40:1–43:7" [Hebrew], in *Studies in Bible and Exegesis, Vol. V: Presented to Uriel Simon* (ed. M. Garsiel et al.; Ramat Gan: Universitat Bar Ilan, 2000), 117–18 n. 29; idem, *Jeremiah: Introduction and Commentary* [Hebrew] (Tel Aviv: 'Am 'Oved, 2001), 724.

74. The silence of the Bible on events that occurred in Judah after the murder of Gedaliah cannot be interpreted as evidence of the view that life in Judah ceased. On this subject, see Lipschits, ed., *Can We Define the Material Culture of the Sixth Century in Judah?* [Hebrew] (Abstracts from the Conference Held in Tel Aviv University; Tel Aviv: Tel Aviv University Press, 1998), 467–87; idem, "History of the Benjaminite Region," 161–65; Jill A. Middlemas, *The Troubles of Templeless Judah* (OTM; New York: Oxford University Press, 2005), 36–37.

The conclusion from all the above is that there is agreement between the biblical description of the days of the destruction and the archaeological finds. The Babylonians dealt a harsh blow to the kingdom of Judah, the harshest blow in the history of the kingdom. They destroyed Jerusalem, as well as many of the urban, military, economic, and administrative centers. They deported the king and all the religious, economic, social, and political elite, and Judah lost its independence.[75] From the demographic point of view, based on all the available archaeological data, one can estimate that, as a result of the long war and as part of its effect and outcome, there was approximately a 60 percent decline in population, from about 110,000 people to about 40,000.[76]

3.1. Ammon in the Sixth Century B.C.E.: What Can We Learn about the Fate of Judah under Babylonian Rule?

The new finds and recent studies presented above support and strengthen the "middle path" presented by the current author elsewhere.[77] They offer the option of focusing on the search for the "half full cup." In this case, the comparison of the archaeological situation in Judah with that in Ammon enables us to view the processes in a neighboring country without benefit of biblical descriptions and without theological influence or any historical interpretation.

Rabbath-Ammon during the Babylonian period is an archaeological and historical blank. We have no information about the fate of this capital city. However, in contrast to the continuation of the settlement in the area immediately south and north of Rabbath-Ammon, we can reconstruct a deliberate destruction of the main sites on the western border of the kingdom and along the main road from the west to Rabbath-Ammon (Tell

---

75. Lipschits, *Can We Define the Material Culture*, 467–87.

76. Lipschits, "Demographic Changes in Judah," 323–79; idem, *Fall and Rise of Jerusalem*, 267–71; cf. Charles E. Carter, *The Emergence of Yehud in the Persian Period: A Social and Demographic Study* (JSOTSup 294; Sheffield: Sheffield Academic Press, 1999), 246–48.

77. See, e.g., Lipschits, "History of the Benjaminite Region," 155–90; idem, "The Rural Settlement in Judah in the Sixth Century B.C.E.: A Rejoinder," *PEQ* 136 (2004): 99–107; idem, *Fall and Rise of Jerusalem*; idem, "The Babylonian Period in Judah: In Search of the Half Full Cup (A Response to the Panel Discussion: In Conversation with Oded Lipschits, *The Fall and Rise of Jerusalem*)," *JHS* 7 (2007): 39–47.

Mazar, Tell es-Sa'idiyeh, and Tel Nimrin).[78] Similar to what happened in Judah (the Babylonian destruction of the western borders and cities in the Shephelah), this archaeological situation in the western border sites of the kingdom of Ammon can be interpreted as part of the "opening of the door" to the heart of the kingdom by the Babylonian army. As in Judah, in Ammon too there was a continuation of the rural settlement from the end of the Iron Age to the Persian period. From the results of Tell el-'Umeiri excavations and the survey conducted as part of the Madaba plains project, scholars have demonstrated that a large area south of the capital of Rabbath-Ammon was not destroyed by the Babylonians and even flourished throughout the Babylonian and the Persian periods.[79] In Ammon, as in Judah, one can discern different geopolitical and demographic processes in the different areas of the kingdom. One can reconstruct a continuation of the rural settlement in the area around 'Umeiri and Ḥesban, south of Rabbath-Ammon and perhaps also in the Baq'ah region, north of Ammon. Farms and small villages continued to exist in those areas, characterized by diverse agricultural installations, mainly winepresses.[80] As at Mizpah in Benjamin, at about 580 B.C.E., after the Babylonian expedition against Ammon and under Babylonian rule, Tell el-'Umeiri was built as the new administrative center of the Madaba plains region.[81] Furthermore, the size of the settlement in 'Umeiri was diminished, and it appears that the smaller settlement took on a highly specialized administrative and political function[82] very similar to that assumed for Mizpah.[83] The one

---

78. Lipschits, "The Rural Settlement in Judah," 41.

79. Ibid., with further literature.

80. Larry G. Herr, "Organization of Excavation and Summary of Results at Tall al-'Umayri," in *Madaba Plains Project 3: The 1989 Season at Tell el-'Umeiri and Vicinity and Subsequent Studies* (ed. L. G. Herr et al.; Berrien Springs, Mich.: Andrews University Press, 1997), 16.

81. Larry G. Herr, "Organization of the Excavation and Summary of Results on the Tell," in *Madaba Plains Project 2: The 1987 Season at Tell el 'Umeiri and Vicinity and Subsequent Studies* (ed. L. G. Herr et al.; Berrien Springs, Mich.: Andrews University Press, 1991), 8–14 (12–13).

82. Ibid., 12–13.

83. See Jeffrey R. Zorn, "Tell en-Nasbeh: A Re-evaluation of the Architecture and Stratigraphy of the Early Bronze Age, Iron Age and Latter Periods" (Ph.D. diss.; University of California Berkeley, 1993), 151–83; idem, "Tell en-Naṣbeh and the Problem of the Material Culture of the Sixth Century," in Lipschits and Blenkinsopp, *Judah and the Judeans in the Neo-Babylonian Period*, 418–33.

Neo-Babylonian style seal that was found in 'Umeiri[84] can be interpreted as a reflection of the Babylonian influence on this administrative center, if not as evidence of actual presence at the site, and it can be compared with the abundance of Babylonian material in Tell en-Naṣbeh.[85] In addition, the seventy-five seals and seal impressions that were found at Tell el-'Umeiri, emphasizing its administrative nature,[86] are similar in function and number to the *m(w)ṣh* and *gb'n gdr* stamp impressions, which date to the sixth century B.C.E. and reflect organized economic and administrative activity in the Babylonian province of Judah.[87]

Thus the destruction of the main cities and administrative, urban, and military centers was parallel in Judah and Ammon, and should not be understood as an indication of a total destruction and demographic gap. Both destructions should be interpreted as focused and intentional, according to the interests and intents of the empire, albeit with many diverse and even difficult consequences. One must take care nonetheless to differentiate very cautiously between varying regions in the kingdom, and not to draw conclusions from one region to another, and especially not to generalize when it comes to the rural settlements and to indications of administrative, economical, and cultural continuity existing in some regions and not in others.[88]

Both from the situation in Ammon and from the new finds and recent studies of the material culture, administration, and economy in sixth-century B.C.E. Judah, it is clear that continuity in material culture can be well attested in the rural areas that continued to survive after the destruction of the urban, military, and administrative centers, and that these regions

---

84. See Larry G. Herr, "The Ammonites in the Late Iron Age and Persian Period," in *Ancient Ammon* (ed. Burton MacDonald and Randall W. Younker; SHANE 17; Leiden: Brill, 1999), 231.

85. See Zorn, "Tell en-Naṣbeh and the Problem of the Material Culture," 433–40.

86. See Larry G. Herr, "The Inscribed Seal Impression," in *Madaba Plains Project 1: The 1984 Season at Tell el 'Umeiri and Vicinity and Subsequent Studies* (ed. L. T. Geraty, et al.; Berrien Springs, Mich.: Andrews University Press, 1989), 369; idem, "Organization of the Excavation," 12.

87. Lipschits, "History of the Benjaminite Region," 178–83; idem, *Fall and Rise of Jerusalem*, 174–81.

88. See, for example, the discussions of Stern (e.g., "The Babylonian Gap: The Archaeological Reality," 273–77), which combine in his survey different regions, including Assyrian provinces in the northern part of the land, with different regions in Judah. Compare this to Vanderhooft's discussion in *Neo-Babylonian Empire*, 106.

functioned as the places where many aspects of the material culture were preserved and continued through the "dark ages." The general agreement on the settlement continuum in the area of Benjamin during the sixth century B.C.E.,[89] and the new data on the similar continuum in the Rephaim Valley and the area south of Jerusalem, are the best indications for the place where the "people that remained in the land" continued to live, with the same pottery and other indications for the material culture that are well known from the period before the destruction of Jerusalem in 586 B.C.E.

In light of the above, the question is, what can we learn from the new discoveries and the new studies on Judah in the sixth century B.C.E. about the role of archaeological research in biblical studies and historical reconstructions?

4. WHAT IS BEHIND THE ARCHAEOLOGICAL RECONSTRUCTIONS OF THE "BABYLONIAN GAP" AND THE "EMPTY LAND"?

The archaeological study of the end of the kingdom of Judah has usually been based on destruction layers, especially in Jerusalem, but also in other cities such as Lachish, military fortresses such as Arad, industrial villages (kinds of royal estates) such as En-gedi, and other large and medium-sized towns and agricultural settlements. The results of these excavations and surveys have usually been interpreted as clearly affirming that Judah was almost entirely destroyed and that its population disappeared from most of the kingdom's territory.

A direct line can be drawn from William Foxwell Albright's 1949 statement "There is not a single known case where a town of Judah was continuously occupied through the exilic period"[90] to the assessments of David Jamieson-Drake[91] of a "complete societal collapse" and "almost complete dissolution" and to the title of Stern's 2004 essay, "The Babylonian Gap: The Archaeological Reality," and the conclusion in the chapter on the Babylonian period in his 2001 book: "A review of the archaeological evidence from sixth-century B.C.E. Judah clearly reflects the literary (i.e.,

---

89. Stern, "The Babylonian Gap: The Archaeological Reality," 273.

90. William F. Albright, *The Archaeology of Palestine* (Baltimore: Penguin, 1949), 142.

91. David W. Jamieson-Drake, *Scribes and Schools in Monarchic Judah: A Socio-archaeological Approach* (JSOTSup 109; Sheffield: Almond, 1991), 75, 146.

biblical) evidence for the complete destruction of all the settlements and fortified towns by Nebuchadnezzar II's armies in 586 B.C.E."[92]

Archaeologists have claimed that "this view is based upon purely archaeological considerations and is not motivated by hidden ideological considerations,"[93] and have usually used these archaeological "facts" as a basis for a historical reconstruction of the "Babylonian gap" and the "empty land" during the sixth century B.C.E., until the time of the return from the exile at the beginning of the Persian period. Are these, however, "purely archaeological considerations"? Can archaeology really differentiate between the material culture from the end of the First Temple period and material culture that was used by "the people who remained in Judah" in the years afterwards, especially at sites that were not destroyed by the Babylonians?

It seems to me that this archaeological "fact" of a total destruction at the beginning of the sixth century B.C.E. is merely an outcome of historical preconceptions about this period based on a traditional interpretation of the biblical description.[94] Bustenay Oded was right to claim that scholars supporting the "myth of the empty land" as a by-product of the thesis about "mythical ancient Israel" have common presumptions, especially regarding the reliability of the biblical description concerning the destruction and deportation, which is part of a late myth, invented as a political claim.[95] He is right in his attempt to demonstrate how much their thesis of the creation of the "myth" is unacceptable and not well founded on archaeological grounds, and even not on biblical grounds. However, it seems to me that just as in the case of the different emphases in 2 Kgs 25:12, 22, the "school" of scholars supporting the "Babylonian gap" and reconstructing a "real" empty land in Judah during the "exilic period" are likewise studying the archaeological finds and interpreting the texts with common presumptions, focusing on general impressions from the statements made by exiles and returnees in order to substantiate their right to the land, rather than using the more delicate research on the different voices and descriptions of this period.

---

92. See Stern, *Assyrian, Babylonian, and Persian Periods*, 323, and the citations in Blenkinsopp, "The Bible, Archaeology and Politics," 178.

93. Stern, "The Babylonian Gap: The Archaeological Reality," 273.

94. See, e.g., Stern, *Assyrian, Babylonian, and Persian Periods*, 353, 581; Oded, "Myth of the Empty Land," 59–66.

95. Oded, "Myth of the Empty Land," 57–58.

It seems to me that the fundamental problem with the archaeological reconstruction of the "empty land" is that until now there has been no archaeological way to differentiate between the material culture of the early or middle sixth century B.C.E. in Judah and the material culture of the last generations before the destruction. In many respects, since archaeologists have not expected to find the material culture from the sixth century B.C.E., this material culture was not discovered, located, or identified. Gabriel Barkay was right when he claimed that "it seems that the destruction of the Temple and the fall of Jerusalem influenced modern scholarship, which fixed the date of the end of the Iron Age according to a historical fact and not on the basis of the archaeological picture."[96] Indeed, it would appear that historical considerations are what stand behind the generalized dating of the destruction layers in all sites in Judah in approximately 587/6 B.C.E., and that these considerations have caused a lack of appropriate attention to the possibility that a large population continued to exist in Judah even after the destruction of Jerusalem. Even in the analysis of the finds from the survey in Benjamin,[97] where there is general consensus among scholars that during the sixth century B.C.E. many settlements continued to exist, the pottery dated to the late First Temple period was considered as representing only the period before 586 B.C.E., and the decline in settlement was considered as "undoubtedly related to the destruction of Judah in the early sixth century B.C.E."[98] Paradoxically, these archaeological assertions have provided material for historical studies, which are based on dating the strata of destruction to create a historical profile of the Babylonian destruction throughout the land of Israel.[99]

Furthermore, no archaeologist could or has even tried to demonstrate from the archaeological perspective any kind of "mass return" at the beginning of the Persian period, as described in the introductory section to Ezra-Nehemiah. This "mass return" had to be well attested in any case of

---

96. Gabriel Barkay, "The Iron Age III: The Babylonian Period" [Hebrew], in *Is It Possible to Define the Pottery of the Sixth Century B.C.E. in Judea?* (ed. O. Lipschits; Tel Aviv: Tel Aviv University Press, 1998), 25.

97. See Magen and Finkelstein, *Archaeological Survey in the Hill Country of Benjamin.*

98. See ibid., 27. For a critique of these conclusions and a renewed discussion of the finds of the survey, see Lipschits, "History of the Benjaminite Region," 180–84; Lipschits, *Fall and Rise of Jerusalem*, 245–49.

99. See Vanderhooft, *Neo-Babylonian Empire*, 106–7.

"mass deportation" and "empty land," as indicated in Ezra 1–6, according to which some 50,000 immigrants returned to Judah at the very beginning of the Persian period with the support of the imperial authorities.

The current indications, as presented above, for the continuity in material culture, economy, and administration, not only from the late Iron Age to the "exilic period," but also to the Persian period, force us to see the sixth century B.C.E. as a period when despite the destructions and deportations, despite the gap in the history of Jerusalem and the temple, despite the move of the social and religious center of gravity from Judah to Babylon, Judahite life continued in Judah, and in many aspects continued in a way very similar to what we know about Judah before the 586 B.C.E. destruction.

It seems to me that while studying the Babylonian period a very detailed and careful examination of different regions is essential from the methodological point of view. By studying archaeological material in this way, even the most enthusiastic supporters of the "empty land" and the "Babylonian gap" theses could not assume that Judah was a truly vacant area.[100] Stern explicitly emphasized that by the term "empty," he refers "to a land that was virtually depopulated."[101]

---

100. Ibid., 104–10, 206; Stern, "The Babylonian Gap," 51; idem, *Assyrian, Babylonian, and Persian Periods*, 321–26; idem, "The Babylonian Gap: The Archaeological Reality," 276; Oded, "Myth of the Empty Land," 66–71.

101. See Stern, "The Babylonian Gap: The Archaeological Reality," 274. From this aspect, the "ultra-conservative thesis" presented by Faust in a series of papers (e.g., Judah in the Sixth Century B.C.E.: A Rural Perspective," 37–53; idem, "Social and Cultural Changes in Judah during the 6th Century B.C.E. and Their Implications for Our Understanding of the Nature of the Neo-Babylonian Period," 157–76; idem, "Settlement Dynamics and Demographic Fluctuations in Judah from the Late Iron Age to the Hellenistic Period and the Archaeology of Persian-Period 'Yehud,'" 23–51; idem, "Judah in the Sixth Century B.C.E.: Continuity or Break?" 339–47) carries many problems and does not stand the test of the historical, archaeological, and biblical critiques. Faust presented the most extreme theory regarding the "empty land" in Judah, ignoring the data presented above on rural settlement in the Rephaim Valley and its surroundings, discussing mainly sites that were explored in salvage excavations without separating the Negev, Southern Judean hills, and the southern Shephelah—which undoubtedly suffered from a demographic crisis at the beginning of the sixth century B.C.E., and became very soon after part of a different province of Idumaea—from the northern Judean hills and the region of Benjamin. He ignored the vast data on the fate of the area of Benjamin, hypothesizing without any basis that although the urban settlement in this region continued uninterrupted, the rural settlement suffered from the events

5. Conclusions

Putting aside unacceptable theories that deny the destruction of Jerusalem and its consequences, what then is the essential difference between the scholars who belong to the "empty land" and "Babylonian gap" school and the way I have presented the situation in Babylonian Judah in this essay?

I believe that like the two voices that can be found in the biblical description of this period—on the one hand agreeing that Judah was not entirely void of population, but on the other hand at odds about where the "true Judah" actually was—so, too, the problem with the interpretation of the archaeological finds is the question of focus and scope. Is the cup half full or half empty? Scholars concur that the Babylonians caused major destruction in Judah, deported part of the population, turned the vassal kingdom into a province, and moved its capital from Jerusalem to Mizpah. The problem is the scope of the destruction caused by the Babylonians, the scope of the deportation, and the scope of the population that was left behind.

I hope that the "middle path" I have suggested here again—this time backed up by additional archaeological data discovered in recent years, especially at Ramat Raḥel and with some further studies that shed new light on the history, administration, economy, and material culture of Judah in the sixth century B.C.E.—will open the way for further refined observations both in biblical and archaeological research, and will give this important period in the history of Judah and its land the place in the sun it rightly deserves.

Bibliography

Aharoni, Yohanan. *Excavations at Ramat Raḥel: Seasons 1959 and 1960*. Serie archeologica 2. Rome: Università degli studi, Centro di studi semitici, 1962.

———. *Excavations at Ramat Raḥel: Seasons 1961 and 1962*. Serie archeologica 6. Rome: Università degli studi, Centro di studi semitici, 1964.

Aharoni, Miriam, and Yohanan Aharoni. "The Stratification of Judahite Sites in the 8th and 7th Centuries B.C.E." *BASOR* 224 (1976): 73–90.

---

of 586. Furthermore, in all these papers, Faust used as a control group a very limited and defined area—the Samarian foothills—an area that was part of the Samarian province since the late eighth century B.C.E., and was one of the most demographically and politically stable regions. It is no wonder that there is continuity in this area between the end of the Iron Age and the Persian period. But the question is whether the history of this region has any relevance to the history of the rural settlements in Judah.

Albertz, Rainer. *Israel in Exile: The History and Literature of the Sixth Century B.C.E.* Translated by David Green. SBLSBL 3. Atlanta: Society of Biblical Literature, 2003.

Albright, William F. *The Archaeology of Palestine.* Baltimore: Penguin, 1949.

Ariel, Donals Tzvi, and Yair Shoham. "Locally Stamped Handles and Associated Body Fragments of the Persian and Hellenistic Periods." Pages 137–69 in *Excavations at the City of David 1978–1985, IV.* Edited by D. T. Ariel. Qedem 41. Jerusalem: Institute of Archaeology, Hebrew University of Jerusalem, 2000.

Avigad, Nahman. "Two Hebrew Inscriptions on Wine Jars." *IEJ* 22 (1972): 1–9.

Barkay, Gabriel. "Burial Caves and Burial Practices in Judah in the Iron Age." Pages 96–104 in *Graves and Burial Practices in Israel in the Ancient Period.* Edited by I. Singer. Jerusalem: Izhak Ben Zvi, 1994.

———. "The Iron Age III: The Babylonian Period" [Hebrew]. Page 25 in *Is It Possible to Define the Pottery of the Sixth Century B.C.E. in Judea?* Edited by O. Lipschits. Tel Aviv: Tel Aviv University Press, 1998.

———. "Royal Palace, Royal Portrait? The Tantalizing Possibilities of Ramat Raḥel." *BAR* 32 (2006): 34–44.

Barstad, Hans M. "After the 'Myth of the Empty Land': Major Challenges in the Study of Neo-Babylonian Judah." Pages 3–20 in *Judah and the Judeans in the Neo-Babylonian Period.* Edited by Oded Lipschits and Joseph Blenkinsopp. Winona Lake, Ind.: Eisenbrauns, 2003.

———. *The Myth of the Empty Land: A Study in the History and Archaeology of Judah during the "Exilic" Period.* SO 28. Oslo: Scandinavian University Press, 1996.

Ben-Arieh, Sarah. "Salvage Excavations near the Holyland Hotel, Jerusalem." *Atiqot* 40 (2000): 1–24.

Bianchi, Francesco. "Le rôle de Zorobabel et de la dynastie davidique en Judée du VIe Siècle au IIe Siècle av.J.-C." *Transeu* 7 (1994): 153–65.

———. "Zorobabele re di Giuda." *Hen* 13 (1991): 133–50.

Blenkinsopp, Joseph. "The Bible, Archaeology and Politics; or, the Empty Land Revisited." *JSOT* 27 (2002): 169–87.

———. "The Judean Priesthood during the Neo-Babylonian and Achaemenid Periods: A Hypothetical Reconstruction." *CBQ* 60 (1998): 25–43.

Carter, Charles E. *The Emergence of Yehud in the Persian Period: A Social and Demographic Study.* JSOTSup 294. Sheffield: Sheffield Academic Press, 1999.

———. "The Province of Yehud in the Post-exilic Period: Soundings in the Site Distribution and Demography." Pages 106–45 in *Second Temple Studies 2: Temple and Community in the Persian Period.* Edited by Tamara C. Eskenazi and Kent H. Richards. JSOTSup 175. Sheffield: JSOT Press, 1994.

Cinamon, Gilad. "The Tumuli South-West of Jerusalem and Their Significance to the Understanding of Jerusalem's Countryside in the Iron Age II" [Hebrew with English abstract]. M.A. thesis. Tel Aviv University, 2004.

Edelstein, Gershon. "A Terraced Farm at Er-Ras." *Atiqot* 40 (2000): 39–63.

Faust, Avraham. "Jerusalem's Countryside during the Iron Age II-Persian Period Transition" [Hebrew]. Pages 83–89 in *New Studies on Jerusalem: Proceedings of the Seventh Conference.* Edited by A. Faust and E. Baruch. Bar Ilan: Bar Ilan University Press, 2002.

———. "Judah in the Sixth Century B.C.E.: A Rural Perspective." *PEQ* 135 (2003): 37–53.

———. "Judah in the Sixth Century B.C.E.: Continuity or Break?" *ErIsr* 29 (2009): 339–47.

———. "Settlement Dynamics and Demographic Fluctuations in Judah from the Late Iron Age to the Hellenistic Period and the Archaeology of Persian-period 'Yehud.'" Pages 23–51 in *A Time of Change: Judah and Its Neighbours in the Persian and Early Hellenistic Periods.* Edited by Y. Levin. London: T&T Clark, 2007.

———. "Social and Cultural Changes in Judah during the 6th century B.C.E. and Their Implications for Our Understanding of the Nature of the Neo-Babylonian Period." *UF* 36 (2004): 157–76.

Feig, Nurit. "The Environs of Jerusalem in the Iron Age II" [Hebrew]. Pages 387–409 in *The History of Jerusalem: The Biblical Period.* Edited by S. Ahituv and B. Mazar. Jerusalem: Yad Yitshak Ben Tsevi, 2000.

———. "Excavations at Beit Safafa: Iron Age II and Byzantine Agricultural Installations South of Jerusalem." *Atiqot* 44 (2003): 191–238.

———. "New Discoveries in the Rephaim Valley, Jerusalem." *PEQ* 128 (1996): 3–7.

Feig, Nurit, and Omar Abed-Rabo. "Khirbet er-Ras" [Hebrew]. *Excavations and Surveys in Israel* 103 (1995): 65–66.

Finkelstein, Israel. "The Archaeology of the Days of Manasseh." Pages 169–87 in *Scripture and Other Artifacts: Essays on the Bible and Archaeology in Honor of Philip J. King.* Edited by Michael D. Coogan, J. Cheryl Exum, and Lawrence E. Stager. Louisville: Westminster John Knox, 1994.

Fox, Nili Sacher. *In the Service of the King: Officialdom in Ancient Israel and Judah.* Cincinnati: Hebrew Union College Press, 2000.

Greenberg, Raphael, and Gilad Cinamon. "Stamped and Incised Jar Handles from Rogem Ganim and Their Implications for the Political Economy of Jerusalem, Late 8th–Early 4th Centuries B.C.E." *TA* 33 (2006): 229–43.

Greenhut, Zvi. "Production, Storage and Distribution of Grain during the Iron Age and Their Linkage to the Socio-Economic Organization of the Settlement in Israel" [Hebrew]. Ph.D. diss. Tel Aviv University, 2006.

Greenhut, Zvi, and Alon De Groot. "Moẓa—A Bronze and Iron Age Village West of Jerusalem" [Hebrew with English Abstract]. *Qad* 123 (2002): 8–17.

Gross, Boaz, and Yuval Goren. "A Technological Study of the Lion Stamped Handles—Preliminary Results" [Hebrew]. Pages 11–12 in *New Studies on the Lion Stamped Jar Handles from Judah.* Edited by O. Lipschits and I. Koch. Tel Aviv: Tel Aviv University Press, 2010.

Herr, Larry G. "The Ammonites in the Late Iron Age and Persian Period." Pages 219–37 in *Ancient Ammon.* Edited by Burton MacDonald and Randall W. Younker. SHANE 17. Leiden: Brill, 1999.

———. "The Inscribed Seal Impression." Pages 369–74 in *Madaba Plains Project 1: The 1984 Season at Tell el 'Umeiri and Vicinity and Subsequent Studies.* Edited by L. T. Geraty et al. Berrien Springs, Mich.: Andrews University Press, 1989.

————. "Organization of Excavation and Summary of Results at Tall al-'Umayri." Pages 7–20 in *Madaba Plains Project 3: The 1989 Season at Tell el-'Umeiri and Vicinity and Subsequent Studies.* Edited by L. G. Herr *et al.* Berrien Springs, Mich.: Andrews University Press, 1997.

————. "Organization of the Excavation and Summary of Results on the Tell." Pages 8–14 in *Madaba Plains Project 2: The 1987 Season at Tell el 'Umeiri and Vicinity and Subsequent Studies.* Edited by L. G. Herr et al. Berrien Springs, Mich.: Andrews University Press, 1991.

Hoffman, Yair. *Jeremiah: Introduction and Commentary* [Hebrew]. Tel Aviv: 'Am 'Oved, 2001.

————. "Literature and Ideology in Jeremiah 40:1–43:7" [Hebrew]. Pages 103–25 in *Studies in Bible and Exegesis, Vol. V: Presented to Uriel Simon.* Edited by M. Garsiel et al. Ramat Gan: Universitat Bar-Ilan, 2000.

Jamieson-Drake, David W. *Scribes and Schools in Monarchic Judah: A Socio-Archeological Approach.* JSOTSup 109. Sheffield: Almond, 1991.

Janzen, J. Gerald. *Studies in the Text of Jeremiah.* HSM 6. Cambridge: Harvard University Press, 1973.

Kloner, Amos. *Survey of Jerusalem: The Southern Sector.* Jerusalem: Israel Antiquities Authority, 2000. [Hebrew and English]

Koch, Ido, and Oded Lipschits. "The Final Days of the Kingdom of Judah in Light of the Rosette-Stamped Jar Handles" [Hebrew]. *Cathedra* 137 (2010): 7–26.

Lapp, Nancy L., ed. *The Third Campaign at Tell el-Ful: The Excavations of 1964.* AASOR 45. Cambridge: American Schools of Oriental Research, 1981.

Lapp, Paul W. "Tell el-Full." *BA* 28 (1965): 2–10.

Lemaire, André. "Nabonidus in Arabia and Judah in the Neo-Babylonian Period." Pages 285–98 in *Judah and the Judeans in the Neo-Babylonian Period.* Edited by Oded Lipschits and Joseph Blenkinsopp. Winona Lake, Ind.: Eisenbrauns, 2003.

————. *Nouvelles inscriptions araméennes d'Idumée au musée d'Israël.* Supplément 3 à *Transeu.* Paris: Gabalda, 1996.

————. "Populations et territoires de Palestine à l'époque perse." *Transeu* 3 (1990): 31–74.

Lipschits, Oded, ed. *Can We Define the Material Culture of the Sixth Century in Judah?* [Hebrew]. Abstracts from the Conference Held in Tel Aviv University. Tel Aviv: Tel Aviv University Press, 1998.

Lipschits, Oded. "The Babylonian Period in Judah: In Search of the Half Full Cup (A Response to the Panel Discussion: In Conversation with Oded Lipschits, *The Fall and Rise of Jerusalem).*" *JHS* 7 (2007): 39–47.

————. "Demographic Changes in Judah between the Seventh and the Fifth Centuries B.C.E." Pages 323–79 in *Judah and the Judeans in the Neo-Babylonian Period.* Edited by Oded Lipschits and Joseph Blenkinsopp. Winona Lake, Ind.: Eisenbrauns, 2003.

————. *The Fall and Rise of Jerusalem.* Winona Lake, Ind.: Eisenbrauns, 2005.

————. "The History of the Benjaminite Region under Babylonian Rule." *TA* 26 (1999): 155–90.

————. "Judah, Jerusalem and the Temple (586–539 B.C.E.)." *Transeu* 22 (2001): 129–42.

———. "Nebuchadrezzar's Policy in 'Ḥattu-Land' and the Fate of the Kingdom of Judah." *UF* 30 (1999): 467–87.

———. "Persian Period Finds from Jerusalem: Facts and Interpretations." *JHS* 9 (2009): 2–30.

———. "The Rural Settlement in Judah in the Sixth Century B.C.E.: A Rejoinder." *PEQ* 136 (2004): 99–107.

———. "The 'Yehud' Province under Babylonian Rule (586–539 B.C.E.): Historic Reality and Historiographic Conceptions" [Hebrew]. Ph.D. diss. Tel Aviv University, 1997.

Lipschits, Oded, and Yuval Gadot. "Ramat Raḥel and the Emeq Rephaim Sites—Links and Interpretations." Pages 2:88–96 in *New Studies in the Archaeology of Jerusalem and Its Religion: Collected Papers*. Edited by D. Amit and G. D. Stiebel. 2 vols. Jerusalem: Israel Antiquities Authority, 2008.

Lipschits, Oded, Yuval Gadot, Benjamin Arubas, and Manfred Oeming. "Palace and Village, Paradise and Oblivion: Unraveling the Riddles of Ramat Raḥel." *NEA* 74 (2011): 2–49.

———. "Ramat Raḥel and Its Secrets" [Hebrew]. *Qad* 138 (2009): 58–77.

———. *What the Stones Are Whispering: 3000 Years of Forgotten History at Ramat Raḥel* [Hebrew]. Forthcoming.

Lipschits, Oded, Omer Sergi, and Ido Koch. "Judahite Stamped and Incised Jar Handles: A Tool for Studying the History of Late Monarchic Judah." *TA* 38 (2011): 5–41.

———. "Royal Judahite Jar Handles: Reconsidering the Chronology of the *lmlk* Stamp Impressions." *TA* 37 (2010): 3–32.

Lipschits, Oded, and David S. Vanderhooft. *Yehud Stamp Impressions: A Corpus of Inscribed Stamp Impressions from the Persian and Hellenistic Periods in Judah.* Winona Lake, Ind.: Eisenbrauns, forthcoming.

Machinist, Peter. "Palestine, Administration of (Assyro-Babylonian)." *ABD* 5:79.

Magen, Yitzhak, and Israel Finkelstein. *Archaeological Survey in the Hill Country of Benjamin.* Jerusalem: Israel Antiquities Authority Publications, 1993.

Malamat, Abraham. "The Last Wars of the Kingdom of Judah." *JNES* 9 (1950): 218–28.

Middlemas, Jill A. *The Troubles of Templeless Judah.* OTM. New York: Oxford University Press, 2005.

Milevski, Ianir. "Settlement Patterns in Northern Judah during the Achaemenid Period, according to the Hill Country of Benjamin and Jerusalem Surveys." *BAIAS* 15 (1996–1997): 7–29.

Miller, J. Maxwell, and John H. Hayes. *A History of Ancient Israel and Judah.* Philadelphia: Westminster, 1986.

Na'aman, Nadav. "An Assyrian Residence in Ramat Raḥel?" *TA* 28 (2001): 260–80.

———. "The Kingdom of Judah under Josiah." *TA* 18 (1991): 3–71.

———. "Royal Vassals or Governors? On the Status of Sheshbazzar and Zerubbabel in the Persian Empire." *Hen* 22 (2000): 35–44.

Oded, Bustenay. "Where Is the 'Myth of the Empty Land' To Be Found? History Versus Myth." Pages 55–74 in *Judah and the Judeans in the Neo-Babylonian Period.*

Edited by Oded Lipschits and Joseph Blenkinsopp. Winona Lake, Ind.: Eisenbrauns, 2003.

Pritchard, James B. *The Water System of Gibeon*. Museum Monographs. Philadelphia: University of Pennsylvania, 1961.

Sack, Ronald H. "Nebuchadnezzar II and the Old Testament: History Versus Ideology." Pages 221–34 in *Judah and the Judeans in the Neo-Babylonian Period*. Edited by Oded Lipschits and Joseph Blenkinsopp. Winona Lake, Ind.: Eisenbrauns, 2003.

Sass, Benjamin. "The Lion Stamp Impressions from Sixth Century B.C.E. Babylon and Their Connection to the Lion Stamp Impressions from Judah" [Hebrew]. Pages 13–14 in *New Studies on the Lion Stamped Jar Handles from Judah*. Edited by O. Lipschits and I. Koch. Tel Aviv: Tel Aviv University Press, 2010.

Sinclair, Lawrence A. "Bethel Pottery of the Sixth Century B.C." Pages 7–76 in *The Excavations of Bethel (1934–1960)*. Edited by James L. Kelso and William Foxwell Albright. AASOR 39. Cambridge: American Schools of Oriental Research, 1968.

Stern, Ephraim. *The Assyrian, Babylonian, and Persian Periods (732–332 B.C.E.)*. Vol. 2 of *The Archaeology of the Land of the Bible*. New York: Doubleday, 2001.

———. "Assyrian and Babylonian Elements in the Material Culture of Palestine in the Persian Period." *Transeu* 7 (1994): 51–62.

———. "The Babylonian Gap." *BAR* 26.6 (2000): 45–51, 76.

———. "The Babylonian Gap: The Archaeological Reality." *JSOT* 28 (2004): 273–77.

———. *Material Culture of the Land of the Bible in the Persian Period, 538–332 B.C.* Warminster: Aris & Phillips, 1982.

Torczyner, Harry. *Lachish I: The Lachish Letters*. London: Oxford University Press, 1938.

Vanderhooft, David S. *The Neo-Babylonian Empire and Babylon in the Latter Prophets*. HSM 59. Atlanta: Scholars Press, 1999.

Weinberg, Joel P. "Demographische Notizen zur Geschichte der nachexilischen Gemeinde in Juda." *Klio* 54 (1972): 45–59.

Weinberg, Shmuel S. "Eretz Israel after the Destruction of the First Temple: Archaeological Report" [Hebrew]. *PNAS* 4 (1970): 202–16.

Williamson, H. G. M. "The Governors of Judah under the Persians." *TynBul* 39 (1988): 59–82.

Wright, G. E. *Biblical Archaeology*. Philadelphia: Westminster, 1957.

Zorn, Jeffrey R. "Mizpah: Newly Discovered Stratum Reveals Judah's Other Capital." *BAR* 23 (1997): 29–38, 66.

———. "Tell en-Nasbeh: A Re-evaluation of the Architecture and Stratigraphy of the Early Bronze Age, Iron Age and Latter Periods." Ph.D. diss. University of California Berkeley, 1993.

———. "Tell en-Naṣbeh and the Problem of the Material Culture of the Sixth Century." Pages 413–47 in *Judah and the Judeans in the Neo-Babylonian Period*. Edited by Oded Lipschits and Joseph Blenkinsopp. Winona Lake, Ind.: Eisenbrauns, 2003.

Zorn, Jeffrey R., Joseph Yellin, and John Hayes. "The *M(W)ṢH* Stamp Impressions and the Neo-Babylonian Period." *IEJ* 44 (1994): 161–83.

Deportation and Demography in Sixth-Century b.c.e. Judah

Avraham Faust

1. Introduction

At least since Charles C. Torrey, the extent of the Babylonian deportations and the conditions in Judah thereafter have been a central problem in biblical scholarship.[1] Torrey believed that the exile was insignificant. Writing in 1910, he claimed: "[S]o far as the Jews of the Babylonian deportation are concerned, it is not likely that they ever exercised any considerable influence on the Jews in Judea."[2] Elsewhere he added: "[T]he fact is, of course, that Nebuchadrezzar and his officers carried away only those on whom they could lay their hands," and they were relatively few in number. According to Torrey, the exile affected only a very small part of the population, and most inhabitants returned to their homes and continued to live their life in the same way as before the Babylonian conquest.[3]

William F. Albright attempted to refute this view by pointing to the fact that many sites were indeed destroyed and that the country suffered greatly during the Babylonian conquest.[4] As a consequence of the dis-

---

1. For an extended discussion of this, as well as other issues relating to the reality in Judah during the sixth century and the evolving debate, see Avraham Faust, *Judah in the Neo-Babylonian Period: The Archaeology of Desolation* (Atlanta: Society of Biblical Literature, forthcoming).

2. Charles C. Torrey, *Ezra Studies* (Chicago: University of Chicago Press, 1910; repr., New York: Ktav, 1970), 288.

3. See, e.g., ibid., 285–300; idem, *Pseudo-Ezekiel and the Original Prophecy* (YOSR 18; New Haven: Yale University Press, 1930), 24–44; idem, *The Chronicler's History of Israel: Chronicles-Ezra-Nehemiah Restored to Its Original Form* (New Haven: Yale University Press, 1954), xxv.

4. William F. Albright, *The Archaeology of Palestine* (Harmondsworth, U.K.: Peli-

cussion over the reality after the destruction of Jerusalem, Torrey's views
were not adopted by mainstream scholarship. Still, although they are not
accepted today (at least in the form he presented them), they have been
quite influential, even if only indirectly, and they appear to fuel part of the
current controversy over the "myth of the empty land."[5]

2. AN EMPTY LAND?

The argument that the number of the exiled was quite small has been
a dominant theme in the "myth of the empty land" debate and among
proponents of the "continuity theory." According to this position, Judah
was not devastated following the Babylonian campaign, and life for most
Judeans continued pretty much as before 586 B.C.E.[6] The land supposedly
could not have been *completely empty* because the Babylonians would not
have deported the *entire* population.[7]

Already in 1988, Niels P. Lemche stressed that "the sources all agree
that a remnant was left behind."[8] Although the remnant consisted of the

can, 1960), 141–42. There are, as we shall see below, some ironic aspects to this debate,
which to a large extent involved scholars speaking past each other.

5. See, e.g., Hans M. Barstad, *The Myth of the Empty Land: A Study in the History and Archaeology of Judah during the "Exilic" Period* (SO 28; Oslo: Scandinavian
University Press, 1996), 21–22; Robert P. Carroll, "Exile? What Exile? Deportation and
Discourse of Diaspora," in *Leading Captivity Captive: "The Exile" as History and Ideology* (ed. Lester L. Grabbe; JSOTSup 278; European Seminar in Historical Methodology 2; Sheffield: Sheffield Academic, 1998), 101–18.

6. See, e.g., Barstad, *Myth of the Empty Land*; idem, "After the Myth of the Empty
Land: Major Challenges in the Study of Neo-Babylonian Judah," in *Judah and Judeans
in the Neo-Babylonian Period* (ed. Oded Lipschits and Joseph Blenkinsopp; Winona
Lake, Ind.: Eisenbrauns, 2003), 3–20; Israel Finkelstein and Neil A. Silberman, *The
Bible Unearthed: Archaeology's New Vision of Ancient Israel and the Origin of Its Sacred
Texts* (New York: Simon & Schuster, 2001), 306–8; Joseph Blenkinsopp, "There Was
No Gap," *BAR* 28.3 (2002): 37–38, 59; idem, "The Bible, Archaeology and Politics; or
The Empty Land Revisited," *JSOT* 27 (2002): 169–87; Niels P. Lemche, *Ancient Israel:
A New History of Israelite Society* (The Biblical Seminar 5; Sheffield: JSOT Press, 1988).

7. See, e.g., Barstad, *Myth of the Empty Land*, 18, 30, 33–34, 37–38, 40, 42–43,
62–63, 68, 79–80; Oded Lipschits, *Jerusalem between Destruction and Restoration:
Judah under Babylonian Rule* (Jerusalem: Yad Ben-Zvi, 2003), 219; idem, *The Fall
and Rise of Jerusalem: Judah under Babylonian Rule* (Winona Lake, Ind.: Eisenbrauns,
2005), 59–62, 69, 187, 367–72.

8. Lemche, *Ancient Israel*, 175–76.

poorest segment of Judahite society, it "may have included as much as 90% of the population."

One of the most outspoken and eloquent representatives of the continuity thesis is Hans M. Barstad. He noted:

> It is unfortunate that scholars have shown a tendency to neglect Torrey because of his more extreme views. ... [M]uch recent scholarship has proved Torrey right with regard to the necessity of stressing continuity rather than a complete break in Judean archaeology, history and tradition between the period prior to Nebuchadnezzar's invasion and the period following the disastrous events of 586. ... The *ideological* "exile," which formed a natural part of the biblical tradition, later became an inherent part of our scholarly *historical* tradition, from which we now are having great difficulties freeing ourselves.[9]

At a later point in his book Barstad goes on to suggest that only the royalty, elite, and skilled laborers were exiled:

> [O]bviously, we should not deny that several deportations took place. What we must renounce, however, is the claim that these deportations affected life in Palestine in the way that much scholarly consensus appears to believe they did. The land left by the Babylonians was not a desolate and empty country lying in ruins. ... [T]he view that the Babylonians brought into exile "the whole of" the Judean people is preposterous on any account.[10]

Similarly, Joseph Blenkinsopp proposes that the destruction was partial: "In both Judah and Philistia, Babylonian punitive expeditions were directed at the central foci of revolt, and it is difficult to see what point would have been served by wholesale devastation of the country."[11]

Likewise, Oded Lipschits rejects the idea "that *all of the kingdom's territories* were destroyed or that *the population in its entirety* was deported. ... Total devastation of the entire region would also have been contrary to Babylonian interests."[12]

---

9. Barstad, *Myth of the Empty Land*, 22. I must stress that the above quote does not suggest that Barstad accepts Torrey's views in full. This is clearly not the case, and Barstad seems merely to be trying to do Torrey justice.

10. Ibid., 79–80.

11. Blenkinsopp, "The Bible, Archaeology and Politics," 187.

12. See, e.g., Lipschits, *Fall and Rise of Jerusalem*, 69, emphasis added.

In sum, Lemche, Barstad, Blenkinsopp, Lipschits, and others stress that the land could not have been *empty* and that not *all* the population could have been exiled.

3. TOTAL EXILE?

I agree that it is unlikely that so many people were exiled as to leave the country empty. But such had never really been maintained. By attributing the demographic decline in the sixth century B.C.E. solely to Mesopotamian deportations, the proponents of the continuity theory construct a straw man that enables them to present the views of other scholars as unreasonable and extreme. Yet several points deserve to be made in response.

First of all, it should be noted that almost all scholars, including those who are usually accused of following (and even producing) "the myth of the empty land," stressed that the land was not empty. John Bright, for example, wrote that "the popular notion of a total deportation which left the land empty and void is erroneous and to be discarded."[13] Likewise, Philip J. King and Lawrence E. Stager argue: "Of course, there must have been some 'am ha'areṣ who remained," adding that the widespread destruction does "not imply that the countryside was totally uninhabited between 586–538."[14] Similar quotes could be brought from practically every archaeologist discussing the sixth century B.C.E.[15] Albright, and following him Bright, estimated the population at the time to include as many as 20,000 people![16] It should be stressed that all these scholars believed that the land was devastated and that the Babylonian blow was catastrophic, but they do not assume that the country was empty.

---

13. John Bright, *A History of Israel* (2nd ed.; Philadelphia: Westminster, 1972), 343–44.

14. Philip J. King and Lawrence E. Stager, *Life in Biblical Israel* (LAI; Louisville: Westminster John Knox, 2001), 257.

15. See, e.g., Kathleen M. Kenyon, *Archaeology in the Holy Land* (London: Methuen, 1965), 298; Amihai Mazar, *The Archaeology of the Land of the Bible, 10,000–586 BCE* (ABRL; New York: Doubleday, 1990), 548; Albright, *The Archaeology of Palestine*, 140–41; Ephraim Stern, "The Babylonian Gap," *BAR* 26.6 (2000): 45–51, 76 (51); idem, *The Assyrian, Babylonian and Persian Periods (732–332 B.C.E.)* (vol. 2 of *Archaeology of the Land of the Bible*; ABRL; New York: Doubleday, 2001), 350.

16. William F. Albright, *The Biblical Period from Abraham to Ezra* (New York: Harper & Row, 1963), 87; Bright, *A History of Israel*, 334.

Second, and more importantly for our purposes, none of the scholars who view the sixth century as a period of great demographic decline attribute this decline solely, or even primarily, to *forced migration* or *deportation*. The claim that past scholars assumed not only that the land was empty but that all the population had been *deported* is therefore a straw man. Clearly, the entire population was not exiled. But does this mean that most of the population was left behind and prospered? Of course not. Because there are other mechanisms of population contraction, deportation is not the only factor that one must consider with when assessing the demographic reality in Judah during the sixth century.

Admittedly, forced migrations were a common practice and would have had some demographic importance.[17] Yet more significant demographically were various other processes and mechanisms that brought about the great demographic decline of the sixth century—a decline that is identified by most scholars and practically all archaeologists.[18] In what

17. E.g., Bustenay Oded, *Mass Deportations and Deportees in the Neo-Assyrian Empire* (Wiesbaden: Reichert, 1979).

18. These identifications begin with Carl Watzinger, *Denkmaler Palastinas* (Leipzig: Hinrichs, 1935), vol. 2, and continue through William F. Albright, *From the Stone Age to Christianity: Monotheism and the Historical Process* (Baltimore: Johns Hopkins University Press, 1940); idem, *The Archaeology of Palestine*; Kenyon, *Archaeology in the Holy Land*; Yohanan Aharoni, *The Land of the Bible: A Historical Geography* (2nd ed.; Philadelphia: Westminster, 1979). See also more recent archaeologists such as Yigal Shiloh, "Judah and Jerusalem in the 8th–6th Centuries BCE," in *Recent Excavations in Israel: Studies in Iron Age Archaeology* (ed. Seymour Gitin and William G. Dever; ASOR; Winona Lake, Ind.: Eisenbrauns, 1989); Lawrence E. Stager, "Ashkelon and the Archaeology of Destruction: Kislev 604 BCE," *ErIsr* 25 (1996): 61*–74*; King and Stager, *Life in Biblical Israel*; Mazar, *Archaeology of the Land of the Bible*; Gabriel Barkay, "The Iron Age II–III," in *The Archaeology of Ancient Israel* (ed. Amnon Ben-Tor; New Haven: Yale University Press, 1992), 302–73; Ze'ev Herzog, *Archaeology of the City: Urban Planning in Ancient Israel and Its Social Implications* (Tel Aviv: Institute of Archaeology, Tel Aviv University Press, 1997), 278; William G. Dever, *Did God Have a Wife? Archaeology and Folk Religion in Ancient Israel* (Grand Rapids: Eerdmans, 2005), 291–94; Daniel Master, "Comments on Oded Lipschits, *The Fall and Rise of Jerusalem*," *JHS* 7 (2007): 28–33; John S. Holladay, "'Home Economics 1407' and the Israelite Family and Their Neighbors: An Anthropological/ Archaeological Exploration," in *The Family in Life and Death: The Family in Ancient Israel: Sociological and Archaeological Perspectives* (ed. Patricia Dutcher-Walls; LHBOTS 504; New York: T&T Clark, 2009), 87–88; Israel Finkelstein, "The Territorial Extent and Demography of Yehud/Judea in the Persian and Early Hellenistic Periods," *RB* 117 (2010): 39–54; Stern, *The Assyrian, Babylonian and Persian Periods*. For a summary, see Avraham

follows, I identify these other processes and mechanisms that contributed to the fall in population that is commonly observed in sixth-century Judah.

4. The Mechanisms of Demographic Decline

Aside from deportation, wartime casualties (including executions following the defeat), epidemics, famine, and refugeeism are among the common causes that scholars have identified when assessing population decline in wartime.[19]

Death in Battle: The death toll in wars in antiquity was usually quite high. With the lack of any real evacuation, effective medicine, and sterile conditions, many wounds ended in death.[20] Such was the case more in siege warfare. The number of casualties among the defenders was considerable, especially if they ultimately lost the war, as in the case of Judah.[21] Notably, conditions even deteriorated after the war (see more below).

Famine and Epidemics: Warfare, especially siege warfare, usually brought famine in its wake.[22] The poor conditions in the besieged cities, where dead could not be disposed of easily, contributed to the spread of epidemics, and this in turn resulted in more deaths.[23]

Executions: In the aftermath of battle, the conquerors often executed many of the survivors, especially members of the royalty, military com-

---

Faust, "Settlement Dynamics and Demographic Fluctuations in Judah from the Late Iron Age to the Hellenistic Period and the Archaeology of the Persian-Period Yehud," in *A Time of Change: Judah and Its Neighbors During the Persian and Early Hellenistic Periods* (ed. Yigal Levin; Library of Second Temple Studies 65; London: Continuum, 2007), 23–51.

19. E.g., Saul S. Weinberg, "Post-exilic Palestine: An Archaeological Report," *Proceedings of the Israel Academy of Sciences and Humanities* 4 (1969): 84; Stern, *The Assyrian, Babylonian and Persian Periods*, 323; David W. Jamieson-Drake, *Scribes and Schools in Monarchic Judah: A Socio-Archaeological Approach* (SWBA 9; Sheffield: Sheffield Academic, 1991), 75, 145–47; Bright, *A History of Israel*, 334.

20. For the treatment of wounds in the Greco-Roman world, see Christine F. Salazar, *The Treatment of War Wounds in Graeco-Roman Antiquity* (Leiden: Brill, 2000).

21. Cf. Israel Eph'al, *Siege and Its Ancient Near Eastern Manifestations* (Jerusalem: Magnes Press, 1996), 37–39; Paul Bentley Kern, *Ancient Siege Warfare* (Bloomington: Indiana University Press, 1999).

22. Eph'al, *Siege and Its Ancient Near Eastern Manifestations*, 57–64; cf. also 2 Kgs 6:28–29; Lam 2:20; 4:10.

23. Eph'al, *Siege and Its Ancient Near Eastern Manifestations*, 64–65.

manders, leaders, and the like.[24] This can be seen, for example, in the reliefs from Sennacherib's palace in Nineveh that depict the conquest of Lachish.[25] These measures seem to have been a deliberate and calculated policy, and should not be explained away as isolated events or exaggerations of the artists. H. W. F. Saggs argued that in order to maintain stability in the region, the Assyrians had to "persuade" their potential foes or rebels that it would be futile to oppose Assyria.[26] They accomplished this by tactics of psychological warfare. Demonstration of power, including unusual cruelty, was consciously directed not only toward those who suffered directly, "but also upon those who heard of it at a distance." Saggs added "the Assyrian king, in perpetrating actions, sometimes atrocities ... put the enemies into panic. ... This represented a conscious use by the Assyrians of terrorism not for sadistic purposes, but for psychological warfare."

Long-Range Factors: We should also not underestimate the impact of war on what Jacob Wright calls the Life Support Systems of a territory. An invading army conventionally laid the countryside to waste. What it did not intentionally destroy was often inadvertently ruined, due to the simple fact that hostilities interfered with the delicate rotation of tilling, planting, and harvesting.[27] The collapse of the administration and the lack of organization in production even further increased the problem of famine.[28]

5. THE IMPACT OF DEATHS

The overall death toll among the population was great. The thousands of burials unearthed at Lachish and Ashdod provide a glimpse of this reality.

---

24. See Kern, *Ancient Siege Warfare*, 69–71, 73, 75.

25. See Richard D. Barnett, "The Siege of Lachish," *IEJ* 8 (1958): 161–64; David Ussishkin, *The Conquest of Lachish by Sennacherib* (Publications of the Institute of Archaeology 6; Tel Aviv: Tel Aviv University Press, 1982).

26. H. W. F. Saggs, *The Might That Was Assyria* (London: Sidgwick & Jackson, 1984), 248.

27. See Jacob L. Wright, "Warfare and Wanton Destruction: A Reexamination of Deuteronomy 20:19–20 in Relation to Ancient Siegecraft," *JBL* 127 (2008): 423–58.

28. E.g., Jamieson-Drake, *Scribes and Schools*, 145–47; cf. Joseph A. Tainter, "Problem Solving: Complexity, History, Sustainability," *Population and Environment* 22 (2000): 3–41 (12). For the effect on the countryside, see also Kern, *Ancient Siege Warfare*, 73.

At both sites, mass burials, probably dated to the eighth century B.C.E., were unearthed.[29]

At Ashdod, in locus 1151 alone, remains of 2434 human beings were unearthed, 22.1 percent of which (i.e., 538 individuals) were less than fifteen years old at the time of death.[30] In another locus (1114) the remains of 376 people were found, the majority of whom died below the age of fifteen years. In other loci (1115, 1113, 1006) additional skeletons were found (all in all remains of about 61–62 individuals), many of whom with evidence that they had been beheaded. Moshe Dothan attributed the massacre to Sargon's conquest of the city in the late eighth century.[31] Israel Eph'al notes that those who were decapitated were usually buried separately, and it is likely that they were executed only after the cessation of fighting.[32] Since the entire area of the city was not excavated, it is possible that more burials are still lying below the ground, but even the above figures reveal the dreadful results of the siege and the executions that followed.

At Lachish mass burials were discovered in a few caves during the excavations conducted in the 1930s.[33] Remains of more than 1,500 individuals were thrown into the caves (caves 107, 108, 116, 120), probably as a result of a massacre following the conquest of the city by Sennacherib.[34] Again, it is likely that many skeletons remain to be unearthed.

Although the data presented above relate to Neo-Assyrian conquests, the fate of the defenders was probably the same in other epochs. The Babylonians may have been even "more oppressive" than the Assyrians, as Marc Van de Mieroop argues.[35]

---

29. Eph'al, *Siege and Its Ancient Near Eastern Manifestations*, 37–38.

30. Ibid., 37; Nicu Haas, "Anthropological Observations on the Skeletal Remains Found in Area D," *Atiqot* 9–10 (1962–1963): 212–14.

31. Moshe Dothan, *Ashdod II–III: The Second and Third Seasons of Excavations (1963, 1965)* (Atiqot 9–10; Jerusalem: The Department of Antiquities and Museums, 1971), 21.

32. Eph'al, *Siege and Its Ancient Near Eastern Manifestations*, 37 n. 67.

33. Ibid., 37–38.

34. Ussishkin, *Conquest of Lachish*, 56–58; though other wars cannot be ruled out, e.g., the destruction of the Late Bronze Age city (Eph'al, *Siege and Its Ancient Near Eastern Manifestations*, 38).

35. Marc Van De Mieroop, *A History of the Ancient Near East, ca. 3000–323 BC* (Malden, Mass.: Blackwell, 2007), 277.

6. Demographic Decline after the War

Clearly, death in the war was a major cause for population decrease. But there are yet other post-war factors that lead to population decline. The collapse of an administration and social infrastructure, along with the exile of the elite, led to even more drastic conditions of famine in the years and decades after the war. This was especially the case in areas that specialized in production of specific agricultural products.[36]

Refugees: The devastation of cities and villages led to a process in which many of the survivors fled the region and migrated to safer and more hospitable places.[37]

Insecurity: Under such circumstances, safety was seriously undermined. The conquering army could remain in the region for some time, looting, killing, and raping.[38] In these conditions of lawlessness (given the above mentioned devastation and decline), gangs emerged.[39] The crime in turn resulted in increased deaths, famine, and, consequently, additional migration.

Deportation: Finally, there is the factor of deportation and forced migration. Deportation was practiced by many empires, including the Assyrians and Babylonians.[40] The deportees included most often the elite and skilled laborers. Their absence contributed to demoralization, demise of organization, famine, and insecurity.

7. Conclusions

In sum, deportation is only one factor—and probably not the most important demographically—that must be considered when discussing demographic change after war. It must be noted that the evidence from

---

36. E.g., wine, oil, and even grains; see Jamieson-Drake, *Scribes and Schools*, 75–76, 145–47.

37. For the period under discussion, see, e.g., Jer 41–44.

38. See, e.g., Kern, *Ancient Siege Warfare*, 81.

39. Joseph A. Tainter, "Post-collapse Societies," in *Companion Encyclopedia of Archaeology* (ed. Graeme Barker; 2 vols.; London: Routledge, 1999), 2:1023.

40. Oded, *Mass Deportations and Deportees*; idem, *The Early History of the Babylonian Exile (8th–6th Centuries B.C.E.)* (Haifa: Pardes, 2010); see also Daniel L. Smith, *The Religion of the Landless: The Social Context of the Babylonian Exile* (Bloomington, Ind.: Meyer-Stone, 1989), 29–31; Amelie Kuhrt, *The Ancient Near East, c. 3000–330 BC* (Routledge History of the Ancient World; London: Routledge, 1995), 532–34.

Mesopotamia seems to indicate high numbers of deportees.[41] Yet no matter how extensive deportations may have been, they were only of secondary importance in comparison to the range of other factors identified above. It is these factors that one must bear in mind in future discussions of the great demographic decline in Judah in the sixth century.

It deserves to be repeated: the population of Judah was not exiled *in toto* in the sixth century B.C.E. But such was never claimed in past scholarship. Anticipating the arguments I have presented here, Bright wrote back in 1972:

> Aside from those deported to Babylon, thousands must have died in battle or of starvation and disease (c.f., Lam. 2: 11f., 19–21; 4:9f.), some—and surely more than we know of (II Kings 25:18–27)—had been executed, while others (cf., Jer., ch 42f.) had fled for their lives.[42]

While various claims and counterclaims were raised in the subsequent debate over the reality in Judah after the Babylonian campaigns, no one really claimed that the entire population was deported (and the land completely empty) nor has anyone, except the proponents of the continuity thesis, assumed that the deportation might be the sole or primary cause for the population decline. The repeated claims that it is impossible that all the population was exiled so as to leave the country empty are therefore completely irrelevant for the study of the demography in Judah in the sixth century, and they do not contribute to our understanding of the reality during this important period.

Bibliography

Aharoni, Yohanan. *The Land of the Bible: Historical Geography*. 2nd ed. Philadelphia: Westminster, 1979.

Albright, William F. *From the Stone Age to Christianity: Monotheism and the Historical Process*. Baltimore: The Johns Hopkins Press, 1940.

———. *The Archaeology of Palestine*. Harmondsworth, U.K.: Pelican, 1960.

———. *The Biblical Period from Abraham to Ezra*. New York: Harper and Row, 1963.

Barkay, Gabriel. "The Iron Age II–III." Pages 302–73 in *The Archaeology of Ancient Israel*. Edited by Amnon Ben-Tor. New Haven: Yale University Press, 1992.

41. See, e.g., Oded, *Mass Deportations and Deportees*; idem, *Early History of the Babylonian Exile*.

42. Bright, *A History of Israel*, 334.

Barnett, Richard D. "The Siege of Lachish." *IEJ* 8 (1958): 161–64.

Barstad, Hans M. "After the Myth of the Empty Land: Major Challenges in the Study of Neo-Babylonian Judah." Pages 3–20 in *Judah and Judeans in the Neo-Babylonian Period*. Edited by Oded Lipschits and Joseph Blenkinsopp. Winona Lake, Ind.: Eisenbrauns, 2003.

———. *The Myth of the Empty Land: A Study in the History and Archaeology of Judah during the "Exilic" Period*. SO 28. Oslo: Scandinavian University Press, 1996.

Blenkinsopp, Joseph. "The Bible, Archaeology and Politics; or The Empty Land Revisited." *JSOT* 27 (2002): 169–87.

———. "There Was No Gap." *BAR* 28.3 (2002): 37–38, 59.

Bright, John. *A History of Israel*. 2nd. ed. Westminster Aids to the Study of Scripture. Philadelphia: Westminster, 1972.

Carroll, Robert P. "Exile? What Exile? Deportation and Discourse of Diaspora." Pages 101–18 in *Leading Captivity Captive: "The Exile" as History and Ideology*. Edited by Lester L. Grabbe. JSOTSup 278. European Seminar in Historical Methodology 2. Sheffield: Sheffield Academic, 1998.

Dever, William G. *Did God Have a Wife? Archaeology and Folk Religion in Ancient Israel*. Grand Rapids: Eerdmans, 2005.

Dothan, Moshe. *Ashdod II–III: The Second and Third Seasons of Excavations (1963, 1965)*. Atiqot 9–10. Jerusalem: The Department of Antiquities and Museums, 1971.

Eph'al, Israel. *Siege and Its Ancient Near Eastern Manifestations*. Jerusalem: Hebrew University Magnes Press, 1996.

Faust, Avraham. *Judah in the Neo-Babylonian Period: The Archaeology of Desolation*. Atlanta: Society of Biblical Literature, forthcoming.

———. "Settlement Dynamics and Demographic Fluctuations in Judah from the Late Iron Age to the Hellenistic Period and the Archaeology of the Persian-Period Yehud." Pages 23–51 in *A Time of Change: Judah and Its Neighbors during the Persian and Early Hellenistic Periods*. Edited by Yigal Levin. Library of Second Temple Studies 65. London: Continuum, 2007.

Finkelstein, Israel. "The Territorial Extent and Demography of Yehud/Judea in the Persian and Early Hellenistic Periods." *RB* 117 (2010): 39–54.

Finkelstein, Israel, and Neil A. Silberman. *The Bible Unearthed: Archaeology's New Vision of Ancient Israel and the Origin of its Sacred Texts*. New York: Simon and Schuster, 2001.

Haas, Nicu. "Anthropological Observations on the Skeletal Remains Found in Area D." *Atiqot* 9–10 (1962–1963): 212–14.

Herzog, Ze'ev. *Archaeology of the City: Urban Planning in Ancient Israel and Its Social Implications*. Tel Aviv: Institute of Archaeology, Tel Aviv University Press, 1997.

Holladay, John S. " 'Home Economics 1407' and the Israelite Family and Their Neighbors: An Anthropological/Archaeological Exploration." Pages 61–88 in *The Family in Life and Death: The Family in Ancient Israel: Sociological and Archaeological Perspectives*. Edited by Patricia Dutcher-Walls. LHBOTS 504. New York: T&T Clark, 2009.

Jamieson-Drake, David W. *Scribes and Schools in Monarchic Judah: A Socio-archaeo-logical Approach*. SWBA 9. Sheffield: Sheffield Academic, 1991.

Kenyon, Kathleen M. *Archaeology in the Holy Land*. London: Methuen, 1965.

Kern, Paul Bentley. *Ancient Siege Warfare*. Bloomington: Indiana University Press, 1999.

King, Philip J., and Lawrence E. Stager. *Life in Biblical Israel*. LAI. Louisville: Westminster John Knox, 2001.

Kuhrt, Amélie. *The Ancient Near East: c. 3000–330 BC*. Routledge History of the Ancient World. London: Routledge, 1995.

Lemche, Niels P. *Ancient Israel: A New History of Israelite Society*. The Biblical Seminar 5. Sheffield: JSOT Press, 1988.

Lipschits, Oded. *The Fall and Rise of Jerusalem: Judah under Babylonian Rule*. Winona Lake, Ind.: Eisenbrauns, 2005.

———. *Jerusalem between Destruction and Restoration: Judah under Babylonian Rule*. Jerusalem: Yad Ben-Zvi, 2003.

Master, Daniel. "Comments on Oded Lipschits, *The Fall and Rise of Jerusalem*." *JHS* 7 (2007): 28–33.

Mazar, Amihai. *The Archaeology of the Land of the Bible, 10,000–586 BCE*. ABRL. New York: Doubleday, 1990.

Mieroop, Marc Van De. *A History of the Ancient Near East, ca. 3000–323 BC*. Malden, Mass.: Blackwell, 2007.

Oded, Bustenay. *The Early History of the Babylonian Exile (8th–6th Centuries B.C.E.)*. Haifa: Pardes, 2010.

———. *Mass Deportations and Deportees in the Neo-Assyrian Empire*. Wiesbaden: Reichert, 1979.

Saggs, H. W. F. *The Might That Was Assyria*. London: Sidgwick & Jackson, 1984.

Salazar, Christine F. *The Treatment of War Wounds in Graeco-Roman Antiquity*. Leiden: Brill, 2000.

Shiloh, Yigal. "Judah and Jerusalem in the 8th–6th Centuries BCE." Pages 97–105 in *Recent Excavations in Israel: Studies in Iron Age Archaeology*. Edited by Seymour Gitin and William G. Dever. ASOR. Winona Lake, Ind.: Eisenbrauns, 1989.

Smith, Daniel L. *The Religion of the Landless: The Social Context of the Babylonian Exile*. Bloomington, Ind.: Meyer-Stone, 1989.

Stager, Lawrence E. "Ashkelon and the Archaeology of Destruction: Kislev 604 BCE." *ErIsr* 25 (1996): 61–74.

Stern, Ephraim. *The Assyrian, Babylonian and Persian Periods (732–332 B.C.E)*. Vol. 2 of *Archaeology of the Land of the Bible*. ABRL. New York: Doubleday, 2001.

Stern, Ephraim. "The Babylonian Gap." *BAR* 26.6 (2000): 45–51, 76.

Tainter, Joseph A. "Post-collapse Societies." Pages 988–1039 in vol. 2 of *Companion Encyclopedia of Archaeology*. Edited by Graeme Barker. 2 vols. London: Routledge, 1999.

———. "Problem Solving: Complexity, History, Sustainability." *Population and Environment* 22 (2000): 3–41.

Torrey, Charles C. *The Chronicler's History of Israel: Chronicles-Ezra-Nehemiah Restored to Its Original Form*. New Haven: Yale University Press, 1954.

———. *Ezra Studies*. Chicago: University of Chicago Press, 1910. Repr., New York: Ktav, 1970.

———. *Pseudo-Ezekiel and the Original Prophecy*. YOSR 18. New Haven: Yale University Press, 1930.

Ussishkin, David. *The Conquest of Lachish by Sennacherib*. Publications of the Institute of Archaeology 6. Tel Aviv: Tel Aviv University Press, 1982.

Watzinger, Carl. *Denkmäler Palästinas*. Leipzig: Hinrichs, 1935.

Weinberg, Saul S. "Post-exilic Palestine: An Archaeological Report." *Proceedings of the Israel Academy of Sciences and Humanities* 4 (1969): 78–97.

Wright, Jacob L. "Warfare and Wanton Destruction: A Reexamination of Deuteronomy 20:19–20 in Relation to Ancient Siegecraft." *JBL* 127 (2008): 423–58.

The Deportation of Jerusalem's Wealth and the Demise of Native Sovereignty in the Book of Kings

Jacob L. Wright

1. Introduction

The Hebrew Bible devotes considerable space to the subject of deportation. Genesis begins by depicting the deity driving "the Adam" out of the garden of Eden (Gen 3:22–24) and later scattering the world's population "over the face of all the earth" (11:8–9).[1] Much of the book treats the factors and decisions that lead the patriarchs and matriarchs to leave the promised land, beginning with Abraham and Sarah migrating to Egypt (12:10–20) and ending with the sons of Jacob taking up residence in the land of Goshen (50:14–26). The rest of the Pentateuch depicts Israel's return to the birthplace of their ancestors. Deportation figures prominently in the law codes of the Pentateuch (Lev 26:32–45 and Deut 28:63b–68). Demonstrating the validity of these covenantal curses, the history narrated in the Former Prophets recounts how foreign invaders carry off the populations of Israel and Judah or force them to flee to other lands. Similarly, much of the Latter Prophets relates to the expulsion of Israel and Judah (as well as

---

1. This essay is an excerpt of larger study of the temple vessels, the first paper on which I had the honor of presenting at the Claremont School of Theology in April 2006. It is dedicated to the memory of Peter R. Ackroyd (1917–2005) in appreciation for his lucid, commonsensical, and perceptive studies of continuity in biblical writings. See his "The Temple Vessels—A Continuity Theme," in *Studies in the Religion of Ancient Israel* (ed. P. A. H. de Boer; VTSup 23; Leiden: Brill, 1972), 166–81, and his inaugural lecture as the Samuel Davidson Chair of Old Testament Studies at King's College, London, published as *Continuity: A Contribution to the Study of the Old Testament Religious Tradition* (Oxford: Blackwell, 1962).

of other peoples) from their native country and subsequent return to it. The same may also be said for much of the Writings, especially the books of Chronicles, Ezra-Nehemiah, Ruth, Daniel, and the Psalms. Therefore, in choosing to focus for the past several years on displacement and deportation, the Warfare in Ancient Israel Section at the SBL Annual Meeting selected a subject of concern not only to current cross-cultural studies but also to the biblical authors.

Forced and voluntary migrations represent radical discontinuity. Admittedly, all destruction brings rupture. But by deporting a people or creating conditions that compel much of the populace to migrate, conquerors create a social, psychological, and historical breach of much more profound proportions than if they had only ravaged a territory and left its population to struggle amidst the ruins. Not surprisingly, the discontinuity that accompanies displacement often generates projects of history writing in which authors seek to chart lines of continuity that connect a people, community, family, or individual to a (spatial and temporal) homeland. This has been the case in Jewish history over the ages, especially after the expulsion of Jews from Spain in 1492, the Holocaust in Europe, and the founding of the State of Israel, when many Sephardi and Mizrahi Jews abandoned their homes throughout the Middle East. In all these cases, migration elicited the composition of various histories and biographies. By reconstructing the past or a previously inhabited space, one rescues it from oblivion.

Because the biblical authors are so deeply concerned with the unity of the people of Israel and the primordial bond that attaches them to their ancestral land, the discontinuity that accompanies population displacement poses a major problem with which they seek to come to terms in various ways—not least through the composition of historical narratives. In what follows, I examine the book of Kings, which represents the end of at least three different histories postulated in contemporary scholarship.[2] I begin by examining the emphasis on radical discontinuity in the book of Kings, arguing that the final paragraphs in 2 Kgs 25 are supplementary. I then delineate a pattern in which the disbursement of accumulated wealth

---

2. Earlier histories written after the destruction of Israel and deportation of its population may be isolated in (versions of) Genesis and Exodus-Joshua. See Reinhard G. Kratz, *The Composition of the Narrative Books of the Old Testament* (London: T&T Clark, 2005), and Konrad Schmid, *Genesis and the Moses Story: Israel's Dual Origins in the Hebrew Bible* (Winona Lake, Ind.: Eisenbrauns, 2010). For the three histories postulated by scholarship, see below.

corresponds to the demise of native sovereignty. This pattern provides a backdrop for a treatment of the final chapters of Kings, which depict the destruction of Jerusalem and the plundering of its wealth. After discussing the differences that one can trace in ancient Near Eastern sources between *destroying* and *deporting* gods or cultic objects, I conclude by comparing the radical discontinuity in Kings with the historiographical endeavor in Chronicles (as well as in Ezra-Nehemiah and 1 Esdras) to posit a durable—metallic—continuity in the form of the temple vessels that were deported intact so that they could be returned one day.

2. THE TABLES TURNED

The final chapter of Kings depicts a resounding defeat of the kingdom of Judah in all facets of its existence: the execution of Zedekiah's sons; the deportation of him together with the royal family and ruling elite; the destruction of the temple, palace, and the surrounding city; and the despoilation of Jerusalem's wealth. These themes express the book's overriding interest in narrating both the rise and demise of the states of Israel and Judah.

What is striking about the conclusion to this history is the silence with regard to the nation as a whole. As such, the conclusion contrasts starkly with the dominant role assigned to "the people of Israel" at the beginning of the narrative—whether one locates that beginning in Genesis (the so-called "Primary History" or "Enneateuch"), in Deuteronomy/Joshua (the traditional view of the Deuteronomistic History), or in the first chapters of Samuel (a new approach to the Deuteronomistic History).[3] In all three of these narrative configurations, the point of departure for the establishment of the centralized kingdom is the united activity of the people of Israel.[4]

---

3. The third configuration is the one I adopt in the present study. It originated with a suggestion made by Ernst Würthwein in *Studien zum deuteronomistischen Geschichtswerk* (BZAW 227; Berlin: de Gruyter, 1994), 1–11. Würthwein's suggestion has been embraced in various ways by many continental scholars such as Reinhard Kratz, Konrad Schmid, Reinhard Müller, Jan Gertz, and Uwe Becker.

4. For the united activity of Israel at the beginning of Samuel–Kings, see the narratives that assume a centralized Israelite cult in 1 Sam 1–3 or common war efforts in 1 Sam 4. The remainder of this history has two large overarching themes: (1) the rise and demise of Israel's territorial sovereignty and (2) the relationship between Israel and Judah. The earliest portions of book of Kings may be sought in the chronistic

For the authors of the "Primary History" (Genesis–Kings), a strong centralized kingdom has undeniably many advantages, yet it also constitutes a grave danger inasmuch as it threatens to eclipse the nation. The advantages of statehood are illustrated in the way in which David and Solomon bring tranquility and welfare to the people from the enemies who encompass them. Conversely, the danger of statehood is illustrated by the way in which a "people's army" or force of "citizen-soldiers," who fight voluntarily for their land, family, and god, is gradually superseded by a professional, standing army consisting of subjects (and foreign mercenaries) whom the king conscripts or pays to fight *his* wars.[5] In the end, the kingdoms of Israel and Judah are destroyed and nothing remains of this greater people of Israel.[6]

-----

passages that synchronize the political histories of Israel's and Judah's royal dynasties (the second of the two overarching themes). These passages assert a relationship between Israel and Judah, even if this relationship did not yet have the national and religious proportions it has in other (later) texts. However, after being joined to the Saul-David-Solomon narrative in the book of Samuel, and especially in its present function within the Primary History of Genesis-Kings, the synchronicity of the rulers of Israel and Judah in the book of Kings assumed a new, and originally unenvisioned, historiographical function. Now rather than merely presenting the kingdoms of Israel and Judah as coexisting in a special political-historical relationship, the synchronistic history of the dual monarchic houses is to be read as evidence of the *disintegration* of Israel's national and religious unity: what was once a single unified people fighting spontaneously for its god-given land has become now two kingdoms with professional armies fighting each other. The national disintegration anticipates and coincides with the parallel theme of the demise of state power (from Saul-David-Solomon, on the one end, to the deportations of Israel's and Judah's kings and populations, on the other end).

5. The "people's army" is depicted throughout Numbers, Deuteronomy, Joshua, Judges, and the first sections of Samuel, while the professional royal forces begin to emerge (hand-in-hand with the monarchy) in Samuel and then are taken for granted in Kings.

6. Previous scholarship has largely failed to take seriously the imbalance between the beginning of the history, with the people of Israel dominating the narrative, and the end, which narrates the destruction of the kingdom in a few short passages and says very little about the people as a whole. Many scholars seem to assume that the narrative corresponds fundamentally to the course of Israel's and Judah's history. Yet others are now responding to this untenable assumption and demonstrating the extent to which the abundant space assigned to the people of Israel in the beginning of these histories (in each of the three configurations mentioned above) owes itself to a creative historiographical move to emphasize the peoplehood of Israel. By presenting Israel as

The final passages of Kings make this point by presenting the Babylonians deporting professional soldiers, arms manufacturers, and royal officials (2 Kgs 24:14–16; 25:11–12).[7] Only some of the peasants are left behind. Yet this remnant does not represent the nation. After the deportation of the elites who serve in the employ of the king, the account concludes: "and thus Judah was exiled from its land" (v. 21b).[8]

From a diachronic perspective, this summary statement in 25:21b may represent the original conclusion to the history.[9] If so, the two para-

---

nation preexisting the states of Israel and Judah, the authors affirm, on the one hand, a fundamental unity of Israel, and on the other, the primacy of peoplehood as a survival strategy in anticipation of and in response to the defeat of the state. See Jacob L. Wright, "A Nation Conceived in Defeat," *Azure* 42 (5771/2010): 83–101.

7. For a different interpretation of חרש and מסגר, see Jacob L. Wright, "Surviving in an Imperial Context: Foreign Military Service and Judean Identity," in *Judah and the Judeans in the Achaemenid Period: Negotiating Identity in an International Context* (ed. Oded Lipschits, Gary N. Knoppers, and Manfred Oeming; Winona Lake, Ind.: Eisenbrauns, 2011), 508. Yet it seems more likely that these two groups are not "civilian artisans" but rather arms manufacturers given their placement right after the reference to soldiers and the statement in 2 Kgs 24:16. See also 1 Sam 13:19.

8. Unless otherwise indicated, all translations are my own. Notice how MT Jeremiah, when reproducing 2 Kgs 25, adds a paragraph in 52:28–30 (missing from LXX) that shifts the focus on the deportation of the elites in Kings to "the people" as a whole (see also the twice-mentioned "Judeans"). The addition of this passage, which may derive ultimately from a source, mirrors the wider *demotic* interest of Jeremiah. In contrast, Samuel–Kings is much more focused on the emergence and fate of Israel's monarchies and the stratified society they generate. This explains why the people as whole do not receive much attention in the final chapters. Nevertheless, various passages throughout Kings do refer to the fate of the general populace (in contrast solely to the elites), especially in descriptions of deportation. See 1 Kgs 14:11–14; 15:29; 16:6, 9; 17:6, 11, 23.

9. Contra Ernst Würthwein, *Die Bücher der Könige: 1. Kön. 17–2. Kön. 25* (ATD 11.2; Göttingen: Vandenhoeck & Ruprecht, 1984), 478–79. Compare the very similar concluding statement in the account of Israel's deportation: "So all Israel was exiled from its land to Assyria until this day" (2 Kgs 17:23b). The absence of "until this day" in 25:21b suggests that the authors are writing after exiles had already begun to return to Judah; otherwise they would have included the statement in reference to Judah as well. I find it difficult to accept the suggestions offered by Jeffrey Geoghegan in *The Time, Place, and Purpose of the Deuteronomistic History: The Evidence of "Until This Day"* (BJS 347; Providence, R.I.: Brown University Press, 2006). The use of the phrase in ch. 17 and its absence in ch. 25 witness to an ideology that the inhabitants of the kingdom of Israel never returned (see 17:24–41), an ideology reflected also in Ezra

graphs attached to it would constitute supplements.[10] I propose that these paragraphs were appended simultaneously.

The first paragraph (25:22–26) contradicts the foregoing account by presenting a population of aristocrats and notables in the land. It tells how Nebuchadnezzar appointed Gedaliah as the population's leader, who along with other Judeans and Chaldeans is eventually massacred by a member of the Judean royal family and "captains of the forces." In response, "all the people, high and low, and captains of the forces" take flight to Egypt. The reason for introducing this paragraph seems to have been twofold: first, to show that in the end the land was completely deprived of any Judean community, and second, to direct the reader's attention away from Judah and the (emerging) diasporic center in Egypt.

Not surprisingly, the second paragraph (25:27–30) identifies Babylon as the locus of restoration. It is there that the deported King Jehoiachin, during the first year of the reign of Evil-Merodach (Amēl-Marduk, a.k.a. Nabû-šuma-ukîn), is released from prison. The passage postdates the receipt of rations to the reign of Nebuchadnezzar's successor so as to present a sequence of defeat and restoration: first destruction and deportation, then the assassination of Gedaliah and the flight of the remaining population to Egypt, and finally Jehoiachin's rehabilitation at Babylon.[11]

4:2. The point here is that the composition of the book of Kings could have persisted long after 586 B.C.E.

10. For this position or a variant of it, see, inter alia, James A. Montgomery, *A Critical and Exegetical Commentary on the Book of Kings* (ICC 10; New York: Scribner, 1951), 564; John Gray, *I and II Kings* (OTL; Philadelphia: Westminster, 1963), 701–6; Walter Dietrich, *Prophetie und Geschichte* (FRLANT 108; Göttingen: Vandenhoeck & Ruprecht, 1972), 142; K.-F. Pohlmann, "Erwägungen zum Schlußkapitel des deuteronomistischen Geschichtswerkes. Oder: Warum wird der Prophet Jeremia in 2. Kön. 22–25 nicht erwähnt?" in *Textgemäß: Aufsätze und Beiträge zur Hermeneutik des Alten Testaments: Festschrift Ernst Würthwein* (ed. A. H. J. Gunneweg and Otto Kaiser; Göttingen: Vandenhoeck & Ruprecht, 1979), 94–109; Mordechai Cogan and Hayim Tadmor, *II Kings* (AB 11; New York: Doubleday, 1988), 324, 327–30; Mark A. O'Brien, *The Deuteronomistic History Hypothesis: A Reassessment* (OBO 92; Freiburg: Universitätsverlag, 1989), 270–73; Steven L. McKenzie, *The Trouble with Kings: The Composition of the Book of Kings in the Deuteronomistic History* (VTSup 42; Leiden: Brill, 1991), 152.

11. From the Weidner Tablets we know that Jehoiachin was already receiving rations in 592 B.C.E. One could harmonize the cuneiform data with the biblical account by postulating that the Babylonian court released Jehoiachin before 592 but later—for an unknown reason—placed him in prison until 562/61 B.C.E. when Evil-

Although perhaps not intended by its author, this concluding passage forms an *inclusio* with the introductory portions of the book of Kings, which portray, in considerable detail, the table of Solomon. The grandeur displayed in the king's feasting is explicitly tied to the security of his royal domain (see esp. 1 Kgs 4:20–5:8; also 3:15; 8:2, 65; 10:4–5, 10; et passim). In this way the royal table illustrates the *demise* of Judean autonomy: On one end of the book is a native king who enjoys ostentatious commensality as the fruit of expansive sovereignty. The greatness of his kingdom even attracts to his table foreign rulers from exotic lands, such as the Queen of Sheba (1 Kgs 10). At the other end of the book is the deported king who no longer serves as a host, but is instead *hosted* by the foreign conqueror. The tables are now turned. Despite the prospect of prosperity under these new mensal conditions, the Judean king's power is nevertheless severely confined in comparison to the dominion enjoyed by the feasting Solomon portrayed at the beginning of the book.[12]

When read in the context of Samuel–Kings, the addition of the final paragraph in Kings brings to the surface the theme of the royal table in the depiction of the earliest days of the monarchy. First Samuel 20 depicts how Saul keeps a close eye on his potential political opponents by assigning them seats at his table; when a royal servant, such as David, withdraws from the court without permission, leaving thereby his seat unoccupied, he arouses suspicion that he may be off mustering the opposition for a coup d'état.[13] Later, after David had usurped Saul's throne, he performs an act of benefaction for the house of Saul by not only restoring to Mephibosheth,

---

Merodach released him. This approach is adopted by Rainer Albertz, "In Search of the Deuteronomists," in *The Future of the Deuteronomistic History* (ed. Thomas Römer; BETL 147; Leuven: Leuven University Press, 2000), 15 n. 52. A more tenable, less harmonistic approach, is that the author assigned the "rehabilitation" of Jehoiachin to the reign of a new king, in keeping with an established convention of history writing, and to a late date in order to make room for other events (the destruction of Jerusalem, the deportations, the assassination of Gedaliah, etc.). In this way, the author could present a clear periodization of doom followed by boon.

12. See Jacob L. Wright, "Commensal Politics in Ancient Western Asia: The Background to Nehemiah's Feasting (Part I)," *ZAW* 122 (2010): 212–33.

13. For this aspect of "court society" (*Hofgesellschaft*), which represents an attempt to concentrate aristocracy and potential political opponents close to the king and divert them from political aspirations through commensality and court culture, see Norbert Elias, *Die höfische Gesellschaft: Untersuchungen zur Soziologie des Königtums und der höfischen Aristokratie* (Berlin: Luchterhand, 1969), and A. J. S. Spaw-

son of Jonathan, Saul's estate but also by granting him a perpetual place at
the royal table (2 Sam 9). This same narrative continues into the first chapters of the book of Kings with David's admonition to Solomon to reward
the sons of Barzillai the Gileadite by allowing them "to be among those
who eat at your table" (1 Kgs 2:7).[14] Later we read that there were officials appointed for each month to provision Solomon's table (1 Kgs 4–5,
esp. 5:7 [Eng. 4:27]).[15] Such conscription of labor and goods is both the
precondition and expression of monarchic domination,[16] and corresponds
domestically to the pacification of a state's foreign enemies. It is therefore
not surprising that the notice about the provisioning of Solomon's table
appears in an account of this king's extensive territorial sovereignty and
unsurpassed security (chaps. 4–5). In all these accounts, the table serves as
a symbol of monarchic power.[17]

Against the backdrop of these texts, we can more precisely delineate
how the final passage of Kings affirms continuity amidst the radical rupture
and discontinuity that accompanied the destruction of the Judahite state
and the deportation of its population.[18] With respect to the *discontinuity*,

---

forth, ed., *The Court and Court Society in Ancient Monarchies* (Cambridge: Cambridge
University Press, 2007).

14. Already 2 Sam 19 juxtaposes the table theme (in relation to Mephibosheth)
with Barzillai.

15. These officials are to be identified with either the 12,000 charioteers mentioned in the immediately preceding line or, in an earlier version of the account, the
twelve appointed officials (נצבים) listed in 5:7–19 (Eng. 4:7–19).

16. Archeologists and anthropologists have often viewed monumental architecture and standing armies as indispensable indicators of full statehood. But monumental architecture and armies presuppose the conscription of bodies. The ancient Near
Eastern epigraphic record attests abundantly to the great amount of attention state
administrations accorded to conscription (the earliest form of taxation). That also biblical authors could identify conscription as the epitome of centralized state control is
demonstrated by 1 Sam 8.

17. One could add to these texts those that present prophets eating at the table of
the king: 1 Kgs 13:7–32 and 18:19. As an indispensable institution of "court society,"
the king's table represents centralization, control, and thereby a potentially corrupting
influence. Insofar as a faithful prophet must guard his neutrality, he usually does not
receive his bread from the king (but see, however, Nathan in 1 Kgs 1). First Kings 17
thus presents Elijah being fed not only by a widow but also by ravens, which according
to later Jewish tradition brought bread from the table of Ahab (or kosher food from
the table of Jehoshaphat). See also 1 Kgs 18:13.

18. In view of the larger ideological agendas (identified in this paragraph) that

the table is not located in the homeland but rather in Babylon, and the Judahite king is now no longer a host but rather just a guest, even if he is one who enjoys special favor. Yet there is also *continuity*: Throughout the foregoing chapters, the narrative focuses primarily on the kings of Israel and Judah. It is therefore not surprising that the narrator here points to a member of the Davidic dynasty as an auspicious sign for the future. Together with the preceding passages, this paragraph orients the reader to Babylon and away from the land of Judah (25:21) and from the Egyptian diaspora (25:22–26). It is in Babylon where history continues. The continuity is identified, however, not with the entire Davidic line but rather particularly with the branch that descends from Jehoiachin. It was he, not Jehoiakim or Zedekiah, who—anticipating the role of Zerubbabel, Ezra, Nehemiah, Esther, and others—managed to secure the benefaction of the imperial court.[19] Yet even if his descendants promise to bring a boon for their people, they could do so only under much different political conditions. Instead of enjoying native autonomy, now Judah's (present and future) kings would have to answer to a higher king.[20]

Hence, Samuel–Kings affirms continuity between the pre- and post-destruction periods in a particular line of the Davidic dynasty. Yet, insofar as 25:21b represents the original conclusion of this history, the continuity would be affirmed only in a secondary appendix (25:27–30).[21] In contrast,

---

informed the composition of the final passages in Kings, we must avoid the facile assumption that the book must have been completed during the lifetime of Jehoiachin. After all, the Judean king is no longer alive in this passage: instead of employing the standard phrase "until this day," the narrator reflects back upon "all the days of his life" (2 Kgs 25:30b).

19. Also Chronicles identifies continuity through this line, linking him to Zerubbabel and many generations thereafter (1 Chr 3:10–24). The addition of the final paragraph in Kings may grow out of the same social context in Babylon, although perhaps from a somewhat earlier time period.

20. Notice how 2 Kgs 25:27–30 consistently refers to Jehoiachin and his peers as "kings" (with "thrones"), and places them in relation to "the king" of Babylon. This language suggests that the author of the passage was promonarchic (in contrast to the antimonarchic stance in, for example, Ezra–Nehemiah).

21. In identifying historical-political continuity as the emphasis in this passage, I am departing from a popular interpretation—initiated by Gerhard von Rad, Hans Walter Wolff, and Erich Zenger—that reads the passage more theologically, as an expression of the author's "hope," his "faith," his confidence in the promises of the God of Israel, etc. Furthermore, if this passage is secondary, then one must use it very carefully when describing the view (or what Wolff called the "kerygma") of *the author*

the preceding passages (many of which seem to belong to the primary stratum of the narrative) depict the utter annihilation of the monarchy and society built up by Israel's first great kings and their successors.

3. Paying for Peace

The narrative in Samuel–Kings gravitates ineluctably toward this catastrophic end. Similarly to the way in which 2 Kgs 25:27–30 uses the table as a symbol of monarchic power, a series of texts in Kings describes how the wealth accumulated in the reigns of David and Solomon is gradually diminished, along with the native political strength that brought this wealth to Jerusalem.

The process of deterioration begins already during the reign of Rehoboam, right after the division of the kingdom, when the Egyptian ruler Shishak marches against Jerusalem (1 Kgs 14:25–28). The account in Kings suggests that it was the wealth assembled in Jerusalem by Solomon that induced the campaign in the first place. (In contrast, the Egyptian account is not even cognizant of Jerusalem.[22])

Two chapters later we are told that Asa sent Judah's remaining wealth abroad in an attempt to ensure the kingdom's domestic security (1 Kgs 15:16–22).[23] The point of departure for the account was, I propose, two

---

of the Deuteronomistic History (either of the whole work or of "Dtr2"). Instead, it seems more tenable to view the composition of the text as one voice in a wide-ranging conversation, which nevertheless has contours that distinguish it from other histories such as Chronicles.

22. On this issue, see the discussion of past scholarship in Kevin A. Wilson, *The Campaign of Pharaoh Shoshenq I into Palestine* (FAT 2/9; Tübingen: Mohr Siebeck, 2005), and subsequent to Wilson's discussion, the following articles: Israel Finkelstein and Alexander Fantalkin, "The Shoshenq I Campaign and the 8th-Century BCE Earthquake: More on the Archaeology and History of the South in the Iron I–IIA," *TA* 33 (2006): 18–42; Israel Finkelstein and Eliazer Piasetzky, "The Iron I–IIA in the Highlands and Beyond: 14C Anchors, Pottery Phases and the Shoshenq I Campaign," *Levant* 38 (2006): 45–61; James K. Hoffmeier, "The Campaign of Pharaoh Shoshenq I into Palestine," *BASOR* 349 (2008): 88–91; and Kenneth A. Kitchen, "The Campaign of Pharaoh Shoshenq I into Palestine," *JSS* 54 (2009): 274–76.

23. First Kings 15:16–22 appears to have emerged secondarily between 15:14 and 15:23. (For the supplementary character of 15:15, see n. 27 below.) Both of these supplements reflect a growing interest in the wealth of the temple that can be detected elsewhere in Kings and that is responsible for much of the significant literary growth that the book underwent.

separate traditions: on the one hand, that the Aramean ruler Ben-hadad annexed the Upper Galilee (v. 20; see 2 Kgs 15:29 and discussion below), and on the other hand, that the Judahite king Asa had conscripted the entire population for a major construction project on the southern border of Israel and northern border of Judah (Geba of Benjamin and Mizpah, v. 22b). These two traditions were synthesized in such a way that Judah—a negligible political power at the time—is presented as soliciting Aramean aggression against Israel's northern border.[24] The account not only presents a financial incentive offered by Judah as the motivation for a major strategic move by one of the most powerful states in the southern Levant. It also portrays an especially horrific political scenario: Judah responds to Israel's hostilities by using all its wealth to initiate foreign hostility against its own kin.[25]

The account of the war between Aram and Israel in 1 Kgs 20 furnishes a foil for other accounts in the book related to the forfeiture of wealth in war. In this account, Ben-hadad lays siege to Samaria and demands from Ahab all his silver and gold, as well as wives and children. The authors tell in a witty manner how Ahab manages—thanks to his adherence to the words of the prophet—to rout the armies of Ben-hadad on two different occasions.

Another encounter between Judah and Aram is reported in the reign of Jehoash (2 Kgs 12:18–19).[26] After seizing the city of Gath, Hazael of Aram directs his aggression against Jerusalem. In response, Jehoash offers Hazael "all the votive gifts [קדשים] that Jehoshaphat, Jehoram, and Ahaziah, his ancestors, the kings of Judah, had dedicated, as well as his own votive gifts, all the gold that was found in the treasuries of the house of YHWH and of

---

24. According to the historiographical synthesis, Israel first attempts to blockade Judah by fortifying Ramah. Asa then retaliates by offering Ben-hadad all the silver and gold from the treasuries of the temple and palace and petitioning him to breach his pact with Baasha. Ben-hadad acquiesces and sends his army commanders against the northern regions of Israel. This act is a ploy to divert Baasha's attention from Judah. Freed from the chokehold by Israel, Asa proceeds to fortify Judah, using the very same construction materials from Baasha's project at Ramah to build Gebah and Mizpah! In this way the authors have adeptly brought together two originally independent notices to create a neat story.

25. This fratricidal aspect is picked up by the author who recounts the massacres during the time of Gedaliah in the book of Jeremiah; see Jer 41:9. See also the Chronicler's interpretation of the account (2 Chr 15:1–16:10).

26. The account, along with 12:5–17, seems to have emerged secondarily between 12:4 and 20.

the palace."[27] Pacified by this generous payment, Hazael withdraws from Jerusalem. Judah is left in peace, but only for the time being (see 2 Kgs 16:5–9 and discussion below). In the meantime, the Aramean king, and later his son Ben-hadad, focus their aggression on Israel (2 Kgs 13).

Jerusalem's wealth is forfeited not only to foreign powers but also to Israel (2 Kgs 14:8–14).[28] When the Judahite king Amaziah beckons Jehoash of Israel to a military contest (perhaps reflecting the breach of a vassal relationship), the armies of Israel trounce the Judahite forces at Beth-shemesh. Jehoash later breaks down a portion of the ramparts in Jerusalem and then confiscates "all the gold and silver, and all the vessels that were found in the house of YHWH and in the treasuries of the palace" (v. 14). He deports hostages along with this booty and returns to Samaria (v. 14). The account unmistakably anticipates the final conquest of Jerusalem by the Babylonians, attributing the very same measures adopted by Nebuchadnezzar to an Israelian king.

The political scenario between Asa and Ben-hadad (1 Kgs 15) is recapitulated in the period of Assyria's initial encroachment on Israelite and Judahite soil (2 Kgs 16:5–9, 17–18).[29] Once again Israel is presented as a

---

27. The immediately preceding passage in 12:5–17, which may represent a redactional supplement, introduces the subject of the wealth in relation to the temple. For the "votive gifts," see 1 Kgs 15:15, and compare the placement of this verse directly before the account of Asa's stripping Jerusalem's wealth to pay Ben-hadad (15:16–22). For the deportation of vessels from Jerusalem by Jehoash, compare the interest in the Assyrian-Babylonian Chronicles (ABC) in the reciprocal abduction of gods. Thus ABC 1 begins: "The third year of Nabû-nasir, king of Babylon: Tiglath-Pileser [III] ascended the throne in Assyria. In that same year the king of Assyria went down to Akkad, plundered Rabbilu and Hamranu, and abducted the gods of Šapazza" (*u ilāni*[MEŠ] *šá* [URU]*Šá-pa-az-za i-ta-bak*)." See A. K. Grayson, *Assyrian and Babylonian Chronicles* (Locust Valley, N.Y.: Augustin, 1975), 71.

28. The author of this passage appears to have brought together two separate notices: v. 7 and vv. 15–16 (the latter is out of place). Similarly to what was witnessed above with respect to 1 Kgs 15, the author of vv. 8–14 explains, midrashically, how these events are related: After Amaziah witnesses victory over the Edomites (v. 7), he feels strong enough to take on Israel. In contrast to many other expansions, this one is more directly related to the dominant theme of relations between Israel and Judah; nevertheless, it is synthesized with the theme of the forfeiture of the temple wealth (v. 14). The same goes for 2 Kgs 16:5–9; see below.

29. Ahaz cuts off (ויקצץ) the frames of the stands and removes various objects of precious metal "because of the king of Assyria" (vv. 17–18). The passage is not only tightly connected to vv. 5–9 (before the introduction of vv. 10–16); it also anticipates

military aggressor against Judah, yet this time with the Arameans as their allies. In order to save his skin, the Judahite king Ahaz turns to Assyria. He petitions Tiglath-pileser III—the founder of the Neo-Assyrian Empire—to "rescue/save" him from the king of Aram and the king of Israel. Ahaz sends a "bribe" of silver and gold from the treasuries of the temple and palace in Jerusalem. Just as Ben-hadad responds to Asa, Tiglath-pileser acquiesces to Ahaz's proposition (compare the formulation in 1 Kgs 15:20 and 2 Kgs 16:9). He attacks Damascus and kills Rezin. With the military coalition disrupted, Israel ceases its aggression against Judah.[30]

This passage once again identifies Judah as the prime mover in geopolitical affairs. As in the case of the Aramean seizure of Israel's northern territories (1 Kgs 15), Assyria conquers Damascus (the inaugural moment in the history of the Neo-Assyrian Empire) not for any strategic reasons connected to its own imperial interests, but because it received a handsome bribe from Judah. Yet what prompts the authors of Kings to reconstruct the historical facts in this manner was likely not an interest in undermining the daunting power of the Neo-Assyrian Empire by showing how its founder took his cue from the much less powerful Judah. Indeed, the book looks unfavorably on the relationship Ahaz establishes with Assyria, revealing it not as an expression of political strength or genius but rather as the inception of a dangerous dependency.[31]

The pattern persists into the reign of Ahaz's son Hezekiah. Seeking to sever his ties to the Assyrians, this ruler succeeds only in bringing about great suffering: Sennacherib comes up against Judah and seizes all its fortified towns; in the end, only Jerusalem is saved. Before leaving, the Assyrian king demands an exorbitant amount of tribute, which the Judahite

---

the Babylonian treatment of the temple furnishings in 2 Kgs 24:13 (see ויקצץ there, which appears only in these two passages in Kings).

30. In the first encounter with Assyria narrated in the book (2 Kgs 15:17–20), Menahem of Israel pays Pul of Assyria a thousand talents of silver. (Compare the very similar rationale for Panamuwa's payment to Tiglath-pileser in *KAI* 215.) Here the theme of "paying for peace" appears in relation to Israel, not Judah. This fact helps explain why the king extracts the wealth not from a temple or palace but rather from "all the wealthy landowners." The method of exaction/taxation is similar to that adopted by Jehoiakim in paying tribute to Neco (which amounts only to a tenth of the sum paid by Menahem; see 2 Kgs 23:32–35).

31. See, e.g., the immediately following episode (2 Kgs 16:10–16), in which Ahaz goes up to Damascus to render tribute to Tiglath-pileser, witnesses an altar, and sends a model of it to Jerusalem with orders to build a replica of it.

king pays by, once again, stripping the temple and palace of its silver and gold (2 Kgs 18:13–16).[32] The account of Hezekiah's reign concludes by recounting a visit by Babylonian messengers whom Hezekiah entertains by showing them all the wealth in his storehouses (20:12–19).[33] Upon hearing of Hezekiah's actions, the prophet Isaiah proclaims an oracle: "Days are coming when all that is in your houses, and that which your ancestors have stored up until this day, shall be carried off to Babylon. Nothing shall be left" (20:17).

So, according to this history, what originally triggered the fateful incursions of the Arameans, Assyrians, and Babylonians was the misuse of Jerusalem's wealth by Judah's kings.[34]

---

32. This passage, or at least 18:13–14, appears to belong to the primary stratum. It may have originally been connected directly to 19:36. (As such, it would agree with Sennacherib's annals.) If confined solely to 18:13–14, the interest in the fate of the temple wealth in vv. 15–16 would be due to a secondary amplification. That vv. 15–16 are supplementary explains two problems: 1) Tribute is normally delivered over a period of time, not immediately. (Sennacherib's annals even claim that Hezekiah sent an emissary to pay the tribute!) However, vv. 15–16 suggest that he paid the tribute immediately. The narrative would not contain this problem if 19:36 followed directly on 18:13–14. 2) The language in these verses is encountered in other secondary passages discussed here. Unfortunately, the very popular, two-source theory has left little room for a supplementary analysis that explores how the Hezekiah narrative has been successively reinterpreted and expanded by later readers.

33. As many agree, the passage likely represents an addition to the account. Later Jewish interpretation (Esth. Rab. 3:1) synthesizes this account with the preceding account of Hezekiah's sickness (20:1–11) by presenting the Babylonians, famous for their interest in astronomy, coming to Jerusalem after the strange phenomenon of the sun retreating ten intervals (20:10–11). The midrashic synthesis is anticipated in v. 12b: "for he heard that Hezekiah had been sick." (Compare Burnaburiash's letter asking Akhenaten why he had not sent messengers to visit him while he was sick.) This clause may, however, have been added by a late hand; Josephus noticeably omits it. If it is indeed a gloss, what prompts the visit of the Babylonians would not have to be the news of Hezekiah's sickness or the Babylonians' astronomical curiosity, but rather an interest in Hezekiah's wealth and his attractiveness as an alliance partner after his deliverance from Sennacherib.

34. Surprisingly little has been written specifically on this theme (the privation of Jerusalem's wealth) in the book of Kings. Although concerned with different issues than those treated here, the articles by H. Tadmor and M. Cogan ("Ahaz and Tiglath-Pileser in the Book of Kings: Historiographic Considerations," *Bib* 60 [1979]: 499–508) and Nadav Na'aman ("The Deuteronomist and Voluntary Servitude to Foreign Powers," *JSOT* 65 [1995]: 37–53) make significant advances toward delineating this

4. THE FINAL DESTRUCTION

The "paying-for-peace" pattern delineated in the preceding section provides a context in which we may interpret the last chapters of Kings. Immediately before turning to the subject of Babylon's engagement in Judah, the narrative describes the tribute that Pharaoh Neco imposes on Judah and Jehoiakim's decision to tax the land in order to pay it (2 Kgs 23:33–35).[35] It then proceeds to report the deportation of Jehoiachin and his court (his mother, servants, officers, and eunuchs; 24:12). Thereafter it recapitulates the statement about the king's deportation, adding groups from the military and general population (vv. 14–16). Yet sandwiched between these paragraphs is a notice describing the deportation of Jerusalem's *wealth*: "[Nebuchadnezzar] carried off all the treasures of YHWH's house, and the treasures of the King's house; he cut in pieces all the vessels of gold in the temple of YHWH, which King Solomon of Israel had made" (24:13). Similarly, in the account of the final destruction in the time of Zedekiah, the details relating to the fate of the king and the general population encircle a passage describing the plundering of what remained of Jerusalem's precious metals (25:13–17).[36]

These passages ascribe to Nebuchadnezzar an interest in the intrinsic, pecuniary worth of the objects he seizes from the temple and palace, not their symbolic value. During the reign of Jehoiachin, the Babylonian king carries away "all the treasures" (כל אוצרות) of the temple and palace. With

---

important theme. Although often overlooked by readers, wealth constitutes a major subject of interest throughout the rest of the Bible. Genesis devotes extensive attention to the amassing of wealth by the patriarchs. A conspicuous theme in Exodus portrays the Israelites taking a great amount of Egyptian wealth with them as they leave (see 3:21–22; 11:2–3; 12:35–36). The Latter Prophets not only allude to wealth in their social critiques but also in many places envision the wealth of the nations being brought to Zion.

35. Notice the attention that the author devotes to the process of collecting the capital: "Jehoiakim gave the silver and the gold to Pharaoh, but he taxed [הֶעֱרִיךְ] the land in order to meet Pharaoh's demand for money. He exacted the silver and the gold from the people of the land, from all according to their assessment, to give it to Pharaoh Neco" (23:35).

36. Both 24:13 and 25:13–17 likely belong to a secondary stratum of the narrative. These passages are consistent inasmuch as the account of Zedekiah refers mostly to copper/bronze because the gold had already been deported in large part during the reign of Jehoiachin (24:13).

respect to the golden vessels that "Solomon had made" for the temple, he strips or cuts them up (ויקצץ). In so doing, he reduces the cultic function of these vessels to their raw metallic value (24:13), similar to "treasures." Later the Babylonian soldiers "break into pieces" all the large objects from the temple (the bronze pillars, the stands, and the bronze sea) and carry their bronze, along with the smaller portable items, to Babylon (25:13–15a). A telling statement in this passage expresses the interest in the intrinsic worth of the objects: "The captain of the guard took for gold what was made of gold, and for silver what was made of silver" (25:15b). This statement is followed by lines that stress the substantial quantity of metal in the massive objects that "Solomon had made for the house of YHWH" (25:16–17).

The destruction of the temple inventory corresponds to the destruction of the temple itself and the surrounding city. It is indeed remarkable that the destruction of the temple is mentioned in passing: "[Nebuzaradan] burned the house of YHWH, the house of the King, and all the houses of Jerusalem; every great house he burned down. All the army of the Chaldeans who were with the captain of the guard broke down the walls around Jerusalem" (25:9–10). Rather than being of independent cultic or social-institutional significance, the temple appears here as part of society that is destroyed—a society that owes its existence to, and revolves around, the king.[37]

In keeping with long-established Egyptian and West Asian conventions, the construction of temples and their inventories is a royal task. As a way of performing kingship, a ruler builds temples and sponsors the production of cultic vessels and other paraphernalia.[38] Temples often constitute monuments of territorial conquest and control. They can also establish the center of a realm in relation to its periphery, and occasionally they demarcate borders. In addition, they frequently function (along with

---

37. Notice how 2 Kgs 25:18–21 describes the execution of Seraiah, the chief priest, and Zephaniah, the second priest, along with guardians of the threshold and conscription officers in charge of mustering the army. The passage suggests that the Babylonians identified the temple and its chief personnel, whose fate is the same as the king's sons, with the palace and its insurgent politics.

38. See Victor Hurowitz, "I Have Built You an Exalted House": Temple Building in the Bible in Light of Mesopotamian and Northwest Semitic Writings (JSOTSup 115; Sheffield: JSOT Press, 1992), 256–59. Cf. Esarhaddon's indictment of the Babylonians for using the Esagila's gold to purchase Elamite military support.

the palace) as the repository of a kingdom's wealth—a kind of national bank or treasury.

Given their spatial-symbolic valence, the demolition of temples—along with the deportation and/or destruction of gods and other cultic items found within them—constitutes one of the most effective methods of conquering and remapping territories.[39] Abundant material evidence witnesses directly to the violent treatment of monuments and statues.[40] In addition, cuneiform sources often refer to forms of iconoclasm. Some of the oldest documentary witnesses stem from the end of the Ur III period, relating to the Elamite destruction of the statues of the Ba'u.[41] The "Lamentation over the Destruction of Sumer and Ur" decries the occupation and destruction of Nanna's chief sanctuary: "The É.kiš.nu.gál of Nanna is inhabited by the enemy. Its heavy … they shatter, its divine statues that filled the shrines they cut into pieces."[42] In a much later text, Ashurbanipal describes how he laid waste to Susa, "the great and holy city, abode of their gods." He carried off its massive wealth, leveled its ziggurat, smashed its shining copper horns. He also demolished Elam's temples, and "scattered their gods and goddesses to the winds," before sowing their lands with salt.[43] The Bavian Inscription of Sennacherib, which describes the Assyrian destruction of Babylon in 689 B.C.E. through flooding (hydraulic warfare), tells how the Assyrian soldiers smashed the local gods.[44]

---

39. With respect to the close association between kings, temples, and the cultic images/symbols that they housed, Steven Holloway notes for the Neo-Assyrian treatment of conquered rulers: "The frequent collocation of the deportation of divine statues and the deportation of captured kings represented the decisive removal of the nuclear symbols of statehood" (Steven W. Holloway, *Aššur Is King! Aššur Is King!" Religion in the Exercise of Power in the Neo-Assyrian Empire* [CHANE 10; Leiden: Brill, 2002], 195–96).

40. A 2011 symposium at the Oriental Institute of the University of Chicago, organized by Natalie May, focused on the subject of "Iconoclasm and Text Destruction in the Ancient Near East and Beyond." The papers are presently being prepared for publication.

41. See Hanspeter Schaudig, *Explaining Disaster: Tradition and Transformation of the "Catastrophe of Ibbi-Sîn" in Babylonian Literature* (AOAT 370; Münster: Ugarit-Verlag, forthcoming 2012), 70.

42. *ANET* 618:412–414 (Michalowski 407b–408).

43. See Maximilian Streck, *Assurbanipal und die letzten assyrischen Könige bis zum Untergang Niniveh's* (VAB 7; Leipzig: Hinrichs, 1916), 2:30–47, 50–58.

44. DINGIR.MEŠ *a-šib lìb-bi-šu* ŠU[II] UN.MEŠ-*ia ik-šu-su-nu-ti-ma ú-šab-bi-ru*, "My people seized the gods from there and smashed (them)." See Eckart Frahm, *Ein-*

A relief from Khorsabad (figs. 1–2, at the end of this essay) shows the soldiers of Sargon II sacking the Urartian temple of Ḫaldi and dismembering a statue of a king. Hanspeter Schaudig compares this image to Esaĝil Chronicle line 36: "At his [Marduk's] command, the hostile gods are bound, and dressed in soiled garments; they are cut to pieces like *mēsu*-trees."[45] Wood from *mēsu*-trees was conventionally used for divine images. Thus, the gods who oppose Marduk are returned, by means of the same cutting through which they became gods, back to raw wood.

We may compare these texts to others from the Bible that enjoin or describe the desecration of sacred spaces and cultic objects. For example, with respect to "the seven nations," Deuteronomy commands Israel to "break down their altars, smash their pillars, hew down their sacred poles, and burn their idols with fire" (Deut 7:5).[46] When David vanquishes the Philistines at Baal-perazim, the enemy abandons their gods and David commands them to be burned (1 Chr 14:12). The parallel text in 2 Sam 5:21 reports that David and his men did not destroy the images; instead, they abducted them (נשא "deport, carry off"; see also 2 Chr 25:14–15).[47]

The deportation of gods and temple inventories is depicted in a wide range of texts and images from ancient Western Asia. In the Mesha Stele, the Moabite king describes how he dedicated the Israelite city of Nebo to Ashtar Kemosh. He claims not only to have slain seven thousand of its inhabitants but also to have "taken the [ves]sels [כלי] of Yhwh and dragged them before Kemosh" (ll. 17–18). Although abduction of gods

---

leitung in die Sanherib-Inschriften (AfOB 26; Vienna: Institut für Orientalistik, 1997), text 122; Grant Frame, *Babylonia 689–627 B.C.: A Political History* (Instanbul: Nederlands Historisch-Archaeologisch Instituut, 1992), 52–63.

45. *epšu pîšu ikkammû ilānū nakrūtu labšū aršūti uktapparū kīma mēsî.* See Schaudig, *Explaining Disaster*, 68–71.

46. See also Deut 7:25: "The images of their gods you shall burn with fire. Do not covet the silver or the gold that is on them and take it for yourself, because you could be ensnared by it; for it is abhorrent to Yhwh your God." Similarly, Deut 12:2–3. In 2 Kgs 23:4, Josiah commands all the *vessels* made for Baal, Asherah, and host of heaven to be brought out of the temple of Yhwh, burned in Kidron, and the ashes "carried off" (נשא) to Bethel.

47. How the Chronicler came to read נשא as שרף is suggested in b. Avoda Zara 44a and Radak ad loc., where נשא is interpreted as "burn" in keeping a possible meaning of the lexeme elsewhere. See Morton (Mordechai) Cogan, *Imperialism and Religion: Assyria, Judah and Israel in the Eighth and Seventh Centuries B.C.E.* (SBLMS 19; Missoula, Mont.: Scholars Press, 1974), 116.

is attested very early in Mesopotamian history (and indeed many of our most important Babylonian images were found in Susa, whence they had been deported by Elamite rulers), some of the richest material stems from the records for Assyrian kings, beginning with Tiglath-pileser I.[48] This Middle-Assyrian ruler presented the gods he captured as captives or trophies that he dedicated to his own gods.[49] In keeping with the demands of an expanding empire, Neo-Assyrian courts adopted a utilitarian ideology that sought to effect a dispositional change on the part of the defeated. Hence, instead of portraying the gods of the vanquished as war trophies, it became more common to depict these gods as abandoning their kings/ cities/lands. For example, Sennacherib proclaims with respect to seven cities on the border of Qummuḫ: "Their gods abandoned them, rendering them helpless."[50] In some of these propagandistic texts, the gods not only abandon their own people but also even choose to join the Assyrian conquerors or desire to undertake a voyage to pay homage to the gods of Assyria.[51] Thus Sennacherib's deportation of the Marduk statue after

---

48. Several very good discussions of this material are already available: Cogan, *Imperialism and Religion*, 9–42, 119–21; Frame, *Babylonia 689–627 B.C.*; Holloway, *Aššur Is King*, 122–51; John Kutsko, *Between Heaven and Earth: Divine Presence and Absence in the Book of Ezekiel* (Biblical and Judaic Studies 7; Winona Lake, Ind.: Eisenbrauns, 2000), 103–24, 157–70; Angelika Berlejung, "Notlösungen: Altorientalische Nachrichten über den Tempelkult in Nachkriegszeiten," in *Kein Land für sich allein: Studien zum Kulturkontakt in Kanaan, Israel/Palästina und Ebirnâri für Manfred Weippert zum 65. Geburtstag* (ed. Ulrich Hübner and Ernst Axel Knauf; OBO 186; Freiburg: Universitätsverlag, 2002), 196–230; Schaudig, *Explaining Disaster,* as well as idem., "Death of Statues and Rebirth of Gods," in *Iconoclasm and Text Destruction in the Ancient Near East and Beyond* (ed. Natalie N. May; Oriental Institute Seminars 8; Chicago: Oriental Institute, forthcoming).

49. *itti ilānišunu ana* ᵈ*Adad rā'imīya ašruk,* "(Copper vessels from Qummuḫ) along with their gods, I presented to Adad, who loves me." For this example and others, see Cogan, *Imperialism and Religion*, 27.

50. *ilānīšun izibūšunūtima ušabšū rēqūssun.* See discussion in ibid., 11 n. 13.

51. See ibid., 16–22; and Kutsko, *Between Heaven and Earth,* 108–9. Compare the Republican Roman *evocatio deorum* in which the tutelary deity of an enemy city was "called out"—that is petitioned to abandon the city and inhabit a new temple in Rome. See Gabriella Gustafsson, "Evocatio Deorum: Historical and Mythical Interpretations of Ritualised Conquests in the Expansion of Rome" (Ph.D. diss., Uppsala University, 2000).

sacking Babylon in 689 B.C.E. is reinterpreted as the desire of Marduk
himself to abandon Babylon for Assur.[52]

This ideological move to attribute the abduction to voluntary self-exile
explains why Neo-Assyrian iconography depicts Assyrian soldiers trans-
ferring the gods of the subjugated in such a ceremonious and reverential
manner. Compare the more haphazard manner of transport portrayed in
the upper register of figure 2 with the formal processions depicted in figures 3–5. In one we witness soldiers sacking a city (and eunuchs weighing
and registering the metallic wealth; compare 2 Kgs 25:13–17), and in the
other we witness a formal process corresponding to the ideology of divine
abandonment.[53]

It is between these two options—destruction and deportation—that
our biblical histories are situated.[54] Chronicles, Ezra-Nehemiah, and
1 Esdras seek to affirm a fundamental, and physical, continuity between
the First and Second Temple periods.[55] Chronicles therefore confines
destruction to the cultic images of Judah's enemies.[56] With respect to
the inventory of the Jerusalem temple, in contrast, Chronicles describes
it being deported intact to Babylon, deposited in a sanctuary, and safeguarded there until it could be returned to the temple during the reign
of the Persian kings.[57] Ezra-Nehemiah and 1 Esdras correlate the homecoming of the deported population with the repatriation of the vessels by

---

52. See the literature cited in Kutsko, *Between Heaven and Earth*, 111, n. 44–45.

53. The scene in the upper register of fig. 2 corresponds to the "Letter to Aššur,"
which records in minute detail the wealth that was seized from the Ḫaldi temple.

54. In some cases, as in the biblical passages discussed above, both destruction
and deportation are reported. Thus, Ashurbanipal claims in the Rassam Cylinder (V
119–120) to have "smashed their gods, and pacified the divine heart of the lord of
lords [Ashur]. His [Ummanaldasi, king of Elam] gods, his goddesses, his property,
his goods, his people, great and small, I carried off to Assyria." See literature cited in
Kutsko, *Between Heaven and Earth*, 113 n. 53.

55. In addition to these histories, the deportation and return of the vessels is
presupposed or depicted in various ways in Jer 27–28, Dan 1 and 5, 2 Macc 2:1–8, 2
Bar. 6:7–9, 4 Bar. 3:7–19, Liv. Pro. 2:11–19, Midr. Rab. Num. 15.10, 'Abot R. Nat. 41,
b. Hor. 12a, b. Ker. 5b, b. Yom. 54a, and in countless later sources. In dispensing with
the emphasis on utter destruction in Kings, this literature echoes ancient practices of
deportation and repatriation of cultic objects (also known as "godnapping," see below).

56. The destruction (in addition to the deportation) of vessels reported in 2 Chr
36:19 represents, as explained above, an attempt to make sure that no vessels remained
in the land so that it could fully enjoy its Sabbaths (v. 21).

57. On these differences between Kings and Chronicles, see Ackroyd, "The Temple

depicting the community returning in order to restore the vessels to the temple in Jerusalem. We may compare this correlation of people and vessels to the Neo-Assyrian images that juxtapose the departure of gods with the deportation of the populace (see figs. 3 and 4).[58]

In sharp distinction from the emphasis on continuity in Chronicles, Ezra-Nehemiah, and 1 Esdras, the history in Samuel–Kings emphasizes discontinuity. It presents, in its first part, David vanquishing Israel's enemies and laying the groundwork for his son's construction of the temple. While Solomon transfers some of the temple's inventory from the tent (1 Kgs 8:4), he and David sponsor the greater part of the furnishings and cultic vessels (1 Kgs 7:45–48, 51).[59] The temple thus represents not only the culmination of conquest (like the tabernacle in Exodus) but also a monument to territorial sovereignty. As an institution, it is an integral part of a monarchic society (or what we would classify today as a "state"), which includes a palace (with a court and royal table), a fortified capital, garrisons, a professional military, an arms industry, and a highly stratified administration.[60] The history of Samuel–Kings narrates numerous episodes, studied in section 3 above, in which the kings of Judah relinquish the wealth of the temple (and palace) as they forfeit the sovereignty established by David and enjoyed by Solomon. These intermediate episodes presage the final destruction of Jerusalem and the deportation of its

---

Vessels," as well as Isaac Kalimi and James D. Purvis, "King Jehoiachin and the Vessels of the Lord's House in Biblical Literature," *CBQ* 56 (1994): 449–57.

58. It is remarkable that these images (and a series of others not reproduced here) consistently omit representations of the kings or court, focusing instead on representations of families from the population. The absence of the king and elites, on the one hand, and the frequency with which women and children are portrayed, on the other hand, may reflect an attempt to illustrate how the Assyrian armies have reduced the societies to their most basic natural elements. Figure 5 lends support to this interpretation.

59. As David grows in military might, he receives gifts of precious metals and "vessels" from conquered peoples and allies, and "dedicates" these to YHWH (2 Sam 8:9–12).

60. This conception of monarchic society informs much of Samuel–Kings but is spelled out most succinctly and straightforwardly in 1 Sam 8. For arms manufacturers, see n. 7 above. The deportation of these professionals, along with the standing army, is reported in 2 Kgs 24:14–16. It is noteworthy that the account of the destruction a decade later refers to a conscripted army and the officers who oversaw it (2 Kgs 25:19). The standing army had apparently not recovered after being significantly decimated during the deportations of 597 B.C.E.

wealth.[61] Such destruction and confiscation of wealth is depicted in figures 1–2.[62]

5. Conclusions

It is not surprising that the exaggerated, tendentious depiction of complete destruction in the final passages of Kings prompted some of its readers to "set the record straight" by composing counter-histories that avoid the implications of radical discontinuity in Judahite history. Such "historical revisionism" may be found already in the final paragraphs of Kings (2 Kgs 25:22–30), which affirms a *royal-dynastic* continuity to the former epoch by pointing to the imperial favor bestowed upon Jehoiachin and his branch of the Davidic line, which survived the Babylonian deportations. Yet other circles apparently found this solution to be deficient. While perhaps not conceived solely with the question of continuity in view, Chronicles, Ezra-Nehemiah, and 1 Esdras seek to counterbalance the emphasis on discontinuity. Significantly, they do so by seizing on the vessels—one of the symbols of *discontinuity* in Samuel–Kings.

---

61. Not only do these episodes anticipate the final destruction of Jerusalem and deportation of its wealth, but as I have attempted to show in this section, a series of texts attributes the demise of the kingdoms of Israel and Judah (partially) to the misuse of Jerusalem's wealth by Judah's kings. Throughout the footnotes, I have pointed out that many of the passages may be assigned to secondary strata. I would suggest that we distinguish between an older group of texts (1 Kgs 14:25–28; 2 Kgs 12:18–19; 18:13–14; 23:33–35) and a younger one (1 Kgs 15:16–22; 2 Kgs 14:8–14; 16:5–9; 18:15–16; 20:12–19). Many from the younger group relate to wars between Israel and Judah, while those from the older group often treat cases of foreign aggression. Several of these texts (1 Kgs 15:16–22; 2 Kgs 14:8–14; and 16:5–9) synthesize, in a highly sophisticated manner, two dominant themes in Samuel–Kings: (1) the enmity between Israel and Judah, and (2) the forfeiture of Judah's wealth (corresponding to the larger interest of the book in depicting the demise of native sovereignty).

62. The Babylonian interest in deporting the wealth of Jerusalem that is depicted in Kings corresponds to a noted tendency in Babylonian inscriptions; see David Vanderhooft, *The Neo-Babylonian Empire and Babylon in the Latter Prophets* (HSM 59; Atlanta: Scholars Press, 1999), 44–47. In contrast, Neo-Assyrian iconography and texts refer much more often to the deportation of gods and symbolic/ritual items. Yet they too manifest a great interest in the wealth that their armies confiscate or that their vassals pay in tribute; see Jürgen Bär, *Der assyrische Tribut und seine Darstellung: Eine Untersuchung zur imperialen Ideologie im neuassyrischen Reich* (AOAT 243; Kevelaer: Butzon & Bercker, 1996).

What was it about the vessels that the authors of these histories devote so much attention to them? One reason was an established ancient Near Eastern practice of not only deporting gods (or cultic inventories) but also *returning* them. Such acts of imperial benefaction in the form of repatriation, often studied under the rubric of "godnapping," are reported widely in sources from the Neo-Assyrian, Neo-Babylonian, Persian, and Hellenistic periods.[63] The biblical authors reflect knowledge of this practice and adapt it to their historiographical and ideological needs.

Another reason was the much different contours that the society of Judah had assumed after the destruction of the Iron Age kingdom. In a time when the conditions were not propitious for a strong native king, the temple assumed the central place previously occupied by the palace. The authors of Chronicles establish historical warrant for this development by presenting the construction of the temple as the chief claim to fame for the two most powerful kings in Israel's history (David and Solomon). Likewise, Ezra-Nehemiah and 1 Esdras assign this role to the Persian kings, who take it upon themselves to rebuild the temple. Yet questions of legitimacy nevertheless arose. All three histories respond to these critical voices by establishing an essential continuity between the Second Temple and the First Temple by pointing to the vessels. These portable objects, made of precious, durable metals, bear the temple's primordial essence. And for this reason, they must be kept intact, deported to Babylon, and safeguarded there until they can be returned and deposited in the chambers of newly built temple.[64]

Yet the history in Samuel–Kings pursues a different objective. Its authors are concerned to delineate how Israel and Judah ultimately forfeit every shred of native political sovereignty in the land. The vessels constitute a filament of continuity leading back to the glorious reign of Solomon, who is portrayed in the first portion of the book, and then explicitly identified in these final texts, as the one who sponsors the construction of the

---

63. The term was coined by Alasdair Livingstone. For research on the phenomenon, see the literature cited above in n. 48.

64. One may compare the vessels to the ark, which in (both Chronicles and Kings) conveys the essence of Sinai and the tabernacle to the temple. Indeed, it may be said that the vessels assume the role of the ark in the absence of the latter. Intriguingly, 1 Esdras, which begins with Josiah's directions to the Levites bearing the ark (1:3–4), states that the Babylonians took the vessels from "the ark of God" and transported them to Babylon (1:54). In this way, the essence of the ark is transferred to Babylon and then finally back to the new temple (see ch. 2 and following).

vessels and then later deposits them in the temple. In the end, a foreign power cuts up these same vessels and reduces them to their raw intrinsic value, thereby effectively eliminating what Solomon had once (symbolically) achieved.

By concluding their history with this sober, unadorned depiction of defeat, deportation, and discontinuity, the authors compel their readers to confront the questions: What now? Will a people survive the destruction of this kingdom? Will the nation prove stronger than the state?

BIBLIOGRAPHY

Ackroyd, Peter R. *Continuity: A Contribution to the Study of the Old Testament Religious Tradition*. Oxford: Blackwell, 1962.

———. "The Temple Vessels—A Continuity Theme." Pages 166–81 in *Studies in the Religion of Ancient Israel*. Edited by P. A. H. de Boer. VTSup 23. Leiden: Brill, 1972.

Albertz, Rainer. "In Search of the Deuteronomists." Pages 1–17 in *The Future of the Deuteronomistic History*. Edited by Thomas Römer. BETL 147. Leuven: Leuven University Press, 2000.

Bär, Jürgen. *Der assyrische Tribut und seine Darstellung: Eine Untersuchung zur imperialen Ideologie im neuassyrischen Reich*. AOAT 243. Kevelaer: Butzon & Bercker, 1996.

Berlejung, Angelika. "Notlösungen: Altorientalische Nachrichten über den Tempelkult in Nachkriegszeiten." Pages 196–230 in *Kein Land für sich allein. Studien zum Kulturkontakt in Kanaan, Israel/Palästina und Ebirnâri für Manfred Weippert zum 65. Geburtstag*. Edited by Ulrich Hübner and Ernst Axel Knauf. OBO 186. Freiburg: Universitätsverlag, 2002.

Botta, Paul-Émile, and M. E. Flandin. *Monument de Ninive*. Paris: Imprimerie Nationale, 1849.

Cogan, Morton (Mordechai). *Imperialism and Religion: Assyria, Judah and Israel in the Eighth and Seventh Centuries B.C.E.* SBLMS 19. Missoula, Mont.: Scholars Press, 1974.

Cogan, Mordechai, and Hayim Tadmor. *II Kings*. AB 11. New York: Doubleday, 1988.

Dietrich, Walter. *Prophetie und Geschichte*. FRLANT 108. Göttingen: Vandenhoeck & Ruprecht, 1972.

Elias, Norbert. *Die höfische Gesellschaft: Untersuchungen zur Soziologie des Königtums und der höfischen Aristokratie*. Berlin: Luchterhand, 1969.

Finkelstein, Israel, and Alexander Fantalkin. "The Shoshenq I Campaign and the 8th-Century BCE Earthquake: More on the Archaeology and History of the South in the Iron I–IIA." *TA* 33 (2006): 18–42.

Finkelstein, Israel, and Eliazer Piasetzky. "The Iron I–IIA in the Highlands and Beyond: 14C Anchors, Pottery Phases and the Shoshenq I Campaign," *Levant* 38 (2006): 45–61.

Frahm, Eckart. *Einleitung in die Sanherib-Inschriften*. AfOB 26. Vienna: Institut für Orientalistik, 1997.

Frame, Grant. *Babylonia 689–627 B.C. A Political History*. Instanbul: Nederlands Historisch-Archaeologisch Instituut, 1992.

Geoghegan, Jeffrey. *The Time, Place, and Purpose of the Deuteronomistic History: The Evidence of "Until This Day."* BJS 347. Providence, R.I.: Brown University Press, 2006.

Gray, John. *I and II Kings*. OTL. Philadelphia: Westminster, 1963.

Grayson, A. K. *Assyrian and Babylonian Chronicles*. Locust Valley, N.Y.: Augustin; 1975.

Gustafsson, Gabriella. "Evocatio Deorum: Historical and Mythical Interpretations of Ritualised Conquests in the Expansion of Rome." Ph.D. diss., Uppsala University, 2000.

Hoffmeier, James K. "The Campaign of Pharaoh Shoshenq I into Palestine." *BASOR* 349 (2008): 88–91.

Holloway, Steven W. *"Aššur Is King! Aššur Is King!": Religion in the Exercise of Power in the Neo-Assyrian Empire*. CHANE 10. Leiden: Brill, 2002.

Hurowitz, Victor. *'I Have Built You an Exalted House': Temple Building in the Bible in Light of Mesopotamian and Northwest Semitic Writings*. JSOTSup 115. Sheffield: JSOT Press, 1992.

Kalimi, Isaac, and James D. Purvis. "King Jehoiachin and the Vessels of the Lord's House in Biblical Literature." *CBQ* 56 (1994): 449–57.

Kitchen, Kenneth A. "The Campaign of Pharaoh Shoshenq I into Palestine." *JSS* 54 (2009): 274–76.

Kratz, Reinhard G. *The Composition of the Narrative Books of the Old Testament*. London: T&T Clark, 2005.

Kutsko, John. *Between Heaven and Earth: Divine Presence and Absence in the Book of Ezekiel*. Biblical and Judaic Studies 7. Winona Lake, Ind.: Eisenbrauns, 2000.

Layard, Austen Henry. *The Monuments of Nineveh*. London: John Murray, 1849.

———. *A Second Series of Monuments of Nineveh*. London: John Murray, 1853.

Montgomery, James A. *A Critical and Exegetical Commentary on the Book of Kings*. ICC 10. New York: Scribner, 1951.

McKenzie, Steven L. *The Trouble with Kings: The Composition of the Book of Kings in the Deuteronomistic History*. VTSup 42. Leiden: Brill, 1991.

Na'aman, Nadav. "The Deuteronomist and Voluntary Servitude to Foreign Powers," *JSOT* 65 (1995): 37–53.

O'Brien, Mark A. *The Deuteronomistic History Hypothesis: A Reassessment*. OBO 92. Freiburg: Universitätsverlag, 1989.

Pohlmann, K.-F. "Erwägungen zum Schlußkapitel des deuteronomistischen Geschichtswerkes. Oder: Warum wird der Prophet Jeremia in 2. Kön. 22–25 nicht erwähnt?" Pages 94–109 in *Textgemäß. Aufsätze und Beiträge zur Hermeneutik des Alten Testaments: Festschrift Ernst Würthwein*. Edited by A. H. J. Gunneweg and Otto Kaiser. Göttingen: Vandenhoeck & Ruprecht, 1979.

Schaudig, Hanspeter. "Death of Statues and Rebirth of Gods." In *Iconoclasm and Text Destruction in the Ancient Near East and Beyond*. Edited by Natalie N. May. Oriental Institute Seminars 8. Chicago: Oriental Institute, forthcoming 2012.

———. *Explaining Disaster: Tradition and Transformation of the "Catastrophe of Ibbi-Sîn" in Babylonian Literature*. AOAT 370. Münster: Ugarit-Verlag, forthcoming.

Schmid, Konrad. *Genesis and the Moses Story: Israel's Dual Origins in the Hebrew Bible*. Winona Lake, Ind.: Eisenbrauns, 2010. Spawforth, A. J. S., ed. *The Court and Court Society in Ancient Monarchies*. Cambridge: Cambridge University Press, 2007.

Streck, Maximilian. *Assurbanipal und die letzten assyrischen Könige bis zum Untergang Niniveh's*. VAB 7. Leipzig: Hinrichs, 1916.

Tadmor, Hayim, and Mordechai Cogan. "Ahaz and Tiglath-Pileser in the Book of Kings: Historiographic Considerations." *Bib* 60 (1979): 499–508.

Vanderhooft, David. *The Neo-Babylonian Empire and Babylon in the Latter Prophets*. HSM 59. Atlanta: Scholars Press, 1999.

Wilson, Kevin A. *The Campaign of Pharaoh Shoshenq I into Palestine*. FAT 2/9. Tübingen: Mohr Siebeck, 2005.

Wright, Jacob L. "Commensal Politics in Ancient Western Asia: The Background to Nehemiah's Feasting (Part I)." *ZAW* 122 (2010): 212–33.

———. "A Nation Conceived in Defeat." *Azure* 42 (5771/2010): 83–101.

———. "Surviving in an Imperial Context: Foreign Military Service and Judean Identity." Pages 505–27 in *Judah and the Judeans in the Achaemenid Period: Negotiating Identity in an International Context*. Edited by Oded Lipschits, Gary N. Knoppers, and Manfred Oeming. Winona Lake, Ind.: Eisenbrauns, 2011.

Würthwein, Ernst. *Die Bücher der Könige: 1. Kön. 17–2. Kön. 25*. ATD 11:2. Göttingen: Vandenhoeck & Ruprecht; 1984.

———. *Studien zum deuteronomistischen Geschichtswerk*. BZAW 227. Berlin: de Gruyter, 1994.

Figs. 1–2. Inset from Khorsabad relief depicting Assyrian soldiers dismembering an image (likely of a ruler) during Sargon II's sacking of the sanctuary of the god Ḫaldi at Muṣaṣir. As seen in fig. 2, the scene is presented against the backdrop of other soldiers carrying off ritual objects made of precious metals, which eunuchs are weighing. From Paul-Émile Botta and M. E. Flandin, *Monument de Ninive* (Paris: Imprimerie Nationale, 1849), vol. 2, pl. 140.

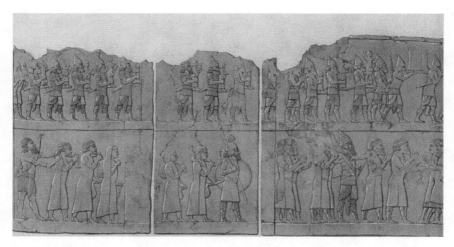

Fig. 3. Relief from the Southwest Palace of Sennacherib at Nineveh, showing the deportation of images (in the upper register) juxtaposed with the deportation of the populace (in the lower register). The identity of the deportees is not clear. From Austen Henry Layard, *A Second Series of Monuments of Nineveh* (London: John Murray, 1853), pl. 30.

Fig. 4. Another relief from Senacherib's Southwest Palace in Nineveh juxtaposing the deportation of the Judahite population from Lachish with the deportation of the symbols of sovereignty and ritual objects (royal chariot, throne, incense burners). Photo taken by author at British Museum; BM 124907.

Fig. 5. Relief from Nineveh showing soldiers carrying off Marduk and an eagle representing Ninurta or Enlil from the Šapazza in Babylon. The image resembles figs. 3–4 insofar as it also juxtaposes fathers, mothers, and children. From Austen Henry Layard, *The Monuments of Nineveh* (London: John Murray, 1849), pl. 67a.

Assyrian Representations of Booty and Tribute as a Self-Portrayal of Empire

Marian H. Feldman

Neo-Assyrian art includes numerous images of the seizure of foreign items. While these images carry documentary weight, they also contain constitutive aspects that helped fashion an imperial self-portrait through the depiction of otherness.[1] In this essay, I argue that the strong, coherent, and consistent style produced by the Assyrian state was not simply the expression of a growing empire; rather, it was part of an active strategy for maintaining a memory of conquest over the vanquished "other," and at the same time neutralizing the other so it could no longer threaten Assyria. I approach style as one mode of engaging with and representing the other and argue that the stylistic rendering of the other in a consistent manner across imperial Assyrian arts renders the other powerless while show-casing the memory of its capture. Such a reading requires that we break with the notion of style as a one-to-one emanation of a cultural entity and instead accept style as part of a selective process of identity forma-tion. Paradoxically, the rendering of otherness acted to establish norms of "being imperial Assyria" that emptied the other of its own stylistic identity through a process of stylistic Assyrianization. In making this argument, I will draw on several different strands of scholarship in complement to the visual record of the reliefs. These include Akkadian terminology, studies of alterity in the Neo-Assyrian empire, and the Assyrian reception of foreign luxury goods.

---

1. I would like to thank the committee of the Warfare in Ancient Israel Section (chaired by Brad E. Kelle) for inviting me to participate in the 2009 Society of Biblical Literature Annual Meeting and to contribute a chapter to this volume. Thanks are also due to Stephanie Langin-Hooper and Brian Brown for reading drafts of this article and providing stimulating feedback about this topic to me.

1. Images of Assyrian Booty and Tribute

The Assyrians are well known for their military exploits, which led to the deportation of vast populations and the acquisition of enormous wealth. From the perspective of ancient Israel, the capture of Lachish occupies a central place in this narrative. The siege, part of Sennacherib's third campaign of 701 B.C.E., is known from both Assyrian and biblical sources. For example, 2 Kgs 18:13–14 recounts:

> In the fourteenth year of King Hezekiah, Sennacherib king of Assyria came up against all the fortified cities of Judah and took them. And Hezekiah, king of Judah, sent to the king of Assyria at Lachish, saying, "I have done wrong. Withdraw from me; whatever you impose on me I will bear." And the king of Assyria required of Hezekiah, king of Judah, three hundred talents of silver and thirty talents of gold. And Hezekiah gave him all the silver that was found in the house of the Lord and in the treasuries of the king's house. (RSV)

From Sennacherib's self-styled Palace without Rival (the Southwest Palace in Nineveh), a series of reliefs from a single small room (XXXVI) graphically displays this event, ending with the image of the enthroned Sennacherib (see figs. 1–3 at the end of the essay).[2] Before him a caption reads: "Sennacherib, king of the world, king of Assyria, sat in a *nemēdu*-throne and the booty of the city of Lachish passed in review before him."[3] Both the Assyrian and biblical texts include mention of the wealth obtained by the Assyrians as part of the outcome of this military activity. The Nineveh relief caption emphasizes in particular Sennacherib's visual inspection (review) of Lachish's booty.

In Sennacherib's reliefs, this booty is itself given visual form, occupying space between the scene of the actual siege and the image of the seated king. What exactly is Sennacherib shown viewing? Closest to the king are men prostrating themselves before the throne. Others—first men and then

---

2. John Malcolm Russell, "Sennacherib's Lachish Narratives," in *Narrative and Event in Ancient Art* (ed. P. J. Holliday; Cambridge: Cambridge University Press, 1993), 55–73.

3. ^{md}30-PAP.MEŠ-SU MAN ŠU MAN KUR *aš+šur* / *ina* GIŠ.GU.ZA *né-me-di ú-šib-ma* / *šal-la-at* URU *la-ki-su* / *ma-ḫa-ar-šu e-ti-iq*. Cited according to John Malcolm Russell, *The Writing on the Wall: Studies in the Architectural Context of Late Assyrian Palace Inscriptions* (Winona Lake, Ind.: Eisenbrauns, 1999), 287–88.

women—follow behind, walking along with Assyrian soldiers, their hands raised up before their faces. Interspersed among them is a scene of an Assyrian soldier felling a Lachishite with his dagger, and beyond them are two further individuals stretched out as they are flayed. Following these we see groups of men carrying sacks and boxes over their shoulders or leading oxen who pull carts filled with more sacks, on top of which sit women and small children. Other women walk, carrying children and more sacks. A camel carries a heavy load on its back, and Assyrian soldiers descend from the besieged city with a chariot, weapons, and furnishings. All this, presumably, falls within the scope of the acquiring gaze of the triumphant king, who sits enthroned reviewing his booty.

This is only one of many images of Assyrian imperial acquisition of wealth, which were depicted not only in the format of carved stone palace reliefs but also on bronze door bands, ivory furniture inlays, and other items of differing size and medium.[4] It is not possible to review all these images here, and indeed, to circumscribe these scenes as a group is itself not without problem. Sennacherib's Lachish reliefs, however, provide a useful avenue into several questions regarding the representation of booty and tribute, starting with the conjunction of the textual reference to booty, known in Akkadian as *šallatu*, and the visual rendering of this presumed *šallatu*.

2. Booty, Tribute, Gods, and Deportees

Terminologically, it is important to note the distinction between tribute and booty. Tribute can be understood as a compulsory "gift" signaling surrender and ongoing loyalty. Booty, however, denotes goods that have been forcefully seized through military action against a city. The Assyrian texts predominately use the word *šallatu* to refer to "booty" as opposed to *maddattu*, which means "tribute." The word comes from the stem š-l-l, "to take forcibly," and clearly indicates the involuntary and violent nature of the seizure. The term is also consistently used to refer to captured people, whom we would call deportees. Liverani has noted that "the term *šallatu* is notoriously ambiguous, its meaning encompassing a generic 'booty' and a specific human booty, i.e. '(civilian) prisoners,' and the distinction is

---

4. Jürgen Bär, *Der assyrische Tribut und seine Darstellung: Eine Untersuchung zur imperialen Ideologie im neuassyrischen Reich* (Kevelaer: Butzon & Bercker; Neukirchen-Vluyn: Neukirchener, 1996).

not always clear."[5] Likewise, *CAD* comments: "In royal inscriptions where *šallatu* occurs beside *bušû*, etc., or in late texts, beside *ḫubtu*, it is often difficult to distinguish whether the latter refers to goods and *šallatu* to persons, or whether *šallatu* is a more general term for booty, including objects, livestock, gods, and prisoners."[6] Such range and diversity of items apparently under the rubric of *šallatu* finds a visual parallel in the Lachish reliefs. There, objects, livestock, and prisoners all appear to be encompassed by Sennacherib's visual review of booty as described in the accompanying caption. *Maddattu*, though perhaps less inclusive than *šallatu*, also covers a range of animate and inanimate items, such as gold, silver, garments, wine, horses, and cattle.[7]

Differences in usage between the terms "booty" and "tribute" fluctuated over the course of the Neo-Assyrian period. In the ninth-century annals of Ashurnasirpal II and Shalmaneser III, lists designated as tribute include much more detailed descriptions of worked luxury items and precious materials such as gold, silver, or ivory, whereas records of booty dwell more on quantities of people, cavalry, and livestock, tending to refer only in generic terms to palace treasures or property.[8] In the later periods from Sargon II on, written descriptions of tribute become less frequent, while those of booty become much more elaborate and detailed, such as Sargon's description of the sack of the Urartian temple of Haldi at Muṣasir in his letter to Ashur.[9] Yet both terms seem to blur categories of things that we today would keep separate. On the one hand, the Assyrians used different terms—*maddattu* and *šallatu*—to distinguish between the means by which items were acquired (rhetorically speaking, this is a distinction between things given "peaceably" and things taken by force). On the other hand, both terms grouped together a broad range of acquisitions from gods to humans and nonhumans. For the purposes of this essay, I refer generically to *wealth* in order to include the full range of these items as well as both booty and tribute.

5. Mario Liverani, *Topographical Analysis* (vol. 2 of *Studies on the Annals of Ashurnasirpal II*; Rome: Università di Roma "La Sapienza," Dipartimento di Scienze Storiche, Archeologiche e Antropologiche dell'Antichità, 1992), 155.

6. *CAD* 17.1:252, *šallatu* A.

7. *CAD* 10.1:13–14, *maddattu* 1.

8. Allison Karmel Thomason, *Luxury and Legitimation: Royal Collecting in Ancient Mesopotamia* (Aldershot, U.K.: Ashgate, 2005), 123–24.

9. Ibid., 124.

The use of a single term, *šallatu* or *maddattu*, to refer to a spectrum of acquisitions that we today would keep separate—gods, humans, and non-humans—points to differences in perception and classificatory schemes between us and the ancient Assyrians. It suggests a different organizational concept of the world—not simply bifurcated between human and non-human or between animate and inanimate, but much more situationally determined: the objectification of gods, humans, and goods as booty or tribute, and at the same time, the animation of these very things as potentially threatening or powerful forces. (In Sennacherib's Lachish caption, the booty, as the subject of the verb *etēqu*, literally "passes by" in review.[10]) Thus, when we consider representations of booty and tribute, we should include among our subjects this same broad spectrum of entities, including gods and humans, whose status in particular as *šallatu* was based primarily on their having been forcibly extracted. That is, when we analyze images such as the Lachish reliefs, we should consider the depiction not only of the weapons and furnishings that the Assyrian soldiers remove from the city, but also the men, women, children, and animals.

3. ALTERITY IN THE ASSYRIAN IMPERIAL IDEOLOGY

When we expand our representational corpus to include human and divine entities, we enlarge and enrich the rhetorical corpus from which to draw inferences concerning Assyrian visual strategies in their encounters with the other. Working from the premise that social groups create their identities in part through opposition to something else, Megan Cifarelli has examined Assyrian depictions of foreigners as evidence of Assyrian interaction with and response to cultural difference.[11] For the most part, foreigners are depicted in a limited range of contexts—as tributaries, in battle, or as captives/deportees. Ethnic type-markers, such as physiognomy, hairstyle, and dress, identify these individuals as non-Assyrians; although, they are integrated into larger compositions through their rendering in the Assyrian court style, to be discussed below. Yet according to Cifarelli, the depiction of their poses and gestures signals a negative valuation when understood within the cultural context of Assyrian social norms. The specific poses and gestures, such as slouching, crouching, and placing the fists

---

10. *CAD* 4:386, *etēqu* A1d.

11. Megan Cifarelli, "Gesture and Alterity in the Art of Ashurnasirpal II of Assyria," *The Art Bulletin* 80 (1998): 210–28.

before the nose, would have been inherently read by Assyrians as sinister, abnormal, or subservient in contrast to the upright postures of depicted Assyrians. She further argues that this negative valuation of alterity was a critical component in the developing ideology of the expanding Assyrian state, which came into place early in its historical trajectory, as exemplified by the slouching tributaries depicted on the façade of Ashurnasirpal II's throne room at Nimrud.[12]

Cifarelli's research indicates that otherness was rarely if ever coded positively in the case of foreign human beings. Given the inclusion of captives among items of booty, we might extend her conclusions about the representations of foreigners, many of whom would be classified as *šallatu*, to include the full range of booty and tribute, which means also gods and goods. We might, therefore, propose that a sinister or threatening aspect inhered in many foreign items, endowing them with a potentially powerful efficacy that required Assyrian intervention.

4. Foreign Goods in Assyria

Such threatening power may be evident in an avoidance of integrating foreign items into the everyday life of the Assyrian court. The wealth accumulated by the Assyrians through their military campaigns, carefully recorded in the annals and depicted in narrative imagery, survives archaeologically best in the physical remains of carved ivories found in the Assyrian heartland that originated from the western areas of Syria and Phoenicia (referred to here generally as the Levant). The largest collections of this material have been excavated over the last 150 years at the ninth-century capital of Nimrud.[13] While there is much debate about the date of both the production and deposition of these ivories, it is clear that even after Nimrud's demotion from the rank of capital under Sargon II around 720 B.C.E., it continued to function as a major administrative center, housing the spoils of Assyrian power in at least two ninth-century buildings: the Northwest Palace built by Ashurnasirpal II (883–859 B.C.E.) and Fort

---

12. Ibid., 214–18.

13. For a review of discoveries, see Georgina Herrmann and Stuart Laidlaw, *Ivories from the North West Palace (1845–1992)* (Ivories from Nimrud 6; London: British Institute for the Study of Iraq, 2009), 27–29.

Shalmaneser, erected as a military arsenal (*ekal mašarti*) by his successor Shalmaneser III (858–824 B.C.E.).[14]

The problem of differentiating stylistic groups among the Levantine ivories is thorny. However, it has been evident since the first discoveries that there exists an Assyrian class of ivories that is appreciably distinct from the others in its favored techniques (typically incised), motifs (courtly scenes associated with the monumental palace reliefs, including scenes of booty and tribute), and style.[15] Although these Assyrian-style ivories occur in far fewer numbers than the Levantine ones, Georgina Herrmann, in her cataloguing of the Nimrud ivories, has discerned noticeably different distribution patterns for the Assyrian and Levantine groups.[16] Assyrian-style ivories tend to be found in major public or reception areas. For example, near the throne base in Room B of the Northwest Palace, Max Mallowan found a series of incised ivories in the Assyrian style that closely follow the art of the better known throne room reliefs.[17] These may have decorated either a throne or an associated piece of furniture. In contrast, aside from wells and other sites of vandalism, Levantine ivories are found predominately in the storerooms of Fort Shalmaneser or in small relatively secure rooms in out-of-the-way parts of buildings, such as rooms A, V, W, and HH in the Northwest Palace.

Based on this distribution pattern, Herrmann suggests that the Assyrian royal court did not appreciate the aesthetic qualities of the Levantine ivories that they accumulated in such vast quantities.[18] She proposes that the Assyrian king used only furniture decorated with Assyrian-style ivories, as indicated by the throne room examples. While Herrmann takes these patterns as evidence for a general lack of interest in ivory as a high-value material by the Assyrians, it is of further note that despite the vast quantities of Levantine-style ivories in the Assyrian heartland, these foreign goods have virtually no stylistic impact on Assyrian art. Early on during the emergence of Assyria as a territorial state in the ninth century, some motival and artistic concepts enter the Assyrian artistic repertoire

---

14. Joan Oates and David Oates, *Nimrud: An Assyrian Imperial City Revealed* (London: British School of Archaeology in Iraq, 2001).

15. Max Mallowan and Leri Glynne Davies, *Ivories in Assyrian Style* (Ivories from Nimrud 2; London: British School of Archaeology in Iraq, 1970).

16. Herrmann and Laidlaw, *Ivories from the North West Palace*, 27–52.

17. Ibid., 36–37.

18. Ibid., 113.

from the West (for example, the North Syrian idea of carving on orthostats and use of protective doorway figures) but not stylistic features.[19] Rather, a distinctly Assyrian style, which can be traced back to the Middle Assyrian period, is already in place during this time.[20]

5. STYLISTIC ASSYRIANIZATION

If we understand style as a selective process and not just something that happens or that is automatically bound to a monolithically defined culture, then the strongly Assyrian style can be seen as part of a strategy of self-representation that actively demarcates between Assyrian and other.[21] I argue here that style functions as one mode (among many) of engagement with the other—a mode, moreover, that effectively deals with the paradox of needing both to destroy the other and to maintain the memory of the destruction itself and the object of destruction.

In a book on collecting practices in Mesopotamia, Allison Thomason argues that the Assyrians transformed the cultural styles of depicted items of tribute and booty through a process of the "period eye."[22] That is, because the Assyrian artists were trained to execute their works in an Assyrian style, they innately transposed this style onto the representation of even non-Assyrian-style things. However, if we accept that the incorporated training of a strongly Assyrian artistic style occurred as part of the maintenance and transmission of an Assyrian imperial identity that saw itself at least in part in opposition to cultural alterity, then we must assign a greater role of agency than the concept of the "period eye" allows. In fact, Thomason's characterization of this process as "Assyrianization"

<hr>

19. Brian Brown, "Monumentalizing Identities: North Syrian Urbanism, 1200–800 BCE" (Ph.D. diss., University of California, Berkeley, 2008), 220–23.

20. Holly Pittman, "The White Obelisk and the Problem of Historical Narrative in the Art of Assyria," *The Art Bulletin* 78 (1996): 334–55; Marian H. Feldman, "Assur Tomb 45 and the Birth of the Assyrian Empire," *BASOR* 343 (2006): 21–43.

21. For the active qualities of style, see, e.g., Irene J. Winter, "The Affective Properties of Styles: An Inquiry into Analytical Process and the Inscription of Meaning in Art History," in *Picturing Science, Producing Art* (ed. C. A. Jones and P. Galison; New York: Routledge, 1998), 55–77; Marian H. Feldman, "Darius I and the Heroes of Akkad: Affect and Agency in the Bisitun Relief," in *Ancient Near Eastern Art in Context: Studies in Honor of Irene J. Winter by Her Students* (ed. J. Cheng and M. H. Feldman; Leiden: Brill, 2007), 265–93.

22. Thomason, *Luxury and Legitimation*, 141.

comes closer to capturing the active and ongoing nature of this tradition-building mechanism.[23] Indeed, it is this notion of process—the making of something other into something Assyrian—connoted by the term *Assyrianization* that I see as central to understanding the representations of foreign booty and tribute.

This Assyrianization is particularly evident in a relief from the reign of Tiglath-Pileser III (745–727 B.C.E.) showing the capture of foreign gods (fig. 4).[24] Here, divine attributes (that is, motifs) such as the lightening fork and axe clearly belong to the West Semitic weather god, as can be seen in any of a number of stelae from that region,[25] but the stylistic rendering of the human form is entirely Assyrian. Just enough of the attributes are depicted to signal its foreignness and otherness, revealing the deliberative nature of this strategy. Yet the depiction is stylistically merged into the larger, all-encompassing field of an imperial Assyrianism. Captured by the Assyrians and brought back to the center, the gods have been emptied of their own cultural essence and Assyrianized in their very stylistic rendering. The tributaries depicted on Ashurnasirpal II's throne room façade in the Northwest palace at Nimrud show this strategy occurring already at an early date in the mid-ninth century.

Likewise, representations of furniture maintain certain distinctively foreign attributes, such as the curving back of a couch, but are translated by and large into Assyrianized stylistic forms. This process of Assyrianization seen in the depiction of foreign gods and goods can be related to the same negative valuation of alterity ascribed by the Assyrians to foreign peoples, since all of them—gods, people, and things—belonged to the same category of booty or tribute. The potentially threatening element of otherness needed to be tamed and brought under the control of Assyria through a process of Assyrianization that was physically expressed through a strong, coherent style that clearly differentiated itself from Assyria's neighbors. Moreover, the fact that items of foreign furniture similar to pieces actually

---

23. Ibid.

24. Richard D. Barnett and Margarete Falkner, *The Sculptures of Assur-nasir-apli II (883–859 B.C.), Tiglath-Pileser III (745–727 B.C.), Esarhaddon (681–669 B.C.) from the Central and South-West Palaces at Nimrud* (London: The Trustees of the British Museum, 1962), 29–30, pls. LXXXVIII, XCIII.

25. See, e.g., Guy Bunnens, *A New Luwian Stele and the Cult of the Storm-God at Til Barsib-Masuwari* (Mission archéologique de l'Université de Liège en Syrie, Tell Ahmar 2; Leuven: Peeters, 2006).

found in the storehouses of Assyria are represented through this same artistic strategy indicates that this process of Assyrianization was not due to any ignorance on the part of the artists, as such items could have been available for inspection and copying had this been important to the Assyrian court.

One might ask, then, if otherness was considered so threatening to the Assyrians, why represent it at all? Would not absence best deflect its power? Yet to do so would also erase the memory of Assyria's mastery over the other. The other must be present in order to keep alive the memory of its own conquest. This paradoxical aspect of representing the other explains why style is such an effective means of co-opting and neutralizing that which is threatening about alterity. By retaining enough physical attributes (rendered as motival traits) to identify the other as foreign, artists could preserve and nurture the memory of victory. At the same time, the Assyrianization of the other, that is, the other's incorporation through visual similarity of form into that which is normatively Assyrian, neutralizes its potency.

In sharp contrast to the Assyrian encounter with most foreign styles, Assyria's complicated relationship with Babylonia presents a rather different picture, and helps highlight the selective nature of this artistic strategy. In this case, Babylonian stylistic features were purposely adopted and incorporated into Assyrian art for exactly the opposite purpose, which is to self-identify with Babylonia, to which Assyria saw itself as a cultural successor. This was achieved using the same means but with the opposite effect, that is, through the cultural assimilation of the Babylonian artistic style (a *Babylonianization*). This can be seen, for example, in a stela of Ashurbanipal from Babylon that uses the rounded, volumetric style of the Babylonian sculptural tradition rather than the flat linear style of the Assyrian one.[26] The erection in Babylon of this stela, which recounts Ashurbanipal's rebuilding of that city, made this piece especially potent, but one can also see Babylonian stylistic influence in the more rounded forms of the figures in Ashurbanipal's reliefs at Nineveh.

I would like to end by turning to one of the most evocative representations of foreign wealth from the Neo-Assyrian period: Ashurbanipal's so-called garden scene from the North Palace at Nineveh (fig. 5). Pauline Albenda was one of the first scholars to point to this relief as more than a bucolic pastoral scene, arguing that the material luxury surrounding

---

26. Béatrice André-Salvini, ed., *Babylone: À Babylone, d'hier et d'aujourd'hui* (Paris: Musée du Louvre, 2008), 139, cat. no. 95.

the Assyrian king should be read, along with the decapitated head of his Elamite enemy hanging from a nearby tree, as trophies of successful military conquests.[27] Among these items she identifies an Egyptian *menat-* necklace, an Elamite or Babylonian bow and quiver, horse trappings that may point to Iran, in addition to the pyxis on the table in front of Ashurbanipal and the couch upon which he reclines, both of which are suggestive of the Levant. Even Ashurbanipal's queen, seated to one side, a rare depiction of female Assyrian royalty, may signal a foreign bride such as those with West Semitic names buried in the eighth-century Queens' tombs under the Northwest Palace at Nimrud.[28] Yet like the images of captured gods and plundered furnishings, the various items are all rendered in the distinctly Assyrian court style. Indeed, this visual Assyrianization is so successful that one scholar has recently argued that Ashurbanipal's couch is actually an Assyrian-made piece of furniture since the tell-tale Levantine "woman at the window" plaques shown on its legs look like Assyrian images of eunuchs.[29] However, when taken with all the other pieces of evidence, including the intermixing of plants that would not grow together in the same ecological niche, it is clear that we see here in this single image the capture and Assyrianization of the foreign cultures over which Assyria held power—extending from the plant realm to the domain of material goods and luxuries, to the very people themselves.

---

27. Pauline Albenda, "Grapevines in Ashurbanipal's Garden," *BASOR* 215 (1974): 5–17; idem, "Landscape Bas-Reliefs in the Bit-Hilani of Ashurbanipal, Part 1," *BASOR* 224 (1976): 49–72; idem, "Landscape Bas-Reliefs in the Bit-Hilani of Ashurbanipal, Part 2," *BASOR* 225 (1977): 29–48.

28. Oates and Oates, *Nimrud*, 78–90.

29. Ellen Rehm, "Assyrische Möbel für den assyrischen Herrscher!" in *Crafts and Images in Contact: Studies on Eastern Mediterranean Art of the First Millennium BCE* (ed. C. E. Suter and C. Uehlinger; OBO 210; Fribourg: Academic; Göttingen: Vandenhoeck & Ruprecht, 2005), 187–206. Rehm, however, does not consider the other aspects of the scene that point to foreign associations as detailed by Albenda. She reads this image with a literalness that is untenable, if only because of the impossibility of the vegetation growing together naturally. If one accepts the vegetation as a manipulation of natural situations (whether only at the representational level or also at the level of the botanical gardens planted by the Assyrian kings), then one also has to consider this aspect for all other elements in the image. While she is correct to point to significant differences between the Levantine representations of the "woman at the window" motif and that on the relief (explainable by the process of Assyrianization discussed in this essay), her comparisons with Assyrian representations of eunuchs are unconvincing.

6. Conclusions

The careful crafting and curation of a distinctive Assyrian style became an active strategy in dealing with the twofold problem of the other, which the conquerors had on the one hand to tame, yet on the other hand to memorialize. The Assyrians did not annihilate the other, nor did they completely destroy the material products of the other; in fact, they hoarded their foreign wealth and celebrated their encounters with the other through the depiction of elaborate narrative representations. This served to preserve the memory of victory through the physical presence of captured things. But at the same time, they needed to neutralize the power of the other so it could no longer pose a threat to the expanding state. A rhetorical stylization of the other into something quintessentially Assyrian (in style but not in "content") offered a particularly effective strategy. A similar effect was accomplished by the Assyrian acquisition of foreign luxury items, such as the Levantine ivories, which were not physically destroyed but hidden in storerooms, only to be displayed periodically in military parades that paradoxically emphasized their invisibility—their existence as hoarded treasuries—through the brief, controlled, and entirely Assyrian environment of their viewing.[30]

The reliefs considered in this essay were never innocent snapshots of an objective reality (as no image ever is); rather, they were representations that selectively presented particular elements. Such narrative depictions were not simply propaganda (though they most likely served this function as well), but fully integrated into the lived experiences of the elite imperial classes, as seen in the consistency of the style and subject matter found across scale and media. Just as this world of representation was closely controlled, so was the style of its rendering. Style, taken as a selective and constitutive process, is deeply implicated in the formation, maintenance, and transformation of collective memories and group identities. The

---

30. For example, an inscription of Esarhaddon (680–669 B.C.E.) from Nineveh describing activities taking place at his Nineveh *ekal mašarti* (arsenal), similar to that of Fort Shalmaneser at Nimrud, says, "May I—every year without interruption—take stock there during the month of the New Year's Festival, the first month, of all steeds, mules, donkeys and camels, of the harness and battle gear of all my troops, and of the booty (*šallatu*) taken from the enemy" (Oates and Oates, *Nimrud*, 216; Alexander Heidel, "A New Hexagonal Prism of Esarhaddon (676 B.C.)," *Sumer* 12 [1956]: 9–37 [col. iv, ll. 32–38]).

Assyrian style, its coherence and consistency, and its use to render foreign items, can therefore be understood as a critical, though often overlooked, component of the Assyrian imperial identity.

BIBLIOGRAPHY

Albenda, Pauline. "Grapevines in Ashurbanipal's Garden." *BASOR* 215 (1974): 5–17.
———. "Landscape Bas-Reliefs in the Bit-Hilani of Ashurbanipal, Part 1." *BASOR* 224 (1976): 49–72.
———. "Landscape Bas-Reliefs in the Bit-Hilani of Ashurbanipal, Part 2." *BASOR* 225 (1977): 29–48.
André-Salvini, Béatrice, ed. *Babylone: À Babylone, d'hier et d'aujourd'hui.* Paris: Musée du Louvre, 2008.
Bär, Jürgen. *Der assyrische Tribut und seine Darstellung: Eine Untersuchung zur imperialen Ideologie im neuassyrischen Reich.* Kevelaer: Butzon & Bercker; Neukirchen-Vluyn: Neukirchener, 1996.
Barnett, Richard D., and Margarete Falkner. *The Sculptures of Assur-nasir-apli II (883–859 B.C.), Tiglath-Pileser III (745–727 B.C.), Esarhaddon (681–669 B.C.) from the Central and South-West Palaces at Nimrud.* London: The Trustees of the British Museum, 1962.
Brown, Brian. "Monumentalizing Identities: North Syrian Urbanism, 1200–800 BCE." Ph.D. diss., University of California, Berkeley, 2008.
Bunnens, Guy. *A New Luwian Stele and the Cult of the Storm-God at Til Barsib-Masuwari.* Mission archéologique de l'Université de Liège en Syrie, Tell Ahmar 2. Leuven: Peeters, 2006.
Cifarelli, Megan. "Gesture and Alterity in the Art of Ashurnasirpal II of Assyria." *The Art Bulletin* 80 (1998): 210–28.
Feldman, Marian H. "Assur Tomb 45 and the Birth of the Assyrian Empire." *BASOR* 343 (2006): 21–43.
———. "Darius I and the Heroes of Akkad: Affect and Agency in the Bisitun Relief." Pages 265–93 in *Ancient Near Eastern Art in Context: Studies in Honor of Irene J. Winter by Her Students.* Edited by J. Cheng and M. H. Feldman. Leiden: Brill, 2007.
Heidel, Alexander. "A New Hexagonal Prism of Esarhaddon (676 B.C.)." *Sumer* 12 (1956): 9–37.
Herrmann, Georgina, and Stuart Laidlaw. *Ivories from the North West Palace (1845–1992).* Ivories from Nimrud 6. London: British Institute for the Study of Iraq, 2009.
Liverani, Mario. *Topographical Analysis.* Vol. 2 of *Studies on the Annals of Ashurnasirpal II.* Rome: Università di Roma "La Sapienza," Dipartimento di Scienze Storiche, Archeologiche e Antropologiche dell'Antichità, 1992.
Mallowan, Max, and Leri Glynne Davies. *Ivories in Assyrian Style.* Ivories from Nimrud 2. London: British School of Archaeology in Iraq, 1970.

Oates, Joan, and David Oates. *Nimrud: An Assyrian Imperial City Revealed*. London: British School of Archaeology in Iraq, 2001.

Pittman, Holly. "The White Obelisk and the Problem of Historical Narrative in the Art of Assyria." *The Art Bulletin* 78 (1996): 334–55.

Rehm, Ellen. "Assyrische Möbel für den assyrischen Herrscher!" Pages 187–206 in *Crafts and Images in Contact: Studies on Eastern Mediterranean Art of the First Millennium BCE*. Edited by C. E. Suter and C. Uehlinger. OBO 210. Fribourg: Academic; Göttingen: Vandenhoeck & Ruprecht, 2005.

Russell, John Malcolm. "Sennacherib's Lachish Narratives." Pages 55–73 in *Narrative and Event in Ancient Art*. Edited by P. J. Holliday. Cambridge: Cambridge University Press, 1993.

———. *The Writing on the Wall: Studies in the Architectural Context of Late Assyrian Palace Inscriptions*. Winona Lake, Ind.: Eisenbrauns, 1999.

Thomason, Allison Karmel. *Luxury and Legitimation: Royal Collecting in Ancient Mesopotamia*. Aldershot, England: Ashgate, 2005.

Winter, Irene J. "The Affective Properties of Styles: An Inquiry into Analytical Process and the Inscription of Meaning in Art History." Pages 55–77 in *Picturing Science, Producing Art*. Edited by C. A. Jones and P. Galison. New York: Routledge, 1998.

Fig. 1. The siege of Lachish, drawing of Slabs 7–8, Room XXXVI, Southwest Palace, Nineveh, by Sir Austen Henry Layard. British Museum, WAA, Or. Dr., I, 59; photo © The Trustees of the British Museum.

Fig. 2. The siege of Lachish, drawing of Slabs 9–10, Room XXXVI, Southwest Palace, Nineveh, by Sir Austen Henry Layard. British Museum, WAA, Or. Dr., I, 59; photo © The Trustees of the British Museum.

Fig. 3. The siege of Lachish, drawing of Slabs 11–12, Room XXXVI, Southwest Palace, Nineveh, by Sir Austen Henry Layard. British Museum, WAA, Or. Dr., I, 59; photo ©The Trustees of the British Museum.

Fig. 4. Relief of city siege (above) and Assyrian soldiers carrying captured cult statues (below), reign of Tiglath-Pileser III, gypsum, from Nimrud. British Museum, WA 118934+118931; photo © The Trustees of the British Museum.

Fig. 5. Relief of Ashurbanipal reclining in his garden, North Palace, Nineveh. British Museum, WA 124920; photo © The Trustees of the British Museum.

A Fragmented History of the Exile

Bob Becking

In the history of ancient Israel, two periods of exile, the Assyrian and the Babylonian, can be detected that are named for the deporting nation. In this contribution, I will not discuss the concept of exile and its negative overtones or the roots of that image in mental history. I will confine myself to the scarce pieces of evidence from which a fragmented history of both the Assyrian and the Babylonian exiles can be constructed.

1. Assyrian Exile

According to 2 Kgs 17:6, Israelites were deported to Assyria, settled in Halah and Habor, on the river of Gozan, and in the cities of the Medes. The deportation is also mentioned in two Summary Inscriptions of Sargon II.[1] Traces of Israelite exiles are found in the assigned areas. In the Habur region, Israelites worked at agricultural estates, often owned by the crown. In Assyria itself some of them were incorporated into the Assyrian army, especially the cavalry. The various documents reflect the Assyrian policy of mingling deportees from different ethnicities into a melting pot in order to preclude new rebellions. They also indicate that the exiled Israelites, although possessing no political power, lived to a certain degree in liberty.[2] No clear evidence for a return from exile for these northern groups exists, although texts such as Nah 2:1–3 (Eng. 1:15–2:2) and Mic 5:5–6 hint at the dream of a return from exile. It has generally been assumed that the descendants of the Assyrian exile disappeared into the ethnic melting pot of the Neo-Assyrian Empire. Interestingly, however, inscriptions found at

---

1. Bob Becking, *The Fall of Samaria: An Historical and Archaeological Study* (SHANE 2; Leiden: Brill, 1992), 25–31.
2. Ibid., 61–93.

Dur Katlimmu from the earliest years of the Neo-Babylonian reign still show the presence of Israelites in the Habur region.[3]

2. Babylonian Exile

2.1. The Time Frame of the Exile

By performing a "Google" search on the Internet, one can find the following remark: "Babylonian captivity, in the history of Israel, the period from the fall of Jerusalem (586 B.C.) to the reconstruction in Palestine of a new Jewish state (after 538 B.C.)."[4] Comparable remarks can be found in other dictionaries on the web or in a library, although for the second event sometimes a slightly later date is given. The first date cited could give the impression that the capture of Jerusalem by the Babylonians was a surprising event without prehistory. The second part of the statement implies a quick and massive return from exile—as early as Cyrus's conquest of Babylon—leading to the reinstallation of a Jewish state. This second group of remarks on the past is highly questionable. It is my purpose here to make clear that such hard boundaries, though traditional, are less than accurate.

2.2. The Conquest of Jerusalem: Why and When?

Evidence for the conquest of Jerusalem is to be found in the Hebrew Bible and in a fragment in a Babylonian Chronicle. In 2 Kgs 24 we read of a first conquest by Nebuchadnezzar, King of Babylon, who answered the rebellion of Jehoiakim with a military attack (2 Kgs 24:13). The narrator in the book of Kings continues with a few more theological remarks in which the siege of Jerusalem is construed as a result of transgressions against Yhwh. Jehoiakim unfortunately dies and is succeeded by his son Jehoiachin, who is captured and deported to Babylon. This report has a counterpart in a Babylonian Chronicle:The seventh year: In the month Kislev the king of Akkad mustered his army and marched to Hattu. He campaigned ag[ainst]

---

3. See Bob Becking, "West Semites at Tell Šēh Hamad: Evidence for the Israelite Exile?" in *Kein Land für sich allein: Studien zum Kulturkontakt in Kanaan, Israel/ Palästina und Ebirnâri für Manfred Weippert zum 65. Geburtstag* (ed. E. A. Knauf and U. Hübner; OBO 186; Freiburg: Universitätsverlag; Göttingen: Vandenhoeck & Ruprecht, 2002), 153–66.

4. http://www.infoplease.com/ce6/history/A0805628.html.

the city of Judah and on the second day of the month Adar he captured the city and seized the king. A king of his own [choice] he appointed in the city. He took a vast tribute and took it to Babylon.[5] As has generally been accepted, the two Judean kings referred to in this inscription are Jehoiachin and Zedekiah. This historical note connects the first year of Jehoiachin's imprisonment with Nebuchadnezzar's seventh regnal year in the Babylonian system of counting years. On that basis, the event can be dated in the time frame of spring 598 to spring 597 B.C.E.[6] A second conquest is only mentioned in the book of Kings. Second Kings 25:1–7 narrates in vivid detail the tragic events. The absence of any mention of this event in Babylonian inscriptions cannot function as an argument against its historicity, especially since the Babylonian Chronicles are rather fragmented.

The conquest of Jerusalem and the beginning of the deportation of exiles to Babylon was the outcome of an historical process in which the Babylonians sought to strengthen their control over the area near the Egyptian border, while some political factions in Jerusalem overestimated their own military strength, as well as the ability of Egypt to come to their aid.[7]

2.3. The Gedaliah Incident

Jeremiah 40:7–41:15 narrates a political murder. Nebuchadnezzar had appointed a certain Gedaliah as governor over those Judahites who remained in the land after the conquest of Jerusalem. The very detailed report in the book of Jeremiah has a parallel in the much shorter note in

---

5. BM 21946 = Babylonian Chronicle V; see most recently Jean-Jacques Glassner, *Mesopotamian Chronicles* (SBLWAW 19; Atlanta: Society of Biblical Literature, 2004), 230–31. Note that in 2 Kgs 24:12 the capture is dated in the eighth year of Nebuchadnezzar. The difference between "seventh" and "eighth" can be explained either by assuming antedating in the book of Kings, or by supposing an autumn year system in this portion of Kings.

6. See Richard A. Parker and Waldo H. Dubberstein, *Babylonian Chronology 626 B.C.–A.D. 75* (Brown University Studies 19; Providence, R.I.: Brown University Press, 1956), 27.

7. See Rainer Albertz, *Israel in Exile: The History and Literature of the Sixth Century B.C.E.* (trans. David Green; SBLSBL 3; Atlanta: Society of Biblical Literature, 2003); Oded Lipschits, *The Fall and Rise of Jerusalem: Judah under Babylonian Rule* (Winona Lake, Ind.: Eisenbrauns, 2005).

the book of Kings (2 Kgs 25:22–26). The Jeremiah account contains the following material not included in 2 Kings:

(1) Jeremiah offers various names of persons who were presumably involved in the incident. (2 Kings mentions only the main characters).

(2) Jeremiah narrates a temporary migration of Judahites to the territories of Ammon, Edom and Moab. (This detail is missing in 2 Kings).

(3) The author of Jeremiah informs his readers about a political background for the assassination. Johanan, the son of Kareah, together with a group of leaders,warn Gedaliah about his coming fate: "and said to him, 'Are you at all aware that Baalis king of the Ammonites has sent Ishmael son of Nethaniah to take your life?' But Gedaliah son of Ahikam would not believe them" (Jer 40:14).

(4) Jeremiah reports Ishmael's slaughter of a group of mourning pilgrims on their way to Jerusalem (Jer 41:4–8).

Strangely enough, no remark on the Gedaliah incident appears in 2 Chronicles. A reference in Josephus, *Ant.* 10.9.7, suggests that the deportation of a group of Ammonites in the twenty-third year of Nebuchadnezzar should be construed as the Babylonian answer to the assassination of Gedaliah.[8] Josephus, however, composed his *Antiquities* in the first century C.E., and can therefore not be taken as a reliable source.

Significantly, the three personal names involved in this incident—*Gdlyhw*, "Gedaliah," *Yšm'l*, "Ishmael," and *B'lyš*, "Baalisha"—all occur in contemporary epigraphic sources.[9] From a historiographic point of view, two problems are involved:

---

8. Ulrich Hübner, *Die Ammoniter: Untersuchungen zur Geschichte, Kultur und Religion eines transjordanischen Volkes im 1. Jahrtausend v. Chr.* (ADPV 16; Wiesbaden: Harrasowitz, 1992), 203–5.

9. Note a seal from Lachish: "Belonging to Gedalyahu, who is over the house" (Samuel H. Hooke, "A Scarab and Sealing from Tell Duweir," *PEQ* 67 [1935]: 195–97). The name Ishmael occurs frequently both in the Old Testament and in inscriptions from the Iron Age II–III. From the Ammonite territory, two inscriptions with the

(1) The problem of identification and the probability of a certain proposal.[10] Since various persons are known with the same name, it is not prima facie clear that the individuals referred to in the seals and inscriptions are identical with the biblical persons.[11]

(2) A name is not a story. Although the presence of a name indicates the historicity of that person, the stories narrated about him or her in the Hebrew Bible, for instance, are not by implication historical.

2.4. Bethel and Mizpah

The reports from the books of Kings and Jeremiah hint at the importance of Mizpah in the post-conquest period. The assassination of Gedaliah is set at Mizpah. This is an interesting feature in view of a noteworthy thesis developed by Joseph Blenkinsopp in the course of a recent and ongoing discussion.[12] In his view, it seems to be a reasonable hypothesis that "following the elimination of the Jerusalem Temple, the old Bethel sanctuary, having survived the Assyrian conquest and the reforming zeal of Josiah, obtained a new lease on life by virtue of the favored status of the Benjamin region and the proximity of Bethel to the administrative center at Mizpah."[13] In other words, he assumes that, in the "exilic" period, Bethel served as a religious center, while Mizpah functioned as the administra-

---

name "Baalisha" were found. See L. G. Herr, "The Servant of *Baalis*," *BA* 48 (1985): 169–72; Bob Becking, "The Seal of Baalisha, King of the Ammonites, Some Remarks," *BN* 97 (1999): 13–17.

10. See Lawrence J. Mykytiuk, *Identifying Biblical Persons in Northwest Semitic Inscriptions of 1200–539 B.C.E.* (SBLAcBib 12; Atlanta: Society of Biblical Literature, 2004).

11. Bob Becking, *From David to Gedaliah: The Book of Kings as Story and History* (OBO 228; Freiburg: Universitätsverlag; Göttingen: Vandenhoeck & Ruprecht, 2007), 141–65.

12. Joseph Blenkinsopp, "The Judaean Priesthood during the Neo-Babylonian and Achaemenid Periods: A Hypothetical Reconstruction," *CBQ* 60 (1998): 25–43; idem, "Bethel in the Neo-Babylonian Period," in *Judah and the Judeans in the Neo-Babylonian Period* (ed. Oded Lipschits and Joseph Blenkinsopp; Winona Lake, Ind.: Eisenbrauns, 2003), 93–107.

13. Blenkinsopp, "Bethel in the Neo-Babylonian Period," 99.

tive center. His thesis includes a discussion of Hebrew Bible material, such as Judg 20–21, which he takes as reflecting the exilic circumstances in the Benjamite territory. Blenkinsopp admits that the archaeological data at our disposal are inconclusive in many details. Nevertheless, his proposal is worth pondering, although new archaeological evidence is very much needed.[14]

2.5. Egyptian Diaspora

In the aftermath of the Gedaliah incident, the biblical texts report a group of Judahites hiding in Bethlehem and planning to flee to Egypt:

> And they set out, and stopped at Geruth Chimham near Bethlehem, intending to go to Egypt because of the Chaldeans; for they were afraid of them, because Ishmael son of Nethaniah had killed Gedaliah son of Ahikam, whom the king of Babylon had made governor over the land. (Jer 41:17–18)

After heavy debates on the question of whether such a move would be an act of disobedience to God,[15] an important group of Judahites—including the prophet Jeremiah—decided to live in diaspora in Egypt. According to Jer 44, they settled at Migdol, Taphanhes, Memphis, and in the land of Pathros.

There exist only glimpses of evidence that could shed light on the early Egyptian diaspora.[16] Jeremiah 44 narrates a conflict between the prophet Jeremiah and persons from the Yahwistic elite in Egypt on the desirability of venerating the "Queen of Heaven."[17] A trace of this veneration might

---

14. See Jill Middlemas, *The Troubles of Templeless Judah* (OTM; New York: Oxford University Press 2005), 133–44; for criticism see Klaus Koenen, *Bethel: Geschichte, Kult und Theologie* (OBO 192; Freiburg: Universitätsverlag; Göttingen: Vandenhoeck & Ruprecht, 2003), 59–64; Melody D. Knowles, *Centrality Practiced: Jerusalem in the Religious Practice of Yehud and the Diaspora in the Persian Period* (SBLABS 16; Atlanta: Society of Biblical Literature, 2006), 48–50.

15. Narrated in Jer 42.

16. Later, in Hellenistic times, an important group of Jews lived in Egypt. It is unclear, however, whether they were the descendants of this first group seeking refuge in Egypt.

17. See Bob Becking, "Jeremiah 44: A Conflict on History and Religion," in *Religious Polemics in Context: Papers Presented to the Second Conference of the Leiden*

be found in an Aramaic letter from Hermopolis from the fifth century B.C.E. that reads in its blessing formula, "Blessing for the temple of Bethel and that of the Queen of Heaven."[18] Since the deity Bethel can be seen as a synonym for YHWH,[19] the Aramaic letter probably refers to a group of Yahwists in Egypt still venerating the "Queen of Heaven."

It is far from certain whether the "Yehudites" from Elephantine were descendants of this first group moving to Egypt. Elephantine is the Greek name for a small island in the Nile not far from present day Assuan.[20] In the Persian Period, this island was on the southernmost border of the Achaemenid Empire. At the beginning of the twentieth century C.E., German and French archaeologists discovered a great variety of ostraca and papyri from the Persian period. These texts inform us of several things. On the island, as well as on the banks of the Nile, a garrison was encamped in order to defend the border. In this garrison, two more or less ethnically distinct groups are detectable: the *Yehudayya* and the *'Aramayya*. The second group are certainly Arameans. The first group are often construed as Jews. In my view, this is an anachronism. In the fifth century B.C.E.— the age of the Elephantine material—Judaism had not yet developed from Yahwism into the form we know from Hellenistic times onward. Therefore, I prefer to label them as Yehudites. I construe them as soldiers that were recruited either from the Persian province of Yehud or from areas in Babylonia where new settlements are known from the Babylonian and Persian period, such as *al Ya-hu-du*, "City of Judah," or *al ša ᴾna-šar*, "Eagleton."[21]

Institute for the Study of Religion (LISOR) Held at Leiden, 27–28 April 2000 (ed. T. L. Hettema and A. van der Kooij; STAR 11; Assen: Van Gorcum, 2004), 255–64.

18. E. Bresciani and M. Kamil, *Le lettere aramaiche de Hermopoli* (Roma: Accademia Nazionale dei Lincei, 1966), 1, 4.

19. See, e.g., Bob Becking, "Die Gottheiten der Juden in Elephantine," in *Der eine Gott und die Götter: Polytheismus und Monotheismus im antiken Israel* (ed. Manfred Oeming and Konrad Schmid; ATANT 82; Zürich: Theologischer Verlag Zürich, 2003), 203–26.

20. See generally Bezalel Porten, *Archives from Elephantine: The Life of an Ancient Jewish Military Colony* (Berkeley: University of California Press, 1968); Becking, "Die Gottheiten der Juden in Elephantine," 203–26.

21. Laurie E. Pearce, "New Evidence for Judaeans in Babylonia," in *Judah and the Judeans in the Persian Period* (ed. Oded Lipschits and Manfred Oeming; Winona Lake, Ind.: Eisenbrauns, 2006), 399–411.

2.6. Assignment Lists

Turning our attention from Egypt back to Babylonia, I want to pursue the question of whether traces of the deported Judahites can be found. Excavations in Babylon have revealed the existence of so-called "assignment lists." These texts list names of prisoners at the Babylonian court who were allowed rations of food.[22] Among other persons, these documents refer to [Ia]-'ú-kinu/Ia-ku-ú-ki-nu (*Yahu-kin), his five sons, and some other Judeans as regular recipients of portions of food at the instruction of the Babylonian king.[23]

The lists under consideration date to the thirteenth year of king Nebuchadnezzar, which is 592 B.C.E. These documents show that the Babylonian court maintained Jehoiachin during his exile or imprisonment. The texts do not hint at some sort of release or amnesty as is narrated in the final four verses of 2 Kgs 25. These assignment lists also make clear that the Babylonians adopted a custom known from Assyrian inscriptions. These earlier inscriptions make clear that according to the Assyrian worldview, prisoners at the court had a right to live. Food and even women had to be given to them.[24] The assignment lists reveal that the Judean royal family and its entourage were imprisoned at the Babylonian court.

2.7. Amnesty for Jehoiachin

In its present form, the book of Kings ends with a note on the release of the exiled Judean king Jehoiachin from prison (2 Kgs 25:27–30). He had reigned in Jerusalem for three months, unfortunately during Nebuchadnezzar's siege and conquest of the city. This event took place in the seventh year of the Babylonian king. His release can thus be dated in the spring of 562 or 561. Second Kings 25:27 relates that the release from prison took place bišnat malkô of Evil-merodach. The Hebrew expression refers to the period preceding the first full regnal year of a king. This expression is parallel to ršyt mmlkt, "the beginning of his reign." Both are equivalents of

---

22. Ernst F. Weidner, "Jojachin, König von Juda in Babylonischen Keilschrifttexten," *Mélanges syriens* 2 (1939): 923–35; see also Albertz, *Israel in Exile*, 67, 87.

23. Weidner, "Jojachin, König von Juda," 923–35.

24. See H. W. F. Saggs, "Assyrian Prisoners of War and the Right to Live," in *Vorträge gehalten auf der 28. Rencontre Assyriologique in Wien 6.–10. Juli 1981* (ed. H. Hirsch and H. Hunger; AfOB 19; Horn: Berger, 1982), 85–93.

Akkadian *rēš šarruti*. In sum, the data on the regnal and other years underscore the plausibility of the release from prison of Jehoiachin in spring 561.

Second Kings also contains an interesting detail with regard to the date of Jehoiachin's release. In the narrative world of the book of Kings, the release is dated to the twenty-seventh day of the twelfth month of the accession year of Evil-Merodach.[25] It should be noted that this is only a few days before the (spring) New Year Festival in the reign of Evil-Merodach. I will not present here a complete picture of all the details of the *Akitu*-festival as it was celebrated around the new year in Babylon or the religious and interpretative implications of a *Thronsbesteigungsfest* for several texts in the Hebrew Bible. It is of great importance to remark, however, that the spring equinox was an appropriate time for rearrangements in the royal administration. Court dignitaries who had acted favorably were promoted, others were demoted. The Babylonian Epic of Creation, *Enuma Eliš*, narrates that Marduk, the head of the Babylonian pantheon, granted amnesty to a group of deities that had rebelled against him. The *Enuma Eliš* was not only a narrative text on the beginnings of the universe, however. There is a clear connection between this creation epic and royal ideology. The deeds of the gods functioned as a mirror for the behavior of kings and their courts. In the same way that Marduk granted amnesty to his former enemies, a just Babylonian king was incited to release his imprisoned enemies. The epic's theme of amnesty was an invitation to act accordingly in real life. Together with the assignments lists, the amnesty for Jehoiachin hints at a slightly more positive image of the exile. This slightly more positive image is also evoked by the next piece of evidence.

2.8. "Eagleton" and "New Jerusalem"

The presence of "Jews in Iraq"—a double anachronism—in the preclassical period is known from the documents in the Murashu archives and is reflected in some late biblical books such as Esther and Daniel. The Murashu archives date to the reign of Darius II (424–404 B.C.E.). They contain numerous personal names with a Yahwistic theophoric element, such as *Abî-Jahô*. From a methodological point of view, it would be incorrect to make a one-to-one connection between the Judeans deported by

---

25. 2 Kgs 25:27; see also Jer 52:31, which has it two days earlier. This would have been 2 April, or 31 March of the year 561 B.C.E.; see Parker and Dubberstein, *Babylonian Chronology*, 28.

Nebuchadnezzar and the persons with a Yahwistic theophoric element in their names in the Murashu archive by construing the latter as the descendants of the former. On the other hand, however, these document show that about a century after the conquest of Babylon by Cyrus the Great, persons with a Yahwistic theophoric element in their names were still living in Mesopotamia.

Recently, some cuneiform documents have been found to provide further important data on the situation under Cyrus.[26] One document is dated to the seventh year of Cyrus, 532 B.C.E. The document records the administration of the receipt of one shekel of silver. This shekel was the payment of the *ilku*-tax by Bunanitu, the widow of Achiqar, the governor, to Abda-Yahu. Both *Ab-da-ia-hu-ú* and his father *Ba-rak-ka-ia-ma* have clear Judean names. The document was written in URU *ša* ᴾ*na-šar*, "the City-of-Nashar," or, to see it anachronistically, "Eagleton," which was likely located in the area of Borsippa.[27] Another document of great importance for the construction of the history of the exile refers to the sale of a bovine by Hara, the daughter of Talimu, to *né-ri-ja-a-ma* DUMU of ŠEŠ(*ahi*)-*ia-a-qa-am* ("Nerî-Jahu, the son of Achiqam"). The transaction took place in *al Ya-hu-du*, "the city of Judah/Yehud," in Babylonia, in 498 B.C.E.[28] The indication "the city of Judah/Yehud" or "New Yehud"[29] reflects the politics of the Neo-Babylonians to bring deportees together in specific ethnic groups. The cities in which these persons were brought were named after their area of origin. Evidence exists for exiled communities referred to as Ashkelon, Gaza, Neirab, Qadeš, Qedar, and Tyre.

The most important, perhaps obvious, conclusion that can be drawn from these texts is that not all the descendants of the exiled Judeans immediately returned to Jerusalem after the conquest of Babylon by Cyrus. Laurie Pearce, who has published an article on this topic,[30] is currently, in cooperation with Cornelia Wunsch, preparing an edition of the larger

---

26. Francis Joannès and André Lemaire, "Trois tablettes cunéiformes à onomastique ouest-sémitique," *Transeu* 17 (1999): 17–34.

27. So Pearce, "New Evidence for Judaeans in Babylonia," *pace* Joannès and Lemaire, "Trois tablettes cunéiformes," 28.

28. On this tablet, see Wilfred G. Lambert, "A Document from a Community of Exiles in Babylonia," in *New Seals and Inscriptions: Hebrew, Idumean, and Cuneiform* (ed. M. Lubetski; Sheffield: Sheffield Phoenix, 2007), 201–5.

29. Ibid., 205.

30. Pearce, "New Evidence for Judaeans in Babylonia."

corpus from which these texts stem. The inscriptions indicate the following items:

(1) The exiled Judeans—or at least the majority of them—remained a separate ethnic group in Babylonia.

(2) Many of them were settled in newly reclaimed agricultural areas.

(3) A group descending from Judean exiles lived at an acceptable level of prosperity and had its own—albeit limited—organization.

(4) After the conquest of Babylon by Cyrus, not all descendants of these exiles returned to Yehud.

It is remarkable that during the time of this text corpus the Judeans and their descendants acted in various roles in transactions that were important enough to be registered. The Judeans are not only listed among the witnesses, but also mentioned as buyers and sellers of goods and properties. Before arriving at some premature conclusions, it should be noted "that all of the transactions are in the context of work done as obligations to royal lands. These are not the transactions of entirely free people working in a true capitalistic market economy."[31] Next to that, it becomes clear that both "Eagleton" and "New Yehud" were newly established locations that were of importance for the production of food for the increasing population in the Babylonian and later Persian Empire. As we will now see, this reality does not tally with the traditional image of exile or the myth of a mass return.[32]

2.9. The Myth of the Empty Land

A historical myth is a social construction of the past that functions within the value system of a community or society and serves some ideologies within that society. Our world is full of historical myths.[33] In the traditional

31. Laurie Pearce in private communication, January 2007.
32. It might be possible to connect the Yehudites from "Eagleton," "New Yehud," and the vicinity with the addressees of the letter to the exiles in Jer 29:5–7.
33. See Jean-Jacques Wunenberger, "Mythophorie: formes et transformations du mythe," *Religiologiques* 10 (1994): 49–70.

historiography of the Babylonian exile, the "myth of the empty land" has been a standard element finding its base in the remark of 2 Chr 36:21 that the land laid desolate for seventy years. The idea of the empty land assumed that during the Babylonian period the territory of the former kingdom of Judah was uninhabited. Everyone important had been exiled with the court to Babylonia. In 597 B.C.E., Nebuchadnezzar had emptied Jerusalem, according to 2 Kgs 24:14–15. Nevertheless, there were still persons living in Jerusalem, so that after the second conquest, Nebuzaradan, the captain of the Babylonian guard, could carry the rest of the people into exile (2 Kgs 25:11–12). These reports in the book of Kings gave rise to the idea that only a few socially unimportant persons were left in the land.

Hans Barstad has deconstructed this view and unmasked it as a historical myth. His analysis of the textual data and the archaeological evidence showed that the land was not empty. The territory of the former kingdom of Judah remained inhabited, and these surviving groups have contributed more to the emergence of the Hebrew Bible than generally assumed.[34] His view is mainly based on an evaluation of archaeological data that indicate continuity of activities in the territory under consideration.

While Barstad's analysis has been challenged unconvincingly, in my opinion, by some scholars who disagreed on the dating of the archaeological evidence, it remains valid.[35] Moreover, in my view, the more general archaeological observations are of great importance. It is remarkable that during the Babylonian period, the number of inhabitants in the area of Bethel and Mizpah is quite constant, while the habitation of Jerusalem dropped to a minimum. Related evidence will be displayed below in the framework of unmasking another historical myth: the idea of a mass return from exile.

---

34. Hans M. Barstad, *The Myth of the Empty Land: A Study in the History and Archaeology of Judah During the "Exilic" Period* (SO 28; Oslo: Scandinavian University Press, 1996); reprinted and revised in Hans M. Barstad, *History and the Hebrew Bible: Studies in Ancient Israelite and Ancient Near Eastern Historiography* (FAT 61; Tübingen: Mohr Siebeck, 2008), 90–134.

35. See, e.g., David S. Vanderhooft, *The Neo-Babylonian Empire and Babylon in the Latter Prophets* (HSM 58; Atlanta: Scholars Press, 1999); Bustenay Oded, "Where Is the 'Myth of the Empty Land' To Be Found? History Versus Myth," in Lipschits and Blenkinsopp, *Judah and the Judeans in the Neo-Babylonian Period*, 55–74; Lisbeth S. Fried, "The Land Lay Desolate: Conquest and Restoration in the Ancient Near East," in Lipschits and Blenkinsopp, *Judah and the Judeans in the Neo-Babylonian Period*, 21–54.

2.10. Traces of Return in Persian Documents?

The traditional image of the Babylonian exile has as its final feature the idea of a return from exile and the formation of a Jewish state soon after the conquest of Babylon by Cyrus the Great in 539 B.C.E. This part of the image is mainly based on a naïve reading of the opening verses of the book of Ezra, according to which YHWH stirred up the spirit of King Cyrus of Persia and as a result the exiles were allowed to return to Jerusalem in Judah and to rebuild their temple with financial support from their former neighbors (Ezra 1:1–4). I will neither introduce here all the interpretative problems connected with the book of Ezra, nor solve them, but only state that, in my opinion, the first six chapters of Ezra cannot be used as trustworthy historical information. A more significant question, then, is whether there are indications of a return to Yehud in Persian documents.

The Cyrus Cylinder is often seen as extrabiblical evidence for the historicity of the decree of Cyrus in Ezra 1. The inscription has been interpreted as showing a liberal policy of respect toward other religions. The inscription would show that Cyrus's policy toward the descendants of the Judean exiles was not unique but fit the pattern of his rule.[36] Amelia Kuhrt, however, has made clear that the inscription is of a propagandistic and stereotypical nature. The text reflects the worldview of the Marduk priests of the Esaǧila temple in Babylon. They present Cyrus as a "good prince" replacing the "bad prince" Nabonidus. The return of divine images and people related in lines 30–34 of the Cyrus Cylinder, if not mere propaganda, refers to measures taken on a local scale. It concerns divine images from cities surrounding Babylon, brought back to the shrines from which they were exiled by Nabonidus. This passage has nothing to do with Judeans, Jews, or Jerusalem.[37]

The famous Behistun inscription of Darius relates in its various versions his rebellion and rise to power, but does not contain historical data on the return to Jerusalem or the rebuilding of the temple.[38] It must, however, be noted that written documents from the Achaemenid Empire are rather scarce. The absence of any reference to Yehudites would hint at the relative

---

36. E.g., T. C. Young, "Cyrus," *ABD* 1:1231–32.

37. Amélie Kuhrt, "The Cyrus Cylinder and Achaemenid Imperial Policy," *JSOT* 25 (1983): 83–97; see also Josef Wiesehöfer, *Das antike Persien von 550 v. Chr. bis 650 n. Chr.* (Münich: Artemis & Winkler, 1994), 71–88; Albertz, *Israel in Exile*, 98–100.

38. Wiesehöfer, *Antike Persien*, 33–43; Albertz, *Israel in Exile*, 100–102.

unimportance of Yehud and the Yehudites for the Persian administration, and there is clearly an absence of any evidence for the return from exile. As discussed above, the texts referring to "Eagleton," "New Yehud," and their vicinity show that the descendants of the exiled Judeans continued to live in southern Babylonia at least until the reign of Darius II.[39]

2.11. The Myth of the Mass Return

The idea of a massive and immediate return from exile, as reflected in the lists in Ezra and Nehemiah and in the anthem in Ps 126, can be challenged. If the mass return from exile was an historical fact, then one might expect that the archaeological traces would show an increase in the population of Jerusalem and its vicinity in the early Persian Period. Recent estimates based on archaeological surveys hint in another direction. The general picture that emerges is that of a demographic decrease in the early sixth century B.C.E. followed by a very slow increase during the Persian Period. As Lipschits formulates: "The 'return to Zion' did not leave its imprint on the archaeological data, nor is there any demographic testimony of it."[40] The evidence available cannot be connected to a theory of mass return in the sixth century. It hints toward the direction of the assumption of a process of waves of return that lasted for over a century.[41]

2.12. Climate Change

The period of the Babylonian exile coincides with a period of global warming of an even greater magnitude than we are experiencing today, followed by a drastic decline of temperature in the early Persian period.[42]Phrased

---

39. Joannès and Lemaire, "Trois tablettes cunéiformes"; Pearce, "New Evidence for Judaeans in Babylonia."

40. Oded Lipschits, "Demographic Changes in Judah Between the Seventh and the Fifth Centuries B.C.E.," in Lipschits and Blenkinsopp, *Judah and the Judeans in the Neo-Babylonian Period*, 323–76 (365).

41. For more details, see Bob Becking, ' "We All Returned as One': Critical Notes on the Myth of the Mass Return," in Lipschits and Oeming, *Judah and the Judeans in the Persian Period*, 3–18.

42. Data derived from the Greenland Ice Sheet Project http://www.gisp2.sr.unh .edu/; for an application to the Holocene, see D. A. Meese et al., "The Accumulation Record from the GISP2 Core as an Indicator of Climate Change throughout the Holocene," *Science* 266 (1994): 1680–82; S. O. Rasmussen et al., "Synchronization of the

otherwise: The "forced migration" to Babylon and the "exilic period" coincided with a process of rapid warming, while the period of "return from exile" up to the time of the mission of Ezra in 398 B.C.E. was characterized by a likewise rapid decrease of temperature.

To understand the impact of climate change on the history of the exile, it should be noted that the culture of ancient Mesopotamia depended heavily on agriculture. Martin Parry has convincingly shown the interconnections between climate change and agriculture.[43] There were large urban areas where trade was of great importance. During the Iron Age, agriculture was made possible thanks to the yearly flooding of the Euphrates and Tigris rivers. The floods came in late spring or early summer when the ice in the northern and northwestern mountains was melting. This age-old system of irrigation distributed the water over the fields. All this evidence concurs with the demographic data available. Julia Bowden has shown that after a minor decline just before 500 B.C.E., the population of Mesopotamia increased steadily and heavily from 480 B.C.E. onward.[44] The course of human history is, of course, by no means solely dependent on circumstances provoked by climate. In any culture, technological developments are of great importance to cope with the various realities. Wunsch, for instance, hints at the importance of the improvement of the cedar plough that turned out to be instrumental in improving agriculture in Mesopotamia from the Neo-Babylonian period onward—an observation that underscores this point.[45]

2.13. The Temple Rebuilt

The evidence in the biblical books of Haggai, Zechariah, Ezra, and Nehemiah has generally been interpreted as an indication that the temple for YHWH in Jerusalem was rebuilt in the final decades of the sixth century

---

NGRIP, GRIP, and GISP2 Ice Cores across MIS 2 and Palaeoclimatic Implications," *Quaternary Science Reviews* 27 (2008): 18–28.

43. Martin L. Parry, *Climatic Change, Agriculture and Settlement* (Folkestone: Dawson, 1978).

44. See John Barton and Julia Bowden, *The Original Story: God, Israel, and the World* (Grand Rapids: Eerdmans, 2005).

45. Cornelia Wunsch, "Exposure and Appropriation: Judeans in Babylonia and the Babylonian Legal System," in *The Judeans in the Achaemenid Age: Negotiating Identity in an International Context* (ed. G. Knoppers, O. Lipschits, and M. Oeming; Winona Lake, Ind.: Eisenbrauns, forthcoming).

B.C.E., most probably around 515. This idea had been challenged already in the sixteenth century C.E. by the Dutch scholar Josephus Justus Scaliger. Recently, Diana Edelman has convincingly argued that the second temple was not rebuilt before the middle of the fifth century B.C.E. In other words, the Darius mentioned in the biblical texts should be construed as Darius II.[46]

3. The Balance of the Evidence

The evidence displayed shows that only a fragmented history of the exilic period can be written. Too many pieces are missing to make a coherent portrait. A few things, nevertheless, are apparent:

(1) The land of Judah did not lie desolate during the Babylonian period.

(2) Mizpah and Bethel most probably functioned as administrative and religious centers for the people that remained.

(3) Many exiled Judeans were settled in agricultural areas in order to supply the urbanized areas of Babylon with food.

(4) These Judeans reached an acceptable standard of living and apparently were free to continue their religion.

(5) The return from exile should not be construed as a massive event; the descendants of the exiled Judeans returned in waves and many remained in Babylonia.

(6) The temple for YHWH was only rebuilt in the middle of the fifth century B.C.E.

I will not deny that the conquest of Jerusalem, the burning of the temple, and the end of the Davidic dynasty caused pain and sorrow. The

---

46. Diana Vikander Edelman, *The Origins of the "Second" Temple: Persian Imperial Policy and the Rebuilding of Jerusalem* (London: Equinox, 2005). Q: PAGE NUMBERS?

general picture of the exilic period, however, is not as dramatic as has often been assumed.

BIBLIOGRAPHY

Albertz, Rainer. *Israel in Exile: The History and Literature of the Sixth Century B.C.E.* Translated by David Green. SBLSBL 3. Atlanta: Society of Biblical Literature, 2003.

Barstad, Hans M. *History and the Hebrew Bible: Studies in Ancient Israelite and Ancient Near Eastern Historiography.* FAT 61. Tübingen: Mohr Siebeck, 2008.

The Myth of the Empty Land: A Study in the History and Archaeology of Judah during the "Exilic" Period. SO 28. Oslo: Scandinavian University Press, 1996.

Barton, John, and Julia Bowden. *The Original Story: God, Israel, and the World.* Grand Rapids: Eerdmans, 2005.

Becking, Bob. *The Fall of Samaria: An Historical and Archaeological Study.* SHANE 2. Leiden: Brill, 1992.

———. *From David to Gedaliah: The Book of Kings as Story and History.* OBO 228. Freiburg: Universitätsverlag. Göttingen: Vandenhoeck & Ruprecht, 2007.

———. "Die Gottheiten der Juden in Elephantine." Pages 203–26 in *Der eine Gott und die Götter: Polytheismus und Monotheismus im antiken Israel.* Edited by Manfred Oeming and Konrad Schmid. ATANT 82. Zürich: Theologischer Verlag Zürich, 2003.

———. "Jeremiah 44: A Conflict on History and Religion." Pages 255–64 in *Religious Polemics in Context: Papers Presented to the Second Conference of the Leiden Institute for the Study of Religion (LISOR) Held at Leiden, 27–28 April 2000.* Edited by T. L. Hettema and A. van der Kooij. STAR 11. Assen: Van Gorcum, 2004.

———. "The Seal of Baalisha, King of the Ammonites, Some Remarks," *BN* 97 (1999): 13–17.

———. "'We All Returned as One': Critical Notes on the Myth of the Mass Return." Pages 3–18 in *Judah and the Judeans in the Persian Period.* Edited by Oded Lipschits and Manfred Oeming. Winona Lake, Ind.: Eisenbrauns, 2006.

———. "West Semites at Tell Šēh Hamad: Evidence for the Israelite Exile?" Pages 153–66 in *Kein Land für sich allein: Studien zum Kulturkontakt in Kanaan, Israel/ Palästina und Ebirnâri für Manfred Weippert zum 65. Geburtstag.* Edited by E. A. Knauf and U. Hübner. OBO 186. Freiburg: Universitätsverlag; Göttingen: Vandenhoeck & Ruprecht, 2002.

Blenkinsopp, Joseph. "Bethel in the Neo-Babylonian Period." Pages 93–107 in *Judah and the Judeans in the Neo-Babylonian Period.* Edited by Oded Lipschits and Joseph Blenkinsopp. Winona Lake, Ind.: Eisenbrauns, 2003.

———. "The Judaean Priesthood during the Neo-Babylonian and Achaemenid Periods: A Hypothetical Reconstruction." *CBQ* 60 (1998): 25–43.

Bresciani, E. and M. Kamil. *Le lettere aramaiche de Hermopoli.* Roma: Accademia Nazionale dei Lincei, 1966.

Edelman, Diana Vikander. *The Origins of the "Second" Temple: Persian Imperial Policy and the Rebuilding of Jerusalem.* London: Equinox, 2005.

Fried, Lisbeth S. "The Land Lay Desolate: Conquest and Restoration in the Ancient Near East." Pages 21–54 in *Judah and the Judeans in the Neo-Babylonian Period.* Edited by Oded Lipschits and Joseph Blenkinsopp. Winona Lake, Ind.: Eisenbrauns, 2003.

Glassner, Jean-Jacques. *Mesopotamian Chronicles.* SBLWAW 19. Atlanta: Society of Biblical Literature, 2004.

Herr, L. G. "The Servant of *Baalis*," *BA* 48 (1985): 169–72.

Hooke, Samuel H. "A Scarab and Sealing from Tell Duweir," *PEQ* 67 (1935): 195–97.

Hübner, Ulrich. *Die Ammoniter: Untersuchungen zur Geschichte, Kultur und Religion eines transjordanischen Volkes im 1. Jahrtausend v. Chr.* ADPV 16. Wiesbaden: Harrasowitz, 1992.

Joannès, Francis and André Lemaire, "Trois tablettes cunéiformes à onomastique ouest-sémitique," *Transeu* 17 (1999): 17–34.

Knowles, Melody D. *Centrality Practiced: Jerusalem in the Religious Practice of Yehud and the Diaspora in the Persian Period.* SBLABS 16. Atlanta: Society of Biblical Literature, 2006.

Koenen, Klaus. *Bethel: Geschichte, Kult und Theologie.* OBO 192. Freiburg: Universitätsverlag. Göttingen: Vandenhoeck & Ruprecht, 2003.

Kuhrt, Amélie. "The Cyrus Cylinder and Achaemenid Imperial Policy," *JSOT* 25 (1983): 83–97.

Lambert, Wilfred G. "A Document from a Community of Exiles in Babylonia." Pages 201–5 in *New Seals and Inscriptions: Hebrew, Idumean, and Cuneiform.* Edited by M. Lubetski. Sheffield: Sheffield Phoenix, 2007.

Lipschits, Oded. "Demographic Changes in Judah Between the Seventh and the Fifth Centuries B.C.E." Pages 323–76 in *Judah and the Judeans in the Neo-Babylonian Period.* Edited by Oded Lipschits and Joseph Blenkinsopp. Winona Lake, Ind.: Eisenbrauns, 2003.

———. *The Fall and Rise of Jerusalem: Judah under Babylonian Rule.* Winona Lake, Ind.: Eisenbrauns, 2005.

Meese, D. A., et al. "The Accumulation Record from the GISP2 Core as an Indicator of Climate Change throughout the Holocene." *Science* 266 (1994): 1680–82.

Middlemas, Jill. *The Troubles of Templeless Judah.* OTM. New York: Oxford University Press 2005.

Mykytiuk, Lawrence J. *Identifying Biblical Persons in Northwest Semitic Inscriptions of 1200–539 B.C.E.* SBLAcBib 12. Atlanta: Society of Biblical Literature, 2004.

Oded, Bustenay. "Where Is the 'Myth of the Empty Land' To Be Found? History Versus Myth." Pages 55–74 in *Judah and the Judeans in the Neo-Babylonian Period.* Edited by Oded Lipschits and Joseph Blenkinsopp. Winona Lake, Ind.: Eisenbrauns, 2003.

Parker, Richard A., and Waldo H. Dubberstein. *Babylonian Chronology 626 B.C.–A.D. 75.* Brown University Studies 19. Providence: Brown University Press, 1956.

Parry, Martin L. *Climatic Change, Agriculture and Settlement*. Folkestone: Dawson, 1978.

Pearce, Laurie E. "New Evidence for Judaeans in Babylonia." Pages 399–411 in *Judah and the Judeans in the Persian Period*. Edited by Oded Lipschits and Manfred Oeming. Winona Lake, Ind.: Eisenbrauns, 2006.

Porten, Bezalel. *Archives from Elephantine: The Life of an Ancient Jewish Military Colony*. Berkeley: University of California Press, 1968.

Rasmussen, S. O., et al. "Synchronization of the NGRIP, GRIP, and GISP2 Ice Cores across MIS 2 and Palaeoclimatic Implications." *Quaternary Science Reviews* 27 (2008): 18–28.

Saggs, H. W. F. "Assyrian Prisoners of War and the Right to Live." Pages 85–93 in *Vorträge gehalten auf der 28. Rencontre Assyriologique in Wien 6.–10. Juli 1981*. Edited by H. Hirsch and H. Hunger. AfOB 19. Horn: Berger, 1982.

Vanderhooft, David S. *The Neo-Babylonian Empire and Babylon in the Latter Prophets*. HSM 58. Atlanta: Scholars Press, 1999.

Weidner, Ernst F. "Jojachin, König von Juda in Babylonischen Keilschrifttexten," *Mélanges syriens* 2 (1939): 923–35.

Wiesehöfer, Josef. *Das antike Persien von 550 v. Chr. bis 650 n. Chr.* Münich: Artemis & Winkler, 1994.

Wunenberger, Jean-Jacques. "Mythophorie: formes et transformations du mythe," *Religiologiques* 10 (1994): 49–70.

Wunsch, Cornelia. "Exposure and Appropriation: Judeans in Babylonia and the Babylonian Legal System." In *The Judeans in the Achaemenid Age: Negotiating Identity in an International Context*. Edited by G. Knoppers, O. Lipschits, and M. Oeming. Winona Lake, Ind.: Eisenbrauns, forthcoming.

Young, T. C. "Cyrus," *ABD* 1:1231–32.

PART 2
SOCIOLOGY AND IDENTITY

THE CASCADING EFFECTS OF EXILE: FROM DIMINISHED RESOURCES TO NEW IDENTITIES

Frank Ritchel Ames

1. INTRODUCTION

Exile is a persistent human phenomenon and a prominent motif in the Hebrew Bible.[1] The Primary History, the Bible's first story, begins with an account of the banishing of humankind's newly created and immediately rebellious prototypical ancestors (Gen 3:23–24) and ends with the razing of the temple in Jerusalem and a deportation to Babylon (2 Kgs 25:1–12).[2] The exile motif, writ large and small, punctuates the rest of the Bible, and the history and memory of exile informs the self-understanding of those who identify with Israel. Arguably, the Babylonian exile defines early Judaism and is, in the words of Daniel L. Smith, Judah's "most sociologically significant event."[3] From the perspective of the Hebrew Bible, all of

---

1. This discussion incorporates material presented in two earlier papers: Frank Ritchel Ames, "Forced Migration and Israelite Families: Ancient and Modern Patterns" (paper presented at the Society of Biblical Literature Annual Meeting, Boston, 22 November 2008), 1–23; and idem, "Forced Migration and the Visions of Zechariah" (paper presented at the Society of Biblical Literature Annual Meeting, New Orleans, 23 November 2009), 1–24.

2. On reading the Primary History as a literary unit related to exilic and postexilic experience, see David Noel Freedman, *The Unity of the Bible* (Distinguished Senior Faculty Lecture Series; Ann Arbor: University of Michigan Press, 1993); and Ehud Ben Zvi, "Looking At the Primary (Hi)story and the Prophetic Books as Literary/ Theological Units Within the Frame of the Early Second Temple: Some Considerations," *JSOT* 121 (1998): 26–43.

3. Daniel L. Smith, "The Politics of Ezra: Sociological Indicators of Postexilic Judaean Society," in *Second Temple Studies 1: Persian Period* (ed. Philip R. Davies; JSOTSup 117; Sheffield Academic Press: Sheffield, 1991), 73–97 (75).

humanity stands East of Eden, and many can say with Moses, "I have been a stranger in a strange land" (Exod 2:22 KJV). Exile played a crucial role in the formation of early Judaism.

Exilic experience is a large-scale phenomenon today as well:

> At the end of 2009, some 43.3 million people worldwide were forcibly displaced due to conflict and persecution, the highest number since the mid-1990s. This included 15.2 million refugees, 27.1 million IDPs [Internally Displaced Persons] and close to 1 million individuals whose asylum application had not yet been adjudicated by the end of the report-ing period.[4]

The scope of forced displacement in the contemporary world overwhelms, and the trauma of displacement felt by nations, communities, families, and individuals is unfathomable. The trauma is psychological, sociologi-cal, and environmental. It disorients individuals and destabilizes groups, and has both short- and long-term effects.

This essay describes the effects of exile and locates representations of the effects in two pericopes in the Hebrew Bible, the story of Ruth and the letter of Jeremiah in Jer 29:4–23. The description offered is eclectic and comparative and brings social observations to bear on literary representa-tions to enrich the analysis of both. I argue that the diminished resources and security and increased morbidity and mortality of exile foster exten-sion and inclusivity in surviving families. The effects of forced displace-ment cascade from the deprivations of exile to the pragmatics of survival to the restructuring of families to new ideals and identities. It is assumed that the experiences and strategies of ancient and modern smallholders, though not identical, are comparable.[5] It is also assumed that textual rep-resentations of human behaviors tend to be unimaginative and offer sem-blances of real life. Regardless of the genre—whether the texts are novellas or letters, or whether the events represented are historical or fictional—the actions and interactions of the characters conform to familiar social pat-

---

4. UNHCR, *2009 Global Trends: Refugees, Asylum-seekers, Returnees, Internally Displaced and Stateless Persons* (Geneva: Division of Programme Support and Man-agement, Field Information and Coordination Support Section, United Nations High Commissioner for Refugees, 2010), 2.

5. Carol L. Meyers, "The Family in Early Israel," in *Families in Ancient Israel* (ed. Leo G. Perdue et al.; The Family, Religion, and Culture; Louisville: Westminster John Knox, 1997), 4.

terns. Even highly imaginative fictions exhibit remarkably unimaginative social patterns, and it is this social-literary verisimilitude—a narrative quality that cannot be avoided by writers and is needed by readers—that undergirds the use of eclectic, comparative approaches. Turning first to social observations, what are the effects of exile?

2. THREE SOCIAL EFFECTS

The first effect is diminishment of resources and security. Exile separates people from their property, including food and water, clothing and furnishings, tools, documents, and artistic, religious, and nostalgic items, as well as animals, which are a form of wealth and a source of food, clothing, entertainment, warmth, and tools. The use of land, housing, and moveable property is lost to the displaced, along with the material contributions that these things make to the welfare of the individual, family, and community. Land provides sustenance, security, and income; housing affords shelter, safety, privacy, and storage; and property offers a wide range of vital benefits.

The loss for the person in exile, of course, is not simply material. Access to personnel and institutions may be blocked. Exile separates family members, friends and neighbors, and community members. Separation fractures social networks and community infrastructures. Exile disrupts a community's complex support system, the benefits of which may not be recognized until they are no longer available to the displaced. The loss of vital resources translates into unmet human needs. Displaced persons take little with them, often no more than things that are worn and that can be carried or bound to a pack animal. Food and water, which are heavy and difficult to transport, are quickly exhausted and, given the size of the population displaced, may not be adequate or safe. Forced displacements in Iraq between February 2006 and March 2007 illustrate the problem: although it was sectarian violence that displaced the 725,000 who fled as part of the "largest population movement[s] since 1948 in the Middle East," they left water, food, shelter, and access to healthcare, education, and employment.[6] The displaced escaped an immediate threat of violence to face the lingering dangers of destitution.

---

6. Norwegian Refugee Council, *Iraq: A Displacement Crisis* (Geneva: Internal Displacement Monitoring Centre, 2007), 12.

Security diminishes during and after relocation, and displacement puts women in particular at risk. One study of modern displacement found that 50 percent of refugee women had been raped, and 94 percent of the sexual assault victims "did not tell their refugee workers of their experience."[7] The reasons for the heightened threat to women during conflict and conflict-induced displacement are complex. Eileen Pittaway and Linda Bartolomei explain,

> During armed conflict, women can become the targets of "ethically motivated gender-specific" forms of violence. Ideological frameworks developed by extreme forms of nationalism and fundamentalism that reify women's image as "bearers of the culture and values" have led to widespread sexual assaults against women as political acts of aggression. Such acts of sexual aggression are often fueled by race- and gender-based propaganda. An additional intersect of race and gender is the forcible impregnation of females from one ethnic group by males from another group as a form of genocide. Women bear the direct impact of these actions. Racism, racial discrimination, xenophobia, and related intolerance have increasingly been used to incite armed conflicts over resources and rights within and between countries around the world.[8]

Elisabeth Rehn and Ellen Johnson-Sirleaf characterize responses to war-related aggression against women as "one of history's great silences."[9] Though every displaced person faces risks, women face additional risks.

The second effect of exile is increased morbidity and mortality. Conflict-induced displacement is hazardous to health.[10] Ironically, the displacement

---

7. Eileen Pittaway and Linda Bartolomei, "Refugees, Race, and Gender: The Multiple Discrimination against Refugee Women," *Refugee* 19 (2001): 24.

8. Ibid., 23.

9. Elisabeth Rehn and Ellen Johnson-Sirleaf, *Women, War, Peace: The Independent Experts' Assessment on the Impact of Armed Conflict on Women and Women's Role in Peace-Building* (Progress of the World's Women 1; New York: United Nations Development Fund for Women, 2002), 19.

10. "Armed conflict between warring states and groups within states have been major causes of ill health and mortality for most of human history. Conflict obviously causes deaths and injuries on the battlefield, but also health consequences from the displacement of populations, the breakdown of health and social services, and the heightened risk of disease transmission. Despite the size of the health consequences, military conflict has not received the same attention from public health research and policy as many other causes of illness and death. In contrast, political scientists have

often proves deadlier than the attack. Mortality during the acute emergency phase of a displacement can reach sixty times normal rates.[11] The baseline crude mortality rate in nonemergency situations in developing countries is less than 0.5 deaths per day among ten thousand persons, and one death per day for children under the age of five years.[12] The emergency threshold is defined as double the baseline rate for the group.[13] Forced displacement increases the mortality rate markedly. When drought in Ethiopia displaced many from the Gode district in Somali, the crude mortality rate reached 6.3 deaths among 10,000 per day, and 12.5 for children under the age of five years.[14] Children under the age of five years usually account for most deaths in conflict-induced displacement. Malnutrition, diarrheal diseases, acute respiratory infection, malaria, and measles account for 60 to 95 percent of reported deaths in famines and complex emergencies. The leading cause of death for children under the age of five is measles.[15]

The third effect of exile is a pragmatic response to diminished resources and security and to increased rates of morbidity and mortality: the composition of households tends to become more extensive and inclusive. To

---

long studied the causes of war but have primarily been interested in the decision of elite groups to go to war, not in human death and misery" (C. J. L. Murray et al., "Armed Conflict as a Public Health Problem," *BMJ* 325 [2002]: 346).

11. Michael J. Toole and Ronald J. Waldman, "Prevention of Excess Mortality in Refugee and Displaced Populations in Developing Countries," *JAMA* 263 (1990): 3296–302.

12. CDC, "Mortality During a Famine—Gode District, Ethiopia, July 2000," *MMWR* 50.15 (20 April 2001): 286. Online: http:// www.cdc.gov/mmwr/PDF/wk/ mm5015.pdf.

13. Robert Lidstone, "Health and Mortality of Internally Displaced Persons: Reviewing the Data and Defining Directions for Research" (paper prepared for The Brookings Institution, University of Bern Project on Internal Displacement, May 2007), 4. For an introduction to morbidity and mortality statistics, see Francesco Checchi and Les Roberts, "Interpreting and Using Mortality Data in Humanitarian Emergencies: A Primer for Non-epidemiologists" (Network Paper 52; London: Humanitarian Practice Network at the Overseas Development Institute, September 2005; online: http://www.forcedmigration.columbia.edu/faculty/LR_HPN.pdf.pdf). According to Checchi and Roberts, "Crude and under-5 mortality rates are key indicators to evaluate the magnitude of a crisis, and a doubling of non-crisis (baseline) mortality is taken to define an emergency situation. However, different views exist on whether absolute or context-specific thresholds should be used" (7).

14. CDC, "Mortality during a Famine," 285–86.

15. Ibid., 287.

compensate for losses, households add individuals who may not have been welcome before displacement. In Iraq, for instance, many immigrants often become a part of an extended family.[16] In modern Israel, households, for economic reasons, tend to become multigenerational.[17] By the time of the second generation, ethnic characteristics exist but have faded within families.[18] In short, when resources diminish and threats increase, families extend.[19] Extension is a pragmatic response to hardship, for "in subsistence systems, the nuclear family is simply not a viable economic unit."[20] Extended and more inclusive families emerge out of desperate living conditions and new proximity. The pragmatics of survival eventually lead to assimilation, and assimilation changes identities and ideologies.

Exile has other effects, but the three broad categories discussed here—diminished resources and security, increased morbidity and mortality, household extension and inclusion—are heuristic and vary in intensity. My description of cascading effects simplifies, but the model provides useful categories for understanding exile and for reading biblical texts.

3. Two Textual Representations

3.1. The Story of Ruth

The cascading effects of forced displacement may be observed in the story of Ruth. The story recounts the plight of a Judean family displaced by natural disaster or—from an emic perspective—a supernatural disaster, for the narrator attributes such phenomena to the intervention of Yhwh, who "had considered his people and [had] given them food" (1:6).[21] In the account, famine drives Elimelech, Naomi, Mahlon, and Chilion from

---

16. Norwegian Refugee Council, *Iraq: A Displacement Crisis*, 11.

17. Ruth Katz and Yoav Lavee, "Families in Israel," in *Handbook of World Families* (ed. Bert N. Adams and Jan Trost; Sage: London, 2005), 497.

18. Lea Shamgar-Handelman, "Family Sociology in a Small Academic Community: Family Research and Theory in Israel," in *Intercultural Variation in Family Research and Theory: Implications for Cross-National Studies* (ed. Marvin B. Sussman and Roma Stovall Hanks; 2 vols.; Haworth Press: New York, 1996), 2: 392.

19. Amy E. Wagner, "Extended Families," in *International Encyclopedia of Marriage and Family* (ed. James J. Ponzetti; 4 vols.; New York: Macmillan, 2002), 2:539–40.

20. K. V. Flannery, "The Origins of the Village Revisited: From Nuclear to Extended Households," *American Antiquity* 67 (2002): 424.

21. Quotations of the Bible are from the NRSV unless otherwise noted.

Judah to Moab (1:1–2). Returning after more than a decade of dislocation, Naomi laments, "I went away full, but the Lord has brought me back
empty" (1:21a). The impoverished state of Naomi and Ruth, the widowed
daughter-in-law who has returned with Naomi, is evident in Ruth's need
to glean barley in a field that is not her own (2:1–23). Though the famine
that drove Elimelech's family from the land has ended, the returning exiles
Naomi and Ruth do not have ready access to the new abundance. The
disaster and dislocation are over, but the impact of the displacement lingers. The author of the story characterizes the famine as an act of God
(1:6, 19–21), and divine providence is an important motif in the story (2:3;
4:1),[22] but one may assume that the famine is probably related to war:

> Populations experiencing famine may or may not displace themselves in
> order to improve food availability. Initially, male family members may
> migrate to cities or neighboring countries to seek employment. During a
> fullscale famine, whole families and villages may flee to other regions or
> countries in a desperate search for food. In most of the major population
> displacements of the past 20 years, however, people have been forced
> to flee because of fear for their physical security caused by war or civil
> strife. Famine in the absence of violence has generated few of the world's
> refugees.[23]

The exposition of the story, 1:1–5, places the famine in a time when
charismatic military leaders governed the tribes of Israel—an era that the
book of Judges characterizes as violent and subject to recurring cycles of
war and peace. Oded Borowski correctly observes that "Israelite traditions
reflect constant preoccupation with the issues of war and peace. In general, war was such a common occurrence that, as far as the Bible was concerned, specific references to times of peace became necessary."[24] Famine
drove the family from its land, and the displacement left the survivors with
nothing. In the language of the text, what was once "full" became "empty"
(1:21a). Exile diminished the resources of Elimelech's family.

---

22. A classic exposition of the theme of providence in the book is offered by
Ronald M. Hals, *The Theology of the Book of Ruth* (Philadelphia: Fortress, 1969).

23. Centers for Disease Control, "Famine-Affected, Refugee, and Displaced Populations: Recommendations for Public Health Issues," *MMWR* 41.13 (24 July 1992);
online: http://www.cdc.gov/mmwr/preview/mmwrhtml/00019261.htm.

24. Oded Borowski, *Daily Life in Biblical Times* (SBLABS 5; Atlanta: Society of
Biblical Literature, 2003), 35.

In addition to the loss of resources, the security of family members is diminished. This experience, though common to exiles, is in the story of Ruth primarily the experience of women: Naomi expresses concern about the security of her daughters-in-law, Orpah and Ruth (1:9; 3:1); Boaz expresses concern about the security of both Ruth and Naomi (2:8–9; 3:17). He orders his men not to bother Ruth (2:9), and Naomi warns Ruth to act with caution around the men in the fields (2:22). Naomi and Ruth, even after arriving at Naomi's own town, are not particularly safe. Ironically, that which concerns Naomi about Ruth gleaning near male harvesters, namely Ruth's attractive appearance, is used to entice Boaz, for Naomi encourages Ruth to adorn herself and to go to Boaz at the threshing floor—an encounter that is fraught with sexual innuendo and danger (3:1–14). Boaz is troubled by the circumstances of their meeting, for he wants to hide Ruth's late-night visit (3:14). Of equal and perhaps greater significance than the potential intrigue of their clandestine meeting are the insecurities imposed on the unattached women by the endogamous culture and its patrilineal inheritance system: marriage outside of family boundaries was discouraged if not prohibited, and women had to bear children to maintain control of inheritable lands.[25] The situation of Naomi and Ruth was difficult, and their lives precarious, for gender, age, and ethnicity conspired against them. Consistent with the experience of other groups subject to forced displacement, the security of the displaced women in the story of Ruth decreases—at least until the plot resolves.

Morbidity and mortality play a significant role in the story's exposition: Naomi's spouse and sons die (1:3–5). Their deaths are an essential element in the plot and, though not explained in the story, are consistent with the realities observed in conflict- and disaster-induced displacement. Woven into the story are the morbidity and mortality of men and children. Naomi's sons do not die as infants, but the story's use of the term יֶלֶד in 1:5 and 4:17 invites readers to think of her sons as Naomi once thought of them: as her babies. Their very names suggest morbidity and mortality: Mahlon and Chilion, "Sickly" and "Mortal."[26]

The response to destitution, insecurity, morbidity, and mortality in the story of Ruth is noble, clever, and pragmatic: the Moabite widow

---

25. Ancient Israelite families were "endogamous, patrilineal, patriarchal, patrilocal, joint, and polygynous" (Philip J. King and Lawrence E. Stager, *Life in Biblical Israel* [LAI; Louisville: Westminster John Knox, 2001], 38).

26. "כליון," *HALOT-SE* 1:479; "מחלון," ibid., 1:569.

Ruth manages to become the wife of Judean landowner Boaz, and Naomi, through the marriage of Ruth to Boaz, acquires a son through whom to gain control of the land of Elimelech (4:7–17). Through a levirate marriage, losses suffered as a result of the famine in Ephrathah and the forced displacement of Elimelech's family are, to the extent possible, remedied for Naomi.[27] Land, safety, wellbeing, and family are regained, and in the midst of the experience, social relationships change. Her family becomes more extensive and inclusive. While displaced in Moab, Naomi's Judean sons marry Moabite women, and one Moabite woman, namely Ruth, migrates to Bethlehem and marries a Judean man. Out of necessity and against preferences for endogamy assumed to be part of the social backstory, the traditional boundaries of the Judean family are crossed. The family in the story is extensive and inclusive. The child of Ruth is the child of Naomi (4:17), and the restored family—a royal family memorialized in the ten-panel linear genealogy of David (4:18–22)—becomes, with the inclusion of Ruth's son, Moabite as well as Judean. In the book, the cascading effects of forced displacement that begin with a pursuit of sustenance end with a transformation of relationships, identity, and, for the reader, ideology. That which was foreign becomes familial; that which was Moabite becomes Israelite.

The events portrayed in the story of Ruth are premonarchic, but the book originated during or after the lifetime of David, who is included in the book's genealogical appendix (4:22), and the provenance of the book is probably postexilic. This is a period in Judah's history shaped by the cascading effects and ideological developments of exilic experience. The exilic and postexilic experience is relevant to interpretation of the book, and the book relevant to the controversies of postexilic times. John J. Collins explains, "Since marriage with foreign women was a contentious issue in postexilic Judah, the book has been construed as a protest against narrow ethnocentrism."[28] Exile fostered exogamy, and exogamy polarized exilic and postexilic Judeans and stirred ideological debate. The book of Ruth is an artifact of the controversy and sanctioned exogamy, a practice that in the story and among exiles mitigates loss of property, security, and family.

---

27. See Frank Ritchel Ames, "Levirate Marriage," *NIDOTTE* 4:902–5.

28. John J. Collins, "Marriage, Divorce, and Family in Second Temple Judaism," in Perdue et al., *Families in Ancient Israel*, 104–62 (106).

3.2. The Letter of Jeremiah

The cascading effects of forced displacement can also be teased out of the letter of Jeremiah (Jer 29:4–23), which is introduced to readers as "the letter that the prophet Jeremiah sent from Jerusalem to the remaining elders among the exiles, and to the priests, the prophets, and all the people, whom Nebuchadnezzar had taken into exile from Jerusalem to Babylon" (v. 1). The use of a letter to communicate with those in exile "constitutes a sophisticated rhetorical strategy" that overcomes distance between prophet and people and, moreover, mitigates a multidimensional separateness that is geographical, social, and ideological is critical for the people.[29] The letter addresses two topics related to exile—the welfare of those exiled and judgment against their oppressors—and it does so in relation to two locations, Babylon and Jerusalem. As Jack R. Lundbom has observed, the letter combines and addresses these topics in four sections that are similar in length (about nine lines) and are arranged to form a chiasm:

A Welfare of *Babylon* (4–9)—9 lines of MT
   B Welfare of *Jerusalem* (10–14)—9 lines of MT
   B' Judgment in *Jerusalem* (16–20)—9+ lines of MT
A' Judgment in *Babylon* (15, 21–23)—8 lines of MT[30]

The rhetoric is crafted without being overly contrived. It is prophetic: it represents the divine voice, Yhwh addressing the Israelite exiles and asserting responsibility for their displacement (v. 4). Instructions and assurances related to their welfare follow in verses 5–14 (sections A and B). Then in verses 15–23 (sections B' and A'), Yhwh pronounces judgment on those who have turned to the lies of false prophets.

The cascading effects of displacement are evident in what the letter says about judgment, which includes the triple threat of "sword, famine,

---

29. Carolyn J. Sharp, *Prophecy and Ideology in Jeremiah: Struggles for Authority in the Deutero-Jeremianic Prose* (OTS; London: T&T Clark, 2003), 106.

30. Jack R. Lundbom, *Jeremiah: A Study in Ancient Hebrew Rhetoric* (2nd ed.; Winona Lake, Ind.: Eisenbrauns, 1997), 137; see also Raymond de Hoop, "Textual, Literary, and Delimitation Criticism: The Case of Jeremiah 29 in [MT] and [LXX]" in *The Impact of Unit Delimitation on Exegesis* (ed. Raymond de Hoop, Marjo C. A. Korpel, and Stanley E. Porter; Pericope 7; Leiden: Brill, 2009), 40–42.

and pestilence" (v. 17): violence that displaces, a diminishing of resources needed for survival, and the heightened morbidity and mortality that plague exile (cf. v. 18). The trauma of these hardships is compounded by scorn, humiliation, and loss of group identity, for the exiled community becomes "an object of cursing, and horror, and hissing, and a derision among all the nations where [Yhwh has] driven them" (v. 18).

The reversal of judgment, which is promised in sections A and B, underscores the effects of displacement from the perspective of relief and restoration: Yhwh promises to restore "fortunes" and "bring back" the exiles (v. 14), who will have land, security, and resources. Yhwh, the letter states, has "plans for [their] welfare and not for harm" (v. 11). The instructions given in section A (vv. 4–9) promote the welfare of the exiles, which—contrary to the expectations of Jeremiah's prophetic opponents— the exiles will achieve in partnership with their Babylonian captors. The letter instructs the exiles to settle down and support rather than oppose Babylon:

> Build houses and live in them; plant gardens and eat what they produce. Take wives and have sons and daughters; take wives for your sons, and give your daughters in marriage, that they may bear sons and daughters; multiply there, and do not decrease. But seek the welfare of the city where I have sent you into exile, and pray to the LORD on its behalf, for in its welfare you will find your welfare. (Jer 29:5–7)[31]

These instructions appear to encourage assimilation and effectively abrogate any prohibition of intermarriage.[32] One could, of course, argue that the text does not specify the nationality or ethnicity of those who are instructed to marry, but, as Carolyn J. Sharp points out, "[E]ven if there is no explicit indication that intermarriage with the Babylonians is being recommended, the danger of exogamy over a period of three generations (the 70-year period insisted on by pro-gôlâ editors) would have been

---

31. The vocabulary of Jer 29:5–7 is reminiscent of Deut 20:5–10. Adele Berlin finds here a subtle intertextual echo that cautions against armed rebellion (Adele Berlin, "Jeremiah 29:5–7, a Deuteronomic Allusion," *HAR* 8 [1984]: 4).

32. Helga Weippert, "Fern von Jerusalem: Die Exilsethik von Jer 29,5–7," in *Zion: Ort der Begegnung* (ed. F. Hahn et al.; BBB 90; Bodenheim: Athenäum-Hain-Hanstein, 1993), 127–39.

obvious."[33] Instances of intermarriage would have increased.[34] Moreover, for the author of the letter, it is integration rather than opposition that promotes the welfare of the community in exile, for the exiles are instructed to seek the welfare of the city of their captors, not merely their own welfare. The letter even commends prayer for the enemy and concludes, "[I]n its welfare you will find your welfare" (v. 7).

Walter Brueggemann correctly recognizes the pragmatic impulse within the prophetic voice when he concludes, "Prophetic faith is powerfully realistic about the political situation of the Jews in exile."[35] The pragmatics of survival mold social structures. Extension and inclusion are grounded in the pragmatics of survival, and there are additional dynamics at work, including ideological dynamics. Human experience, social context, and physical environment transcend and shape ideological perspectives. The letter of Jeremiah links the welfare of Judean and Babylonian enemies, but each, one assumes, has a stake in the security and prosperity of the other, and this promotes extension and inclusion. It fosters new identity and new ideals. Social need becomes theological perspective. John Hill writes,

> The place of exile becomes home, in the deepest sense of that word. The advice in vv. 4–9 about life in Babylon is more than an expression of a pragmatic view of reality, in which conquered exiles realize that they have to make the best of a bad situation. It is the use of images and language from Judah's sacred traditions which gives to vv. 4–9 their startling and radical character. Babylon is described as another Judah. Such a portrait is founded not on an attitude of political pragmatism, but on far more profound theological grounds.[36]

---

33. Sharp, *Prophecy and Ideology in Jeremiah*, 107.

34. "The impression we get is of a high level of integration of the Jewish ethnic minority into the social and economic life of the region by the mid- to late- fifth century B.C. In that international and interethnic environment intermarriage must have been common. Many of the deportees would have taken Jeremiah's advice to seek the welfare of the place to which they had been sent, to build houses, plant gardens, take wives, and raise sons and daughters (Jer 29:5–7), and not all the wives would have been taken from among their own people" (Joseph Blenkinsopp, *Judaism, the First Phase: The Place of Ezra and Nehemiah in the Origins of Judaism* [Grand Rapids: Eerdmans, 2009], 119).

35. Walter Brueggemann, *A Commentary on Jeremiah: Exile and Homecoming* (Grand Rapids: Eerdmans, 1998), 257.

36. John Hill, *Friend or Foe? The Figure of Babylon in the Book of Jeremiah MT* (Biblical Interpretation 40; Leiden: Brill, 1999), 158.

In the letter of Jeremiah, one reads about the hardships of exile, including destitutions and death, and reads instructions to "[t]ake wives and have sons and daughters; take wives for your sons, and give your daughters in marriage, that they may bear sons and daughters; multiply there, and do not decrease" (v. 5), and an ideology evolves.

4. CONCLUSION

Exile has cascading effects. Forced relocation diminishes access to resources, which decreases the security of individuals and families and increases the incidence of disease and death. Women and children face greater risks and losses, though all are subject to dangers and hardships. The deprivations of exile include change of location and loss of property, security, and people. These deprivations have an impact on the identity and ideologies of exiles and exilic communities, which experience an increase in extended families and inclusive marriages and the embrace of supporting ideologies. Ideology yields to the pragmatics of survival. The cascading effects of exile that begin with diminished resources lead to new identities.

BIBLIOGRAPHY

Ames, Frank Ritchel. "Forced Migration and Israelite Families: Ancient and Modern Patterns." Paper presented at the Society of Biblical Literature Annual Meeting. Boston, 22 November 2008.

———. "Forced Migration and the Visions of Zechariah." Paper presented at the Society of Biblical Literature Annual Meeting. New Orleans, 23 November 2009.

———. "Levirate Marriage." NIDOTTE 4:902–5.

Ben Zvi, Ehud. "Looking at the Primary (Hi)story and the Prophetic Books as Literary/Theological Units within the Frame of the Early Second Temple: Some Considerations." JSOT 121 (1998): 26–43.

Berlin, Adele. "Jeremiah 29:5–7, a Deuteronomic Allusion." HAR 8 (1984): 3–11.

Blenkinsopp, Joseph. Judaism, the First Phase: The Place of Ezra and Nehemiah in the Origins of Judaism. Grand Rapids: Eerdmans, 2009.

Borowski, Oded. Daily Life in Biblical Times. SBLABS 5. Atlanta: Society of Biblical Literature, 2003.

Brueggemann, Walter. A Commentary on Jeremiah: Exile and Homecoming. Grand Rapids: Eerdmans, 1998.

Centers for Disease Control. "Famine-Affected, Refugee, and Displaced Populations: Recommendations for Public Health Issues." MMWR 41.13 (24 July 1992). Online: http://www.cdc.gov/mmwr/preview/mmwrhtml/00019261.htm.

———. "Mortality During a Famine—Gode District, Ethiopia, July 2000." MMWR

50.15 (20 April 2001): 285–88. Online: http://www.cdc.gov/mmwr/PDF/wk/mm5015.pdf.

Checchi, Francesco, and Les Roberts. "Interpreting and Using Mortality Data in Humanitarian Emergencies: A Primer for Non-epidemiologists." Network Paper 52. London: Humanitarian Practice Network at the Overseas Development Institute, September 2005. Online: http://www.forcedmigration.columbia.edu/faculty/LR_HPN.pdf.

Collins, John J. "Marriage, Divorce, and Family in Second Temple Judaism." Pages 104–62 in *Families in Ancient Israel.* Edited by Leo G. Perdue, Joseph Blenkinsopp, John J. Collins, and Carol Meyers. The Family, Religion, and Culture. Louisville: Westminster John Knox, 1997.

Flannery, K. V. "The Origins of the Village Revisited: From Nuclear to Extended Households." *American Antiquity* 67 (2002): 417–33.

Freedman, David Noel. *The Unity of the Bible.* Distinguished Senior Facuty Lecture Series. Ann Arbor: University of Michigan Press, 1993.

Hals, Ronald M. *The Theology of the Book of Ruth.* Philadelphia: Fortress, 1969.

Hill, John. *Friend or Foe?: The Figure of Babylon in the Book of Jeremiah MT.* Biblical Interpretation 40. Leiden: Brill, 1999.

Hoop, Raymond de. "Textual, Literary, and Delimitation Criticism: The Case of Jeremiah 29 in [MT] and [LXX]." Pages 29–62 in *The Impact of Unit Delimitation on Exegesis.* Edited by Raymond de Hoop, Marjo C. A. Korpel, and Stanley E. Porter. Pericope 7. Leiden: Brill, 2009.

Katz, Ruth, and Yoav Lavee. "Families in Israel." Pages 486–506 in *Handbook of World Families.* Edited by Bert N. Adams and Jan Trost. London: Sage, 2005.

Katz, Ruth, and Yochanan Peres. "The Sociology of the Family in Israel: An Outline of Its Development From the 1950s to the 1980s." *European Sociological Review* 2 (1986): 148–59.

King, Philip J., and Lawrence E. Stager. *Life in Biblical Israel.* LAI. Louisville: Westminster John Knox, 2001.

Lidstone, Robert. "Health and Mortality of Internally Displaced Persons: Reviewing the Data and Defining Directions for Research." Paper prepared for The Brookings Institution. University of Bern Project on Internal Displacement. May, 2007.

Lundbom, Jack R. *Jeremiah: A Study in Ancient Hebrew Rhetoric.* 2nd ed. Winona Lake, Ind.: Eisenbrauns, 1997.

Meyers, Carol L. "The Family in Early Israel." Pages 1–47 in *Families in Ancient Israel.* Edited by Leo G. Perdue, Joseph Blenkinsopp, John J. Collins, and Carol Meyers. The Family, Religion, and Culture. Louisville: Westminster John Knox, 1997.

Murray, C. J. L., G. King, A. D. Lopez, N. Tomijima, and E. G. Krug. "Armed Conflict as a Public Health Problem." *BMJ* 325 (2002): 346–49.

Norwegian Refugee Council. *Iraq: A Displacement Crisis.* Geneva: Internal Displacement Monitoring Centre, 2007.

Pittaway, Eileen, and Linda Bartolomei. "Refugees, Race, and Gender: The Multiple Discrimination against Refugee Women." *Refugee* 19 (2001): 21–32.

Rehn, Elisabeth, and Ellen Johnson-Sirleaf. *Women, War, Peace: The Independent Experts' Assessment on the Impact of Armed Conflict on Women and Women's Role in Peace-Building.* Progress of the World's Women 1. New York: United Nations Development Fund for Women, 2002.

Shamgar-Handelman, Lea. "Family Sociology in a Small Academic Community: Family Research and Theory in Israel." Pages 377–416 in vol. 2 of *Intercultural Variation in Family Research and Theory: Implications for Cross-National Studies.* Edited by Marvin B. Sussman and Roma Stovall Hanks. New York: Haworth, 1996.

Sharp, Carolyn J. *Prophecy and Ideology in Jeremiah: Struggles for Authority in the Deutero-Jeremianic Prose.* OTS. London: T&T Clark, 2003.

Smith, Daniel L. "The Politics of Ezra: Sociological Indicatiors of Postexilic Judaean Society." Pages 73–97 in *Second Temple Studies 1: Persian Period.* Edited by Philip R. Davies. JSOTSup 117. Sheffield: Sheffield Academic Press, 1991.

Toole, Michael J. and Ronald J. Waldman. "Prevention of Excess Mortality in Refugee and Displaced Populations in Developing Countries." *JAMA* 263 (1990): 3296–302.

UNHCR. *2009 Global Trends: Refugees, Asylum-seekers, Returnees, Internally Displaced and Stateless Persons.* Geneva: Division of Programme Support and Management, Field Information and Coordination Support Section, United Nations High Commissioner for Refugees, 2010.

———. *2009 Statistical Yearbook: Trends in Displacement, Protection and Solutions.* Geneva: Division of Programme Support and Management, Field Information and Coordination Support Section, United Nations High Commissioner for Refugees, 2010.

———. "Refugee Health." (EC/1995/SC.2/CRP.29). Sub-Committee on Administrative and Financial Matters, 11 September 1995. Online: http://www.unhcr.org/excom/EXCOM/3ae68bf424.html.

Wagner, Amy E. "Extended Families." Pages 536–41 in vol. 2 of *International Encyclopedia of Marriage and Family.* Edited by James J. Ponzetti. New York: Macmillan, 2002.

Weippert, Helga. "Fern von Jerusalem: Die Exilsethik von Jer 29,5–7." Pages 127–39 in *Zion: Ort der Begegnung.* Edited by F. Hahn et al. BBB 90. Bodenheim: Athenäum-Hain-Hanstein, 1993.

Lost Space and Revived Memory: From Jerusalem in 586 B.C.E. to New Orleans in 2009

Christl M. Maier

The loss of space—whether by "natural" cause or human evil intent—captures people's minds: on September 11, 2001, or with the impact of Hurricane Katrina in 2005. To cope with their loss, the inhabitants of New York and New Orleans shared their stories, telling the world how the disaster afflicted them and their families. In New Orleans, the loss has invigorated people's memory and generated laments about the city's fate and songs about its former glory, some of which were presented in a session entitled "Lament and Katrina: A Dialogue between Biblical Scholars and Poets," which was held at the SBL Annual Meeting in 2009.[1] Such stories and songs become part of the collective memory once they are ritualized, either told year after year on the day the disaster struck or mentioned in history books. Pictures of the disaster that are displayed publicly or integrated into memorial sites such as the New York firefighters' monument corroborate this memorization process.

As defined by German Egyptologist Jan Assmann, the collective memory of a group or society is the sum of ideas and knowledge gathered to

---

1. The session was organized by the SBL section "Lament in Sacred Texts and Cultures." Scott Ellington presided; the poets were David Brinks, Megan Burns, Bill Lavender, Brenda Marie Osbey, Niyi Osundare, and Jerry W. Ward, Jr.; respondents were Nancy C. Lee and Rebecca Raphael. When Katrina struck, I was living in New Haven, Connecticut. For the SBL meeting in New Orleans in 2009, I traveled from Germany, delivered a version of this paper, and was deeply moved by the songs and stories of these poets. Since I got to know New Orleans only in its partly restored and partly still bruised state, I decided to keep the year 2009 in my title, although the memory of this great city before and after Katrina will surely be carried on.

establish its identity.[2] This memory is revived by "figures of remembrance"[3] that are either cultural assets such as texts, rituals, and monuments, or acts of public communication such as reciting, celebrating, and contemplating. The collective or cultural memory always relates remembrance to the present situation since it understands the present as an outgrowth of the past. A collection of figures of remembrance in literal form, such as the Jewish Tanak or the Christian Bible, is a special form of remembrance that closes the stream of tradition at a given point and fixes part of the memory once and for all.[4]

Like the submergence of New Orleans in 2005, the destruction of Jerusalem in 586 B.C.E. by the Babylonian army greatly influenced the collective memory of the city's population. The book of Lamentations vividly testifies to this destruction of Judah's capital city. By personifying Jerusalem as female, the book is highly effective in generating a close relationship between the city and its population. While studying the personification of Jerusalem throughout the Hebrew Bible, I became aware of the strong symbolism of the female city.[5] In the following, I will assess the role of Jerusalem's personification for the collective memory of Jews and Christians.

1. Lamentations as Literature of Survival

The book of Lamentations offers five poems that are similar to lament psalms. The laments are artistically stylized mostly in acrostic form and follow the limping rhythm of the dirge (Heb. *qînâ*).[6] With this peculiar

---

2. Jan Assmann, "Kollektives Gedächtnis und kulturelle Identität," in *Kultur und Gedächtnis* (ed. Jan Assmann and Tonio Hölscher; STW 724; Frankfurt: Suhrkamp, 1988), 9–19; idem, *Das kulturelle Gedächtnis: Schrift, Erinnerung und politische Identität in frühen Hochkulturen* (5th ed.; Munich: Beck, 2005), 33–42; for an English summary of the topic, see the introduction in idem, *Religion and Cultural Memory: Ten Studies* (trans. R. Livingstone; Stanford, Calif.: Stanford University Press, 2006). Assmann takes the term "collective memory" from Maurice Halbwachs and uses it simultaneously with "cultural memory" in his writings.

3. Assmann, "Kollektives Gedächtnis," 12; idem, *Das kulturelle Gedächtnis*, 37–42. The German term is "Erinnerungsfiguren."

4. Cf. Assmann, *Das kulturelle Gedächtnis*, 93–97, 103–4.

5. See Christl M. Maier, *Daughter Zion, Mother Zion: Gender, Space, and the Sacred in Ancient Israel* (Minneapolis: Fortress, 2008).

6. Lamentations 3 offers three lines beginning with each of the twenty-two Hebrew letters; Lam 5 is not acrostic but keeps to the pattern of twenty-two verses.

form of poetry, the authors obviously tried to overcome the wordless grief "through a recovery of language itself and by giving voice to Jerusalem's experience of suffering."[7] These laments were probably used in public mourning either in Jerusalem at the site of the destroyed temple (cf. Jer 41:5)[8] or in the villages and towns around the destroyed city.[9]

The laments present different speakers who tell about the disaster from different angles. In Lam 1–2, the voice of the poet (1:1–11a; 2:1–10) alternates with the voice of personified Jerusalem named *Daughter Zion* (1:11b–22; 2:11–12, 20–22). In the course of the two chapters, the enormity of Zion's suffering changes the poet's attitude from mere observation to empathy for pain-stricken Zion (2:13–19). In chapter 3, a single male voice laments imprisonment and bodily pain and represents the fate of the exiled members of the community.[10] Chapter 4, returning to the viewpoint of the poet, describes the starvation of the city's inhabitants during the siege. There is also a communal voice, which interrupts the speaker in 3:40–47 and 4:17–22 and utters the fifth lament. This group repents of sins and asks for God's mercy while describing the cruel fate of survivors living under foreign rule and oppression.[11] All of these voices directly address God; they plead, beg, and even insult God, yet there is no divine answer as the phrase, *'ên-lāh mĕnahēm*, "there is none to comfort her" (1:2, 9, 17, 21), underlines.

---

7. Frederick W. Dobbs-Allsopp, *Lamentations* (IBC; Louisville: Westminster John Knox, 2002), 33.

8. Such a liturgical use is argued by Claus Westermann, *Lamentations: Issues and Interpretation* (trans. C. Muenchow; Minneapolis: Fortress, 1994), 62–63.

9. Rainer Albertz (*Israel in Exile: The History and Literature of the Sixth Century B.C.E.* [trans. D. Green; SBLSBL 3; Atlanta: Society of Biblical Literature, 2003]) distinguishes between the *Sitz im Leben* of communal laments such as Ps 44 and Lam 5 in a cultic assembly (141) and of the lament poems of Lam 1, 2, 4, which he imagines to be performed at evening gatherings of the men of the villages (156).

10. Cf. Christl M. Maier, "Body Space as Public Space: Jerusalem's Wounded Body in Lamentations," in *Constructions of Space II: The Biblical City and Other Imagined Spaces* (ed. Jon L. Berquist and Claudia V. Camp; LHBOTS 490; New York: T&T Clark, 2008), 119–38.

11. Although Lam 5 seems to advocate repentance and docility towards God's judgment, Robert Williamson Jr. ("Lament and the Arts of Resistance: Public and Hidden Transcripts in Lamentations 5," in *Lamentations in Ancient and Contemporary Contexts* [ed. Nancy C. Lee and Carleen Mandolfo; SBLSymS 43; Atlanta: Society of Biblical Literature, 2008], 67–80) rightly argues that the last verse reveals a "hidden transcript" that challenges God's wrathful exercise of authority.

Through its character as lyric, the book most probably sought to guide an initial audience of survivors to cope with the loss of space and of fellow humans. Yet the stunning poems were so powerful that they presented a form of remembrance for later generations, too. Although the beginning of the custom is unclear, the book of Lamentations eventually became the prescribed reading for the yearly commemoration of the temple's destruction in the Jewish calendar on Tisha b'Av, the ninth day of the month of Av.[12] The five laments thus became part of the collective memory of Jews and then Christians. Tod Linafelt rightly calls Lamentations a "literature of survival" that embodies a paradox, since it works "to keep alive the memory of death."[13]

In my view, the personification of the city in the female figure of Daughter Zion shaped Israel's collective memory in a twofold way. First, personified Zion attests to a broken relationship between the city, its population, and God, as well as to the survival of part of the population. Second, in sustaining the readers' emotional connection to the space, the female figure generates hope for the survivors of the catastrophe in Judah and in exile, as well as expectations of rebuilding the city.

2. Female Zion Embodying a Ruined Space

The female personification of Jerusalem embodies a human collective and a space at the same time, the inhabitants as well as the gates, buildings, and streets of the city. The name *Zion* traditionally stands for God's elected place, the mountain on which the main sanctuary is located.[14] The title *Daughter Zion* creates a relationship between the space, its population, and God.[15] Within the society of ancient Israel, the daughter

---

12. Cf. Meir Ydit, "Av, the Ninth of," *EncJud* 2:714–16.

13. Tod Linafelt, *Surviving Lamentations: Catastrophe, Lament, and Protest in the Afterlife of a Biblical Book* (Chicago: University of Chicago Press, 2000), 21.

14. The so-called Zion theology is treated in John H. Hayes, "The Tradition of Zion's Inviolability," *JBL* 82 (1963): 419–26; and Ben C. Ollenburger, *Zion, the City of the Great King: A Theological Symbol of the Jerusalem Cult* (JSOTSup 41; Sheffield: Sheffield Academic Press, 1987). The familiarity of the author of Lamentations with the Zion tradition is demonstrated by Frederick W. Dobbs-Allsopp, "R(az/ais)ing Zion in Lamentations 2," in *David and Zion: Biblical Studies in Honor of J. J. M. Roberts* (ed. Bernard F. Batto and Kathryn L. Roberts; Winona Lake, Ind.: Eisenbrauns, 2004), 21–68, esp. 24–27.

15. For a detailed analysis of the metaphor, see Maier, *Daughter Zion*, 60–74.

depends socially and economically on her father. Thus the title conveys that the city needs protection by her divine father. In Lamentations, the daughterly role recedes to the background while the poet presents the city as a weeping widow and mother:

> How lonely sits the city that once was full of people!
> How like a widow she has become, she that was great among the nations!
> She that was a princess among the provinces has become a vassal. (Lam 1:1 NRSV)

In Lam 1–2 the body of Zion stands both for the horrible suffering of the people and the devastation of the city space. Lamentations 1:8–10 describes the enemy's entering of the temple as a rape scene which results in public humiliation:

> Jerusalem sinned grievously, so she has become a mockery;
> all who honored her despise her, for they have seen her nakedness;
> she herself groans, and turns her face away.
> Her uncleanness was in her skirts; she took no thought of her future
> "O LORD, look at my affliction, for the enemy has triumphed!"
> Enemies have stretched out their hands over all her precious things;
> she has even seen the nations invade her sanctuary,
> those whom you forbade to enter your congregation.

The allusion to sexual violence hinges on the correspondence of woman//city, body//temple and genitals//inner sanctuary.[16] The invasion of the city by foreign men is similarly sexualized in Ezek 23:44, "For they have gone into her (the city), as one goes into a prostitute." The public shame inflicted on the woman becomes obvious in the statement that the enemies "have seen her nakedness" (v. 8). This refers to the stripping of the woman, an act closely related to sexual violence or rape in other biblical texts (Isa 47:3; Ezek 16:37). The impurity on Zion's "skirts" (v. 9) describes Zion as menstruating, and thus as ritually impure. Since in Jewish thought sexuality and all fluids connected to it, including menstrual blood, are

---

16. Here I follow the interpretation of Alan Mintz, "The Rhetoric of Lamentations and the Representations of Catastrophe," *Proof* 2 (1982): 4. Frederick W. Dobbs-Allsopp and Tod Linafelt, "The Rape of Zion in Thr 1,10," *ZAW* 113 (2001): 77–81, support this interpretation by adding two parallels to Lam 1:8, 10 from the ancient Near East. For a fuller discussion, see Maier, *Daughter Zion*, 146–47.

barred from the sacred (cf. Lev 15:16–33), the menstruating woman conveys the ultimate counter image to Jerusalem's former status as a sacred space. Thus Lam 1:8–10 narrates the unimaginable violation of the temple by presenting a woman's violated body. At the same time, this image unveils emotions of anger and shame.

In Lam 1:11–16, female Zion raises her voice and describes her inner turmoil in the traumatic situation of defeat. She presents her own body as the battlefield of God's wrath and herself as a victim of war: her feet are fettered, her bones burning; she lies on her back; her neck feels like it is bound by ropes; her heart is overturned; her eyes are full of tears; and her spirits are low. She feels put down, crushed, almost dead, and without hope of help. In Lam 2:20–22, she bemoans her dying inhabitants as a mother mourns for her children. Thus the roles of the assaulted daughter, the forsaken widow, and the mother bereft of her progeny coalesce into one another. The woman's bodily decline corresponds to the devastation of the city and to the deplorable situation of the inhabitants being killed, exiled, or left dying in the streets.

3. How Female Zion Affects the Collective Memory

Lamentations attests to a void in a double sense. First there is a spatial void—the city besieged and razed, emptied and deserted—a void that includes the extinction of people. Second there is an ideological void, as the ideology of Zion's divine election and sacredness has been distorted and the close relationship between God and the community is broken. Thus both the space and its population seem to be lost. Yet the very existence of Lamentations as poems that give voice to the survivors' experience attests to the fact that the city is not totally annihilated and deserted.

In Lam 1–2, the female personification achieves a double representation of pain, the individual pain of any inhabitant as well as the corporate agony of the community.[17] This representation helps the initial audience, survivors of the catastrophe, to embed their individual suffering into the fate of the community. Their personal story becomes part of a larger story and thus gets national significance.

---

17. Knut M. Heim ("The Personification of Jerusalem and the Drama of Her Bereavement in Lamentations," in *Zion, City of Our God* [ed. Richard S. Hess and Gordon J. Wenham; Grand Rapids: Eerdmans, 1999], 130) argues that in a disaster that strikes the whole community, pain is elevated to a different and more complex level.

One may say that female Zion resists her fate. In raising her voice, in mourning her own desolation, in naming God as the perpetrator, Zion assumes the role of the professional mourner and singer of dirges.[18] In ancient Israel, the public dirge is often performed by women (see Jer 9:16–20).[19] By mourning, the female figure attributes agency to a collective subject: although bleeding, the city is not dead; although shattered, she is unwilling to be silent. The images of the raped woman and the mother weeping for her wounded or starving children create a strong relationship between the city and its population. Therefore, the female personification of Jerusalem holds potential for an identification with the place.

A mourning person expects to be comforted by words and gestures of others. In Lamentations, however, God is often addressed (1:9, 11, 20; 2:20; 3:55, 59, 61, 64; 5:1, 19, 21) but never responds. The different voices are on their own to reflect upon the reasons for the disaster. The poet and female Zion openly reveal their despair about God, whose punishment in their view is outrageous and out of proportion (1:12–15; 2:4–5, 11–13, 20–21). Simultaneously, the communal voice contemplates more on human transgressions and even articulates statements of repentance (3:40–47; 4:17–22). Since there is no divine answer in the poems, and no statement of confidence on behalf of the mourners, the book as a whole ends in the open question of whether God has utterly rejected his people (5:22).[20]

---

18. For an assessment of ancient Near Eastern and Israelite mourning rites, see Xuan Huong Thi Pham, *Mourning in the Ancient Near East and the Hebrew Bible* (JSOTSup 302; Sheffield: Sheffield Academic Press, 1999), 16–35. That a dirge may assume a political function in naming the perpetrator or aggressor is attested in lament songs emanating from the wars in Bosnia, Darfur, and other places, which have been collected by Nancy C. Lee, *Lyrics of Lament: From Tragedy to Transformation* (Minneapolis: Fortress, 2010).

19. Nancy C. Lee (*The Singers of Lamentations: Cities under Siege, from Ur to Jerusalem to Sarajevo* [Biblical Interpretation 60; Leiden: Brill, 2002], 53–73), argues for a female poet uttering laments in Jer 4, 8, and 10.

20. Lamentations 5:22 is difficult to translate. A reading as conditional statement without an apodosis is suggested by Linafelt (*Surviving Lamentations*, 60–61). Linafelt reviews the different proposals in "The Refusal of a Conclusion in the Book of Lamentations," *JBL* 120 (2001): 340–43.

Verbalizing pain and telling one's story of suffering often has a cathartic and healing effect.[21] Thus Zion's crying can be understood as an attempt at self-consolation. The wailing body of female Zion signifies both the grief of the suffering individuals and the protest of the survivors against the massiveness of pain and desolation. The disappointment over God, who seemed to be the agent of the disaster, brings the citizens and their city closer together.

Nevertheless, the missing divine response to the laments marks an open wound in the collective memory, which needs to be treated somewhere. About fifty years after the destruction of Jerusalem, an unnamed prophet directly answers Zion's laments by arguing that God chooses to renew the relationship with his city.[22] His message has been collected in Isa 40–55. The prophet announces comfort for the beaten people and the end of misery for Jerusalem (40:1–2). Chapters 49–55 especially describe a renewed relationship between God and Jerusalem, which manifests itself in the re-emergence of Zion's children (49:22–23).

By comparing the relationship between God and Zion to one between a mother and her infant, Isa 49:15 refers back to Zion's compassion for her children in Lam 1:16 and states that God's love is even greater than human love. God's love is so great that he promises the immediate rebuilding of the city and the return of her exiled population. In Isa 54:1–5 the unnamed prophet also announces the resurrection of female Jerusalem from the dust, her adornment as queen, and her rebuilding as a splendid city:

> Sing, O barren one who did not bear;
> burst into song and shout, you who have not been in labor!
> For the children of the desolate woman will be more
> than the children of her that is married, says the LORD.
> Enlarge the site of your tent,

---

21. Heim, "Personification of Jerusalem," 141. For a modern, contemporary example of such a process in Kurdistan, see Kimberley W. Segall, "Lamenting the Dead in Iraq and South Africa: Transitioning from Individual Trauma to Collective Mourning Performances," in Lee and Mandolfo, *Lamentations in Ancient and Contemporary Contexts*, 177–94, esp. 184–85.

22. The idea that Second Isaiah responds to Lamentations is already attested in midrashic writings and rabbinic commentaries (see Linafelt, *Surviving Lamentations*, 63–64). For a detailed analysis of Second Isaiah's answers to Lamentations, see Patricia Tull Willey, *Remember the Former Things: The Recollection of Previous Texts in Second Isaiah* (SBLDS 161; Atlanta: Scholars Press, 1997).

and let the curtains of your habitations be stretched out;
do not hold back; lengthen your cords
and strengthen your stakes.
For you will spread out to the right and to the left,
and your descendants will possess the nations
and will settle the desolate towns.
Do not fear, for you will not be ashamed;
do not be discouraged, for you will not suffer disgrace;
for you will forget the shame of your youth,
and the disgrace of your widowhood you will remember no more.
For your Maker is your husband,
the LORD of hosts is his name;
the Holy One of Israel is your Redeemer,
he God of the whole earth he is called.

The former inhabitants of the city, whether living in the ruins, in surrounding towns, or in exile, can perceive Zion in her new motherly role: she has to enlarge her tents, make room for the home-coming children, and provide them with food and shelter. The anticipated restoration of the city provides positive place-relations for both individuals and the community.

The fact that these oracles of salvation announce a new relationship of God to the city and her populace demonstrates that the female personification of Jerusalem was perceived as a powerful symbol. Thus the image of female Zion has effectively connected the exiled people to their city of origin and revived the spirit of those who have lived in the city's ruins for decades.

4. The Survival of Literature

After the rebuilding of Jerusalem's temple in 520–515 B.C.E. and its city walls in the mid-fifth-century (see Neh 2–7), Lamentations was not erased from the collective memory but served as a constant reminder that the city and its sanctuary depend on God's mercy. The destruction of the Second Temple by the Romans in 70 C.E. invigorated the collective memory of pain and suffering. The ritual of Tisha b'Av with its recitation of all five poems of lament not only commemorates the destruction of Jerusalem in 586 B.C.E. and 70 C.E. but also invigorates the strong connection of the Jewish people to Jerusalem as a space bestowed with divine presence. Thus the female roles of Jerusalem in these laments most efficiently shape the place-relations of Jewish inhabitants in the collective memory. It is no coincidence that the ancient Western wall of the temple precinct is called the Wailing Wall.[23] The Wailing Wall is a symbol of mourning over the loss of the temple—a symbol that gains its significance from the figure of the weeping city in Lamentations.

Besides written poems and laments about the destruction of Jerusalem's temple and city, there must have been a strong oral tradition of commemorating the collective disaster. Although we have no knowledge of this tradition today, analogous processes can be traced in the war zones of our times, in Croatia and Bosnia–Herzegovina in the 1990s or later in Iraq and South Africa. Laments from the former Balkan states found their way into English academic books about trauma and Lamentations.[24] For the latter two countries, Kimberly W. Segall offers striking descriptions of how Kurds and Xhosa were able to transform individual trauma to collective mourning by rituals of lament and public performances.[25]

What role New Orleans will play in the collective memory of the United States in fifty or one hundred years remains to be seen. As we live in a multimedia world, our memory will certainly not only depend on texts but also on pictures, videos, sounds, and music. The smoldering towers of the World Trade Center are already burnt into our mind.[26] Lamentations as part of the collective memory of Jews and Christians is not only significant because it provides powerful laments about a loss of space experienced 2600 years ago. These five laments also shape the imagination of lost space more generally. In her commentary on Lamentations, Kath-

---

23. Jacob Auerbach, Dan Bahat, and Shaked Gilboa, "Western Wall," *EncJud* 21:24–27.

24. In *Singers of Lamentations*, Lee included laments of Croatian and Bosnian women in her interpretation of texts from the biblical book of Lamentations. She published English translations of poems from the Croatian poet Borislav Arapović in *Between Despair and Lamentation* (expanded edition; ed. Nancy C. Lee; trans. Ivana Pozajić Jerić; Elmhurst, Ill.: Elmhurst College, 2002). A selection of these poems also appears in Lee and Mandolfo, *Lamentations in Ancient and Contemporary Contexts*, 163–76.

25. See Segall, "Lamenting the Dead," 177–94.

26. See the collection of pictures, comments, and explanatory texts compiled by photographers and journalists of the New York Times about the collapse of the World Trade Center and the event's political aftermath in *A Nation Challenged: A Visual History of 9/11 and Its Aftermath* (ed. Nancy C. Lee, Lonnie Schlein, and Mitchel Levitas; New York: The New York Times/Callaway, 2002).

leen O'Connor rightly points out that modern readers of these texts who are afflicted by personal suffering can "enter a poetic space that, no matter how distant from our own lives, has strange capacities for assurance and companionship."[27]

In a recent collection of articles there is a poem of Clyde Fant entitled "A Lament for New Orleans," which interweaves the language of the book of Lamentations with the experience of inhabitants of New Orleans who suffered from Katrina and especially from the belated and misguided actions of politicians and relief organizations in the storm's aftermath.[28] It demonstrates both the significance of biblical lament terminology and the persistence of a genre that preserves unofficial views of historical events and will eventually enrich the cultural memory of U.S. citizens. In order to preserve another voice of a New Orleans poet, I close my deliberations on the interrelation between lost space and revived memory with some lines from the poem "Memorial" by Megan Burns:

> a tide of rising songs
> if it goes if we go if we all go
> if a barge slips into a concrete wall
> does anyone recall the sound
> not one free piece of land ever given
> for any small animal to make its way
> you will never be okay again
> the face down faceless floaters
> who are a nameless memory of my city
> gone underground[29]

BIBLIOGRAPHY

Albertz, Rainer. *Israel in Exile: The History and Literature of the Sixth Century B.C.E.* Translated by David Green. SBLStBL 3. Atlanta: Society of Biblical Literature, 2003.

Arapović, Borislav. *Between Despair and Lamentation.* Edited by Nancy C. Lee. Translated by Ivana Pozajić Jerić. Expanded ed. Elmhurst, Ill.: Elmhurst College, 2002.

---

27. Kathleen M. O'Connor, *Lamentations and the Tears of the World* (Maryknoll, N.Y.: Orbis, 2002), 3.

28. Clyde Fant, "A Lament for New Orleans," in Lee and Mandolfo, *Lamentations in Ancient and Contemporary Contexts*, 215–17.

29. Megan Burns, *Memorial + Sight Lines* (New Orleans: Lavender Ink, 2008), 26.

Assmann, Jan. "Kollektives Gedächtnis und kulturelle Identität." Pages 9–19 in *Kultur und Gedächtnis*. Edited by Jan Assmann and Tonio Hölscher. STW 724. Frankfurt: Suhrkamp, 1988.

———. *Das kulturelle Gedächtnis: Schrift, Erinnerung und politische Identität in frühen Hochkulturen.* 5th ed. Munich: C. H. Beck, 2005.

———. *Religion and Cultural Memory: Ten Studies.* Translated by R. Livingstone. Stanford: Stanford University Press, 2006.

Auerbach, Jacob, Dan Bahat, and Shaked Gilboa. "Western Wall." *EncJud* 21:24–27.

Burns, Megan. *Memorial + Sight Lines.* New Orleans: Lavender Ink, 2008.

Dobbs-Allsopp, Frederick W. *Lamentations.* IBC. Louisville: Westminster John Knox, 2002.

———. "R(az/ais)ing Zion in Lamentations 2." Pages 21–68 in *David and Zion: Biblical Studies in Honor of J. J. M. Roberts.* Edited by Bernard F. Batto and Kathryn L. Roberts. Winona Lake, Ind.: Eisenbrauns, 2004.

Dobbs-Allsopp, Frederick W., and Tod Linafelt. "The Rape of Zion in Thr 1,10." *ZAW* 113 (2001): 77–81.

Fant, Clyde. "A Lament for New Orleans." Pages 215–17 in *Lamentations in Ancient and Contemporary Contexts.* Edited by Nancy C. Lee and Carleen Mandolfo. SBLSymS 43. Atlanta: Society of Biblical Literature, 2008.

Hayes, John H. "The Tradition of Zion's Inviolability." *JBL* 82 (1963): 419–26.

Heim, Knut M. "The Personification of Jerusalem and the Drama of Her Bereavement in Lamentations." Page 129–69 in *Zion, City of Our God.* Edited by Richard S. Hess and Gordon J. Wenham. Grand Rapids: Eerdmans, 1999.

Lee, Nancy C. *Lyrics of Lament: From Tragedy to Transformation.* Minneapolis: Fortress, 2010.

———. *The Singers of Lamentations: Cities under Siege, from Ur to Jerusalem to Sarajevo.* Biblical Interpretation 60. Leiden: Brill, 2002.

Lee, Nancy C., Lonnie Schlein, and Mitchel Levitas, eds. *A Nation Challenged: A Visual History of 9/11 and its Aftermath.* Introduction by Howell Raines. New York: The New York Times/Callaway, 2002.

Linafelt, Tod. "The Refusal of a Conclusion in the Book of Lamentations." *JBL* 120 (2001): 340–43.

———. *Surviving Lamentations: Catastrophe, Lament, and Protest in the Afterlife of a Biblical Book.* Chicago: University of Chicago Press, 2000.

Maier, Christl M. "Body Space as Public Space: Jerusalem's Wounded Body in Lamentations." Pages 119–38 in *Constructions of Space II: The Biblical City and Other Imagined Spaces.* Edited by Jon L. Berquist and Claudia V. Camp. LHBOTS 490. New York: T&T Clark, 2008.

———. *Daughter Zion, Mother Zion: Gender, Space, and the Sacred in Ancient Israel.* Minneapolis: Fortress, 2008.

Mintz, Alan. "The Rhetoric of Lamentations and the Representations of Catastrophe." *Proof* 2 (1982): 1–17.

O'Connor, Kathleen M. *Lamentations and the Tears of the World.* Maryknoll, N.Y.: Orbis, 2002.

Ollenburger, Ben C. *Zion, the City of the Great King: A Theological Symbol of the Jerusalem Cult.* JSOTSup 41. Sheffield: Sheffield Academic Press, 1987.

Pham, Xuan Huong Thi. *Mourning in the Ancient Near East and the Hebrew Bible.* JSOTSup 302. Sheffield: Sheffield Academic Press, 1999.

Segall, Kimberley W. "Lamenting the Dead in Iraq and South Africa: Transitioning from Individual Trauma to Collective Mourning Performances." Pages 177–94 in *Lamentations in Ancient and Contemporary Contexts.* Edited by Nancy C. Lee and Carleen Mandolfo. SBLSymS 43. Atlanta: Society of Biblical Literature, 2008.

Tull Willey, Patricia. *Remember the Former Things: The Recollection of Previous Texts in Second Isaiah.* SBLDS 161. Atlanta: Scholars Press, 1997.

Westermann, Claus. *Lamentations: Issues and Interpretation.* Translated by C. Muenchow. Minneapolis: Fortress, 1994.

Williamson, Robert, Jr. "Lament and the Arts of Resistance: Public and Hidden Transcripts in Lamentations 5." Pages 67–80 in *Lamentations in Ancient and Contemporary Contexts.* Edited by Nancy C. Lee and Carleen Mandolfo. SBLSymS 43. Atlanta: Society of Biblical Literature, 2008.

Ydit, Meir. "Av, the Ninth of." *EncJud* 2:714–16.

Rebuilding That Wicked City:
How the Destruction, Exile, and Restoration of New Orleans Elucidates Judah in the Sixth and Fifth Centuries b.c.e.

Michael M. Homan

1. Introduction

My professional work as a Hebrew Bible scholar often focuses on the destruction of Jerusalem at the hands of the Babylonian army in 586 B.C.E. Without this tragedy, and the subsequent fight for cultural survival as Judeans restored their city, there would not be a Hebrew Bible.

As depicted in the books of Ezra and Nehemiah, rebuilding Jerusalem in the sixth century B.C.E. proved to be a very difficult task. For fifty years the leading families of Judah had been in exile in Babylon. Then, with the Persian victory over the Babylonians in 539 B.C.E., and the edict of Cyrus the following year, many former Jerusalemites and their descendants regained hope, and some brave and committed individuals set off to rebuild Jerusalem. They would do their best to preserve and reinvent their pre-exilic culture. Not everyone supported their plan, however. A Persian official named Rehum dictated a letter to King Artaxerxes informing him that the Jews had gone to Jerusalem and, in his words, "they are rebuilding that rebellious and wicked city." Once its walls are complete, "they will not pay tribute, custom, or taxes, and the royal income will be impaired" (Ezra 4:12–13). Of course this hurdle and many others were overcome in time, and the city's infrastructure and even Yhwh's temple were rebuilt, though many who had seen the original temple cried when they witnessed the restored version (Ezra 3:12), presumably because it failed in comparison to the illustrious grandeur of its predecessor.

The rebuilding of Jerusalem was not limited to the city's walls and structures; the culture had to be restored as well. Most of the exiled chose to stay in Babylon, which housed the largest Jewish community for several centuries.[1] But those who returned sought to reconnect with their ancestral traditions. Their efforts may be seen as culminating in the dramatic story of Ezra reading the Torah to the entire community in the square before the Water Gate (Neh 8:1–12). Although their city had not completely recovered at that point, the community had passed an important milestone. Not surprisingly, they marked the achievement with celebrations (Neh 8:9–12).

For the past five years, my personal work has focused on a parallel topic. For those of us living in New Orleans, our world changed on August 29, 2005, when a storm surge from Hurricane Katrina breached the city's poorly constructed levee system in fifty-three places, killing two thousand people and inundating 80 percent of the city with water, which remained for weeks. Rebuilding the city these past five years has been incredibly difficult, due to poor communication, a corrupt, inept government, and a deep and widespread hatred of New Orleans by many people, their behavior not unlike Rehum's. I remained in my New Orleans house during the storm and stayed in my flooded neighborhood for a week, witnessing the complete breakdown of civilization. Due to problems with our insurance company, it took us three long years to rebuild our house, and during that time I also have participated in the restoration of my university (Xavier University of Louisiana in New Orleans), my neighborhood (Mid-City), and the metropolis itself. Many of these events parallel the tragedy of the destruction of Jerusalem in 586 B.C.E., such as exile, theodicy, and the long process of rebuilding documented in Ezra and Nehemiah. Many forces are trying to assimilate the unique culture of New Orleans as we rebuild. But like Ezra and Nehemiah, many of the citizens of New Orleans are fighting to both document and restore our cultural heritage.

---

1. Rainer Albertz, *Israel in Exile: The History and Literature of the Sixth Century BCE* (trans. David Green; SBLSBL 3; Atlanta: Society of Biblical Literature, 2003), 4–38.

2. The Destruction of New Orleans
and the Collapse of Civilization

I remained in my house as the eye of Hurricane Katrina hit land early on August 29, 2005. After the winds died down around noon, my neighbors and I chatted about how we dodged another bullet. But slowly that day, and mysteriously, the water kept rising, until by midnight it had entered all of our homes. Daily during the following week I would venture out of my house and explore my neighborhood either by swimming or by riding in a boat. During that time, I witnessed some amazing acts of charity, such as people canoeing around the neighborhoods bringing food and health-care supplies to people and animals. But during that time I also saw the complete breakdown of civilization. I witnessed terrified people commit violent acts against strangers. I vividly remember one member of the Arkansas National Guard in a boat who was terrified and obviously not used to seeing the cultural diversity of which most New Orleanians are so proud. He was screaming racial slurs and pointing his gun at a woman who was crying frantically as she held her infant child above her head. One of my neighbors was orphaned. She was eight years old at the time, and her mother drowned while holding her daughter's hand. Further down-town, addicts hunting medication had besieged the hospitals.[2] One of my students saw his grandmother for the last time as she was evacuated from the Convention Center by helicopter. He assumes that she passed away, though nobody has ever found her body. The remains of eighty-one indi-viduals, never identified or claimed, are buried in a memorial crypt near my house.[3]

After a week in the flooded city, I accompanied my dogs out of New Orleans and met my family in Jackson, Mississippi. We drove to Nebraska, where we lived for five months. There I first posted my account of what happened during that crazy week, and thanked everyone for their con-cern.[4] I received many supportive emails. One that I remember best was

---

2. Jed Horne, *Breach of Faith: Hurricane Katrina and the Near Death of a Great American City* (New York: Random House, 2006), 85.

3. Laura Maggi, "Katrina Dead Interred at New Memorial." Online: http://www.nola.com/news/index.ssf/2008/08/katrina_dead_interred_at_new_m.html.

4. Michael Homan, "One of the Millions of Hurricane Katrina Stories." Online: http://michaelhoman.blogspot.com/2005/09/one-of-millions-of-hurricane-katrina.html.

from William Propp, my Ph.D. mentor at the University of California, San Diego. He wrote:

> Mike,
> When you were incommunicado, I thought about you every fifteen minutes. When I was told you were trapped in your house, I still thought about you four times an hour. I relaxed when I heard you were safe. But I finally read your blog yesterday; I cannot imagine what you've been through. All the great tragedies of history must be real for you in a way I hope I never know.
> I feel a strong desire to hear your voice. Please send me your phone number and good times to call.
> Yours,
> Bill

I was intrigued by his reference to historical tragedies. I did not lose a family member in the flood, and I would, of course, not want to have experienced firsthand the fall of a city to the Babylonian army. Yet, the experience of witnessing the flood and the subsequent events has made the biblical story of the destruction of Jerusalem more tangible to me, and that has made me a better teacher.

3. By the Rivers of Baton Rouge, Houston, and Mobile: New Orleans in Exile

On August 27, 2005, the residents of New Orleans woke up to the dire news that Hurricane Katrina's course had shifted west and now the massive storm was heading toward the city. Given that there was only a two-day window in which to make arrangements and leave, it is astonishing that about 80 percent of the city's population of 1.3 million evacuated their homes.[5] As news of the breach in the levees and images of their city under water reached evacuees, it slowly became clear that New Orleanians and residents of the Gulf Coast, who had planned to be away from home for just a couple of days, were now going to be without homes for a prolonged period of time. More than one million people, including fifty thousand primary and secondary school students, were redistributed across the nation, making this the largest diaspora in the history of the United

---

5. Aaron Brown, "Hurricane Katrina Pummels Three States." Online: http://transcripts.cnn.com/TRANSCRIPTS/0508/29/asb.01.html.

States.[6] The Red Cross estimated nearly four hundred thousand Hurricane Katrina refugees were in shelters, hotels, homes and other housing in nearly forty states.[7] An estimated two hundred and fifty thousand to three hundred thousand people from the New Orleans area moved to Texas.[8] Many of them had criminal records.[9] Houston's population rose by thirty-five thousand and with this, Houston officials blamed Katrina evacuees for a reported 50-percent rise in crime.[10] This statistic has more recently been debunked, and most now agree that the evacuees only had a modest impact on the crime rate.[11] In addition to Houston, Mobile's population grew by twenty-four thousand, and Baton Rouge's by fifteen thousand. In fact, the African American student population at Louisiana State University in Baton Rouge doubled, causing racial tensions on campus.[12] Though far to the north, Chicago received six thousand evacuees.[13] Hammond, Louisiana received more than ten thousand people, doubling its size. By July of 2006, the U.S. Census showed that the overall population of the state of Louisiana declined nearly 5 percent.[14] While on the one hand residents of the cities in which New Orleanians sought refuge complained

---

6. Anthony E. Ladd, John Marszalek, and Duane A. Gill, "The Other Diaspora: New Orleans Student Evacuation Impacts and Responses Surrounding Hurricane Katrina" (paper presented at the Southern Sociological Society, New Orleans, March 22–26, 2006), 2.

7. Susan Moyer, *Katrina: Stories of Rescue, Recovery, and Rebuilding in the Eye of the Storm* (Champaign, Ill.: Spotlight Press, 2005), 108.

8. Alex Sanz, "Nagin: Count Houston Katrina Evacuees as New Orleans Residents in Census," Online: http://www.khou.com/news/local/Nagin-Houstons-Katrina-evacuees-as-New-Orleans-residents-in-Census-83665532.html.

9. Elizabeth Schubert, "Some Katrina Evacuees at Camp Dawson Have Criminal Records." Online: http://wboy.com/story.cfm?func=viewstory&storyid=5266.

10. Cathy Booth Thomas, "Katrina's Latest Casualty." Online: http://www.time.com/time/nation/article/0,8599,1154134,00.html.

11. Sean P. Varano et al., "A Tale of Three Cities: Crime and Displacement After Hurricane Katrina," *Journal of Criminal Justice* 38 (2010): 42–50.

12. Conisha Holloman, "The 'Class of Katrina' Moves Past Emotional Chapter." Online: http://www.npr.org/templates/story/story.php?storyId=104001215.

13. Mema Ayi, "Katrina Evacuees at Home in Chicago." Online: http://findarticles.com/p/news-articles/chicago-defender/mi_8097/is_20060830/katrina-evacuees-home-chicago/ai_n50616712/?tag=content;col1.

14. Les Christie, "Growth States: Arizona Overtakes Nevada: Texas Adds Most People Overall; Louisiana Population Declines Nearly 5%." Online: http://money.cnn.com/2006/12/22/real_estate/fastest_growing_states/index.htm.

about crime and crowding at schools, stores, and streets, on the other hand officials from these cities aggressively recruited our teachers, police officers, and other trained professionals. San Antonio even tried to steal one of our greatest cultural assets, the New Orleans Saints.[15]

Today New Orleans is decidedly smaller than it was prior to the flood. Population estimates for the city vary from 255,000 to 337,000, representing only 55 to 65 percent of the preflood population.[16] Traditional means of calculating populations through mail delivery and utility use fail here, since people are at various stages of rebuilding and many now use only cell phones. A large percentage of the city's residents lack funding needed to repair their homes. Even today, nearly fifty thousand properties remain in ruins.[17]

As in the aftermath of the edict of Cyrus, not all the city's former inhabitants have returned. Most stayed away and have gradually, though in some cases reluctantly, assimilated. Many cite education as the reason they stayed in their host cities. New Orleanian students in the Texas school systems improved dramatically on standardized test scores in a three-year period.[18] One of our family's closest friends, Lisa M., now lives with her husband Mike and two daughters in Houston, Texas. Prior to the flood, every Sunday they would gather at the home of Mike's mother, with aunts, uncles, cousins, and siblings for a large social gathering of approximately forty people. Now, five years later, this extended family has scattered to seven different states. Lisa and Mike miss New Orleans deeply, but they are not coming back; they claim that Texas has more to offer their daughters who are in public schools. The girls fondly recall unique aspects of growing up in New Orleans, such as the Second Line parades and the spontaneous music. Yet their eyes get wide when describing the resources at their schools, including two swimming pools.

---

15. Associated Press, "Tagliabue, State Working to Keep Saints in Louisiana." Online: http://sports.espn.go.com/nfl/news/story?id=2208747.

16. Coleman Warner, "New Orleans Head Count Gains Steam." Online: http://www.nola.com/news/t-p/frontpage/index.ssf?/base/news-8/1186642536113410.xml&coll=1.

17. Michelle Krupa, "New Orleans Blight Problem Is Too Complex for a One-Size-Fits-All Remedy, Group Says." Online: http://www.nola.com/politics/index.ssf/2010/11/one-size-fits-all_approach_won.html.

18. Brian Thevenot, "Study: Katrina's Exiles Thrived in Texas Schools." Online: http://www.texastribune.org/texas-education/public-education/study-katrinas-exiles-thrived-in-texas-schools/.

4. THEODICY AND SOUR GRAPES FOLLOWING DISASTERS

For some authors of the Hebrew Bible, disasters are readily explained as divine retribution for sin, handed down from a just God. Such is the case for the Deuteronomistic Historian (DtrH), who claims that YHWH used the Assyrians as his instrument when he destroyed Israel for their religious infidelity (2 Kgs 17:7–23). Similarly, DtrH blames the destruction of Jerusalem in 586 B.C.E. on the reigning king, Zedekiah, for "doing evil in the eyes of YHWH" (2 Kgs 24:19). However, it was the rule of Manasseh, more than a century earlier, which ultimately caused YHWH to employ the Babylonians to destroy Jerusalem and the temple. For DtrH, Manasseh's engagement with a wide variety of religious practices (2 Kgs 21:1–18) doomed his kingdom of Judah to a violent destruction many years later (2 Kgs 23:26–27; 24:3–4). While the book of Jeremiah also appears to adhere to a direct cause-effect relationship between disaster and sin, it seems to be uncomfortable with the move to blame the destruction of Jerusalem on a king who reigned five generations earlier. Consequently, Jeremiah argues that God would have spared Jerusalem if there had been one righteous person living within the city's walls (Jer 5:1). Moreover, Jeremiah longs for a day when people are held accountable for their own actions, and not plagued by the "sins of the fathers." To quote a central passage:

> In those days people will no longer say, "The parents eat sour grapes, and the children's teeth set on edge." Instead, everyone will die for their own sin; whoever eats sour grapes, their own teeth will be set on edge (Jer 31:29–30).

Thus Jeremiah predicts a paradisiacal time when the "sins of the fathers" no longer negatively impact a society. Not all biblical authors maintain the direct causal relationship between behavior and disaster. Some biblical writers, including the authors of Habakkuk, Job, and Jonah, seem to argue that bad things can happen to good people, though humans are not capable of understanding why.[19]

---

19. See Habakkuk's question to YHWH in 1:2–4, and the deity's vague answer in 2:2–20. Job maintains his innocence and questions God (Job 23–31), and he is answered by God in chapters 38–41 ("where were you when I laid the foundation of earth?," implying that humans cannot comprehend God's motives and actions). Throughout Jonah, the main character questions God's instructions and decision not

Answers to questions of theodicy following the destruction of New Orleans mirror answers provided for the collapse of Jerusalem more than 2500 years previously. Yet whereas biblical authors focused on a monarch's tolerance for Canaanite religion, some of the earliest voices responding to the devastation of New Orleans blamed the practice of abortion. Even as Hurricane Katrina was making landfall, an organization called "Columbia Christians for Life" issued a statement claiming that the images of the hurricane resembled the image of a six-week-old fetus and implied that God was sending the hurricane because "Louisiana has 10 child-murder-by-abortion centers, and five are in New Orleans."[20] Similarly, Pat Robertson, two weeks later on the Christian Broadcasting Network, proclaimed that the destruction must be viewed as God's wrath in response to the nation's abortion policy.[21] Other commentators who interpreted the flood as divine judgment added to abortion the annual gay pride parade known as "Southern Decadence."[22] Fox News host Bill O'Reilly claimed that instead of God's wrath, the disaster was a wound self-inflicted by African Americans. He stated on his show:

> So every American kid should be required to watch videotape of the poor in New Orleans and see how they suffered, because they couldn't get out of town. And then, every teacher should tell the students, "If you refuse to learn, if you refuse to work hard, if you become addicted, if you live a gangsta-life, you will be poor and powerless just like many of those in New Orleans."[23]

Politicians openly called for the city of New Orleans to be destroyed. Speaker of the House Dennis Hastert stated forty-eight hours after the levee breach that much of the city should be "bulldozed" and that it made

---

to harm the Assyrians. God chastises Jonah for caring about a plant for which he did not labor, implying that God, the creator of everything, is likewise free to choose.

20. T. G., "Is Katrina God's Punishment for Abortion?" Online: http://www.salon .com/news/politics/war_room/2005/08/30/hurricane.

21. J. B., "Religious Conservatives Claim Katrina Was God's Omen, Punishment for the United States." Online: http://mediamatters.org/research/200509130004.

22. Gary Hopkins, "US Fundamentalism: Hurricane Was God's Judgment on New Orleans." Online: http://www.ekklesia.co.uk/content/news_syndication/article_050831.shtml.

23. Michael Eric Dyson, *Come Hell or High Water: Hurricane Katrina and the Color of Disaster* (New York: Basic Civitas Books, 2006), 181.

little sense to rebuild a city where much of it lay below sea level.[24] This statement provoked an angry response from Louisiana Governor Kathleen Blanco, who said in a news conference: "To kick us when we're down and destroy hope, when hope is the only thing we have left, is absolutely unthinkable for a leader in his position." [25]

To be sure, we in New Orleans are plagued by the "sins of the fathers." Slavery, racism, corruption—all of these crimes of past generations have hindered recovery. Certainly the actions and inactions by the Army Corps of Engineers, whose employees built and periodically inspected the New Orleans levee system, impact us on a daily basis. Because of them, our teeth are still set on edge. But there is hope. Americans donated over half a billion dollars during the first week of the flood,[26] and many have been inspired by the tens of thousands of volunteers who have helped rebuild our city.[27]

5. Rebuilding a Culture

In Ezek 37, God shows the prophet a valley of dry bones and asks if the bones can live. The dead, symbolizing the nation of Israel, are, in fact revived. After flesh, muscle and skin attach to the bones, the deceased breathe and come back to life. God tells Ezekiel to tell the newly resurrected: "O my people, I am going to open your graves and bring you up from them; I will bring you back to the land of Israel (Ezek 37:12)." This symbolic prophecy became reality several decades later. As depicted in the books of Ezra and Nehemiah (see above), nearly fifty years after Jerusalem was destroyed, many returned from Babylonian exile and tried to rebuild their city. They faced bureaucratic hurdles from an ineffectual government, and had little support. However, during this period of exile and rebuilding, out of a fear of losing their culture, the people of Jerusalem worked hard to preserve their unique heritage, and one of the most precious products of their efforts was the Hebrew Bible.

---

24. Charles Babington, "Hastert Tries Damage Control after Remarks Hit a Nerve." Online: http://www.washingtonpost.com/wp-dyn/content/article/2005/09/02/AR200 5090202156.html.

25. Ibid.

26. Moyer, *Katrina: Stories of Rescue*, 74.

27. WDSU, "Volunteers Continue Work as Katrina Memories Fade." Online: http://www.wdsu.com/r/24703885/detail.html.

One way that my students have fought to preserve the unique cultural heritage of New Orleans involves collaboration with the non-profit organization Save Our Cemeteries.[28] For the past three years, students taking a course on biblical prophets have teamed up with Save Our Cemeteries to record the names on tombstones at St. Louis Cemetery No. 2. This project is designed to capture a moment in time, as many of the brick tombs and their engraved marble tombstones are rapidly deteriorating. In the process of transcribing texts, students learn a great deal of the history of New Orleans. They learn, for instance, about the Sisters of the Holy Family and its founder Henriette DeLille, who is a candidate for sainthood. Students see the names of victims of the yellow fever plague from the summer of 1853, when nearly 10 percent of the population was decimated. They learn about Dominique You the pirate, and Jordan Noble, the drummer in the Battle of New Orleans. They also see written evidence of our French and Spanish heritage. In transcribing the tomb information, the students are essentially giving new life to the New Orleanian dead.

As we rebuild, it is clear that the "New New Orleans" is different from its pre-Katrina ancestress. The population has clearly tended towards gentrification. Also, the racial makeup of the city has changed. Prior to the levee failure, New Orleans was approximately 70 percent African American. Early on, Bush's Secretary of Housing and Urban Development Alphonso Jackson predicted "New Orleans is not going to be as Black as it was for a long time, if ever again."[29] Large public housing developments were torn down and never rebuilt.[30] Estimates today place the African American population of New Orleans at about 60 percent.[31]

Two events stand out as important milestones for the restoration of New Orleans culture. The first was the reopening of the Superdome on

28. Save Our Cemeteries, http://www.saveourcemeteries.org/. See also Michael Homan, "Service Learning, Biblical Studies, and Resurrecting Flooded Bones in New Orleans," *Society of Biblical Literature Forum*, June 2009; idem, "Dry Bones Tell New Orleans Stories," *Times-Picayune*, Friday, April 16, 2010.

29. Brian Debose, "HUD Chief Foresees a 'Whiter' Big Easy." Online: http://www.washingtontimes.com/news/2005/sep/29/20050929-114710-8545r/.

30. Julia Cass and Peter Whoriskey, "New Orleans to Raze Public Housing." Online: http://www.washingtonpost.com/wp-dyn/content/article/2006/12/07/AR2006120701482.html.

31. Terri Lowenthal and Peter Montgomery, "The Changing Racial and Ethnic Landscape." Online: http://www.civilrights.org/publications/gulf-coast-census/race-ethnicity.html.

September 25, 2006. The pregame ceremony elicited a wide range of emotions, but it was the blocked punt recovered for a touchdown that registered as the climax of exhilaration. According to quarterback Drew Brees, "The crowd went nuts. It was the loudest one-time roar I have ever heard in a stadium. That moment served as a confirmation: this night belonged to New Orleans."[32] The impact of this event was recognized nationally, as it won the 2007 ESPY award for the greatest moment in sports. This scene of devastation, where approximately thirty-five thousand New Orleanians weathered the storm, was now a symbol for recovery. The celebrations may be compared to those described in Neh 8:9–12 (see above), marking the achievement of a major milestone in the rebuilding of Jerusalem.

The second important event was Mardi Gras 2006. Many, including the mayor of New Orleans, advised canceling Mardi Gras that year. They felt that celebrating in the wake of disaster was not appropriate, and images of the residents partying would not play well to the nation, when we desperately needed the nation's help to rebuild. But Mardi Gras rolled, as always, and it was very cathartic. People spoke about this Mardi Gras as being for the residents; it was something we needed. Some of the most politically creative floats paraded that year, many lampooning Michael Brown, FEMA, and other politicians who were hindering our recovery. In New Orleans today, the skeletons of our flooded homes are slowly acquiring flesh, muscle, and skin. As exiles return, our neighborhoods once again breathe healthily, and steadily we are coming back to life. Watching our residents work to rebuild the sacred places of our New Orleans, we are, like Ezekiel, filled with hope for our future.

6. Conclusions about Teaching Hebrew Bible in Post-Katrina New Orleans

In May of 2009, the Xavier students known as "the Katrina class" walked across the stage at graduation. I think about how brave both they and their parents were. They had been at the college only one week when the calls came to evacuate. Then after five months of videos and news about how devastated the city was, they found the courage to return to campus in January of 2006. It was truly inspiring.

---

32. Drew Brees, *Coming Back Stronger: Unleashing the Hidden Power of Diversity* (Carol Stream, Ill.: Tyndale, 2010), 163.

It has been a privilege to teach students about the Hebrew Bible in the years immediately after Hurricane Katrina. My students, especially those from the Gulf South, tell amazing stories about tragedy, exile, and rebuilding. These parallels have helped to get us through some tough moments. There is comfort from the awareness that we are neither alone nor unique in our struggles. There will always be individuals such as Rehum and Hastert who will question the rebuilding of destroyed cities. Tragic events are integral parts of all great cities, and these tragedies remembered often make cultural bonds and urban identities stronger.[33] Cultures can be resurrected from valleys of dry bones. One of my colleagues recalled that on the one-year anniversary of the flood, on a particularly bleak and hopeless day, she stood facing St. Louis Cathedral in Jackson Square. She realized that thousands of New Orleanians before her had stood in that same place over the past centuries and realized that they were ultimately going to get through these tough times. New Orleans, like Jerusalem before it, will survive.

Bibliography

Albertz, Rainer. *Israel In Exile: The History and Literature of the Sixth Century B.C.E.* Translated by David Green. SBLSBL 3. Atlanta: Society of Biblical Literature, 2003.

Associated Press. "Tagliabue, State Working to Keep Saints in Louisiana." Online: http://sports.espn.go.com/nfl/news/story? id=2208747.

Ayi, Mema. "Katrina Evacuees at Home in Chicago." Online: http://findarticles.com/p/news-articles/chicago- defender/mi_8097/is_20060830/katrina-evacuees-home-chicago/ai_n50616712/?tag=content;col.

Babington, Charles. "Hastert Tries Damage Control After Remarks Hit a Nerve." Online: http://www.washingtonpost.com/wp- dyn/content/article/2005/09/02/AR2005090202156.html.

Brees, Drew. *Coming Back Stronger: Unleashing the Hidden Power of Diversity.* Carol Stream, Ill.: Tyndale House, 2010.

Brown, Aaron. "Hurricane Katrina Pummels Three States." Online: http://transcripts.cnn.com/TRANSCRIPTS/0508/29/asb.01.html.

Cass, Julia and Peter Whoriskey. "New Orleans to Raze Public Housing." Online: http://www.washingtonpost.com/wp-dyn/content/article/2006/12/07/AR2006120701482.html.

33. Jacob L. Wright, "The Catastrophic Beginning of the People of Israel," *Azure* 42 (Autumn 2010): 83–101.

Christie, Les. "Growth States: Arizona Overtakes Nevada: Texas Adds Most People Overall; Louisiana Population Declines Nearly 5%." Online: http://money.cnn .com/2006/12/22/real_estate/fastest_growing_states/index.htm.

Cooper, Christopher, and Robert Block. *Disaster: Hurricane Katrina and the Failure of Homeland Security.* New York: Times Books, 2006.

Debose, Brian. "HUD Chief Foresees a 'Whiter' Big Easy." Online: http://www.washingtontimes.com/news/2005/sep/29/20050929-114710-8545r/.

Dyson, Michael Eric. *Come Hell or High Water: Hurricane Katrina and the Color of Disaster.* New York: Basic Civitas Books, 2006.

Holloman, Conisha. "The 'Class of Katrina' Moves Past Emotional Chapter." Online: http://www.npr.org/templates/story/story.php? storyId=104001215.

Homan, Michael. "Dry Bones Tell New Orleans Stories." Online: http://www.nola. com/opinions/index.ssf/2010/04/ dry_bones_tell_new_orleans_sto.html.

———. "One of the Millions of Hurricane Katrina Stories." Online: http://michaelhoman.blogspot.com/2005/09/one-of- millions-of-hurricane-katrina.html.

———. "Service Learning, Biblical Studies, and Resurrecting Flooded Bones in New Orleans." *Society of Biblical Literature Forum* (June 2009). Online: http://www .sbl-site.org/publications/article.aspx?articleId=822.

Hopkins, Gary. "US Fundamentalism: Hurricane Was God's Judgment on New Orleans." Online: http://www.ekklesia.co.uk/content/news_syndication/article_050831.shtml.

Horne, Jed. *Breach of Faith: Hurricane Katrina and the Near Death of a Great American City.* New York: Random House, 2006.

J. B. "Religious Conservatives Claim Katrina was God's Omen, Punishment for the United States." Online: http://mediamatters.org/research/200509130004.

Krupa, Michelle. "New Orleans Blight Problem Is Too Complex for a One-Size-Fits All Remedy, Group Says." Online: http://www.nola.com/politics/index.ssf/2010/11/ one-size-fits- all_approach_won.html.

Ladd, Anthony E., John Marszalek, and Duane A. Gill. "The Other Diaspora: New Orleans Student Evacuation Impacts and Responses Surrounding Hurricane Katrina." Paper presented at the Southern Sociological Society. New Orleans, March 22–26, 2006.

Lowenthal, Terri Ann, and Peter Montgomery. "The Changing Racial and Ethnic Landscape." Online: http://www.civilrights.org/publications/gulf-coast-census/ race-ethnicity.html.

Maggi, Laura. "Katrina Dead Interred at New Memorial." Online: http://www.nola. com/news/index.ssf/2008/08/ katrina_dead_interred_at_new_m.html.

Moyer, Susan. *Katrina: Stories of Rescue, Recovery, and Rebuilding in the Eye of the Storm.* Champaign, Ill: Spotlight, 2005.

Sanz, Alex. "Nagin: Count Houston Katrina Evacuees as New Orleans Residents in Census." Online: http://www.khou.com/news/local/Nagin-Houstons-Katrina-evacuees-as-New- Orleans-residents-in-Census-83665532.html.

Schubert, Elizabeth. "Some Katrina Evacuees at Camp Dawson Have Criminal Records." Online: http://wboy.com/story.cfm?func=viewstory&storyid=5266.

Thevenot, Brian. "Study: Katrina's Exiles Thrived in Texas Schools." Online: http://www.texastribune.org/texas-education/public-education/study-katrinas-exiles-thrived-in-texas-schools/.

Thomas, Cathy Booth. "Katrina's Latest Casualty." Online: http://www.time.com/time/nation/article/0,8599,1154134,00.html.

T. G. "Is Katrina God's Punishment for Abortion?" Online: http://www.salon.com/news/politics/war_room/2005/08/30/hurricane.

Varano, Sean P., Joseph A. Schafer, Jeffrey M. Cancino, Scott H. Decker and Jack R. Greene. "A Tale of Three Cities: Crime and Displacement After Hurricane Katrina." *Journal of Criminal Justice* 38 (2010): 42–50.

Warner, Coleman. "New Orleans Head Count Gains Steam." Online: http://www.nola.com/news/t-p/frontpage/index.ssf?/base/news-8/1186642536113410.xml&coll=1.

WDSU. "Volunteers Continue Work as Katrina Memories Fade." 2010. Online: http://www.wdsu.com/r/24703885/detail.html.

Wright, Jacob L. "The Catastrophic Beginning of the People of Israel." *Azure* 42 (Autumn 2010): 83–101.

Imagining Hope and Redemption: A Salvation Narrative among the Displaced in Sudan

M. Jan Holton

Imagine: You have fled the carnage and death of your homeland in the midst of a devastating war. You have narrowly escaped death but have witnessed the killing of those most precious to you. You may carry emotional wounds from grief and loss, and perhaps the added physical damage from shrapnel, rape, or other abuses. Now you find yourself exiled to a refugee camp in the desolate region of northern Kenya. The future is closed; your children are dead or lost, and home is reduced to an impossible dream. Hunger and insecurity surround you. The world does not seem to know or care about your suffering.

Imagine: One day you discover a book in which your story has already been written. It is the story of a people called Israel, a people who also knew deep suffering and were themselves driven from their homes into exile in a foreign land. But the story doesn't end with the despair and hopelessness you have come to fear it would. Rather, it ends in redemption and hope delivered by a God who never forgets nor forsakes—the same God to whom you have prayed these many long, dark days.

This essay focuses on a pastoral theological perspective on how the biblical account of the Babylonian exile (586 B.C.E.) has influenced the faith narrative of a community of Dinka refugees from South Sudan during their own time of suffering and displacement. The Dinka, one of the largest tribes in South Sudan, fled the civil war that, tragically, has come to define their homeland. They languished in exile, some for more than fifteen years, before a peace agreement was signed in 2005. I propose that for these devout Christians, the biblical narrative of the Babylonian exile is the scriptural foundation for their own salvation narrative, through which they claim their primary sense of agency, purpose, and hope.[1]

I have elsewhere defined Christian pastoral theology as the body of thought and practice that "largely, though not exclusively, tries to reconcile human experience, especially suffering, with the expectations of faith lived and revealed through the Christian tradition in light of the fragility and limitedness of the embodied human creature and the unyielding and unpredictable realities of the lived world toward an end of hope and meaning."[2] Methodologically, biblical studies and pastoral theology traditionally have different beginning points. Biblical studies begins, obviously, with the biblical text. From there one can take a number of different directions to expand upon its meaning. The most obvious of these include historical context and literary form, but also gender, psychology, and culture. Pastoral theology, on the other hand, starts by examining human experience through a multidisciplinary lens that includes theology, psychology, biblical studies, cultural studies, and others. Both methods are hermeneutical endeavors. Biblical studies interprets biblical texts, and pastoral theology interprets human experience in light of theological inquiry. Charles Gerkin, a pioneer in the field of pastoral theology, coined the phrase "living human document" to describe the primary object of focus in the field. Pastoral theologian Bonnie Miller-McLemore suggests that Gerkin ultimately "proposes a dialogical hermeneutical method of psychological and theological investigation of human experience as the primary text of pastoral theology."[3]

The disciplines of pastoral theology and biblical studies find common ground in indigenous African biblical hermeneutics. As we will see, traditional African methods of biblical interpretation bring the biblical text and human experience together into relationship with one another. Reflecting on each in light of the other is necessary to shaping the individual and

---

1. The notion of a salvation narrative at work within the Dinka community was first proposed in an earlier article, M. Jan Holton, "'Our Hope Comes from God': Faith Narratives and Resilience in Southern Sudan," *JPT* 20 (2010): 67–84.

2. M. Jan Holton, *Building the Resilient Community: Lessons from the Lost Boys of Sudan* (Eugene, Oreg.: Cascade, 2010), 3.

3. Bonnie Miller-McLemore, "The Living Human Web: Pastoral Theology at the Turn of the Century," in *Through the Eyes of Women: Insights into Pastoral Care* (ed. Jeanne Stevenson Moessner; Minneapolis: Augsburg Fortress, 1996), 9–26.

communal life of faith. Biblical scholar Knut Holter identifies this method as a comparative study that, he says,

> facilitates a parallel interpretation of certain Old Testament texts or motifs and supposed African parallels, letting them illuminate one another. Traditional exegetical methodology is of course found here, too; however, the Old Testament is approached from a perspective where African comparative material is the major dialogue partner and traditional exegetical methodology is subordinate to this perspective.[4]

This notion of *comparative material* is very often found in the life experience of the everyday African citizen; text moves beyond the written word to the practices and rituals of the community.[5]

1. Setting the Context: Sudan

A brief summary of the events in South Sudan will prove helpful. In 2005, the Comprehensive Peace Agreement between the Government of Sudan in Khartoum and the Sudanese People's Liberation Movement/Army (SPLM/A) of the South brought to a close two decades of civil war that killed over two million people and sent millions more into exile. The more recent genocide in Darfur, though not a part of this conflict, is notable for many reasons, not the least of which is how similar the tactics were to those used in the war with the South. Today, though a fragile peace holds between North and South Sudan, millions of southerners still remain displaced in refugee camps in neighboring countries. Those who have chosen to return to their homeland struggle to meet their basic needs for food, medicine, and shelter. Many have been resettled in countries around the world. Among these are a group formerly known as unaccompanied minors (ages five to fifteen) who were noteworthy for traveling together and surviving the flight from war and journey to the refugee camps largely without the aid of adults. At least ten thousand strong, they were given the name "the Lost Boys of Sudan" by aid agencies and the

---

4. Knut Holter, *Old Testament Research for Africa: A Critical Analysis and Annotated Bibliography of African Old Testament Dissertations, 1967–2000* (BTA 3; New York: Lang, 2002), 88.

5. J. N. K. Mugambi, "African Hermeneutics in a Global Context," in *Interpreting Classical Religious Texts in Contemporary Africa* (ed. Knut Holter; Nairobi: Acton, 2007), 14.

media.[6] In 2001, the United States declared these unaccompanied minors, now young men and some women (Lost Girls), to be a special population eligible for admittance and resettlement. As we will see shortly, the Lost Boys play a profound role in the narrative of exile and redemption that the Dinka have developed.

I first heard of this community and became interested in their plight while I was working with the Catholic Charities Refugee Resettlement Program during the spring of 2001, when sixty Lost Boys arrived for resettlement. In 2003, I traveled to Kakuma Refugee Camp, Kenya, to study the living conditions for refugees in the camp. The material for this essay was gleaned from ethnographic research in 2008 in Bor, Sudan, during which time I conducted interviews among the Abang community, a Dinka clan living near the Nile in Bor.[7] This region of South Sudan holds dual significance as a place of religious importance as well as one of great violence. South Sudan was largely converted to Christianity in the early twentieth century. Bor and the surrounding area are particularly important as one of the first missionary outposts and home to one of the first Sudanese to become an Anglican Bishop, Daniel Deng Atong. Today he is considered by some to be an early prophet who contributed to the spread of Christianity in South Sudan. Bor is also the site of one of the most notoriously violent attacks, known as the Bor Massacre, conducted by factions sympathetic to the Sudanese government, during which more than two thousand Dinka were killed. Later, during the war, Bor became an occupied territory. Because the Dinka are a community with deep roots in the Christian faith, and for whom grief and loss are in the fabric of their identity, it is not surprising that they would turn to the biblical narrative to make sense of the chaos and suffering that surround them.

2. Scripture and the Dinka

The first translation of the New Testament into the local Dinka language occurred in the early 1970s. Due to low literacy rates, however, oral transmission of the biblical narratives remains primary within many faith com-

---

6. The name "Lost Boys" allegedly refers to the young homeless boys in the children's tale by J. M. Barrie, *Peter Pan*.

7. This research was made possible by funding through the Lilly Theological Grants Program. All interviews for this article adhered to the protocol approved by the Human Subjects Committee of the Institutional Review Board at Yale University.

munities. The Old Testament has not yet been translated into Dinka. This presents a predicament for us as outsiders trying to understand the Dinka relationship to the Hebrew Scriptures. On the one hand, there is evidence that early foreign missionaries and even a few local Dinka were biblically and theologically trained, so they would have had access to Old Testament readings. On the other hand, we hear from many of the now grown Lost Boy refugees that it was not until the Dinka reached the churches of the refugee camps in the early 1990s that they discovered full translations of the Old Testament, though they were still in English. I suspect this merely reflects the missionary emphasis on the New Testament in their task of converting local communities. In these early days, stories from the Hebrew Scriptures, to whatever degree they were known, were simply overshadowed by the revelatory news of the New Testament. Once the Hebrew Scriptures were available and read in the context of the increased despair during war and displacement, their importance emerged, offering new insight and meaning through stories that were at once terrible and miraculous—stories of exodus, exile, and God's remarkable love for the Hebrew people.

To understand the power of the biblical narratives in this Sudanese refugee community, we will need to see beyond the historical-critical aspects of these texts. For example, in everyday discourse, refugees will speak of God's actions in the exodus and the exile as if they are bound together by a timeless thread. Certainly, the exodus motif recurs throughout both the Old and New Testaments in numerous places. The intertextual nature of the Dinkas' biblical appropriation shapes their understanding of their experience—God's acts of liberation and redemption are intended to be held together. To separate them based on mythical or historical particularities overlooks the providential power of God to bring good from evil and hope from suffering. I urge that we use caution before dismissing these perspectives as unsophisticated and simplistic. Wisdom derived from the religious experiences of the church in the world, and from her hurting people as they engage Scripture to make sense out of tragedy and despair, is profound and should not be sacrificed in favor of academic knowledge, even if only in the effort to enhance such wisdom.

The Dinka are a storied people who weave the narratives of their deep tribal traditions together with their daily life of both joy and struggle. They seek to make sense out of both by holding them up to the light of the biblical narrative. Much like the world in which they live, seldom do the stories come together in a neat and tidy manner. But this is, nevertheless, how they make meaning out of a sometimes senseless world. Pastoral theologian Andrew Lester, drawing upon narrative theory, proposes that the ability of individuals—and, I think, communities—to develop a future story is a sign of their capacity to hope.[8] Of hope, he says, "The deepest level of hope is an open-ended trusting stance toward existence that perceives a future horizon that transcends [our] finite hopes."[9] Lester goes on to point out the fundamental role of sacred stories to refocus our personal future stories in the context of the larger narrative of God's love and redemption. Even when we are in the midst of chaos, God is active, present, and always involved in moving us toward a hope-filled future abundant with meaning and possibility.[10]

The Dinka, and I would suggest most faith communities, approach Scripture as a lens through which to see their own circumstances and by which to discover how God is at work in the world—in their world. They appropriate the narratives of exodus and exile, for example, because they see their own suffering reflected in these stories. Though not a traditional Western academic approach to biblical interpretation, it is a common style of biblical hermeneutics for most African countries. Interestingly, Gerald West, a South African, and Holter, a Norwegian, are two Western-trained biblical scholars who give authority and voice to these otherwise little-recognized interpretive trends in Africa. As Holter aptly notes, indigenous African scholarship has largely been marginalized from participation in Western academic circles.[11] Consequently, mainstream Western scholarship is relatively unaware of common hermeneutical directions in African biblical scholarship. One of the most important aspects of indigenous African hermeneutics is the lack of distinct categories of secular and religious. In other words, there is no place in the everyday life of an African that is off limits to religious meaning. Religious meaning finds its way into every crevice of African life. Scholar D. R. K. Nkurunziza says, "[African hermeneutics] is destined towards maintaining and sustaining a coherent

---

8. Lester describes the concept of narrative theory as simply "a metaphor for conceptualizing the meaning-making nature of human beings, the process of making sense out of life's ongoing events" (Andrew Lester, *Hope in Pastoral Care and Counseling* [Louisville: Westminster John Knox, 1996], 5).

9. Ibid., 65.

10. Ibid., 69.

11. Knut Holter, *Yahweh in Africa: Essays on Africa and the Old Testament* (Bible and Theology in Africa 1; New York: Lang, 2000), 34.

understanding and living of reality. ... Interpretation is not something occurring in the past but something being lived in the present."[12]

An important task of pastoral theology is to examine the points where our personal and communal stories intersect with the sacred stories of Scripture. Admittedly, the field has a long history of shying away from the kind of comparative interpretation of Scripture that Holter identifies. There is no question that when misapplied, that is, imposed upon others from the outside instead of developing organically within a community, comparative interpretation can be damaging and oppressive. But the Dinka teach us how to recognize that our communal (and personal) experience is connected to a long history of God's people in the world. Their salvation narrative, rooted in their appropriation of the exile narrative of ancient Israel, helps them build a sense of *agency* by recognizing their own responsibilities and accountabilities in relationship with God's desires for them, build a sense of *purpose* by living out the ways these responsibilities and accountabilities call them to action, and, finally, create a *story for their future* that remains open to God's redemptive acts.

3. THE DINKA FAITH NARRATIVE

The Dinka have found their own story deeply embedded within the story of ancient Israel's exile in Babylon. Like Israel, the Dinka believe that God brought the war because South Sudan was unfaithful. The traditional religion of the Dinka centered upon the god known most commonly by the name Nhialic, who, as the creator god, reigned supreme above many other lesser gods. Especially in the early days of Christianity in this region, the Dinka easily merged the two supreme creator gods, Nhialic and YHWH, into one.[13] Even after Christianity began to blossom in the South, many

---

12. D. R. K. Nkurunziza, "African versus Western Hermeneutics," in Holter, *Interpreting Classical Religious Texts*, 32.

13. As with the Old Testament use of the Hebrew word *bara'*, my interviews suggest that the Dinka language also has a verb for creation that pertains exclusively to God. Humans have much power to do and make but not create (Holton, *Building the Resilient Community*, 139 n. 7). Kenyan theologian John Mbiti suggests that the Christian God brought by the missionaries was none other than the very creator God (known by many names throughout Africa); God had already revealed Godself to the African people (see John Mbiti, "Christian Faith and African Religion," in *Third World Liberation Theologies: A Reader* [ed. Deane William Ferm; Maryknoll, N.Y.: Orbis, 1986], 201).

continued to practice spiritual healing rituals and to call upon traditional gods in their time of need. This was especially the case in the many rural villages that dot the countryside of South Sudan.[14] Today, the God of creation remains a common image used among the Dinka and finds its way into the foundation of everyday theological thought. It is the God of creation who has the power both to bring boastful, oppressive nations to their knees and to bring up from the dust the broken and displaced. One refugee from Bor describes how being a part of God's community of creation binds him to ancient Israel and gives him hope: "[It] gives me spiritual hope that the God who created me helped the people in Israel a long time ago. I applied that to myself—he created them and he created me!"

As you will see in the following pages, my interviews reveal how the small Dinka Abang community near Bor, South Sudan, have internalized the narrative of ancient Israel's exile experience to the degree that it has brought meaning to their suffering and helped them form a future story marked by hope and redemption rather than suffering and despair. I have separated their salvation narrative as described to me into four sections: "Exile," which describes the Dinka flight from war and suffering into a foreign land; "Remnant," which reveals how the Dinka understand God's actions through the resettlement of a group of Dinka "children" who are destined to be the future of South Sudan; "Redemption," which describes how God worked through those believed to be Christian nations to bring peace to South Sudan and the beginning of a return for the exiles; and, finally, "Mount Zion," which describes a final moment of celebration for God's work of bringing freedom to South Sudan through the vote for independence.

3.1. Exile, or "Kok"

One Sudanese refugee describes the meaning of exile as being "chased away from my home town and seeking after safety in another country." The duration of one's absence and the distance one must flee are key elements for defining exile for the Dinka. One must go very far away and stay for a long time, says the refugee. The term "aba kok," or refugee, means "I am in exile." The refugees in Kakuma live in desperate conditions, conditions that nevertheless seem quite grand compared to how

---

14. Witchcraft and spiritual healing were also a deeply ingrained part of prewar Dinka life.

new arrivals fare during their first days. Arrivals are housed in open shed-type construction, each with a roof and half walls on three sides. The front is open. There are no separate rooms for privacy. Every family or individual must claim a corner and do the best they can. Latrines are sectioned to one end of the camp. Only then is a building with separate rooms constructed. But even this will only have three or four rooms, and it is being built with women especially in mind. For food, porridge is provided twice a day along with a protein source given at one of the two meals.[15]

The story of war in South Sudan is long and tragic. If we had had today's technology in 1990, we would have been frontline witnesses to the devastating tactics of war that left millions dead and millions more homeless. Much as in Darfur, where the same strategies of destruction were used, we would have heard stories of rape, murder, and kidnapping, villages burned, crops and cattle destroyed. As it was, only occasional reports broke through or made lead stories on the six o'clock news. Arial bombardments and attacks by government forces in tanks, and by armed militia on horseback, plagued the villages of the South. Men, women, and children were killed. Many children were abducted to be sold into slavery. As the bombs fell, southerners ran in every direction. Refugees fled to Ethiopia, Kenya, and Uganda, where the United Nations High Commissioner for Refugees (UNHCR) established refugee camps. Thousands poured over the border into Egypt, which requires no passport or visa for Sudanese citizens. Kakuma Refugee Camp in the northern desert of Kenya, less than one hundred kilometers over the border with Sudan, became a primary holding place for nearly 80,000 refugees, the majority of which were from Sudan. Few suspected that it would become a kind of purgatory in which the Sudanese would be forced to live in exile for more than a decade. I visited Kakuma in 2003. The following describes the general conditions in the camp:

> Here in Kakuma, the heat is brutal. Each breeze carries only swirling dust and little relief. … The grit of the dust and the smells of human waste are overwhelming. … Food rations were given yesterday—lines of children and adults whose stomachs have not known food for days. The portions of raw grains are meager but intended to last two weeks.

---

15. This excerpt is taken from my field notes recorded during a visit to Kakuma Refugee Camp, Kenya, in 2003.

Refugees say they will only last five days. Medicine is limited. Fourteen textbooks must be shared by 120 students. Water is rationed. There is not enough to drink, cook, and bathe. One must choose. To come now to this dry and desolate place seems to hold a grief all its own.[16]

This despairing place was a far cry from the fertile land near the Nile from which the Dinka Bor came and where they once grew crops and raised cattle.[17] One Sudanese refugee I interviewed reflected on this time in Kakuma Refugee Camp, saying,

The local people would rob us at night; we had no hope. There was a shortage of food and water; Sudan was far away. At that time we were suffering in Kenya. [But the preachers said] God was with Israel in Babylon; God will help. Something will happen. God is everywhere you go. One day God will give us something good.

3.2. A Remnant of Children

The preachers said: "It doesn't matter how far you go [from Sudan]." People didn't believe they would ever return; they believed they would be tied to their new countries [of resettlement]. But the preachers said, "Go to those places; don't forget your God who will bring you home." (Sudanese refugee)

Like the exiles in Babylon to whom Jeremiah wrote (Jer 29:4–9), the Dinka struggled to understand when God would bring them home from Kakuma and other refugee camps. When the option arose, as one refugee said, to "hand their children over to another country" for resettlement, perhaps for the rest of their lives, the issue became critical. Preachers preached, and elders fretted over the future of the children—the future of South Sudan. Echoing Jeremiah, the preachers said, "Go, build your homes—but don't forget your God. You will return."

In 2001, the United States was introduced to the Lost Boys of Sudan when the State Department, categorizing them as a *special population*, declared four thousand of the young men, and a few women, eligible for resettlement. The numbers of those declared to be special popula-

---

16. Holton, "Our Hope Comes from God," 74.
17. The Dinka Bor community comes from the Bor region of Sudan and is one of the ten subdivisions of the Dinka tribe (ibid., 8).

tion groups are above and beyond the annual limits for admittance to the United States set by the President each year. This was a tremendously significant event, not only in the lives of the Lost Boys/Girls but in their community as well. It is nearly miraculous when one considers that less than one percent of the world's fifteen million refugees will be resettled in another country. Certainly, they believed, God's hand must be at work in this.[18]

When they realized that so many of their young men (and a lesser number of young women) had been chosen, they recognized it as an extraordinary event. The refugees explain that they believed God had chosen to "save their children" so that through this remnant the future of South Sudan would live. But God would not take them by force. God required that the community make the choice; they must choose to "give their children to America."[19]

When word was received of an impending departure, elders attempted to prepare the youngsters. The boys were given practical and moral instruction that always ended with the mandate that God had given them a job. They were, above all, to remember their God, get an education, remember the needs of the community (clan), and one day return to help rebuild Sudan. One of these young men, now nearly thirty with children of his own, recalls that he was given an audiotape of the elders offering their instructions. He has kept this tape over the last ten years and listened to it often.

The Lost Boys have become a spiritual and economic resource for their clans and home villages. They have indeed *built their homes*. Many have not only completed high school degrees but have gone on to obtain associate or full college degrees. A few have even managed to pursue master's degrees. Monies sent home to family as remittances are used for food,

18. To give a closer point of reference, in 2001 the President of the United States set a limit of a mere 19,000 refugees from the entire continent of Africa who could be admitted for resettlement. Ten years later, those numbers have been reduced even further to a mere 15,000 (United States Department of State, United States Department of Homeland Security, and United States Department of Health and Human Services, *Proposed Refugee Admissions for Fiscal Year 2011: Report to the Congress*, submitted on behalf of the President of the United States to the Committees on the Judiciary, United States Senate and United States House of Representatives. Online: http://www.state.gov/documents/organization/148671.pdf).

19. Holton, "Our Hope Comes from God," 76.

medicine, and the purchase of cattle and other goods that serve to sustain a very fragile economy in South Sudan.

Though this often comes at great cost in terms of the social advancement (in American terms) for the young men, it is difficult to say no to pleas for assistance. In the words of one Lost Boy: "I need to help my people who are suffering, to give myself to them. Even though I haven't served in the war, I want to serve my people."

3.3. A Vision of Redemption

> Those who went to America are our hope from God—we have handed over their lives to God. ... Our peace came from God and our children who went to America. It is all His work. (Refugee from Bor)

> How beautiful upon the mountains are the feet of the messenger who announces peace, who brings good news, who announces salvation, who says to Zion, "Your God reigns." (Isa 52:7)

It is clear that the people still in Kakuma Refugee Camp, those who have been repatriated to South Sudan, and the Lost Boys are all waiting for God to bring the promised redemption. A refugee from Bor now living in the United States said, "When I talk to people back home, [they are] waiting for God to do his job. Some days I say, why does it take so long? But one day it will end; one day good things will happen." They understand, though, that it is not only God who has work to do. Preachers in Bor do not hold back on reminding the people that each person has his or her own job, even the very young and very old—none are exempt.[20]

As I have been working with these Sudanese for the last ten years, this narrative of redemption has continued to unfold, with each vision of redemption becoming more daring than the last. At first, it was to return to their homeland; then they dared to dream of peace. Development has begun to glimmer on the distant horizon. But none of these compares to the vision of a new independent nation called South Sudan. Each of these is a fundamental step for survival. These steps reflect that redemption in a war zone is an ever-evolving and never-finished notion.

To some degree, the Dinka have seen their visions of hope unfold into reality. In 2005, the Comprehensive Peace Agreement was signed, giving

---

20. Ibid., 80.

the South largely autonomous control over its own region and a representative to serve as Vice President in the national government. The Dinka understand God's hand to be at work in the peace accords through what they regard as a Christian nation (namely, the United States) who negotiated on their behalf. As we see in the quote that opens this section, God is working through the Lost Boys and through America: *Our peace came from God and our children who went to America. It is all His work.*

In 2005, refugees began the long process of repatriating to their home villages, and the southern government began the Herculean task of planning for the future. Life continues to be a great struggle. Intertribal violence, banditry, and the occasional resurgence of fighting on the front lines keep fear alive. Food, medicine, and the basic necessities of life are difficult to come by. But the people continue to believe that God will prevail.

The Dinka live in the realization that peace is not the same as freedom. In its most tangible form, redemption is what has become known simply as *the referendum*. The 2005 peace accord included a mandate—the referendum—to vote for the South's secession from North Sudan. The possibility of freedom created a great air of expectation in South Sudan that spread to Sudanese communities in the United States and elsewhere. Expatriate voting locations were set up in countries around the world, including the United States, to accommodate the large Sudanese communities that have settled there. Many of the Lost Boys deeply desired to return to Sudan for the historic vote. Bishop Nathaniel Garrang, a prominent religious leader from Bor, has long been a spiritual guide for the Lost Boys, visiting them to check on their well-being several times since their resettlement ten years ago. In his latest cross-country tour, he encouraged the Lost Boys to return home after the vote for independence when South Sudan will become a nation unto itself. "Come," he says, "even if you do not plan to stay in Sudan."[21] This, they believe, will be the ultimate act of redemption by the God who has seen them through a devastating war and a terrible time in exile. At that time, as citizens of an independent South Sudan, these Dinka will gather to fulfill what was written in Isa 18:7.

---

21. This account of Bishop Garrang's message is told by Lost Boy refugees who met with him during his latest visit to the United States.

3.4. Return to Mount Zion

> At that time gifts will be brought to the Lord of hosts from a people tall
> and smooth, from a people feared near and far, a nation mighty and con-
> quering, whose land the rivers divide, to Mount Zion, the place of the
> name of the Lord of hosts. (Isa 18:7)

This text is among the few Old Testament narratives that the Dinka
have held in their religious history for decades. They give little concern
or attention to any scholarly details concerning authorship. They do not
ponder the difference between First, Second, or Third Isaiah. And yet their
reliance on this passage shows a deep and abiding relationship with Scripture and the God revealed in it.

The Dinka see themselves reflected in Isa 18:7 as "the people tall and
smooth." Missionary and scholar Marc Nikkel says, indeed, "No Old Testament Biblical passage is better known to Sudanese Christians than Isa
18 which speaks explicitly of God's judgment and of his ultimate blessing
upon the people of Sudan."[22] They have been "named" in this Holy Book
and called by God to offer gifts of gratitude for God's redeeming acts.
And offer gifts they will. They will gather at a church near Bor named
Mount Zion, so named because of this very passage. After the vote for
independence through which God's ultimate act of redemption is established, the community will gather, and, in accordance with their tradition, they will kill a bull to offer it as a gift in celebration for all that God
has done for them.

This ritual is a way of physically, emotionally, and spiritually entering into the biblical narrative that frames their own salvation story as the
Dinka people. Anderson and Foley write, "In this quest [for meaning],
ritualization becomes indispensable, for it provides time, space, symbols,
and bodily enactment for disclosing, entering, and interpreting the many
stories that comprise our individual and communal narration and give
shape to meaning in our lives."[23] The ritual of gathering as a community in
the presence of God to feast and give thanks binds them as Dinka. But it

---

22. Marc R. Nikkel, "Aspects of Contemporary Religious Change among the
Dinka," *JRA* 22 (1992): 78–94 (90).

23. Herbert Anderson and Edward Foley, *Mighty Stories, Dangerous Rituals:
Weaving Together the Human and the Divine* (The Jossey-Bass Religion-in-Practice
Series; San Francisco: Jossey-Bass, 1998), 27.

also reaches back to join them in solidarity with their spiritual ancestors, the people Israel with whom they share the story of suffering and exile, but also of the love of a God who creates a future of hope and possibility.

4. CONCLUSION

The ability to imagine a future is a lifeline for a refugee. In this regard, all of us are the same. Imagination is a requirement for hope. If we cannot imagine a future that opens to possibility, we fall into despair and hopelessness. But this is not to say that every vision of the future functions in a healthful and hopeful manner. Lester notes, "Hope is different from fantasy and illusion because it is related to reality. Because hope is realistic in its orientation, creative imagination is not out of touch with the present probabilities when considering future options."[24] The Dinka discovery of the Hebrew Scriptures and the narrative of the exile opened their imagination to envision what God could do. Far from being a future story that gives way to religious fantasy, the Dinka story grounds God's acts of redemption in the realities of war, death, displacement, and loss. While God's work might indeed be mysterious, it moves through the imperfect and utterly unreliable systems—social, political, and economic—already in play around the world.

The Abang community interprets their own experience of displacement through ancient Israel's experience of exile. This has served as a powerful connection to their biblical ancestors in faith and frames a future story filled with hope and possibility rather than the despair and destruction that have marked them for so long. This style of indigenous African biblical interpretation stands outside the norm for both Western biblical studies and pastoral theology. Nonetheless, both can benefit from this comparative biblical hermeneutic that ultimately instills agency, purpose, and hope in the devastated and marginalized community that is still living out its exile and awaiting the time of redemption.

In the Dinka context, a salvation narrative is one told by a community suffering from the violence and despair inherent in conditions of displacement. It describes God's redeeming action on behalf of God's people. The Dinka faith narrative does not leave the people as passive recipients, but rather makes them active participants in the restoration of righteousness

---

24. Lester, *Hope in Pastoral Care and Counseling*, 91.

before God and in the saving of their lives and homeland. The idea of *active participation*, or *agency*, can have a positive effect on the psyches of people who have been rendered helpless by the actions of others. It may even lead to mitigation of the psychological effects of trauma incurred through war, rape, starvation, homelessness, and other detrimental aspects of displacement. By putting their personal stories in the context of the sacred, in this case the exile, they frame their experience with an ultimate purpose. Let me offer a caution here, regardless of how the Dinka may interpret their own experience: I do not suggest a causal connection between God and the death and destruction in times of war. In other words, I do not suggest that God causes suffering to teach lessons. No one can impose such an interpretation upon another community. I do, however, take from the Dinka faith narrative that as one participates *with* God in creating the possibilities for redemption, a sense of purpose and meaning emerges within the community.

> Because of Israel—wow!—we knew God had a plan in our suffering. There will be a time when God will answer our prayers! (Dinka refugee)

As the Dinka vision of redemption continues to clarify itself, the community moves step by step into the future—an open-ended, ever evolving future filled with hope. The possibility demonstrated by a fragile but holding peace, small movements toward development, and a mandated vote for independence are nothing short of remarkable if seen through the lens of the last twenty-five or more years. But when seen through the lens of the Dinka faith framed by Israel's story of long exile and God's ultimate plans for redemption, it is easy to imagine.

Bibliography

Anderson, Herbert, and Edward Foley. *Mighty Stories, Dangerous Rituals: Weaving Together the Human and the Divine.* The Jossey-Bass Religion-in-Practice Series. San Francisco: Jossey-Bass, 1998.

Holter, Knut. *Old Testament Research for Africa: A Critical Analysis and Annotated Bibliography of African Old Testament Dissertations, 1967–2000.* BTA 3. New York: Lang, 2002.

———. *Yahweh in Africa: Essays on Africa and the Old Testament.* BTA 1. New York: Lang, 2000.

Holton, M. Jan. *Building the Resilient Community: Lessons from the Lost Boys of Sudan.* Eugene, Oreg.: Cascade Books, 2010.

———. "'Our Hope Comes from God': Faith Narratives and Resilience in Southern Sudan." *JPT* 20 (2010): 67–84.

Lester, Andrew. *Hope in Pastoral Care and Counseling.* Louisville: Westminster John Knox, 1996.

Mbiti, John. "Christian Faith and African Religion." Pages 199–204 in *Third World Liberation Theologies: A Reader.* Edited by Deane William Ferm. Maryknoll, N.Y.: Orbis, 1986.

Miller-McLemore, Bonnie J. "The Living Human Web: Pastoral Theology at the Turn of the Century." Pages 9–26 in *Through the Eyes of Women: Insights into Pastoral Care.* Edited by Jeanne Stevenson Moessner. Minneapolis: Augsburg Fortress, 1996.

Mugambi, J. N. K. "African Hermeneutics in a Global Context." Pages 13–28 in *Interpreting Classical Religious Texts in Contemporary Africa.* Edited by Knut Holter. Nairobi: Acton, 2007.

Nikkel, Marc R. "Aspects of Contemporary Religious Change among the Dinka." *JRA* 22 (1992): 78–94.

Nkurunziza, D. R. K. "African versus Western Hermeneutics." Pages 29–34 in *Interpreting Classical Religious Texts in Contemporary Africa.* Edited by Knut Holter. Nairobi: Acton, 2007.

United States Department of State, United States Department of Homeland Security, and United States Department of Health and Human Services. *Proposed Refugee Admissions for Fiscal Year 2011: Report to the Congress.* Submitted on behalf of the President of the United States to the Committees on the Judiciary, United States Senate and United States House of Representatives. Online: http://www.state.gov/documents/organization/148671.pdf.

THE IMPACT OF WAR ON CHILDREN: THE PSYCHOLOGY OF DISPLACEMENT AND EXILE

Hugo Kamya

1. INTRODUCTION

Drawing from accounts of children, this essay discusses the vicissitudes of being caught in armed conflicts and the attending psychiatric sequelae. It also attempts to address these symptoms in the context of community, regional, national, and international arenas. The essay will argue that the context of war has created forcible crossings of physical boundaries—a physical exile—and has become the fabric of psychological exile for many children and families. The discussion also details some of the dynamics and factors that lead children to engage in war, linking them to the biblical representations of exile. Three questions are addressed in exploring these topics: (1) What do children or unaccompanied minors know about war experiences? (2) What do they know about the circumstances that have led them into these experiences/territories? and (3) What are important influences for integrating and making meaning of these experiences? The conviction expressed here is that the dynamics of war's impact on children in modern-day settings connect with the experiences of Judean exiles to Babylonia in ways that point toward new dimensions in a social psychology of exile.

2. THE STORIES OF CHILDREN

The centerpiece of this essay's discussion is a collection of data related to modern-day children in contexts of war, especially data related to the context of children in the Sudan. The case of Sudanese children is an especially chilling one. Their stories show what they know about their war-related experiences, the meanings they make from these experiences, and the ways they create those meanings. The data reveal that the children's war experiences provide not only past formative encounters, but also some understanding of the future.

Many children travel, voluntarily or involuntarily, to escape war, and these minors suffer the plight of having witnessed some of the most horrible experiences of war.[1] In many war-torn regions in Africa, tens of thousands of children have been abducted, with over a million people herded into camps and thousands of people killed.[2] For the last twenty years, Sudan has endured a civil war that has left many dead and hundreds of thousands displaced. The stories of children from this context of displacement reveal much about their plight, but raise even more questions.

Consider Mot's story. Mot is a nineteen-year-old young man who was forced to leave his home at the age of ten because of the civil war that was raging in his country. In my interviews with Mot, he told of many traumatic experiences, which included seeing fellow marchers die from drowning and being told to kill a girl who had tried to escape. He described walking on long journeys and crossing many rivers. He watched his fellow travelers being mauled by wild animals. His words are telling:

> Sometimes, we crossed the same river two or three times to escape being noticed by the enemy. We kept running. We did not know who we were running away from. We could not trust anyone. It was very scary. Some of the children belonged to the enemy and they reported on us. We were too scared to sleep at night. We wondered what would happen to us.[3]

Now consider Chet's story: Chet was only thirteen when he escaped to Ethiopia before his father was killed. At that time, Chet lost contact with his mother. He and his sister then crossed over into Sudan with his uncle. At some point, he suffered a severe chest trauma when he was hit by a large rock. He ended up in a camp in Kakuma, Kenya. Chet described his life in the camp as horrendous. He and his fellow travelers had only one meal a day. Every two weeks, they would receive very small amounts of cornmeal rations, which frequently ran out before the next distribution. Sometimes

---

1. See Janice H. Goodman, "Coping with Trauma and Hardship among Unaccompanied Refugee Youth from Sudan," *Qualitative Health Research* 14.9 (2004): 1177–96.

2. Paul Raffaele, "Uganda the Horror," *Smithsonian* (February 2005): 90–99.

3. Personal interview (September 6, 2004).

their ration was stolen or they had to barter it away among themselves. Several days, they went without food. On some occasions, Chet and three other boys had to decide how to spend five shillings (equivalent to a dime): would they buy a bun or could they spend it on corn that would fill their bellies? These were constant daily struggles for them. They also had to make decisions whether to eat during the day and go to bed on empty stomachs, or save the food for the evening so they could have a good sleep. As Chet describes his ordeal, "Then there were the peacekeepers who protected us during the day but came into our huts to rape us at night. It was bad, very bad indeed."[4]

Chet's story is not unlike other stories that have been documented in the popular media. Recent media stories provide graphic details of the plight that surrounds such displaced children and their families, describing people who have lost limbs[5] and depicting a terrible war zone through which these children have to walk daily, as they look into a future with little or no hope. One such story tells of a fourteen-year-old child abducted by the Lord's Resistance Army in Northern Uganda, as reported initially by the Human Rights Watch in 1997:

> I saw quite a number of children killed. Most of them were killed with clubs. They would take five or six of the newly abducted children and make them kill those who had fallen or tried to escape. It was so painful to watch. Twice I had to help. And to do it, it was so bad, it was very bad to have to do.[6]

Another account of a seventeen-year-old boy, reported by the Human Rights Watch in 2003, tells particularly about what captors forced abducted children to do:

> Whenever they killed anyone, they called us to watch. I saw eleven people killed this way. One of them was a boy who had escaped. They found him in his home, and called him outside. They made him lie down on the

---

4. Ibid.

5. Malcolm Linton, Issatu Kargbo, and Abdul Sankoh, "War Wounds: In Africa, an Ugly Civil War Leaves Permanent Scars," *Time* 154, no. 11 (1999). Online: http://www.time.com/time/magazine/article/0,9171,30536,00.html.

6. Human Rights Watch, "The Scars of Death: Children Abducted by the Lord's Resistance Army in Uganda" (September 1997), 7. Online: http://www.hrw.org/legacy/reports97/uganda.

ground, and they pierced him with a bayonet. They chopped him with a bayonet until he was dead. Seeing this, I felt like I was a dead person not feeling anything and then sometimes I would feel like it was happening to me, and I would feel the pain.[7]

One young man describes his attempt to run away:

There had been rumors that rebels were around and we were very fearful. My grandmother was hiding in the bush. It was morning, and I was behind the hut when I heard a shot. I started running into the bush but there was a rebel behind a tree. I thought he would shoot me. He said, "Stop, my friend, don't try to run away!" Then he beat me with a handle of the gun on my back. He ordered me to direct him, and told me that afterwards I would be released.[8]

He continues as he describes the brutal treatment by the soldiers:

But afterwards it was quite different. That afternoon, we met with a very huge group of rebels, together with so many new captives. We marched and marched. In the bush we came across three young boys who had escaped from the rebels earlier, and they removed the boys' shirts and tied ropes around their throats, so that when they killed them they would make no noise. Then they forced them down and started clubbing their heads, and other rebels came with bayonets and stabbed them. It was not a good sight (fifteen years old).[9]

Another child speaks about his experience with his brother and his mother:

It was seven p.m. We were in the house, and two of us were abducted. It was me and my older brother. My mother was crying and they beat her. She was very weak and I do not know if she is alright at all. They beat us, then they made me carry some radios and carry the commander's gun. It was very heavy and at first I was afraid it would shoot off in my arms, but it was not filled with ammunition. We joined a big group and we walked very far, and my feet were very swollen. If you said that you were hurting they would say, "Shall we give this young man a rest?" But by a "rest" they meant they would kill you, so if you did not wish to die you had to say

---

7. Ibid., 8.
8. Ibid.
9. Ibid.

you did not need a rest. Many children tried to escape and were killed. They made us help. I was afraid and I missed my mother. But my brother was very stronghearted and he told me we must have courage, we will not die, so I kept going. We had to keep hoping. We had to do something to help those who could not.[10]

Finally, the description of one child talks about the raid on their school:

They came to our school in the middle of the night. We were hiding under the beds but they banged on the beds and told us to come out. They tied us and led us out, and they tried to set the school on fire. We walked and walked and they made us carry their property that they had looted. At about six a.m. they made us stop and they lined up in two lines, and made us walk between them while they kicked us. They brought us to a large camp. My duties were mostly to farm. I would dig fields and plant maize beans. I spent most of my time digging. They also trained us in how to be soldiers. I was trained to use mortars and RPGs. There was no water in the camp. Every day we would have to search for water. The food was mostly beans but it was not enough. We ate bitter leaves. People were dying, especially young boys. There were many boys. The girls became wives of the commanders, some to as many as three men. Some rebels were fighting over some of the girls. Some girls were taken and were told they had to be wives of the men in the camp. When the men were sent away to fight the girls would be passed on to other men.[11]

Although seemingly far removed from the experiences of ancient Judeans during the Babylonian exile, the stories of the impact of war and displacement on these Sudanese children point toward a social psychology of exile that may also be significant for the realities and representations of the Babylonian exile. In fact, the dynamics involved in the causes and effects of the Judean exile, as well as the return of at least some groups to the land, combine in some mutually illuminating ways with the dynamics of war's impact on children in these modern-day settings.

---

10. Ibid., 7.
11. Ibid., 10.

3. The Judean Exile in the Sixth Century b.c.e.

Exile at the hands of empire was a reality of Israelite and Judean experience from the late eighth century through the early sixth century b.c.e. In the late 700s, the Assyrians conquered the northern kingdom of Israel, exiled some of the inhabitants, and repopulated the land with people from Babylon and other provinces (2 Kgs 17:1–41). Judah survived as an Assyrian vassal. A century and a quarter later in 597 b.c.e., King Nebuchadnezzar of Babylon descended upon Jerusalem, looted the temple, and exiled King Jehoiachin and Judah's elite citizens to Babylon (2 Kgs 24). When Zedekiah, the last king of Judah, engaged in resistance and rebellion against the Babylonians, Nebuchadnezzar returned again about ten years later in 586 b.c.e. and destroyed the temple, exiled Zedekiah, and deported more of the people to Babylon (2 Kgs 25). In less than a century and a half, the kingdoms of Israel and Judah were repeatedly subjugated at the hands of empires. Through these experiences, many of the people of Israel and Judah found themselves displaced into new environments.

The exile of the people from their land was a forcible crossing of physical boundaries that meant "death, deportation, destruction, and devastation."[12] While biblical writers tend to offer theological explanations for the historical events of their times, one can also note that the movements of the Israelites and Judeans were functions of political realities. Israel and Judah were indeed small kingdoms surrounded by the mightier empires of their time. Naturally, they succumbed to the empires' propensity to dominate the region.

As we have begun to suggest regarding the war experiences of Sudanese children, as devastating as the exile was, biblical texts indicate that it also became a formative experience. Israel now had a chance to reevaluate its history and take specific measures to prevent another exile in the future. At least in some texts, Israel's reflection was rooted in exclusionism. The books of Ezra and Nehemiah underscore Israel going through a moment of self-reflection that is defined by building boundaries around the community of faith. Ironically, while Cyrus may be opening up borders by letting the people return, the people themselves are erecting boundaries around each other. Physical, psychological, cultural, and social boundaries

---

12. Ralph W. Klein, *Israel in Exile: A Theological Interpretation* (OBT; Philadelphia: Fortress, 1979), 2.

are often used as protective measures. While they run the risk of creating more alienation, they also become coping mechanisms and offer new ways of self-naming and identity. Boundaries can offer psychological integrity, but they can also create demonization, dehumanization, and denigration of the other. Of course, what is important is how a group, culture, or community makes sense of such events as forced migration and displacement. I will now return to the stories of the young men and women of Sudan to consider some ways these children and youth made sense of their war-related experiences.

4. Stories That Make Meaning

How war-affected children make meaning of the events in their lives as captured by the stories we have noted is crucial. Too little research has been done on Sudanese who have escaped war, but one recent study has compared South Sudanese refugee children living in Uganda with a group of Ugandan children who had not experienced war.[13] Findings from their study revealed that South Sudanese children experienced significantly more traumatic events, and reported more symptoms of post-traumatic stress disorder (PTSD) and depression and more behavioral problems. Especially relevant to meaning-making is the finding that the South Sudanese children reported the use of particular coping strategies in dealing with their traumatic war experiences.

A study by Elizabeth Coker has examined how South Sudanese use, for example, narrative styles to discuss body illnesses associated with refugee-related trauma.[14] The narratives presented by the Sudanese about their body illnesses echo their immigration experiences of escape as they made long journeys into the unknown. The way these children talk about experiences not only underscores the importance of the experiences but also matches the characteristics observed by many who study narrative responses to trauma, namely, the need to articulate multiple perspectives

---

13. B. Paardekooper, J. T. V. M. de Jong, and J. M. A. Hermanns, "The Psychological Impact of War and the Refugee Situation on South Sudanese Children in Refugee Camps in Northern Uganda: An Exploratory Study," *Journal of Child Psychology and Psychiatry* 40 (1999): 529–36.

14. Elizabeth M. Coker, "'Traveling Pains': Embodied Metaphors of Suffering among Southern Sudanese Refugees in Cairo," *Culture, Medicine, and Psychiatry* 28 (2004): 15–39.

of one's lived experiences in order to identify and amplify indicators of strength and resiliency. This process has been described as "thickening."[15] As narrative practitioners observe, thick descriptions yield rich descriptions. Analysis of interviews reveals that the children's knowledge and retelling of stories varied in cohesiveness. Some children told complex stories while others told bits and pieces of stories. The certainty of their knowledge also varied. Stories were remembered differently at different times. Some stories echoed other stories that have been told by people in similar warlike situations. Overall, the stories showed how vulnerable these children are.

5. The Exile of Children in War

Other recent studies examining treatment approaches for working with the Sudanese children population[16] reveal what has been described as intergenerational consequences of trauma.[17] The children of war experienced a form of exile that went beyond the physical. These children's reports of war suggested overwhelmingly alienating experiences. The reports indicated that children were often recruited at a very young age—some as young as seven years old. They were often forced to join fighting groups. Many were indoctrinated into hating their parents and into the destruction of their environment. In some cases, these children went through elaborate rituals during which scars and body marks were engraved on their skins to initiate them into their new "families." Once they were alienated from

---

15. See Michael White and David Epston, *Narrative Means to Therapeutic Ends* (New York: W. W. Norton, 1990); Alice Morgan, *What Is Narrative Therapy?* (Adelaide, Australia: Dulwich Centre Publications, 2000).

16. See M. Eisenbruch, J. T. V. M. de Jong, and W. van de Put, "Bringing Order Out of Chaos: A Culturally Competent Approach to Managing the Problems of Refugees and Victims of Organized Violence," *Journal of Traumatic Stress* 17 (2004): 123–31; K. Peltzer, "A Process Model of Ethnocultural Counseling for African Survivors of Organized Violence," *Counseling Psychology Quarterly* 12 (1999): 335–51; Frank Neuner, "A Comparison of Narrative Exposure Therapy, Supportive Counseling, and Psychoeducation for Treating Posttraumatic Stress Disorder in an African Refugee Settlement," *Journal of Consulting and Clinical Psychology* 72 (2004): 579–87.

17. Joseph H. Albeck, "Intergenerational Consequences of Trauma: Reframing Traps in Treatment Theory—A Second Generation Perspective," in *Handbook of Posttraumatic Therapy* (ed. Mary Beth Williams and John F. Sommer Jr.; Westport, Conn.: Greenwood, 1994), 106–25.

their biological families—a form of exile—military life provided a surrogate family. These experiences, while portrayed as measures of inclusion, were, in fact, forms of exclusion.

Almost all children reported that they were "forced to join the war," and being forced to join the war was described either as an act of self-defense or an opportunity to find their family members who had been abducted. Some children stated that they wanted to seek revenge for the things that happened to them. The theme of "being lied to" also permeated most responses. For example, the children often acted as mine setters or detectors. One child described how his cousin was ordered to run in front of the fighting group only to be blown up. In some cases, they acted as decoys on all sides of the fighting groups. Typically, they were given the most dangerous tasks. While these actions became the children's reality, some of their accounts clearly suggested that they were abducted or enticed by the fighting groups with promises of food or finding their lost parents and relatives.

Children also reported physical, psychological, and emotional effects related to these war experiences. Almost every account revealed strong feelings of fear, confusion, and loss of meaning in life. Like stories of trauma, the children reported feeling continuously frightened and confused about their environments. The accounts display a clear threat to the children's sense of wellbeing and safety. Most significantly, these accounts showed strong symptoms related to complex PTSD. For these children, the stories revealed trauma not as a past event but as a current event in their lives. Alterations in regulating affect included difficulties modulating feelings, destructive behaviors toward themselves and others, and impulsive and risk-taking behaviors. Some children reported difficulties in maintaining attention and intrusting relationships with others. Others expressed a total disappointment in life and saw a future without hope. One young man described his ordeal in these words:

> I get headaches all the time when I think about these things. I cannot
> sleep at night because I fear that someone is going to come get me. Every
> little thing annoys me. I want to beat up those kids who make fun of me
> and my skin. I do not care what happens. I have seen bad things in my
> life. I cannot trust people. You are good to them and they do bad to you.
> I gave up on life a long time ago.[18]

---

18. Personal interview (May 24, 2005).

6. THE PSYCHOLOGY OF DISPLACEMENT
AND THE FORCES OF REORGANIZATION

Not only do the children's accounts speak to a disconnection from others, they reveal a psychological disconnection within the children themselves from the events that occurred in their lives. Almost every child makes some remark to this effect. One account by this eighteen-year-old stands out:

> I sometimes do not know what is going on in my body. Sometimes, I do not feel it. It is as if I am watching me. Is that not funny? Me, outside myself. I am scared of this feeling. Sometimes, when I look back I think it was just a dream but I also know it was real. There are things happening so fast as I think about everything. Then, some I remember, some I don't.[19]

These accounts echo a deep psychological exile in the lives of these children. The physical exile forced upon the children evokes a psychological exile that they continue to experience.

The children's accounts reveal an attempt to deal with this psychological exile that resonates, in some ways, with the depictions of the Judean return to the land in Ezra and Nehemiah. From a psychological standpoint, the life and stance of the postexilic Jews may be seen as seeking to build forces of re-organization. For the Sudanese children too one can find several themes in which children are continually seeking ways to integrate their war experiences into their life stories. Efforts to integrate these experiences can be understood as efforts at re-organization. Almost all of the children struggled with denial. Denial in some cases was through keeping these experiences walled off and denying that anything ever happened to them. Sometimes the events were walled off, but not the effects that came from the events. Such situations allowed for the admission of feelings. There were other situations, however, where the effects were walled off but not the events.

Despite the tendency toward denial, a strong force toward re-organization evident in the children's accounts is that all the children reported feeling anxiously attached to others, and constantly seeking some place of safety, often within themselves. One child reported how much he talks to himself at night:

---

19. Ibid.

Sometimes I will talk as if someone is listening to me. I like doing that because then no one judges me. It is like having one good friend who will not double cross you.[20]

There were also reported concerns about how the war has affected their families and the generations to follow. Feelings of shame and worry appeared to permeate these accounts. Many children lamented losing family members or not knowing what ever happened to them. Many worried that their life had been negatively affected by having to take journeys with distressed people. Some worried that they would never regain their traditional ways of living, as they recognized that they had traversed borders and transgressed boundaries across which they would never return. One child who got separated from his cousins ended up in a different ethnic group. He said he forgot how to speak his language and is now angry because he will "never be able to speak *Dinka*."[21] Loss of language not only separates them from their traditions, but it also cuts them off from themselves. Several children reported these strong feelings of unfamiliarity as they were driven from their homelands into foreign lands.

There are other children who reported how the events of the war have socialized them to watching violent movies: "If a movie does not have violent scenes, I do not think I would want to watch it again. I like to see someone beat up another really bad."[22] Further concerns were expressed by some of the young men who reported that they fear that the things that have happened to them will be passed on to their children and their children's children. As noted above, this concern, the intergenerational transmission of trauma, represents an often-documented phenomenon.[23]

7. TOWARD A PSYCHOLOGY OF RESTORATION

The social and psychological implications of exile for the children of war in Africa have similarities and dissimilarities to the experiences of the ancient Israelites and Judeans. While some Hebrew Bible texts attribute the Babylonian exile to national sin and Torah disobedience, the African

---

20. Ibid.

21. Ibid.

22. Ibid.

23. Kaethe Weingarten, *Common Shock: Witnessing Violence Every Day—How We Are Harmed, How We Heal* (New York: Dutton, 2003).

children of war did not find themselves in their predicament as a result of national sin. Yet in an exilic moment of being forcibly displaced from their homeland, the children, perhaps like some of the ancient Judeans, sensed the loss not only of their traditional lands but also their familial connections, religion, culture, customs, and language. Indeed, they lost their way of life or those traditional things that held them together. Writing about the experience of Africans crossing into the Americas, Vincent Wimbush describes this experience as a "social death" in which they were cut off from their roots, including their languages and religious heritage.[24] Celia Falicov, writing of the experience of immigrants, calls it a "psychological rootlessness."[25] Unlike the ancient Israelites, whose journey into the future was held together by the memory of their past heritage, the children of war often lack that memory.

The social-psychological dimensions of such exiles and displacements, whether of Sudanese children or ancient Judeans, demand serious consideration. Indeed, the children's stories are not different from stories of people who encounter a variety of traumatic or stressful experiences. To recognize the injury they have suffered is to be in touch with their pain and healing. A movement from the psychology of exile and deportation to a psychology of restoration and healing for these children calls for an empathic attunement to their plight. It calls for a conscientious and intentional response to allow for the restoration of humanity that has been taken away from them. Such work is one small attempt at piecing together and healing fragmented relationships into some new kind of whole for themselves and for their communities. A vital first step is to help the children to tell their stories, as heart-wrenching as they may be. Engaging the children can open opportunities for the telling of their stories. Most importantly, the telling can create a community witnessing to these stories for the children. As one child expressed, "Once you tell you feel that the burden is lifted at least for some time. You do not have to be alone with this thing that happened to you."[26]

---

24. Vincent L. Wimbush, "The Bible and African Americans: An Outline of an Interpretive History," in *Stony the Road We Trod: African American Biblical Interpretation* (ed. Cain Hope Felder; Minneapolis: Fortress, 1991), 82–83.

25. Celia J. Falikov, "Working with Transnational Immigrants: Expanding Meanings of Family, Community, and Culture," *Family Process* 46 (2007): 157–72.

26. Personal interview (May 24, 2005).

The stories of these children embody resilience and hope. By telling these stories, these children are reclaiming themselves and moving toward healing. In the telling, they also experience some redemption from all the years of indoctrination, fear, and confusion. But their stories also invite us to further action. They invite us to address world economic inequalities and imbalances. It is crucial to examine these imbalances that often lead to conflicts such as those in Africa. They invite us, in so doing, to examine educational opportunities available to these children. Many of these children are misunderstood as they negotiate their way into various school systems. Emotional issues related to the trauma in their lives are often misinterpreted as learning disabilities. Some people may be quick to suggest medicating these children. Some of these children end up under the heavy arm of the legal system due to behaviors whose context is not understood. To move toward restoration, we need to provide culturally attuned and responsive services to these children.

Attention to best practices with refugee populations and sensitivity to cultural differences among and between different groups are imperative.[27] Issues of gender equality and the empowerment of women must be addressed. As my samples here have shown, stories of girls and women often get little or no attention. Safety for all peoples as a public health issue must also be examined. Governments, non-governmental organizations, and church and worshiping communities must spend human, social, and cultural capital through activism and political lobbying. For researchers, a commitment to responsible conduct of research is imperative. Research that values participants as subjects rather than objects is necessary. Community-based research on these children must take into account new challenges that include addressing issues of racism, oppression, parenting, housing, job placement, skills training, health issues, family and social supports, and the development of longterm relation-

---

27. See Melvin Delgado, Kay Jones, and Mojdeh Rohani, *Social Work Practice with Refugee and Immigrant Youth in the United States* (Boston: Pearson, 2005); Miriam Potocky-Tripodi, *Best Practices for Social Work with Refugees and Immigrants* (New York: Columbia University Press, 2002); Hugo Kamya, "African Immigrants in the United States: The Challenge for Research and Practice," in *Multicultural Issues in Social Work: Practice and Research* (ed. P. L. Ewalt et al.; Washington, D.C.: NASW Press, 1999), 605–21; idem, "The Stress of Migration and the Mental Health of African Immigrants," in *The Other African-Americans: Contemporary African and Caribbean Immigrants in the United States* (ed. Y. Shaw-Taylor and S. A. Tuch; Lanham, Md.: Rowman & Littlefield, 2007), 255–81.

ships as these children prepare to integrate into a new community from their exile. Valuing and understanding the stories of these children is an imperative for researchers, practitioners, and social activists. In short, the task of addressing the psychological impact of displacement and exile due to war is a first imperative toward a psychology of restoration and humanity for these children.

Bibliography

Albeck, Joseph H. "Intergenerational Consequences of Trauma: Reframing Traps in Treatment Theory—A Second Generation Perspective." Pages 106–25 in *Handbook of Post-traumatic Therapy*. Edited by Mary Beth Williams and John F. Sommer Jr. Westport, Conn.: Greenwood, 1994.

Coker, Elizabeth M. " 'Traveling Pains': Embodied Metaphors of Suffering among Southern Sudanese Refugees in Cairo." *Culture, Medicine, and Psychiatry* 28 (2004): 15–39.

Delgado, Melvin, Kay Jones, and Mojdeh Rohani. *Social Work Practice with Refugee and Immigrant Youth in the United States*. Boston: Pearson, 2005.

Eisenbruch, M., J. T. V. M. de Jong, and W. van de Put. "Bringing Order Out of Chaos: A Culturally Competent Approach to Managing the Problems of Refugees and Victims of Organized Violence." *Journal of Traumatic Stress* 17 (2004): 123–31.

Falikov, Celia J. "Working with Transnational Immigrants: Expanding Meanings of Family, Community, and Culture." *Family Process* 46 (2007): 157–72.

Goodman, Janice H. "Coping with Trauma and Hardship among Unaccompanied Refugee Youth from Sudan." *Qualitative Health Research* 14.9 (2004): 1177–96.

Human Rights Watch. "The Scars of Death: Children Abducted by the Lord's Resistance Army in Uganda." Online: http://www.hrw.org/legacy/reports97/uganda.

Kamya, Hugo. "African Immigrants in the United States: The Challenge for Research and Practice." Pages 605–21 in *Multicultural Issues in Social Work: Practice and Research*. Edited by P. L. Ewalt et al. Washington, D.C.: NASW Press, 1999.

———. "The Stress of Migration and the Mental Health of African Immigrants." Pages 255–81 in *The Other African-Americans: Contemporary African and Caribbean Immigrants in the United States*. Edited by Y. Shaw-Taylor and S. A. Tuch. Lanham, Md.: Rowman & Littlefield, 2007.

Klein, Ralph W. *Israel in Exile: A Theological Interpretation*. OBT. Philadelphia: Fortress, 1979.

Linton, Malcolm, Issatu Kargbo, and Abdul Sankoh. "War Wounds." *Time* (September 5, 1999). Online: http://www.time.com/time/magazine/article/0,9171,30536,00.html.

Morgan, Alice. *What Is Narrative Therapy?* Adelaide, Australia: Dulwich Centre Publications, 2000.

Neuner, Frank. "A Comparison of Narrative Exposure Therapy, Supportive Counseling, and Psychoeducation for Treating Posttraumatic Stress Disorder in an African Refugee Settlement." *Journal of Consulting and Clinical Psychology* 72 (2004): 579–87.

Paardekooper, B., J. T. V. M. de Jong, and J. M. A. Hermanns. "The Psychological Impact of War and the Refugee Situation on South Sudanese Children in Refugee Camps in Northern Uganda: An Exploratory Study." *Journal of Child Psychology and Psychiatry* 40 (1999): 529–36.

Peltzer, K. "A Process Model of Ethnocultural Counseling for African Survivors of Organized Violence." *Counseling Psychology Quarterly* 12 (1999): 335–51.

Potocky-Tripodi, Miriam. *Best Practices for Social Work with Refugees and Immigrants.* New York: Columbia University Press, 2002.

Raffaele, Paul. "Uganda the Horror." *Smithsonian* (February 2005): 90–99.

Weingarten, Kaethe. *Common Shock: Witnessing Violence Every Day—How We Are Harmed, How We Heal.* New York: Dutton, 2003.

White, Michael and David Epston. *Narrative Means to Therapeutic Ends.* New York: W. W. Norton, 1990.

Wimbush, Vincent L. "The Bible and African Americans: An Outline of an Interpretive History." Pages 81–97 in *Stony the Road We Trod: African American Biblical Interpretation.* Edited by Cain Hope Felder. Minneapolis: Fortress, 1991.

PART 3
PSYCHOLOGY AND TRAUMA

READING WAR AND TRAUMA: SUGGESTIONS TOWARD A SOCIAL-PSYCHOLOGICAL EXEGESIS OF EXILE AND WAR IN BIBLICAL TEXTS

Daniel L. Smith-Christopher

1. The Changing Study of Social Psychology and Trauma

A reading of Didier Fassin and Richard Rechtman's *Empire of Trauma* (2009 in English) proves quite illuminating for those of us who are thinking about the implications of socio-psychological analysis of "traumatic events" when working on biblical history, and particularly when we are thinking about the traumatic impact of warfare.[1] In this important work of social history and analysis, the authors discuss the social transformations in European (mainly French) medical and social practices that relate directly to conceiving of, identifying, and ultimately treating, different forms of traumatic experiences. As they state in their introductory material, there was a radical change in how human beings were "seen" when traumatic events seemed to impact individuals:

> For a century this human being suffering from trauma was seen as different from others: weak, dishonest, perhaps a phony or a profiteer. Then a few decades ago she or he became the very embodiment of our common humanity. It is this shift from one truth to another, from a realm in which trauma was regarded with suspicion to a realm in which it carries the stamp of authenticity, that we seek to analyze.[2]

---

1. Didier Fassin and Richard Rechtman, *The Empire of Trauma: An Inquiry into the Condition of Victimhood* (trans. Rachel Gomme; Princeton: Princeton University Press, 2009).

2. Ibid., 23.

The social implications of their historical analysis, which spans the course of the twentieth century, are both provocative and illuminating. For example, they point out that during World War 1 the "dominant paradigm in the psychiatry of war neurosis was still that of forensic medicine, with its suspicion that trauma, hysteria, sinistrosis, and malingering were all motivated by personal advantage."[3] The implications of this insight forced me to realize that I may have been rather unfair in criticizing the insistence of C. C. Torrey in 1910 that the exile "was in reality a small and relatively insignificant affair."[4] Given the context of Torrey's time, when virtually all signs of a psychological impact from warfare were subject to the accusation of "malingering," I may need to revise my thinking (or at least my judgmental tone). In short, Torrey's assessment seems certainly in keeping with European thought about traumatic events (indeed, they were not called "traumatic" as yet), especially in connection with conflict.

Fassin and Rechtman show that the early twentieth century professional assessment of the psychological impact of tragedy or (especially, but not exclusively) warfare typically sought to prove that any such psychological impact was the result of a weak personality or an attempt to collect benefits of some kind. As Fassin and Rechtman suggest,

> The question occupying the health services throughout the war was, therefore, not what events were liable to produce long-term pathological effects, but which soldiers were likely to develop a condition inappropriate to their social standing. Who were the men who were not protected by patriotism? … What was the reason for their weakness, given that the event, the war, could not be the sole cause?[5]

Attitudes slowly changed at the beginning of World War 2, as indicated by the (only moderately) less negative tone of "shell shock," but, as Fassin and Rechtman powerfully assert, it was finally the Holocaust that changed the entire paradigm for assessing trauma:

> The notions of malingering, cowardice, selfishness, overdeveloped narcissism, secondary gains, class interest—all the stigmas attached to traumatic neurosis, could not be applied to these people in striped

---

3. Ibid., 45.

4. Charles C. Torrey, "The Exile and the Restoration," in idem, *Ezra Studies* (Chicago: University of Chicago Press, 1910), 285.

5. Fassin and Rechtman, *Empire of Trauma*, 47.

pajamas who were emerging directly from hell. An entirely different paradigm was called for.[6]

Notably, the authors cite the work of Bruno Bettelheim who appears to be among the first to insist on the importance of the *causative events themselves* in assessing adverse psychological reactions. Eventually, the professional and theoretical ideas about psychological reactions to trauma changed dramatically in the late twentieth century. Fassin and Rechtman's summary is worth quoting at length:

> The ideological revolution produced by the concept of trauma changed the status of the wounded soldier, the accident survivor and, more broadly, the individual hit by misfortune, from that of suspect (as it had been from the end of the nineteenth century) to that of entirely legitimate victim. We have described this spectacular reversal that allows the soldier to claim his rights, even on the very basis of crimes he has committed, and the person who claims to have suffered sexual abuse to gain recognition of her suffering on the basis of her word alone, as marking the end of suspicion. This development both establishes and reinforces a new figure, one that is central to an understanding of contemporary society—the figure of the victim.[7]

My own interest in the emerging disciplines in the social sciences called trauma studies, refugee studies, and forced migration studies all began with my interest more generally in social science approaches to biblical literature, especially associated with my focus on the events of the Babylonian conquest of Jerusalem in 597/587 B.C.E. What began as an interest in understanding possible dynamics of the historical events themselves in relation to the biblical literature evolved toward a more serious interest in comparative work with recent examples of forced migrations around the world.[8] It was a short step into the literature of the emerging fields

---

6. Ibid., 71.

7. Ibid., 278.

8. And now this comparative work is very well developed in, for example, John J. Ahn, *Exile as Forced Migrations: A Sociological, Literary, and Theological Approach on the Displacement and Resettlement of the Southern Kingdom of Judah* (BZAW 417; Berlin: de Gruyter, 2011). Important work is published regularly in the *Forced Migration Review* (Refugee Studies Center, Oxford University), and I highly recommend the series of books on themes of migration studies produced especially by Berghahn Books, which maintains a consistently important list in press for this area of study.

of trauma studies, posttraumatic stress disorder (PTSD) literature, and refugee studies. For me, the more particular interest specifically in trauma studies began with an article I wrote in 2000 in which I was critical of a recent book on Ezekiel precisely because the psychological analysis offered therein, although quite interesting, to my mind almost entirely neglected the central most important material context within which I would argue we must read Ezekiel the person and Ezekiel the book, namely, the conquest of Jerusalem and the events of the exile.[9] What I did not know then, but have come to learn now as a result of reading *Empire of Trauma*, is that the evolution of trauma studies and psychological and medical use of concepts of trauma have themselves gone through a tempestuous history in Europe and the United States throughout the twentieth century and until now. Indeed, it was not until 1980 that the very diagnostic descriptions for PTSD entered the third edition of the *Diagnostic and Statistical Manual* (DSM-III), widely used in the psychological profession. In short, reading scripture through trauma studies has really become possible only in the last few decades because trauma studies, forced migration studies, and refugee studies are all disciplinary inventions of the late twentieth and early twenty-first centuries. Sadly, this development is based on the overwhelming plethora of subject matter for such studies. In a profound sense, reassessments of the Babylonian exile and, indeed, the potential for psychological assessments of the experience of warfare in ancient Israel (one thinks, of course, of the impact of the Assyrian campaigns in the late eighth century B.C.E.) are products of the significant changes in social, psychological, and anthropological analysis of the contemporary world. That biblical studies itself, as a discipline, is closely integrated into wider contemporary cultural and social thought could hardly be better illustrated.

2. CAN WE DO EXEGESIS OF THE TRAUMA OF WAR AND EXILE?

In light of the developments traced above, can we speak of a social psychology of exile and war in the Hebrew Bible? If we can use the literature of

---

Frederick L. Ahearn Jr., ed., *The Psychosocial Wellness of Refugees: Issues in Qualitative and Quantitative Research* (Oxford: Berghahn Books, 2000) is particularly helpful.

9. Daniel L. Smith-Christopher, "Ezekiel on Fanon's Couch: A Postcolonialist Critique in Dialogue with David Halperin's *Seeking Ezekiel*," in *Peace and Justice Shall Embrace: Power and Theopolitics in the Bible: Essays in Honor of Millard Lind* (ed. T. Grimsrud and L. L. Johns; Telford, Penn.: Pandora, 2000), 108–44.

trauma (and the associated disciplines of forced migration, refugee studies, etc., which I will hereinafter presume when I use the label, "trauma studies") to construct a realistic idea of some of the social and psychological impacts of the violence of war, massive displacement, and forced resettlement, can elements of the composite picture constructed from contemporary observations of refugee societies illuminate the study of biblical exilic texts? I want to suggest in this essay that we most certainly can benefit from reading the literature from our colleagues in trauma studies and that the potential results of these kinds of studies for our analyses of biblical literature may be quite provocative.

First, however, perhaps we should ask why the question of doing social-psychological exegesis is a difficult one. Is it not the case that the evidence is open and shut—a biblical text either identifies itself as exilic, and thus discusses historical events or persons datable to a particular period, or not? If there is a psychological, emotional, or personal impact, surely it would be mentioned (for example, in the Book of Lamentations). This expectation of obvious and explicit texts would reduce the amount of material we can work with in thinking about these questions.

There are times, however, when the apparent "evidence" is not so explicit. For example, the stories of Dan 1–6 are usually not dated to the Neo-Babylonian period, or even the early Persian period, not only because of the Hellenistic data in chapters 7–12, but also because of the notable historical mistakes of the stories themselves (Belshazzar was not the son of Nebuchadnezzar, and Darius was not a Mede). Texts either have their facts correct, or they do not, right?

Much of the literature in refugee studies already problematizes these questions. James Scott's work introduced many biblical interpreters to the problem of *intentional misrepresentation* as a tactic of the subordinated.[10] Scott's insights about intentionally "hidden transcripts" have been echoed, and in rather blunt terms, in a fascinating analysis of "refugee cultures." Eftihia Voutira and Barbara Harrell-Bond speak of the realities of refugee life, which is expressed by many refugees themselves with the words, "to

---

10. The two classic works often cited are James C. Scott, *Weapons of the Weak: Everyday Forms of Peasant Resistance* (New Haven: Yale University Press, 1985), and idem, *Domination and the Arts of Resistance: Hidden Transcripts* (New Haven: Yale University Press, 1990). See also Daniel E. Valentine and John C. Knudsen, eds., *Mistrusting Refugees* (Berkeley: University of California Press, 1995).

be a refugee means to learn to lie!"[11] There are lies to qualify for help, lies to qualify as "traumatized" or "not too traumatized," lies to get help for family—indeed, one of the most important divides is between the officials and the refugees. John Knudsen observes, based on his work with Vietnamese refugees in Norway:

> [They] often stress that the brutality of the wars has engendered suspicion, individuality, and distrust rather than forthrightness, cooperation, and trust. Hence even daily communication is described as more indirect than direct.[12]

We are thus faced with the radically counterintuitive possibility that misrepresenting historical circumstances may itself be a symptom of precisely the traumatic circumstances that could easily be denied by a modern reader's "plain reading of the text." It is rich irony when the problem with historical-critical analysis is that it can sometimes *believe the text too much*! We thus may risk reading the Bible rather like southern slave holders who had no idea what their slaves were really talking about when they were singing "Steal Away to Jesus" (i.e., "we are leaving tonight"). Fassin and Rechtman repeat again and again in their survey of attitudes toward conceptualizing trauma in twentieth-century European social and psychological thought that financial realities, suspicions of malingering, and even administrative requirements often led practitioners simply not to see certain realities immediately facing them. Military personnel, for example, were only ready to see psychological problems among soldiers as comparable to workplace accidents in which workers were constantly under suspicion of demanding benefits in lieu of actual work.[13] Let me be clear that I am not saying that this argument establishes, for example, that the stories in Dan 1–6 are *early* postexilic stories any more than signs of trauma might prove that Tobit is really from eighth-century Neo-Assyrian exiles (even though I have always suspected that Dan 1–6 are older folk stories than can be assigned to the Hellenistic period). Rather, I am simply

---

11. Eftihia Voutira and Barbara Harrell-Bond, "In Search of the Locus of Trust: The Social World of the Refugee Camp," in Valentine and Knudsen, *Mistrusting Refugees*, 216.

12. John C. Knudsen, "When Trust Is on Trial: Negotiating Refugee Narratives," in Valentine and Knudsen, *Mistrusting Refugees,* 13–35.

13. Fassin and Rechtman, *Empire of Trauma*, 45–47.

attempting to argue that we ignore the insights of social sciences to our peril and that certain established paradigms of historical-critical analysis of texts can blind us to social realities revealed only by reading outside our disciplinary boundaries.

3. Some Possible Directions for the Biblical Analysis of the Exile in Dialogue with Social Psychology

The social psychology of trauma can raise questions about textual analysis. Recently I have been working on a major project on the book of Micah. I have been wondering about a particular passage that may further illustrate the subject of this essay. Briefly, as background, there is a clear tendency in modern Micah studies to assign only chapters 1–3 to the historical Micah in the late eighth century, and this is followed by the suggestion that chapters 4–5 are exilic or even later.[14] The most obvious indication of this is the reference in 4:10, "You shall go to Babylon, there you shall be rescued." But is the phrase itself only an exilic insertion, or does it indicate a longer addition of material? The following verse is also important for a possible postexilic setting, even though it does not contain any of the typical historical "evidence" cited for dating:

> Now many nations are assembled against you, saying, "Let her be profaned, and let our eyes gaze upon Zion." (Mic 4:11)

וְעַתָּה נֶאֶסְפוּ עָלַיִךְ גּוֹיִם רַבִּים הָאֹמְרִים תֶּחֱנָף וְתַחַז בְּצִיּוֹן עֵינֵינוּ:

Who is doing the "gazing" here? Why is this an issue of concern for the writer? Any discussion of a "gaze" reminds us of the considerable literature

---

14. Francis I. Andersen and David Noel Freedman, *Micah: A New Translation with Introduction and Commentary* (AB 24; New York: Doubleday, 2000), 392. Similar divisions of Micah can be found in many of the classic works. See Delbert R. Hillers, *Micah: A Commentary on the Book of the Prophet Micah* (Hermeneia; Philadelphia: Fortress, 1984); Mignon R. Jacobs, *The Conceptual Coherence of the Book of Micah* (JSOTSup 322; Sheffield: Sheffield Academic Press, 2001); idem, "Bridging the Times: Trends in Micah Studies since 1985," *CurBS* 4 (2006): 293–329; James Limburg, *Hosea–Micah* (IBC; Atlanta: John Knox, 1988); James Luther Mays, *Micah: A Commentary* (OTL; Philadelphia: Westminster, 1976); Wilhelm Rudolph *Micha–Nahum–Habakuk–Zephanja* (KAT 13.3; Gütersloh: Gerd Mohn, 1975); Hans Walter Wolff, *Micah: A Commentary* (CC; Minneapolis: Augsburg, 1990).

on the "male gaze" in previous feminist analysis, and also the extensive discussion about the implications of the feminized Zion being "profaned" (especially in the imagery of Jer 3, for example, where Judah waits for her lovers in the desert, or similarly in Hos 2).[15] I am more interested in the potential for reading this passage through social psychology and therefore the possibility that there may be even more evidence for the postexilic dating of this material based on a social psychological tendency in the language itself. Inspired by feminist insights, I propose that we use the idea of an "imperial gaze," comparable to the "administrator's gaze" or the "psychologist's gaze" upon shell-shocked war veterans in the decades before the development of trauma theory and PTSD.

What, then, is the gaze observing in Micah? It seems the answer is the destruction of Jerusalem, which is expressed here using the term חנף. This term, meaning "to profane, pollute," appears often in Job and Jeremiah as an adjective, "godless." It appears as a verb in Isa 24:5 ("the earth lies polluted"). I am particularly intrigued with the term's combination with the seeing, or gaze, of the nations in Mic 4:11. In this case, the sight of the nations regards the "pollution" of Zion. In their discussion of this verse, Francis Andersen and David Noel Freedman limit their comments to the *religious* impact of the temple being destroyed.[16] But surely this is related to a certain shame and humiliation as well, not only religious ideas. The important idea, I suggest, is the emphasis on "many peoples" or "many nations" (גוים רבים).

Although the feminine noun חרפה ("shame/humiliation") does not appear in Mic 4:11, tracing the use of this term sheds further light on the

---

15. The "Male Gaze" was a term coined by Laura Mulvey in an influential essay published originally in 1973. See also Laura Mulvey, "Visual Pleasure and Narrative Cinema," in *Film Theory and Criticism: Introductory Readings* (ed. Leo Braudy and Marshall Cohen; New York: Oxford University Press, 1999), 833–44. The term builds on other uses of the concept of the gaze—the way in which others are seen, assessed, and evaluated, and thus where and how they are expected to be seen. Studies of indigenous peoples in early photography also suggest quite literally the colonizer's gaze. See James C. Faris, *Navajo and Photography: A Critical History of the Representation of an American People* (Salt Lake City: University of Utah Press, 2003); Jane Lydon, *Eye Contact: Photographing Indigenous Australians* (Durham: Duke University Press, 2005); Michael Graham-Stewart, *Out of Time: Maori and the Photographer 1860–1940: The Ngawini Cooper Trust Collection* (Auckland City, New Zealand: John Leech Gallery, 2006).

16. Andersen and Freedman, *Micah*, 448–57.

notion of the "gaze of the nations," a notion at the heart of the verse. This noun is of course more widely used in the biblical texts than the verb or adjective, but one observation may be especially significant. Sometimes the shame seems to be a phenomenon among a small circle. The shame spoken of in Genesis refers to a woman's shame or humiliation in not having a son or in being married to an inappropriate partner (30:23; 34:14; echoed in Isa 4:1 by the seven women who say "take away our disgrace"). Yet shame falls on the people Israel in Josh 5:9, and in 1 Sam 11:2 (in which Nahash intends to bring disgrace on Israel), and shame can be perceived by an individual in the eyes of his countrymen (see Pss 22:6 [Heb 7]; 31:11 [Heb 12]; 39:8 [Heb 9]; 44:13 [Heb 14]; 69:7, 9, 10, 19, 20 [Heb 8, 10, 11, 20, 21]). But something different may occur in Ps 89, a text that Hermann Gunkel already hesitated to assign to any date before the exile:

> All who pass by plunder him;
> he has become the *scorn* of his neighbors. (v. 41 [Heb 42])
> Remember, O Lord, how your servant is taunted;
> how I bear in my bosom the *insults* of the peoples. (v. 50 [Heb 51])

The emphasis here is on taunts and derision from "many peoples." Isaiah 25:8 refers to shame and disgrace "from all the earth." Jeremiah 24:9 refers to "a disgrace, a byword, a taunt, and a curse in all the places where I shall drive them," and verse 18 returns to this theme of the perspective of all the nations (see also Jer 51:51). This change to being seen by all the nations becomes very prominent in Ezekiel:

> Moreover I will make you a desolation and an *object of mocking* among the nations around you, in the sight of all that pass by. (Ezek 5:14)

And, echoing Jeremiah's list of humiliations, the next verse states:

> You shall be a mockery and a taunt, a warning and a horror, to the nations around you, when I execute judgments on you in anger and fury, and with furious punishments—I, the LORD, have spoken. (5:15)

This notion of being an object of scorn in the eyes of the nations is notable in Ezekiel even in promises that Israel will someday no longer be an object of humiliation (22:4; 36:15, 30). In the tradition of the penitential prayer, this notion of being humiliated in the eyes of the nations turns up, of course, in Dan 9:16 and is repeated in Joel 2:17 and 19.

Does social psychology shed any light on this trend toward a concern for being watched by the nations? In fact, two different tendencies in social psychology are interesting in this regard, not only trauma studies but also the early work on "social facilitation." First, it can be argued that the very *raison d'etre* of social psychology is to study the impact of others on the behavior of the individual. It is hardly surprising, then, that one of the primary areas of investigation is the impact of being watched on individual behavior. One of the ways this is addressed in the literature is to speak of "social facilitation." A good part of this discussion takes as a foundation the 1965 work of R. B. Zajonc, who proposed that simple tasks were impacted when subjects felt that they were being watched, but complex tasks were not.[17] There has been considerable discussion concerning why the presence of others modifies behavior, but that it most certainly does is considered beyond question. One of the pernicious directions this research takes, as one might guess, is management theory. But there are other ways that this basic interest in audience can be taken up.

Michel Foucault was also quite interested in the concept of the gaze—in his case, from powerful political leaders. In his study of discipline, Foucault famously cited Jeremy Bentham's proposed prison design from 1791 known as the "panopticon"—an "all seeing" prison building that was designed so that all prisoners could be seen by a few centrally located prison guards whose image was hidden so that prisoners could never be sure whether they were actually being watched. Bentham had proposed that this constant state of being observed would be therapeutic and restorative. In his 1977 study *Discipline and Punish: the Birth of the Prison*, Foucault was interested in social attempts to increase control by ever more impressive and comprehensive notions of discipline and punishment.[18] Similarly, Erving Goffman's justly famous 1961 work, *Asylums*, spoke of "total institutions"—institutions that attempt to exert complete control over individuals as part of their "treatment."[19] Finally, Joseph Piro, writing in the journal *Educational Studies* reflected on the possibility of seeing

17. Robert B. Zajonc, "Social Facilitation," *Science* 149 (1965): 269–74.

18. Michel Foucault, *Discipline and Punish: The Birth of the Prison* (London: Allen Lane, 1977).

19. Erving Goffman, *Asylums: Essays on the Social Situations of Mental Patients and Other Inmates* (Anchor A277; Garden City, N.Y.: Anchor Books, 1961).

aspects of ancient architecture as attempts to enact a sense of being watched by the empire and/or the imperial gods—as ancient "panopticons." The impact of imperial architecture in the Assyrian and Babylonian heartlands is only recently being considered in social terms and as directly related to the interpretation of texts.[20] Yet part of war is occupation or removal, and both of these acts involve supervision. This supervision hardly ceases after the Assyrian and Babylonian periods. If nothing else, Ezra 1–6 illustrates the constant supervision of local opponents to the rebuilding of Jerusalem and the constant need for permission from Persian authorities.

My suggestions out of this brief survey are tentative but, I hope, provocative. Describing his bizarre call narrative, the writer of Ezekiel refers to "eyes all around" (1:18). Later in the book he speaks of God revealing God's power to the "eyes of the nations" (36:23; 38:16). Exilic texts arguably reveal increased awareness of being watched by the nations. The Greeks, too, of course, commented on the "eyes and ears of the king"—the impressive levels of Persian surveillance. Finally, we have seen that refugee studies speak of the heightened awareness by refugees of the need to manipulate their image in the eyes of the powerful. So, once again, can we speak of a social psychology of exile? I believe that we can. Many exilic texts exhibit a heightened awareness of "being watched" on the part of those who have been violently displaced and resettled by a central power, a power whose authority is often dramatically embodied in a massive Mesopotamian architecture of control—an architecture of watching. So perhaps we *could* refer to "the imperial gaze." Indeed, the entire idea of Etamananki, the shrine of Marduk high on the artificial hill, may have as much to do with the perception of the eyes of a god watching over all as it does with the reproduction of the god's dwelling on a mountain. In reference to the Neo-Assyrian Empire, Amélie Kuhrt writes of reliefs depicting its kings reclining near the severed heads of enemies, as well as Assyrian inscriptions boasting of the dead rebels draped on their city walls, or rebellious rulers entrapped with wild animals in cages suspended at city entrances:

> [The king] was awe-inspiring; the fear that filled his enemies was the terror of those knowing that they will be ruthlessly, but justly, punished. The royal power to inspire fear was visualized as a shining radiance...a

---

20. See John Malcolm Russell, *The Writing on the Wall: Studies in the Architectural Context of Late Assyrian Palace Inscriptions* (Mesopotamian Civilizations 9; Winona Lake, Ind.: Eisenbrauns, 1999).

kind of halo, that flashed forth from the royal face.... It made him fearsome to behold and it could strike his enemies down, so that they fell to their knees before him, dazzled by the fearful glow.[21]

In short, do texts proposed to be exilic reveal an intensified sense of being watched and thus exhibit some of the social psychology of captive, militarily subordinated, and resettled peoples? The stories of Daniel, Joseph, and Esther (and later, Tobit) depend rather heavily on the feeling of being a people watched, supervised, and often found out.

This is certainly not the only example of the potential insights we can gain by reading social psychology in relation to the experience of exile. There are many related questions about warfare generally, and the exile specifically, upon which social science literature, and especially recent work in trauma, forced migration, and refugee studies, can shed light.

We face another question, however. It is all well and good for modern biblical scholars to refer to warfare as disastrous. But were these events faced by the ancient exiles, or ancient warriors, actually traumatizing for the people involved? Were they really disastrous for *them*? As we noted in Torrey's 1910 comments, this was clearly an open question for part of the twentieth century. In order to think about this in the modern context, we need to ask whether we know what a disaster is. Here again the cross-disciplinary literature is suggestive.

Contemporary scholars of disaster tell us that there are certain conditions that must be met before a disaster can be "disastrous"—that is, whether the events contain the potential for traumatizing the victims. Here the generalized studies of disaster may assist us, especially when we can cite disaster theorists such as Claude Gilbert, for example, who has revived older views about how disastersonly become disastrousfor people when the events exceed the ability of the group to cope, redefine, and reconstruct their society and their own psychological identities: "We may speak of disaster when actors in modern societies increasingly lose their capacity to define a situation that they see as serious or even worrying through traditional understandings and symbolic parameters."[22] Writing

---

21. Amélie Kuhrt, *The Ancient Near East c. 3000–330 BC* (2 vols.; Routledge History of the Ancient World; London: Routledge, 1995), 2:517.

22. Claude Gilbert, "Studying Disaster: Changes in the Main Conceptual Tools," in *What Is Disaster: Perspectives on the Question* (ed. E. L. Quarantelli; London: Routledge, 1998), 17.

as recently as 2006, Gilbert Reyes (notably, in the four-volume work entitled *Handbook of International Disaster Psychology*) writes,

> Catastrophes of all kinds, but especially those emanating from natural forces, can lead people to deeply question their most fundamental beliefs: they have the power to transform our individual lives and our collective destiny.[23]

So it would seem logical for us to examine biblical texts that indicate whether the Hebrews were coping with the events using normal mental structures about how the world works, or whether there are signs of stress or social breakdown—both ideologically and in artifacts. The archaeology of military conquest, especially the impact of the Babylonians on Judah, is today revealing ever-increasing levels of the disasters of the sixth century. At least the physical evidence is no longer seriously in question.[24] Hence, it seems fairly clear that these events were traumatizing.

In the contemporary literature on refugee studies there is likewise an interesting tension between those who emphasize the creative ability for populations to reconstruct, or even maintain, pre-crisis identities, and those who emphasize the debilitating conditions of having insufficient stability to maintain identity, culture, and rationality. In the introduction to an important series of essays considering identity, gender, and change in refugee settings, Linda Camino and Ruth Krulfeld observe:

> Despite experiences of being violently or forcibly uprooted and plunged into discord and disorder, refugees demonstrate the strengths of innovation for survival, as well as the vitality to create and negotiate new roles and behavior to achieve both necessary and desired ends. By doing so, they reveal the multilayered, richly contextualized meanings of their lives and traditions as they act to reaffirm self and community.[25]

---

23. Gilbert Reyes, "International Disaster Psychology: Purposes, Principles, and Practices," in *Handbook of International Disaster Psychology* (ed. G. Reyes and G. A. Jacobs; 4 vols. Westport, Conn.: Praeger, 2006), 1:3.

24. For a good summary of the archaeology of disaster in sixth-century Judah, see Oded Lipschits, *The Fall and Rise of Jerusalem: Judah under Babylonian Rule* (Winona Lake, Ind.: Eisenbrauns, 2005).

25. Linda A. Camino and Ruth M. Krulfeld, "Introduction," in *Reconstructing Lives, Recapturing Meaning: Refugee Identity, Gender, and Culture Change* (ed. Linda A. Camino and Ruth M. Krulfeld; Basel: Gordon and Breach, 1994), xv.

One important way that the social reconstruction process has been observed in refugee studies literature is in the forging of new histories in the process of reconstructing identity. Daniel Valentine and John Knudsen observe:

> Several anthropologists working with refugees have found that one of the important components in the recovery of meaning, the making of culture, and the reestablishment of trust is the need and the freedom to construct a normative picture of one's past within which "who one was" can be securely established to the satisfaction of the refugee. The refugee's self-identity is anchored more to who she or he was than what she or he has become. ... "Individualities" constructed in oral autobiographies are deemed irrelevant by many caseworkers whereas for the refugee this is the foundation on which a meaningful world may be rebuilt.[26]

Included among the options of this reconstruction of history, however, is the possibility that cultures can be reconstructed in negative terms—being considered cursed, sinful, or doomed. Future writing on the theological viewpoints of Jeremiah and the Deuteronomic Historian, for example, ought to consider this widely reported phenomenon, especially given the negative evaluation of the previous monarchical history typical of all of these biblical sources.

This attempt to see the best in refugee populations is not a majority perspective. But it is an attempt to honor the ways that people try to cope. Even more serious is the work of refugee theorists who emphasize the destructive behavioral patterns that are frequently observed in crisis. Patrick Matlou, for example, emphasizes the destructiveness of flight and the ensuing divisions and internal factions that can result:

> During the processes of forced migration that so often result, ongoing social structures and institutions undergo significant changes. As the state disintegrates, its monopoly over the instruments of power and the allocation of resources disappears. Warlords, praetorian guards, religious zealots, and crime bosses take over the shattered shells of now weakened states and societies. Development recedes, what progress had been made is lost, and violence becomes the order of the day as the weak are further subjugated.[27]

---

26. Valentine and Knudsen, *Mistrusting Refugees*, 5.
27. Patrick Matlou, "Upsetting the Cart: Forced Migration and Gender Issues,

When one considers the divisions between those Judeans who seemed to gravitate toward Egypt and those who, like Josiah, seemed to prefer dealing with Babylon, such internal divisions sound familiar. Furthermore, in a series of observations that seem deeply suggestive for the shrill oracles of judgment by Ezekiel aimed, at least partially, at fellow exiles, Matlou adds:

> the deprivation and uncertainty that refugees often suffer sometimes lead them into conflict with each other over scarce rewards. In this regard, exile often serves as an arena for the continuation of conflicts begun at home and leads to the intensification of discriminatory practices that were already in place.[28]

As another example, many scholars of Daniel have noted the strange ambiguity in diaspora narratives such as Dan 1–6 in their views of foreign rulers. There appear to be alternating views: some near positive feelings about the emperor (e.g., Darius in chapter 6), but also the fear of spectacular death by burning, maiming, mauling, and impaling. (Virtually all six stories refer to such horrific forms of capital punishment at the whim of the emperor.) Such uncertainty, interestingly enough, turns out to be a conscious strategy in the imperial repertoire of modern terrorist regimes. In his study of Latin American persecution of peasant societies, Stuart Turner notes:

> Brutal actions were carried out on a few individuals in such a way that the wider population was literally terrorized. For this to be successful, the state had to make sure that the population was well informed about the violence taking place and was maintained in a state of fear by a sequence of unpredictable actions involving acts of intimidation alternating with conditional protection.[29]

Thus the occasions of vaguely positive evaluation of emperors in regimes that we know from archaeological and textual evidence to be brutal in their policies toward foreign conquered peoples certainly does not mean that the biblical texts reveal positive feelings about living in the shadows

---

the African Experience," in *Engendering Forced Migration: Theory and Practice* (ed. Doreen Indra; Studies in Forced Migration 5; Oxford: Berghahn Books, 1999), 133.

28. Ibid., 136.

29. Stuart Turner, "Torture, Refuge, and Trust," in Valentine and Knudsen, *Mistrusting Refugees*, 57.

of empires. They merely reveal the ambiguity of living under a regime that calculates public relations as an element of domination.

So can these contemporary theories actually be applied to ancient writings? Caution is expressed by refugee theorists such as Vanessa Pupavac, who writes that the rise of disaster psychology has not been without considerable controversy, especially around the medicalization of psychological responses to trauma in the literature of PTSD. She wonders if the stress on trauma counseling after a disaster is a reflection of Western emphases on individual happiness. Pupavac argues that emotional response is arguably the Western way of determining health, happiness, and well-being, and she wonders if PTSD itself, as a concept, is equally driven by Western psychological ideas about alienation and thus perhaps not always appropriate to non-Western trauma victims:

> Relativism rather than conviction, suspicion rather than belief, and mistrust rather than trust typify the Western outlook today, along with a growing skepticism over the possibility of human progress and its gains. ... These characteristics influence the social and personal effect of disasters.[30]

There is immediate cause for concern here. In their analysis of the development of trauma therapies, Fassin and Rechtman note the problem of cultural prejudice. Even as they acknowledge that changes were evident already in World War 2, they point out that in two cases changes were very slow indeed:

> From the late 1920s onwards, hysteria and shell shock were indeed no longer dishonorable conditions that brought shame on anyone suffering from them. The stigma was not, however, removed from sufferers in all social categories. Two groups remained unaffected by the reevaluation, and they inherited all the earlier stereotypes: there were workers who had suffered occupational accidents, whether they were labeled with trauma neurosis or sinistrosis, and natives of the French colonies, particularly the "Muslims" of North Africa and the "Blacks" of sub-Saharan Africa.[31]

---

30. Vanessa Pupavac, "Humanitarian Politics and the Rise of International Disaster Psychology," in Reyes and Jacobs, *Handbook of International Disaster Psychology*, 1:16.

31. Fassin and Rechtman, *Empire of Trauma*, 53.

This blindness to the suffering of the colonized, of course, points us in the direction of Frantz Fanon, whose classic work on the psychological as well as political and economic impacts of colonialism in Algeria was the entry point for my own thinking about psychological impacts of warfare and colonialism.

Examining the debates about whether trauma studies are "Western," we can immediately see the problem for those of us in biblical studies who are reading over the shoulders of our colleagues in the social sciences. In our attempts to carefully and critically remember that ancient societies are *not* modern societies, and that we must be careful in making comparisons, we run the equally serious risk of denying the human reality of traumatizing experiences of fellow humans, even if those humans experienced these events over 2500 years ago. On the other hand, the application of contemporary insights certainly can risk a tendency to level out the experiences of all peoples into a kind of generic "trauma experience" that denies the unique histories and experiences of the peoples in question—in our case, ancient Near Eastern peoples. The dilemma is not easily resolved, but the hasty retreat from drawing any conclusions from contemporary social science literature is no guarantee of the integrity of our historical analysis—and may well amount to a disingenuous refusal to admit that *we all make social and psychological assumptions* when we interpret historical texts (after all, we are *not* sixth-century Judeans!).

4. PRELIMINARY CONCLUSIONS

It is hard to read modern analyses of trauma and crisis, and especially refugee studies—even studies with rather unpromising sounding titles--without being struck by how many insights are suggestive for analysis of biblical texts from the exilic experiences. For example, I recently picked up Milica Bookman's 2002 book, *After Involuntary Migration: The Political Economy of Refugee Encampments.*[32] While most of this study obviously applies to contemporary research in long-term as well as short-term refugee camps, it is once again striking how often one comes across an insight that stirs one's exegetical thoughts. Her analysis of encampment economics, for instance, raises especially important questions. She asks

---

32. Milica Z. Bookman, *After Involuntary Migration: The Political Economy of Refugee Encampments* (Lanham, Md.: Lexington Books, 2002).

what economic self-sufficiency means in long-term encampments. If self-sufficiency means that encampment populations can survive without outside assistance, it does not mean that these people do not interact with local populations:

> Self-sufficiency does not mean that the encampment has no recourse to the local community, with whom it often trades and with whom it participates in a mutually beneficial exchange relationship. Indeed, it is neither feasible nor desirable to seek self-sufficiency without participation and integration into the local community.[33]

For me, this raises interesting questions about the amount of interaction we may presume between Judean exiles and local Babylonian peoples. This is obviously a critically important issue when it comes to our presumptions about how familiar Judeans would have been with Babylonian stories, legends, myths, and traditions.

Even more interestingly, Bookman asks what people in refugee camps actually purchase when the initial critical issues of food and shelter are stabilized. Vietnamese refugees in Hong Kong bought suitcases (see Ezek 12). Bookman reports that these suitcases were used for storage but also had tremendous symbolic value. After this, it was fish tanks and televisions. Boredom in the camps is a huge problem:

> The enforced idleness of unemployed camp residents is further reinforced by the nature of encampment life that entails wasted time and a lot of waiting time… One waits for food distribution, one waits for the water truck, one waits at the clinic. Not only do unemployed workers lack income with which to participate in the economy but they may also become restive and become prone to criminal and destructive nationalist activity.[34]

Do such suggestions provide an even more interesting context for Ezekiel's street theatre—actions that perhaps suggest weeks of time in the demonstration of his messages? Bookman also comments on the nature of internal conflict. While camps compete with each other for limited host and international resources, the most "ferocious competition takes place within the encampment":

---

33. Ibid., 89.
34. Ibid., 99.

The fundamental characteristics of encampments, namely uprooted-
ness, poverty, scarcity, and isolation, are conducive to producing active
and strong nationalist feeling among the residents. Encampments bring
out the worse elements of nationalism. They enable fringe, extremist
sentiments to become mainstream, both within the camp and outside.
From within, encampments are viewed as prisons that only combative
behavior has a chance of breaking, from outside they are viewed as an
eyesore, a drain of resources, and an impediment to the development of
host areas.[35]

Finally, although refugee studies and trauma studies have tended to
emphasize response to contemporary crises, there is increasing evidence
for long-term, and indeed multi-generational, impacts of such crises.
Attention to the social, economic, and traumatic context at work in circumstances of subordination, disaster, warfare, or political oppression
(either individually or in a group) has also led in recent years to increased
consideration of PTSD as a means of understanding cultural groups who
suffer as entire peoples. Eduardo and Bonnie Duran's brilliant work, *Native
American Postcolonial Psychology*, is an excellent move in this direction,
and has obvious relevance to a fuller reading of Ezekiel and Lamentations.[36]
They note the specific social impact of the First Contact period, followed
by the impact of the Invasive War Period, and then Subjugation and the
Reservation Period, the Boarding School Period, and finally the Forced
Relocation and Termination Period. They refer to the research pointing
out the cross-generational passing of PTSD symptomology, as noted in
children of Holocaust survivors, and discuss the realm of dreaming as
places of pain and of groping for understanding in Native American culture and practice. The implications are too obvious to require elaboration
for biblical studies, with its obsessions about redaction of texts long after
the events discussed.

While living in Israel/Palestine between 1986 and 1988, I became
troubled by a clear Western media bias when reporting on local disasters
in Israel and the West Bank. News reports in the West often featured the
demonstrations of great emotional outbursts of both Arab men and women
in the face of disaster or death. Such emotional displays were often met in

---

35. Ibid., 180.

36. Eduardo Duran and Bonnie Duran, *Native American Postcolonial Psychology*
(SUNY Series in Transpersonal and Humanistic Psychology; Albany: State University
of New York Press, 1995).

Western reporters' eyes with a certain kind of disgust. Albert Memmi, in his classic work on the colonial situation, reflects on precisely this aspect of what some writers have since referred to as the "colonial gaze":

> Even a native mother weeping over the death of her son or a native woman weeping over the death of her husband reminds [the colonizer] only vaguely of the grief of a mother or a wife.[37]

I was once startled to hear a respected historian tell me that ancient Mesopotamians would not have suffered much anxiety over war—"Just look at those people today! They couldn't care less!" Their grief, apparently, was not real grief.

Surely our reading of social science literature would help to mitigate any tendencies to forget that ancient Israelites fought real wars that featured real death and injury and caused real suffering and trauma. As European and American scholars particularly, we need to be cautious about the application of a "colonizer's gaze," a modern version of the "imperial gaze." Refugee, trauma, and forced migration studies can certainly help in assisting what we seewhen we read texts about warfare—including ancient warfare. How we apply these insights to the human condition will have to depend on our critical reading of the texts, of course, but we cannot ignore these realities in that important process.

Bibliography

Ahearn, Frederick L., Jr., ed. *The Psychosocial Wellness of Refugees: Issues in Qualitative and Quantitative Research*. Oxford: Berghahn Books, 2000.

Ahn, John J. *Exile as Forced Migrations: A Sociological, Literary, and Theological Approach on the Displacement and Resettlement of the Southern Kingdom of Judah*. BZAW 417. Berlin: de Gruyter, 2011.

Andersen, Francis I. and David Noel Freedman. *Micah: A New Translation with Introduction and Commentary*. AB 24. New York: Doubleday, 2000.

Bookman, Milica Z. *After Involuntary Migration: The Political Economy of Refugee Encampments*. Lanham, Md.: Lexington Books, 2002.

Camino, Linda A. and Ruth M. Krulfeld, "Introduction." Pages viii–xvi in *Reconstructing Lives, Recapturing Meaning: Refugee Identity, Gender, and Culture Change*. Edited by Linda A. Camino and Ruth M. Krulfeld. Basel: Gordon and Breach, 1994.

---

37. Albert Memmi, *The Colonizer and the Colonized* (Boston: Beacon, 1965), 86.

Duran, Eduardo, and Bonnie Duran. *Native American Postcolonial Psychology*. SUNY Series in Transpersonal and Humanistic Psychology. Albany: State University of New York Press, 1995.

Faris, James C. *Navajo and Photography: A Critical History of the Representation of an American People*. Salt Lake City: University of Utah Press, 2003.

Fassin, Didier, and Richard Rechtman. *The Empire of Trauma: An Inquiry into the Condition of Victimhood*. Translated by Rachel Gomme. Princeton: Princeton University Press, 2009.

Foucault, Michel. *Discipline and Punish: The Birth of the Prison*. London: Allen Lane, 1977.

Gilbert, Claude. "Studying Disaster: Changes in the Main Conceptual Tools." Pages 11–18 in *What Is Disaster: Perspectives on the Question*. Edited by E. L. Quarantelli. London: Routledge, 1998.

Goffman, Erving. *Asylums: Essays on the Social Situations of Mental Patients and Other Inmates*. Anchor A277. Garden City, N.Y.: Anchor Books, 1961.

Graham-Stewart, Michael. *Out of Time: Maori and the Photographer 1860–1940: The Ngawini Cooper Trust Collection*. Auckland City, New Zealand: John Leech Gallery, 2006.

Hillers, Delbert R. *Micah: A Commentary on the Book of the Prophet Micah*. Hermeneia. Philadelphia: Fortress, 1984.

Jacobs, Mignon R. "Bridging the Times: Trends in Micah Studies since 1985." *CurBS* 4 (2006): 293–329.

———. *The Conceptual Coherence of the Book of Micah*. JSOTSup 322. Sheffield: Sheffield Academic Press, 2001.

Knudsen, John C. "When Trust Is on Trial: Negotiating Refugee Narratives." Pages 13–35 in *Mistrusting Refugees*. Edited by D. E. Valentine and J. C. Knudsen. Berkeley: University of California Press, 1995.

Kuhrt, Amélie. *The Ancient Near East: c. 3000–330 BC*. Routledge History of the Ancient World. 2 vols. London: Routledge, 1995.

Limburg, James. *Hosea–Micah*. IBC. Atlanta: John Knox, 1988.

Lipschits, Oded. *The Fall and Rise of Jerusalem: Judah under Babylonian Rule*. Winona Lake, Ind.: Eisenbrauns, 2005.

Lydon, Jane. *Eye Contact: Photographing Indigenous Australians*. Durham: Duke University Press, 2005.

Matlou, Patrick. "Upsetting the Cart: Forced Migration and Gender Issues, the African Experience." in *Engendering Forced Migration: Theory and Practice*. Edited by Doreen Indra. Studies in Forced Migration 5. Oxford: Berghahn Books, 1999.

Mays, James Luther. *Micah: A Commentary*. OTL. Philadelphia: Westminster, 1976.

Memmi, Albert. *The Colonizer and the Colonized*. Boston: Beacon, 1965.

Mulvey, Laura. "Visual Pleasure and Narrative Cinema." Pages 833–44 in *Film Theory and Criticism: Introductory Readings*. Edited by Leo Braudy and Marshall Cohen. New York: Oxford University Press, 1999.

Piro, Joseph M. "Foucault and the Architecture of Surveillance: Creating Regimes of Power in Schools, Shrines, and Society." *Educational Studies: Journal of the American Educational Studies Association* 44 (2008): 30–46.

Pupavac, Vanessa. "Humanitarian Politics and the Rise of International Disaster Psychology." Pages 15–34 in vol. 1 of *Handbook of International Disaster Psychology*. Edited by G. Reyes and G. A. Jacobs. 4 vols. Westport, Conn.: Praeger, 2006.

Reyes, Gilbert. "International Disaster Psychology: Purposes, Principles, and Practices." Pages 1–13 in vol. 1 of *Handbook of International Disaster Psychology*. Edited by G. Reyes and G. A. Jacobs. 4 vols. Westport, Conn.: Praeger, 2006.

Rudolph, Wilhelm. *Micha–Nahum–Habakuk–Zephanja*. KAT 13.3. Gütersloh: Gerd Mohn, 1975.

Russell, John Malcolm. *The Writing on the Wall: Studies in the Architectural Context of Late Assyrian Palace Inscriptions*. Mesopotamian Civilizations 9. Winona Lake, Ind.: Eisenbrauns, 1999.

Scott, James C. *Domination and the Arts of Resistance: Hidden Transcripts*. New Haven: Yale University Press, 1990.

———. *Weapons of the Weak: Everyday Forms of Peasant Resistance*. New Haven: Yale University Press, 1985.

Smith-Christopher, Daniel L. "Ezekiel on Fanon's Couch: A Postcolonialist Critique in Dialogue with David Halperin's *Seeking Ezekiel*." Pages 108–44 in *Peace and Justice Shall Embrace: Power and Theopolitics in the Bible: Essays in Honor of Millard Lind*. Edited by T. Grimsrud and L. L. Johns. Telford, Penn.: Pandora, 2000.

Torrey, Charles C. "The Exile and the Restoration." Pages 285–340 in idem, *Ezra Studies*. Chicago: University of Chicago Press, 1910.

Turner, Stuart. "Torture, Refuge, and Trust." Pages 56–72 in *Mistrusting Refugees*. Edited by D. E. Valentine and J. C. Knudsen. Berkeley: University of California Press, 1995.

Valentine, Daniel E. and John C. Knudsen, eds. *Mistrusting Refugees*. Berkeley: University of California Press, 1995.

Voutira, Eftihia and Barbara Harrell-Bond. "In Search of the Locus of Trust: The Social World of the Refugee Camp." Pages 207–24 in *Mistrusting Refugees*. Edited by D. E. Valentine and J. C. Knudsen. Berkeley: University of California Press, 1995.

Wolff, Hans Walter. *Micah: A Commentary*. CC. Minneapolis: Augsburg, 1990.

Zajonc, Robert B. "Social Facilitation." *Science* 149 (1965): 269–74.

Deuteronomy 7 in Postcolonial Perspective: Cultural Fragmentation and Renewal

William Morrow

The problem that concerns this essay is how to account for the transformation of a pre-Deuteronomic tradition that mandated ethnocide into the demand for genocide in Deut 7. This is a difficult and somewhat speculative enterprise given the fact that there is little consensus in biblical scholarship about the composition history of Deut 7. Here I will propose that the development of this text is best accounted for by the experience of exile in Babylon. My thesis is fairly simple: the traumatic experience of being exiled led a Yʜᴡʜ-alone group to radicalize a pre-existing story which distinguished prophetic commitments to the exclusive worship of Yʜᴡʜ from an indigenous form of Israelite religion it considered illegitimate and foreign. After making a few observations about the composition of Deut 7, I will note that genocidal imagery can arise in subjugated groups as well as in dominant societies. This will lead to a description of some of the defenses that traumatized collectivities can use when threatened by overwhelming experiences of violence and terror. Thereafter, I apply these observations to the composition of Deut 7.

1. The Composition of Deuteronomy 7

Studies on the composition of Deut 7 do not yield a clear picture of its literary history. There is broad agreement that verses 25–26 are secondary,[1]

---

1. For example, Gustav Hölscher, "Komposition und Ursprung des Deuteronomiums," *ZAW* 40 (1922): 173-74; Norbert Lohfink, *Das Hauptgebot: Eine Untersuchung literarischer Einleitungsfragen zu Dtn 5–11* (AnBib 20; Rome: Pontifical Biblical Institute, 1963), 185–86; Gottfried Seitz, *Redaktionsgeschictliche Studien zum Deuteronomium* (BWANT 13; Stuttgart: Kohlhammer, 1971), 74–77; A. D. H. Mayes, *Deu-*

and there is an inconsistency in verse 4 due to the unusual first person reference to the deity. It is difficult, however, to make a firm case for other interventions in the text once it is allowed that the change between singular and plural second person references may be a legitimate feature of its composition,[2] and because the chapter is consciously borrowing from a preexisting tradition. Moreover, taken as it stands, the chapter possesses a certain literary cohesion.[3] Therefore, the following discussion assumes that Deut 7* (the asterisk signifies here the earliest edition of the text) may be regarded as a unitary text with the exception of the three verses mentioned above.

In terms of its relationships with other biblical passages, there is clearly an association with instructions regarding the expulsion of the nations and the destruction of their religious culture in Exod 23:20–33 and 34:11–16. The most extensive parallels are with Exod 23, to the point that some scholars assume that the writer of Deut 7* knew the Exodus passage in its present literary form.[4] It is arguable, however, that dependency between the two texts may run both ways.[5] Therefore, I follow Norbert Lohfink in assuming a continuity of tradition rather than making claims about the literary priority of Exod 23:20–33.[6] This tradition was adapted and expanded in Deut 7*.[7]

A second set of intertextual links is found in parallels to the ḥerem-laws in Deut 13:13–18 and 20:15–18. Neither of these texts belonged to the

---

teronomy (NCB; Grand Rapids: Eerdmans, 1981), 181–82; Félix García López, "'Un Peuple consacré:'Analyse critique de Deutéronome VII," VT 32 (1982): 449–50; Horst Dietrich Preuss, Deuteronomium (EdF 164; Darmstadt: Wissenschaftliche Buchgesellschaft, 1982), 49; Christa Schäfer-Lichtenberger, "JHWH, Israel und die Völker aus der Perspektive von Dtn 7," BZ 40 (1996): 197.

2. On the various functions of the so-called Numeruswechsel in Deuteronomy, see Lohfink, Das Hauptgebot, 244–51.

3. Moshe Weinfeld, Deuteronomy 1–11 (AB 5; New York: Doubleday, 1991), 380; Robert H. O'Connell, "Deuteronomy VII 1–26: Asymmetical Concentricity and the Rhetoric of Conquest," VT 42 (1992): 248–65; Richard Nelson, Deuteronomy (OTL; Louisville: Westminster John Knox, 2002), 98.

4. For example, Michael Fishbane, Biblical Interpretation in Ancient Israel (Oxford: Clarendon Press, 1985), 200–201; Weinfeld, Deuteronomy, 380.

5. Nelson, Deuteronomy, 98.

6. Lohfink, Das Hauptgebot, 176.

7. Baruch J. Schwartz, "Reexamining the Fate of the 'Canaanites' in the Torah Traditions," in Sefer Moshe: The Moshe Weinfeld Jubilee Volume (ed. C. Cohen, A. Hurvitz, and S. M. Paul; Winona Lake, Ind.: Eisenbrauns, 2004), 155–59.

earliest literary form of Deuteronomy (the so-called *Urdeuteronomium*). The command to destroy the Canaanite nations in Deut 20:15–18 is an addition to the original war law in 20:10–14, which makes no distinction between cities near and far. By contrast, verse 15 begins with a formula ("thus you shall deal") that operates as an exegetical device meant to limit the law's original application.[8] Deuteronomy 13 interrupts a more primary connection between the centralization laws in Deut 12:13–28 and their continuation in 14:22–28. It is widely regarded as belonging to a revision of the *Urdeuteronomium*.[9]

A third set of intertextual links exists between Deut 7* and the Deuteronomistic History (DtrH). According to Michael Fishbane, the inability of the Israelites to drive out the Canaanites in the account of Josh 14–18 is illuminated by a prognostication in Deut 7:22: the comment, "The LORD your God will clear away these nations before you little by little; you will not be able to make a quick end of them, otherwise the wild animals would become too numerous for you" works in a retrospective manner to justify Israel's failure to fulfill the command to eradicate the Canaanite nations.[10] It is difficult to determine whether Deut 7* was written prior to the corresponding material in the DtrH or is coeval with its composition. But, in any case, there is a close relationship between Deut 7* and some version of the DtrH.

Although Deut 7* has been variously dated to the late preexilic period,[11] the exile,[12] or the postexilic era,[13] I assume an exilic dating for two rea-

---

8. Alexander Rofé, *Deuteronomy: Issues and Interpretation* (London: T&T Clark, 2002), 155–56; see also Fishbane, *Biblical Interpretation,* 199–20.

9. Christoph Koch, *Vertrag, Treueid und Bund: Studien zur Rezeption des altorientalischen Vertragsrechts im Deuteronomium und zur Ausbildung der Bundestheologie im Alten Testament* (BZAW 383; Berlin: de Gruyter, 2008), 130–33.

10. Biblical translation NRSV; Fishbane, *Biblical Interpretation,* 202–3.

11. For example, Nelson, *Deuteronomy,* 6–8; Rofé, "*Deuteronomy,*" 156. Moshe Weinfeld ("The Ban on the Canaanites in the Biblical Codes and Its Historical Development," in *History and Traditions of Early Israel: Studies Presented to Eduard Nielsen* [ed. André Lemaire and Benedikt Otzen; VTSup 50; Leiden: Brill, 1993], 142–60 [155]) dates the Dtn *ḥerem* legislation more generally to "the 8th-7th century BCE, the time of the crystallization of the book of Deuteronomy." A date in the first half of the eighth century is suggested by Philip D. Stern, *The Biblical Ḥerem: A Window on Israel's Religious Experience* (BJS 211; Atlanta: Scholars Press, 1991), 101–2.

12. For example, Schäfer-Lichtenberger, "JHWH, Israel und die Völker," 199.

13. For example, Yair Hoffman, "The Deuteronomistic Concept of the Herem," *ZAW* 111 (1999): 196–210.

sons. First, the reference to future entry into the land in v. 1 may be read as a perspective from the exilic situation.[14] Second, the structure of Deut 7:17–24 closely resembles the oracle of encouragement directed to a king.[15] The fact that Israel now stands as a recipient of such a communication is commensurate with other indications that, during the exile, rhetoric once reserved for royalty was being applied to the people as a whole.[16] Besides these textual arguments, one may also advance an argument from ethnographic analogy. There is a need to identify a sufficiently forceful national trauma to explain the emergence of the demand for genocide in Deut 7*. This can be located in the experience of Israel's exile, particularly among those who were deported to Babylon.

2. The Genocidal Impulse as a Protest against Ethnocide

The discussion in this section makes a distinction between the concepts of *ethnocide* and *genocide*. Both, in fact, are important for the argument of this paper. Ethnocide involves a deliberate attempt "to destroy the national, ethnic, religious, political, social, or class *identity* of a group, as these groups are defined by the perpetrators" (emphasis original).[17] Unlike genocide, which one would like to imagine is fairly rare in human experience, world history is replete with accounts of ethnocide. They comprise a wide range of phenomena, including such varied policies as the mass

---

14. Schäfer-Lichtenberger, "JHWH, Israel und die Völker," 198–99.

15. Ibid., 212–14. For the form of Deut 7:17–24 as an oracle of holy war, see Gerhard von Rad, *Deuteronomy* (OTL; Philadelphia: Westminster, 1966), 69.

16. Claus Westermann, *Isaiah 40–66* (OTL; Philadelphia: Westminster, 1969), 283–84.

17. The definition is from Steven T. Katz, *The Holocaust in Historical Context: The Holocaust and Mass Death before the Modern Age* (New York: Oxford University Press, 1994), 1:137. Katz prefers the term *cultural genocide* to *ethnocide*, because he regards ethnocide as a term that may obscure the fact that groups not defined by ethnicity, such as class enemies or religious heretics, can also be victims of policies to destroy their social identities. Nevertheless, I use ethnocide following Frank Chalk and Kurt Jonassohn, *The History and Sociology of Genocide: Analyses and Case Studies* (New Haven: Yale University Press, 1990), 23. In part, this is because Katz himself (*Holocaust in Historical Context*, 1:131–33) is prone to use the term *genocide* without qualification to refer to deliberate attempts at mass murder of a defined group of people. It seems advisable, therefore, to reserve the term *genocide* for such actions and find another term for the elimination of a group's identity when there is no intent to physically eliminate the people themselves: *ethnocide*.

deportations carried out by Assyria in the first millennium B.C.E. to programs of intentional deculturation carried out by the Western colonial powers in the nineteenth and twentieth centuries of the Common Era.[18] For example, the deliberate attempts made by the Indian residential or boarding school systems established by the governments of Canada and the United States, with the collusion of the mainline churches, to inculcate the values of the dominant society while denigrating native traditions amounted to a program of ethnocide.[19]

Genocide is a concept that has engendered a fair share of debate and competing definitions.[20] I follow Nicholas Robbins in accepting the definition of Frank Chalk and Kurt Jonassohn: "*Genocide* is a form of one-sided mass killing in which a state or other authority intends to destroy a group, as that group and membership are defined by the perpetrator" (emphasis in the original).[21] Of particular importance in this definition is the concept of intent: genocide involves a deliberate decision to eliminate another group of people by mass killing.[22] For this reason, Deut 7* may be considered to enjoin a program of genocide on its readers, because it intends the unconditional physical elimination of the Canaanite peoples it names.[23]

Genocide can be perpetrated from a variety of motives including the need to eliminate a real or perceived threat or to implement a belief or ideology.[24] Below I will stress the connection between Deut 7* and the need to eliminate a threat and to implement a belief. Here I wish to underscore the

---

18. Katz, *Holocaust in Historical Context*, 1:139–46.

19. Literature on this subject is large and growing. For aboriginal voices holding this opinion see, e.g., Eduardo Duran and Bobbie Duran, *Native American Postcolonial Psychology* (Albany: State University of New York, 1995), 33–34; Bernard Schissel and Terry Wotherspoon, *The Legacy of School for Aboriginal People: Education, Oppression, and Emancipation* (Toronto: Oxford University Press, 2003), 35–39; Roland Chrisjohn, Sherri Young, and Michael Maraun, *The Circle Game: Shadows and Substance in the Indian Residential School Experience in Canada* (rev. ed.; Penticton, British Columbia: Theytus Books, 2006), 59–78.

20. See Chalk and Jonassohn, *History and Sociology of Genocide*, 12–23.

21. Nicholas A. Robbins, *Native Insurgencies and the Genocidal Impulse in the Americas* (Bloomington: Indiana University Press, 2005), 18; see Chalk and Jonassohn, *History and Sociology of Genocide*, 23.

22. Chalk and Jonasohn, *History and Sociology of Genocide*, 26; Katz, *Holocaust in Historical Perspective*, 1:133–35.

23. Jeffrey H. Tigay, *JPS Torah Commentary: Deuteronomy* (Philadelphia: Jewish Publication Society, 1996), 472.

24. Robbins, *Native Insurgencies*, 20.

fact that the genocidal imagination can be activated in subjugated as well as in dominant societies. We are probably most familiar with genocidal actions taken on behalf of a state against a minority. This was paradigmatically true of the *Shoah,* the calculated destruction of Jews during World War 2. But historically there have also been movements by oppressed peoples that have either dreamed of or taken steps to eliminate what they perceived as the intrusive domination of foreigners from their midst by intending their mass elimination. There are illustrations of this fact from aboriginal societies colonized by Europeans in the Americas. Among them one might list the Great Pueblo revolt of 1688, the Great Rebellion of Peru in 1780, and the Caste War of Yucatán in 1847.[25] Mention should also be made of the Ghost Dance movements of 1870 and 1890 in North America. While the Ghost Dance did not lead to native uprisings that perpetrated mass exterminations of enemy-others, destruction of aboriginal cultures as a result of colonialism led to the widespread acceptance of beliefs and hopes that a coming apocalypse would sweep away not only European culture but the whites themselves.[26] The Ghost Dance movement is an important ethnographic analogy for a study of Deut 7*, because it shows that a subjugated people can entertain a genocidal impulse even when it lacks the means or opportunity to carry it out.

Every one of the native movements mentioned above was predicated on a history of domination by a foreign power whose elimination was deemed necessary for a return or revival of a traditional native culture. In other words, the genocidal desire was provoked by a perception that the oppressed group was in danger of becoming a victim of ethnocide.[27] Given the constraints of space, I cannot describe any of these movements in detail. But their instructive value for this paper is that genocide can be the dream of a dominated as well as a dominant social group.

These observations have relevance for the next part of my argument, even as one must also recognize that there are some important differences between the cases just mentioned and the situation in Deut 7*. One of the most significant differences is that the biblical text commands the geno-

---

25. Described in Robbins, *Native Insurgencies,* 23–67.

26. There are many studies of this important nativistic movement in nineteenth-century North America. My remarks rely on Bryan R. Wilson, *Magic and the Millennium: A Sociological Study of Religious Movements of Protest among Tribal and Third-World Peoples* (London: Heinemann, 1973), 283–306.

27. Robbins, *Native Insurgencies,* 164.

cide of a fictive enemy. Scholars have frequently noted that by the time this chapter was written there were no "Canaanite" nations to be eliminated. The demand for the destruction of the original inhabitants of the land of promise as well as their idolatrous material culture has a symbolic value; it represents a metaphor for some other kind of religiously valorized social action.

3. War, Exile, and Trauma

In order to understand the metaphoric value of Deut 7*'s genocidal imagination, I turn to literature on the psychology of collective trauma. As I do not claim to be expert in individual or social psychology, I will attempt to couch my observations in nonclinical language to reflect the fact that I am a layperson in the field of trauma studies. For the sake of variety and because it is a nonclinical term, I will use the phrase "experiences of overwhelming violence" as a synonym for trauma.

Trauma can be defined as (violent) stress that is sudden, unexpected, or nonnormative, exceeds the individual's perceived ability to meet its demands, and disrupts various psychological needs.[28] Within this definition, I am particularly drawn to the concept of disruption. One of the well-known effects of trauma is its capacity to shatter a previously constructed sense of self.[29] Both for groups and individuals seeking recovery, it is of primary importance to find ways to assert control over the violence that is frequently internalized as various forms of self-hatred and ongoing syndromes of disintegrating experiences.

In other words, trauma connotes a sense of "severe dislocation" that disrupts a previously constructed sense of self.[30] The proximity between trauma and dislocation is informative because it allows for a connection between the study of psychological processes and concepts current in postcolonial studies. One of the major metaphors for the colonial experience is "dis-placement." A valid and active sense of agency can be eroded

---

28. I. Lisa McCann and Laurie A. Pearlman, *Psychological Trauma and the Adult Survivor: Theory, Therapy, and Transformation* (Brunner/Mazal Psychosocial Stress Series 21; New York: Brunner/Mazal, 1990), 10.

29. Jeffrey S. Murer, "Constructing the Enemy-Other: Anxiety, Trauma and Mourning in the Narratives of Political Conflict," *Psychoanalysis, Culture & Society* 14 (2009): 113.

30. Ibid., 114.

by migrations and processes of indenture imposed on a colonized people. It may also be destroyed by cultural denigration: conscious and unconscious oppression of the indigenous personality by a supposedly superior racial and cultural model.[31] In any of these cases, the colonized group has effectively lost its place in the world. There is a close relationship, therefore, between the experiences of exile, cultural displacement, trauma, and war. In this respect, Daniel Smith-Christopher has called for a hermeneutic of the exile that is informed by familiarity with "patterns of domination, resistance, and the dynamics of social subordination."[32]

Along with the connotations of displacement, another metaphor for understanding the effects of trauma is provided by the concept of *abjection* in the thought of the French feminist literary critic and psychoanalyst Julia Kristeva. Abjection connotes the visceral abhorrence that human beings feel toward experiences that compromise their sense of self. It is experienced as the intrusion of unwanted ambiguities that threaten a sense of social competence and cultural agency. The effects of abjection can also be described as "boundary failure."[33] In terms of group psychology, an experience of boundary failure as a result of overwhelming violence possesses the capacity to exacerbate pre-existing social tensions that the society had held in check.[34]

Victims of trauma display a large number of coping strategies that are designed to protect themselves from a repetition of the violence they have experienced and to reconstruct some kind of coherent sense of self. In this connection, there are two defensive moves that I think are particularly important for understanding the genesis of Deut 7*. One of these is storytelling; the second involves processes of "othering."

The role of storytelling as a means for recovering from overwhelming experiences of violence is well-known. Narratives provide at least a partial solution to the lack of coherence between the present and the past that is

---

31. Bill Ashcroft, Gareth Griffiths, and Helen Tiffin, *The Empire Writes Back: Theory and Practice in Post-Colonial Literatures* (2nd ed.; London: Routledge, 2002), 8–9.

32. Daniel L. Smith-Christopher, "Reassessing the Historical and Sociological Impact of the Babylonian Exile (597/587–539 BCE)," in *Exile: Old Testament, Jewish, and Christian Conceptions* (ed. J. M. Scott; JSJSup 56; Leiden: Brill, 1997), 36.

33. Martha J. Reineke, *Sacrificed Lives: Kristeva on Women and Violence* (Bloomington: Indiana University Press, 1997), 26–32.

34. Murer, "Constructing the Enemy-Other," 116–17.

brought about by trauma. In this respect, they help to rebuild a shattered sense of self. Certain narratives about the past may also become proxy representations of the unprocessed memories of the calamities that victims have suffered, sometimes by casting them as heroes in a story about a past struggle. In other words, collective narratives of trauma may reinterpret past traditions to make sense of current situations.[35]

The second defensive strategy involves shoring up a sense of self by making boundaries between self and other more rigid. In this respect, stories also become an important marker of insiders and outsiders, defined as those who share the story and those who do not. By the same token, the process of self-making implicit in recovering from trauma also manufactures insiders and outsiders by projecting onto outsiders unacceptable traits of the self. Enemies may be created in the process of recovering from trauma because the enemy-other becomes "a reservoir of unwanted self- and object representations."[36] In other words, the enemy comes to embody those unacceptable parts of the self that a victimized group blames for the violations it has experienced. It is important to note that depersonalization and dehumanization of the enemy will depend on the degree of fragility that the group-self senses about its own boundaries. The more the group feels threatened, the more it is tempted to dehumanize the enemy-other. As explained by political psychologist Erel Shalit, aggression increases with the threat of annihilation.[37]

4. Synthesis and Application to Deuteronomy 7*

It is my thesis that one can understand the composition of Deut 7* as a response to the overwhelming violence of the exile on the part of some of those deported from Judah to Mesopotamia by the Babylonians. In making this proposal, I am well aware that I am taking sides in a vigorous and unresolved scholarly debate about relationships between Deuteronomy and the DtrH by locating the historical context for the composition of Deut 7* in Babylon.[38] But I would observe that the threat of assimilation, of the annihilation of Israel as a covenant community centered on Yhwh,

---

35. Ibid., 114–15.

36. Ibid., 115–16.

37. Erel Shalit, "The Relationship Between Aggression and Fear of Annihilation in Israel," *Political Psychology* 15 (1994): 418.

38. For a review of theories on the composition of the DtrH, see Rainer Albertz,

seems to have been particularly acute to those who suffered the various deportations from Judah to Mesopotamia. Proof for this can be found in the disputation speeches of the Second Isaiah that attempt to counter the exiles' fascination with the religion of Babylon,[39] and also in the prophecies of Ezekiel who, among other things, must answer the despair of the people at having to live among those who worship "wood and stone."[40]

In fact, the exiles experienced several kinds of war-related trauma. Violence increased dramatically in the general environment of Judah and Jerusalem as a result of Babylonian invasions. The first Babylonian conquest took place in March of 597 B.C.E. The Babylonian Chronicle suggests that after a short siege the city was captured and heavily plundered, and its monarch exiled. A second rebellion under the substitute king, Zedekiah, led to a two-year siege of Jerusalem in the early 580s. By its end, there was famine in the city. A few weeks after Jerusalem was captured, the temple, royal palace, and homes of the aristocracy were burned to the ground; the city walls were torn down. Some surviving royal and temple officials, military commanders, and provincial leaders were rounded up and summarily executed. In addition, wide-ranging destruction took place in the countryside, particularly affecting the fortress towns, which were pillaged and despoiled. There is no way to estimate the casualties, but it is safe to assume that a fair percentage of Judah's human resources and leadership was killed off.[41]

Portions of the population of Judah and Jerusalem were forcibly deported by the Babylonian empire in order to suppress the country's capacity to rebel. There are discrepancies among the biblical sources about the number of deportations, their dates, and the size of the populace affected. Conflicting accounts are found in 2 Kgs 24:8–25:21 and Jer 52:1–30. Various attempts have been made to harmonize these texts, but none are satisfactory. Nevertheless, it may be concluded that, by any account, a sizable number of elite citizens, temple and military officials,

---

Israel in Exile: The History and Literature of the Sixth Century B.C.E. (trans. David Green; SBLSBL 3; Atlanta: Scholars, 2003), 274–79.

39. For example, Isa 40:18–20; 44:9–20; 46:5–7; see William S. Morrow, "Comfort for Jerusalem: The Second Isaiah as Counselor to Refugees," *BTB* 34 (2004): 86.

40. Ezek 20:32; see Dalit Rom-Shiloni, "Facing Destruction and Exile: Inner-Biblical Exegesis in Jeremiah and Ezekiel," *ZAW* 117 (2005): 198.

41. J. Maxwell Miller and John H. Hayes, *A History of Ancient Israel and Judah* (Philadelphia: Westminster, 1986), 408–16.

and artisans was involved.[42] Estimates vary as one must also guess about the total size of Judah and Jerusalem at this time. It is possible, however, that Judah's population was reduced to approximately half of what it had been as result of the predations of the Babylonian empire through war, famine, and deportation.[43]

The experience of the Babylonian exile heightened tensions in a sense of collective self that was already conflicted in the late preexilic period. There is substantial evidence that the customs Deut 7* attributes to the Canaanite nations were once part and parcel of Israelite popular religion. That is, a significant part of the population in preexilic Israel was polytheistic and expressed itself in a material culture that included sacred poles, pillars, and other divine images.[44] A protest against this kind of Israelite religion was already developing in the preexilic era under prophetic aegis, with the prophet Hosea being an early and recognizable exponent of what Morton Smith called the "YHWH-alone" movement.[45] It was an iconoclastic faction that insisted on the exclusive veneration of YHWH by Israel.

One expression of this movement is the tradition that Deut 7* adapted. The YHWH-alone movement developed a narrative that imagined Israel's occupation of the land as a divinely accomplished incursion in which the material culture of idolatry was to be destroyed. According to this pre-Deuteronomic expression of YHWH-alone theology, the traditional religion of its ethnic contemporaries was a foreign abomination. By implication, a polytheistic Israelite was no Israelite at all, but an outsider. So already in the preexilic traditions reflected in Exod 23:20–33 one may see elements of social conflict, the creation of a narrative to sustain a particular identity, and the use of pejorative terminology to distinguish the in-group from the out-group.

---

42. Ibid., 419–20.

43. Albertz, *Israel in Exile*, 90.

44. William G. Dever, "The Silence of the Text: An Archaeological Commentary on 2 Kings 23," in *Scripture and Other Artifacts: Essays on the Bible and Archaeology in Honor of Philip J. King* (ed. Michael D. Cogan, J. Cheryl Exum, and Lawrence E. Stager; Louisville: Westminster John Knox Press, 1994), 160; Robert K. Gnuse, *No Other Gods: Emergent Monotheism in Israel* (JSOTSup 241; Sheffield: Sheffield Academic, 1997), 179.

45. Morton Smith, *Palestinian Parties and Politics That Shaped the Old Testament* (New York: Columbia University Press, 1971), 29–30. Smith's views are summarized in Gnuse, *No Other Gods*, 75–77.

Among recent commentators, Nathan MacDonald and Joel Lohr have been particularly insistent on the metaphoric significance of Deut 7. For MacDonald, Deuteronomy's *herem* laws illustrate, by way of contrast, the positive command to love and obey YHWH exclusively.[46] For Lohr, Deut 7 illustrates what it means for Israel to know itself as elected by God because the idea of *herem* is closely connected with holiness: "Through the *herem*, Israel is able to be what God intended Israel to be: a people set apart and devoted to him."[47] I have no quarrel with either MacDonald or Lohr, save for the fact that I do not think they have fully dealt with the increase in the violent imagination that marks Deut 7* against its traditional roots. Surely, the same insights were available to Deuteronomic theologians from a simple reappropriation of the demands for the destruction of the material religious culture of Israel's Canaanite rivals. The demand for the extermination of the Canaanite nations in Deut 7 rather than their expulsion (according to Exod 23 and 34) points to the presence of a particularly conflicted context that the Deuteronomic passage was written to address.

Above I noted that a genocidal imagination might arise in a group that was oppressed by a colonial power and that was feeling the effects of ethnocide. I suggest that similar conditions were operative among Judah's intellectuals during the Babylonian exile. The destruction of the Jerusalem temple, the only place authorized for sacrifice according Deuteronomy, and the loss of access to the land of Israel were tantamount to a deliberate attempt to destroy a collective identity that depended on that institution and that geographical place to mediate its relationship with God. As with other groups in history, faced with the threat of ethnocide, the group responsible for the composition of Deut 7* responded with the dream of genocide.

Boundary failure and the genocidal imagination, therefore, are unsurprising bedfellows. The need to defend against the intrusion of unwanted ambiguities leads to the creation of what Kristeva calls a "sacrificial economy," which is a social strategy characterized by sets of prohibitions meant to protect against the intrusion of boundary-threatening experiences by

---

46. Nathan MacDonald, *Deuteronomy and the Meaning of "Monotheism"* (FAT 2/1; Tübingen: Mohr Siebeck, 2003), 113–17.

47. Joel N. Lohr, *Chosen and Unchosen: Conceptions of Election in the Pentateuch and Jewish-Christian Interpretation* (Siphrut 2; Winona Lake, Ind.: Eisenbrauns, 2009), 172.

separating the cultural agent from them. One of the chief expressions of a sacrificial economy is law.[48]

In fact, biblical law is highly concerned with certain forms of boundary failure. All of the major law codes, for example, deal with problems involving idolatry, slavery, and sex. Illegitimate sexual performances are closely connected with illegitimate worship practices, as can be seen, for instance, in the rhetoric against the Canaanites.[49] The Canaanites, according to the biblical tradition, lost their claim to the land due to moral and religious excesses (see, for instance, Lev 18). As a result, there are strong prohibitions in biblical law meant to avoid the boundary failures signified by both sexual infidelity and idolatry. The threatened consequences for tolerating such experiences of abjection was the loss of land and Israel's loss of competence as an agent in the ancient world: slavery (see, for example, the curses in Deut 28:20–44).

Feeling severely compromised by the intrusion of what it had come to regard as alien to its own values and culture, during the exile a YHWH-alone group was drawn to imagine the possibility of eliminating the agents of that violating foreignness from its midst. Its motivations for articulating Deut 7* arose from three different sources: (a) to stake out its position in a situation of social conflict; (b) to express an increase in defensive aggression; and (c) to articulate a new narrative to assimilate experiences of overwhelming violence.

4.1. Social Conflict

There is evidence for sharp social conflict within Israel during the exilic era. With respect to Ezekiel, a voice from the early exile, Dalit Rom-Shiloni has described the emergence of a rhetoric of hostility between those who remained in the land and those who were exiled. One of the concerns of Ezekiel's prophetic activity was to delegitimize the community left in Jerusalem by accusing them of various sins that estranged them from

---

48. Julia Kristeva, *Powers of Horror: An Essay on Abjection* (European Perspectives; New York: Columbia University Press, 1982), 110–12; Reineke, *Sacrificed Lives,* 67–73.

49. Stephen A. Geller, *Sacred Enigmas: Literary Religion in the Hebrew Bible* (London: Routledge, 1996), 148.

God and denying their claim to be the continuing covenant people.[50] It is not my intent to homogenize the views of Ezekiel and Deut 7*.[51] My purpose is served here simply by noting that strong inter-community rivalries manifested themselves during the exile in which charges of idolatry and apostasy played important roles. That Deut 7* was written out of a conflicted social situation is shown by its concern to avoid intermarriage with representatives of apostate groups. The presence of the prohibition against intermarriage suggests the presence of an ongoing cultural struggle,[52] even as the metaphor of ḥerem represents the noncompromising cultural identity the addressees of Deut 7* were expected to adopt.

One might ask why Deut 7* targets social rivals within Israel (symbolized by the fictitious Canaanites)[53] instead of polemicizing against the actual perpetrators of Judah's exile, namely the Babylonians. Israel's thinkers refused to acknowledge any ultimate cause for the destruction of Jerusalem other than the wrath of Yhwh against his apostate people. As Louis Stuhlman has observed, a sense of social apprehension and the idea that Israel's boundaries can be compromised by dangerous insiders permeates the book of Deuteronomy.[54] Deuteronomy 7* participates in this anxiety, but also offers its readers a remedy for it by calling on them to identify with a group willing to express its exclusive loyalty to Yhwh in the most uncompromising terms.

---

50. Dalit Rom-Shiloni, "Ezekiel as the Voice of the Exiles and the Constructor of Exilic Ideology," *HUCA* 76 (2005): 18-20.

51. Yet I would note that their perspectives were brought together by the writer who added vv. 25–26 to the original text of the chapter, since this passage shows affinities with legal categories also used by Ezekiel. See Schäfer-Lichtenberger, "JHWH, Israel und die Völker," 212.

52. MacDonald, *Deuteronomy and Monotheism*, 117–19.

53. I am by no means the first to suggest that the polemic against the Canaanites in Deuteronomy is a cipher for an inner-Israelite social conflict. See, e.g., Lori L. Rowlett, *Joshua and the Rhetoric of Violence: A New Historicist Analysis* (JSOTSup 226; Sheffield: Sheffield Academic, 1996), 12–13; Mark G. Brett, "Genocide in Deuteronomy: Postcolonial Variations on Mimetic Desire," in *Seeing Signals, Reading Signs: The Art of Exegesis. Studies in Honor of Antony F. Campbell SJ for his Seventieth Birthday* (ed. Mark A. O'Brien and Howard N. Wallace; JSOTSup 415; London: T&T Clark, 2004), 83–84. Both Rowlett and Brett, however, relate the social conflict in which "Canaanite" is used as a metaphor for opponents of the Deuteronomic point of view to the Josianic period.

54. Louis Stuhlman, "Encroachment in Deuteronomy: An Analysis of the Social World of the D Code," *JBL* 109 (1990): 631.

4.2. Increased Aggression

The exile increased the threat of annihilation on the part of the YHWH-alone party as it found itself surrounded by an alien culture, with no physical or political boundaries to protect itself. The perception of an increased threat of annihilation required an increase in aggression toward the metaphorical entity opposed to faithful Israel. This aggression had two sources. On one hand, it represented the energy needed to defend weakened boundaries between self and other; on the other, it stemmed from an internalized violence that had to be displaced if it was not to rebound on the group as self-hatred. In previous work on Second Isaiah, I have shown exiled Israel was living with a significant degree of self-hatred as those who knew themselves as the objects of divine wrath.[55] How can they deflect the intense pain of living as those who were the agents of Israel's destruction, as the generation punished by God for apostasy? One way was to dissociate from the group of idolatrous perpetrators by venting on them the full weight of divine wrath that Israel itself had received.

4.3. Unassimilated Experiences of Violence

A third effect of the exile was to promote the need for a narrative to help process unassimilated experiences of trauma. The destruction of the seven Canaanite nations served as a proxy memory for the violent destruction of the exiles' own culture; only now it is Israel who is in the position of power. In other words, Deut 7* is a revenge fantasy, a common experience of people who have been violated and become the victims of violent actions. Here, the desire for revenge is directed against metaphorical representatives of the part of Israel that is utterly unacceptable to the YHWH-alone party. The writers of Deut 7* believed themselves to be locked in a deadly conflict; the price for not eliminating Canaanite culture was the elimination of Israel by YHWH.[56]

---

55. Morrow, "Comfort for Jerusalem," 83–84.
56. Schwartz, "Reexamining the Fate of the Canaanites," 155.

5. Conclusion

The iconoclastic tradition reflected in Exod 23 and 34, upon which Deut
7* depends, suggests that YHWH himself will create the division between
Israel and the nations by driving them out. As Baruch Schwartz describes it,
according to this tradition Israel really did not have to do anything except
get out of the way: YHWH was going to do for them.[57] It would not be too
far off the mark to claim that in the exile Israel's thinkers came to the conclusion that more was expected of God's people than that. A defense of its
boundaries, in fact, required constant vigilance and the utmost devotion.
The genocidal imagination of Deut 7*, therefore, represents an attempt to
defend the community against an increased threat of ethnocide or cultural
annihilation. For this reason, during the exile in Babylon, a YHWH-alone
party suffering from the trauma of war and captivity radicalized its commitment to a society free of idolatry and devoted exclusively to the god of
Israel by composing Deut 7*.

It ought to be noted, however, that becoming a victim of overwhelming
violence is not necessarily a life sentence. Time may not heal all wounds;
but the symptoms of trauma can be ameliorated through the passage of
the years.[58] Georg Braulik's study of the canonical frame of Deuteronomy
suggests it was written for a group of returnees for whom the metaphor
of complete extermination of the inhabitants of the land was no longer
operative. Passages that explicitly address the return from exile such as
Deut 30 do not envisage the conflictual process represented in Deut 7*.[59]
It would appear, therefore, that through the passage of time trauma symptoms among the Babylonian diaspora diminished. Therefore, one need not
think that Deut 7* represents the last word on the psychology of exiled
Israel even if it played a vital part at some point during the Babylonian
captivity in addressing its wounded sense of self.

---

57. Ibid., 157.

58. Donald Meichenbaum, *A Clinical Handbook/Practical Therapist Manual for
Assessing and Treating Adults with Post-traumatic Stress Disorder* (Waterloo, Ont.:
Institute Press, 1994), 23.

59. Georg Braulik, "Die Völkervernichtung und die Rückkehr ins Verheissungsland: Hermeneutische Bermerkungen zum Buch Deuteronomium," in *Deuteronomy
and Deuteronomic Literature: Festschrift C. H. W. Brekelmans* (ed. M. Vervenne and J.
Lust; BETL 133; Leuven: Peeters, 1997), 37–38.

Bibliography

Albertz, Rainer. *Israel in Exile: The History and Literature of the Sixth Century B.C.E.* Translated by David Green. SBLSBL 3. Atlanta: Society of Biblical Literature, 2003.

Ashcroft, Bill, Gareth Griffiths, and Helen Tiffin. *The Empire Writes Back: Theory and Practice in Post-Colonial Literatures.* 2nd ed. London: Routledge, 2002.

Braulik, George. "Die Volkervernichtung und die Rückkehr ins Verheissungsland: Hermeneutische Bermerkungen zum Buch Deuteronomium." Pages 3–38 in *Deuteronomy and Deuteronomic Literature: Festschrift C. H. W. Brekelmans.* Edited by M. Vervenne and J. Lust. BETL 133. Leuven: Peeters, 1997.

Brett, Mark G. "Genocide in Deuteronomy: Postcolonial Variations on Mimetic Desire." Pages 75–89 in *Seeing Signals, Reading Signs: The Art of Exegesis. Studies in Honor of Antony F. Campbell SJ for His Seventieth Birthday.* Edited by Mark A. O'Brien and Howard N. Wallace. JSOTSup 415. London: T&T Clark, 2004.

Chalk, Frank, and Kurt Jonassohn. *The History and Sociology of Genocide: Analyses and Case Studies.* New Haven: Yale University Press, 1990.

Chrisjohn, Roland, Sherri Young, and Michael Maraun. *The Circle Game: Shadows and Substance in the Indian Residential School Experience in Canada.* Rev. ed. Penticton, British Columbia: Theytus Books, 2006.

Dever, William G. "The Silence of the Text: An Archaeological Commentary on 2 Kings 23." Pages 143–68 in *Scripture and Other Artifacts: Essays on the Bible and Archaeology in Honor of Philip J. King.* Edited by Michael D. Cogan, J. Cheryl Exum, and Lawrence E. Stager. Louisville: Westminster John Knox, 1994.

Duran, Eduardo, and Bobbie Duran. *Native American Postcolonial Psychology.* Albany: State University of New York, 1995.

Fishbane, Michael. *Biblical Interpretation in Ancient Israel.* Oxford: Clarendon, 1985.

Geller, Stephen A. *Sacred Enigmas: Literary Religion in the Hebrew Bible.* London: Routledge, 1996.

Gnuse, Robert K. *No Other Gods: Emergent Monotheism in Israel.* JSOTSup 241. Sheffield: Sheffield Academic, 1997.

Hoffman, Yair. "The Deuteronomistic Concept of the Herem." *ZAW* 111 (1999): 196–210.

Hölscher, Gustav. "Komposition und Ursprung des Deuteronomiums." *ZAW* 40 (1922): 161–255.

Katz, Steven T. *The Holocaust in Historical Context: The Holocaust and Mass Death before the Modern Age.* New York: Oxford University Press, 1994.

Koch, Christoph. *Vertrag, Treueid und Bund: Studien zur Rezeption des altorientalischen Vertragsrechts im Deuteronomium und zur Ausbildung der Bundestheologie im Alten Testament.* BZAW 383. Berlin: de Gruyter, 2008.

Kristeva, Julia. *Powers of Horror: An Essay on Abjection.* European Perspectives; New York: Columbia University Press, 1982.

Lohfink, Norbert. *Das Hauptgebot: Eine Untersuchung literarischer Einleitungsfragen zu Dtn 5–11.* AnBib 20. Rome: Pontifical Biblical Institute, 1963.

Lohr, Joel N. *Chosen and Unchosen: Conceptions of Election in the Pentateuch and Jewish-Christian Interpretation.* Siphrut 2. Winona Lake, Ind.: Eisenbrauns, 2009.

López, Félix García. "'Un Peuple consacré:' Analyse critique de Deutéronome VII." *VT* 32 (1982): 438–63.

MacDonald, Nathan. *Deuteronomy and the Meaning of "Monotheism."* FAT 2/1. Tübingen: Mohr Siebeck, 2003.

Mayes, A. D. H. *Deuteronomy.* NCB. Grand Rapids: Eerdmans, 1981.

McCann, I. Lisa, and Laurie A. Pearlman. *Psychological Trauma and the Adult Survivor: Theory, Therapy, and Transformation.* Brunner/Mazal Psychosocial Stress Series 21. New York: Brunner/Mazal, 1990.

Meichenbaum, Donald. *A Clinical Handbook/Practical Therapist Manual for Assessing and Treating Adults with Post-traumatic Stress Disorder.* Waterloo, Ont.: Institute Press, 1994.

Miller, J. Maxwell, and John H. Hayes. *A History of Ancient Israel and Judah.* Philadelphia: Westminster, 1986.

Morrow, William S. "Comfort for Jerusalem: The Second Isaiah as Counselor to Refugee." *BTB* 34 (2004): 80–86.

Murer, Jeffrey S. "Constructing the Enemy-Other: Anxiety, Trauma and Mourning in the Narratives of Political Conflict." *Psychoanalysis, Culture & Society* 14 (2009): 109–30.

Nelson, Richard. *Deuteronomy.* OTL. Louisville: Westminster John Knox, 2002.

O'Connell, Robert H. "Deuteronomy VII 1–26: Asymmetrical Concentricity and the Rhetoric of Conquest." *VT* 42 (1992): 248–65.

Preuss, Horst Dietrich. *Deuteronomium.* EdF 164. Darmstadt: Wissenschaftliche Buchgesllschaft, 1982.

Rad, Gerhard von. *Deuteronomy.* OTL. Philadelphia: Westminster, 1966.

Reineke, Martha J. *Sacrificed Lives: Kristeva on Women and Violence.* Bloomington: Indiana University Press, 1997.

Robbins, Nicholas A. *Native Insurgencies and the Genocidal Impulse in the Americas.* Bloomington: Indiana University Press, 2005.

Rofé, Alexander. *Deuteronomy: Issues and Interpretation.* London: T&T Clark, 2002.

Rom-Shiloni, Dalit. "Ezekiel as the Voice of the Exiles and the Constructor of Exilic Ideology." *HUCA* 76 (2005): 1–45.

———. "Facing Destruction and Exile: Inner-Biblical Exegesis in Jeremiah and Ezekiel." *ZAW* 117 (2005): 189–205.

Rowlett, Lori L. *Joshua and the Rhetoric of Violence: A New Historicist Analysis.* JSOTSup 226. Sheffield: Sheffield Academic Press, 1996.

Schafer-Lichtenberger, Christa. "JHWH, Israel und die Völker aus der Perspektive von Dtn 7." *BZ* 40 (1996): 194-218.

Schissel, Bernard, and Terry Wotherspoon. *The Legacy of School for Aboriginal People: Education, Oppression, and Emancipation.* Toronto: Oxford University Press, 2003.

Schwartz, Baruch J. "Reexamining the Fate of the 'Canaanites' in the Torah Traditions." Pages 155-59 in *Sefer Moshe: The Moshe Weinfeld Jubilee Volume.* Edited by C. Cohen, A. Hurvitz, and S. M. Paul. Winona Lake, Ind.: Eisenbrauns, 2004.

Seitz, Gottfried. *Redaktionsgeschictliche Studien zum Deuteronomium*. BWANT 13. Stuttgart: Kohlhammer, 1971.

Shalit, Erel. "The Relationship between Aggression and Fear of Annihilation in Israel." *Political Psychology* 15 (1994): 415–34.

Smith, Morton. *Palestinian Parties and Politics That Shaped the Old Testament*. New York: Columbia University Press, 1971.

Smith-Christopher, Daniel L. "Reassessing the Historical and Sociological Impact of the Babylonian Exile (597/587-539 BCE)." Pages 7–36 in *Exile: Old Testament, Jewish, and Christian Conceptions*. Edited by J. M. Scott. JSJSup 56. Leiden: Brill, 1997.

Stern, Philip D. *The Biblical Ḥerem: A Window on Israel's Religious Experience*. BJS 211. Atlanta: Scholars Press, 1991.

Stuhlman, Louis. "Encroachment in Deuteronomy: An Analysis of the Social World of the D Code." *JBL* 109 (1990): 613–32.

Tigay, Jeffrey H. *JPS Torah Commentary: Deuteronomy*. Philadelphia: Jewish Publication Society, 1996.

Weinfeld, Moshe. "The Ban on the Canaanites in the Biblical Codes and Its Historical Development." Pages 142–60 in *History and Traditions of Early Israel: Studies Presented to Eduard Nielsen*. Edited by André Lemaire and Benedikt Otzen. VTSup 50. Leiden: Brill, 1993.

———. *Deuteronomy 1–11*. AB 5. New York: Doubleday, 1991.

Westermann, Claus. *Isaiah 40–66*. OTL. Philadelphia: Westminster, 1969.

Wilson, Bryan R. *Magic and the Millennium: A Sociological Study of Religious Movements of Protest among Tribal and Third-World Peoples*. London: Heinemann, 1973.

Reading into the Gap:
Refractions of Trauma in Israelite Prophecy

David M. Carr

In an evocative article on fantasy in Gen 1–3, Roland Boer reflects at length on the possible presence of an "unrepresentable horror" that might stand behind and generate narratives such as the garden of Eden story.[1] Building on Lacan (especially Zizek's adaptation of Lacan), Boer suggests that biblical narratives such as Gen 2–3 may be shaped as much by what they avoid saying as what they say. Where biblical scholars often discern the agenda of texts like Gen 2–3 in their major emphases, Boer proposes looking at what they mask. Similarly, in a powerful essay on the "exegesis of the unwritten," Dow Edgerton proposes:

> The spaces which are unwritten are anything but empty. They are the places where deeper power lives, where the "more" of living experience refuses to be ruled by the "less" of what can be written. The written is the place of words, but the unwritten is the place where meaning is found. These unwritten spaces pull with the power of a star's gravity, drawing everything into orbit

---

1. Roland Boer, "The Fantasy of Genesis 1–3," *BibInt* 14 (2006): 309–31, especially 317–20 (using Slavoj Zizek's adaptation of Lacan in *Plague of Fantasies* [London: Verso, 1997]). The present essay originated as a contribution to a November 2009 panel in New Orleans, organized by the Consultation on Exile (Forced Migrations) in Biblical Literature. It bears the marks of the request by the organizers to address the question of how the exile shaped the prophetic *Gattung*. In particular I thank John Ahn for the invitation to contribute to the session and the participants and others who provided helpful comments on this work at the presentation. This essay was prepared as part of a broader project published now as *The Formation of the Hebrew Bible: A New Reconstruction* (New York: Oxford University Press, 2011). As a result, several parts of this essay overlap with material regarding exile in that book.

around themselves. It is around the unwritten spaces that the
"texts" rotate. Instead of being what is fixed and central while
the unwritten is marginal, the "texts" are revealed as uncentered
and marginal themselves. They are captured by the power of the
unwritten center. The lived world is stronger than the authorized
world. It is around the lived world that the texts of authoriza-
tion revolve as lesser satellites, although a Ptolemaic imagination
believes otherwise.[2]

These reflections, coming from diverse loci, invite biblical scholars to
the risky enterprise of reading absences as well as presences in biblical
texts, indeed in the Bible as a whole. This project seems "risky," because
it involves suppositions about what might be in a biblical text, but is not.
There are, of course, all kinds of reasons why something is *not* in a given
text, not all of which are particularly significant for exegesis of the text.

With such due caution, I propose to attend to one of the most striking absences in the broader Hebrew Bible corpus: the relative lack in the
Bible of discourse directly about life during the exile or attributed to figures speaking from the exile. For I would argue that an important datum
for study of prophetic literature in the exile period is the fact that—aside
from a couple of prophets (Jeremiah and Ezekiel) whose predestruction
literary legacy extended into very first years of the exile—*we have no prophetic material in the Hebrew Bible that explicitly purports to be from a
prophet working in the exile*. We see this particularly in the Book of the
Twelve, where several figures attributed to the preexilic period occur—
Hosea, Joel, Amos, Obadiah, Micah, and so on—and then the postexilic
figures of Haggai, Zechariah, and Malachi conclude the book. Of course,
the majority of scholars date large portions of the books of Jeremiah and
Isaiah to the period of Babylonian exile, but the biblical books themselves
do not set their prophecy in the exilic period. Moreover, this gap of prophecy corresponds to a gap of narrative in the exilic period. We have virtually no continuous historical narrative from the destruction of the temple
in 587 to Cyrus's decree in 538, certainly nothing for the quarter century
from 562 to 538 B.C.E. If an individual did not speak at all about a comparable portion of their adult life, that would be a pointer to possible trauma

---

2. Dow Edgerton, *Passion of Interpretation* (Louisville: Westminster John Knox,
1992), 107.

during those years.[3] I suggest that *precisely this absence* of explicit attribution of prophecy to the heart of the period of exile is itself one of the impacts of exile on the prophetic *Gattung*: the displacement of authorship of prophetic texts to the preexilic periods and the lack of explicit discussion of the exile except in highly symbolic and ambiguous forms (e.g. the suffering servant or daughter Zion).

Of course, within an individual, a hypothesis of trauma behind a gap in recollection would need to be supported by other evidence. So I propose starting with the definition and diagnosis of trauma, particularly collective trauma of a community, before returning to potential marks of such trauma in literary prophecy of the sort we see in the Bible. The challenge is that trauma is often, by definition, not directly thinkable. As Cathy Caruth, a major writer on literature and trauma, puts it, "The trauma is the confrontation with an event that, in its unexpectedness or horror, cannot be placed within the schemes of prior knowledge. … Not having been fully interpreted as it occurred, the event cannot become … a narrative recovery that is integrated into a completed story of the past." And, she adds, it is "history that *has no place*." It is "speechless terror."[4] This is especially true, I suggest, for the literary tradition of an ancient culture whose texts are a distillate of writing-supported cultural memory to be passed on to future generations. Such texts, in what they say and do not say, reflect the achievements and challenges of the consciousness of the group as a whole.

Thus the trauma of the overall Neo-Babylonian period may not lie so much in the destruction of the temple, about which much is said, or the gradual collapse of the Judean state, however traumatic such events certainly were. Instead, if we read the above-mentioned *absences* of the biblical record, the trauma of exile may have been located as much or more in the in-between time of living in exile. This is trauma defined not on an index of intensity of pain, but of the incomprehensibility of pain—the difficulty or unwillingness of exiles to speak and think directly about their experience of living in diaspora. Instead, I propose, like many forced-migrants

---

3. For a summary of research regarding the issue of *recollection* of trauma, see Richard J. McNally, *Remembering Trauma* (Cambridge: Harvard University Press, 2003), who argues that survivors generally remember trauma, albeit sometimes in quite generalized way. Trauma generally does not lead to forgetting, but to not speaking of certain events.

4. Cathy Caruth, "Introduction: Recapturing the Past," in *Trauma: Explorations in Memory* (ed. Cathy Caruth; Baltimore: Johns Hopkins University Press, 1995), 153.

after them, they lived in a memorialized past, filled with "still life images refusing to yield."[5] Knudsen notes in work with Vietnamese refugees how middle- and upper-class refugees in particular (i.e., refugees whose social status would correspond most to that of the elite exiled Judeans) were particularly focused on establishing their identities in diaspora based on identities from the past—as doctors, professors, government officials, etc. As he puts it,

> To secure a positive feeling of self ("who I am") through identity management, the individual often tries to negotiate on the basis of past, now lost, positions ("who I was") rather than present positions ("who I have become"). Central to these processes of negotiation, as well as the disputes arising from them, is the strategic presentation of self through life histories.[6]

Thus refugees could speak of the past, indeed wanted to speak a lot about it. Nevertheless, Knudsen writes, "When events of the [more recent] past are recalled, whether from Vietnam, the flight, or the camp, they are recounted in very general terms, told in detached or depersonalized ways, with the most painful episodes skimmed over."[7] This sort of selective, generalized memory is a common theme in studies of people who have undergone the traumatic dislocations of forced migration.[8] In the uncertain context of refugee camps or life in diaspora, the identities and events of the more distant past become ever more important, now transformed into the basis for fragile identity building in a hostile environment. These assertions of memory are aimed at undermining the dislocations in social position and identity formation that dominate the diaspora present.

Following the lead of such trauma studies, we find that our access to the impact of exile can only be indirect, through the reverberations in biblical literature of the incomprehensible dimensions of exile. Luckily, such reverberations do not just occur in what is *not* said, but also in certain

---

5. John Chr Knudsen, "When Trust Is on Trial: Negotiating Refugee Narratives," in *Mistrusting Refugees* (ed. E. Daniel Valentine and John Chr Knudsen; Berkeley: University of California Press, 1995), 25.

6. Ibid.

7. Ibid.

8. Even an overview that emphasizes the presence of memory, such as McNally (*Remembering Trauma*, 130–34), notes that generalized memory is typical for those suffering from posttraumatic stress disorder (PTSD) and related syndromes.

patterns of what *is* said. In what follows, I will build on some broad gener-
alizations about the effects of collective trauma on discourse, correlating
repeated features of such discourse of the collectively traumatized with
features we see in prophetic literature that likely dates to the exilic period.
My thesis is that many of the features we now see enshrined in material
associated with the *preexilic* prophets strongly correlates with the dynamics of a traumatized exilic community. In this I am not, by the way, propos-
ing that all this material dates from the exile. Rather I am adding evidence
from trauma studies to buttress and supplement prior theories that the
exile, as a collectively traumatic event, catalyzed the preservation, shaping,
and extension of *preexilic* prophetic texts.

Let me start with an example mentioned already by Daniel Smith-
Christopher, William Morrow, and others in connection with Ezekiel and
Second Isaiah: the struggle of traumatized communities and individuals
with feelings of shame and guilt.[9] This is one of the most commonly mentioned features of the experience of trauma, whether that of individuals or
communities. The distinction between shame and guilt here is important.
It is one thing, and actually somewhat reassuring, to think that a bad *decision,* or set of decisions, led to the agonizing present. You can feel guilty
about the decision, learn from it, and avoid that mistake in the future.
Quite different, however, is the experience of shame, where one's own *self*
is on trial for bringing on the catastrophe. Take, for example, the experience of Cambodian refugees who questioned whether their own culture
was fundamentally to blame for the unspeakable horror of the Khmer
Rouge genocide.[10] In so far as one's own culture or one's self is fundamentally to blame for the agony one finds oneself in, there is no escape.

---

9. Here I have benefited particularly from Daniel Smith(-Christopher), *The
Religion of the Landless: The Social Context of Babylonian Exile* (Bloomington, Ind.:
Meyer-Stone, 1989); idem, "Ezekiel on Fanon's Couch: A Postcolonialist Dialogue
with David Halperin's *Seeking Ezekiel*," in *Peace and Justice Shall Embrace: Power and
Theopolitics in the Bible* (ed. Ted Grimsrud and Loren L. Johns; Telford, Penn.: Pan-
dora Press, 1999), 108–44; idem, "Ezekiel in Abu Ghraib: Rereading Ezekiel 16:37–39
in the Context of Imperial Conquest," in *Ezekiel's Hierarchical World* (ed. Stephen L.
Cook and Corrine L. Patton; SBLSymS 31; Atlanta: Scholars, 2004), 141–57; idem, *A
Biblical Theology of Exile* (OBT; Minneapolis: Fortress, 2002); and William Morrow,
"Vicarious Atonement in the Second Isaiah," in *From Freud to Kohut* (vol. 1 of *Psychol-
ogy and the Bible: A New Way to Read the Scriptures,* ed. J. Harold Ellens and Wayne G.
Rollins; Westport, Conn.: Praeger, 2004), 167–83.

10. Marjorie A. Muecke, "Trust, Abuse of Trust, and Mistrust among Cambodian

As one surveys the material associated with preexilic prophets, the focus on the blame of the community, of course, is huge. Not only do large swaths of the major prophets, Isaiah, Jeremiah and Ezekiel, feature indictments of the people, but so do many of the preexilic minor prophets, such as Hosea, Amos, Micah, and Zephaniah. As scholars have long supposed, such indictments—whenever they were written—were well suited for exiles attempting to come to terms with what had happened to them. Dated to the preexilic past, these prophetic traditions offered concrete diagnoses of where Israel and Judah went wrong. In this way, they helped exiles on the journey from shame to guilt, indicating possible wrong decisions that led to the catastrophe in which they now found themselves. This is the way prophetic literature of ancient Israel textualizes what Robert K. Lifton has described as the feeling of "failed enactment" among survivors of catastrophic trauma—replaying again and again the mistakes of the past in hope of achieving some kind of mental control over the incomprehensible present and recent past.[11]

If the themes of survivor guilt and shame are virtual universals among those who experience trauma, there is another prominent theme: the challenge of reestablishing trust and hope. Precisely in its seeming unpredictability and incomprehensibility, trauma savages a community's trust in itself and its future. Kai Erikson found this a general phenomenon among otherwise quite disparate community traumas such as Three Mile Island, Love Canal, and the Buffalo Creek flood. This is not only a phenomenon relating to natural disaster. Rather, communities like those at Buffalo Creek, Three Mile Island, and, one might add, sixth-century Judah, experienced deep wounds of their trust of basic governmental structures, the dependability of competing social groups, outsiders, and even God. Catastrophe, including betrayal or failure by government, societal subgroups and neighbors, and God, brings a changed sense of self and community formed under the pervading sense of doom, that "something awful is *bound* to happen." The universe no longer seems to follow rules of order and certainty, but instead is characterized by randomness and change, and

---

Refugee Women: A Cultural Interpretation," in Valentine and Knudsen, *Mistrusting Refugees*, 40.

11. Robert K. Lifton, "Understanding the Traumatized Self: Imagery, Symbolization, and Transformation," in *Human Adaptation to Extreme Stress: From the Holocaust to Vietnam* (ed. John P. Wilson, Zev Harel, and Boaz Kahana; New York: Plenum, 1988), 8–9.

this experience, whether faced by survivors of Katrina or by sixth-century Judeans, can paralyze one's ability to move forward. As Erikson puts it, the "hardest earned and most fragile accomplishment of childhood, basic trust, can be damaged beyond repair by trauma."[12]

Much of biblical literature, I would hold, including prophetic litera-ture, was shaped to help Judeans repair such trust, at least on the level of trust of the integrity of their nonstate communal identity, Israel, and the relation of that Israelite entity to God. Already the indictments briefly mentioned above served that purpose, especially since they presented themselves as preserved records of the *past* indictments given by the God of Judah and Israel that thus established God's credibility in being in onto-logical and intellectual control of the catastrophic events that those com-munities experienced. Yet exclusive emphasis on the misdeeds of the com-munity could actually aggravate communal shame and undermine any progress in rebuilding trust in itself. So we see, for example, probable exilic texts in Ezekiel and Jeremiah that promise divine intervention into the hearts of the communal members themselves to rebuild the divine-human relationship—whether the new heart in Ezek 36:26, or the torah written on the heart in Jer 31:31–34. We see the articulation of hope based on God's determination to protect God's name, a hope completely independent of the community's virtue or lack thereof. And we see in prophetic literature, especially in material often referred to as Second Isaiah, a new level of processing of memory of the distant past—stories of creation, ancestors, and exodus—to undergird hope for God's intervention in the near future.

People reconstructing hope in the wake of the trauma of forced displacement often focus in particular on the prospect of *return*. This, for many exiles, is the incarnation of hope. For example, in an essay on "transforming trust," Julie M. Peteet notes that Palestinian refugees in camps in Lebanon preferred to refer to themselves as *returners* rather than refugees.[13] Return, Peteet asserts, is a crucial part of the exile's nar-

---

12. Kai Erikson, "Notes on Trauma and Community," in *Trauma: Explorations in Memory* (ed. Cathy Caruth; Baltimore: Johns Hopkins University Press, 1995), 197. Note also the broader discussion on the tenuousness of hope in Alessandra Lemma, "On Hope's Tightrope: Reflections on the Capacity for Hope," in *The Perversion of Loss: Psychoanalytic Perspectives on Trauma* (ed. Susan Levy and Alessandra Lemma; Whurr Series in Psychoanalysis; London: Whurr, 2004), 108–26.

13. Julie M. Peteet, "Transforming Trust: Dispossession and Empowerment among Palestinian Refugees," in Valentine and Knudsen, *Mistrusting Refugees*, 177.

rative. Similarly, a distinguishing feature of prophecy attributed to the exilic period is the focus on the prospect of return, both the visions of restoration in the post-587 prophecies of Ezekiel and the yet more vivid images of return and restoration found in Second Isaiah. We see no such focalization on return in demonstrably preexilic literature, and postexilic literature focuses instead on the challenges of rebuilding. Yet exilic *prophecy*, particularly that of Second Isaiah, is in large part an articulation of the case that return is immanent. As such it is a rebuilding of specifically *exilic* hope among those experiencing the disintegration of hope during decades of extended displacement.

Such linkage of themes of judgment and hope are not brand new. Yet trauma studies offer insight into the dynamics that would have produced such a focus in the exile on the selection, preservation, and reshaping of prophetic literature both to process experiences of survivor guilt and failed enactment and to attempt—building on the authority of preexilic prophecy—to rebuild bonds of trust and hope that were severely wounded by the experience of destruction and especially exile.

In addition, another feature found by Knudsen and others in their studies of people undergoing collective trauma is the tendency toward dichotomization of social relationships into "us" and "them." For example, the Vietnamese refugees studied by Knudsen faced an incredibly fraught, shifting, and unpredictable social world from the time they boarded a boat carrying them illegally to a neighboring shore to the series of refugee camps in which they stayed on the way to hoped-for asylum in the United States or another country. Where such people might once have lived amidst a more porous and overlapping set of expanding social circles defining near and far social relations, they now were thrown into a context where the only constant social relations were those that defined them more generally as Vietnamese and those that defined the not-Vietnamese nations, aid agencies, etc. with whom they had to work.[14] In an evocative statement of this process in relation to the creation of Cambodianness in the United States, Carol Mortland says, "Exile creates not only homelessness, thus refugeeness, it creates ethnicity, for it is exile that allows, rather forces, a group to see 'difference' … to see 'others.'"[15]

---

14. Knudsen, "Trust on Trial," 21.

15. Carol A. Mortland, "Cambodian Refugees and Identity in the United States," in *Reconstructing Lives, Recapturing Meaning: Refugee Identity, Gender, and Culture*

This process relates to a broader tendency toward enhanced nationalism among forcibly dislocated peoples. In particular, studies of Palestinian refugees have documented how refugee camps for Palestinians have proven fertile grounds for the growth of extremely nationalist elements. Rather than allowing the displaced individuals to disperse into the broader culture, such camps concentrate a vulnerable and frustrated population in one place. Thus concentrated, they are particularly attracted to ideological options that conform to the "us"-versus-foreign-"them" mentality already encouraged by the experience of traumatic forced dislocation. Nationalism becomes an emphatic articulation of their shared identity in a hostile foreign context. In the absence of land, they hold ever more tightly onto the idea of land. In the absence of power, they hold that much more tightly onto dreams of power. The camp is a place of purity of suffering and nationalist identity, while people outside that experience are polluted by contact with the outside world. Within that culturally protected space Palestinian refugees built an ever more essentialized picture of their common past, the "days of paradise" that orient their hope for a brighter future.[16]

Judean exiles did not live in refugee camps, but they do seem to have been settled together, in Ezekiel's Tel-Aviv or the "city of Judah" that appears in some recently published Babylonian legal documents.[17] Such settlements provided an important context for Judean exiles to cultivate a like sense of nationalist identity and a shared sense of a common past. Judging from the biblical record, the common narrative they developed was hardly about days of paradise, but instead both articulated their sense of guilt for their present predicament and grounded their hope for eventual restoration to the land. These common settlements represented a crucial context for the nurturance of feelings akin to nationalism among the Judean refugees, along with antipathy toward a foreign "them" analogous to the hostility toward Israel and the West nurtured in Palestinian refugee camps.

This may bear on the seemingly increased focus, particularly in prophecy of the exilic period, on the nation as a whole on the one hand and on

---

Change (ed. Linda A. Camino and Ruth M. Krulfeld; Basel: Gordon & Breach Science, 1994), 8.

16. Peteet, "Transforming Trust," 179–81.

17. Preliminarily see Laurie E. Pearce, "New Evidence for Judeans in Babylon," in *Judah and the Judeans in the Persian Period* (ed. Oded Lipschits and Manfred Oeming; Winona Lake, Ind.: Eisenbrauns, 2006), 399–412, especially 400–403.

hostility toward outside groups on the other. In other words, the particular dynamics of forced migration and trauma can lead to a reconfiguration of trust and distrust along new and sharpened lines. These lines separate the refugee group *as a whole* from those outside it. "Israel" becomes the defining category of "us," while the mistrust characteristic of refugee experience in general is focused ever more on the "them" of everyone else. This redefinition is found particularly in prophecies picked up by exilic tradents and created by them, privileging oracles about "Israel" in general over those directed more specifically at leaders or groups in Israel. It would explain some of the distinctiveness of literary Israelite prophecy, in its communal audience and focus on collective guilt as compared with archives of Near Eastern prophecy (e.g., Mari, Neo-Assyrian prophecy) that had not gone through the sieve of exilic trauma.

The flip side of this is the xenophobia that has been documented among forcibly displaced peoples. Biblical scholars have long seen reflexes of such hostility toward foreigners in exilic prophetic literature, especially groups such as Edom and Babylon, who were perceived to have inflicted the worst traumas on the Judean exiles. We see this in the imprecation against Edom and gleeful anticipation of Babylonian babies dashed against rocks at the end of Ps 137. We see it also in the oracles against Babylon in Ezekiel and Second Isaiah, and we see it in the redirection of preexilic prophecy, say in the probable Babylon-focused reshaping of oracles in the book of Isaiah, so that an oracle originally directed against the Assyrian king in Isa 14 was redirected against Babylon, and then an early version of the series of foreign oracles was concluded with two oracles against Babylon in Isa 21.

Less often recognized is the way the trauma of social marginalization may have affected more subtle expressions of hostility in exilic prophetic literature. Sometimes forcibly displaced groups avoid expressing hostility toward foreign groups openly, especially given their relative social marginalization. Instead, they use indirection and humor to express antagonism toward the foreigners who control crucial aspects of their lives.[18] These "hidden transcripts" thus do not add to the vulnerability experienced by refugees already mistrustful of most humans around them.[19] We see a

---

18. Knudsen, "Trust on Trial," 21.

19. The term, now much broadened in use, comes from James C. Scott, *Domination and the Arts of Resistance: The Hidden Transcript of Subordinate Groups* (New Haven: Yale University Press, 1990).

good candidate for such parodic protected speech in the polemics against idols in Second Isaiah. There is plenty of prophecy and legislation against idolatry in other parts of the Bible, but it is striking that this discourse takes such a turn toward parody and humor in texts such as Isa 44. To be sure, this text occurs as part of a layer of late exilic texts in Isa 40–55 that include quite open antagonism toward Babylon. Nevertheless, I suggest that the appearance of the parodic turn in exilic-period prophetic texts reflects the impact of such parodic discourse in the broader culture of Judean exiles. It is another way in which the experience of exile may have had an impact on the prophetic *Gattung*. Once the experience of exile was past, we see less parodic discourse about foreigners.

In conclusion, we can best trace the impact of exile on the prophetic *Gattung* by tracing the dynamics of trauma of forcibly displaced peoples on prophetic material from the later exilic period, such as Second Isaiah. To be sure, Ezekiel appears to have been displaced himself, and he is the one prophet explicitly placed in the situation of exile. Yet in many ways the literature attributed to him partakes of the dynamics of the late pre-exilic period: attribution of his material to himself, a primary focus on indictment, differentiation among various groups to whom his prophecy is addressed, lack of reflection yet on exilic lamentation literature, little focus on return.

Second Isaiah, on the other hand, represents in microcosm the impact of the exile on prophecy, both illustrating in itself that impact and modeling the dynamics that impacted biblical prophetic literature more generally. It is not so much that the suffering servant of Isaiah models the symptoms of posttraumatic stress disorder (PTSD), as Morrow proposes.[20] Rather it is more generally in the way Second Isaiah exemplifies a broader tendency to avoid attribution of exilic period prophecy to the exilic period itself, focusing instead on a memorialized past, struggling with lingering feelings of shame and guilt, and both showing open hostility toward Babylon and parodying it, and in the way it exemplifies exilic strategies for rebuilding trust and hope, focusing particularly on the prospect of return.

Furthermore, I have suggested that these tendencies so beautifully illustrated in Second Isaiah also played a role in the broader selection and shaping of preexilic literature. There is no shortage of scholarly theories regarding the exilic reshaping of Isaiah and Jeremiah as well as—according

---

20. Morrow, "Vicarious Atonement," 167–83.

to a more recent theory by James Nogalski, Rainer Albertz and others—
an exilic-period "book of the four prophets" encompassing Hosea, Amos,
Micah and Zephaniah. My comments here simply build on such broader
trends in suggesting that several features of biblical prophecy in general,
indeed features that set it apart from its Near Eastern counterparts, likely
stem from the fact that such prophecy was shaped by the trauma of forced
displacement. Those features include the more generalized focus of much
biblical literary prophecy on broad social categories of "us" versus "them,"
such as the people of Israel as a whole rather than just the king or royal officials, the emphasis in much biblical prophecy on confronting the despair
of traumatic displacement through review of past indictments of Israel for
its social and cultic ills, and the concomitant focus of much prophecy on
persuasive rebuilding of the hope and confidence of the *people* in God's
restoration of them, particularly their return to their homeland.

Jungian psychologists such as John P. Wilson have argued that the literary record of many peoples contain mythic resources by which those
peoples have confronted and survived multiple traumas. For them, such
resources can be found in the rehearsing of the experience of trauma and
healing through hero stories such as Joseph Campbell collected.[21] Part
of the genius of biblical prophetic literature is the way it confronted the
trauma of forced displacement to Babylon. It did not just provide a timely
word to exiled Judeans such as those who inhabited the Babylonian "city
of Judah." It provided a literary distillate for many subsequent generations-
-Judeans suffering under perceived Hellenistic persecution, diaspora Jews
under Rome and later, and Christians as well—to process shame and move
toward guilt, to trust in God's mercy despite perceived shortcomings, and
to envision divine restoration and return. In this sense, the exile had an
impact on the prophetic *Gattung* in ways that assured its ongoing relevance long after the exile. Judean exile was the furnace that refined past
traditions into a proto-canonical form so that they could speak to generations of people confronting unspeakable pain and help them envision a
better day.

In this sense, the lack of explicit discourse about the exile in the Bible
may have been one factor that helped exilic prophetic literature transcend

---

21. John P. Wilson, "Culture, Trauma and the Treatment of Post-Traumatic Syndromes: A Global Perspective," in *Ethnocultural Perspectives on Disaster and Trauma*
(ed. Anthony J. Marsella et al.; International and Cultural Psychology; New York:
Springer, 2008), 351–77.

the period of its origination. However accurate it may be that Isa 40–55, Jer 31–33, and many portions of other prophetic books were shaped during the exile, they do not explicitly speak of that period, and the lack of explicit linkage to the exile in these texts probably *helped* such texts not be limited in relevance and use to that period. Exilic prophetic texts such as Second Isaiah focus much on the distant past (creation, ancestors, exodus, wilderness), and they look forward to the future of God's restoration. Nevertheless, they speak of the traumatic present, if at all, only in highly ambiguous figures such as the servant or daughter Zion. Insofar as such silence and slant in exilic prophetic literature are reflexes of the trauma of events during the Neo-Babylonian period that authors and audiences found too difficult to address directly, these profoundly timebound traumatic dynamics ironically helped these prophetic texts transcend the originating trauma and speak to later experiences as well.

BIBLIOGRAPHY

Boer, Roland. "The Fantasy of Genesis 1–3." *BibInt* 14 (2006): 309–31.

Caruth, Cathy. "Introduction: Recapturing the Past." Pages 151–57 in *Trauma: Explorations in Memory*. Edited by Cathy Caruth. Baltimore: Johns Hopkins University Press, 1995.

Edgerton, Dow. *Passion of Interpretation*. Louisville: Westminster John Knox, 1992.

Erikson, Kai. "Notes on Trauma and Community." Pages 183–99 in *Trauma: Explorations in Memory*. Edited by Cathy Caruth. Baltimore: Johns Hopkins University Press, 1995.

Knudsen, John Chr. "When Trust Is on Trial: Negotiating Refugee Narratives." Pages 13–35 in *Mistrusting Refugees*. Edited by E. Valentine and John Chr. Knudsen. Berkeley: University of California Press, 1995.

Lemma, Alessandra. "On Hope's Tightrope: Reflections on the Capacity for Hope." Pages 108–26 in *The Perversion of Loss: Psychoanalytic Perspectives on Trauma*. Edited by Susan Levy and Alessandra Lemma. Whurr Series in Psychoanalysis. London: Whurr, 2004.

Lifton, Robert K. "Understanding the Traumatized Self: Imagery, Symbolization, and Transformation." Pages 7–31 in *Human Adaptation to Extreme Stress: From the Holocaust to Vietnam*. Edited by John P. Wilson, Zev Harel, and Boaz Kahana. New York: Plenum, 1988.

McNally, Richard J. *Remembering Trauma*. Cambridge: Harvard University Press, 2003.

Morrow, William. "Vicarious Atonement in the Second Isaiah." Pages 167–83 in *From Freud to Kohut*. Vol. 1 of *Psychology and the Bible: A New Way to Read the Scriptures*. Edited by J. Harold Ellens and Wayne G. Rollins. Westport, Conn.: Praeger, 2004.

Mortland, Carol A. "Cambodian Refugees and Identity in the United States." Pages 5–27 in *Reconstructing Lives, Recapturing Meaning: Refugee Identity, Gender, and Culture Change*. Edited by Linda A. Camino and Ruth M. Krulfeld. Basel: Gordon & Breach Science, 1994.

Muecke, Marjorie A. "Trust, Abuse of Trust, and Mistrust Among Cambodian Refugee Women: A Cultural Interpretation." Pages 36–55 in *Mistrusting Refugees*. Edited by E. Valentine and John Chr Knudsen. Berkeley: University of California Press, 1995.

Pearce, Laurie E. "New Evidence for Judaeans in Babylonia." Pages 399–411 in *Judah and the Judeans in the Persian Period*. Edited by Oded Lipschits and Manfred Oeming. Winona Lake, Ind.: Eisenbrauns, 2006.

Peteet, Julie M. "Transforming Trust: Dispossession and Empowerment among Palestinian Refugees." Pages 168–86 in *Mistrusting Refugees*. Edited by E. Valentine and John Chr Knudsen. Berkeley: University of California Press, 1995.

Scott, James C. *Domination and the Arts of Resistance: The Hidden Transcript of Subordinate Groups*. New Haven: Yale University Press, 1990.

Smith, Daniel L. *The Religion of the Landless: The Social Context of Babylonian Exile*. Bloomington, Ind.: Meyer-Stone, 1989.

Smith-Christopher, Daniel. *A Biblical Theology of Exile*. OBT. Minneapolis: Fortress, 2002.

———. "Ezekiel in Abu Ghraib: Rereading Ezekiel 16:37–39 in the Context of Imperial Conquest." Pages 141–57 in *Ezekiel's Hierarchical World*. Edited by Stephen L. Cook and Corrine L. Patton. SBLSymS 31. Atlanta: Scholars, 2004.

"Ezekiel on Fanon's Couch: A Postcolonialist Dialogue with David Halperin's *Seeking Ezekiel*." Pages 108–44 in *Peace and Justice Shall Embrace: Power and Theopolitics in the Bible*. Edited by Ted Grimsrud and Loren L. Johns. Telford, Penn.: Pandora Press, 1999.

Wilson, John P. "Culture, Trauma and the Treatment of Post-traumatic Syndromes: A Global Perspective." Pages 351–77 in *Ethnocultural Perspectives on Disaster and Trauma*. Edited by Anthony J. Marsella, Jeannette L. Johnson, Patricia Watson, and Jan Gryczynski. International and Psychological Perspectives. New York: Springer, 2008.

Zizek, Slavoj. *Plague of Fantasies*. London: Verso, 1997.

A Vocabulary of Trauma in the Exilic Writings

David G. Garber Jr.

Recent biblical scholarship has drawn upon the insights of trauma theory and the study of survivor literature in conversation with various aspects of the biblical material, particularly materials originally formed in response to the destruction of Jerusalem and the exile. Kathleen O'Connor has extensively examined the correlation between trauma and the study of the exile in her work on Jeremiah.[1] Likewise, the book of Ezekiel has seen several treatments of the intersection between exilic studies and trauma theory. Previous attempts to psychoanalyze a historical Ezekiel existed, but Daniel L. Smith-Christopher first connected the study of Ezekiel with refugee studies and with posttraumatic stress disorder (PTSD), and Gail Yee has pursued an analysis of Ezek 23 using trauma theory as an interpretive lens.[2] While trauma theory has helped illumine some aspects of the biblical text, a truly interdisciplinary conversation would also ask

---

1. Kathleen M. O'Connor, "Lamenting Back to Life," *Int* 62 (2008): 34–47; "A Family Comes Undone (Jeremiah 2:1–4:2)," *RevExp* 105 (2008): 201–12; "Teaching Jeremiah," *PRSt* 36 (2009): 273–87; "Reclaiming Jeremiah's Violence," in *Aesthetics of Violence in the Prophets* (ed. Julia M. O'Brien and Chris Franke; New York: T&T Clark, 2010), 37–49.

2. Daniel L. Smith-Christopher, *A Biblical Theology of Exile* (OBT; Minneapolis: Fortress, 2002), 88–89; Gale A. Yee, *Poor Banished Children of Eve: Woman as Evil in the Hebrew Bible* (Minneapolis: Fortress, 2003), 120–22. See also David G. Garber Jr., "Traumatizing Ezekiel, the Exilic Prophet," in *From Genesis to Apocalyptic Vision* (vol. 2 of *Psychology and the Bible: A New Way to Read the Scriptures*; ed. J. Harold Ellens and Wayne G. Rollins; Westport, Conn.: Praeger, 2004), 215–35; Brad E. Kelle, "Dealing with the Trauma of Defeat: The Rhetoric of the Devastation and Rejuvenation of Nature in Ezekiel," *JBL* 128 (2009): 469–90; and Nancy R. Bowen, *Ezekiel* (AOTC; Nashville: Abingdon, 2010).

what biblical scholarship or the biblical text can contribute to the study of trauma in general.

One helpful aspect of trauma theory in analyzing the response to Judah's national crisis involves the impossibility and imperative to testify to the traumatic experience. According to Shoshana Felman, texts that testify to traumatic events are "composed of bits and pieces of a memory that has been overwhelmed by occurrences that have not settled into understanding or remembrance, …events in excess of our frames of reference."[3] In discussing Jeremiah's response to trauma, O'Connor expresses a similar sentiment: "Disasters inflict wounds without words, or at least without words adequate to the harm that has been done."[4] This language loss lies at the core of testimony to traumatic events. According to Dori Laub: "There are never enough words or the right words, there is never enough time or the right time, and there is never enough listening or the right listening to articulate the story that cannot be fully captured in *thought, memory* and *speech*."[5] Laub insists, however: "It is essential for this narrative that *could not be articulated*, to be *told*, to be *transmitted*, to be *heard*."[6] In fact, the only access we have to the memory of the destruction of Jerusalem and the resulting exile comes through text—through words incapable of expressing the damage done to the Judean community, but recorded and preserved nonetheless.

One difficulty with placing trauma theory in conversation with studies of exilic literature arises in the attempt to negotiate the chasm between trauma theory as the product of modern psychological, philosophical, and literary theory and the ancient Judeans' articulation of devastating events. In addition to the conundrum of traumatic testimony exceeding the bounds of semantic reference, the ancients had a different semiotic system, a different vocabulary with which to express the all too universal experience of trauma. Without the psychological categories that modern literary and trauma theorists take for granted, would ancient Judean readers have perceived military defeat in battle in the same ways that modern readers do? Or does their ancient worldview profoundly impact their understanding of catastrophe in a way that can inform current under-

---

3. Shoshana Felman and Dori Laub, *Testimony: Crises of Witnessing in Literature, Psychoanalysis, and History* (New York: Routledge, 1991), 5.

4. O'Connor, "A Family Comes Undone," 201.

5. Felman and Laub, *Testimony*, 78.

6. Ibid., 85.

standings of traumatic testimony? What constitutes an ancient Judean vocabulary of trauma?

In what follows I will explore the use of the Hebrew root חלל as the label for victims of military defeat and as a starting point for constructing a vocabulary of trauma in the exilic literature. I will begin with some basic characteristics of trauma derived from trauma theory, then explore the Greek root for trauma. A brief search of τραυμα and its derivative lexemes in the LXX shows that the LXX translators overwhelmingly used this vocabulary to translate the Hebrew root חלל. I will then investigate the use of חלל in three biblical books that testify to Babylon's destruction of Jerusalem and the resulting exile: Lamentations, Jeremiah, and Ezekiel. Each biblical tradition employs חלל in a manner that is in keeping with the overall rhetoric of the tradition.[7] The book of Ezekiel in particular employs an intricate wordplay using the roots חלל I and חלל II in a way that weaves together two aspects of the book's peculiar response to the destruction of Jerusalem and exile of the Judeans: the expression of victimization itself (חלל II) and Ezekiel's priestly worldview (חלל I). This study of vocabulary can further inform the conversation between trauma theory and biblical studies, providing an example of how the exiled Judeans, whose worldview includes ancient religious perspectives, processed and articulated catastrophic events that fractured their human community.

1. THE VOCABULARY OF TRAUMA

Even within trauma theory, the term "trauma" itself remains as difficult to define as the traumatic experience is difficult to articulate. Victims of trauma are subjected to an outside force that breaks in upon them in an overwhelming fashion. The intensity of trauma exists on a continuum for both individuals and communities. Most trauma theorists focus on extreme trauma, such as calamities that befall the human community due to warfare (atomic attack or genocide) or natural disasters. Cathy Caruth suggests that the extreme psychic trauma resulting from such disasters "involves intense personal suffering, but it also involves the recognition of

---

7. While I recognize the very complex composition history of each of these books, this preliminary investigation will explore the vocabulary of these texts in their final form, recognizing that the portions of the testimony to the traumatic event within them may derive from caretakers of the memory and tradition in successive generations.

realities that most of us have not begun to face."[8] In the wake of such events, human systems of linguistic reference ultimately fail. For example, when writing about the Holocaust, Lawrence Langer suggests that Auschwitz survivors grope for a language "beyond analogy" to bring the experience to "our recognizable earth."[9] In terms of the study of exilic literature, what vocabulary do texts that testify to Judah's calamity in 586 B.C.E. employ to articulate the experience in a way that was recognizable for its survivors?

One possible response to this query can begin by exploring the use of the Greek source for the English word "trauma" within the LXX. The Greek noun τραυμα—usually translated as a "wound," "damage," "blow," or "defeat"[10]—and its variant lexemes τραυματιας and τραυματιζω occur 111 times in LXX. The noun form τραυματιας indicates the victim of a wound, while the verb form τραυματιζω indicates the action of wounding. Approximately 38 percent of these lexemes in the LXX appear within the books of Jeremiah, Lamentations, and Ezekiel (42 of 111), all written in response to the destruction of Jerusalem and resulting exilic experience. Ezekiel contains the most references (31), while Jeremiah includes eight, and Lamentations, three. Of these references to trauma in the LXX, forty-one translate some form of the Hebrew root חלל.[11]

The search for חלל within the Hebrew Bible yields inflated results because of the root's two major meanings in Hebrew, חלל I and חלל II. Variants of the Greek word for "trauma" translate חלל II, typically expressed in English as "pierce," or in the noun form (חָלָל) as "one who is pierced" or "one who is slain." The more common חלל I translates as "to profane," or "to dishonor," or in the *hiphil* stem, "to begin." While חלל II straightforwardly expresses the trauma of a wound (typically with a sword), exilic authors also make significant use of wordplay between the two roots in their use of חלל I.

---

8. Cathy Caruth, "Preface," in *Trauma: Explorations in Memory* (ed. Cathy Caruth; Baltimore: Johns Hopkins University Press, 1995), vii.

9. Lawrence L. Langer, *Versions of Survival: The Holocaust and the Human Spirit* (Albany: State University of New York Press, 1982), 25.

10. LSJ, 1811.

11. The only exceptions occur in Jer 10:19, where τραυμα μου, "my wound," translates חלי "my sickness," a noun derived from the Hebrew root חלה. Ezekiel 32:26 and 32:29 repeat a form of τραυμα in LXX, where חלל only occurs once in the MT of each verse.

The use of חלל within Lamentations is relatively straightforward. Lamentations 2 subtly utilizes the pun between חלל I and חלל II. Lamentations 2:2 uses חלל I to express the degradation of Judah:

> The Lord has destroyed without mercy all the dwellings of Jacob;
> in his wrath he has broken down the strongholds of daughter Judah;
> he has brought down to the ground in dishonor (חִלֵּל) the kingdom and
> its rulers.[12]

The first portion of the verse clearly establishes the traumatic event as the destruction of Judah's fortresses. חלל in the final line is typically translated as "dishonor." Later in the chapter, however, חלל II appears metaphorically, comparing the people of Judah to infants who contemplate the scarcity of food and languish "like the wounded" (כחלל) in the streets as they die in their mothers' arms. The theme of famine also accompanies the two uses of חלל II in 4:9, comparing the slain of the sword (חללי־חרב) to the slain of the famine (חללי רעב), arguing that the former are better off than the latter. In sum, Lamentations uses both forms of חלל to express the wounds of military defeat, famine, and accompanying shame.

The book of Jeremiah uses both forms of חלל thirteen times. Jeremiah 8:21 expresses Jeremiah's lament for the people—including himself as the prophet—who have been dejected: "Because my people is shattered I am shattered; I am dejected, seized by desolation."[13] In Jer 8:23, this shattering leads the prophet to wish that his head be composed of water so his tears could pour a fountain of perpetual tears for his slain people (חללי בת־עמי). At the heart of another lament in Jer 14:18, the prophet connects the dual atrocities of military slaughter and famine that accompany the realities of war as seen in Lamentations. Those slain by the sword (חללי־חרב) on the countryside parallel those sick with famine in the city.[14] In Jer 25, the prophet reiterates that YHWH is responsible for these disasters. Jeremiah 25:33 describes the magnitude of the coming disaster, in which the corpses of those slain by YHWH (חללי יהוה) will litter the entire land like dung. חלל II occurs in its most literal sense in Jer 41:9, describing those that Ishmael slew (חללים) in the *coups d'etat* against Gedaliah. The remaining

---

12. All scripture citations are from the NRSV unless otherwise noted.

13. Jer 8:21 NJPS.

14. Notice the use of the similar root חלה to describe those "sick with famine" (תחלואי רעב).

uses of חלל II occur in oracles against Babylon. In these oracles, the same
YHWH who employed the Babylonian soldiers to defeat the inhabitants of
Jerusalem will punish the Babylonians for their part in the slaughter. In
Jer 51:4 and 51:47 the soldiers of Babylon will fall slain,[15] and in 51:52,
those slain in Babylon will die groaning. Jeremiah 51:49, again using חלל
II, offers the motivation for YHWH's retribution: they will fall for the slain
of not only Israel, but the slain of all the earth, a recompense to all of the
nations that suffered under Babylonian militarism.

Jeremiah uses חלל I sparingly. When it occurs in Jer 16:18, it refers to
the reason that the Israelites will suffer: they have profaned YHWH's land
with their idols' corpses. In fact, the juxtaposition of "profaned" (חללם)
and "corpses of their idols" (נבלת שקוציהם) could be a wordplay evoking
the meaning of חלל II, which as seen above, often refers to those slain in
Israel or in Babylon. Likewise, חלל I appears in Jer 34:16 to express the
profaning of the divine name by the elites in Jerusalem who rescinded the
proclamation of freedom for their slaves (ותחללו את־שמי).[16]

Not surprisingly, given the book's purity concerns, Ezekiel more evenly
balances חלל I and חלל II. The only other location within the Hebrew
canon that contains חלל I with similar frequency is the Holiness Code,
particularly Lev 18–22. The book of Ezekiel especially highlights the connection between defilement and disaster, and this connection, in turn, can
illumine our understanding of how this biblical book articulates traumatic
experience. Before turning to Ezekiel's use of חלל II, an understanding
Ezekiel's use of חלל I can provide a frame of reference for the interrelationship between defilement and violence in the book.

The uses of חלל I fall into three categories: first, a general debasement
or lowering of status; second, YHWH as the one causing the defilement; and
third, YHWH or the sacred objects of YHWH as the objects of defilement. In
the first category, Ezek 21:30 uses חלל I as a general indicator of debasement
or shame to describe the figure identified as the dishonored and wicked
prince of Israel (חלל רשע נשיא ישראל; see also 21:34). Part of Judah's punishment involves dishonor in the face of the nations (22:16). The oracle
against Tyre employs חלל I twice in this manner (28:7 and 28:16), setting
up a wordplay with חלל II in 28:8–9 (see below). Secondly, YHWH causes
defilement in Ezek 7 as an aspect of judgment. Not only will the people face

---

15. Also notice the shame language in Jer 51:47: וכל־ארצה תבוש.

16. חלל I's remaining uses in Jer 25:29 and 31:5 express not profanity, but beginning or putting into use.

the traumas of the sword, pestilence, and famine (7:15) as a punishment for their impurity (7:20), but Yʜwʜ subjects the Judeans to defilement in 7:21–24. In these verses, Yʜwʜ will give the people of Judah into the hands of foreigners who will plunder and defile them (7:21), Yʜwʜ's treasures and the land itself (7:22), as well as the people's sanctuaries (7:24).

The majority of references to חלל I place Yʜwʜ as the object of defilement. Ezekiel 13:19 indicts the women prophets who defile Yʜwʜ (ותחללנה אתי), accepting bribes of barley and bread in return for false pronouncement. The retelling of Israel's history in Ezek 20 contains several instances of חלל I. Here חלל I refers to profaning Yʜwʜ's name (20:9, 14, 22, 39) or Yʜwʜ's sabbaths (20:13, 16, 21, 24; see also 22:8). In Ezek 23:38, the reference to the defilement of the sabbaths (ואת־שבתותי חללו) parallels the desecration of Yʜwʜ's sanctuary (טמאו את־מקדשי), suggesting that חלל and טמא are parallel terms in Ezekiel's rhetoric. In 23:39 חלל I also refers to the desecration of the sanctuary. Ezekiel 22:26 describes the profaning of the sanctuary as an act of violence against Yʜwʜ's teaching (כהניה חמסו תורתי). The violence entails their refusal to distinguish between the profane (חל) and the holy. Yʜwʜ takes this personally, and describes himself as defiled, using the passive form of the verb: "I am profaned in their midst" (ואחל בתוכם). In the climax of the first section of the book, Yʜwʜ expresses intent to desecrate the sanctuary personally:

> I will profane my sanctuary, the pride of your power, the delight of your eyes, and your heart's desire; and your sons and your daughters whom you left behind shall fall by the sword. (Ezek 24:21)

Yʜwʜ will defile the sanctuary in part because the people have already defiled it. Yʜwʜ's defilement of the sanctuary will grieve the people, although Yʜwʜ prohibits them from any communal expression of their sorrow (24:22–23). Even Yʜwʜ's restorative acts in later oracles only serve to restore the divine reputation, repeatedly reminding the House of Israel that they defiled it (36:20–21, 23). In 39:7, Yʜwʜ vows to never again allow anyone to defile the name. (A similar instruction guarding against the profanation of the temple occurs in Ezek 44:7.) In Ezekiel's rhetoric, the restoration of Israel takes place not for Israel's sake, but to preserve Yʜwʜ's name. At every turn, the oracles remind the survivors of the catastrophe of their guilt. All of the punishments that they experience in the form of death, destruction, disease, and deportation occur because they first violated and profaned Yʜwʜ.

Ezekiel uses חלל II in messages of judgment against both Israel and
the nations. It first appears in Ezek 6:4, a pronouncement of YHWH's
destruction of cultic sites (already defiled by the presence of idols). YHWH
declares that he will cast those who are slain (והפלתי חלליכם) before their
false idols. Only after the slain fall (ונפל חלל) in the midst of the destroyed
shrines and cultic objects will they know YHWH's true identity (Ezek 6:7).
Ezekiel 6:13 reiterates this sentiment:

> And you shall know that I am the LORD, when their slain [חלליהם]
> lie among their idols around their altars, on every high hill, on all the
> mountain tops, under every green tree, and under every leafy oak, wher-
> ever they offered pleasing odor to all their idols.

The Judeans' slaughter in these instances reveals the deity's true identity
as well as YHWH's purpose—to purge the nation. In Ezek 9, the prophet
witnesses the slaughter through a visionary experience. A variant translation of חלל I ("to begin") occurs twice in Ezek 9:6, as YHWH instructs the
city's executioners to annihilate anyone not bearing a saving mark on their
forehead: "'Begin [תחלו] at my sanctuary.' So they began [ויחלו] with the
elders who were in front of the house." The next verse amplifies the wordplay. YHWH instructs the executioners to defile the temple, filling the streets
with the slain (חללים). Ulitlizing an alternate word for defile (טמא), perhaps
to avoid confusion, this verse evokes the priestly view of corpses as impure.[17]
Canonically speaking, the previous chapter illustrates that the inhabitants of
Jerusalem had already corrupted the temple complex with their false worship practices. Now YHWH will utterly defile it by filling it with their corpses.

חלל II appears a second time in the first temple vision in Ezek 11. In
Ezek 11:6–7, YHWH indicts the elders of Jerusalem for the corpses of the
people they have slain (הרביתם חלליכם). As punishment for their guilt,
they will suffer exile and will fall by the sword themselves (11:9–10). The
final reference to חלל II in the judgment oracles against Israel fittingly
appears in the oracle of the sword in Ezek 21:13–22. The oracle's language
describes the weapon as "a sword for massacre [חרב חללים], a sword for
great carnage [חרב חלל הגדול]" that presses against the nation (21:19).

The remainder of Ezekiel's references to חלל II lie within judgment
oracles against the foreign nations, particularly Tyre, Egypt, and Edom.
In these oracles YHWH's wrath turns against other nations, describing the

---

17. See, for example, Lev 22:4 and Num 5:2; 6:6, 11.

cosmic consequences when the slain who fall in Tyre will groan (באנק
חלל, 26:15). Forms of חלל I and חלל II occur three times within 28:7–9.
In 28:7, YHWH describes the nations who will debase (חלל, וחללו I) the
splendor of Tyre's false pride. The oracle quickly turns to חלל II to describe
the people of Tyre's death as the "death of the slain" (ממותי חלל, 28:8) by
the hands of those who pierce them (ביד מחלליך, 28:9). The oracle returns
to חלל I describing the humiliation of the prince of Tyre in Ezek 28:16
(ואחללדך מהר אלהים) as well as the reasons for the judgment—the desecration of Tyre's sanctuaries (חללת מקדשיך)—in 28:18. Ezekiel 28:23 reiterates the slaughter of Tyre's citizens in a way reminiscent of the slaughter
of the Israelites, describing the pestilence, bloodshed, and bodies of the
slain that will fall (ונפלל חלל) in the midst of the city. Carol Newsom indicates the semantic play between חלל II ("to pierce, slay") and חלל I ("to
profane, pollute"): "It is precisely the frustration of the reader's expectation
of a form of the word חלל 'to slay' that makes one attend to the implications of the unexpected reference to pollution."[18] Newsom suggests that
the oracle connects death with cultic impurity, since corpses profane sanctuaries and make them unsuitable for divine habitation. She concludes,
"Ezekiel is wryly telling the pretentious king of Tyre that once he is killed
there, Tyre will be defiled and no longer a suitable residence for a god,"[19] a
message that parallels the oracles against Israel in Ezek 1–24 when YHWH
departs Jerusalem because of its profanity.

In much the same manner, Ezekiel describes the future slaughter of
the Egyptians (30:4, 11) and of their Pharaoh, who will groan like the slain
(ונאק נאקות חלל, 30:24). Just as Assyria's great trees lie with the slain in
Sheol (31:17), so also will the slain of Egypt (31:18). The next major cluster
involves the slain of all the nations residing in Sheol in Ezek 32:21–32.
Significantly for Ezekiel, those who are slain parallel the uncircumcised.
Those who suffer YHWH's judgment will be sent to Sheol, which as the
realm of the dead is already impure: "They have come down, they lie still,
the uncircumcised (הערלים), killed by the sword (חללי־חרב)" (32:21).
The parallel structure between the uncircumcised and the slain recurs in
each verse in Ezek 32:24–26, 28–30, and 32. Ezekiel 44:6–7 prohibits the
uncircumcised entry into the sanctuary, lest they profane the offerings, a

---

18. Carol A. Newsom, "A Maker of Metaphors: Ezekiel's Oracles Against Tyre," in
This Place Is Too Small for Us: The Israelite Prophets in Recent Scholarship (ed. Robert
P. Gordon; Winona Lake, Ind.: Eisenbrauns, 1995), 199.

19. Ibid., 200.

prohibition reiterated in 44:9. A final reference to those slain in the oracles against the nations occurs in an oracle against Edom in Ezek 35:8.

2. The Exilic Vocabulary of Trauma and Trauma Theory

The above analysis evokes a few responses in light of the conversation between trauma theory and study of the exile. First, each book incorporates חלל to represent the destruction in a way that complements its own particular rhetorical themes and theological concerns. Lamentations ties חלל directly to the theme of famine. Jeremiah's use of חלל II occurs in laments and oracles against the nations to describe the slain (and in one brief historical record of Ishmael). In his use of חלל I, Jeremiah is primarily concerned with profaning of the land through idolatry or of the name of Yhwh through social injustice. Ezekiel connects the overloaded portrayal of the destruction directly to priestly matters, making the most of the semantic play between חלל I and חלל II. In fact, establishing חלל as a part of Ezekiel's vocabulary of trauma could offer a bridge between two of the current approaches to Ezekiel's perpetual strangeness, attending to the tradition's priestly perspectives while also investigating the book as testimony to trauma.[20] Perhaps the semantic play between חלל I and חלל II is another way that the Ezekiel tradition utilizes "the primary categories of priestly thought (holiness/sovereignty and purity/impurity)" to testify to the trauma of exile.[21]

Second, in addition to using various forms of חלל II to testify to the slaughter that the Judeans suffered, Jeremiah and Ezekiel use חלל I to reinforce the culpability of the community in the trauma that they experienced. Ezekiel does this by suggesting that the Israelites provoked the wrath of Yhwh by profaning Yhwh's name, sanctuary, and sabbaths. Because the people of Judah profaned Yhwh (חלל I), Yhwh will profane their sanctuaries and slay (חלל II) the people. Likewise, for Jeremiah, the people have profaned Yhwh's land by idolatry, and Yhwh's name by practicing social injustice. While Jeremiah does not connect the semantic play between חלל I and חלל II as overtly as Ezekiel, the references to the slain (חלל II) of Judah result from the disobedience to Yhwh that incited the deity to

---

20. On these two approaches to Ezekiel's complexities, see Kelle, "Dealing with the Trauma of Defeat," 470.

21. Ibid., 481.

use the Babylonians to punish them. Both traditions clearly establish the people of Judah as guilty and as deserving the traumas that befall them.

A debate exists within studies of trauma and survivor literature about the role of guilt for the traumatized survivor. Terrence Des Pres, for instance, argues that survival entails the human capacity to endure "the pressure of protracted crisis, to sustain terrible damage in mind and body and yet be there, sane, alive, still human."[22] This leads Des Pres to suggest that guilt has no role in survivor testimony: "With very few exceptions, the testimony of survivors does not concern itself with guilt of any sort. Their books neither admonish nor condemn nor beg forgiveness."[23] For Des Pres, the act of attributing guilt to the survivor as an explanation for his or her plight silences the survivor's authority: "If he is guilty, then the survivor's suffering, all the sorrow he describes, is deserved."[24] In short, Des Pres leaves little to no room for self-blame in survivor testimony. Robert J. Lifton, on the other hand, insists "no survival experience … can occur without severe guilt."[25] In his study of Hiroshima survivors, Lifton suggests the trauma produced a *"communal reinforcement of guilt*—the creation of a 'guilt community' in which self condemnation is 'in the air.'"[26] The exilic literature found in Jeremiah and Ezekiel (and to a lesser extent in Second Isaiah)[27] processes the community's trauma theologically, defining their experience as the deserved punishment for their sins. This confuses patterns in the study of human-caused traumatic events, which typically place witnesses into three categories: victims, perpetrators, and bystanders. In Jeremiah and Ezekiel, YHWH is the victim of Judah's disobedience (characterized as violence) as well as the perpetrator of violence against Judah. The people of Judah are clearly the victims of violence, but are also culpable in their own victimization. Likewise the foreign nations—some of whom are bystanders and some co-perpetrators (the Babylonians)—will also become victims of divine wrath. Traumatic testimony formed within

---

22. Terrence Des Pres, *The Survivor: An Anatomy of Life in the Death Camps* (Oxford: Oxford University Press, 1980), v.

23. Ibid., 44.

24. Ibid., 41.

25. Robert Jay Lifton, *Death in Life: Survivors of Hiroshima* (New York: Random House, 1968), 489.

26. Ibid., 6–7, 494.

27. See, for example, the use of חלל I in Isa 43:38 and חלל II in Isa 47:6.

the system of this ancient religious perspective does not permit straight-forward categorization.

This leads to a third observation. Both Jeremiah and Ezekiel use חלל II in particular in their oracles against foreign nations. In Jeremiah, חלל is used when predicting the ultimate downfall of the Babylonians. While Ezekiel does not condemn the Babylonians, who were the sword in Yhwh's hand, Ezekiel does use חלל in dooming other nations such as Tyre, Egypt, and Edom, employing as much vitriol as Jeremiah uses against Babylon.[28] The other nations who were responsible for military carnage or oppression in the ancient Near East will suffer a fate similar to Judah's. Additionally, the semantic play between חלל I and חלל II, accompanied by Ezekiel's use of the uncircumcised in the oracle against Egypt, reinforces the perception that the foreign nations are inherently profane. Perhaps establishing these oracles as the response of a traumatized community to the nations they hold partially responsible for their suffering might give current interpreters an entrance into the study of these portions of scripture that have too often been caricatured as simple xenophobia.[29]

Building a vocabulary of trauma in the exilic literature, using חלל as one point of inception, can perhaps lead to a deeper understanding of the crisis that Judah faced in the sixth century B.C.E., and of the impact of that crisis on future generations that bore its memory. Developing this vocabulary of trauma, however, should not be a reductionist enterprise. Rather than solving the disturbing and even terrifying exilic texts, a serious consideration of them as trauma literature amplifies their peculiarities, causing even current readers to attend to ancient Judah's traumatic testimony. In a statement on the ethics of heeding traumatic testimony, Caruth suggests:

> The difficulty of listening and responding to traumatic stories in a way that does not lose their impact, that does not reduce them to clichés or turn them all into versions of the same story, is a problem that remains central to the task of therapists, literary critics, neurobiologists, and film-makers alike.[30]

---

28. Other uses of חלל in the oracles against the nations include Isa 23:9 (חלל I) and 34:3 (חלל II), Nah 3:3 (חלל II), and Zeph 2:12 (חלל II).

29. For a discussion of perceived xenophobia in the oracles against the nations, see Joseph Blenkinsopp, *Ezekiel* (Interpretation; Louisville: John Knox, 1990), 108–9.

30. Caruth, *Trauma*, vii.

Perhaps we should add biblical scholars to that list. By attending to each piece of literature in the aftermath of Judah's demise as traumatic testimony, current interpreters may begin the difficult task of listening to them with a new perspective. By coupling the study of this literature with the insights of other movements within biblical scholarship, and by analyzing the vocabulary and rhetoric of the variety of responses within the biblical material, perhaps we can avoid reducing the diversity of responses to destruction and exile within the Hebrew Bible to the point of cliché.

BIBLIOGRAPHY

Blenkinsopp, Joseph. *Ezekiel*. Interpretation. Louisville: John Knox, 1990.

Bowen, Nancy R. *Ezekiel*. AOTC. Nashville: Abingdon, 2010.

Caruth, Cathy. "Preface." Pages vii–ix in *Trauma: Explorations in Memory*. Edited by Cathy Caruth. Baltimore: Johns Hopkins University Press, 1995.

Des Pres, Terrence. *The Survivor: An Anatomy of Life in the Death Camps*. Oxford: Oxford University Press, 1980.

Felman, Shoshana, and Dori Laub. *Testimony: Crises of Witnessing in Literature, Psychoanalysis, and History*. New York: Routledge, 1991.

Garber, David G. Jr. "Traumatizing Ezekiel, the Exilic Prophet." Pages 215–35 in *From Genesis to Apocalyptic Vision*. Vol. 2 of *Psychology and the Bible: A New Way to Read the Scriptures*. Edited by J. Harold Ellens and Wayne G. Rollins. Westport, Conn.: Praeger, 2004.

Kelle, Brad E. "Dealing with the Trauma of Defeat: The Rhetoric of the Devastation and Rejuvenation of Nature in Ezekiel." *JBL* 128 (2009): 469–90.

Langer, Lawrence L. *Versions of Survival: The Holocaust and the Human Spirit*. Albany: State University of New York Press, 1982.

Lifton, Robert Jay. *Death in Life: Survivors of Hiroshima*. New York: Random House, 1968.

Newsom, Carol A. "A Maker of Metaphors: Ezekiel's Oracles Against Tyre." *Int* 38 (1984): 151–64. Reprinted as pages 191–204 in *This Place Is Too Small for Us: The Israelite Prophets in Recent Scholarship*. Edited by Robert P. Gordon. Winona Lake, Ind.: Eisenbrauns, 1995.

O'Connor, Kathleen M. "A Family Comes Undone (Jeremiah 2:1–4:2)." *RevExp* 105 (2008): 201–12.

———. "Lamenting Back to Life." *Int* 62 (2008): 34–47.

———. "Reclaiming Jeremiah's Violence." Pages 37–49 in *Aesthetics of Violence in the Prophets*. Edited by Julia M. O'Brien and Chris Franke. New York: T&T Clark, 2010.

———. "Teaching Jeremiah." *PRSt* 36 (2009): 273–87.

Smith-Christopher, Daniel L. *A Biblical Theology of Exile*. OBT. Minneapolis: Fortress, 2002.

Yee, Gale A. *Poor Banished Children of Eve: Woman as Evil in the Hebrew Bible.* Minneapolis: Fortress, 2003.

Reversing Fortune: War, Psychic Trauma, and the Promise of Narrative Repair

Janet L. Rumfelt

1. Introduction

Aristotle observed that happiness, at least in part, requires certain "external goods"[1]—friendship, health, and wealth—and their possession is in large measure a matter of fortune, which is notoriously fickle: "[M]any changes occur in life, and all manner of chances, and the most prosperous may fall into great misfortunes in old age ... and one who has experienced such chances and has ended wretchedly no one calls happy."[2] Though Aristotle did not allow chance to cast the final vote in determining happiness, he nevertheless recognized the fragility of human existence by acknowledging its susceptibility to the whims of fortune. His remarks call attention to the hard reality that the kind of lives we lead, in large measure, depends on the lots we draw in the genetic, economic, and socio-historical lottery.

The prevalence of chance might lead one to conclude that human beings provide a maximum role for fortune in their assessment of the world and their place in it, but psychological research demonstrates the opposite: human beings tend to minimize the role of randomness in life, thereby preserving belief in its overall goodness and fairness. Melvin J. Lerner was among the first to call attention to this phenomenon, and it became the cornerstone of his "just world theory."[3] At first blush, Lerner's

---

1. Aristotle, *Nicomachean Ethics* 1.1099b (in *The Complete Works of Aristotle* (ed. Jonathan Barnes; 2 vols.; Bollingen Series 71; Princeton: Princeton University Press, 1984), 2:1738.

2. Aristotle, *Nicomachean Ethics* 1.1100a (ibid.).

3. Melvin J. Lerner, *The Belief in a Just World: A Fundamental Delusion* (New York: Plenum, 1980). See also Melvin J. Lerner and Carolyn H. Simmons, "Observer's

contention may seem incredible. After all, most people acknowledge that bad things happen to good people, and indeed his critics maintain that belief in a just world is not a general human propensity but is rather attributable to personality characteristics and other sociological factors.[4] While there is no doubt some truth to their assertions, Lerner's thesis is existentially compelling, for he asks us to contemplate what it would be like to live in a world devoid not only of ultimate justice that is deferred to an afterlife, but also of immanent or temporal justice.[5] What would happen to human functioning if, for example, we believed that crime really does pay or that in fundamental ways evil triumphs over good? Lerner observes that most people, in the face of nihilism, resort to some kind of belief in the fundamental justice of the world.[6]

Yet the experience of trauma shatters the resiliency of just-world beliefs, leaving the beneficent lens in ruins. Life after trauma is "uncanny." In explaining the uncanny, Sigmund Freud riffed on Daniel Sanders's definition of *Heimlich*, which defined canny as "belonging to the house" and "homely."[7] Thus for Freud, the uncanny or the "*Unheimlich*" was displacement, the dis-ease of not feeling at home. In this essay, I explore the consequences of trauma's rupturing effects on those displaced by war. I

Reaction to the 'Innocent Victim': Compassion Or Rejection?" *Journal of Personality and Social Psychology* 42 (1966): 203–10. For a summary of follow-up studies, see Jürgen Maes, "Immanent Justice and Ultimate Justice: Two Ways of Believing in Justice," in *Responses to Victimizations and Belief in a Just World* (ed. Leo Montada and Melvin J. Lerner; New York: Plenum, 1998), 9–40.

4. Zick Rubin and Letitia Anne Peplau, "Belief in a Just World and Reactions to Another's Lot: A Study," *Journal of Social Issues* 29 (1973): 73–93; idem, "Who Believes in a Just World?" *Journal of Social Issues* 31 (1975): 65–89.

5. Piaget noted that the belief in immanent justice is jettisoned as part of normal childhood development (Jean Piaget, *The Moral Judgment of the Child* [trans. Marjorie Gabain; London: Paul, Trench, Trübner, 1932]).

6. Lerner distinguishes between "preconscious" and "rational" just-world beliefs, arguing that while most adults give voice to the role of randomness on a conscious level, they nevertheless minimize its impact when confronted with victims of chance by devaluing the victim or emphasizing future compensation—tactics that leave just-world beliefs in place (Lerner, *The Belief in a Just World,* 31–53). Krantz analyzed the role of chance in "everyday narratives" and noted that the tendency to allow for luck depended on the positive or negative outcome (David L. Krantz, "Taming Chance: Social Science and Everyday Narratives," *Psychological Inquiry* 9 [1998]: 87–94).

7. Sigmund Freud, *The Uncanny* (trans. David McLintock; London: Penguin Books, 2003), 125–26.

argue that they endure a triple displacement. They are *physically* displaced from their homes (either internally or externally), *psychically* displaced from their cognitive assumptions about the beneficence of the world, and *relationally* displaced from others insofar as their traumatic experience poses a challenge to friends' and family members' assumptions concerning the justness of the world—assuming they are not themselves the victims of violence. The cumulative effect of these displacements is an existential crisis of meaning with a subsequent loss of a sense of mastery and control that ruptures subjectivity and one's place in the world.

But where trauma unhinges victims and their loved ones from the existentialist ground of their being, narrative offers the promise of repair. While many have called attention to narrative's healing role, I suggest that two different kinds of stories enable re-placement by reversing these ruptures. First, survivors engage in a hermeneutics of retrieval with the aim of getting the facts of the traumatic event straight. For many victims, the event does not seem real; thus, survivors are unhinged from the reality of their experience. Narration, precisely because it is an embodied and relational activity, bears witness to the reality of the event. Second, survivors engage in a hermeneutics of reversal. In developing this concept, I draw on José Medina's revision of J. L. Austin's speech act theory, called "The New Austin," to show how narratives can reverse psychic and relational displacements.[8] While standard readings of Austin maintain that stable, public conventions are necessary for felicity (i.e., successful or happy speech acts), Medina argues that the deliberate violation of felicity conditions provides fertile ground for renegotiating the boundaries of conventional practice and personal identity. I appropriate this insight to show that survivors can re-narrate their lives in a way that reverses misfortune, both on a personal and sociological level.[9] On the personal level, it is in the narration of their experience that they move from victim to advocate insofar as their story challenges listeners to acknowledge the role that chance plays in life. Why is such an admission important? Because the recognition of fortune's capriciousness creates the best opportunity for reversing its sociological effects. Acknowledging that our lot in life is, to a

---

8. José Medina, "How to *Undo* Things With Words: Infelicitous Practices and Infelicitous Agents," *Essays in Philosophy* 8 (2007): 1–15.

9. It is important to note that this reversal does not undo the damage done by trauma, but promotes healing by reversing the ruptures incurred by the trauma.

certain degree, predicated on the lots we draw enables us to create societies in which we strive to mitigate misfortune's injustices.

2. "Assumptive Worlds"

Just-world beliefs constitute what Ronnie Janoff-Bulman calls our "fundamental assumptions" about life, which include (1) the benevolence of the world, (2) its meaningfulness, and (3) self-worth.[10] Taken together, these beliefs reflect the convictions that the world, people, and self are basically good and that life makes sense insofar as benefits and burdens are distributed in proportion to an individual's just deserts.[11]

Along similar lines, Robert Stolorow points out that everyday existence is constituted by ordinary "absolutisms," the sense that things will work out, more or less, as planned.[12] Drawing on psychoanalytic theory and Heideggerian philosophy, he likens these assumptions to a "naive realism" or an "optimism" about life that enables one to believe that the world is basically safe and predictable.[13]

The kinds of beliefs discussed by Janoff-Bulman and Stolorow are akin to what Colin Murray Parkes has labeled an "assumptive world," which "is the only world we know and it includes everything we know or think we know. It includes our interpretations of the past and our expectations of the future, our plans and our prejudices."[14] Thus "assumptive worlds" function as paradigms that organize human experience.[15]

------

10. Ronnie Janoff-Bulman, *Shattered Assumptions: Towards a New Psychology of Trauma* (New York: Free Press, 1992), 6; see also idem, "Rebuilding Shattered Assumptions After Traumatic Life Events: Coping Processes and Outcomes," in *Coping: The Psychology of What Works* (ed. C. R. Snyder; New York: Oxford University Press, 1999), 302–23.

11. Lerner, *The Belief in a Just World*, 11–19.

12. Robert D. Stolorow, *Trauma and Human Existence: Autobiographical, Psychoanalytic, and Philosophical Reflections* (Psychoanalytic Inquiry Book Series; New York: Routledge, 2007), 16.

13. Ibid.

14. Colin Murray Parkes, "Psycho-Social Transition: A Field of Study," *Social Science and Medicine* 5 (1971): 101–15, here 102.

15. Jeffrey Kauffman, "Introduction," in *Loss of the Assumptive World: A Theory of Traumatic Loss* (ed. Jeffrey Kauffman; The Series in Trauma and Loss; New York: Brunner-Routledge, 2002), 2.

Such beliefs are fantastical, and indeed both Janoff-Bulman and Stolorow refer to them as "illusions" and "delusions" respectively; nevertheless, Janoff-Bulman points out that while "not everyone holds these basic assumptions. ... it appears that most people do."[16] The durability of these belief systems is attributable to their adaptive function insofar as they enable us to believe "that things will work out well, that we are safe and protected."[17]

Research also suggests that the psychic origins of the "assumptive world" are deeply rooted, derived from "good enough" early childhood relationships and experiences.[18] Janoff-Bulman argues that "fundamental beliefs" are "positively biased overgeneralizations" developed during childhood and mapped across time to different experiences.[19] Allan Schore, based on his neurological study of children, maintains that childhood experiences

> shape the development of a unique personality, its adaptive capacities as well as its vulnerabilities and resistances against future forms of pathologies. Indeed they profoundly influence the emergent organization of an integrated system that is both stable and adaptable, and thereby the formation of the self.[20]

---

16. Janoff-Bulman, *Shattered Assumptions*, 6, 21; and Stolorow, *Trauma and Human Existence*, 15–16. See also the study of Turkish guest workers in Germany by Barbara Reichle, Angela Schneider, and Leo Montada, "How Do Observers of Victimization Preserve Their Belief in a Just World Cognitively or Actionally? Findings from a Longitudinal Study," in Montada and Lerner, *Responses to Victimizations and Belief in a Just World*, 55–64.

17. Janoff-Bulman, *Shattered Assumptions*, 18.

18. Regina Pally draws on cognitive science to demonstrate that the "relative permanence" of the subcortical limbic circuits (i.e., the neurological networks developed during childhood and primarily responsible for affect regulation) serves an adaptive function. "[I]t is circuit permanence that allows children to form and maintain attachments to their parents over the long period of their development and to seek familiar reliable resources of safety and comfort" (Regina Pally, *The Mind-Brain Relationship* [London: Karnac Books, 2000], 15).

19. Janoff-Bulman, *Shattered Assumptions*, 25.

20. Allan N. Schore, *Affect Regulation and the Origin of the Self: The Neurobiology of Emotional Development* (Hillsdale, N.J.: Erlbaum, 1994), 1.

Thus the "assumptive world" owes its generally benevolent tenor to the "good enough caregiving" provided during childhood.[21]

Other researchers have also pointed to the role that religion plays in constructing just-world beliefs.[22] While the biblical text does not speak with a monolithic voice, many texts promote and support the idea that the world is governed by a moral structure. The opening narratives of the Hebrew Bible are illustrative of this point. Adam and Eve are expelled from the garden of Eden because of their disobedient behavior (Gen 3). The first natural disaster recorded in the Bible—the flood—is depicted as punishment for human wrongdoing, and Noah and his family are only spared on account of his righteousness (Gen 6). Sodom and Gomorrah are destroyed because of the sin of their inhabitants (Gen 19). The paradigmatic event— the exodus from Egypt—begins when God responds to the Israelites' cries over the injustice of slavery (Exod 2).

Other texts also speak to a fundamental morality operant in the universe. Ezekiel 34:15–16 depicts God as righteous shepherd:

> I myself will graze my flock, and I Myself will let them lie down—declares the Lord GOD. I will look for the lost, and I will bring back the strayed; I will bandage the injured, and I will sustain the weak; the fat and the healthy ones I will destroy. I will tend them rightly. (Tanakh)

While these verses allow for a degree of immanent injustice (i.e., some are injured, lost, and weak), they nevertheless point to an ultimate justice, a time in which God will right injustices.

---

21. Janoff-Bulman, *Shattered Assumptions,* 12–17. See also John Bowlby, *Attachment and Loss* (New York: Basic Books, 1969), and idem, *Separation: Anxiety and Anger* (New York: Basic Books, 1973). It is important to point out that childhood trauma often prohibits the development of a positive "assumptive world." On this point, see Sandra L. Bloom, "Beyond the Beveled Mirror: Mourning and Recovery From Childhood Maltreatment," in Kauffman, *Loss of the Assumptive World,* 139–70.

22. Rubin and Peplau, "Belief in a Just World"; idem, "Who Believes in a Just World?" Some studies suggest that there might not be a causal relationship between religion and just-world beliefs. Benson's studies failed to find such a correlation. Other researchers have suggested that this might owe more to the limitations of the questions than the lack of perceived causation (D. E. Benson, "Why Do People Believe in a Just World? Testing Explanations," *Sociological Spectrum* 12 [1992]: 73–104; and John H. Ellard and Melvin J. Lerner, "What Does the Just World Scale Measure: Dimension or Style?" (paper presented at the Annual Convention of the American Psychological Association, Anaheim, Calif., 27 August 1983).

But it is the book of Job that best characterizes this viewpoint. In the poetic portion of the book, Job's three friends, Zophar, Bildad, and Eliphaz, offer him counsel after calamity befalls him. Eliphaz reminds him:

> Evil does not grow out of the soil,
> Nor does mischief spring from the ground;
> For man is born to [do] mischief,
> Just as sparks fly upward. ...
> See how happy is the man whom God reproves;
> do not reject the discipline of the Almighty.
> He injures, but He binds up;
> He wounds, but His hands heal. (Job 5:6–7, 17, Tanakh)

The logic is clear: misfortune is not random; its origins are in human misconduct. To put the logic in colloquial terms, bad things happen to bad people.

Taken together, these texts constitute an "assumptive world" in which God rewards good behavior and punishes bad. As with their secular counterparts, the function of sacred "assumptive worlds" is pragmatic: they enable people to make sense of their world and the situations in which they find themselves, but in this case by promoting belief in an ultimate and divine, even if not always immediate, justice.

3. The Storied Nature of "Assumptive Worlds"

"Assumptive worlds," however, are not merely pragmatic tools, reducible to epistemic paradigms. Rather, they are storied frameworks. Alisdair MacIntyre calls attention to the centrality of narrative:

> It is through hearing stories about wicked stepmothers, lost children, good but misguided kings, wolves that suckle twin boys, youngest sons who receive no inheritance but must make their own way in the world and eldest sons who waste their inheritance on riotous living and go into exile to live with the swine, that children learn or mislearn both what a child and what a parent is, what the cast of characters may be in the drama into which they have been born and what the ways of the world are. Deprive children of stories and you leave them unscripted, anxious stutterers in their actions as in their words. Hence, there is no way to give us an understanding of any society, including our own, except through

the stock of stories which constitute its initial dramatic resources.
Mythology, in its original sense, is at the heart of things.[23]

His point is that concepts are not intelligible apart from the storied framework in which they gain their sense. Moral principles, for example, are
abstracted from narratives. As applied to this current discussion, it means
that "fundamental assumptions" about the world only make sense within
a storied framework.

Theodore Sarbin's definition of narrative provides further elucidation:

> The narrative is a way of organizing episodes, actions, and accounts of
> actions; it is an achievement that brings together mundane facts and fan-
> tastic creations; time and place are incorporated. The narrative allows
> for the inclusion of actors' reasons for their acts, as well as the causes of
> happening.[24]

Life is a series of unfolding moments; it is the narrative frame that enables
us to weave these moments together. Significantly, it also enables a selec-
tivity in which we incorporate only those moments that make meaningful contributions to our story. In the introduction, I mentioned that
stories re-place us; they are able to do so because they locate us in time
and place. They provide both a retrospective and present-future orientation, which is to say that they help us understand the past, and in turn,
we draw on this understanding to orient us in the present and propel
us toward the future.[25] Conversely, our understandings in the present
also enable us to re-inscribe the past. Thus narrative provides a frame in
which experience and its interpretation are interwoven into a dynamic
storyline that makes sense of the past, grounds us in the present, and
opens us to the future.

---

23. Alasdair C. MacIntyre, *After Virtue: A Study in Moral Theory* (Notre Dame,
Ind.: University of Notre Dame Press, 1981), 216.

24. Theodore R. Sarbin, *Narrative Psychology: The Storied Nature of Human Conduct* (New York: Praeger, 1986), 9.

25. My ideas are drawn from readings of Martin Heidegger, *Being and Time*
(trans. Joan Stambaugh; New York: State University of New York Press, 1996), and
from Stolorow, *Trauma and Human Existence*.

4. Storied Selves

It is by now commonplace to note that human subjectivity is linguistically constituted. It is not merely language that constitutes subjectivity, but stories. MacIntyre's discussion of narratives is helpful in this regard. He maintains that if we want to figure out what we ought to do, we must first ask a prior question, "Of what story or stories do I find myself a part?"[26] We come to know who we are and what we are to do by locating ourselves within inherited, storied frameworks. Our self is inextricably bound up with the stories from which we come. Importantly, then, we are not the sole authors of our narratives; we inherit—by chance—the familial and cultural storied frameworks by which we come to understand ourselves and our place in the world.

But MacIntyre's emphasis on the inherited aspect of story, while important, diminishes human autonomy. Marilyn Friedman points out that while we cannot choose the stories that we are born into, we can choose the communities and thus the communal narratives of which we find ourselves a part. In making this distinction between narratives of birth and narratives of choice, Friedman calls attention to the possibility of altering one's identity by choosing to participate in different communities and hence locating oneself within new frameworks. I would suggest that Friedman's augmentation of MacIntyre does not go far enough. It is not only possible to adopt different narratives, but it is also possible to alter the storyline itself.

5. "Assumptive Worlds" and Cognitive Stasis

Alteration to the storyline is no simple matter. Popular literature and even scholarly philosophies sometimes fall prey to the notion that human beings can simply take up another story, much like one puts hats on and takes them off.[27] But to change the storyline is to alter one's "fundamental assumptions" about the way the world works. It is for this reason that "assumptive worlds" tend toward cognitive stasis.

---

26. MacIntyre, *After Virtue*, 216.

27. See the discussion of the "self-creation" produced by psychoanalysis in Richard Rorty, "Freud and Moral Reflection," in *Essays on Heidegger and Others* (Philosophical Papers 2; New York: Cambridge University Press, 1996), 143–63.

This tendency was first observed by Jerome Bruner and Leo Postman in their now famous study involving the identification of anomalous playing cards.[28] Subjects consistently misclassified anomalous playing cards by classifying them within known suit categories.[29] Similar observations were made by Jean Piaget, who observed that children processed new information by assimilating it into preexisting schemas, or through accommodation, which required adjustments to the existing schemas.[30] Though he maintained that children strive to find equilibrium between assimilation and accommodation, Janoff-Bulman draws on a large body of empirical study to demonstrate that when faced with new information, "we are biased towards assimilation rather than accommodation."[31] Subsequently, "assumptive worlds" have a conservative bias; their storyline tends toward rigidity rather than flexibility.

6. Trauma and Displacement

That said, the "assumptive world" is not immune from the vicissitudes of life. This is especially true with respect to trauma, which, as Janoff-Bulman has noted, shatters "fundamental assumptions" and thereby displaces victims.

The *DSM-III* and the *DSM-III-R* defined trauma as "outside the range of usual human experience," thereby differentiating it from more ordinary ruptures like chronic illness that threatens life or the death of a loved one from a prolonged illness.[32] This distinction is blurred in the *DSM-IV* and the *DSM-IV-R*, both of which allow for a more inclusive understanding. Trauma is now understood to be:

---

28. Jerome Bruner and Leo Postman, "On the Perception of Incongruity: A Paradigm," *Journal of Personality* 18 (1949): 206–23.

29. See Thomas S. Kuhn, *The Structure of Scientific Revolutions* (2nd ed.; Chicago: University of Chicago Press, 1996), 62–65.

30. Jean Piaget and Margaret Cook, *The Origins of Intelligence in Children* (trans. Margaret Cook; 2nd ed.; New York: International Universities Press, 1959), 210–62.

31. Janoff-Bulman, *Shattered Assumptions,* 30. See Colin Murray Parkes and Robert Stuart Weiss, *Recovery From Bereavement* (New York: Basic Books, 1983), 9.

32. American Psychiatric Association, *Diagnostic and Statistical Manual of Mental Disorders: DSM-III* (Washington, D.C.: American Psychiatric Association, 1980), §309.89, and idem, *Diagnostic and Statistical Manual of Mental Disorders: DSM-III-R* (Washington, D.C.: American Psychiatric Association, 1987), §309.81.

direct personal experience of an event that involves actual or threatened death or serious injury, or other threat to one's physical integrity; or witnessing an event that involves death, injury, or a threat to the physical integrity of another person; or learning about unexpected or violent death, serious harm, or threat of death or injury experienced by a family member or other close associate.[33]

Traumatic events now include violent and nonviolent threats to existence. The definition includes those who directly experience trauma, those who witness someone else's trauma, and those who hear about the traumatic experiences of a close friend or family member. Thus trauma, rather than being extraordinary experience, turns out to be an inevitable aspect of human existence with extraordinary implications.

Though trauma is inevitable, war is not an inevitable trauma, and its rupturing effects are particularly severe. While this discussion is primarily focused on the psychic and relational displacements of trauma, it is important to recognize the enormity of the material challenges faced by internally displaced persons and refugees, including housing, health care, nutrition, and employment.[34] Refugees face additional challenges in that they may also have to learn new languages, political systems, and cultures mores.

This physical displacement mirrors their psychic and relational displacement, intensifying the uncanniness of the situation. Internally displaced persons and refugees struggle to feel at home in body, mind, and in relationships with those who have not experienced trauma. Though more empirical research needs to be done, a study conducted on the psychiatric and cognitive effects of war in the former Yugoslavia confirms Janoff-

---

33. American Psychiatric Association, *Diagnostic and Statistical Manual of Mental Disorders: DSM-IV* (Washington, D.C.: American Psychiatric Association, 1994), §309.81; and idem, *Diagnostic and Statistical Manual of Mental Disorders: DSM-IV-TR* (Washington, D.C.: American Psychiatric Association, 2000), §309.81.

34. The United Nation's Internal Displacement Monitoring Centre estimates that there are over 27 million internally displaced persons due to conflict. For country-by-country statistics, see Internal Displacement Monitoring Centre, "Global Statistics,"online: http://www.internal-displacement.org/8025708F004CE90B/%28htt pPages%29/22FB1D4E2B196DAA802570BB005E787C?OpenDocument. As of 2009, the United Nations Refugee Agency estimates that there are over 48 million forcibly displaced refugees worldwide (UNHCR, "Refugee Figures," online: http://www.unhcr. org/pages/49c3646c1d.html).

Bulman's insight concerning the shattering effects of trauma, for survivors did indeed report having "less faith in the benevolence of people and a just world than did the controls."[35] Put another way, they could no longer trust their previous "fundamental assumptions" about the world and their place in it. One displaced survivor of Auschwitz poignantly described it this way in her oral testimony:

> I am not like you. You have one vision of life and I have two. ... I have lived on two planets. ... Hitler chopped off part of the universe and created annihilation zones and torture and slaughter areas. You know, it's like part of the planet was chopped up into a normal [part]—so called normal; our lives are really not normal—and this other planet, and we were herded into that planet from this one, and herded back again [while] having nothing—virtually nothing in common with the inhabitants of this planet. And we had to relearn how to live again. ... we have these ... double lives.[36]

Her testimony gives voice to trauma's psychic and relational sequelae. Her existence has been reduced to a permanent, liminal state in which she is unable to go back to the "planet" before Auschwitz, but also unable to move forward into the "planet" after Auschwitz. She is displaced, neither here nor there, frozen between two worlds, and unable to relate to those who did not share her shattering experiences.

A survivor of the 1994 Rwandan genocide, who was infected with HIV/AIDS from a gang rape, describes her life in similar categories. "I only half survived. I am still carrying death in me; not only the death that AIDS will bring. Others say they escaped from the sword, but the sword is still in my heart. Even in death, I do not believe I will find rest."[37] She, too, is between two worlds, the world before the traumatic rape and genocide and the world after, and she cannot find her place in the world after because the trauma from the past—the sword in her heart—forecloses on

---

35. Metin Başoğlu et al., "Psychiatric and Cognitive Effects of War in Former Yugoslavia: Association of Lack of Redress for Trauma and Posttraumatic Stress Reactions," *JAMA* 294 (2005): 588.

36. Cited in Lawrence L. Langer, *Holocaust Testimonies: The Ruins of Memory* (New Haven: Yale University Press, 1991), 54–55; Tape T12870—Testimony of Isabella L.

37. Anne-Marie Bucyana, "Oral Testimony," online: http://www.kigalimemorial-centre.org/old/survivors/anne-marie.html.

the present and future, so much so that she cannot even imagine that death will provide a respite from the suffering.

7. The Promise of Narrative Repair

The rupture of trauma is a narrative (as opposed to nervous) breakdown, rupturing the self in the form of the loss of one's organizing principles and the rupturing of one's relationships with others. "The worlds of traumatized persons are fundamentally incommensurable with those of others, the deep chasm in which an anguished sense of estrangement and solitude takes form."[38] This shattering is immobilizing, leaving survivors without a story that enables them to move into their worlds by making sense of the world, their place it, and their relationships with others.[39] But the construction of new narratives holds out the promise of repair.

Two types of posttraumatic stories help mend the breaches. The first is the hermeneutics of retrieval. Susan Brison and Hilde Lindeman Nelson suggest this story is told for the sake of the survivor as a means of bearing witness to the historicity and veracity of the experience.[40] Holocaust survivor Primo Levi often compared himself to Coleridge's "Ancient Mariner":

> I acted exactly like that ancient sailor, grabbing people in the street. ... I well remember talking freewheel in a train with people I did not know. Among them was a priest. He was astonished, upset, and he asked me why, why do you address people you don't know and I told him I had no choice, how could I refrain, how could I cease this urge within me to tell the tale.[41]

---

38. Stolorow, *Trauma and Human Existence*, 16.

39. Susan Brison, a philosopher and rape survivor, argues that trauma immobilizes because it leaves one in a present "that has no meaning" (*Aftermath: Violence and the Remaking of a Self* [Princeton: Princeton University Press, 2002], 104). I agree that trauma immobilizes, but describe the details of the paralysis differently. The problem is that the present and future are eclipsed by the past. It is in this respect that time stops; all that exists is the past, understood according to a fixed storyline that endlessly repeats itself without reprieve.

40. Brison, *Aftermath*, 106–10; and Hilde Lindemann, *Damaged Identities, Narrative Repair* (Ithaca, N.Y.: Cornell University Press, 2001), 111–12.

41. Anthony Rudolf, "Primo Levi in London (1986)," in *The Voice of Memory: Primo Levi, Interviews 1961–1987* (ed. Marco Belpoliti and Robert Gordon; New York: The New Press, 2001), 27.

Susan Brison, a philosopher and rape survivor, explains that mastery is the purpose of this kind of narration: "the retroactive attempt to master the trauma through involuntary repetition is carried out, intrapsychically, until a listener emerges who is stable and reliable enough to bear witness to it."[42]

The second kind of story, the hermeneutics of reversal, is of primary importance for this current discussion. Here, I draw on Medina's "New Austin" to show how the deliberate violation of felicity conditions can reverse the personal misfortune of the survivor and lessen the sociological impact of misfortune's injustices.

Before demonstrating how narratives can reverse misfortune, I must first discuss Medina's "New Austin," which pivots on whether the meaning of words is derived from "their continuation with or from their breakage with customs, institutions, and traditions, from doing or from undoing things within them."[43] The standard account of Austin has it that relatively stable public practices are the necessary conditions for a successful speech act. Thus, for example, in order to name a ship, certain public conventions must be adhered to, not the least of which is that one has been invited to do so by the "appropriate persons" and under the "appropriate circumstances."[44] On this reading, meaning is tied to continuation with customary conventions.

Further, all speech acts are subject to the "ill" of infelicity, which can occur whenever there is a "misfire" or an "abuse" of the felicity conditions.[45] An abuse happens whenever the proper conventions are in place, but the speaker's motives are insincere. For example, if the locution: "I promise" is uttered insincerely, with no intention of keeping the promise, then the speech act fails and is infelicitous. A misfire occurs when conventional felicity conditions are in place, but are violated. If, for example, someone performs a marriage ceremony, but does not have the authority to do so, then the pronouncement misfires, rendering the act infelicitous. Abuses end in hollow utterances, while misfires result in voided acts.

---

42. Brison, *Aftermath*, 110.

43. Medina, "How to *Undo* Things with Words," 2.

44. John L. Austin, *How to Do Things With Words* (2nd ed.; ed. J. O. Urmson and Marina Sbisà; Cambridge: Harvard University Press, 1975), 34–38.

45. Ibid., 18–19. It should be noted that the distinction between these is not iron-clad.

The standard account of Austin maintains that infelicitous acts are accidental. Medina's insight is that this reading "has misconceived the normative significance of the infelicities that speech acts are subject to."[46] Rather than construe them as accidents, he insists that they are constitutive of felicitous acts.[47] This means that unhappy speech acts are the condition for the possibility of happy ones. But Medina's contention goes even further. In his construction of "the New Austin," infelicitous acts provide fertile ground for renegotiating the boundaries of the conventional practices and of personal identity.

In standard readings, felicity conditions are dependent on the reification of public conventions, which has the effect of stabilizing, indeed stagnating, these conventions, and leaves little space for the renegotiation of the felicity conditions themselves. The consequent effect is that traditional practices and customs remain in place. But Medina insightfully locates a new way of reading Austin in his essay "A Plea for Excuses," where Austin notes that the issue of excuses entails an examination of "cases where there has been some abnormality or failure; and as so often, the abnormal will throw light on the normal, will help us penetrate the blinding veil of ease and obviousness that hides the mechanisms of the natural successful act."[48] Thus infelicitous speech acts reveal the hidden mechanisms of normalization that are at work in public conventions. That being the case, Medina notes that the deliberate "practice of infelicity" can function to challenge the stasis of felicity conditions. In other words, the repeated and deliberate performance of infelicitous acts calls for a reappraisal of the normative felicity conditions.

This new interpretation of Austin enables us to see how posttrauma narratives can create linguistic space for reversing misfortune. In the hermeneutics of reversal, the survivor actively challenges the normative felicity conditions of posttrauma narratives, which though unstated, are nevertheless operative. In comparing Holocaust written memoirs to oral histories, Lawrence Langer noted that their trajectories differed. The former most often ended with liberation from the camps or the end of the war, triumphant themes that reaffirmed readers' expectations. In contrast, oral testimonies often ignored chronology and avoided trium-

---

46. Medina, "How to *Undo* Things With Words," 2.

47. Ibid., 3.

48. John L. Austin, "A Plea for Excuses," in *Philosophical Papers* (ed. J. O. Urmson and G. J. Warnock; New York: Oxford University Press, 1979), 179–80.

phant themes.[49] It is in the interviewers' responses and questions that the unstated but operative felicity conditions manifest themselves. One survivor, in discussing the disconnect she felt between herself and other people, gave voice to her knowledge of the harsh realities of life, of her "extreme pessimism" with regard to faith in other people. The interviewer interrupted her to say, "Mrs. W., you are one of the greatest optimists I've ever met."[50] Another interviewer led a discussion of survival with this statement, "You were able to survive because you were so plucky."[51] These conditions also manifest themselves in the contemporary context. In a 2001 interview with Elie Wiesel, Oprah Winfrey commented that the Holocaust "was a reminder of the triumph of the human spirit."[52] Taken together these examples reveal that the felicity conditions require that a story—even a traumatic one—ought not disrupt the listener's "fundamental assumptions" about the overall beneficence and goodness of life.

In the hermeneutics of reversal, the survivor deliberately violates these conditions by acknowledging the role that chance plays in life. Elie Wiesel's remarks demonstrate how this might work: "The only role I sought was witness. I believed that, having survived by chance, I was duty bound to give meaning to my survival, to justify each moment of my life. I knew the story had to be told. Not to transmit an experience is to be betray it."[53] Through re-narration, they reverse their status as victims to that of advocates insofar as they give voice to human fragility and vulnerability.

This prepares the way for the second stage of reversal. Janoff-Bulman raises an interesting question at the end of one of her essays. After noting that most survivors are able to acknowledge the role that chance plays in life, she also notes that they are nevertheless able to construct meaningful lives after trauma. She wonders how it might be possible "to reap the benefits of a more valued existence without going through the pain of victimhood."[54] I suggest that it is possible by attuning ourselves to the sto-

---

49. Langer, *Holocaust Testimonies*, 57.

50. Ibid., 59.

51. Ibid., 63.

52. Oprah Winfrey, "Oprah Talks to Elie Wiesel," *O, The Oprah Magazine* (November 2000): 234–36.

53. Cited in K. Tal, *Worlds of Hurt: Reading the Literature of Trauma* (Cambridge: Cambridge University Press, 1996), 120.

54. Ronnie Janoff-Bulman, "From Terror to Appreciation: Confronting Chance after Extreme Misfortune," *Psychological Inquiry* 9 (1998): 101.

ries that survivors tell and allowing their narratives of misfortune to challenge our own "fundamental assumptions." Thus, their narration reverses fortune by inviting others to create social conditions that mitigate fortune's capriciousness. If we acknowledge chance, we are more likely to strive to rectify its unequal distribution of burdens and benefits in order to create a more just society.

In telling their stories, victims are no longer frozen in time; rather, they are advocates, ones who tell a story in the present about the past so as to create a better future. Displaced victims may not be able to return to their homes, nor even to their homelands. They may not be able to return to their "homely," pre-trauma, just-world assumptions, nor to the relational ease cultivated when people share assumptions about the world, but they can construct a narrative with a conceptual basis in which they can feel at home, and where they can invite others to join with them in creating a society that is more just because it recognizes and mitigates fortune's injustices. As Jacques Lacan noted, "It is by touching, however lightly, on man's relation to the signifier—in this case by changing the procedures of exegesis—that one changes the course of history by modifying the moorings of his being."[55]

Bibliography

American Psychiatric Association. *Diagnostic and Statistical Manual of Mental Disorders: DSM-III*. Washington, D.C.: American Psychiatric Association, 1980.

———. *Diagnostic and Statistical Manual of Mental Disorders: DSM-III-R*. Washington, D.C.: American Psychiatric Association, 1987.

———. *Diagnostic and Statistical Manual of Mental Disorders: DSM-IV*. Washington, D.C.: American Psychiatric Association, 1994.

———. *Diagnostic and Statistical Manual of Mental Disorders: DSM-IV-TR*. Washington, D.C.: American Psychiatric Association, 2000.

Aristotle. "Nicomachean Ethics." Pages 1729–867 in vol. 2 of *The Complete Works of Aristotle: The Revised Oxford Translation*. Edited by Jonathan Barnes. 2 vols. Bollingen Series 71. Princeton: Princeton University Press, 1984.

Austin, John L. *How to Do Things With Words*. Edited by J. O. Urmson and Marina Sbisà. 2nd ed. Cambridge: Harvard University Press, 1975.

———. "A Plea for Excuses." Pages 175–204 in *Philosophical Papers*. Edited by J. O. Urmson, and G. J. Warnock. New York: Oxford University Press, 1979.

---

55. Jacques Lacan, "The Instance of the Letter in the Unconscious," in *Encrits: A Selection* (trans. Bruce Fink; New York: Norton, 2002): 165.

Başoğlu, Metin, M. Livanou, C. Crnobarić, T. Franciskovič, E. Suljić, D. Durić, and M. Vranesić. "Psychiatric and Cognitive Effects of War in Former Yugoslavia: Association of Lack of Redress for Trauma and Posttraumatic Stress Reactions." *JAMA* 294 (2005): 580–90.

Benson, D. E. "Why Do People Believe in a Just World? Testing Explanations." *Sociological Spectrum* 12 (1992): 73–104.

Bloom, Sandra L. "Beyond the Beveled Mirror: Mourning and Recovery from Childhood Maltreatment." Pages 139–70 in *Loss of the Assumptive World : A Theory of Traumatic Loss*. Edited by Jeffrey Kauffman. New York: Brunner-Routledge, 2002.

Bowlby, John. *Attachment and Loss*. New York: Basic Books, 1969.

———. *Separation: Anxiety and Anger*. New York: Basic Books, 1973.

Brison, Susan J. *Aftermath: Violence and the Remaking of a Self*. Princeton: Princeton University Press, 2002.

Bruner, Jerome, and Leo Postman. "On the Perception of Incongruity: A Paradigm." *Journal of Personality* 18 (1949): 206–23.

Bucyana, Anne-Marie. "Oral Testimony." Online: http://www.kigalimemorialcentre. org/old/survivors/anne-marie.html.

Ellard, John H., and Melvin J. Lerner. "What Does the Just World Scale Measure: Dimension or Style?" Paper presented at the Annual Convention of the American Psychological Association, Anaheim, Calif., 27 August 1983.

Freud, Sigmund. *The Uncanny*. Translated by David McLintock. London: Penguin Books, 2003.

Heidegger, Martin. *Being and Time*. Translated by Joan Stambaugh. New York: State University of New York Press, 1996.

Internal Displacement Monitoring Center. "Global Statistics." Online: http://www. internal-displacement.org/8025708F004CE90B/%28httpPages%29/22FB1D4E2 B196DAA802570BB005E787C?OpenDocument.

Janoff-Bulman, Ronnie. "From Terror to Appreciation: Confronting Chance after Extreme Misfortune." *Psychological Inquiry* 9 (1998): 99–101.

———. "Rebuilding Shattered Assumptions after Traumatic Life Events: Coping Processes and Outcomes." Pages 302–23 in *Coping: The Psychology of What Works*. Edited by C. R. Snyder. New York: Oxford University Press, 1999.

———. *Shattered Assumptions: Towards a New Psychology of Trauma*. New York: Free Press, 1992.

Kauffman, Jeffrey, "Introduction." Pages 1–9 in *Loss of the Assumptive World: A Theory of Traumatic Loss*, ed. Jeffrey Kauffman. The Series in Trauma and Loss. New York: Brunner-Routledge, 2002.

Krantz, David L. "Taming Chance: Social Science and Everyday Narratives." *Psychological Inquiry* 9 (1998): 87–94.

Kuhn, Thomas S. *The Structure of Scientific Revolutions*. 2nd ed. Chicago: University of Chicago Press, 1996.

Lacan, Jacques. "The Instance of the Letter in the Unconscious." Pages 138–68 in *Encrits: A Selection*. Translated by Bruce Fink. New York: Norton, 2002.

Langer, Lawrence L. *Holocaust Testimonies: The Ruins of Memory*. New Haven: Yale University Press, 1991.

Lerner, Melvin J. *The Belief in a Just World: A Fundamental Delusion*. New York: Plenum, 1980.

Lerner, Melvin J., and Carolyn H. Simmons. "Observer's Reaction to the 'Innocent Victim': Compassion Or Rejection?" *Journal of Personality and Social Psychology* 42 (1966): 203–10.

MacIntyre, Alasdair C. *After Virtue : A Study in Moral Theory*. Notre Dame, Ind.: University of Notre Dame Press, 1981.

Maes, Jürgen. "Immanent Justice and Ultimate Justice: Two Ways of Believing in Justice." Pages 9–40 in *Responses to Victimizations and Belief in a Just World*. Edited by Leo Montada and Melvin J. Lerner. New York: Plenum, 1998.

Medina, José. "How to *Undo* Things with Words: Infelicitous Practices and Infelicitous Agents." *Essays in Philosophy* 8 (2007): 1–15.

Nelson, Hilde Lindemann. *Damaged Identities, Narrative Repair*. Ithaca, N.Y.: Cornell University Press, 2001.

Pally, Regina. *The Mind-Brain Relationship*. London: Karnac Books, 2000.

Parkes, Colin Murray. "Psycho-Social Transition: A Field of Study." *Social Science and Medicine* 5 (1971): 101–15.

Parkes, Colin Murray, and Robert Stuart Weiss. *Recovery From Bereavement*. New York: Basic Books, 1983.

Piaget, Jean. *The Moral Judgment of the Child*. Translated by Marjorie Gabain. London: Paul, Trench, Trübner, 1932.

———. *The Origins of Intelligence in Children*. Translated by Margaret Cook. 2nd ed. New York: International Universities Press, 1959.

Reichle, Barbara, Angela Schneider, and Leo Montada. "How Do Observers of Victimization Preserve Their Belief in a Just World Cognitively or Actionally? Findings From a Longitudinal Study." Pages 55–64 in *Responses to Victimizations and Belief in a Just World*. Edited by Leo. Montada and Melvin J. Lerner. New York: Plenum, 1998.

Rorty, Richard. "Freud and Moral Reflection." Pages 143–63 in idem, *Essays on Heidegger and Others*. Philosophical Papers 2. New York: Cambridge University Press, 1996.

Rubin, Zick, and Letitia Anne Peplau. "Belief in a Just World and Reactions to Another's Lot: A Study." *Journal of Social Issues* 29 (1973): 73–93.

———. "Who Believes in a Just World?" *Journal of Social Issues* 31 (1975): 65–89.

Rudolf, Anthony. "Primo Levi in London (1986)." Pages 23–33 in *The Voice of Memory: Primo Levi, Interviews 1961–1987*. Edited by Marco Belpoliti and Robert Gordon. New York: The New Press, 2001.

Sarbin, Theodore R. *Narrative Psychology: The Storied Nature of Human Conduct*. New York: Praeger, 1986.

Schore, Allan N. *Affect Regulation and the Origin of the Self: The Neurobiology of Emotional Development*. Hillsdale, N.J.: Erlbaum, 1994.

Stolorow, Robert D. *Trauma and Human Existence: Autobiographical, Psychoanalytic, and Philosophical Reflections*. Psychoanalytic Inquiry Book Series. New York: Routledge, 2007.

Tal, K. *Worlds of Hurt: Reading the Literature of Trauma*. Cambridge: Cambridge University Press, 1996.

UNHCR. "Refugee Figures." Online: http://www.unhcr.org/pages/49c3646c1d.html.

Winfrey, Oprah. "Oprah Talks to Elie Wiesel." *O, The Oprah Magazine* (November 2000): 234–36.

PART 4
TEXTS AND COMPARISON

THE PROSE AND POETRY OF EXILE

Samuel E. Balentine

Historical sense and poetic sense should not, in the end, be contradictory, for if poetry is the little myth we create, history is the big myth we live, and in our living, constantly remake.

— Robert Penn Warren[1]

History as far as I can see is not the arrangement of what happens, in sequence and in truth, but a fabulous arrangement of surmises and guesses held up as a banner against the assault of withering truth.

— Sebastian Barry[2]

1. INTRODUCTION

"There were two ways to mark the tragedy of the sixth century catastrophe in the immediate aftermath," Jill Middlemas says. "One was to mourn it, and another was to record it."[3] The Hebrew Bible typically turns to prose for the latter, to poetry for the former. The distinction has to do with different generic forms, but also with more than this. Prose narratives are generally offered as normative and factual accounts of events that happened, their cause and their effect. The progression of thought is linear, sequential, and contextually embedded in historical contingencies. Poetry is generically terse, figurative, and decontextualized. Its paratactic and elliptical style typically omits conjunctions; the connections between jux-

---

1. Robert Penn Warren, *Brother to Dragons: A Tale in Verses and Voices* (New York: Random House, 1953), xiii.

2. Sebastian Barry, *The Secret Scripture* (London: Faber & Faber, 2006; repr., New York: Penguin, 2008), 55.

3. Jill Middlemas, *The Templeless Age: An Introduction to the History, Literature, and Theology of the "Exile"* (Louisville: Westminster John Knox, 2007), 28.

taposed lines (or cola) are left open, unexplained, inviting a multiplicity of meaning.

Beyond these obvious distinctions, prose and poetry also convey different perspectives on time. Prose privileges "chronological time," especially the impact of the past on the present and future. Poetry attunes itself to "durational time," what Walter Benjamin calls the "empty time" that is "filled up by the presence of the now (*Jetztzeit*)."[4] Chronological time is primarily the preoccupation of historiographers, whose objectives are to compile, preserve, and interpret the "evidence" of the past. Especially in the wake of pivotal crises, the act of providing a temporal record of events serves explanatory aims, either by valorizing the past as a determinative prologue—for good or ill—to the future (the way it was explains the way it is) or by valorizing the present as seeding a future that may be superior to the past (what is and can be overcomes and corrects past shortcomings). Durational time is primarily the preoccupation of poets, whose figurations linger over the "now," loosening temporal connections that either explain the present or dispel the future. This resistance to closure is simultaneously an insistence that the import of the present not be minimized or erased when "history exercises its rights."[5] Gabrielle M. Spiegel has helpfully connected durational time with "liturgical time," and specifically with the poetry and prayers of the synagogue that give vivid expression to the claims of the present on those who depend on ritual and recitation to sustain their identity.[6]

Another distinction between prose and poetry should not be overlooked, even though the limitations of this essay permit only a brief mention. Prose accounts of historical events tend to be conservative in ori-

---

4. I appropriate the terms "chronological time" and "durational time" from Lawrence Langer, *Admitting the Holocaust: Collected Essays* (Oxford: Oxford University Press, 1995), 15, 22, *et passim*. For the Benjamin citation, see Walter Benjamin, "Theses on the Philosophy of History," no. XIV. Online: http://www.sfu.ca/~andrewf/CONCEPT2.html.

5. I slightly emend the words of Pierre Vidal-Naquet (*The Jews: History, Memory and the Present* [ed. and trans. David A. Curtis; New York: Columbia University Press, 1996], 57), who has noted that the weight of Jewish memory of the holocaust blocks "history from exercising its rights." Here, as throughout this paragraph, my thinking has been informed by Gabrielle M. Spiegel, "Memory and History: Liturgical Time and Historical Time," *History and Theory* 41 (2002): 149–62. For Spiegel's use of Vidal-Naquet's language cited here, see p. 152.

6. Spiegel, "Memory and History," 151–53.

entation. By privileging the past as prologue to the present and future, they summon attention to determinative facts that inform and potentially resolve questions about the status quo. Conformity to history's irreversible timeline for the way things happen, not rebellion from it, is the religious and political response prose perspectives hope to generate and sustain. Poetic accounts of historical events tend to be more liberal in orientation. Sustained focus on present experiences, essentially uncoupled from causal historical explanations, fills the "empty time" between past and future with questions about normative truths. Dissent, not conformity, is the religious and political response that poetry often voices and empowers, because the status quo has been found wanting.[7] As Spiegel has discerned, liturgical time creates sacred space for a "poetics of sacrilege that consoles even as it borders on blasphemy."[8]

2. "So Judah Went into Exile out of Its Land" (2 Kgs 25:21): Historical Narratives and Metanarratives

The prose and poetic accounts of exile represent multiple voices in response to the time when Israel's "history" with God—from the garden of Eden to the temple in Jerusalem—comes to a punctiliar end. When the dust clears enough for the historical record to continue, decades later in Ezra-Nehemiah and Chronicles, the narrative resumes with the return to

---

7. On the religious and political ramifications of writing history and "alternate history," see the seminal essay by Gavriel Rosenfeld, "Why Do We Ask 'What If?' Reflections on the Function of Alternate History," *History and Theory* 41 (2002): 90–103.

8. Spiegel, "Memory and History," 153. Spiegel appropriates the phrase "poetics of sacrilege" from Jeremy Cohen, "The Hebrew Crusade Chronicles in the Twelfth-Century Cultural Context" (paper presented at the meeting of the American Historical Association, San Francisco, 1994). She extends her argument with a citation from Sidra D. Ezrahi on the caustic "sacred parody" that arises when authors deploy an "ironizing appropriation of the consecrated past or of constitutive texts that still manages to preserve their normative valence. By incorporating the anger, and even the blasphemy, into the normative response to catastrophe, the language of sacred parody remains contained yet infinitely expandable; scriptural and liturgical texts can be appropriated while registering the enormity of the violation of central precepts" (Sidra D. Ezrahi, "Considering the Apocalypse: Is the Writing on the Wall only Graffiti?" in *Writing and the Holocaust* [ed. Berel Lang; Ithaca, N.Y.: Holmes & Meier, 1988], 141); cited in Spiegel, "Memory and History," 153.

Jerusalem. Inside the "narrative wreckage,"[9] a dominant metanarrative, stitched together from diverse deuteronomistic, prophetic, and priestly traditions, emerges in the literature of Yehud.[10] Ongoing research has made it increasingly clear that various aspects of this metanarrative are counterfactual, especially claims for a total depopulation of Judeans, a total destruction of Judah's economic infrastructures, and a full return and restoration of national identity for all those who had been exiled.[11] Close scrutiny of these and other issues during the last two decades has required significant revision of previous scholarly models that settled for monolithic views of what was generally described simply as "the exile."[12] Other essays in this volume address these issues; I will not pursue them here.

For the purpose of this essay, it is more important to reflect on how the "grammar" and ideology of this metanarrative generates perspectives of closure on what happened in sixth-century Judah.[13] Though drawing upon diverse traditions, the metanarrative creates a coherent "historical"

---

9. Kathleen O'Connor, *Lamentations and the Tears of the World* (Maryknoll, N.Y.: Orbis, 2002), 7.

10. For an overview of the major texts, see John Kessler, "Images of Exile: Representations of the 'Exile' and 'Empty Land' in Sixth to Fourth Century Yehudite Literature," in *The Concept of the Exile in Ancient Israel and Its Historical Contexts* (ed. Ehud Ben Zvi and Christoph Levin; BZAW 404; Berlin: de Gruyter, 2010), 309–51. Kessler locates representative texts on a continuum, from those affirming the inclusion of only the 597 exiles (Jer 24 and Ezek 11:14–21), to those open to the inclusion of subsequent deportees (Ezek 33:21–29); from texts describing a complete exile as the result of Israel's disobedience (Lev 26:14–45; Deut 28:1–68; 2 Kgs 25:22–26; Ezra-Nehemiah), to those anticipating a complete return to the land of all deportees consonant with God's renewed mercy (Zech 1–8; Isaiah; and Micah).

11. Ehud Ben Zvi, "The Voice and Role of Counterfactual Memory in the Construction of Exile and Return: Considering Jeremiah 40:7–12," in Ben Zvi and Levin, *The Concept of Exile in Ancient Israel*, 168–88.

12. The emerging characterization of exile as a "forced migration" that evokes different "generation-units" of migrant stories is worthy of special mention. See John J. Ahn, *Exile as Forced Migrations: A Sociological, Literary, and Theological Approach on the Displacement and Resettlement of the Southern Kingdom of Judah* (BZAW 417; Berlin: de Gruyter, 2010); idem, "Forced Migration Studies as a New Approach to the Study of the Exilic Period," in *By the Irrigation Canals of Babylon: Approaches to the Study of Exile* (ed. John Ahn and Jill Middlemas; LHBOTS 526; London: T&T Clark International, forthcoming). Note also the ongoing work of the Society of Biblical Literature consultation group on "Exile (Forced Migrations) in Biblical Literature."

13. Ehud Ben Zvi, "Total Exile, Empty Land and the General Intellectual Discourse in Yehud," in Ben Zvi and Levin, *Concept of Exile in Ancient Israel*," 163; idem,

account by accenting several dominant motifs. (1) First and foremost is the emphasis on the entropy of sin and disobedience. The perpetual inclination to abrogate God's requirements for covenant fidelity requires a just God to enact stipulated punishment. Absolved of potential complaints of caprice, a just and justified God enacts a forewarned destruction of the land, its people, and their identity. Drawing upon traditions deeply embedded in social memory (e.g., Lev 26:14–45; Deut 28:1–68), Ezekiel makes the case succinctly: "They shall realize that it was not without cause [$lō$ 'el-$ḥinnām$; literally, 'not for no reason'] that I the Lord brought this evil upon them" (Ezek 6:10; cf.14:23). (2) The metanarrative, especially its prophetic components, seeks to overcome the historical contingency of human sin with a summons to hope in God's abiding, noncontingent, forgiveness and mercy. As Deutero-Isaiah insists, the present, "new," experience of exile cannot and will not supplant the "old" visions of God's capacity to be God (e.g., Isa 40:1–11; 43:1–7; 45:12–13; 49:19–26; cf. 60:1–22; 66:10–16). (3) In a biblical culture where history always competes with revelation,[14] the metanarrative deftly identifies its reading of history with "the word of God." "Thus says the Lord of hosts, the God of Israel" [to Jeremiah]. ... "I am determined to bring disaster on you, to bring all Judah to an end" (Jer 44:2, 11; cf. Mic 4:6–7); "The word of the Lord came" to Ezekiel saying, "I will gather you from the peoples ... and I will give you the land of Israel" (Ezek 11:14, 17; cf. 33:23–29).[15] As Ehud Ben Zvi has discerned, assessments of history that bear the imprimatur of God's word create imaginably livable, albeit sometimes utopian, worlds that are ultimately invulnerable to destruction. The metanarratives of exile insist that such worlds, unbearably severe as they may have been, do not "allow for a final separation ... between YHWH and Israel."[16]

When the historical narrative resumes in Ezra-Nehemiah and Chronicles, the exile is over. Reverberations continue, of course, but they gradually become softer, more infrequent, less controlling. When placed on a timeline that moves inexorably forward, exile to a large extent becomes a parenthesis in history, a pause, however pivotal it may have been for those

---

"Reconstructing the Intellectual Discourse in Ancient Yehud," *Studies in Religion/Sciences Religieuses* 39 (2010): 7–23, esp. 14–15.

14. See Spiegel, "Memory and History," 152.

15. On these and other commonalities in the constructed metanarrative of exile, see Ben Zvi, "Reconstructing the Intellectual Discourse," 9–11.

16. Ben Zvi, "The Voice and Role of Counterfactual Memory," 173 n.18.

who experienced it, following which the major narrative about God and Israel picks up where it left off. Ezra-Nehemiah reports that knowledge of God was not lost during the Babylonian hiatus. Ezra, a "scribe skilled in the law [*torah*] of God" instructs a community still summoned by and responsive to the "statues and ordinances" that had long formed the basis for its identity as the people of God (Ezra 7:6, 10). Both Ezra and Nehemiah lead the community in prayers of repentance and confession, as Solomon himself had once modeled, confident in the sustaining mercies of the "great and awesome God who is keeping covenant and steadfast love" (Ezra 9:6–15; Neh 9:6–37; cf. 1 Kgs 8:46–47,49).[17] Chronicles not only resumes the pre-exilic narrative, it substantially retells it. Its genealogies, which move from Adam to Saul (1 Chr 1–9), provide prologue for the reigns of David and Solomon, with emphasis on their preparation and building of the temple (1 Chr 10–2 Chr 9; roughly 43 percent of 1–2 Chronicles). The last section focuses on post-Solomonic kings (2 Chr 10–36). The account of the exile (2 Chr 36:17–21), four verses condensed from 2 Kgs 25, concludes with Cyrus's edict of return and a summons to continue worship in the temple: "Whoever is among you of all his people, may the Lord his God be with him! Let him go up" (2 Chr 36:23). Significantly, the summons is not to go up to the second temple, which presumably had been rebuilt, but to return to worship in the first temple, now destroyed but envisioned as a virtual

---

17. These penitential prayers (including Dan 9) are widely regarded as reflecting Deuteronomistic perspectives on piety. See, e.g., Samuel E. Balentine, *Prayer in the Hebrew Bible: The Drama of Divine-Human Dialogue* (OBT; Minneapolis: Fortress, 1993), 103–17. The literature on this prayer genre has grown significantly in the last two decades. See Mark Boda, *Praying the Tradition: The Origin and Use of Tradition in Nehemiah 9* (BZAW 277; Berlin: de Gruyter, 1999); Rodney Werline, *Penitential Prayer in Second Temple Judaism: The Development of a Religious Institution* (SBLEJL 13; Atlanta: Scholars Press, 1998); Judith Newman, *Praying by the Book: The Scripturalization of Prayer in Second Temple Judaism* (SBLEJL 14; Atlanta: Scholars Press, 1998); Richard J. Bautch, *Developments in Genre between Post-exilic Penitential Prayers and Psalms of Communal Lament* (SBLAcBib 7; Atlanta: Society of Biblical Literature, 2003); Mark Boda, Daniel K. Falk, and Rodney Werline, eds., *The Origins of Penitential Prayer in Second Temple Judaism* (vol. 1 of *Seeking the Favor of God*; SBLEJL 21; Atlanta: Society of Biblical Literature, 2006); idem, *The Development of Penitential Prayer in Second Temple Judaism* (vol. 2 of *Seeking the Favor of God*; SBLEJL 22; Atlanta: Society of Biblical Literature, 2007).

reality. Solomon's prayer that the Lord bring Israel back to the land (2 Chr 6:25; 1 Kgs 8:34) has been answered.[18]

Both the dominant narrative and the metanarrative that keeps it alive agree on one fundamental issue. The exile has come and gone. Life goes on with the abiding promise that "Israel may yet be what it *is*."[19] Ben Zvi's observation, though specifically focused on Chronicles, may also serve as an apt summation of the historian's perspective on exile: "At the deepest level, from the perspective of Chronicles the worst calamity in the memory of its readership did not change anything of substance."[20]

3. THE POETRY OF EXILE: MOURNING THAT CANNOT BE TRAPPED IN HISTORY[21]

The poetry that emerges in the wake of exile constitutes what may be called a "lexicon of trauma."[22] The literature includes Deutero-Isaiah, portions of

---

18. Leslie Allen, "The First and Second Books of Chronicles," in *The New Interpreter's Bible* (ed. Leander Keck et al.; Nashville: Abingdon, 1999), 3:657.

19. I appropriate this citation from Simon J. DeVries (*1 and 2 Chronicles* [FOTL 11; Grand Rapids: Eerdmans, 1989], 20, emphasis added), who applies it to Chronicles in a somewhat different way than I have done, although not unrelated.

20. Ben Zvi, "Reconstructing the Intellectual Discourse of Ancient Yehud," 15.

21. See O'Connor, *Lamentations and the Tears of the World*, 6.

22. Trauma theory has long been appropriated in psychoanalysis, and more recently in literary theory and historiography, especially of the Holocaust, e.g., Judith Herman, *Trauma and Recovery: The Aftermath of Violence—From Domestic Abuse to Political Terror* (New York: Basic Books, 1997); Shoshana Felman and Dori Laub, *Testimony: Crises of Witnessing in Literature, Psychoanalysis and History* (New York: Routlege, 1992); Shoshana Felman and Martha Evans, *Writing and Madness: Literature/Philosophy/Psychoanalysis* (Stanford: Stanford University Press, 2003); Cathy Caruth, *Unclaimed Experience: Trauma, Narrative, and Experience* (Baltimore: Johns Hopkins University Press, 1996); Dominick LaCapra, *Writing History, Writing Trauma* (Baltimore: Johns Hopkins University Press, 2001). For its appropriation by biblical scholars, especially as a hermeneutical tool for interpreting exilic and postexilic literature, see, e.g., Paul M. Joyce, "Lamentations and the Grief Process: A Psychological Reading," *BibInt* 1 (1993): 304–20; Tod Linafelt, *Surviving Lamentations: Catastrophe, Lament, and Protest in the Afterlife of a Biblical Book* (Chicago: Chicago University Press, 2000); Hugh Pyper, *An Unsuitable Book: The Bible as Scandalous Text* (BMW 7; Sheffield: Sheffield Phoenix, 2005), 89–100; Kathleen O'Connor, "The Book of Jeremiah: Reconstructing Community after Disaster," in *Character and Ethics in the Old Testament: Moral Dimensions of Scripture* (ed. M. Daniel Carroll R. and Jacqueline E. Lapsley; Louisville: Westminster John Knox, 2007), 81–92; idem, "Lamenting Back

Jeremiah and Ezekiel, the "Jerusalem lament" psalms,[23] Lamentations and, as I will argue, Job.[24] With the collapse of the Jerusalem temple, these texts construct a rhetorical "house for sorrow,"[25] a shelter for mourning irretrievable losses that rupture history's timeline with the invincible question "Why?" For those whose circumstances compel them to ask this question, exile constitutes life in Sheol,[26] a death in the midst of life impermeable to God's presence. A modern analogue may be instructive, even if freighted with implications that no analogue may be able to bear. Life in exile, life in Sheol, is like the durational "empty now" of life in Auschwitz,

> a no man's land of the mind, a black box of explanation; it sucks in all historiographic attempts at interpretation, it is a vacuum taking meaning only from outside history. ... Only *ex negativo*, only through the constant attempt to understand why it cannot be understood, can we measure what sort of occurrence this breach of civilization was. As the most extreme of extreme cases, and thus as the absolute measure of history, this event is hardly historicizable.[27]

---

to Life," *Int* 62 (2008): 34–47; idem; "Building Hope Upon the Ruins," in *The Bible in the American Future* (ed. Robert Jewett, Wayne L. Alloway, and John G. Lacy; Eugene, Oreg.: Cascade, 2009), 146–62; idem, "Reclaiming Jeremiah's Violence," in *The Aesthetics of Violence in the Prophets* (ed. Chris Franke and Julia M. O'Brien; New York: T&T Clark, 2010), 37–49; idem, *Jeremiah: Pain and Promise* (Minneapolis: Fortress, forthcoming); Samuel E. Balentine, "Traumatizing Job," *RevExp* 105 (2008): 213–28.

23. Pss 44, 69, 74, 79, 102, 137. See Adele Berlin, "Psalms and the Literature of Exile: Psalms 137, 44, 69, and 78," in *The Book of Psalms: Composition and Reception* (ed. Peter W. Flint and Patrick D. Miller; VTSup 99; Leiden: Brill, 2005), 65–86; idem, *Lamentations: A Commentary* (OTL; Louisville: Westminster John Knox, 2002), 25; idem, "On Writing a Commentary on Lamentations," in *Lamentations in Ancient and Contemporary Cultural Contexts* (ed. Nancy C. Lee and Carleen Mandolfo; SBLSymS 43; Atlanta: Society of Biblical Literature, 2008), 5.

24. For my preliminary reflections on this literature, with focused attention on Job, see Balentine, "Traumatizing Job," 213–28.

25. Alan Mintz, "The Rhetoric of Lamentations and the Representation of Catastrophe," *Proof* 2 (1989): 2. See further, idem, *Hurban: Responses to Suffering in Hebrew Literature* (2nd ed.; Syracuse: Syracuse University Press, 1996).

26. Berlin, "On Writing a Commentary," 9.

27. Dan Diner, "Historical Understanding and Counterrationality: The *Judenrat* as Epistemological Vantage," in *Probing the Limits of Representation: Nazism and the "Final Solution"* (ed. Saul Friedlander; Cambridge: Harvard University Press, 1992), 128, as cited in Spiegel, "Memory and History," 154.

Inside this "black box of explanation," where words can do little more than approximate what is felt, exile tempts even poetry to silence.[28]

Exile did not in fact silence poetry. Instead it seeded multiple, some-times conflicting, voices that insisted on giving speech to pain and suffer-ing. Two examples must suffice; the first, the voice of the *geber* in Lam 3; the second, the voice of the *geber* in Job 16.

Lamentations 3, like Lam 1, 2, and 4, is structured as an alphabetic acrostic. As with most other acrostic forms in the Hebrew Bible, Lam 3 is rooted thematically in the idea of retributive justice, a poetic reflection on and defense of God's righteous judgment.[29] The speaker is a *geber* (v. 1; cf. vv. 27, 35, 39) who bears witness to the affliction he has seen and experienced "under the rod of God's wrath." The identity of this *geber* is unclear,[30] but the term is typically used of a strong man, a warrior, per-haps a royal figure,[31] who fights gallantly to protect and defend his people. Whether historicized as a particular individual or personified as the voice

---

28. This is a slight emendation of George Steiner's statement that faced with the deep truth of Auschwitz, poetry "is tempted by silence" (George Steiner, *Language and Silence: Essays on Language, Literature, and the Inhuman* [New York: Athenaeum, 1986], 123).

29. Nancy C. Lee, *The Singers of Lamentations: Cities under Siege, from Ur to Jeru-salem to Sarajevo* (BInS 60; Leiden: Brill, 2002), 164–66. Of the four acrostic poems in Lamentations, Lam 3 is the most extensive, with sixty-six lines, three lines for each letter in the Hebrew alphabet. Kathleen O'Connor's discernment of the function of the acrostic form is apt: "The acrostic form is symbolic. It imposes a familiar order on the swirling chaos of the world. It implies that suffering is so enormous, so total, that it spreads from a to z, aleph to taw. There are no letters left for suffering" ("Voices Argu-ing About Meaning," in Lee and Mandolfo, *Lamentations*, 29).

30. For discussion of the interpretive options, see the standard commentaries, e.g., Bertil Albrektson, *Studies in the Text and Theology of the Book of Lamentations with a Critical Edition of the Peshitta Text* (Studia Theologica Lundensia 21; Lund: CWK Gleerup, 1963); Delbert Hillers, *Lamentations* (AB 7a; Garden City, N.Y.: Doubleday, 1972); Robert Gordis, *The Song of Songs and Lamentations* (New York: Ktav, 1974); Iain Provan, *Lamentations* (NCB; Grand Rapids: Eeerdmans, 1991); O'Connor, *Lam-entations and the Tears of the World*; idem, *Lamentations* (NIB 6; Nashville: Abingdon, 2001); Johan Renkema, *Lamentations* (HCOT; Leuven: Peeters, 1998); Frederick W. Dobbs-Allsopp, *Lamentations* (Interpretation; Louisville: Westminster John Knox, 2002); Berlin, *Lamentations*. See further, Magne Saebø, "Who Is 'the Man' in Lam-entations 3? A Fresh Approach to the Interpretation of the Book of Lamentations," in *Understanding Poets and Prophets: Essays in Honour of George Wishart Anderson* (ed. A. Graeme Auld; JSOTSup 152; Sheffield: JSOT Press, 1993), 294–306.

31. Dobbs-Allsopp, *Lamentations*, 108–9.

of exile,[32] the *geber* speaks as a Job-like figure who knows firsthand how brutal an angry God can be. Numerous intertextual connections between the *geber*'s lament and Job's lament in Job 16:7–17 provide the sort of details from a victim's perspective that often slip through the cracks of historical reportage:[33]

Lamentations 3		Job 16:7–17
vv. 5–9	besieging a city	v. 14
vv. 10–11	God as attacking animal[34]	v. 9
vv. 12–13	attacking with bows and arrows	vv. 12–13
v. 13	slashing vital organs	v. 13b
vv. 15, 19	pours out my gall	v. 13c
vv. 16, 29	laid in the dust	v. 15
v. 30	striking the cheek	v. 10b
v. 43	God shows no mercy	v. 13b
v. 46	gaping mouths	v. 10a
vv. 48, 49	eyes weeping	v. 16

Following the *geber*'s opening lament (3:1–19), he moves to an affirmation of hope (vv. 21, 24) in the fundamental goodness and compassion of a God "who does not willfully afflict or hurt human beings" (3:33).

---

32. Berlin, *Lamentations*, 84–85.

33. For the thematic connections below, see Samuel E. Balentine, *Job* (SHBC; Macon, Ga.: Smyth & Helwys, 2006), 256. Whether the Joban author is intentionally interacting with Lam 3 or both texts are drawing upon a common stock of language for the divine violence manifest in exile is an open question. My working assumption is that the Joban author is reflecting the Lamentations text in order to contrast the responses to exile of the *geber* of Lam 3 and the *geber* of Job. See below.

34. In Lam 3, God is not specifically referenced until v.18. God never speaks, although God's response is indirectly quoted in v. 57. However, numerous references to God throughout the remainder of the poem make clear that from the *geber*'s perspective, God is the agent of cause (cf. vv. 22, 24, 25, 31, 35, 37, 40, 41, 50, 55, 59, 61, 64).

Much of this portion of the *geber*'s speech echoes the counsel of Job's friends, who similarly admonish Job to remember that suffering is a sign of God's disciplining love (Job 5:17), that the God who hurts also heals (Job 5:18), and that God does not pervert justice (Job 8:3). Such affirmations, deeply embedded in the orthodoxy of Deuteronomistic, prophetic, and sapiential traditions, disclose nevertheless the existential dilemma of life contorted by the realities of exile. If God does not willingly hurt or afflict, then either God is acting against God's own compassionate nature, or God has been "trapped" into an unwanted but required punitive action by human sinfulness.[35]

The *geber*'s response to this conundrum is to summon his fellow sufferers to introspection, confession of sin, and a plea for forgiveness (3:40–42). Even though enemies have inflicted the grievous suffering of exile "for no reason" (*ḥinnām*; 3:52; cf. Ezek 6:10; 14:23; Job 1:9; 2:3), even though God has pursued the people in anger and killed them without pity (3:43), even though God may refuse to accept their supplications (3:42, 44), the *geber* summons his audience to a resolute trust in God's ultimate grace. Even if such trust seems hopeless, the gap between who God is and who God should be may be bridged with urgent cries for help. One day, if God is God, then God will respond by saying, "Do not fear!" (3:57). Subverting the "why" question that ricochets through the exile threatening all status quo explanations, the *geber* of Lam 3 recommends that all complaints about God's capriciousness be silenced: "Why should any who draw breath complain about the punishment of their sin?" (3:39).[36]

Of the multiple voices in Lamentations mourning the brokenness and loss of exile—Daughter Zion, the poetic narrator, the community—the *geber* offers himself as the model of piety the crisis demands. "My experience is your experience!"[37] he says to a people who are in danger of losing their relationship to God. "Let us lift up our hearts as well as our hands to

---

35. See O'Connor, *Lamentations and the Tears of the World*, 52.

36. Mark Boda has argued that Lam 3, along with Jer 14–15, constitutes an early link in the development of postexilic penitential prayers (see n. 17), which question the appropriateness of protest or complaint in the wake of exile. See Mark Boda, "The Priceless Gain of Penitence: From Communal Lament to Penitential Prayer in the 'Exilic' Liturgy of Exile," in Lee and Mandolfo, *Lamentations*, 90–98.

37. Frederick W. Dobbs-Allsopp, "Tragedy, Tradition, and Theology in the Book of Lamentations," *JSOT* 74 (1997): 41.

God in heaven" (3:41). When faced with the realities of the exile, "follow the *geber*!"[38]

The connections between Lam 3 and Job 16 invite a question at just this point. *Which geber* should the community follow in the wake of exile? Should they emulate the *submissive piety* of the *geber* who speaks in Lam 3 or the *defiant piety* of the *geber* who speaks in Job 16?[39] Job, too, lingers over the physical brutality he has experienced at the hands of God. Drawing heavily upon the same lament traditions that inform Lam 3, he knows the pain that pushes conventional language beyond normal boundaries; at best, words can only approximate the intensity of hurt, the urgency of help. God strikes at his cheeks (v. 10), seizes his neck (v. 12), ruptures his kidneys (v. 13), and breaks open his skeleton (v. 14). Job is well acquainted with the conventional interpretation that such suffering summons him to confess his sins, acknowledge God's justice, and thereby to be healed and restored by God's sovereign grace. His friends repeatedly urge him to embrace this "if-then" model of piety (Job 8:5–7; 11:13–20; 22:21–27; 33:23–28). Job, however, insists that he cannot repent of sins he has not committed. There is no violence (*ḥāmās*) in his hands (16:17). Pray for restoration he will, but his prayers will be "pure," attuned more to the counsel of Shakespeare's Duke of Albany, eyewitness to Lear's tragic demise, than to "theologians" who whitewash the truth with lies (cf. Job 13:4): "The

---

38. Renkema, *Lamentations*, 476. As recent commentators have noted, it is important not to read the *geber*'s summons to penitence in isolation from the rest of Lam 3 or from the rest of the book in which it is embedded. Lamentations 3 constitutes the single voice of hope in the book, but it is framed and perhaps rhetorically overwhelmed by other voices that seem unable to embrace the *geber*'s model. See especially, Linafelt (*Surviving Lamentations*, 35–61), who demonstrates that the inconsolable Zion figure who speaks in Lam 1–2 offers an important alternative to the submissive *geber* of chapter 3. One may argue that neither the *geber* nor his audience can finally muster the confidence to believe the "orthodox view of suffering" as requisite divine punishment for sin (Provan, *Lamentations*, 23). In this sense, the poetry of mourning in Lamentations both embraces the closure of exile as linearly calibrated in historical narratives and metanarratives—covenantal disobedience → divine punishment → repentance → forgiveness → restoration → return—and challenges its efficacy.

39. Although Job does not refer to himself as a *geber* in Job 16, he introduces himself this way in Job 3:3. Further, in the divine speeches, God twice challenges Job to gird up his loins like the *geber* he claims to be and as such to respond to God's challenge (Job 38:3; 40:7). It is not insignificant that in Job 16:14, Job refers to God as a *gibbōr*, a "warrior" who comes after him relentlessly, thus setting the stage for a *geber* versus *geber* confrontation.

weight of this sad moment we must obey / Speak what we feel, not what we ought to say" (*King Lear* 5.3).

The *geber* of Lam 3 laments *toward repentance*. Once suffering is understood as God's just punishment, then appeals to God's merciful forgiveness constitute requisite piety. Job laments *toward justice*; conventional models of repentance do not work for him, because he is innocent. Innocent suffering, suffering God inflicts on the blameless and upright "for no reason" (Job 2:3), explodes the summons to contrition by making a moral claim on God's justice and righteousness. All efforts to close the gap between God's covenantal commitments to the faithful and God's willingness to hurt innocent human beings (Lam 3:33) are stymied until and unless God changes God's way of being God.

Toward this end, Job extends conventional forms of lament by insisting on a radically litigious faith partnership with God. Invoking the image of the murdered Abel, whose blood cries out from the earth for justice (Job 16:18; cf. Gen 4:8–10), Job pleads for a world, designed and now violated by God's own actions, to rise up in defense of the moral order on which it depends. Like Abraham, Job determines to stand face to face, *geber* à *geber* (cf. Job 16:14), with the Creator of the cosmos, and to demand that God do what is just (Gen 18:25), that God act like God.

For such an encounter, Job also summons a "witness" (v. 19, *ʿēd*) in heaven to recognize the legitimacy of his cry for justice and to argue his case "with God" (v. 21). The identity of this witness is not disclosed, but a close reading of the text suggests that Job envisions a third party who will serve as an intermediary between himself and God, someone who will side with him in God's court and bear witness to the truth of his claim. However this witness may be interpreted,[40] it is clear there is a vast chasm between what Job hopes for and what his friends believe he will receive. While Job "pours out tears to God," his friends scorn him (v. 20). When he hopes for an advocate to defend him, they warn him that no "holy ones" will come to his rescue (5:1). When he insists that he is innocent and that God's assaults on him are unjust, his friends argue that his only legitimate defense is to "agree" with God and plead guilty (22:21). Modeling the friends' counsel, the *geber* in Lam 3 repents and moves, however haltingly, to an affirmation

---

40. The "witness" in Job 16:19 must be considered alongside Job's appeal for an "arbiter" (*môkîaḥ*) in 9:33, his hope for a "redeemer" (*gōʾēl*) in 19:25, and Elihu's invitation to hope for an angelic "mediator" (*mēlîṣ*) in 33:23. For discussion of the interpretive options, see Balentine, *Job*, 257–60.

of God's justice: 'You have taken up my cause, O Lord, you have redeemed my life. You have seen the wrong done to me" (Lam 3:55–56). Refusing the friends' counsel, Job laments, not to prove himself sufficiently penitent to remain in God's company, but rather to insist that God must remain in the company of the righteous as the moral agent of justice. At this juncture in the Joban dialogues, such defiance seems futile. Job's spirit is broken (17:1). "Even now" (16:19), as he hopes for the "witness" who does not appear, Job walks down a path of no return, destined to finish his days in the land of Sheol, hopeless and abandoned (16:22; cf.17:13–16).

4. "The Days Are Long, and Every Vision Has Perished" (Ezek 12:22): Concluding Reflections

On the other side of the prose narratives and metanarratives, exile is a historical memory. On the chronological timeline, exile has a beginning point, the destruction of Jerusalem, and an ending point, the return to Yehud. The reportage of the events that have occurred, each one sequentially followed by the next, provides a norming and coherent cause-and-consequence explanation. Covenantal disobedience triggers covenantal punishment; it was "not for no reason" (Ezek 6:10; 14:23) that God brought this calamity on Judah. Confession and repentance trigger God's sustaining mercies; the abiding word of God constructs history as the venue for divine revelation. Inside and alongside this narrative, poetic voices struggle to articulate a traumatized present, a gap within history, between past and future, that refuses the closure of coherency. In response to thundering "why" questions, the dominant narratives continue to summon acceptance, in the geber's embrace of penitence in Lam 3 as the bridge that leads from God's wrath to God's mercy, and in the friends' counsel that Job follow the same route. Other voices envision a different response, embodied in Job's refusal to "join words together" like others do (Job 16:4), his restless, raw, demand that history's timeline not erase his quest for justice.

Both the geber's hope in Lam 3 and the geber's hoplessness in Job 16 are structurally framed by other voices that provide context or rhetorical boundaries, depending on how they are read. Daughter Zion's inconsolable weeping, punctuated repeatedly by the refrain that there is no one to comfort her (Lam 1:2, 7, 9, 16, 17, 21), concludes with a fervent imperative that God look at her suffering, that God understand what God has done to her. Neither here nor in the rest of the book does God respond to her cries (Lam 2:20). Lamentations ends with a communal lament that presses the question that will not go away, despite the *geber*'s insistence that it be set aside (3:39): "Why have you [Lord] forgotten us completely? Why have you forgotten us these many days?" (5:21). As Tod Linafelt has noted, "The book is left opening out into the emptiness of God's nonresponse," a "structural unfinishedness" that awaits completion before the next chapter of history can be written.[41]

The Joban dialogues, in Job 16 as throughout, are introduced by a matter-of-fact prose report that God is complicit in the deaths of Job's seven sons and three daughters "for no reason" (Job 2:3), which stands the conventional "not for no reason" assessment of such calamities on its head.[42] On the other side of the dialogues, the prose account resumes with an all's-well-that-ends-well summation of Job's story (Job 42:7–17). The ending of the book of Job, like the ending of Lamentations, has a "structural unfinishedness," an ending that leaves its readers wondering whether the words "for no reason," which are attributed to God, convey a *traumatized concession* to reality, a change forced upon the narrative by a truth that history can no longer conceal or explain, or whether these words convey a *traumatizing assertion*, a psychic shot across the bow of all would-be dissenters that is designed to shock them into (in)voluntary compliance.[43]

In his essay on the distinctions between biblical prose and poetry, Patrick D. Miller raises this question: "What does poetry mean *theologically*? ... What does poetry do or not do as part of the Bible's claim to speak about God?"[44] After surveying the various ways poetic speech transcends the limits of "explanatory, bound prose speech," Miller ends his essay by quoting the words of the British cosmologist John Barrows: "No

---

41. Linafelt, *Surviving Lamentations*, 60–61.

42. See further, Samuel E. Balentine, "For No Reason," *Int* 57 (2003): 349–69; idem, *Job*, 58–60.

43. See further, Balentine, "Traumatizing Job." The ending of the book, especially the conventional rendering of Job 42:6 as Job's ultimate capitulation to orthodoxy's summons to repentance, merits serious reconsideration. For my interpretation, see Samuel E. Balentine, "'What Are Human Beings That You Make So Much of Them?' Divine Disclosure From the Whirlwind: 'Look at Behemoth,'" in *God in The Fray: A Tribute to Walter Brueggemann* (ed. Tod Linafelt and Timothy K. Beal; Minneapolis: Fortress, 1998), 259–78; idem, *Job*, 696–99.

44. Patrick D. Miller, "The Theological Significance of Poetry," in *Language, Theology, and the Bible: Essays in Honour of James Barr* (ed. Samuel E. Balentine and John Barton; Oxford: Clarendon, 1994), 214.

non-poetic view of reality can be complete."[45] "When Judah went into exile out of its land" and "every vision comes to nothing," as Ezekiel puts it (Ezek 12:22), the burden of living faithfully in the interim fell not only to the historians but also to the poets. A final caveat concerning what biblical poetry contributes to this shared endeavor to navigate the exile is in order, this from a modern poet's perspective on the challenge and what it demands:

> [P]lain speech is the mother tongue ...
> [but] one clear stanza can take more weight
> Than a whole wagon load of elaborate prose.[46]

BIBLIOGRAPHY

Ahn, John J. *Exile as Forced Migration: A Sociological, Literary, and Theological Approach on the Displacement and Resettlement of the Southern Kingdom of Judah.* BZAW 417. Berlin: de Gruyter, 2010.

———. "Forced Migration Studies as a New Approach to the Study of the Exilic Period." In *By the Irrigation Canals of Babylon: Approaches to the Study of Exile.* Edited by John Ahn and Jill Middlemas. LHBOTS 526. London: T&T Clark International, forthcoming.

Albrektson, Bertil. *Studies in the Text and Theology of the Book of Lamentations with a Critical Edition of the Peshitta Text.* Studia Theologica Lundensia 21. Lund: CWK Gleerup, 1963.

Allen, Leslie. "The First and Second Books of Chronicles." Pages 3:297–660 in *The New Interpreter's Bible.* Edited by Leander Keck et al. 12 vols. Nashville: Abingdon, 1999.

Balentine, Samuel E. "For No Reason." *Int* 57 (2003): 349–69.

———. *Job.* SHBC. Macon, Ga.: Smyth & Helwys, 2006.

———. *Prayer in the Hebrew Bible: The Drama of Divine-Human Dialogue.* OBT. Minneapolis: Fortress, 1993.

———. "Traumatizing Job." *RevExp* 105 (2008): 213–28.

———. "'What Are Human Beings That You Make So Much of Them?' Divine Disclosure from the Whirlwind: 'Look at Behemoth.'" Pages 259–78 in *God in the Fray: A Tribute to Walter Brueggemann.* Edited by Tod Linafelt and Timothy K. Beal. Minneapolis: Fortress, 1998.

---

45. Ibid., 230, quoting John D. Barrows, *Theories of Everything: The Quest for Human Explanation* (London: Oxford University Press, 1991).

46. Czeslaw Milosz, "A Treatise on Poetry [Preface]," in *New and Collected Poems (1931–2001)* (New York: Harper Collins, 2001), 109.

Barrows, John D. *Theories of Everything: The Quest for Human Explanation*. London: Oxford University Press, 1991.

Barry, Sebastian. *The Secret Scripture*. London: Faber & Faber, 2006. Repr., New York: Penguin, 2008.

Bautch, Richard J. *Developments in Genre between Post-exilic Penitential Prayers and Psalms of Communal Lament*. SBLAcBib 7. Atlanta: Society of Biblical Literature, 2003.

Benjamin, Walter. "Theses on the Philosophy of History." Cited 24 January 2011. Online: http://www.sfu.ca/~andrewf/CONCEPT2.html.

Ben Zvi, Ehud. "Reconstructing the Intellectual Discourse in Ancient Yehud." *Studies in Religion/Sciences Religieuses* 39 (2010): 7–23.

———. "Total Exile, Empty Land and the General Intellectual Discourse in Yehud." Pages 155–68 in *The Concept of Exile in Ancient Israel*. Edited by Ehud Ben Zvi and Christoph Levin. BZAW 404. Berlin: de Gruyter, 2010.

———. "The Voice and Role of Counterfactual Memory in the Construction of Exile and Return: Considering Jeremiah 40:7–12." Pages 168–88 in *The Concept of Exile in Ancient Israel*. Edited by Ehud Ben Zvi and Christoph Levin. BZAW 404. Berlin: de Gruyter, 2010.

Berlin, Adele. *Lamentations: A Commentary*. OTL. Louisville: Westminster John Knox, 2002.

———. "On Writing a Commentary on Lamentations." Pages 3–11 in *Lamentations in Ancient and Contemporary Cultural Contexts*. Edited by Nancy C. Lee and Carleen Mandolfo. SBL SymS 43. Atlanta: Society of Biblical Literature, 2008.

———. "Psalms and the Literature of Exile: Psalms 137, 44, 69, and 78." Pages 65–86 in *The Book of Psalms: Composition and Reception*. Edited by Peter W. Flint and Patrick D. Miller. Leiden: Brill, 2005.

Boda, Mark. *Praying the Tradition: The Origin and Use of Tradition in Nehemiah 9*. BZAW 277. Berlin: de Gruyter, 1999.

———. "The Priceless Gain of Penitence: From Communal Lament to Penitential Prayer in the 'Exilic' Liturgy of Exile." Pages 90–98 in *Lamentations in Ancient and Contemporary Cultural Contexts*. Edited by Nancy C. Lee and Carleen Mandolfo. SBLSymS 43. Atlanta: Society of Biblical Literature, 2008.

Boda, Mark, Daniel K. Falk, and Rodney Werline, eds. *The Development of Penitential Prayer in Second Temple Judaism*. Vol. 2 of *Seeking the Favor of God*. SBLEJL 21. Atlanta: Society of Biblical Literature, 2007.

———. *The Origins of Penitential Prayer in Second Temple Judaism*. Vol. 1 of *Seeking the Favor of God*. SBLEJL 21. Atlanta: Society of Biblical Literature, 2006.

Caruth, Cathy. *Unclaimed Experience: Trauma, Narrative, and Experience*. Baltimore: Johns Hopkins University Press, 1996.

Cohen, Jeremy. "The Hebrew Crusade Chronicles in the Twelfth-Century Cultural Context." Paper presented at the meeting of the American Historical Association. San Francisco, 1994.

DeVries, Simon J. *1 and 2 Chronicles*. FOTL 11. Grand Rapids: Eerdmans, 1989.

Diner, Dan. "Historical Understanding and Counterrationality: The *Judenrat* as Epistemological Vantage." Pages 128–42 in *Probing the Limits of Representation:*

Nazism and the 'Final Solution.' Edited by Saul Friedlander. Cambridge: Harvard University Press, 1992.

Dobbs–Allsopp, Frederick W. *Lamentations.* Louisville: Westminster John Knox, 2002.

———. "Tragedy, Tradition, and Theology in the Book of Lamentations." JSOT 74 (1997): 29–60.

Ezrahi, Sidra D. "Considering the Apocalypse: Is the Writing on the Wall only Graffiti?" Pages 137–53 in *Writing and the Holocaust.* Edited by Berel Lang. Ithaca, N.Y.: Holmes & Meier, 1988.

Felman, Shoshana, and Martha Noel Evans. *Writing and Madness: Literature/Philosophy/Psychoanalysis.* Stanford: Stanford University Press, 2003.

Felman, Shoshana, and Dori Laub. *Testimony: Crises of Witnessing in Literature, Psychoanalysis and History.* New York: Routlege, 1992.

Gordis, Robert. *The Song of Songs and Lamentations.* New York: Ktav, 1974.

Herman, Judith. *Trauma and Recovery: The Aftermath of Violence—From Domestic Abuse to Political Terror.* New York: Basic Books, 1997.

Hillers, Delbert. *Lamentations.* AB 7a. Garden City, N.Y.: Doubleday, 1972.

Joyce, Paul M. "Lamentations and the Grief Process: A Psychological Reading." *BibInt* 1 (1993): 304–20.

Kessler, John. "Images of Exile: Representations of the 'Exile' and 'Empty Land' in Sixth to Fourth Century Yehudite Literature." Pages 309–51 in *The Concept of the Exile in Ancient Israel and Its Historical Contexts.* Edited by Ehud Ben Zvi and Christoph Levin. BZAW 404. Berlin: de Gruyter, 2010.

LaCapra, Dominick. *Writing History, Writing Trauma.* Baltimore: Johns Hopkins University Press, 2001.

Langer, Lawrence. *Admitting the Holocaust: Collected Essays.* Oxford: Oxford University Press, 1995.

Lee, Nancy C. *The Singers of Lamentations: Cities Under Siege, from Ur to Jerusalem to Sarajevo.* BInS 60. Leiden: Brill, 2002.

Linafelt, Tod. *Surviving Lamentations: Catastrophe, Lament, and Protest in the Afterlife of a Biblical Book.* Chicago: Chicago University Press, 2000.

Middlemas, Jill. *The Templeless Age: An Introduction to the History, Literature, and Theology of the "Exile."* Louisville: Westminster John Knox, 2007.

Miller, Patrick D. "The Theological Significance of Poetry." Pages 213–30 in *Language, Theology, and the Bible: Essays in Honour of James Barr.* Edited by Samuel E. Balentine and John Barton. Oxford: Clarendon Press, 1994.

Milosz, Czeslaw. "A Treatise on Poetry [Preface]." Pages 107–51 in *New and Collected Poems (1931–2001).* New York: Harper Collins, 2001.

Mintz, Alan. *Hurban: Responses to Suffering in Hebrew Literature.* 2nd ed. Syracuse: Syracuse University Press, 1996.

Mintz, Alan. "The Rhetoric of Lamentations and the Representations of Catastrophe." *Proof* 2 (1982): 1–17.

Newman, Judith. *Praying by the Book: The Scripturalization of Prayer in Second Temple Judaism.* SBLEJL 14. Atlanta: Scholars Press, 1999.

O'Connor, Kathleen. "The Book of Jeremiah: Reconstructing Community after Disaster." Pages 81–92 in *Character and Ethics in the Old Testament: Moral Dimensions of Scripture*. Edited by M. Daniel Carroll R. and Jacqueline E. Lapsley. Louisville: Westminster John Knox, 2007.

――――. "Building Hope Upon the Ruins." Pages 146–62 in *The Bible in the American Future*. Edited by Robert Jewett, Wayne L. Alloway, and John G. Lacy. Eugene, Oreg.: Cascade, 2009.

――――. *Jeremiah: Pain and Promise*. Minneapolis: Fortress, forthcoming.

――――. "Lamenting Back to Life." *Int* 62 (2008): 34–47.

――――. "Lamentations." Pages 6:1011–72 in *The New Interpreter's Bible*. Edited by Leander Keck et al. 12 vols. Nashville: Abingdon, 2001.

――――. *Lamentations and the Tears of the World*. Maryknoll, N.Y.: Orbis, 2002.

――――. "Reclaiming Jeremiah's Violence." Pages 37–49 in *The Aesthetics of Violence in the Prophets*. Edited by Chris Franke and Julia M. O'Brien. New York: T&T Clark, 2010.

Provan, Iain. *Lamentations*. NCB. Grand Rapids, Mich.: Eeerdmans, 1991.

Pyper, Hugh. *An Unsuitable Book: The Bible as Scandalous Text*. BMW 7. Sheffield: Sheffield Phoenix, 2005.

Renkema, Johan. *Lamentations*. HCOT. Leuven: Peeters, 1998.

Rosenfeld, Gavriel. "Why Do We Ask 'What If?' Reflections on the Function of Alternate History." *History and Theory* 41 (2002): 90–103.

Saebø, Magne. "Who Is 'the Man' in Lamentations 3? A Fresh Approach to the Interpretation of the Book of Lamentations." Pages 294–306 in *Understanding Poets and Prophets: Essays in Honour of George Wishart Anderson*. Edited by A. Graeme Auld. JSOTSup 152. Sheffield: JSOT Press, 1993.

Spiegel, Gabrielle M. "Memory and History: Liturgical Time and Historical Time." *History and Theory* 41 (2002): 149–62.

Steiner, George. *Language and Silence: Essays on Language, Literature, and the Inhuman*. New York: Athenaeum, 1986.

Vidal-Naquet, Pierre. *The Jews: History, Memory and the Present*. Edited and translated by David A. Curtis. New York: Columbia University Press, 1996.

Warren, Robert Penn. *Brother to Dragons: A Tale in Verses and Voices*. New York: Random House, 1953.

Werline, Rodney. *Penitential Prayer in Second Temple Judaism: The Development of a Religious Institution*. SBLEJL 13. Atlanta: Scholars Press, 1998.

Sites of Conflict: Textual Engagements of Dislocation and Diaspora in the Hebrew Bible

Carolyn J. Sharp

1. Introduction

Texts produced in cultural contexts of colonization do not simply "represent" exile and oppression. To varying degrees, they can collude in the colonizer's ongoing exercise of power on the subaltern imagination. In this essay, I consider ways in which some postexilic Hebrew Bible texts mimic or refuse dynamics of domination in their own textual performances of authority and vulnerability.

"By the rivers of Babylon—there we sat and there we wept when we remembered Zion. … For there our captors asked us for songs, and our tormentors asked for mirth, saying, 'Sing us one of the songs of Zion!'" (Ps 137:1, 3). What kind of sacred language can withstand the dehumanizing threat under which the colonized subject lives? How can the subaltern speak at all, much less sing? Calculating from 597 B.C.E., Babylon's subjugation of Judah lasted less than sixty years, but its impact on the Judean cultural imagination was staggering. The Babylonian exile was no single event, but rather an escalating series of experiences of political disenfranchisement. Judah was compelled to witness the deaths or deportations of several kings in rapid succession, multiple deportations of clerical and political leaders and some of the general populace, destruction of the capital city Jerusalem and its temple, installation of a hated puppet governor, and continued plundering of Judean economic and cultural resources.[1]

---

1. See Jon L. Berquist, "Postcolonialism and Imperial Motives for Canonization," in *The Postcolonial Biblical Reader* (ed. R. S. Sugirtharajah; Oxford: Blackwell, 2006), 78–95. Berquist writes, "The empire exists only insofar as it *continues* to extract resources. Empires construct multiple modes of extraction. Conquest is a straight-

The Babylonians' military and political subjugation of Judah was a protracted and complex experience, and it generated multifarious literary
responses over the decades that followed the fall of Jerusalem.

Leaders who are forced to inhabit a subaltern position must offer
some kind of response if their community is to avoid cultural annihilation. Yet in order to speak at all, the colonized subject must tolerate a kind
of "double-mindedness," as Jon Berquist notes. Every subaltern has to
negotiate a "complex multiplication of loyalties, interests, and alliances,"
and the demands of this negotiation may yield a painful hybridity for the
individual and for the whole community.[2] Hybridity may be exploited for
its creative potential, but it can also fracture the psyche of the subaltern.
Some responses resist the conqueror, but others, tragically, project their
anxiety and rage onto a safer target: fellow citizens in the subaltern state. It
is politically and psychologically less risky to demonize the familiar than
to cede control to the terrifying Other—in the case of sixth-century Judah,
the monstrous Babylonians.[3] Fracture and internecine conflict are normal
responses (although of course not the only responses) to experiences of
trauma and powerlessness in the unsafe space of subalternity. Texts produced under colonialism may be "discourses of resistance," but these textual acts of resistance can themselves be toxic, producing new subalterns
and new kinds of deformation as pathological by-products of the experience of subjugation.[4]

---

forward example of resource extraction. ... Methods such as taxation are slower and
more subtle than conquest, but no less imperialistic. ... The empire may use its army
along with other more bureaucratic measures to intensify local production in order to
increase extraction" (79–80, emphasis original).

2. Jon L. Berquist, "Psalms, Postcolonialism, and the Construction of the Self,"
in *Approaching Yehud: New Approaches to the Study of the Persian Period* (ed. Jon L.
Berquist; Atlanta: Society of Biblical Literature, 2008), 196–97.

3. The distinction between the "monstrous" invader and its victims does blur, as
cultural theorist Amy Kalmanofsky notes. The predations of monster Babylon render
the people of Judah themselves "monstrous" in their woundedness; see her "The Monstrous-Feminine in the Book of Jeremiah," *Lectio Difficilior* 1 (2009), online: http://
www.lectio.unibe.ch/09_1/kalmanofsky_the_monstrous_feminine.html; and more
generally her *Terror All Around: Horror, Monsters, and Theology in the Book of Jeremiah* (LHBOTS 390; New York & London: T&T Clark, 2008). An ideological critic
might also suggest that the predations of Babylon create the "monstrous" accommodationist politics of the Deutero-Jeremianic prose and the hyper-sexualized theological
fetishism of Ezekiel.

4. R. S. Sugirtharajah, "Charting the Aftermath: A Review of Postcolonial

In what follows, I will explore three ancient Judean responses to dislocation and subalternity. Some might argue that there is an ironic dimension to my use of "subaltern" to describe the producers of sacred texts in ancient Judah, for scribes were vested and powerful members of their communities: vested by virtue of their literacy in the largely illiterate milieu of the ancient Near East and powerful by means of their connections to the royal court, in many cases. But under Babylonian hegemony, Judean elites were indeed forced into a position of subalternity, just as displaced persons today may have enjoyed significant stature in their contexts of origin but are compelled to inhabit subaltern statuses due to forced migration or political repression.[5] My ideological-critical analysis of two dictions in Jeremiah and Ezekiel will illustrate ways in which subaltern communities use "splitting" to reconfigure the enemy in familiar terms, at a potentially devastating cost to the subalterns' own subjectivity. I argue that a third response, Lamentations, operates in a dialogical mode that allows for expressions of anger, powerlessness, and hope without pathologizing the author's own community.

Criticism," in Sugirtharajah, *Postcolonial Biblical Reader*, 7–32, notes the complexities involved in defining collusion with or victimization by imperial ideologies and practices. He writes, "Those engaged in postcolonial discourse are ... constantly confronted with two questions. One, whether one should rake up the past and blame earlier generations and make their present successors feel guilty for the misdeeds of their forebears. The other side of all this is to make all victims innocent and virtuous. The issue is not that one is at fault, and the other is blameless. The issue is how one makes use of the past and who benefits from it" (25).

5. The hybridity and fluidity of elite/subaltern status(es) have made the definition of "subaltern" a matter of ongoing debate in postcolonial studies. One may be a king in the terms set by one's indigenous culture, yet under the colonizer's regime even "kings" must rely on scraps from the ruler's table (as Jehoiachin in Jer 52:31–34). Jim Masselos addresses this issue in his "The Dis/appearance of Subalterns: A Reading of a Decade of Subaltern Studies," *South Asia* 15 (1992): 105–25; reprinted in *Reading Subaltern Studies: Critical History, Contested Meaning, and the Globalisation of South Asia* (ed. David Ludden; Delhi: Permanent Black, 2001), 187–211. Masselos notes in his review of the work of Ramachandra Guha, "Élites were dispersed and heterogeneous; significantly, their members might at regional and local levels either be part of the élite or, according to circumstance and situation, be classified as subaltern" (189).

2. Ideological Criticism of Subaltern Hebrew Bible Texts

The book of Jeremiah was forged in the crucible of the Babylonian invasion and occupation of Judah. Its texts "describe" the horrific events of that traumatic time, but this is no unbiased historical reportage. Jeremiah as a book is riven by two competing political ideologies—ideologies that are transparently evident on even a surface reading of the text. The dominant ideology shaping the prose of the book insists that the diaspora group in Babylon constitutes the "true" Judah, a remnant that alone will be the seed for God's future work of replanting; those Judeans back in Judah and who fled to Egypt from Babylon's predations are, in the perspective of this ideology, despicable sinners whom God will exterminate. At the heart of this ideology lies an accommodationist politics that advocates military submission to Babylon and prayer for the welfare of the overlord (Jer 29:7). Submerged but still visible within Jeremiah is another ideology, one that valorizes staunch resistance to Babylon (for example in Jer 35, the story of the Rechabites) and foresees inevitable destruction for Babylon and the whole earth; this perspective does not privilege any one group within the subaltern Judean community.[6]

The figure of Jeremiah himself may be read as a contested icon in the cultural and political struggles of exilic and early postexilic Judah. There are multiple layers of text inscribed in Jeremiah, attesting to the liveliness of this tradition in its compositional, redactional, and text-critical dimensions. The attentive reader of Jeremiah will notice the alternation of first- and third-person voice in narratives about the prophet; stark differences in focus, rhetoric, and tone from the short poetic oracles to the verbose prose sections that dominate the latter two-thirds of the book; conflicting ways of articulating the scope and purpose of God's punishment of Judah; and a self-consciousness within the book (see Jer 36) about erasure, rewriting, and supplementation, perhaps related to the variant texts of Jeremiah that are preserved in the Old Greek and Masoretic traditions.

Thus Jeremiah is complicated, politically and culturally. Textual contestations and internecine conflict seethe throughout the book. My attention here will be on the dominant voice within the Jeremiah prose: that of

---

6. See Carolyn J. Sharp, *Prophecy and Ideology in Jeremiah: Struggles for Authority in the Deutero-Jeremianic Prose* (OTS; London: T&T Clark, 2003) and Karl-Friedrich Pohlmann, *Studien zum Jeremiabuch: Ein Beitrag zur Frage nach der Entstehung des Jeremiabuches* (FRLANT 118; Göttingen: Vandenhoeck & Ruprecht, 1978).

expatriate Judeans in Babylon. The diaspora traditionists represent power and agency in a way that cements their own authority and disenfranchises their fellow Judeans in Judah and Egypt. Explaining a vision of good and rotting figs, the God of the Judean diaspora thunders,

> Like these good figs, so I will regard as good the exiles from Judah whom I have sent away from this place to the land of the Chaldeans. I will set my eyes upon them for good, and I will bring them back to this land. I will build them up, and not tear them down; I will plant them, and not pluck them up. ... But ... like the bad figs that are so bad they cannot be eaten, so will I treat King Zedekiah of Judah, his officials, the remnant of Jerusalem who remain in this land, and those who live in the land of Egypt. I will make them a horror, an evil thing ... a disgrace, a by-word, a taunt, and a curse in all the places where I shall drive them. And I will send sword, famine, and pestilence upon them, until they are utterly destroyed from the land that I gave to them and their ancestors. (Jer 24:4–10)

Or consider the disenfranchisement performed by this rhetoric:

> I swear by my great name, says the LORD, that my name shall no longer be pronounced on the lips of any of the people of Judah in all the land of Egypt. ... All the people of Judah who are in the land of Egypt shall perish by sword and by famine, until not one is left. (Jer 44:26–27)

The political body constructed in Jeremiah is a fractured and divided body. Jeremiah is indelibly marked by struggles for power and venomous hatred for compatriots who have become the Other in place of the actual enemy, Babylon. Thus Jeremiah—the tradition— becomes a textual site of conflict that continually enacts its own exiling of part of its community. The subaltern community mimics that which is destroying it.

Jeremiah's contemporary, the priest Ezekiel, creates a subaltern discourse with a different "body" in mind: the covenantal body. Ezekiel's theology requires an utterly transcendent God in an otherworldly chariot. This God, distant and terrifying and unreachable, is impervious to defilement from unworthy worshippers. As for the people of Judah who are God's partners in covenant, Ezekiel attacks them with florid oracles of judgment cast in harshly sexualized terms. This prophet is revolted by what he sees as the shameful loathsomeness of his people. Ezekiel operates within a priestly conceptual world in which ritual and moral purity are among the highest of theological values. Ezekiel's God roars, "Be holy, as I am holy!" (Lev 19:2); but alas, Judah has remained flagrantly idolatrous. Ezekiel's view of Judah's subjugation is entirely monocular: Judah has defiled herself and her land with "abominations" cultic and moral, so diaspora and death are fitting consequences.

The dominant metaphor in Ezekiel's figuration of subaltern Judah is that of a nymphomaniacal adulterous wife who acts like a prostitute.[7] Being addressed through such a rhetorical figure would have emasculated and shamed Ezekiel's audience, the male leaders responsible for guarding the cultural boundaries of the "social body" of Judah.[8] Traumatized[9] and unable to resist Babylon directly, Ezekiel constructs Judah's covenantal body as a fetishistic object of rape, battery, and murder. Consider these texts:

> At the head of every street you [Jerusalem] built your lofty place and prostituted your beauty, offering yourself to every passer-by and multiplying your whoring. ... Because your lust was poured out and your nakedness uncovered in your whoring with your lovers, and because of your abominable idols ... I will gather all your lovers ... [and] deliver you into their hands. ... They shall strip you of your clothes and take your beautiful objects and leave you naked and bare. They shall bring up a mob against you, and they shall stone you and cut you to pieces with their swords. (Ezek 16:25, 36, 39–40)

> I will deliver you into the hands of those whom you hate, into the hands of those from whom you turned in disgust; and they shall deal with you in hatred, and take away all the fruit of your labor, and leave you naked and bare. ... They shall repay you for your lewdness, and you shall bear

---

7. Nymphomania, adultery, and prostitution are distinct sex-related behaviors and should not be blurred together in analysis. Ezekiel manages to draw on dimensions of all three in his characterizations of Judah and Jerusalem: the prophet charges that his people have been obsessive and indiscriminating about their choice of "lovers," they have betrayed the covenantal relationship, and they have acted as if they were soliciting wages for their infidelity.

8. See Kenneth A. Stone, *Sex, Honor and Power in the Deuteronomistic History* (Sheffield: Sheffield Academic Press, 1996), 27–49; Alice A. Keefe, *Woman's Body and the Social Body in Hosea* (JSOTSup 338/GCT 10; London: Sheffield Academic Press, 2001).

9. The prophet's initial self-report is that he was overwhelmed and bitter to the point of catatonia (Ezek 3:14–15).

the penalty for your sinful idolatry, and you shall know that I am the Lord GOD. (Ezek 23:28–29, 48–49)

Ezekiel, too, is a textual site of conflict. The prophet is so revolted by belonging to a defiled communal body that his text continually (re)performs its own people's public shaming and dismemberment.

Thus we see bitter internecine conflict in Jeremiah: one group within the anxious subaltern community turns ferociously on its own people, cannibalizing the possibility for united resistance over against the colonial power. And we see hyperbolic fetishizing of the Judean "body" in Ezekiel: the subaltern community is coerced into voyeuristically staring at its own shame rather than repudiating the cruelty of the enemy. Both of these rhetorics constitute aggressively overcompensatory attempts to counter the vulnerability of the subaltern state. The dictions of Jeremiah and Ezekiel betray more of the horrendous cost of colonization than their ancient authors could ever have dreamed.

Might there be a kind of biblical subaltern speech that is able to move beyond overcompensatory violence against the traumatized diaspora community?

3. DIALOGUE AS RESISTANCE

Yes. Lamentations is a multivocal text, as is Jeremiah, and it is concerned with the devastation and shame of Zion, as is Ezekiel. But this poetic book enacts its discourse in a radically different way than those prophetic books do. Lamentations is, first and most obviously, lament: it offers expressions of wrenching grief, tenuous hope, anger, and yet more grief. In Lamentations, we hear the pathos-drenched observations of an observer, the plaintive cries of Zion herself, the bitter musings of a shamed Judean male, and the urgent exhortations of the subaltern community as a whole. No voice silences another; no voice dominates. God never speaks; as Kathleen O'Connor has noted, "God's silence leaves each voice, each testimony, standing, unrefuted, and unresolved."[10] There is no divine voice to trumpet one totalizing explanation, no theological metanarrative that would dare to "solve" the horrific suffering that Judah has experienced. Instead, we

---

10. Kathleen M. O'Connor, "Voices Arguing about Meaning," in *Lamentations in Ancient and Contemporary Cultural Contexts* (ed. Nancy C. Lee and Carleen Mandolfo; SBLSymS 43; Atlanta: Society of Biblical Literature, 2008), 28.

are invited into the tensive interplay of unresolvable and open dialogue. "Judah has gone into exile with suffering and hard servitude; she lives now among the nations, and finds no resting place," the narrator sighs (Lam 1:3). "Is it nothing to you, all you who pass by? Look and see if there is any sorrow like my sorrow," Zion wails (Lam 1:12). "I am the man who has seen affliction under the rod of God's wrath. ... He has besieged me and enveloped me with bitterness and tribulation," a male Judean cries (Lam 3:1, 5). "Restore us to yourself, O LORD, that we may be restored; renew our days as of old," pleads the subaltern community as a whole (Lam 5:21). In Lamentations, no voice controls the interplay of meanings by making stentorian pronouncements. Suffering, uncertainty, and hope: all are true, and all are allowed to be what they are.

The dialogical form of Lamentations has important implications for the political and theological identity formation of its audiences. As F. W. Dobbs-Allsopp observes, "The theology of Lamentations is ... pluralistic, equivocating, and fragmentary."[11] Lamentations refuses hegemonic discourse. Because the book declines to perform violent monological speech, its readers are freed to do the same. Lamentations' dialogical expressions of powerlessness and hope build community rather than brutally dividing it. Lamentations takes responsibility for past sin[12] while neither scapegoating one group nor fetishizing guilt.

4. CONCLUSION

Jeremiah, Ezekiel, and Lamentations bear agonistic witness to the pervasive effects of colonization, displacement, and diaspora on Judean culture. Both Jeremiah and Ezekiel manifest aggressive signs of what in the realm

---

11. Frederick W. Dobbs-Allsopp, *Lamentations* (IBC; Louisville: Westminster John Knox, 2002), 23. He continues: "Individual truths are allowed to surface and be experienced on their own, but are also ultimately required to be considered as part of a larger whole, which acts as a strong deterrent to the domination of any single perspective.... Tensions between contrasting positions are intentionally created, and the poet routinely fails to grant closure to these tensions. ... It [viz., this poetic style] stresses responsiveness and attention to complexity, and discourages the search for single and all-encompassing answers" (25–26).

12. Lamentations strongly protests the disproportionateness of the divine punishment, and here and there claims innocence (3:52, 59; 5:7), but also acknowledges that Judah and its leaders were guilty (1:8–9, 18, 22; 2:14; 3:42; 4:13–14).

of psychology is called "splitting,"[13] a polarizing move that is an adaptive and potentially pathological defense against trauma. The (Deutero-) Jeremianic prose splits the political body of the subaltern community into "good figs" and "bad figs," beloved, faithful Judeans in Babylon over against rebellious Judeans back in Judah and in Egypt. Ezekiel splits the covenantal body—God and people—into a distant and transcendent God and a thoroughly shamed, hypersexualized Judah that survives only to testify to its own loathsomeness.[14] These examples show us that "history from below"—that celebrated notion from postcolonial historiography—ought not be romanticized as a necessarily valiant rewriting of power dynamics on behalf of the oppressed. Subaltern speech can replicate dynamics of marginalization and generate terrible new disenfranchisements. "History from below" can be ugly.

But Lamentations offers another diction for those struggling to negotiate the traumatic effects of colonization and displacement. Lamentations models the broken community "hearing one another into speech."[15] Lamentations is a discourse of resistance, make no mistake.[16] But this book

---

13. See the discussion of the dissociative maneuver known as "splitting" in Pamela Cooper-White, *Shared Wisdom: Use of the Self in Pastoral Care and Counseling* (Minneapolis: Fortress, 2004), esp. 15, 48–49, and 108–109. Cooper-White draws in particular on the work of Sigmund Freud, Melanie Klein's "Notes on Some Schizoid Mechanisms," *International Journal of Psycho-Analysis* 27 (1946): 99–110, and Heinz Kohut's "The Two Analyses of Mr. Z," *International Journal of Psycho-Analysis* 60 (1979): 3–27.

14. Regarding the pressures on the exiled Ezekiel and the diaspora traditionists responsible for much of the Deutero-Jeremianic prose, we may find relevant an observation of Rosalind O'Hanlon in "Recovering the Subject: Subaltern Studies and Histories of Resistance in Colonial South Asia," *Modern Asian Studies* 22 (1988): 189–224; reprinted in Ludden, *Reading Subaltern Studies*, 135–86. O'Hanlon writes, "What an important and complex field is this production of the self in the colonial context, particularly of the self of the colonised. For we have not only the approved selves which the coloniser attempts to produce for the native and to constitute as the sole area of legitimate public reality, but the continual struggle of the colonised to resolve the paradoxes which this displacement and dehumanisation of indigenous processes of identification sets up in his daily existence" (156).

15. The phrase is famously associated with Nelle Morton (1905–1987), an anti-racism activist, educator, and feminist theologian. Prominent among her written works is *The Journey Is Home* (Boston: Beacon Press, 1985).

16. See Robert Williamson Jr., "Lament and the Arts of Resistance: Public and Hidden Transcripts in Lamentations 5," in Lee and Mandolfo, *Lamentations*, 67–80. On Williamson's reading, Lam 5 resists the hegemony of YHWH: "With this public

articulates its pain and rage by means of a dialogical, openended sensibility that does not create new subalterns.

The violence generated by the Babylonian diaspora runs deep in the Hebrew Bible. In Ps 137, the "song" sung by the Judean exiles ends with a distorted desire to butcher Babylonian infants. In Ezra-Nehemiah, we see the performance of a reactionary nativism that ruthlessly tears ethnic "Others" from the arms of their Israelite loved ones. From the chilling execution of Achan and his family in Josh 7[17] to the hyperbolically excessive slaughter in the book of Esther,[18] we see postexilic Israel responding to the insider/outsider dilemma with virulent new inscriptions of violence. But Lamentations, along with other texts such as Job and the Servant Songs in Isaiah, bears witness to the resilience of the Judean cultural imagination even in its experiences of most severe dislocation. Because of those few brave texts, we see that even in desperate discourses of resistance, it is possible to refuse to mimic dynamics of domination. And such a refusal is sacred indeed.

BIBLIOGRAPHY

Berquist, Jon L. "Postcolonialism and Imperial Motives for Canonization." Pages 78–95 in *The Postcolonial Biblical Reader*. Edited by R. S. Sugirtharajah. Oxford: Blackwell, 2006.

———. "Psalms, Postcolonialism, and the Construction of the Self." Pages 195–202 in *Approaching Yehud: New Approaches to the Study of the Persian Period*. Edited by Jon L. Berquist. Atlanta: Society of Biblical Literature, 2007.

---

speaking of the hidden transcript as a challenge to YHWH's excessively wrathful exercise of authority, Israel claims the possibility of a future. Lamentations offers no guarantee that YHWH will relent and restore Jerusalem. Nonetheless, the book ends with an act of dignity on the part of Israel, a public challenge to the one who has caused its degradation" (79).

17. On the Achan narrative as an overcompensatory response to the threat of the "Other" in Israel's midst, see Danna Nolan Fewell, "Joshua," in *The Women's Bible Commentary* (ed. Sharon H. Ringe and Carol A. Newsom; Louisville: Westminster John Knox, 1992), 63–66; and Lori Rowlett, "Inclusion, Exclusion and Marginality in the Book of Joshua," *JSOT* 55 (1992): 22–23.

18. On the scholarly arguments about the slaughter in Esther, and my own position that the narrative ironizes any diaspora strategy that mimics colonial violence, see Carolyn J. Sharp, *Irony and Meaning in the Hebrew Bible* (Bloomington: Indiana University Press, 2009), 65–81.

Cooper-White, Pamela. *Shared Wisdom: Use of the Self in Pastoral Care and Counseling*. Minneapolis: Fortress, 2004.

Dobbs-Allsopp, Frederick W. *Lamentations*. IBC. Louisville: Westminster John Knox, 2002.

———. "Lamentations from Sundry Angles: A Perspective." Pages 13–25 in *Lamentations in Ancient and Contemporary Cultural Contexts*. Edited by Nancy C. Lee and Carleen Mandolfo. SBLSymS 43. Atlanta: Society of Biblical Literature, 2008.

Fewell, Danna Nolan. "Joshua." Pages 63–66 in *The Women's Bible Commentary*. Edited by Sharon H. Ringe and Carol A. Newsom. Louisville: Westminster John Knox, 1992.

Kalmanofsky, Amy. "The Monstrous-Feminine in the Book of Jeremiah." *Lectio Difficilior* 1 (2009). Online: http://www.lectio.unibe.ch/09_1/kalmanofsky_the_monstrous_feminine.html.

———. *Terror All Around: Horror, Monsters, and Theology in the Book of Jeremiah*. New York: T&T Clark, 2008.

Keefe, Alice A. *Woman's Body and the Social Body in Hosea*. JSOTSup 338/GCT 10. London: Sheffield Academic Press, 2001.

Klein, Melanie. "Notes on Some Schizoid Mechanisms." *International Journal of Psycho-Analysis* 27 (1946): 99–110.

Kohut, Heinz. "The Two Analyses of Mr. Z." *International Journal of Psycho-Analysis* 60 (1979): 3–27.

Masselos, Jim. "The Dis/appearance of Subalterns: A Reading of a Decade of Subaltern Studies." *South Asia* 15 (1992): 105–25. Reprinted as pages 187–211 in *Reading Subaltern Studies: Critical History, Contested Meaning, and the Globalisation of South Asia*. Edited by David Ludden. Delhi: Permanent Black, 2001.

Morton, Nelle. *The Journey Is Home*. Boston: Beacon Press, 1985.

O'Connor, Kathleen M. "Voices Arguing about Meaning." Pages 27–31 in *Lamentations in Ancient and Contemporary Cultural Contexts*. Edited by Nancy C. Lee and Carleen Mandolfo. SBLSymS 43. Atlanta: Society of Biblical Literature, 2008.

O'Hanlon, Rosalind. "Recovering the Subject: Subaltern Studies and Histories of Resistance in Colonial South Asia." *Modern Asian Studies* 22 (1988): 189–224. Reprinted as pages 135–86 in *Reading Subaltern Studies: Critical History, Contested Meaning, and the Globalisation of South Asia*. Edited by David Ludden. Delhi: Permanent Black, 2001.

Pohlmann, Karl-Friedrich. *Studien zum Jeremiabuch: Ein Beitrag zur Frage nach der Entstehung des Jeremiabuches*. FRLANT 118. Göttingen: Vandenhoeck & Ruprecht, 1978.

Rowlett, Lori. "Inclusion, Exclusion and Marginality in the Book of Joshua." *JSOT* 55 (1992): 15–23.

Sharp, Carolyn J. *Irony and Meaning in the Hebrew Bible*. Bloomington: Indiana University Press, 2009.

———. *Prophecy and Ideology in Jeremiah: Struggles for Authority in the Deutero-Jeremianic Prose*. OTS: London: T&T Clark, 2003.

Stone, Kenneth A. *Sex, Honor and Power in the Deuteronomistic History*. Sheffield: Sheffield Academic Press, 1996.

Sugirtharajah, R. S. "Charting the Aftermath: A Review of Postcolonial Criticism."
    Pages 7–32 in *The Postcolonial Biblical Reader*. Edited by R. S. Sugirtharajah.
    Oxford: Blackwell, 2006.
Williamson, Robert, Jr. "Lament and the Arts of Resistance: Public and Hidden Tran-
    scripts in Lamentations 5." Pages 67–80 in *Lamentations in Ancient and Contem-
    porary Contexts*. Edited by Nancy C. Lee and Carleen Mandolfo. SBLSymS 43.
    Atlanta: Society of Biblical Literature, 2008.

The Emasculation of Exile: Hypermasculinity and Feminization in the Book of Ezekiel

T. M. Lemos

Masculinity is not a given.[1] It must be shaped and cultivated, created and re-created by cultural discourses, inscribed and reinscribed by social hierarchies and social actions. It experiences triumphs, it endures crises—and none of these pinnacles is greater, it seems, than that experienced when a man or a group of men conquers another, subjecting the vanquished to physical violence and public humiliation, strengthening their claims to masculine honor while at the same time depriving the conquered of their own masculine status. In the ancient Near East, the victorious proclaimed their glories upon stelae and portrayed them upon reliefs, boasting of their strength and prowess, of the favor their gods had bestowed upon them. But how did the vanquished express the despoliation of their manhood, the shame of status newly fallen, the agony of stripes, both emotional and physical, newly struck and so slow in healing? The book of Ezekiel, and chapter 23 in particular, offers one a very interesting and in many ways unique response to this question. There are few ancient Near Eastern texts written by the conquered, and while the book of Ezekiel in some ways serves as the tortured counterpart of hypermasculinized Mesopotamian and Egyptian royal inscriptions, in other ways it presents a vision of gendered suffering even more graphic than the royal inscriptions might lead one to expect. Ezekiel presents us with a masculine dyad of conqueror/ conquered in which the Israelites, through their feminization, occupy the debased bottom tier. Unable to satisfy their own standards of masculinity, the Israelite exiles, in the mind of Ezekiel, are effectively men no more.

---

1. I thank Matthew Neujahr and Andrea Stevenson Allen for their helpful comments on this paper.

In two infamous passages in the book of Ezekiel, the city of Jerusalem, and through it Judah as a whole, is represented metaphorically as a
whorish and wayward woman. In chapter 16, Jerusalem is Yahweh's wife, a
woman saved from destitution by Yahweh yet one who repeatedly commits
adultery against him with other men. In chapter 23, in the metaphor of the
two sisters, Samaria is represented as a whorish woman named Oholah,
and Jerusalem as her sister Oholibah. According to Ezekiel, Jerusalem is
even more brazen in her whorings than was her sister, and the language
with which he describes her insatiable desires for foreign men is striking.
Verses 12–21 say of Oholibah:

> After the Assyrians she lusted, governors and prefects, warriors dressed
> in opulence, horse-riding cavalry, desirable young men all of them. ...
> She increased her whoring when she saw men graven upon the wall,
> images of Chaldeans engraved in crimson, belts on their loins, flow-
> ing turbans on their heads, with the appearance of chariot warriors all
> of them—a likeness of Babylonians whose native land is Chaldea. She
> lusted after them when her eyes saw them, and she sent messengers to
> them in Chaldea. The Babylonians came to her, to the bed of love, and
> they defiled her with their whoring. ... Yet she multiplied her whoring
> further, reminiscing over the days of her youth when she had whored in
> the land of Egypt and lusted after her lovers there, whose flesh was that
> of donkeys and whose emission[2] that of horses. So you longed for the
> obscenity of your youth when the Egyptians pinched your nipples and
> fondled your young breasts.[3]

Unlike Ezek 16, which describes Jerusalem's passions as being "indiscrimi-
nate" ("you poured out your whorings on any passerby"),[4] in Ezek 23, the
whore Jerusalem is described as sleeping only with powerful foreign men—
with Egyptians, Assyrians, and Babylonians.[5] Each of these sets of lovers

---

2. "Stick" or "branch" is also possible as a translation here. The word is זרמה, but
Koehler-Baumgartener sees a metathesis of ר and מ, and thus reads זמורה, "branch,"
i.e., "penis." See Ludwig Köhler, Walter Baumgartner, and Johann Jakob Stamm, *The
Hebrew and Aramaic Lexicon of the Old Testament* (Study Ed.; trans. M. E. J. Richardson; Leiden: Brill, 2001), 1: 282.

3. Translations my own unless otherwise noted.

4. As Cynthia R. Chapman puts it; see her *The Gendered Language of Warfare
in the Israelite-Assyrian Encounter* (HSM 62; Winona Lake, Ind.: Eisenbrauns, 2004),
124.

5. While the Egyptians, Assyrians, and Chaldeans are also specifically mentioned

is depicted as being irresistibly masculine—the Assyrians are warriors, physically attractive, sitting regally astride horses, and the Chaldeans, too, are soldiers alluring in their officer's dress.[6] The Egyptians' masculinity, like that of the Assyrians, is associated with the equine, but it is not merely that the Egyptians *ride* stallions. No, the bodies of the Egyptians themselves are compared to horses; Ezekiel bluntly states that their genitalia is like that of donkeys and their ejaculate like that of stallions. Much of the scholarship on this passage has been distracted by attempts to paint Ezekiel as pornographic,[7] without asking in the first place in what ways such graphic language was typical or atypical of ancient Near Eastern texts. The portrayal of foreign men here has several features—it describes genitalia; it is animalizing; and it relates to foreign conquerors. I will examine each of these qualities in order to ascertain why Ezekiel says what he does in chapter 23. What purpose does this graphic language serve for Ezekiel?

The language in Ezek 23, particularly that regarding the Egyptians, seems grotesque, a fact that has been noted by various commentators. Walther Zimmerli writes that "with forceful sharpening of the diction the lasciviousness of the Egyptians is described."[8] Paul M. Joyce calls the verses a "dramatic symbolization of the Egyptians' reputation for lewdness."[9] Referring to Ezek 16:26—which mentions the large "flesh," that is, penises, of the Egyptians—Daniel I. Block states the language is "obscenely physical," and

---

as lovers in Ezek 16, it does not appear that these were Jerusalem's only lovers, nor is one told why Jerusalem was attracted to these men/nations, as is the case in ch. 23.

6. The attractiveness of the foreigners is described not only in vv. 12–16, quoted above, but also in vv. 5–6 and 23.

7. See T. M. Lemos, "'They Have Become Women': Judean Diaspora and Postcolonial Theories of Gender and Migration," in *Social Theory and the Study of Israelite Religion: Essays in Retrospect and Prospect* (ed. Saul Olyan; SBLRBS; Atlanta: Society of Biblical Literature, forthcoming), as well as Robert P. Carroll, "Desire under the Terebinths: On Pornographic Representation in the Prophets—A Response," in *A Feminist Companion to the Latter Prophets* (ed. Athalya Brenner; FCB 8; Sheffield: Sheffield Academic Press, 1995), 275–307, who also critiques this tendency.

8. Walther Zimmerli, *Ezekiel 1: A Commentary on the Book of the Prophet Ezekiel Chapters 1–24* (trans. Ronald E. Clements; Hermeneia; Philadelphia: Fortress , 1979), 487.

9. Paul M. Joyce, *Ezekiel: A Commentary* (LHBOTS 482; London: T&T Clark, 2007), 162. Notably, the only evidence he provides for this alleged reputation is another verse from Ezekiel—16:26. Moshe Greenberg (*Ezekiel 21–37: A New Translation with Introduction and Commentary* [AB 22A; New York: Doubleday, 1997], 480) makes a similar comment, again providing no evidence save Ezek 16:26.

he calls what one finds in Ezek 23 "crude bestial imagery."[10] Finally, Margaret S. Odell writes: "As the archetypal enemy of Yahweh, Egypt is portrayed in mythically bestial terms in 29:2 and 32:2; here Ezekiel employs imagery that is more in keeping with the sexual imagery of the chapter. Returning to the days of her youth, Oholibah makes a reckless descent into chaos, as Ezekiel couples the imagery of human fondling with the sights and sounds of a stable."[11] These and other commentators note, too, how these verses paint Oholibah's desires as repulsive; her lust is profligate and beyond that of even other transgressive women.

Certainly the portrayals of Jerusalem in both chapter 16 and 23 are so exaggerated and the city/woman is spoken of with such disgust and such violence that it is quite clear how Ezekiel wished his audience to respond to her. But is it as clear that he meant to portray the *Egyptians* and the other foreign lovers of Jerusalem as "bestial" and repugnant? Counter to what is stated or implied by the scholars above, I would suggest that whether Ezekiel meant for the descriptions of Jerusalem's lovers to denigrate these foreign groups is a more complicated question than one might initially suppose. Of course, in other chapters in the book, especially in the oracles against Egypt in chapters 29 and 32, that nation is spoken of in very negative terms; however, I would caution against homogenizing or flattening out the nuances of different passages in this work. In order to understand the graphic language on its own terms, it is fruitful to look not only to other parts of Ezekiel but to other ancient Near Eastern texts that speak of sexuality and/or that compare human beings to animals.

Examining Mesopotamian potency incantations is quite instructive in this case. These incantations were meant to address male sexual dysfunction,[12] and many relate directly to the equine sexual language in Ezek 23. For example, one incantation reads: "Incantation. Wild ass! Wild ass! Wild bull! Wild bull! … Ram who has an erection for mating!"[13] Another reads: "Wild ass who had an erection for mating, who has damp-

---

10. Daniel I. Block, *The Book of Ezekiel: Chapters 1–24* (NICOT; Grand Rapids: Eerdmans, 1997), 495, 747.

11. Margaret S. Odell, *Ezekiel* (SHBC; Macon, Ga.: Smyth & Helwys, 2005), 302–3.

12. See Robert D. Biggs, *Šà.zi.ga, Ancient Mesopotamian Potency Incantations* (Locust Valley, N.Y.: Augustin, 1967), 1–8. Most of these incantations, while generally existing in first-millennium copies, likely date to the Middle or even the Old Babylonian period.

13. Ibid., 12.

ened your ardor? Violent stallion whose sexual excitement is a devastating flood, [w]ho has bound your limbs?"[14] These are just two of several incantations that mention donkeys and/or stallions, sometimes together with bulls and lions, as paragons of sexual vigor.[15] Finally, there are also incantations that refer to great penis length or thickness as desirable, as in: "May your penis become as long as a *mašgašu*-weapon!"[16] This is relevant because Ezek 23:20 obviously conveys penis *size* through the comparison of Egyptians' members with the genitalia of donkeys, and because Ezek 16:26 describes the Egyptians as being "great of flesh." There is also Mesopotamian art that is pertinent to this chapter. While graphic sexual materials are uncommon in Assyria, lead inlays do survive from the Middle Assyrian period that explicitly portray various sexual scenes. In more than one of these, the male's penis is "outsized," as Julia Assante puts it.[17] In Babylonia, where erotic materials were more common, penises were also sometimes portrayed as exaggerated in size.[18] One finds graphic portrayals of sexuality and/or genitalia in Egyptian texts and art as well. Egyptian creation accounts in fact speak of the sun god commencing the work of creation through solitary sexual acts. For example, Spell 527 from the Pyramid texts, which were found on the walls of Old Kingdom royal pyramids, reads, "Atum evolved growing ithyphallic, in Heliopolis. He put his penis in his grasp that he might make orgasm with it, and the two siblings were born—Shu and Tefnut."[19] Ithyphallic portrayals of deities (e.g., Osiris, Geb, Min) are relatively common, and one illustration even shows Geb fellating himself as his forefather Atum is also described as having done.[20] The penises of the gods in these depictions are, perhaps unsur-

---

14. Ibid., 17.

15. Ibid., 22, 27.

16. Ibid., 33.

17. Julia Assante, "The Lead Inlays of Tukulti-Ninurta I: Pornography as Imperial Strategy," in *Ancient Near Eastern Art in Context: Studies in Honor of Irene J. Winter* (ed. Jack Cheng and Marian Feldman; CHANE 12; Leiden: Brill, 2007), 375, 393, 395.

18. Julia Assante, "The Erotic Reliefs of Ancient Mesopotamia" (Ph.D. diss., Columbia University, 2000), 82.

19. Translated by James P. Allen (*COS* 1.3:7). Notably, Papyrus Bremner-Rhind, a text compiled in the Ptolemaic period, relates an account of divine auto-fellatio: "I [Atum] am the one who acted as husband with my fist: I copulated with my hand, I let fall into my own mouth, I sneezed Shu and spat Tefnut." See James P. Allen's translation in *COS* 1.9:14.

20. See, for example, Gay Robins, "Male Bodies and the Construction of Mascu-

prisingly, incredibly large. The Turin Erotic Papyrus, from the Ramesside period, correspondingly portrays human sexuality in numerous very
graphic scenes.[21] While this text is generally seen as satirical, it is still
worth noting that the males involved in the sex scenes are depicted with
extremely large members.

It bears keeping in mind that there is even a biblical text implying
that large penis size was considered more desirable and more masculine
than the alternative. In 1 Kgs 12, when "all the assembly of Israel" comes
to Rehoboam to ask him to lighten the load his father Solomon had laid
upon them, Rehoboam's advisors encourage him to say to them, "my little
finger"—or "my little thing," depending on how one chooses to render the
problematically vocalized קָטָנִּי—"is thicker than my father's loins" (v. 10).[22]
Regardless of one's particular translation, the sense of this statement seems
clear enough, and it lends support to seeing the Israelites as having had the
same conception of penis size that Egyptians and Mesopotamians apparently had—large size was preferable. Certainly, the contrast between Ezekiel's portrayal of foreign men and his portrayal of the conquered Judeans
is striking in this regard: the Assyrians and Babylonians are officers and
horsemen, and the Egyptians—to use a crude but relevant phrase from our
own culture—are "hung like horses," while the conquered Israelites are not
men at all. They have become women, or rather *a woman*, and a wayward
one at that.

As was discussed previously, Mesopotamian potency incantations
invoke animal sexuality in cases where male sexual potency is lacking.
These incantations present large genital size and equine-like prowess as
desirable, a fact which should lead one to call into question whether or not
Ezekiel's comparison of foreign men to animals in chapter 23 is meant to

linity in New Kingdom Egyptian Art," in *Servant of Mut: Studies in Honor of Richard Fazzini* (ed. Sue H. D'Auria; Probleme der Ägyptologie 28; Leiden: Brill, 2008), 208–15; and Lana Troy, "Engendering Creation in Ancient Egypt: Still and Flowing Waters," in *A Feminist Companion to Reading the Bible: Approaches, Methods and Strategies* (ed. Athalya Brenner and Carole Fontaine; Sheffield: Sheffield Academic Press, 1997), 245.

21. On this text, and on the graphic sexual ostraca found at Deir el-Medina, see Jaana Toivari-Viitala, *Women at Deir el-Medina: A Study of the Status and Roles of the Female Inhabitants in the Workmen's Community During the Ramesside Period* (Egyptologische Uitgaven 15; Leiden: Nederlands Instituut voor het Nabije Oosten, 2001), 143–53.

22. See Mordechai Cogan, *1 Kings: A New Translation with Introduction and Commentary* (AB 10; New York: Doubleday, 2001), 348–49.

convey repulsiveness and a "bestial" character, or rather something else, something more complex and less denigrating. In my view, Ezek 23 does not reflect merely ancient Near Eastern ideas about genitalia and the positive valuation placed upon large genitalia, but also a cultural discourse spanning the larger Near Eastern region of animalization *as* masculinization. In a comparative treatment of foreigners in Mesopotamian, Egyptian, and Chinese sources, Mu-chou Poo writes, "It seems that the most condescending way possible for the Mesopotamians to express their contempt toward the foreigners or enemies was by referring to them as animals."[23] This statement is not entirely satisfactory, however. While it is true that foreigners are frequently denigrated by being compared to animals, or by having language applied to them that involves animals in some way, it is equally true that both Egyptian and Mesopotamian kings very regularly expressed their power and skill by comparing *themselves* to animals in their own royal inscriptions. For example, in Mesopotamian texts of the Neo-Assyrian era, animalizing language is frequently applied to enemies, foreign or otherwise, but is just as frequently applied to Assyrian kings. The annals of Sennacherib repeatedly use animalizing language. The annals state, in the voice of Sennacherib, that the people of Bît-Yakin ran off "before my powerful weapons like wild asses."[24] Sennacherib boasts, too, that he cuts down the field marshal of the Elamites and his nobles "like fat steers who have hobbles put on them."[25] He also says that his enemies "fled like young pigeons that are pursued" and ran off "like hinds," and that he slaughters them "like wild animals," among other statements of this kind. [26] Yet he also says of himself, "In the midst of the high mountains I rode on horseback where the terrain was difficult. ... Where it became too steep, I clambered up on foot like the wild-ox."[27] He states later in the text, "Like a young gazelle I mounted the high(est) peaks" and "like a lion I raged";[28] "the terror of my battle overturned them (lit. their bodies) like

23. Mu-chou Poo, *Enemies of Civilization: Attitudes toward Foreigners in Ancient Mesopotamia, Egypt, and China* (Albany: State University of New York Press, 2005), 50–51.

24. Daniel David Luckenbill, *The Annals of Sennacherib* (University of Chicago Oriental Institute Publications 2; Chicago: University of Chicago Press, 1924), 38.

25. Ibid., 45.

26. Ibid., 47, 51–52, 77.

27. Ibid., 26.

28. Ibid., 36, 44, 50.

a bull" and "I, like a strong wild-ox, led the way."[29] And Sennacherib is not
the only Assyrian king to describe himself in these ways.[30]

A very similar situation obtains in Egyptian sources: while foreigners
are sometimes denigrated through animalizing language, such language
is applied seemingly much more often to kings in their own royal texts.
Ramesses II's inscription recording the battle of Qadesh states that, among
his enemies, he was "like a fierce lion in a valley of wild game."[31] Ramesses
II calls himself not only a lion, but "a bull poised in the arena," and states
that he was "prepared to fight like an eager bull," "entered into the battle-
lines, fighting like the pounce of a falcon," and was "after" his enemies "like
a griffon."[32] The Gebel Barkal Stela of Thutmose III states that the king
is a "stout-hearted bull"; he "smit[es] southerners and behead[s] north-
erners ... slaughtering Asian Bedouin and overthrowing defiant desert
dwellers."[33] A final example of the many available is from the second Beth-
Shean stela of Seti I, who is said to be "like a young bull, powerful lion,
falcon of Khepri"; he is "valiant like a falcon and a strong bull wide-strid-
ing and sharp-horned."[34] In these inscriptions, animalizing comparisons
relate directly to masculine traits these kings wish to present themselves
as possessing—bravery, physical strength, and prowess in battle. These are
not traits the kings wish to possess in moderation; no, they wish to have
these qualities to an extraordinary degree, and they compare themselves
to the most powerful animals they know of to express how they are in fact

---

29. Ibid., 47, 71.

30. For example, Adad-Nerari II presents a veritable litany of royal declarations,
many of which clearly double as boasts of superior masculinity and in the midst of
which one finds leonine imagery: "I am king, I am lord, I am powerful, I am important, I am praise-worthy, I am magnificent, I am strong, I am mighty, I am fierce, I am
enormously radiant, [I am a hero], I am [a lion], I am a virile warrior, I am foremost,
I am exalted, I." See Albert Kirk Grayson, *Assyrian Royal Inscriptions: Part 2: From
Tiglath Pileser I to Ashur-nasur-apli II* (RANE 2; Wiesbaden: Harassowitz, 1976), 85.

31. "The Battle of Qadesh—The Poem, or Literary Record," translated by K. A.
Kitchen (*COS* 2.5:33). Strikingly, he asks of the sun god, "What are they to you, O
Amun, these Asiatics, despicable and ignorant of God!" (*COS* 2.5: 34). Later in the
text, he relates what he said to his shield-bearer: "What are these effeminate weaklings
to you, for millions of whom I care nothing?" (ibid., 2.5:36)

32. *COS* 2.5:33, 35, 37.

33. "The Gebel Barkal Stela of Thutmose III," translated by James K. Hoffmeier
(*COS* 2.2B:14–15).

34. "Second Beth-Shan Stela [Year Lost]" (*COS* 2.4D:28).

beyond other men in having these qualities. If one may generalize about ancient Near Eastern royal inscriptions as a whole, it appears that these inscriptions convey no sense that masculinity could be conceived of as excessive in royal figures. Kings did not value in themselves temperance of character, but rather raging like a lion, fighting like a bull, terrifying and killing one's enemies like a wild animal. There is no excess of fearsome masculinity possible—only glorious abundance.

Considering the frequency with which animalizing language is applied to kings in ancient Near Eastern royal texts and the central role it plays in the braggadocio of these kings, as well as what one sees in Mesopotamian potency incantations, one must ask the question of whether or not ancient Israelites, or ancient Babylonians or Egyptians, would have interpreted the descriptions of foreigners in Ezek 23 as "bestial." In light of the fact that this animalizing language is used from Egypt to Mesopotamia and that it persists over many hundreds of years, it is likely that Israelites not only knew of this language and the gender discourses of which it formed a part, but themselves shared the conceptions of masculinity that produced and were produced by them. Of course, no royal inscriptions of the type that exist for ancient Egypt or Mesopotamia survive from ancient Israel, and biblical texts provide fewer examples of men being aggrandized through comparisons with animals.[35] Yet some examples may still be found. In Jacob's blessing over his sons in Gen 49, verses 8–9 acclaim Judah and utilize leonine imagery to do so: "Judah, your brothers will praise you; your hand shall be on the neck of your enemies. … Judah is a lion's cub; from the prey, my son, you have gone up. He crouches, he lies down like a lion,

---

35. Chapman has argued that in Israelite prophetic texts the contest of masculinity is not between Israel's kings and foreign kings, but between Israelite's god and foreign kings (*Gendered Language*, 142). I agree that this is frequently the case, and this being so, it is worth noting that animalizing language is sometimes applied to Yahweh himself. See, e.g., Isa 31:4, where the prophet states that Yahweh will come down to fight on Mount Zion "like a lion or young lion" who is not afraid of shouting; Jer 50:44; Hos 5:14; 11:10; 13:7–8; and Amos 3:8, though in some of these cases Yahweh is acting against the Israelites. Noteworthy, too, is Yahweh's old title יעקב אביר (likely "Bull of Jacob"), used in Gen 49:24; Ps 132:2; Isa 49:26; 60:16. In Isa 10:13, the word אביר by itself is applied to Yahweh, and in Isa 1:24 אביר ישראל is used. On this title, see, for example, Frank Moore Cross, *Canaanite Myth and Hebrew Epic: Essays in the History of the Religion of Israel* (Cambridge: Harvard University Press, 1973), 4, 15; and Mark S. Smith, *The Early History of God: Yahweh and the Other Deities in Ancient Israel* (2nd ed.; Grand Rapids: Eerdmans, 2002), 49–50, 84.

like a northern lion[36]—who will rouse him up?" David's lament over Saul
and Jonathan in 2 Sam 1 states, "Saul and Jonathan … they were swifter
than eagles, they were stronger than lions." Also, like Egyptian and Assyrian kings, David boasts of how he has slain lions in 1 Sam 17:36.[37] One sees
this, too, in Judg 14, which tells of how the mighty Samson tears apart a
lion with his bare hands. This feat is in fact the first of many that establish
Samson as hypermasculine, a man beyond other men. Interestingly, the
passages in which one finds perhaps the most direct comparisons to the
language in ancient Near Eastern royal inscriptions are found in 1 and 2
Maccabees, which postdate most biblical materials by hundreds of years.
First Maccabees 3:4 states of Judah Maccabee, "He was like a lion in his
deeds, like a lion's cub roaring for prey." Second Maccabees 11:11 also says
of Judah, "They hurled themselves like lions against the enemy, and laid
low eleven thousand of them and sixteen hundred cavalry, and forced all
the rest to flee. Most of them got away stripped and wounded, and Lysias
himself escaped by disgraceful flight."[38]

One might counter these biblical examples by pointing to others that,
like the comparisons of foreigners to animals in ancient Near Eastern
texts mentioned above, demonstrate that animalizing language could be
used in ancient Israel in multiple ways, both positive and negative. For
instance, just a few lines after the use of leonine imagery to extol Judah's

---

36. The word used, לביא, is normally translated "lioness," but Ludwig Köhler suggested that it refers to the Asiatic lion, while ארי or אריה refers to the African lion. See
Ludwig Köhler, "Lexikologisch-Geographisches," *ZDPV* 62 (1939): 115–25, especially
122–25. While Brent Strawn (*What Is Stronger Than a Lion? Leonine Image and Metaphor in the Hebrew Bible and the Ancient Near East* [OBO 212; Fribourg: Academic
Press; Göttingen: Vandenhoeck & Ruprecht, 2005], 311–19) sees this differentiation as
"unwarranted," he agrees that the word means "lion," not "lioness."

37. See the "Armant Stela of Thutmose III," translated by James K. Hoffmeier
(*COS* 2.2C:18–19), where Thutmose III boasts of killing seven lions and one hundred
and twenty elephants, as well as having "carried off" twelve wild bulls; "The Memphis and Karnak Stelae of Amenhotep II," translated by Hoffmeier (*COS* 2.3:19–22),
where the pharaoh boasts of killing or capturing various wild animals; and "Annals:
Aššur Clay Tablets," translated by K. Lawson Younger, Jr. (*COS* 2.113B:265–66), where
Shalmaneser III relates having killed lions, bulls, and elephants. Also, Aššurbanipal
is portrayed hunting lions on his palace reliefs (Chapman, *Gendered Language*, 73).
Ancient Near Eastern kings are thus *like* lions, but able to capture and kill lions and
thereby demonstrate that their strength is even greater than that of one of nature's
most fearsome beasts.

38. Translations of 1 and 2 Maccabees are from the NRSV.

power in Gen 49, one reads the following: "Issachar is a bony donkey ... he bent his shoulder to bear the load and became a forced laborer." One sees, then, that even comparisons to one particular animal, the donkey, could convey very different sentiments—in Gen 49, the strength and subservience of an *arbeitstier*, and in Ezek 23, potent (or rampant) sexuality.[39] This fact complicates one's interpretation of the latter chapter. But this much is clear: animalizing language in itself was not problematic to the Egyptians, Assyrians, or Israelites. If it were, Egyptian and Assyrian monarchs would not be so frequently the object of such comparisons on their own royal inscriptions, neither would biblical texts use animalizing language in the positive ways they sometimes do. What is disparaging or complimentary is not that an analogy is made between human and animal, but rather what particular comparison is made and for what reason. Stating that an enemy flees like a bird or a wild ass is negative because of the behavior described, not because of the comparison to a bird or donkey. When the annals of Thutmose III say of defeated foreign troops that they were caught as fish in the bight of a net, it is not the comparison to a fish that is necessarily negative, but rather being caught and rendered helpless by one's enemy.[40]

Does one find, then, a positive or negative use of a comparison to donkeys and horses in Ezek 23? Since this passage expresses the large size of genitalia and abundance of sexual emissions, I think it more likely, considering the evidence discussed here as a whole, to see the passage as expressing the impressiveness of Egyptian sexuality and masculinity. The ancient Near Eastern and biblical evidence points rather clearly in the direction of seeing large genitals as preferable and masculinity as something that cannot exist in excess. There is no sense of hypermasculinity as a negative trait that one gets from reading the royal inscriptions of the ancient Near East. However, these inscriptions certainly do express the idea that masculinity can be deficient. This deficiency is most clearly described in texts that speak of conquest and of vanquished men, which is precisely what the exiled Israelites were. Both Egyptian and Mesopotamian royal texts seem to see men as falling into two categories—the conquerors and the conquered, the hypermasculine and the emasculated. This is, of course, part of their rhetoric—that those who are conquered by them will become

---

39. Judah is referred to as a wild ass in Jer 2:24 as part of Jeremiah's metaphor of Israel-as-whore. There, the sexual connotations, applied to a metaphorical woman rather than to a man, are negative.

40. "The Annals of Thutmose III," translated by Hoffmeier (*COS* 2.2:11).

so lowly as to be non-men. Cynthia Chapman has examined very convincingly the discourses of gender in Neo-Assyrian royal inscriptions and
detailed the symbolism of masculinity and emasculation in both text and
image. She writes:

> The royal performance of masculinity in Assyrian written and visual
> battle narratives involved displaying strength, courage, and heroism on
> the battlefield. Because the king had to present an image that he was no
> ordinary male, it was not enough for him simply to be strong, coura-
> geous, and heroic; he had to win the contest of masculinity by proving
> that he was "without rival" on the battlefield. ... Real and potential male
> "rivals" represented a serious threat to the Assyrian king. As such, his
> inscriptions and reliefs went to great lengths to discredit the masculin-
> ity of male rivals through the two related motifs of the fleeing and the
> surrendering king. ... Furthermore, through the imposition of curses on
> surrendering vassals, the Assyrian king discredited a male rival through
> images of feminization.[41]

Perhaps the most glaring instance of a feminizing curse can be found
in Esarhaddon's Succession Treaty, which reads, "May all the gods who are
called by name in this treaty tablet spin you around like a spindle-whorl,
may they make you a woman before your enemy."[42] Chapman writes of this
and other texts that make similar statements: "At its most basic level, a man's
behaving 'like a woman' involved showing fear. ... Some of the associated
commonplaces tied to the metaphor of men 'becoming women' included
'becoming a prostitute,' losing one's land, failing to sire an heir, and losing
one's bow."[43] The feminization or desired feminization of enemies is not
limited to evidence from the Neo-Assyrian period. The Middle Assyrian
king Tikulti-Ninurta I likewise asks Ishtar to "change his enemy from a
man to a woman and to cause his manhood to dwindle away."[44] Ramesses
II similarly refers to his enemies as "effeminate weaklings" on the Qadesh
inscription.[45] In Israelite sources as well, one finds language strikingly similar to that in Esarhaddon's treaty in Isa 19:16, Jer 50:37 and 51:30, and in

---

41. Chapman, *Gendered Language*, 58–59.

42. Lines 616–17. See Simo Parpola and Kazuko Watanabe, *Neo-Assyrian Treaties
and Loyalty Oaths* (SAA 2; Helsinki: Helsinki University Press, 1988), 56.

43. Chapman, *Gendered Language*, 48–49.

44. Assante, "Lead Inlays," 384.

45. See n. 31 above.

Nah 3:13. The latter of these texts reads, "Look at your people[46]: they are women in your midst. The gates of your land are opened wide to your foes; fire has devoured the bars of your gates." To be conquered, then, was to be vulnerable and weak, and to be weak was to become a "woman."

While Nahum is speaking of Nineveh, the implications for the exiled Israelites and for reading Ezekiel are clear. Not only the Israelites but the Babylonians who had conquered them, as well as the Egyptians of whom Ezekiel spoke in such graphic terms, would have understood well the connotations of Ezek 23. While the foreigners embody a laudable, esteemworthy image of masculinity, the Judean exiles are emasculated to the point of feminization—and properly so, in light of their humiliating defeat and the loss of their land. This is not merely a case of cultural appropriation, however. Ezekiel does not coopt the masculine ideals of his conquerors as part of his traumatized presentation of his people—rather, the ideals that underlie his presentation of Jerusalem and her lovers are *Israelite* ideals as well.[47] Chapters 16 and 23 reflect native Israelite cultural conceptions, conceptions that were extremely widespread throughout the ancient Near East and that saw conquered men in uniformly negative terms. Masculinity necessitated strength, bravery, and most important of all, victory. When they were defeated, the Israelites showed themselves to be more feeble than their enemies. They were controlled and abused by others and thus lost all claim to masculine honor. By their own standards of masculinity, they were disgraced and emasculated. In the midst of their Babylonian conquerors, they had become "women."

I do not deny that Ezekiel expresses revulsion through the vivid metaphors in chapters 16 and 23. This revulsion is felt toward himself and the other Judean exiles as conquered men. As is so consistently the case in Israelite prophetic texts, Ezekiel blames the people themselves for the terrible violence inflicted upon them. They transgressed against Yahweh; they were unfaithful, and so they were punished. His disgust is so strong that he chooses to couch it in a sexualized metaphor that Israelite and other ancient Near Eastern men, and perhaps most women as well, would have found disturbing and enraging. He is not alone among prophets in using this metaphor, but his presentation is striking in its graphic sexual

---

46. A translation of "soldiers" is also possible here. See Chapman, *Gendered Language*, 107.

47. Chapman makes a similar point in *Gendered Language*, 142.

imagery and in its violence.[48] But I would argue that, besides a powerful sense of disgust, there is something else in these passages as well—an
acknowledgement of the superior claim to masculinity held by the Egyptians, the Assyrians, and the Babylonians, the handsome foreigners that
Jerusalem found so irresistible. Ezekiel does not deny that the Judeans'
vanquishment debased them, only that their god was vanquished and
debased along with them. Ezekiel reframes only the theological understanding of their defeat, not the nature of defeat itself. Yahweh's honor may
have been threatened by his whorish wife Jerusalem, but the Israelite god
acts to punish her shamelessness with a retribution both brutal and public.
The book of Ezekiel does not deny that defeat is shaming—it instead reinforces this idea by expressing that defeat is a justified shaming executed by
the hand of Yahweh. Its human agents are the lovers of Jerusalem, whose
masculinity surpasses that of the Judeans not only in Ezekiel's metaphor
but in life, as it was in life and not in metaphor alone that Judah was conquered by them.

There are many striking features to be found within the book of Ezekiel, but perhaps one of the most noteworthy is that this book stands as
one of very few texts in the ancient Near East that was written by a conquered individual.[49] Certainly, there are many examples of Egyptian and
Mesopotamian kings boasting of their conquests, but very few accounts
produced by the conquered themselves—not by later generations, but by
those who had themselves been marched into exile. Ezekiel offers us a
window into the experiences of such men, and what one sees is not a
contestation of lowly status, but an affirmation of it, not a rebuttal against
emasculation but rather an assertion of feminization. Remarkably, Eze-

---

48. Of course, the language is crude at times in Jeremiah as well, particularly in
Jer 3:2, but still Jeremiah does not go so far as to discuss genital size or the fondling
of naked breasts.

49. Another example may be found in the dozens of messages of Rib-Hadda/
Rib-Addi, the king of Gubla (Gebal, i.e., Byblos), found among the Amarna letters.
This king writes repeatedly to the king of Egypt, begging for troops and aid to be sent
to him so that he could fight off the neighboring groups who were in the process of
conquering his territory. These letters, of course, present a very different case from
what we find in Ezekiel, but it is interesting to note the range of emotions found in
this correspondence, emotions ranging from desperation to righteous indignation to
resentment bordering on petulance, and perhaps more than anything else a tenacious
persistence. See William L. Moran, *The Amarna Letters* (Baltimore: Johns Hopkins
University Press, 1992), 138–230.

kiel in some ways goes even further in expressing the hypermasculinity of foreign conquerors than they themselves do—he speaks of them as being sexually potent in the very language the Mesopotamians used to describe potency in their incantations. Egyptian and Assyrian kings may boast that they are like bulls, but not that their penises are like those of stallions. They may portray themselves as well dressed and powerful, but they do not, like Ezekiel, speak outright of their being sexually alluring or sexually potent.

Ezekiel portrays the Mesopotamians and Egyptians in the way these groups idealized masculinity and the way they idealized themselves on royal inscriptions—as beautifully dressed and thus wealthy, as officers and thus of high status, and as victorious soldiers and thus masculine. Ezekiel accepts and reproduces the rhetoric of these inscriptions because he shares the masculine ideals of the Assyrians and Babylonians, and by these standards, his own standards, the Judeans' masculinity was found wanting. Texts such as Ezekiel, written by a vanquished, debased man and for an audience of vanquished, debased people, are exceedingly rare in the ancient world. It is the words of Thutmose and Sennacherib that survive for us, not the words of those whom Thutmose and Sennacherib tortured and massacred. These kings stripped the conquered naked, cut off their limbs and their testicles,[50] and left their bodies strewn across the field of battle; in doing all this, they symbolically equated their victims with women and animals.[51] They transformed them into symbols of emasculation. Symbolism, however, is not reality. In the material world, a dead man is still a *man* no matter what you do to him. But in the world of texts, it is different; elisions and transformations of all kinds can occur, and in some cases, these far outlive the physical body. In a sense, then, in his traumatized self-hatred and blinding sense of shame at what he and his kind had undergone, Ezekiel did what the stripping, raping, and killing of the Assyrians and the Babylonians could not do, though Tikulti-Ninurta may have entreated Ishtar for it to be so—he transformed men into women, the highest classes of Judean elites into the whorish wife of Yahweh.

---

50. See Luckenbill, *The Annals of Sennacherib*, 45, for that king's boast that he tore out his enemies' testicles "like the seeds of cucumbers of Siwan."

51. See T. M. Lemos, "Shame and Mutilation of Enemies in the Hebrew Bible," *JBL* 125 (2006): 225–41.

BIBLIOGRAPHY

Assante, Julia. "The Erotic Reliefs of Ancient Mesopotamia." Ph.D. diss. Columbia University, 2000.

——. "The Lead Inlays of Tukulti-Ninurta I: Pornography as Imperial Strategy." Pages 369–407 in *Ancient Near Eastern Art in Context: Studies in Honor of Irene J. Winter*. Edited by Jack Cheng and Marian Feldman. CHANE 12. Leiden: Brill, 2007.

Biggs, Robert D. *Šà.zi.ga, Ancient Mesopotamian Potency Incantations*. Locust Valley, N.Y.: J. J. Augustin, 1967.

Block, Daniel I. *The Book of Ezekiel: Chapters 1–24*. NICOT. Grand Rapids: Eerdmans, 1997.

Carroll, Robert P. "Desire Under the Terebinths: On Pornographic Representation in the Prophets—A Response." Pages 275–307 in *A Feminist Companion to the Latter Prophets*. Edited by Athalya Brenner. FCB 8. Sheffield: Sheffield Academic Press, 1995.

Chapman, Cynthia R. *The Gendered Language of Warfare in the Israelite-Assyrian Encounter*. HSM 62. Winona Lake, Ind.: Eisenbrauns, 2004.

Cogan, Mordechai. *1 Kings: A New Translation with Introduction and Commentary*. AB 10. New York: Doubleday, 2001.

Cross, Frank Moore. *Canaanite Myth and Hebrew Epic: Essays in the History of the Religion of Israel*. Cambridge: Harvard University Press, 1973.

Grayson, Albert Kirk. *Assyrian Royal Inscriptions Part 2: From Tiglath Pileser I to Ashur-nasur-apli II*. RANE 2. Wiesbaden: Otto Harassowitz, 1976.

Greenberg, Moshe. *Ezekiel 21–37: A New Translation with Introduction and Commentary*. AB 22A. New York: Doubleday, 1997.

Joyce, Paul M. *Ezekiel: A Commentary*. LHBOTS 482. London: T&T Clark, 2007.

Köhler, Ludwig. "Lexikologisch-Geographisches." *ZDPV* 62 (1939): 115–25.

Köhler, Ludwig, Walter Baumgartner, and Johann Jakob Stamm. *The Hebrew and Aramaic Lexicon of the Old Testament*. Study Edition. Translated by M. E. J. Richardson. Leiden: Brill, 2001.

Lemos, T. M. "Shame and the Mutilation of Enemies in the Hebrew Bible." *JBL* 125 (2006): 225–41.

——. "'They Have Become Women': Judean Diaspora and Postcolonial Theories of Gender and Migration." In *Social Theory and the Study of Israelite Religion: Essays in Retrospect and Prospect*. Edited by Saul Olyan. SBLRBS. Atlanta: Society of Biblical Literature, forthcoming.

Luckenbill, Daniel David. *The Annals of Sennacherib*. University of Chicago Oriental Institute Publications 2. Chicago: University of Chicago Press, 1924.

Moran, William L. *The Amarna Letters*. Baltimore: Johns Hopkins University Press, 1992.

Odell, Margaret S. *Ezekiel*. SHBC. Macon, Ga.: Smyth & Helwys, 2005.

Parpola, Simo, and Kazuko Watanabe. *Neo-Assyrian Treaties and Loyalty Oaths*. SAA 2. Helsinki: Helsinki University Press, 1988.

Poo, Mu-chou. *Enemies of Civilization: Attitudes Toward Foreigners in Ancient Mesopotamia, Egypt, and China*. Albany: State University of New York Press, 2005.

Robins, Gay. "Male Bodies and the Construction of Masculinity in New Kingdom Egyptian Art." Pages 208–15 in *Servant of Mut: Studies in Honor of Richard Fazzini*. Edited by Sue H. D'Auria. Probleme der Ägyptologie 28. Leiden: Brill, 2008.

Smith, Mark S. *The Early History of God: Yahweh and the Other Deities in Ancient Israel*. 2nd ed. Grand Rapids: Eerdmans, 2002.

Strawn, Brent A. *What Is Stronger Than a Lion? Leonine Image and Metaphor in the Hebrew Bible and the Ancient Near East*. OBO 212. Fribourg: Academic Press; Göttingen: Vandenhoeck & Ruprecht, 2005.

Toivari-Viitala, Jaana. *Women at Deir el-Medina: A Study of the Status and Roles of the Female Inhabitants in the Workmen's Community During the Ramesside Period*. Egyptologische Uitgaven 15. Leiden: Nederlands Instituut voor het Nabije Oosten, 2001.

Troy, Lana. "Engendering Creation in Ancient Egypt: Still and Flowing Waters." Pages 238–69 in *A Feminist Companion to Reading the Bible: Approaches, Methods and Strategies*. Edited by Athalya Brenner and Carole Fontaine. Sheffield: Sheffield Academic Press, 1997.

Zimmerli, Walther. *Ezekiel 1: A Commentary on the Book of the Prophet Ezekiel Chapters 1–24*. Translated by Ronald E. Clements. Hermeneia. Philadelphia: Fortress, 1979.

Daughter Zion as *Homo Sacer*: The Relationship of Exile, Lamentations, and Giorgio Agamben's Bare Life Figure

Amy Meverden

Inasmuch as the refugee, an apparently marginal figure, unhinges the old trinity of state-nation-territory, it deserves instead to be regarded as the central figure of our political history. We should not forget that the first camps were built in Europe as spaces for controlling refugees, and that the succession of internment camps—concentration camps—extermination camps represents a perfectly real filiation. One of the few rules the Nazis constantly obeyed throughout the course of the "final solution" was that Jews and Gypsies could be sent to extermination camps only after having been fully denationalized (that is, after they had been stripped of even that second-class citizenship to which they had been relegated after the Nuremberg laws). When their rights are no longer the rights of the citizen, that is when humans are truly *sacred*, in the sense that this term used to have in Roman law of the archaic period: doomed to death.[1]

1. Introduction

The interdisciplinary climate of contemporary biblical studies allows for an important partnership with the field of critical theory, a discipline that uses social sciences and humanities to examine and to criticize society and culture.[2] Recent trends in both critical and political theory engage power

---

1. Giorgio Agamben, *Means without End: Notes on Politics* (trans. V. Binetti and C. Casarino; Minneapolis: University of Minnesota Press, 2000), 22.

2. "Critical Theory has a narrow and a broad meaning in philosophy and in the history of the social sciences. 'Critical Theory' in the narrow sense designates several generations of German philosophers and social theorists in the Western European

constructions through the study of biopolitics, the relationship of power
between the political sovereign and the human being.[3] One example of the
implications of biopolitics in archaic and contemporary political landscapes
appears in the work of the Italian philosopher, Giorgio Agamben.[4] He draws
from Foucault's study of biopolitics that the conception of sovereignty as
power over the human existence is implicit in the earliest stages of Western
political existence. Working from the depiction in archaic Roman law of the
homo sacer (the *bare life* figure), one who cannot be sacrificed but whose
body is expendable without consequence, Agamben discusses the history of
the political sovereign in Western thinking, tracing this to the existing state
of biopolitics. Agamben builds upon ancient Western conceptions of sovereignty, subsequently moving the conversation into contemporary political
phenomena such as the Nazi concentration camp and Guantanamo Bay.
This essay discusses *homo sacer* from outside of the Western political landscape, comparing sovereign power and bare life with the ancient Near Eastern context. Using the example of the exiled people of Israel as depicted in

---

Marxist tradition known as the Frankfurt School. According to these theorists, a 'critical' theory may be distinguished from a 'traditional' theory according to a specific
practical purpose: a theory is critical to the extent that it seeks human emancipation,
'to liberate human beings from the circumstances that enslave them' (Horkheimer
1982, 244). Because such theories aim to explain and transform *all* the circumstances
that enslave human beings, many 'critical theories' in the broader sense have been
developed. They have emerged in connection with the many social movements that
identify varied dimensions of the domination of human beings in modern societies. In both the broad and the narrow senses, however, a critical theory provides the
descriptive and normative bases for social inquiry aimed at decreasing domination
and increasing freedom in all their forms" (James Bohman, "Critical Theory," *The
Stanford Encyclopedia of Philosophy* [ed. Edward N. Zalta; spring 2010; online: http://
plato.stanford.edu/archives/spr2010/entries/critical-theory/]).

3. The study of biopolitics originates in Michel Foucault's construction of bio-
power: a concept that articulates the manner in which the political sovereign employs
"numerous and diverse techniques for achieving the subjugation of bodies and the
control of populations." Michel Foucault, *The History of Sexuality, Volume 1: An Introduction* (trans. R. Hurley; New York: Vintage Books, 1978), 140.

4. The term "political landscape" replaces words such as "state" throughout this
paper, taking cues from Adam T. Smith's assertion that the focus on the state as the
archetypal typology of political construction fails to capture the fullness and diversity
of early complex polities. Referring to a political landscape opens the designation to
space, geography, societal/political construction, and many other factors comprising a
political entity. See Adam T. Smith, *The Political Landscape: Constellations of Authority
in Early Complex Polities* (Berkeley: University of California Press, 2003), 80.

the book of Lamentations, this essay engages power dynamics between the bare life figure of Daughter Zion and the sovereign power, which may be the Neo-Assyrian army, the Deity, or a combination of both.

2. AGAMBEN's *HOMO SACER*

The point of access for Agamben is ancient Western politics, about which he observes, "The fundamental categorical pair of Western politics is not that of friend/enemy but that of *bare life*/political existence, *zoē/bios*, exclusion/inclusion."[5] Agamben explains that the idea of *homo sacer* or bare life occupies an exceptional place in archaic Roman law, quoting *De verborum significatione* (*On the Significance of Words*) by second-century C.E. Roman grammarian Pompeius Festus, who wrote the following under the heading *sacer mons*:

> The sacred man is the one whom the people have judged on account of a crime. It is not permitted to sacrifice this man, yet he who kills him will not be condemned for homicide; in the first tributarian law, in fact, it is noted that "if someone kills the one who is sacred according to the plebiscite, it will not be considered homicide." This is why it is customary for a bad or impure man to be called sacred.[6]

The bare life figure is one whose life cannot be sacrificed, but whose life is expendable without consequence. Agamben explains that the violence, "the unsanctionable killing that, in his case, anyone may commit—is classifiable neither as sacrifice nor as homicide, neither as the execution of a condemnation to death nor as sacrilege."[7] This places the bare life figure outside of the juridical realms of religion and politics: "It indicates, rather, a life that may be killed by anyone—an object of a violence that exceeds the sphere of both law and of sacrifice."[8] The bare life model presents a stratum outside of the domain of sacred and secular jurisdiction, occupying a neutral space, where the community has the opportunity to cast aside

---

5. Giorgio Agamben, *Homo Sacer: Sovereign Power and Bare Life* (trans. D. Heller-Roazen; Stanford, Calif.: Stanford University Press, 1998), 8.

6. Ibid., 71.

7. Ibid., 82.

8. Ibid., 86.

blame and save itself from expending the energy to grieve or avenge the bare life figure.

What defines the bare life figure, then, is the double exclusion to which the figure is exposed: the figure is neither sacrificed nor murdered, essentially killed without satiation or consequence. When exempt from the sanctioned realms of divine and human law, this double exclusion allows for human action that is neither sacred nor profane. Agamben states that limits in the human sphere are traditionally understood within the rubric of divine sanction. Thus he renders the example of the bare life figure a complicated exception. He attempts further explanation for the construction of the bare life figure:

> We may even then advance a hypothesis: once brought back to his proper place beyond both penal law and sacrifice, *homo sacer* presents the originary figure of life taken into the sovereign ban and preserves the memory of the originary exclusion through which the political dimension was first constituted. The political sphere of sovereignty was thus constituted through a double exclusion, as an excrescence of the profane in the religious and of the religious in the profane, which takes the form of a zone of indistinction between sacrifice and homicide. *The sovereign sphere is the sphere in which it is permitted to kill without committing homicide and without celebrating a sacrifice, and sacred life—that is, life that may be killed but not sacrificed—is the life that has been captured in this sphere.*[9]

Abandoned without consequence to the community or recognition of its humanity through recompense, the *bare life* figure holds no account or recognition of its expendable life within religious, social, or political realms.

Certain characteristics of the *homo sacer* figure may vary according to context, but the following essential qualities appear in the *bare life* designation. First, the sacred quality of the bare life figure, that which sets the figure apart for condemnation to death, involves the judgment issued by the sovereign power (in the Roman text, literally, *enforced by the people*) against the *homo sacer*. The sovereign power imposes guilt upon the bare life figure, invoking political authority within the established juridical norms of the political landscape. The judgment issued by the sovereign power marks the individual as a bare life figure: sacred and set apart for death. Important to this concept of judgment is the sovereign power's abil-

---

9. Ibid., 83.

ity to render an individual guilty based on the sovereign's own dictum: the crime may simply be occupying a space, demographic, or status within the sovereign power's political landscape.

Although the sovereign power marks the bare life figure as set apart for death, the second essential quality of the bare life figure is that it cannot be sacrificed. When the bare life figure is given the status of sacrificial offering, the life serves a sacred purpose in relation to the institutional cult. As set apart for sacrifice, the individual is no longer a bare life figure, but a sacrificial figure, whose death satiates a deity or political entity. The life of the sacrificial figure is honorable in that it commemorates and satisfies with the offering of its death. The sacrificial figure does not stand in liminal space: the function of the sacrifice is directed at a particular political, religious, or social expectation. The death of the bare life figure does not commemorate a sacrifice or satiate a deity/political entity; its life is set apart solely for death.

The third quality of the bare life figure is its expendability without consequence. The bare life figure may be killed without consequence to the entity responsible for its death, whether this entity is the sovereign power or someone else. This quality reinforces the notion that the bare life figure is set apart solely for death. The quality of expendability reinforces the abject state of the bare life figure in that its body's existence is inconsequential.

One final quality of the bare life figure is its excluded social/political status within the political landscape. What is not clear from the ancient text describing the *homo sacer* is its status within the political landscape. Is the bare life figure an individual with citizenry, status, or rights within the political landscape, which are taken from the individual upon conviction by the sovereign power, or is this figure a refugee, alien, or one of other, lesser status? The text suggests that the bare life figure occupies space outside of citizenry and political rights, a space allowing for the easy expendability of its body by the sovereign power.

Implicit in the construction of the bare life figure is the role of the sovereign power. The sovereign power is the political entity whose authority controls the beings within its sovereign domain. Agamben states that inherent in the construction of sovereignty exists the paradox that "the sovereign is, at the same time, outside and inside the juridical order," or to speak as the sovereign, "I, the sovereign, who am outside the law, declare that there is nothing outside the law."[10] The sovereign power is the one with

---

10. Ibid., 15.

the authority to grant exception, and ultimately, the power to exclude.[11] The notion of exclusion links to the idea of *homo sacer* in that the bare life figure is defined by exclusion: exclusion from satiating a religious deity or cause through the act of sacrifice, exclusion from receiving vindication upon being put to death by another being (sovereign or otherwise), and exclusion from life, being a convicted, sacred human. The sovereign power controls inclusion and exclusion within the political landscape, rendering the bare life figure a liminal entity as one who cannot be sacrificed and is expendable without consequence.

3. Daughter Zion as *Homo Sacer*

The book of Lamentations describes the downfall of the kingdom of Judah and Jerusalem's experience in the midst of three waves of deportation by the Babylonian army from 597 to 581 b.c.e. Lamentations is a city lament[12] that characterizes the city of Jerusalem as Daughter Zion, a female person-ification that also appears in Psalms, Isaiah, Jeremiah, Micah, Zephaniah, and Zechariah. Unanimously categorized as a poetic text, the book of Lam-entations is often viewed as less important than other books in terms of the historicity of its images and depictions of exile, since some scholars per-ceive these images to be poetic hyperbole or the fabrication of an author's experience of emotional despair.[13] Daniel Smith-Christopher highlights the importance of understanding the felt reality of the exile in books such as Ezekiel and Lamentations, as doing so guards the reader against render-ing "chains and fetters, swords and suffering into sanitized metaphors that insulate the modern reader from the trauma of the historical exile as an event in the life of the Hebrews."[14] Reading the images of abject existence, images of conquest, displacement, rape, starvation, and cannibalism "is once again to recover Lamentations as a measure of the psychological and spiritual crisis of the exile."[15] Tension must be held between understanding the genre of Lamentations as a poetic city lament, and recognizing that the

---

11. Ibid., 17.

12. F. W. Dobbs-Allsopp, *Lamentations* (IBC; Louisville: Westminster John Knox, 2002), 7.

13. Daniel L. Smith-Christopher, *A Biblical Theology of Exile* (OBT; Minneapolis: Fortress, 2002), 76.

14. Ibid., 104.

15. Ibid.

images Lamentations describes recount many historically attested traumas of siege warfare.[16] According to Smith-Christopher, "To read these texts without some sense of the trauma of exile is tantamount to blaming the victims at the very least, and perhaps grossly misunderstanding much of the power of the text in its social context."[17] Smith-Christopher's emphasis on the power of the text in its social context is the focus of the following section, as images of Daughter Zion in exile depict the abject state of Israel as it suffers the devastating effects of siege warfare by the sovereign power, the Babylonian army.

While many figures in the Hebrew Bible portray either the guilty or the abject qualities of the bare life figure (abject encompassing inability to be sacrificed, expendability without consequence, and exclusion), such as the slayer who seeks asylum in cities of refuge in Deut 4:41–43 (guilty), or the Levite's concubine in Judg 19 (abject), the construction of one who stands both guilty and abject, whose death fails to satiate any grievance through sacrifice, whose death warrants no recompense, and whose inclusion is not recognized by the sovereign power, exists in the exiled image of Daughter Zion. First, Daughter Zion is guilty and admits her own guilt at the outset of Lamentations: "The LORD is in the right, for I have rebelled against his word, but hear, all you peoples, and behold my suffering; my young women and young men have gone into captivity" (1:18 NRSV). Second, Daughter Zion is unable to be sacrificed, as her condemnation and exile do not satiate the Deity or serve as a sacrifice to the sovereign power. Third, Daughter Zion is expendable without consequence. The Babylonian Empire receives no indictment or punishment by the Deity for the disposal of Daughter Zion's inhabitants. Finally, Daughter Zion is excluded and rendered a displaced person and refugee in Babylon. Even those inhabitants left in Jerusalem experience exclusion at the destruction of Babylonian siege warfare, sponsored by the Deity, which demolished the city and its temple (Lam 2:6–7).

Within the book of Lamentations, the abject construction of Daughter Zion and her physicality are central to the imagery of exile. Kathleen O'Connor observes, "By making Jerusalem a woman, the poetry gives her

---

16. Neo-Assyrian war reliefs depict kings seated on thrones surrounded by corpses of enemies, evoking images of trauma and horror to inflict terror onto the enemy. Amélie Kuhrt, *The Ancient Near East, c. 3000–330 B.C.* (2 vols.; London: Routledge, 1995), 2:517.

17. Smith-Christopher, *Biblical Theology of Exile*, 104.

personality and human characteristics that evoke pity or disdain from readers. ... Her female body is the object of disgrace and shaming, and her infidelities become shocking, intimate betrayals."[18] More than simply utilizing gendered imagery,[19] Lamentations depicts Daughter Zion as a woman who is simultaneously raped while her children are taken from her (1:10) and as a woman enduring such extreme starvation that she consumes her own offspring (4:10).

In Lamentations, the first bare life image of Daughter Zion as a woman who is simultaneously raped while her children are taken from her occurs in 1:10: "Enemies have stretched out their hands over all her precious things; she has even seen the nations invade her sanctuary, those whom you forbade to enter your congregation." The meaning of "precious things" (machmād/machmod) in verses 7, 10, and 11 is noteworthy and debated. Claus Westermann suggests that the word machmād describes the pillaging of temple treasures, but F. W. Dobbs-Allsopp and Tod Linafelt suggest that this word refers to the rape of Daughter Zion, since "precious things" carries a sexual connotation, with the euphemism of the temple representing a woman's body.[20] While this interpretation is certainly illuminating and useful, the reading posed by Charles William Miller presents another alternative.[21] Miller suggests that machmād in verses 10–11 means more than simply temple treasures or a woman's body; it refers to her children. Arguably, both theories apply to verse 10 that the "precious things" taken by the enemies are children in 10a (so Miller), and the sexual connotation of sanctuary invasion is physical rape in 10b (so Dobbs-Allsopp and Linafelt). Furthermore, the rendering of "precious things" as children in Lam 1:11 connects with Lam 4:10's discussion of children and starvation: "All her people groan as they search for bread; they trade their treasures for food to revive their strength. Look, O LORD, and see how worthless I have

---

18. Kathleen M. O'Connor, *Lamentations and the Tears of the World* (Maryknoll, N.Y.: Orbis, 2002), 14.

19. Cynthia Chapman writes on the gendered imagery of warfare, with important insight into the depiction of Israel as Daughter Zion, which for space constraints was not included in this essay. See Cynthia R. Chapman, *The Gendered Language of Warfare in the Israelite-Assyrian Encounter* (HSM 62; Winona Lake, Ind.: Eisenbrauns, 2004), 60–72.

20. Frederick W. Dobbs-Allsopp and Tod Linafelt, "The Rape of Zion in Thr 1,10," *ZAW* 113 (2001): 77–81.

21. Charles William Miller, "Reading Voices: Personification, Dialogism, and the Reader of Lamentations 1," *BibInt* 9 (2001): 393–408.

become" (1:11). Miller asserts that the rendering of *machmād* as "precious ones" or "children" follows the theme of Israel's utter desolation:

> One may observe, therefore, a significant movement in this speech from the opening line, where a foe stretches out his hand to commit gratuitous acts of violence against Jerusalem's precious things (that is, her people), to the closing line, where Jerusalem's people are so desperate for food that they are willing to sell, or perhaps eat, their own precious things (that is, their children) to stave off hunger.[22]

The fears expressed in Lam 1:11 that the heirs to the land, cult, traditions, and Deity are in danger of being consumed due to famine and starvation, come to fruition in 2:20 and 4:10. Lamentations 2:20 presents the first image of cannibalism: "Look, O LORD, and consider! To whom have you done this? Should women eat their offspring, the children they have borne? Should priest and prophet be killed in the sanctuary of the Lord?" Similarly, 4:9–10 depicts a warfare scene enacted by the sovereign power in its devastation of the city and of the livelihood of its inhabitants: a cannibalistic image of mothers cooking and consuming their own children:

> Happier were those pierced by the sword than those pierced by hunger, whose life drains away, deprived of the produce of the field. The hands of compassionate women have boiled their own children; they became their food in the destruction of my people.

Lamentations prompts the reader to react with horror to this extreme and grisly act through the language in chapter 1, which describes the "precious ones" as the most prized possessions of Daughter Zion. At first, the reader pities Daughter Zion for enduring the captivity of her children into the Babylonian exile, but the true horror happens when the account depicts mothers cooking and consuming their offspring.

Carol Meyers comments on the abject state of mothers who consume their offspring by stating, "Perhaps the greatest horror associated with the deprivations of war or other disaster is the way some people will eat human flesh in order to survive. That horror is particularly powerful if it involves parents cannibalizing their children."[23] Meyers notes that Leviticus and

---

22. Ibid., 399.

23. Carol Meyers, "Mother (and Father) Cannibalizing Their Daughters (and Sons)," in *Women in Scripture: A Dictionary of Named and Unnamed Women in the*

Deuteronomy contain the formulaic ancient Near Eastern curses concluding both books, which are standard threats describing what will befall those
who disobey the treaty between deity and humanity. Meyers concludes her
article with a poignant statement: "What could be a more fitting threat to
society than the specter of a woman, the creator of life, taking back into her
body as food the very ones to whom she has given birth!"[24]

Lamentations presents cannibalism of one's own offspring as the ultimate state of abject existence. The sovereign power exerts such force over
Daughter Zion through military siege that she is forced into the abject
states of sacrifice, expendability, and exclusion. Daughter Zion's children
are not sacrificed to the Deity as an offering to satiate or offer reparation;
they perish out of starvation or are eaten by their mothers due to the
extreme conditions inflicted upon the bare life figures by the sovereign
power. Daughter Zion's children are expendable without consequence.
They are led away to Babylon for servitude or eaten by their mothers; their
existence is inconsequential to the sovereign power. Lastly, Daughter Zion
is an exclusionary figure. Daughter Zion is left behind while her children
are taken away in exile to Babylon, she is raped and ravaged by the Babylonian army without rights to her own body, and she performs a social/
religious taboo of consuming her own children, all acts excluding Daughter Zion from agency and power. Ultimately, Daughter Zion depicts the
abject existence of the bare life figure at the hands of the sovereign power
through the images of rape and of losing her children to displacement
through exile, starvation, and cannibalism.

4. Who Is the Sovereign Power?

Identifying the sovereign power and bare life figure within a political
landscape may not be as straightforward as one initially perceives. Arguably, the people of Israel take on the role of the sovereign power in the
conquest narrative in the book of Joshua, which recounts that the armies
of Israel are instructed to adhere to the ban, *ḥērem*, devoting people,
livestock, and war plunder to destruction. In the account, Israel renders
the inhabitants of Canaan bare life figures whose bodies are expendable

---

Hebrew Bible, the Apocryphal/Deuterocanonical Books, and the New Testament (ed.
Carol Meyers, Toni Craven, and Ross S. Kraemer; Grand Rapids: Eerdmans, 2000),
214.

24. Ibid., 215.

without consequence. In another example, Israel as sovereign power over the political landscape of its northern and southern kingdoms displays a lack of regard for the inhabitants of the land, and Israel is accused of failing to care for its orphans, widows, and refugees (aliens)—the bare life individuals within its midst (Jer 7; 22). Certainly Israel has its own record of serving in the role of political sovereign, but in the book of Lamentations, Daughter Zion is the bare life figure, suffering under the hegemony of the sovereign power.

When one considers the political climate of the Babylonian exile, first impressions suggest that if Daughter Zion is the bare life figure, the political sovereign power is the Babylonian Empire. Just as the Roman Empire serves as the sovereign power over the *homo sacer*, so the Babylonian Empire serves as the sovereign power over Daughter Zion. The effects of siege warfare, the relocation of the elite populous, the plundering and destruction of the city and the temple, the destruction of crops and methods of livelihood left the remaining lowest classes of Judahites homeless, destitute, ailing, and suffering from extreme thirst and starvation.

However, the book of Lamentations directs its grievances to the Deity and not directly against the Babylonian Empire (Lam 1:12–16). The text frequently makes direct address to the Deity, acknowledging its sovereignty over the situation at hand (Lam 2:1–10). The experience of the Deity punishing the people by inflicting trauma is an interpretation of sovereign power that continues in present times, with condemnation of New Orleans by religious radicals for its "debauchery" through the devastation inflicted by Hurricane Katrina in 2005 or of Haiti for its practice of Voodoo, which radicals assert ushered in the Haiti Earthquake of 2010 as an act of judgment. Even in the contemporary era, the Deity is viewed as the source of trauma. One is left to wonder what is more traumatic: the sovereign power of the political authority or the sovereign power of the Deity? One could posit the idea of a double-sovereign, a sovereign power comprised of both the Deity and the political authority, but the difficulty in creating a binary relationship between religious and political authority is that rarely do such binary relationships exist in the ancient Near East. The political sovereign is the manifestation of the Deity of a particular landscape. The human political authority acts on behalf of the divine within the same construction of sovereign power.[25] While one cannot choose between the Deity or

---

25. Kuhrt, *Ancient Near East,* 2:507.

the Babylonian Empire as *the* sovereign power, Lamentations depicts siege warfare by the Babylonian Empire as divine judgment. In the same way that the sovereign power exercises agency over the body of the individual, the Deity is complicit with the Babylonian Empire, both serving the role of the sovereign power in dictating the fate of Daughter Zion as the bare life figure.

5. Conclusion

Central to Agamben's concern in engaging the sovereign power/bare life dichotomy is his regard for ethical, not purely political, study. Agamben scholar Leland de la Durantaye observes, "That ethics and politics should not be treated as separate and distinct disciplines is one of the guiding ideas in Agamben's philosophy."[26] Agamben's concern for the manner in which the sovereign power has the ability to exclude and to dehumanize the body by marking it as the *homo sacer* renders this construction useful for political landscapes outside of the ancient Roman context. Agamben's description of the power dynamics between the sovereign power and bare life figure, like the depiction of the exiled Daughter Zion in Lamentations, calls to mind the struggles of one contemporary bare life figure: the refugee or displaced person.

The comparison between the bare life figure and Lamentations shows the importance of the book as a text of the bare life experience, and not merely a hyperbolic text rife with flowery imagery of psychological despair. The images of siege warfare, namely, the ravaging of women's bodies through rape, displacement, starvation, and infant consumption, relate the text to both ancient and contemporary bare life figures. The cries of despair from Lamentations resonate with cries from the bare life figure in the Roman Empire, as well as with the cries of the bare life figure suffering from displacement and abject treatment at the hands of the sovereign power in contemporary times.

Bibliography

Agamben, Giorgio. *Homo Sacer: Sovereign Power and Bare Life*. Translated by D. Heller-Roazen. Stanford, Calif.: Stanford University Press, 1998.

---

26. Leland de la Durantaye, *Giorgio Agamben: A Critical Introduction* (Stanford, Calif.: Stanford University Press, 2009), 13.

———. *Means Without End: Notes on Politics.* Translated by V. Binetti and C. Casarino. Minneapolis: University of Minnesota Press, 2000.

Boyman, James. "Critical Theory." In *The Stanford Encyclopedia of Philosophy.* Edited by Edward N. Zalta. Spring 2012. Online: http://plato.stanford.edu/archives/spr2010/entries/critical-theory.

Chapman, Cynthia R. *The Gendered Language of Warfare in the Israelite-Assyrian Encounter.* HSM 62. Winona Lake, Ind.: Eisenbrauns, 2004.

Dobbs-Allsopp, F. W. *Lamentations.* IBC. Louisville: Westminster John Knox, 2002.

———. "Tragedy, Tradition, and Theology in the Book of Lamentations." *JSOT* 74 (1997): 29–60.

Dobbs-Allsopp, Frederick W., and Tod Linafelt. "The Rape of Zion in Thr 1,10." *ZAW* 113 (2001): 77–81.

Durantaye, Leland de la. *Giorgio Agamben: A Critical Introduction.* Stanford, Calif.: Stanford University Press, 2009.

Foucault, Michel. *The History of Sexuality, Volume I: An Introduction.* Translated by R. Hurley. New York: Vintage Books, 1978.

Gorst-Unsworth, Caroline. "Psychological Sequelae of Torture: A Descriptive Model." *British Journal of Psychiatry* 157 (1990): 475–80.

Kuhrt, Amélie. *The Ancient Near East, c. 3000–330 B.C.* 2 vols. London: Routledge, 1995.

Meyers, Carol. "Mother (and Father) Cannibalizing Their Daughters (and Sons)." Pages 214–15 in *Women in Scripture: A Dictionary of Named and Unnamed Women in the Hebrew Bible, the Apocryphal/Deuterocanonical Books, and the New Testament.* Edited by Carol Meyers, Toni Craven, and Ross S. Kraemer. Grand Rapids: Eerdmans, 2000.

Miller, Charles William. "Reading Voices: Personification, Dialogism, and the Reader of Lamentations 1." *BibInt* 9 (2001): 393–408.

O'Connor, Kathleen M. *Lamentations and the Tears of the World.* Maryknoll, N.Y.: Orbis, 2002.

Smith, Adam T. *The Political Landscape: Constellations of Authority in Early Complex Polities.* Berkeley: University of California Press, 2003.

Smith-Christopher, Daniel L. *A Biblical Theology of Exile.* OBT. Minneapolis: Fortress, 2002.

Exiling in America:
The American Myth and the Spectral Christ

Shelly Rambo

Current public debates about illegal immigration reveal a rhetorical bat-tleground over what constitutes American identity. Who is rightly an American? Who belongs here? In the midst of these debates, images of the founding spirit and vision of America surface; biblical images of ancient Israel surface as well. From its colonial beginnings, settlers imaged the new frontier as the promised land, their westward expansion as providen-tially ordained, and their identity as God's chosen people—the New Israel. A particular version of the history of ancient Israel is deeply woven into the fabric of America's national identity. In public discourse about who belongs, there is a surge of appeals to the origins of the country, espe-cially to its Christian foundations. For biblical scholars and theologians, it is timely to exegete the distinctively American version of these biblical stories, a version that has mixed the symbols and images of ancient Israel and the Jesus story in such a way as to produce a sacred version of national identity.[1] The danger of this national identity is that exile and exiling prac-tices are constitutive of the American myth.

Cultural historian Richard Slotkin notes that when the myth of Amer-ica is exposed as vulnerable to historical contingencies, two things can occur. This revelation, on the one hand, can open up a process of re-sto-rying our common life; on the other hand, it can spur attempts to declare a single story of pristine origins. The idea behind the latter is that if we can retrieve the true origins of the country, we can secure it against the historical contingencies. The danger of these retrievals lies in the surge

---

1. See Richard T. Hughes, *Myths We Live By* (Champaign: University of Illinois Press, 2004), and idem, *Christian America and the Kingdom of God* (Champaign: University of Illinois Press, 2009).

of exiling practices that enforce American identity to secure it at its most fragile point. The acts of displacing and exiling persons reveals the violent underbelly of the biblical narrative of America.

In this essay I reexamine the dynamics operating in this dominant American myth. I argue that, when the myth is at its most fragile, the underside of this story can be enacted—its exiling underside. I introduce the notion of the spectral, emerging within the field of literary criticism, to think about ways of disrupting and opening up the story of America. A spectral reading of the myth reveals, in the words of the poet Langston Hughes, an "America that never was America to me."[2] For a country that has patterned its story according to the biblical narrative of ancient Israel, an exiling narrative is the spectral underside of a self-professed New Israel. As new attention is being given to the biblical exile, I offer here a window into a spectral Christology that meets national dis-ease and opens to new ways of storying those exiled in America.

1. The Myth of America

> Like other modern nations, America was an imagined community. It was also a process of symbol making through which the norms and values of a modern culture were rationalized, spiritualized, and institutionalized.[3]

The writings of Puritans like Cotton Mather and John Winthrop suggest that America discovered itself in the Bible.[4] Sacvan Bercovitch, a scholar of

---

2. Langston Hughes, "Let America Be America Again," *The Collected Poems of Langston Hughes* (ed. Arnold Rampersad and David Roessel; New York: Vintage Books, 1994), 189.

3. Sacvan Bercovitch, *Rites of Assent: Transformations in the Symbolic Construction of America* (New York: Routledge, 1993), 12–13.

4. For works that represent the biblical imagery underlying the Puritan vision of America, see John Winthrop, "A Model of Christian Charity," in *God's New Israel: Religious Interpretations of American Destiny* (ed. Conrad Cherry; Englewood Cliffs, N.J.: Prentice-Hall, 1971), 39–43. See also Cotton Mather, *Magnalia Christi Americana, Books I and II* (ed. Kenneth B. Murdock with Elizabeth W. Miller; Cambridge, Mass.: Belknap Press, 1977). In his 1989 farewell address to the nation, Ronald Reagan invoked the Puritan vision: "In the past few days when I've been at that window upstairs, I've thought a bit of the 'shining city upon a hill.' The phrase comes from John Winthrop, who wrote it to describe the America he imagined. What he imagined was important because he was an early Pilgrim, an early freedom man. He journeyed here on what today we'd call a little wooden boat; and like the other Pilgrims, he was

Puritan literature, shows how the story of ancient Israel shaped the typology of the New World. He writes: "In the strange New World, the Puritans sanctified their society by the Bible's figures and types."[5] They founded their story in the larger biblical story of exodus and promise, of displacement and fulfillment. In *The Search for Christian America* Mark Noll, Nathan Hatch, and George Marsden note that Winthrop and the Puritans understood themselves in the following way: "They were becoming a people of God with a political identity, and so they stood in precisely the same relationship to God as did Old Testament Israel."[6] The biblical narrative gave spiritual purpose to the journey from old England to the new England. They interpreted their migration as an errand; the new settlers were not just moving from one place to another, but from a depraved Old World to the New Canaan.[7]

Although the American story was aligned with the exodus story of ancient Israel, the figure of Christ hovered over the frontier as well. In *Magnalia Christi Americanas*, Cotton Mather placed Christ at the center of history, his figure casting a shadow backward across the Hebrew Scriptures and forward to the end of time. Jesus was the figure of redemption, providing a way of reading the end of history while in the midst of history. It was as if the settlers bore the confidence of knowing their end, perceiving their present struggles through the lens of the biblical Kingdom of God already fulfilled in Christ. They never understood themselves as overtaking the western lands, but as reclaiming them as the land promised to them by God. Bercovitch writes:

> In other words, they used the biblical myth of exodus and conquest to justify imperialism before the fact. The Puritans sometimes appear as isolationists, but basically they were as eager as any other group of emi-

---

looking for a home that would be free" (online: http://www.ronaldreagan.com/sp_21 .html).

5. Sacvan Bercovitch, "The Biblical Basis of the American Myth," in *The Bible and American Arts and Letters* (ed. Giles Gunn; SBLBAC 3; Philadelphia: Fortress; Chico, Calif.: Scholars Press, 1983), 221.

6. Mark A. Noll, Nathan O. Hatch, and George M. Marsden. *The Search for Christian America* (Westchester, Ill.: Crossway Books, 1983), 34.

7. Bercovitch, *Rites of Assent*, 32.

grants for land and gain. The difference was that they managed more effectively to explain away their greed.[8]

Taking on the story of themselves as exiles of the old England, they never interpreted their displacement of indigenous peoples in the new land as such. The figure of Christ provided an alternative reading of their actions.

Bercovitch offers warnings about this American rendering of the biblical story. He notes that the American myth is peculiarly vulnerable to history, precisely because core to its myth is the notion of an overarching redemptive history; though living in it, they were able to transcend it.[9] The consequence of this is that while there was spiritual meaning and purpose infused in the American mythos, the story fostered inattention to historical contingencies. Redemption history mapped by America served to cover over the realities of history. Bercovitch notes that the history of the Israelites cannot sufficiently guide America. The danger, he says, is that when the contingencies of history are taken seriously, the American myth is continually questioned for its capacity to respond to those contingencies. He asks: "What happens when history severs the symbol from the nation, the logos from the logocracy? ... What happens when history separates 'America,' divine plan and all, from the United States?"[10] He notes that this will be a crisis point, a confrontation with the reality of the United States as opposed to the "America" of mythic origins. He writes: "What if the country were to be recognized for what it was, not a beacon to mankind ... but as just one more nation in the wilderness of this world?"[11] This "what if" is both an invitation and a warning.

As a cultural historian, Richard Slotkin moves in a similar direction in his trilogy surveying American literature. He traces the development of America through what he identifies as its dominant American myth—the myth of the frontier. First scripted according to the wilderness journey of the ancient Israelites, the myth of westward expansion, manifest destiny, and defeat of the savage natives supported the early ideology of America. Slotkin explains the relationship between myth and ideology in this way:

---

8. Sacvan Bercotich, *The Puritan Origins of the American Self* (New Haven: Yale University Press, 1975), 32.

9. Ibid., 35–71.

10. Bercovitch, "Biblical Basis," 228.

11. Bercovitch, *Rites of Assent,* 65.

Ideology is a basic system of concepts, beliefs and values that defines a society's way of interpreting its place in the cosmos and the meaning of its history. ... Myths are stories drawn from a society's history that have acquired through persistent usage the power of symbolizing that society's ideology and of dramatizing its moral consciousness.[12]

Myths story the nation. "The primary function of any mythological system," Slotkin says, is to "provide a people with meaningful emotional and intellectual links to its own past."[13] In the case of America, the story was given force by the sacred symbols.

Slotkin says that there are moments, however, when the myth breaks down, when the story no longer provides meaning. Crisis events such as bad harvests, plagues, and defeat in war call into question the validity of the guiding myth and call for a revisioning of the images and symbols. He identifies these as moments of cognitive dissonance. When this happens, Slotkin tells us, "a more or less deliberate and systematic attempt may be made to analyze and revise the intellectual moral content of the underlying ideology."[14] Vietnam was one such crisis that severely punctured the myth of the frontier. The events presented a crisis in America's mythology. Yet instead of a revisioning, Slotkin says, there was a shocking recrudescence of the frontier myth in the Reagan and Bush administrations.[15] The frontier symbols were problematically resuscitated, fueling a surge of patriotism without an aligning ideological grounding. According to Slotkin, these symbols did not help to make sense of the dis-ease of Americans who felt that the most fundamental principles of national ideology were in question. Instead of adjusting beliefs to the changing realities, we witnessed a repackaging of a mythic American past. The cost was that we failed to make meaning of the history.

---

12. Richard Slotkin, *Gunfighter Nation: The Myth of the Frontier in Twentieth-Century America* (Norman, Okla.: University of Oklahoma Press, 1998), 5.

13. Ibid., 638.

14. Ibid., 6.

15. Ibid., 652–53. Webster's online dictionary defines *recrudescence*, as "[a] return of something after a period of abatement." In the extended definition, it is described as the reappearance of a disease after it had been in remission (http://www.websters-online-dictionary.org/definitions/recrudescence). I will draw upon this imagery in the second half of the essay, noting that one of the aspects of the spectral is its appearance within contexts of *dis-ease*.

Slotkin wrote *Gunfighter Nation* in 1992. In 2009, journalist and war correspondent Chris Hedges fills in this picture in his book *The Empire of Illusion*. Hedges says that this moral revisioning process has been hijacked by our manufacturing of images. He writes:

> The country I live in today uses the same civic, patriotic, and historical language to describe itself, the same symbols and iconography, the same national myths, but only the shell remains. The America we celebrate is an illusion.[16]

New and meaningful myths cannot arise if we are held captive to the illusion of America. And violence is enacted in the process. Myths can, Slotkin says, reach out of the past to cripple, to incapacitate, and to strike down the living. Hedges's reflections on a post-9/11 America at war suggest that 9/11 serves as a present-day Vietnam, in which the myths of national identity are hollow and need to be revised. The recrudescence of the rhetoric of the founding fathers enacts practices of policing identity: Who is a true patriot?[17] In the charged religious climate of a post-9/11 world, the accompanying question is "Who is the true Christian?"

These authors expose the ways in which the myth of America can go awry, when it stops speaking meaningfully for, and to, human experiences. When the myths are resuscitated rather than revised, violence can occur. Recrudescent myths can be forced upon experiences and enforced in ways that attempt to secure those in power at the experience of the most vulnerable. In thinking about the resurgence of appeals to founding origins and to the claim of America's Christian character, these authors position us to think about the underside of these retrievals. The underside emerges precisely because American identity is perceived to be under attack. Increased enforcement of the category of the "illegal" corresponds with the perceived threat to those who define themselves as "legal."[18] To think

---

16. Chris Hedges, *The Empire of Illusion: The End of Literacy and the Triumph of Spectacle* (New York: Nation Books, 2009), 142.

17. The United States instituted the USA Patriot Act in the wake of the terrorist attacks of September 11, 2001. Signed into law on October 26, 2001, this legislation set into motion a surge of deportations of illegal immigrants who were suspected of terrorist-related acts.

18. For an excellent analysis of such enforcement in relation to US practices at Guantanamo Bay, see Judith Butler, *Precarious Life: The Powers of Mourning and Violence* (London: Verso Books, 2004).

about this threat, I want to turn to the concept of the spectral, to offer a lens through which to view the American frontier and its exiles.

2. SPECTRALITY

> History cannot be written without ghosts: the narratives of history must necessarily include ghosts—they will also be written by ghosts.[19]

The notion of the spectral has emerged in recent scholarship on several fronts. In continental philosophy, the term arises from Jacques Derrida's reflections in *Specters of Marx*.[20] While his reflections have been controversial among Marxists, his hauntology has provided a way of rethinking ontology, providing a figure that expresses the destabilization of being at the heart of deconstruction. The spectral, the ghost, the haunting, speaks to a "shadowy third" in which binaries no longer hold.[21] For Derrida the ghost is a deconstructive figure hovering in the between—between the dead and the living, between the past and the present, and between the material and the spiritual. The ghost represents, in Colin Davis's words, "a structural openness or address directed towards the living by the voices of the past or the not yet formulated possibilities of the future."[22]

Hauntology resonates with literary interpretations of trauma, in that the return of the past in the present reflects the problem at the heart of trauma: How is it that the past invades the present, appearing in the form of symptoms, or fragments, flashes, that cannot be registered as memories or as somatic memories inaccessible to language or straightforward cognitive retrieval? The event returns, but it does so in a form that is both familiar and unfamiliar. In postcolonial studies, hauntings signal the apparition of "once-hidden colonial histories."[23] Etymologically, haunting refers to providing a home, getting home; a spirit looking for a home, a

---

19. David Punter, "Spectral Criticism," in *Introducing Criticism at the 21st Century* (ed. Julian Wolfreys; Edinburgh: Edinburgh University Press, 2002), 262.

20. Jacques Derrida, *Specters of Marx: The State of the Debt, the Work of Mourning and the New International* (trans. Peggy Kamuf; New York: Routledge, 1994).

21. Jeffrey Andrew Weinstock, ed., *Spectral America: Phantoms and the National Imagination* (Madison, Wis.: University of Wisconsin Press, 2004), 4.

22. Colin Davis, "Hauntology, Spectres and Phantoms," *French Studies* 59 (2005): 379.

23. Michael F. O'Reilly, "Postcolonial Haunting: Anxiety, Affect, and the Situated Encounter," *Postcolonial Text* 3 (2007): 3.

resting place, or a residence. The specters of the colonial heritage return; the repressed colonial scene returns, but it does so in new forms that are difficult to recognize—transnational forms of hierarchy and oppression.[24]

In each of these, the spectral signals two things. First, the spectral signals dis-ease in the present. It points to shifts in how we interpret ourselves over time, especially in how we understand our relationship to history. Second, the spectral has ethical significance. The spectral return has an aspect of summons, of a reckoning that unearths the past violence; a "truth" that has been suppressed returns. The ghosts not only bring to light the past; they also demand something in the present. Avery Gordon refers to this as a "something to be done."[25] Gordon aptly points out that our accounts of history leave much unaccounted for. Ghosts provide a way of figuring the undertow of the story of history. In *Spectral America*, Jeffrey Weinstock suggests that this emphasis on the spectral says something about a current mood in our country. The current fascination with ghosts, he says, "arises out of a general postmodern suspicion of meta-narratives accentuated by millennial anxiety."[26] Attention to ghosts arises at the beginning of a new millennium, when America feels unsettled and anxious about its future. Ghosts return when the master story loses its omnipotence. The ghosts speak to the suppressed truths of the historical pasts that were often hidden under the cloak of the master story. Although the myth of America might be revealed as a dominant story that enacted the "exclusions and invisibilities of American history," it is naïve to think that this story can be replaced by other stories.[27] It is, in fact, deeply woven into American cultural identity. The ghosts tell us that master stories linger, inhabiting us in unanticipated ways. This interplay between the master narrative and the truths arising that unsettle the "truth" of that master narrative constitutes the spectral.

Fueled by both dis-ease and demand, the spectral reveals something important arising from the critical juncture that both Bercovitch and Slotkin name. At this juncture between retrenching and revising the American myth, between resuscitating old symbols and reimagining new ones, the spectral witnesses to violent practices on the underside of any domi-

---

24. Ibid., 2.

25. Avery F. Gordon, *Ghostly Matters: Haunting and the Sociological Imagination* (Minneapolis, Minn.: University of Minnesota Press, 2008).

26. Weinstock, *Spectral America*, 5.

27. Ibid., 6.

nant myth. The nostalgia spurred by anxiety threatens to turn into seemingly securing, yet violent, practices of national identity. Slotkin notes that America "is at a 'liminal' moment in our cultural history."[28] In this moment, the spectral can function to disturb the illusions of America and call for new myths, new ways of narrating our collective life. The truths of the past cannot be contained; there never was one story. The ghosts whisper, "America never was America to me."

3. A Spectral Reading

In his 1938 poem, "Let America Be America Again," poet and novelist Langston Hughes opens with what appears to be nostalgia for an America of the past: "Let America be the dream it used to be. Let it be the pioneer on the plain / Seeking a home where he himself is free."[29] The poet calls up the myth of the frontier, drawing on classic national symbols of pioneers, of the land of the free, of the "land that I love." Yet in parentheses following each of the three patriotic stanzas invoking the myth of America, the poet offers a statement in the singular. Following stanza one, he writes: "(America never was America to me)." "(It never was America to me)" follows stanza two, and "(There's never been equality for me/Nor freedom in this 'homeland of the free')" follows stanza three.[30] The tripartite invocations sound like a prophetic call for America to return to its origins, to turn back to what is true about itself. Turning back suggests that America has lost its way and that, if it just turns to the past, it will find itself again.

Yet the apparent intentions of the poet come to a halt with the parentheses. The story of the nation and its pristine past is disrupted by this lone voice. America as it once was did not account for this speaker who arises from the margins of the poem to expose the mythic past. The effect of these stanzas and parenthetical lines is to reveal America as an exclusive term, thereby provoking the question, "Whose America?" This lone voice presents another history, the parenthetical note in America's master story. If we read these lines through a spectral lens, we can think of the ghosts of the past, the silenced voices on the underside of history, calling out here. The repetition—"never was"—punctures the pristine myth. Following these stanzas, two questions appear in italics. These lines respond to this

28. Slotkin, *Gunfighter Nation*, 654.
29. Hughes, "Let America Be America Again," 189.
30. Ibid., 189–90.

voice, calling back: "*Say, who are you that mumbles in the dark? / And who are you that draws your veil across the stars?*"[31] It is as if the poet is speaking to the parenthetical voice, calling it out of hiding. The parenthetical refusals to transform into the first person—"I am." Hughes goes on to identify them as the poor white, the Negro, the native ("the red man"), and the immigrant. He names these, the humble, the hungry, and the lowest, as the dreamers, giving them voice: "I am the farmer, bondsman to the soul. / I am the worker sold to the machine. / I am the Negro, servant to you all."[32] Those who were never counted in the dream of America suddenly become dreamers here. The voice shifts again, as if the original narrator returns. "O, let America be America again— /the land that never has been yet— / And yet must be—the land where every man is free."[33] Having heard these voices, the call changes, not to a vision of the past but to a renarrated land named for those whose work literally made America.

There is a truthtelling in this poem, a reckoning, in which ghosts of the past refuse the gloss of mythic pasts. Appeals to the American dream will now come with an accompanying question: Whose dream? When America is called the land of the free, we ask, "At whose expense?" This spectral disturbance also bears an invitation to re-mythologize. Remaking America calls for new symbols and new images. The land, the endless plain, the grassy stretch, cannot be contained in this myth of the frontier. Hughes's poem figures the spectral voices as always present, yet hidden, in the enclosed parentheses of a dominant national narrative. Featuring the voices of the exiles, Hughes shows the ways in which the myth of America is supported by the figures of those who were not counted as Americans. The underside of the myth is that the myth is only possible through exclusionary practices.

4. The Spectral Christ in America

In the Puritan writings, the story of America is a mixture of symbols from the Hebrew and Christian scriptures. Jesus is often figured in those Puritan accounts as the redemptive figure hovering over the American landscape, casting his shadow over the past and the future, as if to read redemption back through history and forward to the millennium. In John Gast's clas-

---

31. Ibid., 190.
32. Ibid.
33. Ibid., 191.

sic picture of westward expansion, "American Progress," a large glowing angelic figure is suspended above the frontier.[34] Her name is America, and her body faces west, signaling a forward, progressive movement; she is both guardian and guiding angel to the settlers below. Gast provides a visual representation of manifest destiny. But other figures are also underfoot; the displaced native peoples are shown fleeing the scene, as the stagecoaches and trains—the marks of civilization—threaten to overtake them. In this figure, the theological concepts of sovereignty and providence, primal innocence and divine blessing are conveyed. These are almost inextricable from the American myth. If Gast's painting were overtly theologized in accordance with the Puritan ideology, we could read this angelic feminine figure as the figure of Jesus, the Christ, hovering over America.

In a classic reading, Gast provides a visual depiction of a divinely ordained theology that operates above the land; it is a Christology that can provide divine justification for violence on the ground below. Yet if we conceive of the spectral Christ not as the fulfillment of the story of America but as the Christ who, in Hughes's language, "has not yet been," the Christ who "has yet to be," we can image a theology that calls into question the practices of a self-proclaimed Christian nation. The spectral Christ haunts American Christianity. This is the haunting figure, the Savior who never was a Savior to many who lived in the United States. Read through a spectral lens, this spectral being conjures up a different theology of the frontier. She hovers over the dis-ease, making demands. This ghostly Christ witnesses to the redemptive shadow cast over the American landscape. In his name, violence was wielded. The spectral Christ witnesses the underside of the myth of American progress in whose name the land below is ravaged. This figure, instead of hovering over the land as a protective figure blessing the westward journey, is conjuring up the voices silenced by the settler story. The hovering is not a providential presence but a reckoning absence.

The concept of the spectral is emerging in the works of Christian theologians attentive to the colonial dynamics underlying a master story of Christianity.[35] They appeal to the haunting of the Christian story to

---

34. American painter John Gast painted "American Progress" in 1872. Online: http://www.webpages.uidaho.edu/~rfrey/422gast.htm.

35. Mark Lewis Taylor, *The Theological and the Political: On the Weight of the World* (Minneapolis: Fortress, 2011); Mayra Rivera, "Ghostly Encounters: Spirits, Memory, and the Holy Ghost," in *Planetary Loves: Spivak, Postcoloniality, and Theol-*

develop a theology that speaks to issues such as forced migration, deportation, and war. Calling attention to those exiled in the name of America, I invite us to imagine a spectral Christ who reckons with America, hovering at the margins of the master narrative, whispering "(Jesus never was Jesus to me)." In liberation theology, Jesus is often figured as the exiled one. In what is often referred to as a "theology from below," he is interpreted as the immanent God who is revealed in the movement of communities in solidarity with the oppressed. By contrast, a "theology from above" emphasizes a transcendent God, figured as the Christ who mediates salvation. A hovering, spectral Christ is neither of these, but instead occupies a liminal position. A spectral Christology haunts these familiar divisions, as if to invoke the Christ who has yet to find form but demands a form congruent with historical realities. This Christ might be envisioned as the spectral body roaming the American territory, witnessing the undertow of the myth of America, and conjuring up new ways of being.

Bibliography

Bercovitch, Sacvan. "The Biblical Basis of the American Myth." Pages 219–29 in *The Bible and American Arts and Letters*. Edited by Giles Gunn. SBLBAC 3. Philadelphia: Fortress; Chico, Calif.: Scholars Press, 1983.

———. *The Puritan Origins of the American Self*. New Haven: Yale University Press, 1975.

———. *Rites of Assent: Transformations in the Symbolic Construction of America*. New York: Routledge, 1993.

Butler, Judith. *Precarious Life: The Powers of Mourning and Violence*. London: Verso Books, 2004.

Davis, Colin. "Hauntology, Spectres and Phantoms." *French Studies* 59 (2005): 373–79.

Derrida, Jacques. *Specters of Marx: The State of the Debt, the Work of Mourning and the New International*. Translated by Peggy Kamuf. New York: Routledge, 1994.

Gordon, Avery F. *Ghostly Matters: Haunting and the Sociological Imagination*. Minneapolis: University of Minnesota Press, 2008.

Hedges, Chris. *The Empire of Illusion: The End of Literacy and the Triumph of Spectacle*. New York: Nation Books, 2009.

Hughes, Langston. "Let America Be America Again." Pages 189–91 in *The Collected Poems of Langston Hughes*. Edited by Arnold Rampersad and David Roessel. New York: Vintage Books, 1994.

ogy (ed. Stephen D. Moore and Mayra Rivera; New York: Fordham University Press, 2011), 118–35.

Hughes, Richard T. *Christian America and the Kingdom of God.* Champaign: University of Illinois Press, 2009.

———. *Myths We Live By* . Champaign: University of Illinois Press, 2004.

Mather, Cotton. *Magnalia Christi Americana, Books I and II.* Edited by Kenneth B. Murdock with Elizabeth W. Miller. Cambridge, Mass.: Belknap Press, 1977.

Noll, Mark A., Nathan O. Hatch, and George M. Marsden. *The Search for Christian America.* Westchester, Ill.: Crossway Books, 1983.

O'Reilly, Michael F. "Postcolonial Haunting: Anxiety, Affect, and the Situated Encounter." *Postcolonial Text* 3 (2007): 1–15.

Punter, David. "Spectral Criticism." Pages 259–78 in *Introducing Criticism at the 21st Century.* Edited by Julian Wolfreys. Edinburgh: Edinburgh University Press, 2002.

Rivera, Mayra. "Ghostly Encounters: Spirits, Memory, and the Holy Ghost." Pages 118–35 in *Planetary Loves: Spivak, Postcoloniality, and Theology.* Edited by Stephen D. Moore and Mayra Rivera. New York: Fordham University Press, 2011.

Slotkin, Richard. *Gunfighter Nation: The Myth of the Frontier in Twentieth-Century America.* Norman, Okla.: University of Oklahoma Press, 1998.

Taylor, Mark Lewis. *The Theological and the Political: On the Weight of the World.* Minneapolis: Fortress, 2011.

Weinstock, Jeffrey Andrew, ed. *Spectral America: Phantoms and the National Imagination.* Madison, Wis.: University of Wisconsin Press, 2004.

Winthrop, John. "A Model of Christian Charity." Pages 39–43 in *God's New Israel: Religious Interpretations of American Destiny.* Edited by Conrad Cherry. Englewood Cliffs, N.J.: Prentice-Hall, 1971.

"There Was No Place for Cholly's Eyes to Go": (Black-on-Black) Crime and (Black Male) Displacement in Toni Morrison's *The Bluest Eye*

Nghana Lewis

By the rivers of Babylon we sat and wept
When we remembered Zion. ...
How can we sing the songs of the Lord
While in a foreign land? (Ps 137:1, 4, NIV)

The history and structure of the Jewish diaspora, along with the related themes of forced exile, resistance, resilience, and liberation, have long been used as models for shaping and analyzing black people's experiences in America.[1] Psalm 137, in its expression of the paradox of despair, which, on one hand, indicates that the conditions of displacement from their homeland strip exiles in Babylonian captivity of the will to sing and, on the other hand, voices these conditions in song, is among the most widely invoked biblical passages in black expressive culture.[2] The frequency of this invocation has, on one level, been attributed to the centrality of the oral tradition in general and songs in particular to the preservation of values and beliefs transported by enslaved Africans to the Americas."[3] On another level, the

---

1. See Barbara Christian, "Fixing Methodologies: *Beloved*," in *Female Subjects in Black and White: Race, Psychoanalysis, Feminism* (ed. Elizabeth Abel, Barbara Christian, and Helene Moglen; Berkeley: University of California Press, 1997), 364; and Adam Zachary Newton, *Facing Black and Jew: Literature as Public Space in Twentieth-Century America* (Cambridge: Cambridge University Press, 1999), 14.

2. George Bornstein, "The Colors of Zion: Black, Jewish, and Irish Nationalism at the Turn of the Century," *Modernism/Modernity* 12.3 (2005): 370.

3. W. E. B. Du Bois, *The Souls of Black Folk* (New York: Penguin, 1996; orig., 1903), 17.

invocation has served as a reminder of the historical effects of displacement on black people.[4]

From the arrival of the first enslaved Africans to the Americas in the late fifteenth century C.E. through today, displacement is a concept that has factored centrally into the self and community formation processes of black people. As early as 1783, free and newly emancipated blacks who remained loyal to the British government throughout the Revolutionary War organized en masse to negotiate with English authorities for their return to Africa, the continent from which most of their ancestors arrived in the Americas as slaves.[5] A little over a hundred years later, at the dawning of the twentieth century, the Pan-Africanist philosophy of Marcus Garvey called for both literal and symbolic repatriation among people of African descent throughout the world in opposition to racism and colonialism, the legacies of American slavery and European imperialism. The self-imposed exiles of luminaries W. E. B. Du Bois and James Baldwin, coupled with the momentum fostered by the Black Power and Black Arts Movements of the 1960s and 1970s, mark the latter half of the twentieth century as an especially significant period in the evolution of black people's experiences of displacement. Like Native, Jewish, and Irish Americans, blacks' experiences of displacement are paradoxically characterized by a sense of "upheaval, dislocation and loss of connection" as well as sustained efforts to claim and affirm cohesive cultural identities and histories in articulation with discreet geographic locations.[6] It is no surprise, therefore, that displacement is a concept that fundamentally drives black American cultural production and thus is traceable in the most time-honored novels of the black literary tradition.

This essay offers new ways of thinking about the concept of displacement in shaping black people's experiences through an analysis of Toni Morrison's classic 1970 novel *The Bluest Eye*. Although this article may seem far afield from the others in the present volume, my analysis here provides another resource by which biblical scholars can reconsider the

---

4. Frederick Douglass, "What to the Slave Is the Fourth of July?" Online: http://teachingamericanhistory.org/library/index.asp?document=162.

5. Graham Russell Hodges, Susan Hawkes Cook, and Alan Edward Brown, *The Black Loyalist Directory: African Americans in Exile after the American Revolution* (New York: Garland, 1996), xii.

6. Alicia Kent, *African, Native, and Jewish American Literature and the Reshaping of Modernism* (New York: Palgrave, 2007), 115.

variegated dynamics of displacement that attend to the historical realities and literary representations of the Babylonian exile. The kind of wide-ranging interdisciplinary perspective provided by reading this essay in the context of more explicit examinations of Judean experience can provide biblical scholars with new sets of questions and new prerogatives, especially for exploring the literary representations of exile scattered throughout the biblical literature and the often under-considered social and psychological aspects of all experiences of displacement and deportation.

That *The Bluest Eye* explores the concept of displacement manifested in its widely analyzed opening with the primer text, "Here is the house. It is green and white. It has a red door. It is very pretty. Here is the family. Mother, Father, Dick, and Jane live in the green-and-white house. They are very happy."[7] Repeated three times in the opening, this text becomes increasingly incoherent, as the words run together, effecting, in the second iteration, a kind of stream-of-consciousness and, in the third iteration, a dizzying, disorienting sense of disruption, dislocation, and downward spiraling. The primer text provides the larger context within which characters struggle to situate themselves, and this struggle is the vantage point from which much of *The Bluest Eye*'s criticism of mainstream American standards of language, style, beauty, and location is offered. Indeed, as told, the story is fundamentally a series of childhood memories compiled and conveyed through the first person narrator Claudia MacTeer and through the third person omniscient point of view. Claudia's memories of growing up in an environment where "love, thick and dark as Alaga syrup, eased up into" the cracked windows of her bedroom and permeated throughout her house gives relief to signature strategies of resistance and resilience deployed in response to black people's historic experiences of displacement.[8]

However, Claudia's context starkly contrasts with the environments into which other central characters in the novel are born. As readers, we are, for example, drawn into Pecola Breedlove's story through Claudia's memories of Pecola's desire to see the world through the blue eyes of white baby dolls, Shirley Temple, and the little white girl on Mary Jane candy wrappers. Cat Moses argues that the initial privileging of Claudia's point of view indicates that the novel is as much about "a young black woman's

---

7. Toni Morrison, *The Bluest Eye* (New York: Washington Square Press, 1970), 7.
8. Ibid., 14.

survival" during the era of Jim Crow as it is about the racial antagonism and hostility of this historical period that led to the physical violation, emotional breakdown, and spiritual defeat of the child Pecola.[9] Expanding the focal point of the novel still further, Marilyn Mehaffy argues that Pauline Breedlove, Pecola's mother, images an important critique of the trade card industry which, from the latter part of the nineteenth century through the first half of the twentieth century, mass marketed "the United States as a specifically white, consumer nation" through visual narratives of black women conforming to the myth of the southern mammy.[10] So entrenched are the perspectives of female characters in the critical history of *The Bluest Eye* that Geraldine, among the "brown girls" from the South to whom only a few pages in the novel are devoted, has given fodder to the notion that *The Bluest Eye* issues an indictment to the 1954 Supreme Court opinion in *Brown v. Board of Education*, a watershed opinion that paradoxically used social science theories of black cultural deficiencies to argue for the integration of public schools.[11] My reading of *The Bluest Eye* departs from convention by focally shifting from the female's to the male's point of view in an effort to broaden understanding of the multiple, complex ways the novel anchors thinking about black people's experiences of displacement *within* black communities. Fueled by the gains of the civil rights, black arts, and black power movements of the 1960s and 1970s, *The Bluest Eye* contributed upon its release to the naming and undoing of the historically debilitating psychological effects on black people of white standards of physical beauty, desirability, and location.[12] Morrison conceded this rhetorical objective in a 1974 interview for *Black World*, when she observed, "The concept of physical beauty as a *virtue* is one of the dumbest, most pernicious and destructive ideas of the Western world, and we should have nothing to do with it. Physical beauty has nothing to do with our past, present or future. Its absence or presence was only important to *them*, the white people who used it for anything

---

9. Cat Moses, "The Blues Aesthetic in Toni Morrison's *The Bluest Eye*," *African American Review* 33.4 (1999): 623.

10. Marilyn Mehaffy, "Advertising Race/Raceing Advertising: The Feminine Consumer(-Nation), 1876–1900," *Signs* 23.1 (1997): 133.

11. Christopher Douglas, "What *The Bluest Eye* Knows about Them: Culture, Race, and Identity," *American Literature* 78 (2006): 144.

12. Farah Jasmine Griffin, "Thirty Years of Black American Literature and Literary Studies: A Review," *Journal of Black Studies* 35 (2004): 169.

they wanted."[13] The persistence of white normative standards in advertising, movie and television industries, and public education today, affirms the novel's continued relevancy to discussions of the function of race as a physical, cultural, and social construct. By focally shifting to the male point of view, however, I argue that seeing race in *The Bluest Eye* casts important light on other problems related to the social and cultural positioning and location of black people to which the novel spoke in 1970 and continues to speak in the new millennium. The most important of these, especially for the examination of representations of forced displacement in literary works, are black male identity and black-on-black crime. The character that brings these related phenomena into sharpest focus is Cholly Breedlove.

Cholly's experiences of displacement provide frameworks for analyzing problems which, although intricately connected to the legacy of American racism, threatened to cripple, if not completely destroy, black communities from within. The social unrest that defined America throughout the 1960s and 1970s has conventionally been represented in terms of black people's struggle to achieve the same opportunities as their white counterparts for participation in political processes, as well as equal protection under the law. Although subject to relatively less scholarly attention, the 1960s and 1970s have also been read against the backdrop of efforts undertaken by veteran leaders and emerging scholars of the post-civil rights black American experience to identify and come to terms with the destructive effects of displacement on the identity formation of young black men. In 1962, sociologist Kenneth B. Clark issued a report to President Lyndon B. Johnson's Committee on Juvenile Delinquency titled *Youth in the Ghetto: A Study of the Consequence of Powerlessness and a Blueprint for Change.* This ethnographic study examined the conditions in which black youth in Harlem, New York were living as background for the development of a comprehensive program to assist in wresting these youth from what Clark characterized as "institutionalized pathology. ... Self-perpetuating pathology," in which, Clark insisted, one pathology "breeds another." Children born into this environment are "more likely to come into a world of broken homes and illegitimacy; drug addiction, and criminal violence. Neither instability nor crime can be controlled by police

---

13. Toni Morrison, "Behind the Making of *The Black Book*," *Black World* 23 (February 1974): 89.

vigilance or by reliance on the alleged deterring forces of legal punishment, for the individual crimes are to be understood more as symptoms or
the contagious sickness of the community itself than as the result of inherent criminal or deliberate viciousness."[14] A little over ten years after Clark
issued his report, civil rights activist Roosevelt Dunning coined a term for
the problem Clark described, when he alleged, "For too long, treatment of
the subject of black-on-black crime could be likened to the retarded child
of the family in past years. In public, he was spoken of in whispers, and
tolerated by his family as a cross to bear. Had that public or that family
had the understanding and fortitude to confront the problem, I believe
that years of torment could have been averted. In the context of black-on-
black crime, I contend that you, as concerned, responsible citizens, have
the inherent capability of dealing with this cancer that threatens to engulf
our community."[15] If Morrison was not familiar with the particulars of
Clark's and Dunning's findings, she was at least familiar with their general
objectives. For as activists Jean Carey Bond and Patricia Peery pointed out
in the same year that *The Bluest Eye* was published, "In black communities
all over the country today, intelligent and imaginative people are discussing the political, economic, and culture aspects of the Black Liberation
Struggle."[16] *The Bluest Eye* contributes to this dialogue by pointing out the
ways in which black-on-black crime prohibits black people from experiencing true freedom. This interpretation of the novel extends in large part
from a close reading of Cholly's characterization.

That Morrison cultivates this discourse through Cholly Breedlove
makes sense. Historically, the primary victims and perpetrators of black-
on-black crime have been young black men. In fact, black-on-black
crime is a term that has come to be nearly synonymous with black male
youth violence. Implicit in the term is the notion that such acts of violence are highly localized, occurring within communities that are racially

---

14. Kenneth B. Clark, *Youth in the Ghetto: A Study of the Consequence of Powerlessness and a Blueprint for Change* (New York: Harlem Youth Opportunities, 1964),
81.

15. Roosevelt Dunning, "Black-on-Black Crime: Why Do We Tolerate the Lawless?" sermon delivered at St. John's Baptist Church, New York, N.Y., December 7,
1975; repr. in *Vital Speeches of the Day* 42 (1975–1976): 215–18.

16. Jean Carey Bond and Patricia Perry, "Is the Black Male Castrated?" in *The
Black Woman: An Anthology* (ed. Toni Cade Bambara; New York: Washington Square
Press, 1970), 141.

homogenized, socioeconomically destitute, politically disenfranchised, and socially dispossessed. The term also implicates larger issues of displacement and isolation that have historically given definition to the particular experiences of black American male youth. The most up-to-date community-contextual and individual-level data from the National Longitudinal Study of Adolescent Health indicate that black males disproportionately fall victim to, or perpetrate, black-on-black crime as a result of encounters with violence well before they reach the age of employment, and that these encounters typically take place within a two-mile radius of their primary dwellings. Data from a psychological study which looked at the relationship between chronic exposure to violence and post-traumatic stress disorder (PTSD) among a nonrandom sample of black youth aged seven to eighteen, found that black boys were more likely than black girls to be victims of and witnesses to violent acts.[17] A related study concluded that exposure to violence increased black male youths' "susceptibility to developmental harm and posttraumatic stress,"[18] as well as the likelihood of perpetrating a violent crime.[19] Psychologists, sociologists, and economists alike have attributed the dismal plight of the black male in America today to compounded effects of American racism, the absence of "competent and self-actualized" black images in American popular culture, and the result of willful self-neglect and abuse in the absence of strong social networks and kinship support.[20] In a 2007 address before a Joint Economic Committee hearing in Washington, D.C., Ronald Mincy, professor of social policy at Columbia University, reported that disproportionate rates of unemployment, high school dropout, and incarceration among black men between the ages of sixteen and twenty-five have a direct corollary in black male youth's predisposition

---

17. Kathleen Fitzpatrick and Jan Boldizar, "The Prevalence and Consequences of Exposure to Violence among African American Youth," *Journal of the American Academy of Child Adolescent Psychiatry* 32 (1993): 425.

18. James Garbarino, *Raising Children in a Socially Toxic Environment* (Chicago: Jossey-Bass, 1999), 49.

19. Robert Durant, Robert Pendergrast, and Chris Cadenhead, "Exposure to Violence and Victimization and Fighting Behavior by Urban Black Adolescents," *Journal of Adolescent Health* 15 (1994): 313.

20. Ronald B. Mincy, "Testimony of Ronald B. Mincy, Joint Economic Committee, March 8, 2007, Washington, D.C." Online: http://jec.senate.gov/archive/Hearings/03.08.07%20African-American%20Male%20Unemployment/Testimony%20-%20Mincy.pdf.

to early encounters with and perpetuation of violence.[21] What is striking to me, therefore, about a novel that is clearly interested in addressing
the relationship among displacement, identity formation, and violence
among black youth is that little to no substantive scholarly consideration
has been given to the specific effects of violence on Cholly, *The Bluest
Eye*'s primary black male character.

Ironically, it was in a discussion of her Pulitzer prize-winning novel
Beloved that Morrison characterized the foundation upon which I would
argue that any understanding of the importance of the interchange among
black male behavior, identity formation, displacement, and black-on-
black crime in *The Bluest Eye* must build. Morrison said that when she
began writing *Beloved*, she thought she was writing a "very contemporary
story. I wanted to write about self-murder," she explained, "the ways in
which we can sabotage ourselves with the best of all possible intentions."[22]
When mapped onto a character who, because of his sex, race, and minor
status can neither alter nor sufficiently comprehend the social, economic,
and historical forces shaping his life, the harrowing situations in which we
encounter Cholly in the novel are more numbing than shocking. Signifying on several classic representations of black manhood and discourses on
black masculinity in the canon of American literature, including Richard
Wright's *Black Boy/American Hunger*, Ralph Ellison's *Invisible Man*, and
James Baldwin's *Blues for Mister Charlie*, Morrison's characterization of
Cholly does not duplicate narrative techniques that allow Wright's, Ellison's, and Baldwin's protagonists to achieve self-actualization both apart
from and in relation to their communities. Instead, Cholly embodies and
voices the "ghastly," "unspeakable" crimes, the acceptance of which Baldwin once said, "would lead, literally, to madness,"[23] as a means of confronting and remedying conditions that both literally and symbolically trap
disproportionate numbers of black male youth in vicious cycles of self-
destruction. A close examination of the basic elements underlying Cholly's
characterization reveals how these processes work.

---

21. Ibid.

22. Bonnie Angelo, "The Pain of Being Black: An Interview with Toni Morrison,"
in *Conversations with Toni Morrison* (ed. Danille K. Taylor-Guthrie; Jackson: University Press of Mississippi, 1994), 255–56. Online: http://www.time.com/time/commu-
nity/pulitzerinterview.html.

23. James Baldwin, *Blues for Mr. Charlie* (2nd ed.; New York: Vintage, 1995), xiv.

Cholly's experiences, like Claudia's and Pecola's, underscore the coalescing impact on their identity formations of the larger and specific contexts into which black children in America are born. In Cholly's case, the struggle to situate himself in the mainstream is compounded by his inability, over the course of his life, to find sanctuary in the context of his immediate family or extended black community. The effects of tripled displacement and isolation thus render Cholly vulnerable, and his vulnerability both propels and explains his violence. Among critics, Cholly has been assessed in the context of his physical abuse of his wife Pauline and sexual abuse of his daughter Pecola. The focal shift to Cholly's point of view allows his characterization to resonate beyond the discursive frameworks of domestic violence and incest to speak to the crisis of black-on-black crime which, by its very definition, mandates consideration of the cross-currents of racialized violence. That *The Bluest Eye* is concerned to address black-on-black crime is apparent, given the interrelations among issues of isolation, identity formation, and violence in the novel's construction of community as well as the role the larger community plays in sealing Pecola's tragic fate. However, this nexus has largely been unaccounted for in critical assessments of Cholly's fate.

The handful of critics who have given Cholly more than casual consideration view him as an equally pitiable and contemptible character. As one critic states, "Cholly is the poor, uneducated black American male doomed to the underclass. ... Unfathered, unsocialized, and 'castrated' early in his youth by an encounter with white men ... he is a social derelict, as much outside the system of race, class, and gender privilege as Pecola."[24] At the same time, argues another, because Cholly breaks "the rules of the community" by raping Pecola, he must be made to "pay for his transgression."[25] Critics have dealt extensively with the scene of Pecola's rape, viewing it as the force that ultimately drives her into the state of madness that we find her in at the novel's conclusion. It is perhaps in so closely attending to the effects of this event on Pecola that critics have neither adequately nor accurately accounted for its effects on Cholly. At the end of the novel,

---

24. Rafael Pérez-Torres, "Tracing and Erasing: Race and Pedagogy in *The Bluest Eye*," in *Approaches to Teaching the Novels of Toni Morrison* (ed. Nellie Y. McKay and Kathryn Earle; New York: The Modern Language Association of America, 1997), 24.

25. Kathryn Earle, "Teaching Controversy: *The Bluest Eye* in the Multicultural Classroom," in McKay and Earle, *Approaches to Teaching the Novels of Toni Morrison*, 31.

we know that Cholly is dead, but his death is never explicitly or implicitly linked to his violation of Pecola. Instead the original scene is recalled,
extended, and assessed near the end of Pecola's dialogue with her mad self
in a manner that symbolically implicates the entire Breedlove family in the
initial violation:

I wonder what it would be like.
Horrible.
Really?
Yes. Horrible.
Then why didn't you tell Mrs. Breedlove?
I did tell her!
*I don't mean about the first time, I mean about the second time, when you
were sleeping on the couch.*
I wasn't sleeping! I was reading!
You don't have to shout.
You don't understand anything, do you? She didn't even believe me when
I told her.
So that's why you didn't tell her about the second time?
She wouldn't have believed me then either.
You're right. No use telling her when she wouldn't believe you.
That's what I'm trying to get through your thick head.
O.K. I understand now. Just about.
What do you mean, just about?
You sure are mean today.
You keep on saying mean and sneaky things. I thought you were my
friend.
I am. I am.
Then leave me alone about Cholly.
O.K.
There's nothing more to say about him, anyway. He's gone, anyway.
Yes. Good riddance.
Yes. Good riddance.
And Sammy's gone too.
And Sammy's gone too.
So there's no use talking about it. I mean them.
No. No use at all.
It's all over now.
Yes.[26]

---

26. Morrison, *The Bluest Eye*, 201.

Pecola's memories of herself and her mother, father, and brother transmit ideas about the role the family plays in regulating and protecting her body. Explicit in this passage is Pecola's express remorse for the violation to which she is subjected not only at her father's hand but also by her mother's failure to believe and protect her. Tragically, the finality of the tone on which the exchange closes connotes feelings not of relief and security but of loneliness and abandonment. The sentiment works doubly to recall events that evidence the multiple forms of abuse to which Cholly, like Pecola, is subjected in early childhood.

Cholly stands in striking opposition to Pecola, however, because he is forsaken by both his mother and his father at birth. Unlike Pecola, Cholly is looked upon with contempt by the entire community. As the oft-quoted passage explains, "The Breedloves did not live in a storefront because they were having temporary difficulty adjusting to the cutbacks at the plant. They lived there because they were poor and black, and they stayed there because they believed they were ugly. ... No one could have convinced them that they were not relentlessly and aggressively ugly. Except for the father Cholly, whose ugliness (the result of despair, dissipation, and violence directed toward petty things and weak people) was behavior, the rest of the family ... wore their ugliness, put it on, so to speak, although it did not belong to them."[27] The parenthetical statement has the effect of clarifying the authenticity of Cholly's ugliness and rooting it in *his* actions toward others.

When we review the sequence of events that lead Cholly to Lorrain, Ohio, however, to become the subject of other people's uncritical observation, a second, closer reading of the parenthetical statement above suggests that Cholly's ugliness results from the bad things he's done to others and the bad things others have done to him. Cholly experiences the first of these things four days after entering the world when, as the narrator explains, "his mother wrapped him in two blankets and one newspaper and placed him on a junk heap by the railroad."[28] The instinctive will of a child to know compels Cholly to ask questions of his Great Aunt Jimmy that repeatedly expose him to the trauma not only of parental separation but also of parental neglect. At the age of four, Cholly musters the courage "to ask his aunt who and where his father was,"[29] only to have her dismiss

---

27. Ibid., 38.
28. Ibid., 132.
29. Ibid., 133.

both the merit of the question and Cholly's apparent motive for asking the question:

> "How come you all didn't name me Samson?" Cholly's voice was low.

> "What for? He wasn't nowhere around when you was born. Your mama didn't name you nothing. The nine days wasn't up before she throwed you on the junk heap. When I got you I named you myself on the ninth day. You named after my dead brother. Charles Breedlove. A good man. Ain't no Samson never come to no good end."[30]

Extensive scholarly attention has been given to the historic role of naming and renaming among black Americans.[31] Aunt Jimmy's refusal to provide for Cholly's naming after his father recalls the truncation of enslaved black people's histories effected by their renaming upon their arrival to the United States. Aunt Jimmy doubles the assault through the stigma that she vicariously attaches to Cholly through his father. In other words, she essentially fates him to "come to no good end."[32] This reading is fortified when we remember that at this stage in the narrative's development, Cholly is a child. He is in his formative years of emotional and psychological development. Aunt Jimmy cuts off Cholly's lifeline to his biological father—and the longer paternal line extending from the father—in a manner that repeats the abuse of Cholly's father—and mother. Aunt Jimmy's refusal to engage Cholly, to nurture his sense of family, also effectively silences him, stunting his social and cultural maturation until Cholly meets Blue, two years later.

Blue becomes a kind of surrogate father to Cholly, filling crucial gaps in his social and cultural education by telling him "old-time stories about how it was when the Emancipation Proclamation came. How the black people hollered, cried, and sang. And ghost stories about how a white man cut off his wife's head and buried her in the swamp, and…how he talked his way out of getting lynched once, and how others hadn't."[33] He initiates Cholly's first rite of passage into the black community by taking him to the

---

30. Ibid., 106.

31. Michael Awkward, "Roadblocks and Relatives: Critical Revision in Toni Morrison's *The Bluest Eye*," in *Critical Essays on Toni Morrison* (ed. Nellie Y. McKay; Boston: G. K. Hall, 1988), 58.

32. Morrison, *The Bluest Eye*, 106.

33. Ibid., 133–34.

church picnic and breaking and eating ice-cold watermelon—a symbolic breaking of bread—with Cholly.

Cholly's time with Blue marks the beginning of a fundamental development in his consciousness and status from cultural outsider to cultural insider. Increasingly, Cholly registers awareness of the link between black cultural values and practices and the broader social dynamics this relationship gives rise to, as evidenced in the passage that recounts his thoughts upon viewing his dead aunt's body:

> Cholly had not yet fully realized his aunt was dead. Everything was so interesting. Even at the graveyard he felt nothing but curiosity, and when his turn had come to view the body at the church, he had put his hand out to touch the corpse to see if it were really ice cold like everybody said. But he drew his hand back quickly. Aunt Jimmy looked so private, and it seemed wrong somehow to disturb that privacy.[34]

Personal, ethical, and social boundaries relax to enable the performative and transformative aspects of the funeral ritual to envelop Cholly. It is in this frame of mind—this inchoate state of cultural development—that Cholly's experience of another rite of passage into manhood—through sexual intercourse—is abruptly, and brutally, interrupted. The relevant passage deserves exact quoting.

> There stood two white men. One with a spirit lamp, the other with a flashlight. There was no mistake about their being white; he could smell it. Cholly jumped, trying to kneel, stand, and get his pants up all in one motion. The men had long guns.
> "Hee hee hee heeeee." The snicker was a long asthmatic cough.
> The other raced the flashlight all over Cholly and Darlene.
> "Get on wid it, nigger," said the flashlight one.
> "Sir?" said Cholly, trying to find a buttonhole.
> "I said, get on wid it. An' make it good, nigger, make it good."
> There was no place for Cholly's eyes to go. They slid about furtively searching for shelter, while his body remained paralyzed. The flashlight man lifted his gun down from his shoulder, and Cholly heard the clop of metal. He dropped back to his knees. Darlene had her head averted, her eyes staring out of the lamplight into the surrounding darkness and looking almost unconcerned, as though they had no part in the drama

---

34. Ibid., 143.

taking place around them. With a violence born of total helplessness, he pulled her dress up, lowered his trousers and underwear.

"Hee hee hee hee heeee."

Darlene put her hands over her face as Cholly began to simulate what had gone on before. He could do no more than make-believe. The flashlight made a moon on his behind.[35]

This scene is as crucial and indispensable a scene in *The Bluest Eye* as the scene of Cholly's violation of Pecola. As many critics have pointed out, it functions to clarify at least part of Cholly's psychology: how it is, in other words, that he could violate his daughter. Yet even as critics recognize the scene for what it is, a rape, there has not been as precise an assessment of the multiple levels on which the scene operates, particularly against the backdrop of the larger narrative context in which it is embedded. The moment is clearly traumatic. Cholly is compelled from a position of consenting sexual agent to a violated and violating sexual object. The moment is also, perhaps not so clearly, ritualistic. This rite of passage marks Cholly's initiation into the stark, violent reality of American racism. He is, in the moment, a representative "every(black)man," or any black man, who in the era of Jim Crow could be subjected to this type of injustice and dehumanization, without any expectation or hope of legal recourse. It is crucial, therefore, that Cholly experience some form of symbolic or actual therapy that can carry him through, or assist him in negotiating at least the psychological, if not the physical, trauma that he endures.

Cholly sets off, therefore, in search of an image of "what his own self looked like. He only knew he was fourteen years old, black, and already six feet tall," the narrator explains.[36] But urged on by a developing sense of cultural awareness, he leaves in search of his father. The journey culminates with Cholly being further traumatized, this time by his father's "vexed and whiny voice" telling Cholly to "get the fuck outta my face!" The weight of the moment is so heavy that Cholly literally deficates on himself "like a baby."[37] The narrative again, importantly, genuflects before a ritualistic performance, this time of Cholly's symbolic rebirth and capitulation to a wayward lifestyle:

---

35. Ibid., 147–48.
36. Ibid., 122.
37. Ibid., 157.

Finding the deepest shadow under the pier, he crouched in it, behind one of the posts. He remained knotted there in a fetal position, paralyzed, his fists covering his eyes, for a long time. No sound, no sight, only darkness and heat and the press of his knuckles on his eyelids. He even forgot his messed up trousers. ... Cholly began to smell himself. He stood up and found himself weak, trembling, and dizzy. He leaned for a moment on the pier post, then took off his pants, underwear, socks, and shoes. He rubbed handfuls of dirt on his shoes; then he crawled to the river edge. He had to find the water's beginning with his hands, for he could not see clearly. Back near his post, he took off his shirt and wrapped it around his waist, then spread his trousers and underwear on the ground. He squatted down and picked at the rotted wood of the pier. Suddenly he thought of his Aunt Jimmy. ... With a longing that almost split him open, he thought of her handing him a bit of smoked hock out of her dish. He remembered just how she held it—clumsy-like, in three fingers, but with so much affection. No words, just picking up a bit of meat and holding it out of him. And then the tears rushed down his cheeks, to make a bouquet under his chin.[38]

A quick review of the next fourteen years of his life reveals that Cholly's baptism results in his being born into a life characterized by solicitation, profligacy, addiction, and violence. His arrival in Lorrain, marks the period when, according to the prostitute Marie, boys stopped being boys. "Folks started getting born old," she explains.[39] At first, Cholly tries to situate himself productively within the black community. At every turn, however, he is denied the right of placement, or passage, into this community. The displacement within the black community that Cholly experiences is compounded and worsened by the feelings of isolation and impotency that he relives with every effort he makes to provide his family a sense of normalcy in their day-to-day living. This fact is driven home by the memories that basic home items conjure for Cholly. "Occasionally," the narrator observes, "an item provoked a physical reaction: an increase of acid irritation in the upper intestinal tract, a light flush of perspiration at the back of the neck as circumstances surrounding the piece of furniture were recalled."[40] The sofa, for example, causes memories to surface that overlap with his physical violation by the white men in the woods, under-

---

38. Ibid., 157–58.
39. Ibid., 44.
40. Ibid., 36.

scoring the extent to which Cholly continues to relive the traumatizing effects of this encounter.

When the scope of Cholly's history is mapped, several important conclusions about the character can be drawn at the end of the novel when we know that he is dead, but don't know how or why he dies. First, Cholly was, as the narrator lyrically observes, "dangerously free. Free to feel whatever he felt—fear, guilt, shame, love, grief, pity. Free to be tender or violent, to whistle or weep."[41] He was also an adult whose emotional and cultural development were traumatically stunted in childhood. As a consequence, he finally lacked the resources needed to come to terms with the abuses to which he had been subjected for the greater part of his life. Cholly's violation of his daughter is tragic. It also tragically mirrors the multiple traumas Cholly experienced as a child, signifying the vicious cycle of abuse to which black children coming of age without the protection and nurturing of their communities are subjected. It is no surprise, therefore, that the adult Cholly becomes not only the target of the community's anger and hatred but also the embodiment of its greatest fears and transgressions.

By focally shifting to the male point of view and the insight it offers into problems arising from within the black community, I do not mean to deny the historic impact of structural racism on the plights of black people in America. Rather, I offer this reading with the hope that it will stimulate deeper, more meaningful debates about interwoven issues of identity formation and location that have historically shaped black people's experiences. These debates will undoubtedly bear on our nation's ability to formulate effective strategies for addressing and resolving the crisis of black-on-black crime, which displaces, disenfranchises, and destroys disproportionate numbers of young black men in America today.

Bibliography

Angelo, Bonnie. "The Pain of Being Black: An Interview with Toni Morrison." Pages 255–56 in *Conversations with Toni Morrison*. Edited by Danille K. Taylor-Guthrie. Jackson: University Press of Mississippi, 1994. First published in *Time* (May 22, 1989): 120–22.

Awkward, Michael. "Roadblocks and Relatives: Critical Revision in Toni Morrison's *The Bluest Eye*." Pages 57–68 in *Critical Essays on Toni Morrison*. Edited by Nellie Y. McKay. Boston: G. K. Hall, 1988.

---

41. Ibid., 159.

Baldwin, James. *Blues for Mr. Charlie*. 2nd ed. New York: Vintage, 1995. Originally published 1964.

Bond, Jean Carey, and Patricia Perry. "Is the Black Male Castrated?" Pages 141–48 in *The Black Woman: An Anthology*. Edited by Toni Cade Bambara. New York: Washington Square Press, 1970.

Bornstein, George. "The Colors of Zion: Black, Jewish, and Irish Nationalism at the Turn of the Century." *Modernism/Modernity* 12.3 (2005): 369–84.

Christian, Barbara. "Fixing Methodologies: *Beloved*." Pages 363–71 in *Female Subjects in Black and White: Race, Psychoanalysis, Feminism*. Edited by Elizabeth Abel, Barbara Christian, and Helene Moglen. Berkeley: University of California Press, 1997.

Clark, Kenneth B. *Youth in the Ghetto: A Study of the Consequence of Powerlessness and a Blueprint for Change*. New York: Harlem Youth Opportunities, 1964.

Douglas, Christopher. "What *The Bluest Eye* Knows about Them: Culture, Race, and Identity." *American Literature* 78 (2006): 143–68.

Douglass, Frederick. "What to the Slave Is the Fourth of July?" Online: http://teachingamericanhistory.org/library/index.asp?document=162.

Du Bois, W. E. B. *The Souls of Black Folk*. New York: Penguin, 1996.

Dunning, Roosevelt. "Black-on-Black Crime: Why Do We Tolerate the Lawless?" Sermon delivered at St. John's Baptist Church, New York, N.Y, December 7, 1975. Reprinted in *Vital Speeches of the Day* 42 (1975–1976): 215–18.

Durant, Robert, Robert Pendergrast, and Chris Cadenhead. "Exposure to Violence and Victimization and Fighting Behavior by Urban Black Adolescents." *Journal of Adolescent Health* 15 (1994): 311–18.

Earle, Kathryn. "Teaching Controversy: *The Bluest Eye* in the Multicultural Classroom." Pages 27–33 in *Approaches to Teaching the Novels of Toni Morrison*. Edited by Nellie Y. McKay and Kathryn Earle. New York: The Modern Language Association of America, 1997.

Fitzpatrick, Kathleen, and Jan Boldizar. "The Prevalence and Consequences of Exposure to Violence among African American Youth." *Journal of the American Academy of Child Adolescent Psychiatry* 32 (1993): 424–30.

Garbarino, James. *Raising Children in a Socially Toxic Environment*. Chicago: Jossey-Bass, 1999.

Griffin, Farah Jasmine. "Thirty Years of Black American Literature and Literary Studies: A Review." *Journal of Black Studies* 35 (2004): 165–74.

Hodges, Graham Russell, Susan Hawkes Cook, and Alan Edward Brown. *The Black Loyalist Directory: African Americans in Exile after the American Revolution*. New York: Garland, 1996.

Kent, Alicia. *African, Native, and Jewish American Literature and the Reshaping of Modernism*. New York: Palgrave, 2007.

Mehaffy, Marilyn. "Advertising Race/Raceing Advertising: The Feminine Consumer(-Nation), 1876–1900." *Signs* 23.1 (1997): 131–74.

Mincy, Ronald B. "Testimony of Ronald B. Mincy, Joint Economic Committee, March 8, 2007, Washington, D.C. Online: http://jec.senate.gov/archive/

Hearings/03.08.07%20African-American%20Male%20Unemployment/Testimony%20-%20Mincy.pdf.

Morrison, Toni. "Behind the Making of *The Black Book*." *Black World* 23 (February 1974): 86–90.

———. *The Bluest Eye*. New York: Washington Square Press, 1970.

Moses, Cat. "The Blues Aesthetic in Toni Morrison's *The Bluest Eye*." *African American Review* 33.4 (1999): 623–37.

Newton, Adam Zachary. *Facing Black and Jew: Literature as Public Space in Twentieth-Century America*. Cambridge: Cambridge University Press, 1999.

Pérez-Torres, Rafael. "Tracing and Erasing: Race and Pedagogy in *The Bluest Eye*." Pages 21–26 in *Approaches to Teaching the Novels of Toni Morrison*. Edited by Nellie Y. McKay and Kathryn Earle. New York: The Modern Language Association of America, 1997.

Contributors

Rainer Albertz
Westfälische Wilhelms-Universität Münster

Frank Ritchel Ames
Rocky Vista University College of Medicine

Samuel E. Balentine
Union Presbyterian Seminary

Bob Becking
Universiteit Utrecht

Aaron A. Burke
University of California Los Angeles

David M. Carr
Union Theological Seminary in the City of New York

Avraham Faust
Bar-Ilan University

Marian H. Feldman
University of California Berkeley

David G. Garber Jr.
Mercer University

M. Jan Holton
Yale University

Michael M. Homan
Xavier University of Louisiana

Hugo Kamya
Simmons College

Brad E. Kelle
Point Loma Nazarene University

T. M. Lemos
Huron University College at the University of Western Ontario

Nghana Lewis
Tulane University

Oded Lipschits
Tel Aviv University

Christl M. Maier
Philipps-Universität Marburg

Amy Meverden
Union Theological Seminary in the City of New York

William Morrow
Queen's University

Shelly Rambo
Boston University

Janet L. Rumfelt
Regis University

Carolyn J. Sharp
Yale University

Daniel L. Smith-Christopher
Loyola Marymount University

Jacob L. Wright
Emory University

Index of Primary Texts

GREEK AND LATIN AUTHORS

RABBINIC AND MEDIEVAL JEWISH TEXTS

Index of Modern Authors

CPSIA information can be obtained at www.ICGtesting.com
Printed in the USA
LVOW101137270112

265829LV00001B/51/P